GERMAN CROSS STITCH PATTERN.

RUSSIAN CROSS STITCH PATTERN.

ITALIAN CROSS STITCH PATTERN.

Encyclopedia
of Victorian Needlework

[DICTIONARY OF NEEDLEWORK]

S. F. A. CAULFEILD
AND
BLANCHE C. SAWARD

IN

TWO VOLUMES

Volume II

M-Z

AND SUPPLEMENT

DOVER PUBLICATIONS, INC.

NEW YORK

Published in Canada by General Publishing Company, Ltd., 30 Lesmill Road, Don Mills, Toronto, Ontario.
Published in the United Kingdom by Constable and Company, Ltd.

This Dover edition, first published in 1972, is an unabridged republication of the second edition (1887) of the work originally published by A. W. Cowan, London, in 1882 under the title *The Dictionary of Needlework: An Encyclopedia of Artistic, Plain, and Fancy Needlework*.

For this reprint edition, the work has been divided into two volumes, whereas the original work was published in six separately bound divisions. Some of the plates that originally appeared in color are here reproduced in black and white.

A Table showing the location of the color and halftone plates has been prepared especially for this reprint edition.

International Standard Book Number: 0-486-22801-0
Library of Congress Catalog Card Number: 79-182103

Manufactured in the United States of America
Dover Publications, Inc.
180 Varick Street
New York, N.Y. 10014

M.

Machine Work.—The several varieties of ordinary stitching which may be accomplished by means of small machines, hand-worked by the needlewoman, for Buttonholing, Darning, Fringing, Gauging, Kilting, and Knitting, and by the several kinds of ordinary Plain Sewing Machines, for all of which see their various headings. (*See* PLAITER and KILTER.)

Macramé Lace (also called FILET DE CARNASIÈRE). —This useful and easily made lace is a revival, under the name of Macramé, of the Italian Knotted Points (Punto a Groppo), which were much used in Spain and Italy for ecclesiastical linen, church vestments, and other trimmings, from the end of the fifteenth to the seventeenth century. This lace is first mentioned in the Sporza Inventory (1493); and in a painting by Paul Veronese, of the Supper of Simon the Canaanite, now in the Louvre, it adorns the tablecloth there depicted. The word Macramé is Arabic, and is used in the East to denote an ornamental fringe to any material; at Genoa, where Macramé Lace is chiefly made, the name was at first given to homespun huckaback towelling with plain fringed edges, and only gradually became the designation of the lace worked in likeness of these plain knotted fringes. The art of making Macramé has been taught during the whole of the present century in the schools and convents along the Riviera, but it was not until 1843 that any but the most simple designs were manufactured; at that date, a piece of old Knotted Point coming into the possession of one of the workers, she managed to unpick it, and learn from it the complicated knots.

The basis of all Macramé Lace is Knots, which are made by the fingers tying tightly together short ends of thread, either in horizontal or perpendicular lines, and interweaving the knots so made so as to form a design, sometimes slightly raised, but generally flat. From the nature of the work, the patterns thus made are simple, and are geometrical in form, it being almost impossible to form figures or flowers by such a process. Macramé is celebrated for its durability and excellence; the finer kinds, made with black and white silk threads, can be used as insertions or edgings to ladies' garments; the coarser, formed of écru coloured or black Maltese thread and twine, make mantel and table borders, and other furniture trimmings.

The materials required are as follows: A cushion, large black-headed pins, a crochet hook, or fine knitting needle, and a pattern; Italian twine, or Adams' silks, or Walter and Evans' flax, and Maltese thread of three sizes—coarse, medium, and fine. The coarse thread is used for large furniture pieces of lace, the medium for that required for ordinary uses, and the fine for dress trimmings. Make the Cushion as an oblong, flat-shaped pillow, 12in. long by 8in. wide; stuff it with sand to render it heavy, cover it with good Ticking, and arrange the lines woven in the Ticking evenly along the length of the Cushion, as they can then be used as guides for the horizontal lines of the work. An ornamental cover of scarlet ingrain twill, or blue silk, can be arranged over the Ticking cover,

if the latter is not considered ornamental enough, but it is not necessary. Prepare a piece of fine linen or silk, similar in shape to the Covers used in other Pillow Lacemaking, and use this to pin over the lace while in progress, so as to keep it clean. The pins should be strong and good; they are required to pin the lace to the cushion. The crochet hook and knitting needle are very useful, especially to a beginner, in forming the knots, as they can be insinuated under the threads, without disarranging them, in places where the figures cannot go. Within the last year, a Tension Frame and Loom, known as Anyon's Patent, have been invented. These are used instead of the Cushions, and are made as long wooden frames, fitted with levers and screws that hold the horizontal threads, or foundation bars, in position, and keep them stretched. A clip is fitted to the Loom to work the Solomon Knot; it is used to draw the centre strands over the top of it, and hold them firmly while the knot is completed. The use of either Frame or Loom expedites the making of the lace, and renders the work much more firm.

The patterns used in Macramé are not, as in other laces, traced upon parchment, and pinned on to the pillow beneath the threads, as the lace is so simple that it is easily worked from a paper pattern, placed at the side of the worker, or from written directions. The difficulties to be mastered are these: To pin the cords which run along the length of the lace at even distances upon the Cushion, to work each Knot of the same tightness, to draw each Knot close up to the last, to preserve the same distance apart, when repeating the pattern, as kept at first, and to keep every thread lying straight down the cushion, in the order in which it was first arranged.

KNOTS OR STITCHES.—The stitches are all formed either of Knots or Loops, arranged as Bars, Cords, Fillings, or Knots. They should be mastered before any design is attempted, as the whole beauty of the lace depends upon their being made close and tight, and placed apart at set intervals; and a beginner will have quite enough to do to keep them even, while forming a pattern, without having to trouble over how they are made. The stitches are known as Bars, Cords, Diamonds, Fillings, Knots, Open Knottings, Leaders, Rows, and Stars, and are made as follows:

Bars.—The Bar is used to form the lighter portions of the design. It is made with two, three, or four threads, according to the thickness required, and in the following varieties:

To make a *Chain Boulée*, or *Single Bar*: Pick up two threads lying close together, hold one in each hand, and keep the left-hand thread tight; pass the right-hand thread round the left as a loop, in making which bring the end of the thread out over the first part of the loop, push the loop up to the top of the thread, then hold the right-hand thread tight in the right hand, and loop the left-hand thread round it, and run the loop up to the top of the thread. Repeat these two loops until the length required for the Bar is obtained; the usual number of loops are nine, but these are increased or decreased according to the thickness of the thread used. The Chain Bar is illustrated in the Macramé pattern, Fig. 597.

To make a *Double*, or *Knotted Bar* : Take four threads lying close together, hold two in the left hand and two in the right, and loop the right over the left, and then the left over the right, as in Chain Bar.

To make a *Flat Solomon Bar* : Take four threads close together, and pin down to the lower part of the cushion the two centre ones; then take the left-hand thread (*see* Fig. 589), and pass it over the two pinned down threads and under the fourth, or last thread (*see* Fig. 590), take the fourth thread, twist it round the one put underneath it, put it under the two secured threads, and bring it out over the first, or left-hand thread (*see* Fig. 590); then hold the fourth and first threads, one in each hand, and run them up the secured threads to the top. Now reverse the movement; take the thread now on the right hand, and put it over the two secured threads and under the left-hand thread, which loop round it, and put under the secured threads and out over the right-hand

FIG. 589. MACRAMÉ—FLAT SOLOMON BAR.

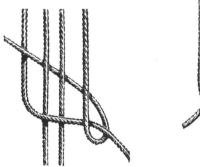

FIG. 590. MACRAMÉ—FLAT SOLOMON BAR.

FIG. 591. MACRAMÉ—FLAT SOLOMON BAR.

thread, draw the knot so made up close to the first knot. Repeat these two movements for the length of the Bar. A finished Solomon Bar is shown in Fig. 595.

To make a *Ridge*, or *Twisted Bar* : Take four threads, and work like the first part of a Solomon Bar, and go on repeating this movement until the right length of Bar is made. The Ridge, or Twist, will come after two knots have been made. This Bar is much used in the Raised Macramé. The Twisted Bar is shown in Fig. 595.

Cord.—The cord is the horizontal line that runs the whole length of the lace, and which is used in many patterns two or three times. To work: Before commencing the pattern, count the number of the straight horizontal lines running the entire length that are required, and for each, wind upon a separate flat card a doubled thread that is rather longer than the length the lace is to be made. Where the design requires a Cord, take one of these cards, Knot the ends of the doubled thread, and pin down to the left-hand side of the Cushion, laying the cord as close as possible to the last Row worked, and straight across the Cushion from left to right; there stick a big pin into the cushion, and wind the doubled thread tightly round it, so as to make the line across the thread quite taut, and then firmly

pin the card to the Cushion. The Cord being placed, cover it with the lace threads. Take the first thread lying on the left side of the work, loop it over the Cord (*see* Fig. 592), and pull it through again to the front with the help of the Crochet hook; pull it up quite tight, and close to the last line of work, and then loop it over the Cord again in the same manner. Take up the next thread and repeat, and continue to the end of the lace. The beauty of the Cord depends upon the evenness with which the loops are made upon it, and the perfect regularity of the line it forms, and this depends upon the tightness of the laid thread and the firmness of every loop made. Short, slanting lines in the lace, made without the introduction of the double thread, are formed by using one of the lace threads as a Cord, for which see *Leaders*.

Diamonds.—These are made with the short threads, and of Macramé Knots; they are formed in the working of the lace by taking one thread, slanting it to the right or left, and covering it with Knots made with the rest of the threads looped over it. The slanted thread is known as the LEADER, and when a set number of Macramé Knots have been made over it, it forms one side of a diamond, which figure is completed by three other threads being slanted and covered in the same manner. Diamonds are made with 6, 8, 12, or 16 threads, and with Single, Double, and Treble Leaders.

To make a *Single Diamond* : Take eight threads, number them from left to right, and pick up thread No. 4 in the left hand and hold it tight, slanting it from right to left, to form the LEADER on the top side of Diamond that slopes from the centre outwards. Hold thread No. 3 in the right hand, get it under the Leader, and make with it two loops or the MACRAMÉ KNOT on the Leader; push these loops well up to the top of the Leader. Pick up No. 2 thread, and make a Macramé Knot, and do the same with No. 1 thread; push all the Knots up to the top of the Leader, and then pin the Leader down to the Cushion. Now pick up No. 5 thread, hold it in the right hand, and slant it to the right to form the top of the Diamond on the right side, and slant outwards, pass thread No. 6 under it, and make the Macramé Knot on the Leader, and repeat to thread No. 8. Form the other two angles of the Diamond by reversing the slanting of the Leaders, sloping them inwards instead of outwards, and make the Macramé Knots upon them as before, using thread 8 before thread 7, and thread 1 before thread 2. Single Diamonds can be made with any even number of threads, but 8 or 6 are the usual number.

To make *Double Diamonds* : Take sixteen threads, divide them in the middle, and wind the last eight out of the way. Make thread 8 into the LEADER, cover it with the other threads, as described in Single Diamond, and pin it down; then take thread 7 (the first one used upon the Leader) and form that into a Leader by slanting it, and covering it with MACRAMÉ KNOTS in the same way; keep it close up to the first Leader, and, when that is reached, unpin it, and form a Macramé Knot with it

FIG. 592. MACRAMÉ —CORD.

upon the second Leader; pin this Leader down to the cushion, and take the eight threads numbered from 9 to 16: Make No. 9 thread the Leader, and slant it outwards and cover it as before; pin it down and take thread No. 10, slant it and make it a Leader, and cover it as before, not forgetting to work the first Leader on to it at the last with a Macramé Knot. Finish the Diamond by reversing the slant of the Leaders, using the same threads for Leaders, and reversing the order of the Macramé Knots. Tie the Leaders together where they meet in the centre of the Diamond.

To make *Treble Diamonds*: Take sixteen or more threads, and work exactly like Double Diamonds, but make three LEADERS instead of two, by using threads 6 and 11 as Leaders, and reverse them in the same way as for Double Diamonds. In working Diamonds, the centre threads, before being used to cover the reversed Leaders, are frequently knotted together; these are either made in *Open Knotting* or in *Ornamental Knot*.

Edging.—The usual finish to Macramé is made as follows: Having worked all the lace, comb out and straighten the ends of the threads that hang down, and cut them to an equal length, so as to form a Fringe. Should a thick Edging, and not a Fringe, be required, bend the threads to the right, and BUTTONHOLE over them, so as to form a thick cord that follows the outline of the lace. Cut out, after every second Buttonhole, two ends of thread, so as to absorb all gradually, and yet keep the cord even throughout its length. Ornament the edge thus made with PICOTS.

Fillings.—These are made in the centres of Diamonds, either with Macramé, Ornamental, or Solomon Knots, or with Open Knotting. *See* these headings.

Genoese Groppo.—See *Ornamental Knot*.

Heading.—The part to which the lace threads are first fixed is known as the Heading, and there are two ways of attaching them. The one most used is formed with the cord as follows: Prepare a doubled thread, rather longer than the length required for the lace, and wind it upon a Card. Knot the ends together, and pin the Knot to the upper part of the Cushion, on the left side. Unwind the doubled thread until it reaches the right side of the Cushion, and stick a big pin in there, on a line with the first pin, wind the thread tightly round it, and then pin the card to the Cushion. Take a skein of thread, cut it across at each end, or only in one place, according to the width of the lace required, draw out one of the threads, double it in half, put the loop thus formed under the stretched Cord or Doubled Thread (*see* Fig. 593), draw it through with the crochet hook, slip the two ends through the loop, and draw up tight, so that a Knot is formed upon the horizontal Cord; pin this Knot down. Continue to loop the threads on to the Cord until there are sufficient for a pattern (it is a mistake to put on a greater number), and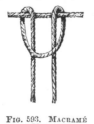

FIG. 593. MACRAMÉ —HEADING.

loop them on slightly apart, so that they lie flat upon the Cushion, and can be worked without interfering with each other. When the whole of the lace is made, the doubled thread supporting the threads can be drawn out the loops then form an open Heading.

The second manner of forming a Heading is as follows: Fix a line of black-headed pins along the upper part of the Cushion, from left to right, and a quarter of an inch apart. On to each of these pins fasten two doubled threads taken from the cut skein, and with their four ends work a SOLOMON KNOT. After the Solomon Knot has fastened the threads together, lay a CORD and work over it. This last Heading gives rather a better edging than the first.

Join Threads.—If a thread is to be inserted on a Leader or Cord, fasten it on as for the heading; if a thread requires renewing, make, with a new thread, a MACRAMÉ KNOT on a LEADER, and absorb the short end of the thread in the work. In other parts of the lace, tie the thread on with an Ordinary Knot.

Knot.—These are of three kinds—Macramé, Ornamental, and Solomon, and are described under those headings.

Leaders.—These are the threads that are slanted, either to form Diamonds or Stars. Take these threads from the ones forming the width of the lace, and when they have been covered with MACRAMÉ KNOTS to the length required, work them again into the pattern without distinguishing them in any way.

Macramé Knot.—This is the Knot from which the lace takes its name, and is worked with two, three, or four  threads. To make as shown in Fig. 594: Take three threads, and hold the third one in the right hand, pass it over the two, behind the third thread, and round underneath them, and bring it out over itself, repeat, and draw the knot thus made up to the top of the two threads. When worked with two threads, only one is enclosed; when worked with four threads, three are enclosed, but the knot in all cases is made with two loopings of the last thread.

FIG. 594. MACRAMÉ —KNOT.

Varieties of the Knot are formed by looping the thread three or four times instead of twice, and by working a whole row of these knots, and then commencing a second row as follows: Leave the first threads hanging, and take in the left hand the thread that formed the loops in the last row; make a Macramé Knot with this round the two threads in front of it, and draw up tight as before; continue to the end of the Row, always making the new Knots with the thread that made the knots on the first row, but that inclosed the strands behind the ones now looped together.

Open Knotting.—These stitches are used to fill up the centres of Diamonds, or are worked in rows along the lace. These Knots were used in the KNOTTING worked in the eighteenth century. To make as shown in Fig. 596, on page 334: Take four threads, and number them from the left to the right; take the first, and pass it over the second and third and under the fourth; take the fourth, loop it round the first, under the third and second, and over the first, and draw up; then take the first thread (which is now on the right hand), and put it under the third and second and over the fourth (now on the left hand), then take the fourth thread, loop it round the first, and put it over the second and third and under the loop made by the first thread, and draw it up. While making the knot, keep the centre threads tight, and rather loosen the outer ones. Put a pin through this knot, take the four next threads, make a Knot with them on a line with the last, and pin that down, and continue to the end of the row. For the second row — miss two threads, and make a Knot with two threads from the first, and two threads from the second Knot of the first row, pin down and repeat. For the third row—take on the two threads left

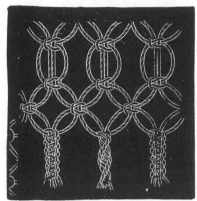

FIG. 595. MACRAMÉ—OPEN KNOTTING.

in the second row, and make the first knot with them, and with two threads from the first Knot on the second row. The difficulty in making Open Knotting, when working it in rows, lies in the necessity of making the Knots in even lines; this is obviated when one of the blue lines on the Ticking can be used as a guide. In Fig. 595 the Open Knotting is finished off with a RIDGE, or TWISTED BAR, and with two SOLOMON BARS.

To make Fig. 596: This Open Knotting is made like the one shown in Fig. 595, but with two Knots instead

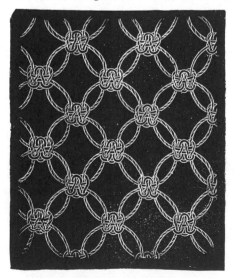

FIG. 596. MACRAMÉ—OPEN KNOTTING.

of one to each thick part. Work as in Fig. 595, and then repeat the Knot there made.

Ornamental Knot.—Used as a Filling in the centre of Diamonds, or to join Stars together, and worked as follows: Take four threads, and number them from the left

to the right; pin down two and three on to the cushion, at some distance from where the knot is being made; then take the four in the right hand, pass it over the two and three, under and over the one, then slip it under the two and three, and bring it out over itself, and draw it up tight. Repeat this until seven to nine knots are made, according to the thickness of the thread used. Take a Knitting needle (No. 10), place it upon the Ornamental Knot, and turn the ends of the knot over the pin, so as to inclose the pin in the Knot, and bring them out underneath the Knot in the place they started from, and there tie two ends on to the thread nearest them on the right side, and two ends on the left side. Smooth them down, and proceed to work the second half of DIAMOND or STAR with the threads used in the Knot. This Ornamental Knot is shown in Figs. 597 and 598.

Rows. — These are made either with horizontal CORDS or with MACRAMÉ KNOTS, worked over two or more perpendicular threads, or with OPEN KNOTTING.

Solomon Knot.—This Knot is much used in the lace to form Bars or centre fillings; the manner of working is fully described in SOLOMON BARS.

Stars.—These are used in the lace, and made with the working threads covered with MACRAMÉ KNOTS like Diamonds, but the first two Leaders, instead of slanting outwards, slant inwards to the centre, in order to form the right shape, and the two Leaders forming the bottom part of the star slant outwards from the centre. The Stars are made as Single, Double, and Treble Stars.

To work a *Single Star*: Take eight threads, number them from the left to the right, take the first as a LEADER, and slant it from left to right, and cover it with MACRAMÉ KNOTS, made with two, three, and four threads; pin it down, and take thread No. 8, slant it from right to left, and cover it with Knots made with seven, six, and five threads, and bring it to the centre, and tie the two Leaders together; then slant the right-hand Leader to the right, and the left-hand Leader to the left, and proceed to cover them in the same manner.

To work *Double Stars*: Take twelve threads, and use the first and the twelfth for LEADERS, work them to the centre as before, here pin them down, and make the second and the eleventh the next Leaders, and work them to the centre; make the last knots upon them with the first Leaders. Make an ORNAMENTAL KNOT with the four centre threads, and secure it, then divide the threads again, and work the second half of the Star, slanting the Leaders from the centre outwards. This Star is shown in the pattern given in Fig. 599.

To work *Treble Stars*: Take twelve threads, and repeat the instructions given for Double Stars, but make a LEADER of third and tenth threads, as well as of first and second, and eleventh and twelfth. Make the ORNAMENTAL KNOT in the centre, and then slant the Leaders outwards. This star is shown in the pattern given in Fig. 598.

PATTERNS.—The following Designs, illustrating the various stitches used in Macramé, will be within the scope of the worker who has learned the Knots. These designs are intended for Furniture Lace, and should be worked with either medium or coarse écru thread; they can be altered into trimming laces by being worked with fine black or white silk.

To work Fig. 597: In this pattern the threads are not Knotted on to a Cord as a Heading, but are arranged upon large-headed pins as follows. Place a row of pins, along a blue line of the Cushion, a quarter of an inch apart; cut a skein of threads at each end, take two threads, and double them over each pin. First row—work a SOLO-

knots in each Bar. Fifth row—Knot six Knots on the first Chain, then take the next two Chain Bars, and pass the fourth thread forming them round the others, as in the first part of MACRAMÉ KNOT; divide the threads again into pairs, and work the Chain Bar six knots to each Bar. Sixth row—make a Solomon Knot on every four threads, and pin it down. Seventh row—work a Cord as in the second row. Eighth row—take eight threads, divide them, and make the top half of a TREBLE STAR;

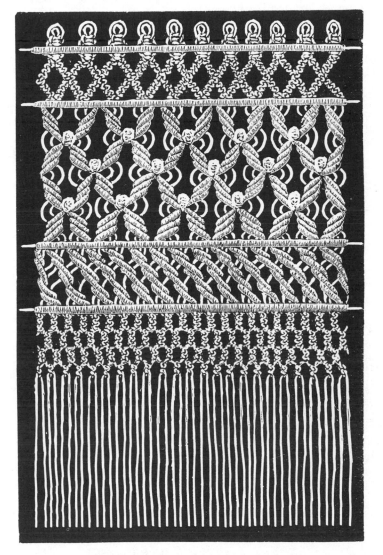

FIG. 597. MACRAMÉ PATTERN (No. 1).

MON KNOT below each pin with the threads on it. Second row—wind a double thread, long enough to work the length of the lace, upon a card. Pin the end of this to the left side of the Cushion, and lay it close along beneath the Solomon Knots as a CORD, and pin the card and the Cord firmly down on the right hand of the Cushion. Then work over the Cord with every thread, as explained in Cord. Third row—work a Solomon Knot with every four threads, and pin each down. Fourth row —work a CHAIN BAR with every two threads, tying six

repeat to the end of the row. Ninth row—make an ORNAMENTAL KNOT in the centre of each Treble Star, using the two centre threads of each half Star. Draw the Ornamental Knot over a knitting needle, bring the ends between the two corners of the Star, and turn them under; tie them in a common knot to the other ends, divide the threads again, and work the lower half of Treble Star; repeat to the end of the row. Tenth row—take the right-hand bottom quarter of the first Treble Star, and the left-hand bottom of the second Star, make an

Ornamental Knot between them, and work the lower half of Treble Star with these threads. Continue to make Ornamental Knots and lower halves of Treble Stars to the end of the row, then take the left-hand bottom quarter of the first Star, and make three slanting lines with it. Eleventh row—make an Ornamental Knot between the two first parts of the Star, and finish by working the lower half to it; repeat to the end of the row. Twelfth row —work a Cord like the second row. Thirteenth row—take the first three threads, and use the first as a LEADER, and slope it from left to right; cover it with a Macramé Knot from each of the other two threads; repeat to the end

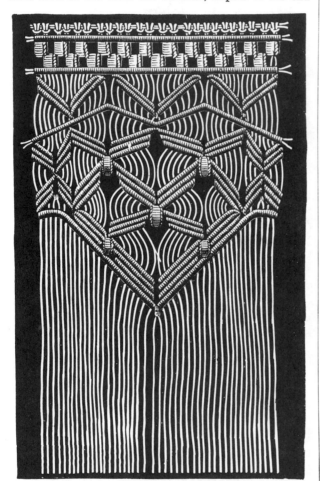

FIG. 598. MACRAMÉ PATTERN (No. 2).

of the row. Fourteenth row—take the first thread as a Leader, slope to the right, and cover with Macramé Knots from four threads. Take the fifth thread, make it a Leader, and cover it with Knots made with the one thread left from the line above it, and two from the next; repeat this last slanting line to the end of the row, always taking the Leader from one slanted line in the previous Knot, and the covering threads from the slanted line before it; repeat this row from the commencement three times. Eighteenth row—work a Cord like the second row. Nineteenth row—make Chain Bars with every two threads of six Knots to each Chain Bar. Twentieth row—miss the

first thread, and make Chain Bars of all the rest, six Knots to each Bar. Twenty-first row like the nineteenth. Twenty-second row like the twentieth, but work four Knots instead of six to each Bar.

To work Fig. 598: Wind a double thread, the length of the lace, upon a card, pin it to the Cushion, and fasten the threads to it, as described in HEADING. First row—fasten a second double thread down, and work the CORD. Second row—take four threads, number them from left to right, and make a MACRAMÉ KNOT with the fourth thread over the other three. Work the Knot until there are four loops upon the thread. Repeat to the end of the row. Third row—take two threads from the first Macramé Knot and two from the second, and make the Macramé Knot with the fourth thread the same number of times as in the previous row; repeat to end. Fourth row—work the Cord. Fifth row—work the upper part of a DOUBLE STAR, using sixteen threads. Sixth row—work the Cord, but instead of making it a horizontal line, arrange it as a diagonal one, and pin it firmly in this shape to the Cushion before covering it with the double loops. Make the first slant of the Cord right across the first Star and upwards, the second into the centre of the second Star and downwards, the third from the centre of the Star upwards to the top, the fourth across the third Star downwards, and repeat from the commencement when carrying on the pattern. Seventh row—take the first eight threads, and work with them the two upper halves of a TREBLE STAR, then take the next sixteen threads, and work with them the two upper halves of a Treble Star, work another Treble Star with sixteen threads, and another Treble Star with eight threads, and repeat from the commencement of the row. Eighth row—work the second or bottom half of a Treble Star with the first eight threads, then take the four centre threads of the sixteen that worked the large Star, and make with them an ORNAMENTAL KNOT; divide these four threads, and work with the sixteen the second, or bottom half, of the Treble Star, repeat the Ornamental Knot and the lower halves of the large Treble Stars with the next sixteen threads, work the small eight-thread Star without a Knot, and repeat the whole pattern from the commencement. Ninth row—make an Ornamental Knot with the threads 23, 24, 25, and 26, and before commencing the pattern, then miss the first eight threads, and, with the next sixteen, make the upper half of a Treble Star and an Ornamental Knot with its four centre threads, then take the next sixteen threads and repeat the upper half of a Treble Star with them, miss the next eight threads, and repeat from the commencement. Tenth row—miss the first sixteen threads, and make the lower half of a Treble Star with the next sixteen, and an Ornamental Knot on each side of them; miss the next twenty-four threads, and repeat the lower half of the Treble Star. Eleventh row—take a double thread, and pin it down to make a Cord; arrange it as follows: lay it horizontally along the ends of the two small Stars, and close to them, then bring it down to the lowest point of the Treble Star worked in the last row, and up again to the commencement of the small Star, and pin it down carefully before covering it with the double loops.

To work Fig. 599: Place along a line in the Ticking of the Cushion large pins a quarter of an inch apart; cut a skein of thread in one place, and hang two threads doubled on to each of the pins. First row—work with every four threads a SOLOMON KNOT. Second row—lay down a double thread and work over it as in CORD. Third

last thread of one group to loop over the first two threads of the next group. Fifth row—lay down the doubled thread and work the Cord. Sixth row — take twelve threads, divide them, and work with them the upper halves of a TREBLE STAR, pinning each Star firmly to the Cushion as worked; repeat to the end of the row, and

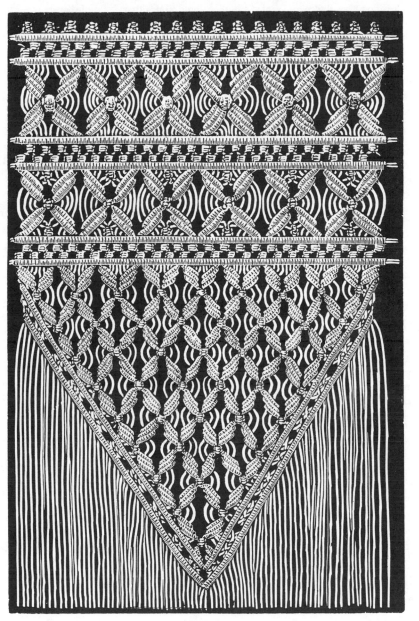

FIG. 599. MACRAMÉ PATTERN (No. 3).

row—take the first three threads, and make the MACRAMÉ KNOT over the first two with the third thread; loop the thread three times over the others; repeat to the end of the row. Fourth row—leave the first two threads, and take the one that was looped over the others, and with it make the three loops over the fourth and fifth threads; repeat these loops to the end of the row, always using the

make six Stars. Seventh row — take the four centre threads of each group of twelve threads, and work an ORNAMENTAL KNOT with them, tie it tight, re-divide the threads, and work the lower half of the Treble Star with them. Eighth, ninth, tenth, and eleventh rows—as the second, third, fourth, and fifth rows. Twelfth row—make a flat Solomon Knot with the four centre threads of each group of twelve threads, then commence with the first thread and work the upper halves of a DOUBLE STAR with the group of twelve threads six times, and in the centre of every Star work with the four centre threads another flat Solomon Knot. Thirteenth row—work the lower half of the Double Star, and then with the four centre threads of each group of twelve work a flat Solomon's Knot. Fourteenth, fifteenth, sixteenth, and seventeenth rows—as the second, third, fourth, and fifth rows. Eighteenth row—take the first eight threads, divide them, and work with them the upper halves of a Treble Star; repeat to the end of the row with eight threads to each Star, and make nine Stars, and then take the four centre threads of each group of eight, and work a Solomon's Knot with them, which pin down to the cushion as made. Nineteenth row—leave the first four threads alone, and then work exactly as the eighteenth row, leaving the last four threads of the ninth Star alone. Twentieth to twenty-sixth rows—repeat the nineteenth row, always leaving the first and last four threads unworked, so that the pattern is reduced finally to the upper half of one Star, which forms a point in the centre, as shown in the illustration. Twenty-seventh row—take the first thread and slant it down to the bottom of the last Star, pin it down there, and work over it as a Cord; then take the last thread of the ninth Star and slant that to meet the first, pin it down, and work over it as a Cord. Twenty-eighth row—make a Solomon Knot with every four threads of the pattern. Twenty-ninth row—repeat the twenty-seventh row, tying the two laid threads together where they meet in the centre of the pattern.

To work Fig. 600: Fasten a row of pins into the Cushion a quarter of an inch apart, cut a skein of thread twice, and hang two doubled threads on to each of the pins. First row — work a MACRAMÉ KNOT on each four threads, reversing the Knot at every other group of threads. Second row—lay down a double thread as a CORD, and cover it with two loops from each thread. Third row—take the first twelve threads, and with the centre four work the OPEN KNOTTING with two knots, illustrated in Fig. 596; then divide the threads in half, and with the first six work the left hand top half of a DOUBLE STAR, and with the last six work the right hand half of the same Star, but cross the second LEADER of that half over the Leader of the first half, and keep it pinned down in that position ready for the next row; repeat to the end. Fourth row—take the threads Nos. 11, 12, 13, and 14, and make the Open Knotting with two Knots, and pin down firmly; repeat to the end of the row, using the last two threads of one group of twelve threads and the first two of another for the Knot, then finish the lower half of the Star; on the Leader crossed over from right hand to left work all the left hand threads except thread No. 6, which make the first Leader on the right hand side, putting it under the crossed Leader; having completed the Star, work with the four centre threads of each group of twelve an Open Knotting Knot, as worked in the third row. Fifth row — lay down a double thread and work a Cord. Sixth row — work an Open Knotting Knot with every four threads. Seventh row — work a Cord. Eighth row — take twenty threads

and make an Open Knotting Knot with the middle four, then with the four on each side of the Knot work a short Cord slanting towards the Knot, pin all down, take No. 1 thread, make it a Leader, and work the left hand top side of a TREBLE STAR, bringing in all the threads as far as No. 10; then, with No. 20 as first Leader, work the right hand top side of Treble Star, bringing in all the threads from No. 20 to No. 11; repeat to the end of the row. Ninth row—work a CHAIN BAR with six Knots with every two threads. Tenth row—knot two Chain Bars together, re-divide them, and work two Chain Bars with eight Knots

FIG. 600. MACRAMÉ PATTERN (NO. 4).

each; repeat to the end of the row. Eleventh row—repeat the tenth row, but only work four Knots to the Chain Bars.

The following pattern, from a piece of Macramé Lace worked in the eighteenth century, can be worked from instructions without a design. It is formed with flat Solomon and Twisted Solomon Bars, and with Open Knotting, and is very easily worked, and extremely elegant. To work: Lay a double thread as a HEADING, cut a skein of thread once, and loop on any number of threads that divide into four, and pin each down just enough apart to

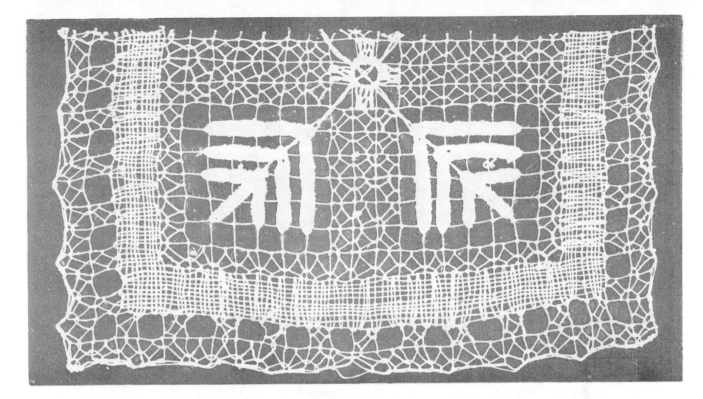

GUIPURE D'ART.

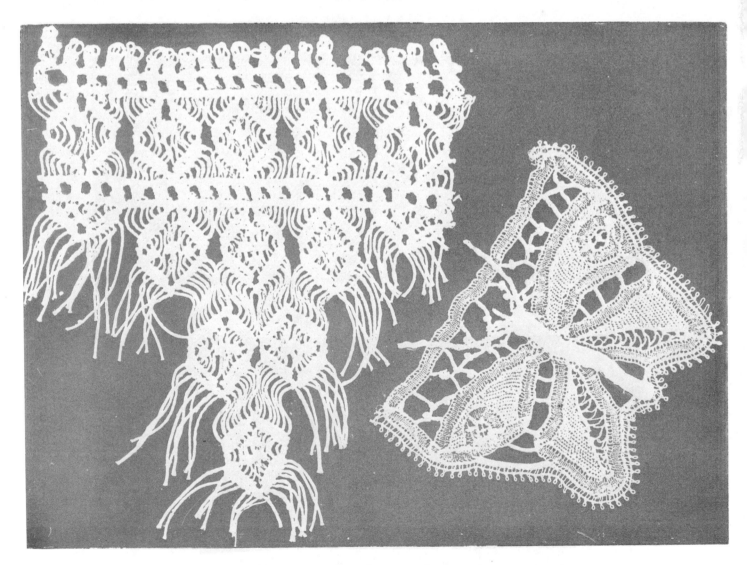

MACRAMÉ.   MODERN POINT.

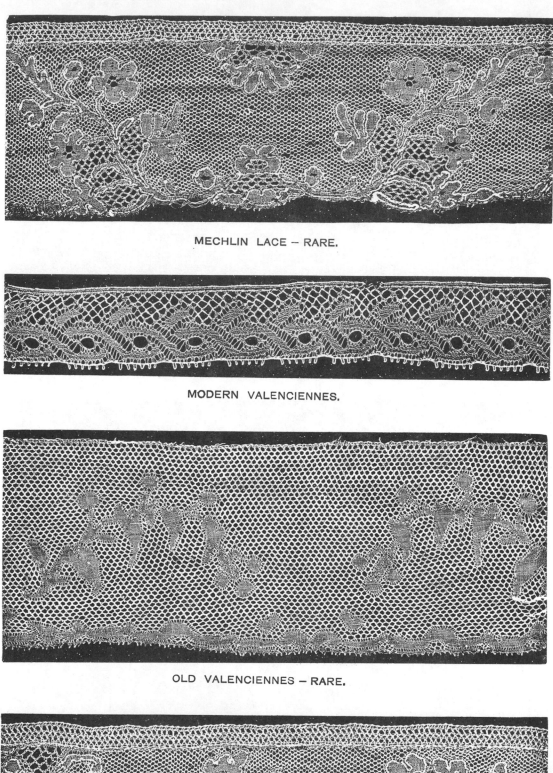

MECHLIN LACE — RARE.

MODERN VALENCIENNES.

OLD VALENCIENNES — RARE.

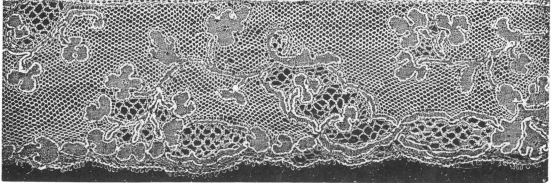

MECHLIN LACE — RARE.

lie flat. First row—lay down a doubled thread and work it as a CORD. Second row—make with every four threads flat SOLOMON BARS, six knots to each Bar. Third row—leave the first two threads, and with the four next make a Solomon Bar with four knots; repeat to the end of the row, always taking two threads from one Bar of the last row and two threads from the next Bar. Fourth row—with the first four threads make a Solomon's Bar with four knots, and repeat to the end of the row. Fifth row—leave the first two threads, and make with the next four threads a Twisted Solomon Bar of eight knots; repeat to the end of the row, always making the Twisted Bar with two threads from one Bar and two threads from another Bar of the preceding row. Sixth row—commence with the first threads and make a Twisted Bar, as in the last row. Seventh row—leave the first two threads, and make Solomon Bars of five knots each. Eighth row—take the first threads and make Twisted Solomon Bars of twelve knots. Ninth row—leave the first two threads, and with the next four make the SINGLE OPEN KNOTTING, illustrated in Fig. 595. Tenth row—take the first two threads, and two from the first Knot, and with them work the Open Knotting, as in the ninth row. Eleventh row—work like the ninth. Twelfth row—Knot every four threads together and cut the ends of the threads straight, allowing two inches for fringe.

Madagascar Lace.—A native production of the island from which it takes its name, and of the neighbouring coasts of Africa. The lace resembles gimp more than lace, and is made of a number of loose threads twisted together, so as to form scallops and loops, and secured in those positions. It possesses no value beyond the fact of its being unlike any lace of European manufacture.

Madapolams.—A coarse description of calico cloth, of a stiff heavy make, originally of Indian manufacture, where it was employed for Quilts. It can be had either dressed or undressed, for underclothing, and measures from 29 to 33 inches in width, or in the double widths it is from 1¼ yards to 33 inches wide. These latter varieties are much employed for Curtains, Quilts, servants' Aprons, &c.

Madeira Lace.—The lace made by the natives of Madeira is not a native production, and the manufactory has only existed for fifty years. The laces made are Maltese, Torchon, and a coarse description of Mechlin.

Madeira Work.—This is white Embroidery upon fine linen or cambric, not differing from Irish Work or Broderie Anglaise in any material degree, but made by the nuns in Madeira, and eagerly sought by all admirers of fine needlework because of the excellence of its workmanship. To make as shown in Fig. 601: Trace the design upon fine cambric, work the outline in BUTTONHOLE STITCH, OVERCAST the EYELETHOLES, and fill in their centres with eight-armed WHEELS. Make the dots in POINT DE POIS, and the leaves in POINT LANCÉ, join the insertion to the edging, and hide the seam thus made by working over it in DOUBLE CORAL STITCH.

Madeira Work Trimmings.—These are hand-sewn Embroideries, executed by nuns in the Island which gives its name to the industry. Edgings, Insertions, Flounces, and children's Dresses, of very excellent quality, are worked on muslin, and imported to this country. It is to be had both in close and open work. Our own Scotch and Irish White Embroidery, especially the latter, is equally good.

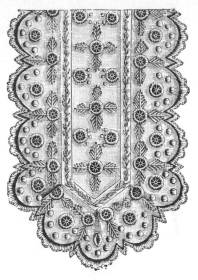

FIG. 601. MADEIRA WORK.

Madras Lace.—A school for lace making has lately been founded in Madras. The lace made is the black and white silk Maltese Guipure.

Madras-net Muslin.—This is a handsome, but coarse make of Muslin, produced in several varieties, some in cream colour, others with coloured designs of a bold character, and others again in uni-colour. They are all 72 inches wide. Those with coloured designs rise, from the price of the cream-coloured Muslins, to more than double their value.

Madras Work.—This work is so called from its being executed upon the brightly coloured silk handkerchiefs that are known as Madras handkerchiefs. When embroidered these handkerchiefs are used either for caps, mats, or workbasket covers, or are made into Chair Backs, by lace being sewn round them. To work: Select a brightly coloured handkerchief, with a deep border, composed of lines of various widths and of contrasting colours, and line it with calico. Work in Embroidery silks over these lines in DOUBLE CORAL STITCH, POINT CROISÉ, TÊTE DE BŒUF, and LATTICE STITCH, selecting silks that contrast in colour with the lines of the handkerchief. Having filled in with these open stitches all the lines that compose the border, select either a dark blue, green, or brown silk, and RUN it along both sides of each line, so as to enclose the fancy stitch decorating the centre.

Make One.—One of the ways in Knitting of enlarging the pattern. *See* KNITTING.

Making Crossings.—*See* CROSS TRACING.

Making up Lace Sprigs. — *See* HONITON APPLICATION.

Malabars.—Cotton Handkerchiefs, printed in imitation of Indian Handkerchiefs, the patterns of which are of a peculiar and distinctive type, and the contrasts of colour brilliant and striking. *See* Monteiths.

Malins Lace.—Another name for Mechlin Lace.

Maltese Lace.—Lace making was carried on in Malta during the sixteenth century, but the lace then produced was of a coarse description, and resembled Mechlin and Valenciennes without their fine grounds. But during the present century the manufacture of Greek Guipures was commenced in the island, and the first black silk plaited laces made of these designs came from Malta. The Lace is a handsome and heavy lace, made both in white silk and thread, and also in the black silk known as Barcelona silk, such as is used in Spain and France for the Spanish Chantilly Blonde Laces. The patterns are all simple, and either arabesque or geometric; they are worked upon the Pillow, are connected together with a Pearled Bar ground made at the same time as the designs, and are

Manteau.—The French name for a cloak, or loose external covering, worn out of doors.

Mantle.—An outer covering somewhat resembling a short cloak, from which it differs in being slightly fitted to the figure, and having either a loose frilling over the elbows, where the arms protrude from under it, or, sometimes, a very short sleeve commencing from the elbow. The size, form, and material of mantles vary with the season, the fashion, or the figure and taste of the wearer. They may be had in silk, velvet, cashmere, lace, and fur. After the Conquest, the cloaks so designated were introduced by the Normans, who wore them—at all seasons of the year—embroidered, lined with costly furs, fringed, and jewelled. The Mantle presented to Henry I. by Robert Bloet, Bishop of Lincoln, was valued at a sum equal to about £1,500 of our present currency. That of Cœur de Lion was of much greater value, and the inventories of our various sovereigns contain entries of their mantles. Those represented in Anglo-Saxon MSS. as worn by the ladies of

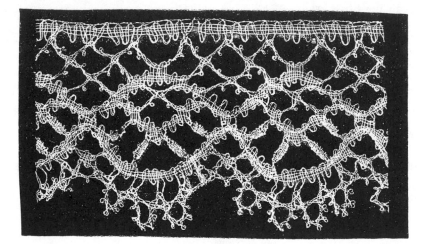

Fig. 602. MALTESE LACE.

formed of Plaiting and Cloth Stitch. The best are decorated with a little raised work, but the usual make is shown in Fig. 602, which consists of a simple Pearled Bar ground, with a pattern formed of Cloth Stitch, and Plaitings. The edge of the lace is distinguished by its lightness. The manufacture of Maltese Lace is not confined to Malta, but is largely carried on in Auvergne, Le Puy, Ireland, Buckinghamshire, and Bedfordshire, while the lace made in Ceylon and Madras resembles Maltese. Handsome shawls and veils, worth £30, were at one time made of this lace, but latterly the manufacture has been limited to narrow trimmings, costing from 1s. 6d. to 10s. a yard.

Manchette.—A French term denoting a cuff; the word *Manche* meaning a sleeve, and the fragmentary character of the sleeve represented by the final diminutive "*ette.*"

Manilla Hemp.—A fibrous material obtained from a plant allied to the Banana, and a native of the Philippine Islands. Mats, cables, and rigging in general are made of it. *See* Hemp.

that time were of the Poncho order, being a square with a hole in the centre, sufficiently large to admit the head of the wearer. Perhaps the earliest mention of them is to be found in the Book of Ruth; and, doubtless, such a form of garment dates back to the period immediately subsequent to the Fall. Amongst the Greeks it was called the *Pallium,* and the Romans the *Toga.* Our own old English name "pall" was a corruption of the Greek *Pallium.*

To make a Crape Mantle needs especial care. When making a small cape, or rotonde, without a lining, cut the piece so that the straight way of the material shall be preserved for the centre of the back. Fold the Crape together in equal halves, and then cut out the Cape upon the desired pattern, and thus avoid a seam down the back. If, however, a join be unavoidable, cut off the thick part of the extreme edge of the Crape at the selvedges, and unite them down the back by means of a Mantua-makers' Hem, which should be left unpressed. To make a Seam on the shoulders a method is adopted that has no name to distinguish it, as follows: Make a Running on the right side of the Crape, leaving the two raw edges standing up on the shoulders. Then fold back the two sides, laying them together, and make a second Running, sufficiently deep from the first as to enclose the raw edges (which may be seen perfectly well through so transparent a material), and to enable the needlewoman to take in the edges, and leave a joining free of loose ends of thread when placed back into position. It is less liable to stretch, and lies flatter for that part than a Mantua Makers' Hem. The extreme edge of the mantle is sometimes finished by a narrow sarsenet ribbon being run on, and then turned up on the inside, so as to give a firm foundation for a mourning fringe, and Crêpe rouleau Heading, as a trimming. If a double Crêpe tuck be used instead of fringe, it is easiest to place the raw edge of the Crape between the two of the Tuck, and TACK through all three sufficiently far in, to allow of afterwards turning the raw edge of the Tuck on the wrong side of the mantle, and SLIP STITCHING it down to make all neat. A fancy fold may then be laid over the cut edge of the Tuck on the mantle's right side.

Mantle Cloths.—A term employed in trade to denote every description of cloth suitable for mantles, cloaks, and all other purposes of exterior clothing for men, and, in many cases, also adapted for women's wear.

Marabout Feathers.—These are procured from a species of Stork, Adjutant, and Paddy or Rice Bird, and may be had in white, grey, or dyed. They are employed as plumes for Head dresses, Bonnets, and Trimmings for Dresses, Fans, Muffs, and Tippets, and are used with gold, silver, and pearls. White Marabout Feathers are more expensive than the grey, and have sometimes been sold for their weight in gold. The best Feathers are taken from the tail and underneath the wings.

Maracaybo Lace.—Better known as Venezuelan Lace, and consisting of Drawn Threads united with Darned Stitches. *See* VENEZUELAN LACE.

Marbled Cloth.—A new material, manufactured in two shades, composed of silk and wool, and interwoven so that the surface is mottled or "dappled." In the sixteenth century "marble-silk" was manufactured, the weft of which was of a variety of coloured threads, so woven as to give the appearance of marble to the web, stained with many hues. Many ecclesiastical vestments made of this description of silk were in use in old St. Paul's; and we read that the Lord Treasurer rode to meet "the old gwyne of Schottes" when she "rod thrught London," "with a C. gret horsse, and their cotes of marbull" on the 6th of November, 1551.

Marcella, or Marsella. — A description of cotton

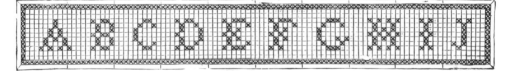

FIG. 603. MARKING IN CROSS STITCH.

Mantua Cushion Point.—A name sometimes given to GENOESE BRAID LACES.

Mantua-makers' Hem.—This is a quick method of Hemming, practised by dressmakers only, by which the Running together of two pieces of material, previous to their being Felled, is rendered unnecessary. The term Mantua-maker owes its origin to the rich silks produced at Mantua, in black and in colours, which were imported into this country in 1685 by the French immigrants, and which appear to have borne the first reputation for excellence. To work: Place the two raw edges together, fold both of them over, and HEM through the double fold of stuff, leaving the Hem so formed as a ridge, instead of a flat one, as it would have been had it been Felled. *See* FELLING.

Marabout.—A peculiar kind of "thrown" silk, frequently made of three threads of raw silk, which, being nearly white as it comes from the cocoon, is capable of receiving the most delicate shades of colour at once, without the discharge of its natural gum. A thin textile, very fine in quality, is produced from it, of which fancy scarves are made, having a white centre and coloured borders. The great delicacy of the strands of this tissue was the origin of such a name being applied to it, as the feathers of the bird so called are notable for their extreme delicacy.

Quilting or coarse Piqué, having a pattern resembling that of diaper in relief. The name is derived from the Marseilles Quilts, of which it is a lighter and cheaper variety. Marcella is sold by the yard for making toilet covers, dressing table mats, and other articles. The width measures from 30 inches to 36 inches.

Marking.—The art of Marking was carried to great perfection before the invention of the numerous modern marking inks, and during the years succeeding home-weaving of linen, when the name was woven into the material as part of the design. To be able to embroider the name of the owner, and the numerals standing for the number of articles possessed, was an accomplishment that no lady of the eighteenth and earlier part of the nineteenth century was without, and the work executed then was frequently of a very beautiful description, and always conspicuous for its neatness and finish. At the present date Marking in England is almost exclusively confined to pockethandkerchiefs, bed linen, and woollen materials; but upon the continent, Initials beautifully worked often form the sole ornamentation of silk cushions, table covers, and work-basket covers.

The marking of linen may be effected in a variety of stitches: in Cross Stitch, Embroidery Stitches, and Chain Stitch; but the orthodox style is after the first-named method. Fig. 603 is a sample of the easiest kind of

Marking. To work: Procure ingrain red cotton, and work upon Linen of a coarse texture, so as to be guided by the threads that are woven in it. Form the letters with CROSS STITCH, and place the stitches at the distance apart shown in the illustration, counting the linen threads as squares.

Fig. 604 shows the numerals used in marking To work: Trace their outlines upon the material, and RUN them with fine Embroidery cotton, then fill the centres with a padding of soft cotton, and work them entirely over in RAISED SATIN STITCH.

of this species is of a pure white, distinguishing it from the Baum, which has a yellow hue. It is a superior description of Fur, and is employed for women's dress. There is also the English Marten.

Maskel Lace.—An old lace, now obsolete.

Mastic Cloth.—A new variety of canvas, designed for embroidery purposes. It is woven in alternate stripes, from four to five inches in width; consisting of Basket woven Canvas, and a species of SATIN SHEETING. Mastic cloth measures 56 inches in width.

FIG. 604. MARKING IN SATIN STITCH.

To work the letters shown in Fig. 605: Trace the outline upon the material, and place the letter across a corner and not straight upon the article. RUN the outlines round with fine Embroidery cotton, and work the dark centres in RAISED SATIN STITCH, HERRINGBONING a light thread over the Satin stitch when complete. Work all the dots in POINT DE POIS, and the flower spray, the leaves, and flower petals in Satin Stitch, the centre of each flower as an EYELETHOLE, and the stems in OVERCAST.

Mat.—A lace maker's term for the close part of a design. In Pillow Laces this is worked in CLOTH STITCH, in Needle made laces with close and even rows of BUTTONHOLE.

Mat Braid.—A thick worsted Braid, woven after the manner of plaiting, of from half an inch to three inches in width. It is to be had in other colours besides black, and is employed as a trimming for coats, dresses, outdoor cloaks, &c.

FIG. 605. MARKING IN EMBROIDERY.

Marking Cotton.—An ingrain coloured sewing cotton, to be had in Turkey-red and blue, and sold in small balls and reels; the numbers running from 40 to 120, by tens.

Marten Fur.—This animal is of the Weasel tribe. There are two kinds of Marten, the Baum, or Pine Marten (*Mustela abietum*), and the Stone Marten (*Mustela saxorum*). This animal is a native of most European countries, and found in mountainous districts, while the manufactured skin is sometimes known as the French Sable. The Fur is of a dark brown at the extremity of the hair, while nearest the skin it is of a bluish white. The throat

Matelassé.—A French term applied to a silk or woollen textile, to denote the peculiar style of its manufacture. Such materials have a raised figured or flowered design on the surface, having a quilted or wadded appearance. This is indicated by the adaptation of the past participle of the verb *Matelasser*, to quilt or wad. Matelassé silk is employed for dresses and mantles, very fine descriptions having been recently produced. Those of wool are employed for a cheaper class of mantles and jackets, but not for dresses. Those of silk are made in white and in colours, and are much used for opera cloaks, as well as real hand-quilted silk and satin.

Mechlin Embroidery.—A term applied to Mechlin Lace, as the thread that was inserted round the outlines of that lace gave it somewhat the look of Embroidery.

Mechlin Grounds.—These are of two kinds, the Circular and the Hexagonal, but both are known as the "Vrai Réseau" by laceworkers, and used in Brussels and other laces as well as in Mechlin. The manner of making these grounds is shown in Figs. 606 and 607, in which they are purposely enlarged, to render them more easily understood.

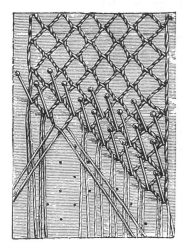

FIG. 606. MECHLIN GROUND—CIRCULAR MESH.

To work the *Circular Mesh* shown in Fig. 606: For each twist two BOBBINS are required, so commence by

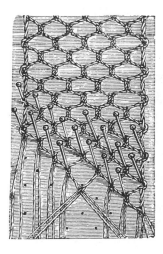

FIG. 607. MECHLIN GROUND—HEXAGONAL MESH.

hanging on four Bobbins at each Pinhole at the top of the pattern; take the two Bobbins at the outside of the left hand Pinhole, twist these three times, and pin them down straight so as to form the edge of the insertion; twist the other two three times, and pin them down in the Pinhole to the right; take up the next four Bobbins, divide them, twist two three times, and pin them down with the pin last stuck, twist the other two in the same way and put up a fresh pin to the right of them; repeat

with the four Bobbins until the first line is formed across the lace. In working the next line, twist and pin down the Bobbins as before, but take one of the Bobbins from one twist and one from the other to twist together, instead of using the same pair together always; the way to do this is shown in the illustration, as is also the line across the lace in which the meshes are made.

To work the *Hexagonal Mesh*, as shown in Fig. 607. This is both a plaited and a twisted ground: Put up two pairs of BOBBINS (four) at each Pinhole at the top of the lace, and work the two side Bobbins as before mentioned to form the outside edge, and twist the others down to the first row of Pinholes, as in Circular Mesh. Then with the four Bobbins work CLOTH STITCH twice or three times backwards and forwards without putting in pins, and forming a close plait. Work the whole row, and then divide the Bobbins that have been plaited together, putting up a pin between each pair; twist each pair twice, the right hand pair to the right, the left hand pair to the left, then take a pair of Bobbins from each side of the mesh and form a plait as before with Cloth Stitch. Work the ground entirely in this way, twisting the threads to form the sides, and plaiting them in Cloth Stitch where the pins are stuck. The manner of working the meshes across the lace is shown in the illustration.

Mechlin Lace.—Before the middle of the seventeenth century all Flemish Pillow Laces were indifferently classed as Mechlin or Malins Laces, and it is only by distinguishing the fabrics made at Antwerp, Mechlin, Lierre, and Turnhout by the flat shiny thread that surrounds their outlines that we know these old Mechlin Laces from the productions of Ypres, Bruges, Dunkirk, and Courtrai. These old Mechlin Laces are shown in Fig. 608, and generally have no grounds, and are frequently called Broderie de Malins by old writers, or "lace without ground." Mechlin Lace was worn by Anne of Austria, but the period of its greatest popularity was during the eighteenth century; it was then the only Lace used for ruffles and cravat ends, and for all purposes except full dress occasions. It was the favourite Lace of Queen Charlotte and Princess Amelia, and was exceedingly popular in England until superseded by Spanish Blondes. The Lace is made in one piece upon the Pillow, the ground being formed with the pattern, and, as both are made of the very finest thread, and require much skill to execute, the fabric is extremely costly. It is an extremely delicate lace and very transparent, and retains its original feature of a shiny plait thread surrounding the outlines of the sprigs and dots that form the design. The stitches are chiefly Cloth Stitch, but occasionally some of the light open Fillings are introduced. Mechlin Lace is always made with a Réseau ground, either of circular or hexagonal-shaped meshes, the old Malines à Bride occasionally met with being productions of neighbouring towns, and not true Mechlin.

Fig. 609, on the following page, is a modern Mechlin Lace design, showing the traced parchment pattern upon which it is worked. To work: Secure the pattern to the Pillow in the ordinary manner, and hang on sixty BOBBINS filled with thread (No. 250), and six filled with double thread (No 60). Use these last to form the plait outlines to the flowers. Work the ground as the Circular Mechlin Ground, the pattern in CLOTH STITCH. Pin the outline plait threads round the outside of the design, and secure them by working over them the threads that form the ground.

Mechlin Lace Wheel.—Used in ancient Needle Point and in Modern Point, and formed with a number of Bars

design, such as pomegranates and their leaves and flowers, passion flowers with their fruit, &c. For Russian canvas: This material is sold, arranged for borderings, with a design already woven into it of a colour contrasting with the ground, therefore it will be sufficient to work over that as a pattern. To work the flowers: Fill them in with shaded floss silk in SATIN STITCH, make FRENCH KNOTS with purse silk for their centres, and secure round them

FIG. 603. MECHLIN LACE—OLD.

crossing each other, with a circle or wheel ornamented with Picots in the centre of the space. To work: Work on a single thread in BUTTONHOLE STITCH a number of Horizontal BARS at equal distances apart. Work the same Bars perpendicularly, but after having worked five or six Buttonhole Stitches past where the horizontal and perpendicular lines meet, commence to form a small circle or wheel in the centre; work half a quarter of the circle in Buttonhole, make a small loop with a pin, and into this three Buttonhole Stitches; then proceed as at the beginning of the circle, and work each quarter the same

as an outline a thread of purse silk, as in COUCHING. For the fruit, Couch down in BASKET STITCH or with plain laid threads, the gold thread to fill in their centres, and secure purse silk round them as an outline. For the leaves and stems, work in Embroidery silks of various shades in CREWEL STITCH, and edge them with a gold cord. Pieces of silk velvet can be introduced into this Embroidery, and APPLIQUÉ on to the ground instead of the elaborate stitches, and the ground can be worked over in TENT STITCH, or left plain, according to the fancy of the worker.

FIG. 609. MECHLIN LACE—MODERN.

as the first one. The loop or Picot is left out in some patterns.

Mediæval Embroidery.—This is a modern Embroidery worked in the same stitches as are used in Church Embroidery, and with Floss and Purse silks and Gold thread, but with less elaborate patterns and upon French or Russian canvas, with the material left exposed as a ground. To work, for French canvas: Select a grey or écru coloured canvas, and trace upon it a conventional flower and fruit

Mediæval Guipure.—A name given to the Knotted Laces now known as MACRAMÉ.

Melton Cloth.—A stout make of cloth suitable for men's wear, which is "pared," but neither pressed nor "finished." It is called after the name of the original manufacturer.

Mending Cottons.—These cottons may be had both white and unbleached, in small skeins of four, six, or eight to the ounce; in bundles of 10lb. or 5lb., or wound upon reels and cards. The numbers run from 8 to 40. Mending cottons may be had in a variety of colours.

Mendings.—These yarns are composed of a mixture of cotton and wool, and designed for the darning of Merino stockings. They are produced in a variety of colours, and medleys of colours, and are sold on small cards or reels.

Menin Lace.—This is a Valenciennes Lace. The variety made at Menin is considered both cheap and good. *See* VALENCIENNES.

Meraline Rayé.—An all-wool material, designed for women's dress for spring and summer wear. It is of about the thickness and weight of cashmere, is 42 inches in width, has a right side with an *armure* design and narrow stripe, and will bear washing.

Mercery.—A term denoting silk merchandise, the vendors of which latter are called Mercers. In former times a dealer in small wares was described as a "Mercer."

Merino.—A thin, woollen, twilled cloth, made of the wool of the Spanish Merino sheep, and employed for ladies' dresses, and for woven underclothing for both sexes. Merino is sometimes a mixture of silk and wool. French Merinos are of superior make and wool, are equally good on both sides, and may be obtained in all colours. This description of cloth was first made in England early in the present century. The seat of the manufacture is at Bradford, Yorkshire, socks and vests of white and grey Merino being chiefly produced in Leicestershire. The stuffs made in Saxony and at Rheims are superior to ours.

Mermaids Lace.—A name sometimes given to fine Venetian Points, from the legend of a lacemaker having copied the seaweed known as Mermaid when making one of the patterns in Venetian Point.

Merveilleux Satin.—A very thick and superior description of Satin. *See* SATIN.

Meshes.—A term used in Netting to denote the completed loops, and in Pillow Lace making, the threads that form a net pattern ground. Also, implements made of ivory, bone, or boxwood, and employed in Embroidery and Netting, are known as Meshes. Those for Raised work in Embroidery vary in width from $\frac{1}{16}$ inch to 2 or 3 inches and upwards. They are to be had with a groove on one side, as a guide for the scissors when cutting the loops. They are employed for the regulation of the looped stitches, and for the formation of the Knots in Netting. There is also a Cutting Mesh, used for highly finished kinds of Raised Work.

Metallic Embroidery.—An ornamental work suitable for cushions, footstools, and table borders. The materials used are velvet for the foundation, stiff gold, silver or bronze gauze, for the design, tulle to cover the gold gauze, and coloured silks and gold cord to embroider the pattern. To work: Stretch the velvet in the EMBROIDERY FRAME, cut out the design in gold gauze, and OVERCAST this to the velvet, SEW tulle upon the gauze, use that to count the stitches, and make ornamental fillings, by RUN LINES, HERRINGBONE, CROSS STITCH, &c., carried down through tulle, gauze and velvet; cut away the tulle beyond the gauze pattern, and COUCH, as outline lines, a line of gold,

and a line of coloured cord, round every part of the pattern.

Métre.—The French name of a measure of length employed in commerce in France. It is equal to 1¼ English yards.

Mexican Embroidery.—This is a variety of Embroidery suitable for ornamenting washing materials, such as linens, muslins, and cambrics. It is worked with ingrain silks or cottons, or Pyrenean wools, is easily and quickly executed, and will stand a good deal of rough usage. It is used for children's dresses and undercloth-

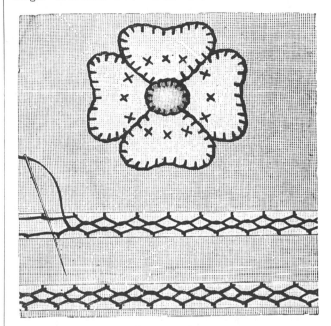

FIG. 610. MEXICAN EMBROIDERY.

ing, corners to d'oyleys, and borders for towels and tablecloths. To work as shown in Fig. 610: Trace the outline upon a cambric material with a very faint line, and place under all the parts to be embroidered a lining cut out of the same material, which simply TACK down. Then outline the design with a line of BUTTONHOLE

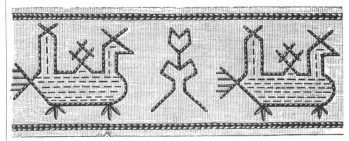

FIG. 611. MEXICAN EMBROIDERY.

STITCHES, and work in the lining with every stitch. Use bright coloured silks or Pyrenean wool for the Buttonhole. Work POINT DE CROIX to fill up the outline design, and fill in the centre of the pattern with a thick, close round of Buttonhole. Finish the design by working over the two bottom rows. These are intended for tucks, and are made by folding the material, and tacking the lining between the folds. The stitch ornamenting the tucks need not be traced; it is made thus: Work a line of loops, at even distances, along the top of the tuck, and then a line along the bottom, taking care that the stitches in each line are between, and not opposite, each other. Then take a fresh thread, and with it draw the two lines together down the centre, and the stitch will be complete. Finish the work by cutting away the lining round the outline of the flower.

Fig. 611 represents Mexican Embroidery with a Raised instead of a Buttonhole outline, used for small figures, grotesque animals, and geometrical designs. To work: Trace the outline upon a thick material, such as well-woven linen or German canvas, which will not require lining, then cover it with a coloured cord. OVERCAST this cord down to the material with coloured cotton of the same tint, and, to finish, fill in the centres of the design with a number of RUN lines. Work the border inclosing the pattern with a line of CHAIN STITCH.

Mezzo Punto.—The Italian name for BEGGARS' LACE and LACET.

Mignardise Crochet.—*See* CROCHET.

Mignonette Lace.—One of the first Pillow Laces made, and a flourishing manufacture during the sixteenth seventeenth, and eighteenth centuries. The lace was light and fine, and often known as Point de Tulle, from the fine texture and beauty of its ground. It was made of Lille thread, and always of narrow widths. The chief places of its manufacture were Lille, Normandy, Paris, and Switzerland. It is mentioned in the celebrated poem known as " La Révolte des Passemens."

Mignonette Netting.—*See* NETTING.

Milanese Lace.—This is made in the Philippine Isles, with Manilla grass. The work is a combination of Drawn Work and open Embroidery, and has not much the appearance of lace. A specimen of it can be seen in the South Kensington collection.

Milan Point.—Lace was made at Milan as early as 1493, and in several varieties. The earliest kinds were the gold and silver thread laces, and the Reticellas; to these succeeded the Milan Points, which were fine laces similar to the Spanish and Venetian Points. The lace made at the present time by the peasantry is Torchon.

Mille-rayé.—A variety of Percale, so named as being descriptive of the pattern, which consists of minute threadlike stripes, alternately black and white. The width of this light printed cotton cloth is 32 inches; it is a washing material, and is suitable for children's frocks, pinafores, &c.

Millinery.—A term denoting the composition of any description of head-dress, whether bonnet, cap, veil, or other decorative or useful head covering. These articles, notably the bonnet and cap, are generally made up with a foundation of a stiff character, such as Buckram, Straw and Ribbon wire; but some consist entirely of lace, ribbons, flowers, feathers, silk, velvet, fur, or a mixture of two or three of these materials. Good taste, an eye for colour, and a light hand, are essential characteristics of a successful milliner. In former times, Millinery was a term

of much wider scope than at present, as the worker had to make up the foundations, or bonnet shapes, on which to arrange the materials employed, as well as to work in straw, and produce both Beaver and Felt Bonnets and Hats. In Paris, this additional branch of Millinery is still carried on in those great houses where fashions in this department are originated. Old-fashioned bonnets used to consist of three parts—the front, or shape; the back, or crown; and the curtain at the back. At present the whole is usually comprised in one, or else in two parts—the crown, and, possibly, a narrow brim attached to the foundation, merely sufficient to admit of some forms of trimming by which that brim is concealed.

When a bonnet is formed of two parts—the Front and the Crown—the method of making it is as follows: Cut a paper pattern, and lay it on the Willow, or Buckram, cutting it by the outline supplied: SEW wired chip round the outer edge of the Front, the wire being inclosed between it and the Front; and then BIND all with a strip of soft silk or muslin, cut on the bias, to cover all unevennesses. Proceed to wire the inside of the Front next to the head—the chip inside, the wire outside, and the Willow foundation between them. The Willow will project beyond the chip and wire, and must then be snipped at regular intervals, to make it expand at the edge, and turned up to fit better to the head, or Crown, which will afterwards be attached to it. Lay a piece of thin muslin smoothly over the Willow Front, upon which place the silk or satin material of the Bonnet, so as to lie the straight way of the web, and pin it on carefully, that it may not be drawn on the bias. Then TACK down the silk on the inside to the chip; in the same way line the Front, finishing the edge by SLIP STITCHING, or else with a plain binding or a cord edge.

The Crown of the Bonnet must be made next, either plain or full. Cut it out of the Willow, or Buckram, from a paper pattern, and join the extreme ends, so as to fit the Front made for it. The upper edge (if a plain Crown) must be stiffened with a wire chip. Crowns with plain round tops may be procured ready-made from a manufacturer. Cover the top with a flat piece of wadding or muslin, then lay the silk covering over it, and Tack it down to the sides. Then cover the sides, and take care so to place the join as that it shall be concealed under some trimming; otherwise, finish it with a Cord, and let the joining at the top, as well as of the side, be finished precisely at the edge of the Front.

The next business is to sew the Crown and Front together, which constitutes one of the chief arts of the trade, all depending on the degree of slant given—either forwards or backwards—to the Crown.

Full or fancy Crowns require to be made on a "dummy," having been first cut out of Buckram to a pattern, and then plaited upon the "dummy" head.

The old-fashioned Drawn Bonnets are no longer seen, excepting for children's wear, although the backs of fancy ones are sometimes Gauged. The Front, when drawn, was made of a length of material, cut the straight way, the selvedge going round the outer rim of the Front. Then a wide Hem was made, in which from three to five runnings were made, to form casings for the wires or canes to be introduced into them; a stiff wire was run into the outermost, the better to maintain the shape desired. Then the wires, canes, or whalebones, were secured at one end, the Gatherings evenly drawn, and then the other ends of the stiffeners were sewn down. The Crown was drawn in the same way, and the circular form obtained, by fixing it to a wired chip. We give these details on the chance of a return to such a style.

To make any description of light, transparent, summer Bonnet, such as Crape, Gauze, Muslin, or Net, the following rules may suffice: Employ a foundation of Paris net (this material is thin and brittle, and needs careful handling), sew a narrow, white, wired chip round the edge of the Front; lay on the transparent covering (cut on the straight), TACK it in position, and BIND the edge with satin, as likewise the chips and joinings of the Crown. These may be equally well concealed by folds of satin instead of bindings.

Bonnets worn in mourning must be made of Crape, or of silk trimmed with it. If of Crape only, cover the Willow foundation with thin black silk, to conceal it, as black Willow is not to be recommended, on account of its brittleness. Make a broad HEM on the Crape bow and strings; the double Hem being about an inch in width.

Caps of Lace must be made on a foundation of stiff, coarse muslin, or of wired chip; but all depends on its shape and size, and the fashion changes so much and so frequently in such articles of dress, that it should be studied in the show rooms and windows of the best houses in the trade, at the opening of each season, as no rules given at the present time might hold good for a year hence in reference to Millinery.

Miltons.—Hard thick cloths, produced in scarlet, blue, and brown, and originally introduced for use in hunting.

Miniver (otherwise *Minever*, or, according to the old spelling, *Mineveer* and *Minevair*).—The name is derived from *menu vair*, the latter word denoting the variety shown by this fur in its colouring. It was a valuable fur, and was much worn as linings to robes and hoods by nobles in the Middle Ages. It was composed of the skin of a species of Squirrel of the genus *Sciurus*, supposed to have been a native of Hungary, grey on the back, and white underneath and on the neck. The extreme end of the tail was black, and it was sewn on the white portion of the fur at equal distances apart, so as to produce small spots all over it. In heraldry this Fur is called *vair*, being one of the eight furs used.

Mink (*Mustela vison*).—This fur resembles Sable in colour, though considerably shorter and more glossy, as well as durable. It is exported in large quantities by the Hudson's Bay Company, and also from the United States, and is employed for tippets, muffs, and cuffs.

Mirecourt Lace.—The lace made at Mirecourt is a description of Lille Lace, but it is only within the last twenty years that it has been in any way better than other manufactures of Lille Lace; since that period it has steadily improved both in workmanship and design. The lace is made upon the Pillow in detached sprigs, and Appliqué upon a ground of fine machine net.

Mitorse Silk.—This is a half-twisted silk, employed for various descriptions of needlework. If skilfully handled, it proves superior to the floss silks, being less liable to become rough and fluffy after a little wear. Thus, for the embroidery of any article of dress it is the best for the purpose, and is very suitable for the working of slippers, stools, &c., in conjunction with wool. Mitorse resembles the silk employed by the Chinese for their double Embroidery.

Mitre.—A word sometimes used in old instruction books upon Stocking Knitting, instead of Gusset, when describing the part of a stocking that is worked after the heel and instep are made. To work: Divide the stitches on to three needles, putting double the amount and four extra on to the needle carrying the front stitches than on the two side needles. KNIT two stitches together upon each side where the pieces forming heel and instep meet, and TAKE IN, in this manner, every third round eight times.

Mitreing.—A term used by Stocking Knitters to denote a gusset. *See* KNITTING, *Socks and Stockings.*

It is also a term used in dressmaking, and is borrowed from architecture, in which it denotes the form given by following the line drawn by two sides of a square, producing an angle of 45 degrees, for the "striking" of which masons employ what is called "a mitre square." The border produced by cutting according to this pattern is employed for flounces and fillings in dress materials and underlinen.

Mittens.—Gloves without fingers, having either an opening for the thumb, or else a partial sheath for it, the rest of the glove ending with the palm of the hand. They are made for Arctic regions with a complete covering for thumb and fingers, but the latter have no separate sheaths, with which the thumbs are supplied. Mittens are to be had in kid leather, Beaver, Chamois, woven Stockingette cloth, also in silk, and knitted by hand. Some mittens in kid leather or woven silk extend up the arm to the elbow, when the sleeve of an evening dress is either short or very open.

Mixtures.—A term applied to any cloths of variegated colouring, such as Knickerbockers and Tweeds.

Mocassin Grass Embroidery.—*See* GRASS EMBROIDERY.

Modern Point Lace.—This lace is an imitation of the old Renaissance Lace, both Pillow and Needle made, and was first attempted about the year 1855. It has been brought to great perfection in France, where it is called Dentelle Renaissance, and it is also known in that country as Dentelle Irlandaise, from the beauty of Irish imitations of real lace.

The materials for this beautiful and useful lace are neither numerous nor expensive, and consist of a lace pattern, tracing cloth on which to copy the design, Toile Ciré, to give firmness to the lace while in progress, needles, linen braids, and linen thread. The braids, with which the outlines of all the designs, and the thick parts of the lace are made, are of various widths and thicknesses, and have sometimes an open edge resembling the pearled edge of Pillow Lace patterns, and at others a perfectly plain edge in imitation of the Tape Guipure Laces. They are sold in many varieties of design, or are made upon the Pillow; when made on the Pillow, the lace becomes a real, and not an imitation lace. The linen thread used is fine, and resembles the Mecklenburgh thread used in real lace; that known as Haythorne's is the thread most in use. The stitches known as Modern Point Stitches are all copies from the stitches used in making Point Lace, Spanish and Venetian Points, Rose Points, Hollie Points, and other Needle-made laces. They are all named and described under their own headings, as not exclusively belonging to this lace in particular. They are as follows: ANTWERP EDGE, ALENÇON BAR, ANGLETERRE BAR, BARCELONA STITCH, BRABANT EDGE, BRUXELLES EDGE, CADIZ, CORDOVA, DIAMOND, ENGLISH and ESCALIER LACE, FAN LACE, FLEURETTE STITCH, HENRIQUE LACE,

the thumb, without turning the braid over, and draw in the inner edge with an Overcast thread. Connect the braid in different parts where no stitches are worked with a BAR. To make a Bar: Pass a thread across the space three times, and BUTTONHOLE to the middle, then work a PICOT, and finish with a Buttonhole as before. Fill in the centre of the braid with POINT DE BRUXELLES STITCH.

To work Fig. 613: Trace the outline as before, tack the braid on, and OVERCAST the edges, make the BARS that connect the lace together, and fill in the thick parts with POINT DE BRUXELLES STITCH, POINT DE VENISE, SORRENTO LACE, POINT D'ESPAGNE, POINT DE BRA-BANÇON, ENGLISH WHEELS, and varieties of the same. Then work all round the braid forming the pattern, and at its outer edge, as a finish, with Point de Venise.

FIG. 612. MODERN POINT LACE.

MECHLIN LACE and WHEELS, OPEN ENGLISH LACE, POINT D'ALENÇON, POINT D'ANGLETERRE, POINT D'ANVERS, POINT DE FILLET, POINT DE FLANDRE, POINT DE REPRISE, POINT DE VALENCIENNES, POINT DE VENISE, POINT D'ESPAGNE, POINT DE GREQUE, POINT DE TURQUE, RAYLEIGH BARS, SORRENTO LACE, BARS, and WHEELS.

To work Modern Point as shown in Fig. 612: Draw the outline of the lace, and TACK the braid over it to the tracing cloth rather loosely, and without any stretching. Form the angles and curves, turn over the braid to prevent any lumpiness, and sew down each edge firmly, without taking the thread through to the tracing cloth. Then OVERCAST the braid round all its edges, and draw in the thread slightly at the inner edge where the corners or curves are formed. To make circles, form them first with

Modes.—A term used in Lacemaking to denote the open work FILLINGS between the thick parts of the design. It is also the French term to signify fashions in dress.

Mohair.—Fabrics are so called which are composed of the hair of the Angora goat, mixed with silk or cotton warps. These fabrics have a peculiar lustre, equal to that of silk, are remarkably regular in texture, and are both soft and fine. Mohair cloth is of very ancient origin, and was much worn in the Middle Ages. The yarn is sold in retail shops, and is chiefly spun and manufactured at Bradford and Norwich. The French purchase it in England for the purpose of lacemaking, and a species of Utrecht velvet is made of it at Coventry. There are many varieties of cloth made of Mohair, the dress materials being watered, striped, and checked.

The Angora goat, according to Mr. Hayes, secretary of

FIG. 613. MODERN POINT LACE.

the National Association of Wool Manufacturers, is the most valuable wool-bearing animal, not even excepting the Cashmere goat, which produces only two or three ounces of the *pushm* used for making Indian shawls. Mohair, the fleece of the Angora, is worth, on an average, 3s. a pound —more than double the price of the best Lincoln wool. It is used for making Utrecht velvets, or "furniture plush," the piles of imitation sealskin, the best carriage and lap robes, braids for binding, black dress goods, as before stated, laces, and for many other purposes, the number of which is only limited by the limited supply —the entire production of the world being only about 4,750,000lb. The English have obtained the highest success in spinning mohair, and it is owing to the stiffness of the fibre that it is rarely woven alone, either the warp or woof being usually of cotton, silk, or wool. A pure mohair fabric is considered nearly indestructible. The whitest variety of hair is imported from Smyrna and Constantinople, but quantities of an inferior description are sent out from other parts of Asia Minor. *See* ANGORA GOATS' HAIR.

Mohair, or Russian Braids.—These braids consist of two cords woven together. They are cut into short lengths, and sold by the gross pieces. The wider braids are in 36 yard lengths, four pieces to the gross, and the numbers run from 0 to 8. The various sizes may be had both in black and in colours.

Mohair Poplin Yarn.—A beautifully even yarn, having a fine lustre, produced for the manufacture of Poplin fabrics. The seat of manufacture of this particular description of yarn is near Bingley, in Yorkshire.

Moire Antique.—A description of silk of a superior quality. It is of double width, and of ordinary make, but stouter. To produce a "watered" effect, this silk is folded in such a manner as that, when heavily pressed, the air contained between the folds should not easily escape; and, when forced out, it drives the moisture employed for the watering before it, the pressure required to effect the purpose amounting to from 60 to 100 tons. Some inferior kinds of Moiré Antique are made having cotton backs. *See* SILKS.

Moleskin.—A description of Fustian, its peculiarity, as compared with others, consisting in the cutting short of the pile before the material is dyed. This material is very strong, and is, therefore, especially suited to the dress of labouring men.

Moleskin Fur.—The Mole, or Mould-warp, is a small insect-eating Mammal, belonging to the genera *Talpa*, *Scalops*, and *Condylura Cristata*. The Fur is exceedingly soft, thick, and fine in quality; and very warm for wear.

Momie Cloth.—This has a cotton warp and woollen weft, or else a silk warp and woollen weft, and has the appearance of very fine Crape. It is made 44 inches in width, and, being dyed black, is very suitable for mourning.

Monteiths.—A description of Cotton Handkerchiefs, which are dyed of one uniform colour, but have a pattern of white spots occurring at regular distances, produced by the discharge of the colour, effected by a particular process. These goods are known by the name of the manufacturers, at Glasgow. Cotton Bandanas are subjected to the same process. A large quantity of Handkerchiefs, dyed Turkey-red, are laid one on the other, and pressed under a perforated plate, when a liquid is poured through the openings, which discharges the colour at those places. This method is so rapid in its operation that, by the hands of four workmen only, 1600 pieces— representing 19,200 yards—of cotton may be thus figured with spots or other devices within a period of ten hours. *See* MALABARS.

Moorish Lace.—This lace is of very ancient origin, and is frequently called "Dentelle de Moresse" in old inventories when described by European writers, and under that name it figures in the poem known as the "Révolte des Passemens," published in 1661. The lace is really Drawn Work, and the art was probably taught to the Moors by the Italian or Greek peasants they captured and made slaves of. The lace is still made in Morocco, and forms an edging to the towels and dresses of the ladies in the harems.

Moreen.—A coarse and stout description of Tammie, only less stiffened, and watered or plain. It is employed for women's petticoats and for upholstery, chiefly for window curtains. There are some of very rich quality, resembling silk damask. The width runs from 26 inches to 27 inches.

Morees.—Manchester-made Muslins, much employed for the African export trade.

Morocco Leather.—This leather is known in France as *Maroquin*, and is made of goat skins tanned with sumach. There is an inferior sort, called Roan, made from sheep skins, which is much thinner, and neither so handsome nor so durable.

Mosaic Art Embroidery.—A modern name given to a species of Braiding combined with Embroidery stitches. To work: Trace a geometrical or conventional design upon black cloth, and stitch down on to all the outlines silk braids of various colours. Then take Embroidery silks matching the braids in tints, and fill in parts of the design with CREWEL and SATIN STITCH, and work over small leaves or flowers in the design in Satin Stitch and in shaded colours.

Mosaic Canvas.—The finest descriptions of canvas employed for Embroidery, whether of silk, thread, or cotton, have acquired the popular appellation of Mosaic.

Mosaic Woolwork.—This is a handwork made in imitation of woven goods and of Tapestry. The work is chiefly done in Yorkshire for trade purposes, and with large bold designs. To make: Prepare a large piece of paper, by ruling upon it a number of perfect squares; upon this draw the design to be executed in its full size, and colour it. Then, if the pattern is large, divide it into lengths ready for use, and lay it by the side of the worker. Have ready two steel bars, the length of the pattern, and fasten them so that they run parallel to each other, and are quite firm. Then take coarse Berlin wool of the shades matching the pattern, carefully match the colours on the pattern with it, tying two colours together where required on one line, and fasten it on to the bars. Stretch it tightly from one bar to another, and arrange it in the proper shades. Having stretched the wool, cover its surface with a strong solution of indiarubber, and cover a piece of stout canvas with the same mixture; lay the canvas upon the wool while both are wet, and press the two together; the wool and the canvas when once glued together will never come apart.

Moskowa Canvas.—This variety of canvas has the appearance of straw. It is woven in fancy patterns, and lines of gold and silver, black and blue thread being introduced in the groundwork. It is made for purposes of embroidery, but is sufficiently handsome to obviate the necessity of grounding.

Mosquito Net.—A coarse cotton net, employed for bed curtains in warm countries where Mosquitos abound. It is likewise employed for purposes of embroidery. It is made in double width.

Mossoul Embroidery.—This work is founded upon Eastern Embroidery, and is a pleasing variety to CREWEL WORK, as it possesses all the artistic attributes of that work. It is useful for table and mantel borders, for chair backs, toilet covers and towels, and is worked with either crewels or silks, upon linen and woollen materials. The patterns are the same as those so familiar to us in Persian and Turkish needlework, and consist of geometrical figures or much conventionalised flower and foliage designs. Any Eastern design can be used, as the distinctive feature of the work consists in its colouring and manner of filling in, not upon its pattern. The colours selected for the embroidery are all artistic, the greens shading to yellow, the reds to pink and yellow, and the browns to red and cinnamon; while magenta, scarlet, and bright blue are excluded. No shading is used, each isolated spray, leaf, or flower being filled in with one tint, and the variety of colour produced by blending together in harmony these various detached shades.

To work: Trace out upon the material a design, which select as much as possible of small detached pieces, forming conventionalised leaves and stems; fill in all these sprays with HERRINGBONE STITCH. Work the Herringbone Stitch so closely together that no part of the material shows between the stitches, and commence working across the part to be filled at its widest end, and work down to its narrowest, carrying the stitches across from side to side without a break. The stitch so worked will produce a plait down the centre of the part filled in, and this plait is the chief feature of the work. Fill in all the design with Herringbone Stitch, and then work round the outlines with ROPE STITCH. This stitch is really Crewel Stitch worked more closely together than usual. The colour used for all the outlines should be of one uniform tint, which should slightly contrast with the colours used in the design. Thus, if yellow-greens and brown-reds form the centres, dark peacock blue should be used for outlining them; or if the centres are formed of orange shades, green or russet brown tints should outline them. Finish off the embroidery with a bordering of DRAWN WORK, which work over with silks matching in tint those used in the design.

Motifs.—A French term, used to distinguish the pattern of a piece of Embroidery from the groundwork or material.

Mother-of-Pearl Work.—*See* NACRE WORK.

Mount Needlework.—*See* EMBROIDERY FRAME.

Mourning Stuffs.—These consist chiefly of Crape, Crape Cloth, Widows' Silk, Barathea, Paramatta, black Cashmere, Merino, Serge, Grenadine, Cotton, and any lustreless woollen stuffs, such as the new serge-like dress material called "Drap-Sanglier."

Mousseline de Laine.—A very fine light woollen cloth, of a muslin-like texture, introduced from France, and subsequently manufactured here, and at a much cheaper cost. An imitation of this fabric has been made, which is a union of cotton with the wool. Mousseline de Laine may be had for dress materials in every colour, with all kinds of designs printed on it, as well as plain; and it is frequently sold under some different name.

Mousseline de Soie.—A very delicate soft silk textile, of a make as open as that of muslin, and having a fringe. It is employed for women's neckerchiefs. It may also be had in the piece, which measures from 28 to 30 inches in width.

Mousseline de Soie Crépée.—A silk muslin, crimped after the manner of crape. At one time it was manufactured as a dress material and trimmings for the purposes of dressmaking and millinery. It measures about 28 inches in width, and is to be had in white and cream colour.

Muff.—A circular oblong covering for the hands, hollow in the middle, to admit both, and dating from the time of Louis XIV., in France, from whence it was introduced into this country. According to Fairholt, two examples are given in a piece of tapestry of that date, formerly in the possession of Crofton Croker, Esq., one being of yellow silk edged with black fur; the other of white fur, decorated with small black tails, probably ermine, and with a blue bow in front. The same author states that they used to be worn by gentlemen as well as women in the seventeenth century, and remained in fashion as an article of men's clothing for nearly a hundred years. In the eighteenth century they were covered with feathers, as many now are, and were also richly decorated with embroidery. They may be worn of every description of fur, or two strips of fur combined with one in the centre of velvet, and of grebe or other feathers. Cheap kinds are to be had of wool in Crochet Work. There are also varieties containing a pocket outside. The size changes with the current fashion.

Mule Twist.—Cotton thread, manufactured by the aid of steam engines, for the weaving of muslins, and the finest cotton goods, and which is rather softer than "water twist." It is so called because made by a machine called a "Mule-jenny," or Mill-jenny, *Mühle* being the German for a Mill, of which our word is a corruption.

Mull Muslin.—A very thin and soft variety of Muslin, employed for morning dresses, and for trimmings. It is undressed, whereas the Swiss Mull is dressed. It runs from 30 to 36 inches in width, the best varieties being of the latter dimensions. Mull Muslin is finer than NAIN-SOOK, is of a pure white colour, and has a perfectly soft finish.

Mummy Cloth.—An imitation of the ancient Egyptian make of flaxen cloth, which was employed for wrapping round mummies. It is now manufactured for purposes of embroidery; and the same make is also used for waist-coating. It is 30 inches in width.

Mungo (otherwise called **Shoddy**).— Wool obtained from disintegrated woollen cloths—old worn-out garments, or clippings left by tailors after cutting out. When thus reduced, cleaned, and prepared, Mungo, or Shoddy, is manufactured into cloth again.

Mushroo.—A costly satin cloth, manufactured in the Deccan, and sent for sale to Madras. It has a silk surface and a cotton back, and is decorated with loom-embroidered flowers in white silk. It is priced at about £2 for a piece of 5 yards, of about 30 inches in width, and weighing 1½lb. There are costlier examples, extensively flowered in gold, with stripes in silk. The productions from Hyderabad are remarkable for the brilliant tones and arrangements of the colours, which are composed in wavy stripes of rich yellow and gold, with pink and white Mushroos, and are superior to our English-made textiles of this description, as the fine kinds bear washing very well, an advantage which they possess equally over French satins. *See* INDIAN SILKS.

Muslin.—A thin, and more or less transparent, cotton textile, of Eastern origin, deriving its name from Mosul, or Moosul, a large town in Turkey in Asia. There are many varieties of Muslin, such as Mull Muslin; a dressed and stiffened variety, called Swiss Mull; another, Foundation Muslin, which is very open in texture, and made both in white and black, for the stiffening of dresses and bonnets; Buke (commonly corrupted into "Book") Muslin, which is sold in a plain, clear, soft, and unstiffened state, or hard and dressed—this kind is used for Tambour Embroidery. There are also Figured Muslins, wrought in the loom, of various widths. Cambric Muslin is an imitation of linen of that make; it is sold coloured for linings, glazed white and black, plain and twilled, figured, striped, and corded. Seerhand Muslin is a kind between Nainsook and Mull, and valued for dresses on account of its retaining its clearness after having been washed. Tamboured Muslins are chiefly made in Scotland. Muslinette is a thick description of Muslin. Leno is a clearer, thinner, and softer material than the Buke, slight and gauze-like in quality, and much employed for window curtains; the threads of the warp and woof differ in size, and the mate-rial cannot be as easily starched as other kinds of muslins. There are also Cord and Fancy Checks, having stripes and cords crossing each other, forming squares, thick threads being introduced into the warp or weft. Nainsook is a thick sort of jacconet, made plain in stripes, the latter running the same way as the warp. India Muslins were introduced into this country about the year 1670, and the manufacture of Muslin was commenced at Paisley in 1700. It is now extensively made at Bolton and Glasgow. At Zurich and St. Gall their manufacture preceded ours, and there are now many factories for it in Germany.

Muslin Appliqué.—*See* APPLIQUÉ UPON NET.

Muslin Embroidery.—*See* EMBROIDERY ON MUSLIN.

Muslinette.—A thick variety of muslin, resembling a Brilliant; employed for infants' clothing, and for dressing gowns. It measures from 30 inches to 36 inches in width.

Muslin Grounds.—This is a description of GINGHAM.

Muslin Trimmings.—These consist of Edgings, Insertions, Scallops, and Flouncings of variegated needle-work. They are made in short lengths, and in pieces of from 24 yards to 36 yards.

Musquash, or Musk Rat (*Tiber zibethicus*).—The fur of this animal resembles that of the Beaver, and used to be employed for hats and bonnets. It is dyed for articles of dress, and other use, and is inexpensive. These animals are found in great numbers in America, inhabiting swamps and rivers. They have a peculiar odour, like that of musk. The fur is used by hat manufacturers, and is dyed by furriers for a variety of articles, such as muffs and boas. It is much used as an imitation Seal skin.

Mysore Silks.—These are fine, soft, undressed silk stuffs, both plain and printed, dyed and undyed. They may be had in all colours, of an Indian character, the designs being chiefly a close running all-over floral ones, although some printed in gold or in silver are a little bolder in pattern, and are printed in black, and in the natural colour of the silk. They all measure 34 inches in width, and are sold at 35s. per piece of about 7 yards. The Mysore silks are of the class termed "cultivated."

N.

Nacre.—The French word for mother-o'-pearl, employed in a certain kind of embroidery.

Nacre Work.—A peculiar kind of work, and one that is little practised in the present day. It was at one time used for embroidering borders to ecclesiastical vestments, and consisted in cutting out pieces of mother-of-pearl, and sewing them on to velvet or silk. To work: Trace out a flower and leaf design upon velvet, and back and frame this in an EMBROIDERY FRAME. Prepare a quantity of small pieces of mother-of-pearl cut into petal and leaf shapes, and bore holes in these. Attach these to the pattern with silk or gold thread, and lay them on flat, but arrange them to imitate the natural curves and lines of the objects they are intended to represent. Form the centres of the flower stems and sprays that are too small to lay the mother-of-pearl over with gold thread, and COUCH this to the velvet.

Napore Silks.—These are all soft, slight, and un-dressed, and are to be had in every variety of essentially Indian colours. The pieces vary but little from 7 yards in quantity, and run about 37 inches in width. They belong to that class of Indian silk called the "cultivated."

Nail.—A measure of length employed for textiles, describing a length of 2¼ inches; four nails make 1 quarter, and four quarters 1 yard.

Nainsook.—A description of Muslin made both plain and striped, the stripe running the way of the warp. It is a kind of Jacconet, or Bengal Muslin. *See* MUSLIN.

Nankeen.—A Chinese cotton cloth, of a natural buff colour, deriving its name from the city of Nankin, where it is chiefly manufactured. An imitation is made in this country, at Manchester and elsewhere; but this, though more even in texture, and equally fine in colour, is found to be inferior when washed, as the colour is obtained by dyeing; whereas the original Chinese Nankeen is made of the natural colour of the raw cotton grown in China, which is buff; in other countries white is common. The broad pieces, called the "Company's Nankeen," are of a superior quality to the narrow ones. Varieties of Nankeen, dyed blue, white, and pink, have been made, but are not often to be seen. On the banks of the Ganges, and in the Southern States of America, a Nankeen-coloured cotton grows, something peculiar in the soil being supposed to produce the buff hue by which it is distinguished. Nankeen was formerly much employed for both men's and women's dress, but is now almost limited to that of children.

Nap.—The pile, woolly substance, or knots which are produced, in the process of weaving, on the surface of certain textiles. All cloths have an uneven roughness unless they are shorn, but all have not a pile, which is expressly made. Women employed for this purpose are called Nopsters.

Napery.—A term employed to designate house linen, but more especially applied to table linen; the French term is *Nappe*, a tablecloth. Hollinshed, in his "Description of England" (1577), says:

> Our innes are also verie well furnished with Naperie, bedding, and tapisserie, especiallie with naperie.

Narrow Cloths.—These cloths are so designated in contradistinction to those known as Broad Cloths. Narrow Cloths are made in both single and double milled Cassimere, and run from 27 inches to 29 inches in width; also in double and treble milled Doeskins, measuring the same number of inches wide as the Cassimere.

Narrowing.—In Crochet, Knitting, and Netting, the size of an article being worked can be Decreased by working two or more of the stitches or loops as one. *See* DECREASE.

Natté Silk.—A French material, having a check pattern, overlaid by a plait, which in the superior qualities is coarse, and in the inferior fine. The name is derived from the French *Natter*, to plait or twist.

Needle.—A pointed instrument, sharp at one end, and perforated at the blunt extremity to receive the thread which it is designed to draw through any description of textile, whether in Plain Sewing or Embroidery. Mention of this implement, and of sewing, may be found in the *Sañhita* of the *Rig Veda* (Wilson's "Rig Veda," II., p. 288; IV., p. 60), and the Vedic word, "*s' úchi*," is identical with that now used to indicate a Needle (*see* "Indo-Aryans," by Rájendralála Mitra, LL.D. and C.I.E.). This notice of Needles dates back as far as six centuries before Christ— "Clothes, and the like, wrought with a Needle, last a

long time" ("Rig Veda," II., 288). In ancient times Needles were made of wood, bone, ivory, bronze, and iron, and were very coarse in quality and dimensions. Of these there are a variety of examples in our museums, some dating back to pre-historic times. Some Needles found in Herculaneum and Pompeii were of bronze. The Needles of modern times appear to have had their origin in Spain, and were thence introduced into this country in the reign of Queen Elizabeth. England was famous for the work of the Needle previous to the introduction or the manufacture of the appliance such as it now is, and the embroideries accomplished, and still preserved, compare well with modern art under better auspices. Rough as Needles were in the days of Edgitha wife of Edward the Confessor, she was pronounced by her historian to be "perfectly mistress of the Needle;" and English work was held in esteem above all other in Europe, even in her day. In the reign of Mary I., steel wire Needles were first made in England, and then by a Spanish negro, who kept his secret during his lifetime; they were afterwards made in the reign of Elizabeth, by one Elias Krause, a German. The great secret was lost after his death, and recovered again about a hundred years after. In the year 1656, Cromwell incorporated the Company of Needlemakers. Needles of English manufacture are now regarded as the best in the world, those of Germany coming next. The chief seat of our manufacture is at Redditch, Worcestershire. Needles pass through 126 hands before they are ready for sale.

Those in general use for hand work are as follows: Darners, Straws, Sharps, Long-eyed Sharps, Ground-downs, Betweens, Blunts, Tapestry, Whitechapel, Chenille, Rug, and Harness. Darners vary much in length and thickness, to suit the quality of the material to be repaired. The eye is long, and is easily threaded by turning back the loose ends of the yarn employed, and retaining them between the finger and thumb, passing them, flatly looped, through the long eye. Straws are used by milliners, for straw bonnets and braids. Long-eyed Sharps are employed for Embroidery in silk and wool, the numbers running from 1 to 10. Another variety of these is the Whitechapel, which are preferable for that purpose to the Long-eyed Sharps. Sharps are in general use for personal and household plain sewing; they may be had in a great variety of sizes, distinguished by numbers, and are sold in papers, either of mixed sizes, or each paper containing one size only. Some of them are gold-eyed, and are considered to be of superior quality, and warranted not to cut the thread. Ground-downs are shorter than the ordinary Sharps. Betweens are shorter than Ground-downs, and Blunts than Betweens. Blunts are thick and strong, and are employed by staymakers, tailors, glovers, shoe-binders, and others who work in leather; the sizes run from 1 to 15. Tapestry Needles are blunt at the point, and have a long and rather oval eye; the numbers in common use run from 14 to 25, but they may be had in other sizes. For use in hot and tropical climates they may be had in gold or silver. Rug Needles are thick, with large eyes and blunt points. Chenille Needles differ from the Tapestry only in having a sharp point, as they are employed for working on canvas, cloth, or silk. Harness Needles are used by Saddlers.

To this list others may be added, such as Machine Needles, made for the especial use of the sewing machines of various makers, such as those respectively of Howe, Grover and Baker, Wheeler and Wilson, Willcox and Gibbs, Thomas, Weir, the Wanzer, the Singer, &c. Besides these, Netting, Knitting, and Crochet Needles should be included in the list. The Knitting Needle is sometimes called a Pin.

Needle Etching.—Synonymous with ETCHING EMBROIDERY.

Needle Point.—A title given indifferently to all kinds of real lace worked with a Needle, and not with Bobbins.

Needle-threader.—A small appliance, made for the use of persons of imperfect sight. It is usually made of ivory. The top portion above the handle is flat, on which a small metal plate is fixed, through which a hole is pierced; a corresponding hole being in the ivory, of larger size, the needle is passed through it, the eye fitting exactly over that in the plate, so that the thread passes through the three holes at once. Other kinds may be had; such, for

FIG. 614. NEEDLE-THREADER.

instance, as that illustrated at Fig. 614. A is the hole through which the thread is to be passed, and so through the eye of the Needle, which is to be placed with the eye exactly even with it; B is the pointed end of the Needle. The central hole is cup-shaped, sloping towards the middle, and so directing the thread into the small opening, which would be unseen to failing sight.

Needlework.—A generic and comprehensive term, including every species of work, whether plain or decorative, that can be executed by means of the Needle, and of whatever description the Needle may be. From the most remote ages the employment of the Needle has formed a source of recreation, of remunerative work, and no less of economy, the useful occupation of time and charity, amongst all classes of women, in all parts of the world.

The rise and progress of the ornamental part of the art, and the different modifications it underwent, down to the time of its final decay, have already been described in the article upon Embroidery; it, therefore, now only remains to enumerate some of the most celebrated Embroiderers and their productions, which have become matters of history. The high honour bestowed upon Needlework in ancient days, when it was considered one of the chief spoils of the conqueror, and a fitting gift to be presented to kings, is fully shown by its frequent mention by the sacred writers, and by Homer, Pliny, Herodotus, and others. The corselet presented by Amasis to Minerva, the spoils of Sisera, the curtains of the Tabernacle, the Peplus of Minerva at Athens, the Needlework sails of Cleopatra's vessels, the web of Penelope, and the works of Helen and Andromache, by the very fact that they were considered worthy of record by such writers, prove how much they were valued. Coming nearer to our times, we

find Needlework of the most beautiful description worked in England, and presented to Pope Adrian IV.; while the Banner of Strasbourg, the Stole of St. Cuthbert, the Glastonbury Cope, the Syon Cope, and many other ecclesiastical garments still in existence (with the exception of the Strasbourg Banner, burnt in 1870), all testify to the labour and art spent in their manufacture. The well-known Bayeux Tapestry is another of these historical pieces, and though its execution does not allow of its ranking with the more elaborate articles first mentioned, it is a remarkable production, both for its antiquity and the number of figures of great size that it contains. Following upon these ancient specimens come the hand-made tapestries, worked during the Middle Ages, as wall hangings, and the numerous altar-cloths and church vestments that embellished the gorgeous ritual of the Romish Church, of which many fragments remain in museums and private collections, and which, but for the mistaken zeal of the Reformers, who expended upon these inanimate objects some of their religious fervour, would be still as perfect as when first made.

The Anglo-Saxon ladies were celebrated, not only in their own country, but on the Continent, for their skill in Needlework, particularly in the Opus Anglicanum, or Opus Anglicum—a stitch in Embroidery that they invented. The four sisters of Athelstan, daughters of Edward the Elder, and Edgitha the Queen of Edward the Confessor, were particularly famed. After them came Matilda, the wife of William the Conqueror, and Adelais, the wife of Henry the First; but the most famous of all English queens is Katherine of Aragon, who came from a land celebrated for its Embroideries and Lace, and who enlivened the many sad hours of her life by instructing her maids of honour, and the poor people living near her palace, in the art of making Lace and Embroidery. We are told by Taylor, the Water Poet, who wrote a poem upon the " Needle's Excellency," in reference to this queen—

> That her days did pass
> In working with the needle curiously.

Her daughter Mary also excelled with her needle, and her works are mentioned by the same poet, who also devotes a couplet to the praise of the Embroidery produced by Queen Elizabeth; but other chroniclers are more inclined to consider that the shirt presented by this Queen to her brother, upon his sixth birthday, worked by herself, was almost her only achievement. Mary II. was the next queen who paid attention to Embroidery, and the beautiful work executed under her supervision still remains at Hampton Court. Queen Charlotte devoted much time to Needlework, frequently embroidering the Court dresses of her daughters, and constantly bestowing articles knitted by herself upon the poor; and at Oatlands, some of the woolwork executed by the Duchess of York is still preserved. Although not belonging to England, we cannot omit to mention two celebrated Embroiderers, whose works are to be found in almost every collection—Mary Queen of Scots, and Marie Antoinette, the wife of Louis XVI. To both these ill-fated ladies the Needle afforded a solace, both before and during their misfortunes, as it has done throughout all ages to women who, though of not so exalted a rank, have yet had as many sorrows. And upon both these queens' tombstones could have been written the epitaph that is inscribed upon a tablet in the Cloisters of Westminster Abbey : "She was excellent with her needle."

Net.—This was at one time made by ladies with the needle, as a foundation to Lace; it was then called Réseau Lace Ground, and will be found described under GROUNDS. Besides this true lace ground, another was made from fine Scotch gauze, which was drawn together by the needle until it assumed a honeycomb shape. The Scotch gauze necessary to this art is no longer manufactured; it consisted of very fine silk threads, woven as clear, but minute, open squares. The thread was taken diagonally across these squares with a kind of Back Stitch, and was twisted round each mesh as it was made.

Net may be had woven as well as hand-made. Machinery for its production was introduced early in the present century, the textile having been previously restricted to pillow work. Regular meshes are formed by the use of four threads of flax or silk, twisted together so as to form hexagonal, octagonal, or diamond-shaped forms. Net is usually rather more than a yard wide, or double width. Of all the varieties produced, the Brussels is the most highly esteemed, and may be obtained 2 yards in width for dressmaking. Three threads are employed in all descriptions of Net, one passing from right to left, another from left to right, and a third twining round the two former threads, so as to form a honeycomb-patterned tissue. The French Net made by machinery consists of single Press Points, when not ornamented called Tulle, and when ornamented called Dentelle. It is made of silk, and is pretty, but inferior. There is also the Trico-Berlin, in which the stitch is removed three needles from its place of looping; Fleur de Tulle, having a mesh of two descriptions; and Tulle Anglois, a double pressed point. The English kinds include a Silk Net in imitation of Blonde, 1 yard 3 inches wide, and machine made; Quilting Silk Net, slightly stiffened with gum; Pillow-thread Net, hand made; and Piece Bobbin Net, machine made, of various widths, from 3—8 and 8—4; the threads are so entwined as to form regular six-sided meshes. The material known as Italian Net is really not a Net in the style of its manufacture, but is a strong gauze, composed of silk and worsted, and produced in various colours for women's dresses. Cotton Net is the cheapest kind of woven Net, and is employed for stiff linings and foundations.

Net Embroidery.—An effective way of ornamenting

FIGS. 615 AND 616. NET EMBROIDERY.

White or Black Net for dress trimmings, caps, and other small articles of dress. To work as shown in Figs. 615,

616, and 617: Trace the design upon calico, and strengthen the calico with a brown paper backing. TACK the Net

FIG. 617. NET EMBROIDERY.

down upon the pattern, and work the various stars over in SATIN STITCH, with filoselles of bright colours, and shades that bear candle light.

To work Fig. 618: This design is for a Necktie end, and is worked with silk cord and filoselle upon Brussels Net.

FIG. 618. NET EMBROIDERY.

Trace the design as before-mentioned, lay the Net over it, and then loop the Cord over the lines so as to follow the pattern outlines. KNOT the cord together, and secure with a BUTTONHOLE STITCH taken through the Net where indicated, and make the centre Wheel and the small Pyramids with filoselle; also work the small Stars and the Buttonhole Edging with the same material.

Netted Lace.—*See* NETWORK.

Netting.—This art is so ancient that no date can be fixed for its invention. That it was practised for fishing and birdcatching purposes by the earliest inhabitants of the earth is without doubt; and there are still to be seen, in the Museum at Berlin, Egyptian Nets, and the implements by which they were made, that are 3000 years old. Besides these commoner specimens of work belonging to the Egyptians, it is evident, from the accounts still extant, and from ancient frescoes, that that nation from the very earliest period produced Netting—or, as it was then called, Caul Work and Network—of a much higher kind than modern workers have ever attained to. The figures painted upon Egyptian monuments are frequently clothed in tunics made of Netting, the loops being formed with gaily coloured silks, or gold and silver threads. Amasis, King of Egypt, presented a corselet to the Temple of Minerva, in the island of Rhodes, composed of the finest Netting, each thread containing 360 distinct threads, and yet the texture was so light and fine that the whole could easily pass through a man's ring. A netted corselet, matching this one in delicacy, was given by the same monarch to Mutianus, the third Roman Consul; but this was embroidered with animals and figures worked with gold thread into the Netting. In the writings of Pliny and Herodotus, the fine flax used by the Egyptians is spoken of with admiration; and Homer, in the "Iliad," mentions the Cauls and Networks of gold worn by the Trojan ladies. In the Bible there is frequent allusion to the art; some of the curtains adorning Solomon's Temple were made of Checker Work, or Netting; and Isaiah enumerates the Cauls of Network and Veils worn by the Jewish women; and when summing up the calamities that were to fall upon Egypt, includes in the general curse those who "weave Networks." We have little mention of Netting during the Roman Empire, and it is not until the thirteenth century that the art was practised in Europe so as to draw attention; Netting was then worked for ecclesiastical purposes, and looked upon as lace. St. Paul's Cathedral, in 1295, possessed a kneeling cushion of Network; and Exeter Cathedral, a few years later, several altar cloths. In the thirteenth and fourteenth centuries Netting was known as Opus Filatorium and Opus Araneum, or Spider Work; the ground only was Netted, the design being Darned or Embroidered upon it. But the plain, unembroidered Netting was frequently made either in silk or flax, and used as Curtains and Bed Hangings. At a later date, Darned Netting was known as Lacis, and was worked more with flax than gold or silk threads; and, in the sixteenth century, this Lacis is frequently mentioned in Wardrobe Accounts, and finds a place in the articles enumerated in the will made by Mary, Queen of Scots, before the birth of her son. Lacis, when not Embroidered or Darned, was called Réseau, or Rezeuil, and differed in no way from Plain Netting; nor do Lacis in any way differ from the modern Guipure d'Art, in which, upon a groundwork of Netting, a pattern is Darned and Embroidered. After the universal adoption of Pillow and fine Needle-made Laces, the Netted and Darned Lace was little used; but occasionally a specimen appears among the relics of palaces and old families, and a coverlet used by Louis XIV., still in existence, is made of a Netted Foundation with Darned Embroidery.

In England, Netting has always been practised for useful purposes, and sixty years ago was much worked for Curtains, Window Blinds, and Drawing-room Covers, either in Darned or Plain Netting. Crochet has lately superseded Netting, on account of its greater portability, but there is no doubt that the ancient art will again revive, and that its light and artistic productions are much superior to the work to which it has given place.

Netting is very easy to do, and likewise possesses the advantage of being extremely strong, each loop that is made being independent, and, if properly knotted, remaining firm, whatever accident happens, either to the ones before or behind it; for the same reason, nothing is more difficult than to undo a piece of Netting when once made, every loop requiring to be separately unpicked and undone with a sharp-pointed knitting needle or stiletto. The beauty of Netting consists in the regular size of the loops made, and the tightness of each individual knot, and this result cannot be obtained unless good materials are used, and the art has been well practised. Bad thread and silk are liable to break when under the strain of being pulled into a knot, and a break in the material necessitates the thread being joined in the working of a row, which is to be avoided, not only for the knot produced by the join always showing, but also by reason of the loop that contains it rarely being made the same size as the ones surrounding it. All joins in the working thread should be made at the first loop in a row, and with a WEAVER'S KNOT. Every loop or knot in Netting counts as a stitch in other work; but it takes four knots to make what is called a complete loop, or mesh, in Netting. These meshes are generally of a diamond shape, and are made with Plain Netting; but Round and Square Meshes are also worked, in order to give a certain variety and relief to the ordinary loop, which, however, is not capable of very much alteration; and varieties in Netting are more often made by working several loops into a loop, or by missing loops and crossing one over the other, than by changing the form of the loop worked. Netting is always made the contrary way to what it will hang when in use, and in some articles, such as curtains and purses, the loops forming the length are all put on the Foundation Loop at once; while in others, such as lawn-tennis nets, one loop is only put upon the Foundation Loop, and the right length made by Increasing in every row. When the article is finished, it should be slightly damped, and then well stretched, and pinned out upon a board, so that every mesh may assume its right position.

The implements used in Netting are few; they consist of a Netting Needle, which is a long piece of ivory, wood,

FIG. 619. NETTING NEEDLE.

or steel (see Fig. 619), split at each end to admit of the thread being wound upon it; Mesh or Spool, of various sizes, also made of ivory, steel, or wood (see Fig. 620), and

FIG. 620. ROUND MESH.

numbered as to sizes in the same way as the needles; Twine, fine Knitting Cotton, or Silk, for making the Netting; and a Stirrup, or Lead Cushion, to which to attach the Netting while working, so as to resist the pressure each Knot in making throws upon the work.

The manner of Netting is as follows: Wind upon the Needle sufficient cotton for one row of Netting, and be careful to use a mesh that will allow the needle to pass easily through the loops as they are made; then attach it to the FOUNDATION LOOP on the

Stirrup and place the latter round the left foot, so regulated as to length that the row to be Netted is about on a level with the waist of the worker. Take the Mesh in the left hand, and place that thumb over it, and the fingers underneath it; hold the needle in the right hand, with about twice its length in cotton between it and the work; hold the Mesh up to the Foundation loop, put the cotton over the Mesh, round the first three fingers, and back on to the Mesh, and over it, so that it is held down with the left thumb: throw the thread outwards round the work from left to right, and place the right hand holding the needle in the palm of the left hand. Push the needle through the under part of the loop on the Mesh, and into the Foundation Loop, the thread held from being drawn up by being round the little finger of the left hand. Draw this Foundation Loop up to the Mesh, release the thread under the thumb, and draw it up as a knot over the Foundation Loop; drop the thread on the third finger and draw up, and drop the thread on the little finger and draw up. The knot that is made with these movements should be close to the mesh, and so firm and strong as not to reply to any attempts to alter its position; it is repeated throughout the work, the loops on the previous row answering to the Foundation Loop. Form each row of Netting with a succession of these knots, and work them always from left to right. When the end of a row is reached, turn the Netting over, and commence to make the next row by working on the Loop last made.

TERMS AND MATERIALS.—The following Terms and Materials are used in Netting:

Cushion.—When the Stirrup is not used to keep the Netting taut, it is necessary to pin the work to a Cushion. The Cushion required is shown with the Foundation Loop in Fig. 621. It is a large Cushion, heavily weighted with lead, covered with cloth, and made so as to resist without yielding when each loop is pulled and knotted in the progress of the work.

Decrease.—This is managed by Netting two or more loops together of the preceding row. To Net two loops together: Work the LOOP as far as putting the netting needle into the loop formed on the preceding row; pass it through two loops instead of one on this row, and finish the loop in the ordinary way.

Foundation Loop.—All Netting, whether worked upon the Stirrup or the Cushion, requires a foundation, on to which the first row is Netted. The Foundation Loop, when the work is finished, is carefully cut, and the first row drawn out and straightened. To make a Foundation Loop for work pinned to a Cushion, as illustrated in Fig. 621: Take a piece of twine the size of the knitting cotton to be used in the Netting, make a loop in it, small or large, according to the length of the work and the consequent number of netted loops that will be required, and then make a very small loop; pin the Foundation Loop down by attaching the small loop to the cushion, and then fasten an end of the knitting cotton to it, and work the first row of loops on to it, as shown in the illustration.

To make a Foundation Loop upon a Stirrup: Pass a loop of strong, fine twine, through the upper end of the

Stirrup, and work the first row of Netting on to it in the same way as before described. Some workers Net a number of rows upon the Foundation before they commence their real pattern; these netted rows are retained

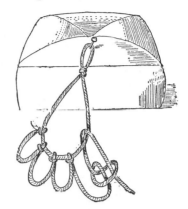

FIG. 621. FOUNDATION LOOP AND CUSHION.

upon the Foundation Loop, and serve as a starting point for many pieces of Netting. It is not necessary to do this, but the loops of the first row are of a more equal size when worked upon such a support.

Increase.—In Netting this is accomplished by making two or more Loops into the one Loop of preceding row. To work: NET a Loop into the Loop on the preceding row in the ordinary way, and then Net another Loop into the same Loop before proceeding to the next one.

Knot. The Knot made by twisting the cotton round the Mesh and fingers is made with every Netted Loop, and is essential to its security. The manner of making it is described in PLAIN NETTING and FISHERMAN'S KNOT.

Long Loop.—Loops in Plain Netting are sometimes made of two different sizes in the same row. This is managed as follows: Net in the ordinary way until the place is reached where a Long Loop has to be Netted, then put the cotton twice round the Mesh instead of once, and make the KNOT as in PLAIN NETTING.

Loop.—A loop in Netting takes the place of a stitch; it is formed over the Mesh, and is secured by a KNOT, as described in PLAIN NETTING, or in FISHERMAN'S KNOT.

Mesh.—The instrument used in Netting to work the Loops upon, and made of bone, steel, or wood, of various sizes, either round or flat, according to the size of the loops to be made. A Mesh was at one time called a Spool, on account of the title Mesh being also given to the loops of Netting when quite completed as Squares, Rounds, or Diamonds.

Needle.—Used to hold the cotton, and made of sizes matching the Meshes.

Round.—When Netting is worked as a continuous looping, without any turning of the work, a Round has been made when each Loop upon a level has been worked. To net a Round: Join the Netting as in CIRCLE, and indicate the last Loop by marking it with a piece of coloured wool; Net until that loop has again to be worked.

Row.—In Netting this term indicates the Loops from one side of the work to the other. To make a Row: Commence on the left-hand side of the Foundation, and Net in every Loop until the last upon the right-hand side is reached. In working curtains, and other large articles, a Row is frequently a yard in length. As the loops forming this yard could not be contained upon one Mesh, slide the first-made ones off on the left side as the new ones are formed on the right, but always leave enough made Loops upon the Mesh to be a guide as to size to the ones being made. Draw the Mesh entirely out when the Row is completed, and commence a new Row. Turn the Netting over in the hand, place the Mesh close to the loop last made, make a new Loop upon it, and work from the left to the right to end of row.

Spool.—See MESH.

Stirrup.—Netting, which is really a succession of Loops secured in position by knots, requires to be kept stretched while in progress, or the Loops made are unequal in size, and the knots are not drawn up tight. This stretching is accomplished by either pinning the Foundation Loop of the Netting to a lead Cushion, or attaching it to the foot with the help of a Stirrup, the last plan being the one usually adopted, and the best. To make a Stirrup: Take a piece of oak or elm, 4 to 5 inches in length, and 1½ inches in width, and bore a hole in the centre through each of its ends. Take 2 yards of ribbon, 1 inch wide, of a strong make, pass each end through a hole, and sew the two ends together, or tie them underneath the piece of wood; put the piece of wood under the left foot, and bring the ribbon up as a loop. Regulate the Long Loop thus formed by the height of the worker, as it should always reach to the knee. If the ends of the ribbon are only tied together, the Stirrup can be shortened during the progress of the work, which is often an advantage. A more ornamental Stirrup can be made by Embroidering a narrow band, to pass over the instep, and attaching that to the ends of wood, and making the loop of ribbon rise from the centre of the embroidery; but for ordinary Netting the plain Stirrup is the best, as the whole of the weight of the foot is upon it.

NETTING PATTERNS.—Although the Loop, or, rather, Knot in Netting appears not to admit of much variety, it can be worked in the various ways here given.

Caroline Netting.—This can either be worked in single fleecy wool and round wooden Meshes, for scarves and shawls, or with fine crochet cotton of a medium size, and with a flat Mesh, 1 inch in width, for curtains and window blinds. To work: First row—Net in PLAIN NETTING, upon the Foundation Loop, enough Loops to make the length of the article required. Second row—work as for Plain Netting, but take up the second Loop upon the needle, and then push the first Loop over it, and net these two Loops as one, Net another and a Plain Loop into the same Loop, a Plain Loop upon the third Loop, and repeat from the commencement for the rest of the row. Third row—Plain Netting. Fourth row—as the second row. Repeat the second and third rows three times; then take a

rather wider Mesh, and Net a plain row with that, and repeat from first row.

Circle.—A Circle in Netting is formed upon the Foundation Loop, which makes the centre of the circle. To work as shown in Fig. 622: Make a very small Foundation Loop, and Net, in PLAIN NETTING, ten Loops into it, and, instead of reversing the work and commencing a new row as in ordinary Netting, Net the next Loop into the first Loop

FIG. 622. NETTING—CIRCLE.

of the ten just made, and draw these together as the first round and commence the second round. After this first drawing together, the Netting will form a Circle by simply working every Loop as reached, but as each Circle is larger in circumference than the preceding one, the Loops must be increased. The Increase is shown in Fig.

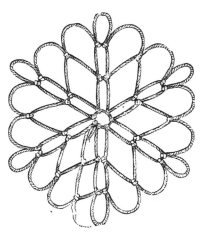

FIG. 623. NETTING—INCREASED CIRCLE.

622, and is thus worked: After the first round, which in Fig. 623 contains six Loops, work two Loops into every Loop for the second round. Third round—Work two Loops into the first Loop, one Loop into the second, and repeat to the end of the round. Fourth round—the Increase, by the time that the fourth round is reached, will have assumed the shape shown in Fig. 623; work into the Loop that is drawn longways in the illustration two Loops wherever it occurs, one Loop into all the other Loops; continue to Increase six times in this manner in every round until the Circle is complete.

Cross Netting.—This is used either for the centres of scarves, shawls, or curtains, or as a border to plain netted articles. Medium sized knitting cotton, and two flat Meshes, one half the size of the other, are required. To work as shown in Fig. 624: First row—take the smallest Mesh, and Net in PLAIN NETTING the length required. Second row—Net in Plain Netting with the largest Mesh. Third row—take the narrow Mesh, Net a Loop, taking the

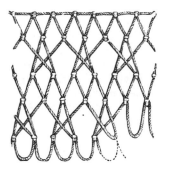

FIG. 624. CROSS NETTING.

second Loop of the last row, then Net the first Loop of the last row, then the fourth, and then the third; continue to the end of the row, always Netting the second Loop on the last row before the one next the Mesh. Fourth row —use the largest Mesh, and Net a plain row. Fifth row —as the third row; this row is not completed in the illustration, so that the crossing of the two Loops in it should be fully indicated.

Diamond Netting.—This is a term applied to Plain Netting, and is worked as such when the loops are made of an uniform size, and following each other in regular succession. Fancy Diamond Netting is worked in three different ways, as follows:—*Single Diamond Netting.*— Work with fine silk or cotton, and Mesh and Needle No. 10. Net the first Loop in ordinary PLAIN NETTING, and the second in the same way, but pass the cotton twice round the Mesh, so as to make this Loop twice the size of the other. Repeat these two Loops to the end of the row. In the next row make the short Loop over the Long Loop of the last row, and work as in the first row. *Treble Diamond Netting.*—Use the same cotton, Mesh, and Needle, as for Single Diamond Netting. First row —make a Plain Netting Loop, but put the cotton twice round the Mesh. Then Net three Plain Netting Loops, and repeat these four Loops to the end of the row. Second row—a plain Loop over the Long Loop in the last row, then a Long Loop and two plain Loops; repeat to the end of the row, and withdraw the Mesh before a long Loop is Netted as a plain Loop. Third row—Net a Plain and a Long Loop alternately, commencing with two plain Loops, should the pattern require it. Fourth row—Net three plain Loops and one Long Loop; repeat to the end of the row. Fifth row—as the second row. *Diamond Netting made*

with Five Loops.—Use the same cotton, Mesh, and Needle as in Single Diamond Netting, and work the Long and the Plain Loop in Plain Netting; take the Mesh out of the work when a Long Loop has to be netted as a Plain Loop, and after this has been done, the pattern forms a diamond of small loops surrounded by an open space formed by the Long Loops; commence by Netting upon the Foundation Loop a number of loops that divide into six, and one over. First row—make a Long Loop with the cotton twice round the Mesh, and five Plain Loops; repeat to the end of the row; finish with a Long Loop. Second row—Plain Loop over the Long Loop, a Long Loop, 4 Plain Loops; repeat to the end of the row. Third row—a Plain Loop, a Long Loop, 4 Plain, the last over the Long Loop; repeat to the end of the row. Fourth row—a Plain Loop, a Plain Loop over the Long Loop, a Long Loop, 3 Plain, the last over a Long Loop; repeat to the end of the row. Fifth row—a Plain Loop, a Plain Loop over a Long Loop,* a Long Loop, 5 Plain, the last over a Long Loop; repeat from * to the end of the row. Sixth row —2 Plain, 1 Plain over a Long Loop, a Long Loop, 2 Plain, the first over a Long Loop; repeat to the end of the row. Seventh row—3 Plain, the last over a Long Loop, a Long Loop, 2 Plain; repeat to the end of the row. Eighth row—4 Plain, the last over a Long Loop, a Long Loop, a Plain Loop; repeat to the end of the row. Ninth row—3 Plain, the last over a Long Loop, 1 Plain; repeat to the end of the row. Tenth row—3 Plain, the last over a Long Loop, 2 Plain, the last over a Long Loop, a Long Loop; repeat to the end of the row. Eleventh row—2 Plain, the last over a Long Loop, 3 Plain, the last over a Long Loop, a Long Loop; repeat to the end of the row. Twelfth row—2 Plain, the last over a Long Loop, 4 Plain, the last over a Long Loop; repeat to the end of the row, but end with a Long Loop instead of a Plain one. Thirteenth row—work as the first, and repeat from there.

English Netting, also called Honeycomb.—Work with any sized Mesh and cotton, according to the article to be made. First row—PLAIN NETTING. Second row—also Plain Netting, but Net the second Loop before the first, the fourth before the third, and so on to the end of the row. Third row—Plain Netting. Fourth row—as the second, but commence with a Plain Loop before beginning the crossing. Fifth row—Plain Netting. Sixth row—as the second row, and repeat from that row.

Fisherman's Knot.—This Knot differs from the one ordinarily used in Plain Netting, and is considered to be stronger. It is used by fishermen for their nets, hence its name; and is also used for hammocks, lawn-tennis nets, and other articles subject to rough treatment and rain. The process of making is shown in Fig. 625, and the Knot when made is thicker than other Knots. To work: Hold the Mesh and the netting needle in the ordinary way, the thumb over the Mesh and the fingers supporting it; pass the thread round the Mesh, but not over the fingers, and put the needle upwards through the Loop that is to be worked, and then draw the Loop up to the Mesh, and keep the thread tight by holding it down with the thumb. Allow the loose thread to fall to the left of the work, and put the needle upward, behind the Loop being worked, and out on the left (*see* Fig. 625), so as to inclose it with the thread, and draw the thread tight. The illustration gives the Knot nearly completed; the

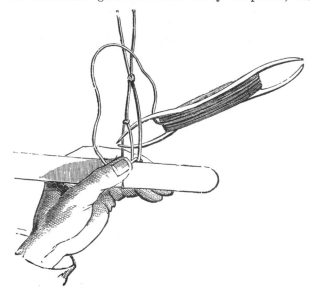

FIG. 625. NETTING—FISHERMAN'S KNOT.

thread in it is passed round the Mesh, through the Loop, and secured with the thumb, and the movement shown is that of the needle being passed at the back of the Loop, and to the left, before the final drawing tight of the Knot.

Fly Netting.—A very pretty and easy kind of Netting, suitable for scarves, shawls, and neckties, and made with wool and silk, or wool and cotton. To work: Wind upon the needle together a strand of wool and silk, so that they unwind as one. Net upon the Foundation Loop enough Loops to form the width required, and work these loops, and all others, in PLAIN NETTING. Continue to net rows of this Plain Netting over an inch sized flat Mesh until the width desired for the article is obtained, then cut the woollen thread round every Knot, and fluff it up, so that it conceals the Knot and makes a little ball; but be careful to leave the silk or cotton strand untouched. Make a Fringe or Edging to the work with some of the patterns given under EDGING and FRINGE.

Grecian Netting.—Used for purses when worked with fine silks, and for curtains and toilet cloths when worked with knitting cotton. The Loop is troublesome at first, and should not be tried by a beginner. Two flat Meshes, one half the size of the other, are required. To work: First row—Net in PLAIN NETTING, and with the largest Mesh. Second row—take the small Mesh, and make the usual Loop over the Mesh which commences a Plain Netting Loop, then pass the netting needle through the under part of the Loop, and bring it out clear of the Mesh; put it through the first Loop on the last row, and into the second, draw the cotton and Needle back through the first Loop, and then twist the second Loop round the first, and Net the first Loop, finishing it as in the ordinary Plain Netting. For the next Loop, Net the little Loop that is formed by twisting the first and the second Loop

together. Repeat these two movements to the end of the row. Third row—as the first. Fourth row—as the second. Repeat the first and second rows to the end of the work.

Hollow Square Netting.—A square of Netting with the centre left hollow is sometimes required as a groundwork for a piece of Guipure d'Art Lace, or for a pincushion cover or cheese cloth, in ordinary Netting. The hollow square is formed in the Netting, as it proceeds, in the following manner: Commence with one Loop upon the Foundation Loop as in SQUARE NETTING, and Net in PLAIN NETTING. INCREASE a Loop at the end of every row, as in Square Netting, until half the length of one side of the outside square is obtained; then divide the Loops, and leave those at the end of the row unworked, and Net the other half as if making OBLONG NETTING on the inside of the square; DECREASE by Netting two Loops together at the inside end, and Increase by Netting two Loops into the end Loop in every row upon the outside of the square. Work in this way until the whole length of one side of the outside square is made, turn the corner as it were, and commence another side by Netting the two outside Loops together, and Increasing in the inside by making two Loops in the outer Loop there in every row. Continue until half the outside line of the square is formed, and then drop the Loops, and pick up those left when the oblong was commenced. Work these in the same manner, Increasing at the outside, Decreasing at the inside, until the length of that side of the outside square is obtained, and then turn the corner, and Decrease on the outside and Increase on the inside, until these Loops are brought down to the level of the others. Work right across the whole number, and Decrease in every row until only one Loop is left on the row. The following example will make the working of this Hollow Square quite clear. To form a Hollow Square with fifteen Loops along the outer side: Commence with one Loop, and Increase in every row until there are twelve Loops in the row; drop the last six, and work six rows, Increasing at the outside of the square, and Decreasing at the inside; turn the corner, and work six rows, Increasing at the inside, and Decreasing at the outside of the square; leave those Loops, and pick up the ones first dropped, which Net down to the others in the same way. For the thirteenth row, work right across the twelve Loops, and Decrease until only one Loop is left in the row.

Honeycomb Netting.—See *English Netting.*

Leaf Netting.—Also known as Puff Netting, and worked so as to raise some of the loops of a row above the others. It is simply Plain Netting worked with different sized meshes, and can be adapted to any of the purposes for which Netting is employed. It looks particularly well worked as a border to netted curtains, or when made for window blinds. To work: Use medium sized crochet cotton and two flat Meshes (one twice the width of the other); a quarter of an inch and a half inch Mesh are good sizes, but all depends upon the destination of the work. First, Second, and Third rows—PLAIN NETTING. With the small Mesh make into the FOUNDATION LOOP as the first row, the number of Loops required for the length, and Net a Loop into each of these for the second and third rows. Fourth row—use the same Mesh, and Work one Loop in Plain Netting in the first Loop, and six Loops in the second Loop, the cotton to be put twice round the Mesh before making any of these six Loops; repeat from the commencement to the end of the row. Fifth and Sixth rows—use the small Mesh and work a Loop into every Loop on the previous row. Seventh row—use the large Mesh, work a Loop into every Loop on the previous row, work the first Loop in Plain Netting, the next six with the cotton twice round the Mesh, and repeat to the end of the row from the commencement. Eighth row—work a Loop into the first Loop, still using the large Mesh, take up the next six Loops, and work them as one Loop into the Second Loop; repeat these two Loops to the end of the row. Ninth and Tenth rows—Plain Netting with the large Mesh into every Loop. Eleventh row—use the large Mesh, and work two Loops in every Loop on the row. Twelfth row—use the large Mesh, and take up two Loops in every Loop on the row. Thirteenth row—as the tenth. Fourteenth and Fifteenth rows—as the eleventh and twelfth. Sixteenth row—repeat from the first row. The leaf, or raised part of this pattern, is contained in rows four to eight; the rest can be altered in any way, so long as the number of Loops, when once arranged, is kept to, and that part of the Netting left flat.

Long Twisted Netting.—This requires working with two Meshes of unequal widths; the larger one should be exactly double the size of the smaller. To work: First row—take the smaller Mesh, and work with it a row of Loops in ROUND NETTING. Second row—take the large Mesh, and work with it a row of PLAIN NETTING Loops. Repeat these two rows alternately to the end of the pattern.

Looped Netting.—This is used for either edgings or to form the whole of shawls, curtains, fire screens, window blinds, and drawing-room covers. The design shown in Fig. 626 is the width of work it is necessary to make for a border, but any width can be made. To work: Use a half-inch or quarter-inch flat Mesh, and knitting cotton

FIG. 626. LOOPED NETTING.

or wool, according to the article to be Netted. First row—Net in PLAIN NETTING the length required. Second row—make four Loops into every Loop of the preceding row. Third row—run the needle through the four Loops worked together in the last row, and work them together in Plain Netting; the illustration shows this third row uncompleted,

with the manner of passing the cotton through the four loops. Fourth row—repeat from the first row.

Mignonette Netting.—This is used for curtains and window blinds, it being extremely easy, and worked with one Mesh. To work: Use medium-sized crochet cotton, and a flat Mesh half an inch in width, or one smaller. First, second, and third rows—PLAIN NETTING. Fourth row—Net into the first Loop one Plain Loop, then put the cotton twice round the Mesh, and Net a LONG LOOP into the same Loop on the last row, and finally Net a Plain Loop into the same Loop; repeat to the end of the row, Netting three Loops into one Loop. Fifth row—Net in Plain Netting all the Long Loops, but leave the Plain Loops. Sixth row—repeat from the second row.

Netting with Beads.—When making ornamental articles with Netting, beads are often worked into the Netting, and are used particularly in Purse Netting and to ornament bags. The beads used are steel, gold, and coloured, the last two kinds wearing the best, steel being apt to tarnish. The beads should be German, selected so as to match each other perfectly as to shape and size, as any unevenness in the make of the beads is instantly detected when they are in position, and destroys the look of the work. Unless perfectly secured, beads will move upon the loop when netted. To work: Use a long Darning Needle instead of a Netting Needle, threaded with silk enough for the row that is to be beaded; thread each bead as required, bring it up in front of the Mesh, and keep it there with the left thumb upon it until the knot of the Loop is made; then pass the needle through the bead again from underneath, and pull the bead close up to the knot just made. Thread another bead, and repeat until the number of beads required are secured.

Oblong Netting.—This shape is much used for making lawn tennis nets, hammocks, and garden nets. It is shown in Fig. 627, and is worked either with Fisherman's Knot or Plain Netting. To work: Commence as for SQUARE NETTING, with a single Loop in the FOUNDATION LOOP; INCREASE by working two Loops into the last

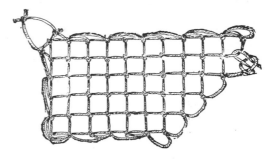

FIG. 627. OBLONG NETTING.

Loop in every row until the depth required for the article is obtained (in the illustration five rows make the necessary depth); tie a piece of bright-coloured wool into the last Loop, and, whenever the side is reached where the wool is, DECREASE by working two Loops as one (see lower part of the illustration); Increase at the other end of the row, whenever it is reached, by working two Loops into the last Loop. If attention is paid to keep the Increase and Decrease regular, a long straight piece of Netting is made. When this is sufficiently long, proceed to form the second short side of the oblong. To do this, Decrease by Netting two Loops together at the end of every row until only one Loop remains.

Open Netting.—A very simple manner of making an alteration in Plain Netting. Work with crochet cotton or silk, and with two flat Meshes, the larger an inch in width, the smaller half an inch in width. First, second, and third rows—PLAIN NETTING, with the small Mesh. Fourth row—Plain Netting, with the large Mesh. Fifth row—repeat from the first row.

Plain, or Diamond Netting.—This loop is the elementary one in Netting, and upon it all the more complicated loops are formed. It is used in all Netting as a foundation for Darning upon Net, or for Guipure d'Art, and its various stages are shown in Figs. 628, 629, and 630, in which the Netting is given without the hands that hold it, in order that the making of the Loop may be fully

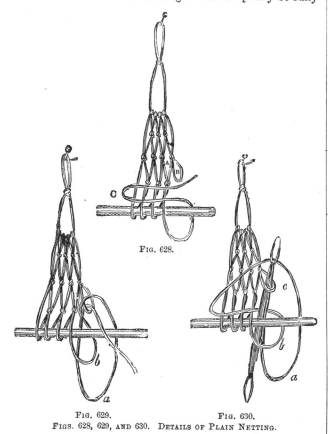

FIG. 628.

FIG. 629.   FIG. 630.
FIGS. 628, 629, AND 630. DETAILS OF PLAIN NETTING.

shown. To work: Having secured the FOUNDATION LOOP to the Stirrup, put the latter over the foot, fill the needle with cotton, and attach the cotton to the Foundation Loop; take the Mesh in the left hand, and the needle in the right hand, holding the Mesh with the thumb over it, and the fingers beneath. Pass the cotton over the Mesh, and round the first three fingers, and hold the Mesh close to the Foundation Loop. Bring the cotton round under the Mesh to the top, and put it under the left thumb and to

the left (shown in Fig. 628 by the letter c); then bring it round to the right, past the letter B in Fig. 628, and round the hand, as shown in Figs. 629 and 630, then by the letter a (this last Loop is held by the little finger of the left hand). The needle, by this action, is brought in front of the Mesh, and into the palm of the hand; it is then passed under the first Loop, between the Mesh and the fingers holding it, and into the Foundation Loop (see Fig. 630, letter c), and over that piece of cotton which is turned back from the left thumb, and then forms Loop a of Figs. 629 and 630. Before pulling the Mesh out of the Foundation Loop, it is necessary to change the position of the right hand; this, while pushing the needle through the cotton and Foundation Loop, is at the lower part of the needle, and must be transferred to the upper, so that it can grasp the needle firmly; make the change, and keep all the turns of the cotton on the left hand steady while doing so, then draw the Foundation Loop up to the Mesh; release the Loop of cotton held down by the left thumb, and pull it tight over the Foundation Loop with a pull upon the needle; let go the Loop over the three fingers, and pull that tight by opening the third and little fingers of the left hand, and enlarging the Loop upon them; and finally let this Loop go, and pull the cotton firmly up with the right hand. The Knot that is formed by these movements should be close up to the Mesh, but not upon it, and should be made by a strand of cotton firmly inclosing a piece of the Foundation Loop, and no true knot is formed unless this is the result. A repetition of these knots make a row in Netting, and the beauty and value of the work depends upon their being made with Loops of an equal size, which can only be accomplished when every knot is made close to the Mesh. It takes two rows to complete the diamond-shaped Loop from which this knot derives its name, the first Loop being shown by the letter B in Fig. 628, and the completed diamond by the letter A in the same illustration.

Puff Netting.—See *Leaf Netting.*

Rose Netting.—The meshes formed by this Netting are shaped like honeycombs, and are surrounded with a double line of thread. This variety is generally used for making fine silk veils, or mittens; but, if worked with Crochet cotton, it will make very lacy-looking curtains, To work in silks, use flat Meshes, sizes No. 9 and 18; if with cotton, a flat Mesh three quarters of an inch wide, and one half that size. First row—use the finer Mesh, and make upon the FOUNDATION LOOP in PLAIN NETTING the number of Loops necessary for the length of the article to be worked. Second row—with the larger Mesh, Net into every Loop in Plain Netting. Third row—draw the first Loop of the last row through the second Loop, and well up it, Net the first Loop in Plain Netting with the smaller Mesh, run the needle into the second Loop where it crosses the first Loop, and pull it out there and Net it as the first Loop. Continue to work in this way for the whole row. The only difficulty is the taking up correctly of the second Loop in the right place inside the first Loop, and not outside it. Fourth row—Plain Netting into every Loop, using the large Mesh. Fifth row—work like the third row with the small Mesh, but miss the first

Loop and draw the second through the third, to diversify the crossing of the Loops. Sixth row—Plain Netting, with the large Mesh. Seventh row—repeat from the third row.

Round Netting.—A Loop considered strong. It is used for purses, mittens, and other articles subject to wear. Round Netting has the appearance of a four-sided honeycomb. To work: Commence by making the Loop over the Mesh, as in the ordinary PLAIN NETTING, put the needle through the under part of the thread on the Mesh, then draw it well out, turn it, and pass its point from above the work into the Loop of the Netting that is to be completed; draw this up to the Mesh, and finish the stitch as in ordinary Plain Netting. As the manner of working Round Netting causes the work to contract, place one-fifth more Loops upon the FOUNDATION LOOP than would be required for the same length when made in the ordinary way.

Square Netting.—The Loop in Square Netting is the same as that used in Plain Netting, but the work, having to form an exact square, is commenced with only one Loop upon the Foundation Loop, instead of the number of Loops corresponding to the length; it is then Increased until two sides of the square are formed, and then Decreased to the one Loop to form the two remaining sides. To work: Work one Loop into the FOUNDATION LOOP in PLAIN NETTING. Into this Loop work two Loops in the next row. In the third row, work two Loops into the last Loop, and continue to INCREASE by always working two Loops into the last Loop of each row until the length required for the square is formed. The Loops of the row across the square will be the same in number as those upon the outside edges. As soon as the length of the square is thus formed, commence to DECREASE by Netting two Loops together at the end of every row. The squares required as foundations to Guipure d'Art are Netted in this manner.

Star Netting.—This Loop can be made either as a finish to, or centre of, a curtain. It presents, when finished, the appearance shown in the small stars of Fig. 632, and its manner of working is considerably en-

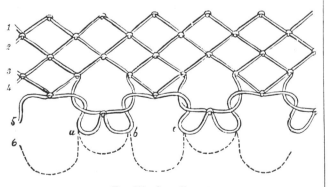

FIG. 631. STAR NETTING.

larged in Fig. 631, so that the complicated part of the Loop may be fully understood. To work as a border: Use Strutt's cotton No. 8, a round Mesh half an inch in circumference, and a steel Netting needle. Net in

PLAIN NETTING the first three rows. Fourth row—Net the first Loop in Plain Netting, the second in the same, but pass the cotton twice round the Mesh, to make a Loop twice the length of the first (this long and short Loop

FIG. 632. STAR NETTING.

is shown in Fig. 631, in row marked 4); repeat the two Loops alternately to the end of the row. Fifth row—pass the cotton round the Mesh, and the needle over and under the long Loop on the preceding row, and Net a Loop, pass the cotton again over the Mesh, and the needle over and under the same long stitch on the preceding row, and Net into the short Loop; repeat throughout the row (the letters *a*, *b*, and *c*, in Fig. 631 show the Loops formed in this row). Sixth row—repeat the fourth row, make the

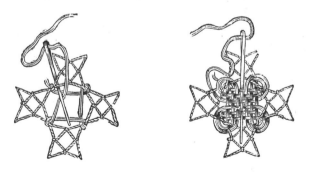

FIG. 633. STAR NETTING.   FIG. 633. STAR NETTING (DETAIL A).

short Loop between the letters *a* and *b* in Fig. 631, and the long between the letters *b* and *c* in the same illustration; therefore, commence the row with a long Loop. Seventh row—as the fifth row. Eighth row—as the fourth.

Figs. 632, 633, and 634 are illustrations of the various devices with which this Star Netting can be ornamented when worked for curtains. The cotton to use for these decorations should be linen thread, No. 80. Fig. 632 shows a large Darned Star carried across four of the open spaces left in the Star Netting. It is worked thus: Thread a needle with the cotton, and carry it backwards and forwards across one of the large spaces four times, always ending in one of the small stars; repeat this filling up so that the four arms of the Star are formed. Fig. 633, Detail A, shows how one of these large spaces can be filled with a thick stitch, which resembles Point de Toile in Guipure d'Art. To work: Loop the needle into the four corners of the square, and continue these Loops, DARNING each thread in and out, as shown in Detail A, until the open space is quite filled up.

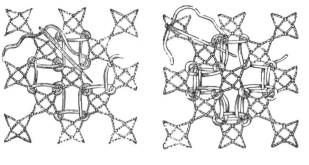

FIG. 634. STAR NETTING.   FIG. 634. STAR NETTING (DETAIL A).

Fig. 634 and Detail A show the same stitch worked so as to form a Maltese cross in a lighter way than in Fig. 633. To work: Loop the thread all round the outside line of the Maltese cross, so as to mark it well out, then repeat the outside line, working the second line over the first, and DARNING the two together, as shown in Fig. 634, Detail A. All these various stitches can be worked, if required, upon the same curtain.

Straight Netting.—In this Netting there is neither Increasing nor Decreasing; the number of loops that are required for the width of the work are Netted on to the Foundation Loop, and are then worked until the length required is obtained. To work: On the FOUNDATION LOOP (see Fig. 635), Net in PLAIN NETTING the number of loops required, and continue to Net

FIG. 635. STRAIGHT NETTING.

these, simply turning the work over in the hand, to work the next row from left to right without breaking off the thread, or Increasing or Decreasing a loop. Straight Netting, if required to be very even, should have two rows worked on the Foundation Loop before the real piece is commenced, as then every loop made will be of equal size, which is not always the case when the work is immediately begun from the Foundation Loop.

NETTED ARTICLES.—The patterns previously given can be used to work the following articles, but, as distinct directions as to number of loops and length of work is necessary, the manner of working is described in detail:—

Antimacassar.—The prettiest kind of Netted Antimacassar is formed with Netted rosettes of two different sizes; these rosettes are worked separately, and are then sewn together. One of the large rosettes forms the centre of the Antimacassar, and is surrounded by six rosettes of the same size; six small rosettes are placed to fill up the space outside these, and twelve large rosettes are sewn above, the six large ones forming the first circle; twelve small rosettes fill in the spaces between these last, and the Antimacassar is finished with twenty-four large rosettes forming the third circle. Thirty-one large rosettes and twelve small ones are required. Boar's-head cotton No. 12; two flat Meshes, $\frac{3}{8}$ and $\frac{3}{16}$ of an inch; and a round Mesh No. 12, are required. The Netting is easier worked attached to a Lead Cushion than to a Stirrup. To work the large rosette: First row—upon a small FOUNDATION LOOP, Net in PLAIN NETTING, on No. 12 Mesh, seven Loops, and join these together as a CIRCLE. Second and Third rounds—as the first round. Fourth round—use the smaller flat Mesh, and Net four loops into each loop upon the third round. Fifth and Sixth rounds—use No. 12 Mesh, and Net a Loop in every Loop upon the last round. Seventh round—use the largest Mesh, and Net two Loops into every Loop of the last round. Eighth and Ninth rounds—as the fifth round. For the small rosette, make a very small Foundation Loop over a pencil, and Net five Loops into it, using No. 12 Mesh; join these as a Circle, and net two more rounds upon them with the same Mesh. Fourth round—use the same Mesh, and Net two Loops into every Loop in the last round. Fifth round—Net with the smaller flat Mesh two Loops into every Loop upon the last round. Sixth and Seventh rounds—use No. 12 Mesh, and Net a Loop into every Loop. The centre of all the rosettes, after they are joined together, should be finished with an ORNAMENTAL WHEEL, such as worked in Modern Point Lace.

Bag.—Use Mesh No. 16, and coarse Netting silk, and Net sixty Loops on to the FOUNDATION LOOP; work the desired length, and draw one end up, and finish with a tassel, and running a ribbon through the other end.

Bag, Pence.—Use fine crimson silk, and Meshes Nos. 15 and 11. Net in PLAIN NETTING nine Loops upon the FOUNDATION LOOP, and join up. First and Second rounds—Net with the small Mesh in Plain Netting. Third round—with the small Mesh, Net two Loops into every Loop. Fourth round—small Mesh, a Loop into every Loop. Fifth round—small Mesh, Net two Loops into the first Loop, and one into the second Loop; repeat to the end of the round. Sixth round—small Mesh, a Loop into every Loop. Seventh round—small Mesh, INCREASE in this round by working two Loops into one eight times; these Increases should not be placed above the ones in the fifth round, but should be worked in the Loops before those. Eighth round—small Mesh, a Loop into every Loop. Ninth round—like the seventh round. Repeat eighth and ninth round seven times. Work forty-six rounds in Plain Netting with the small Mesh. Work a round with the large Mesh. For the next round, use the small Mesh, Net the second Loop before the first, and the fourth before the third; repeat to the end of the round. Work four rounds with the small Mesh in Plain Netting, and finish off with a SCALLOPED EDGING. Run a ribbon through the round worked with the large Mesh.

Cloud.—For a Cloud, single Berlin or Fleecy wool of two colours is required, and three flat Meshes, an inch, half an inch, and a quarter of an inch in width. To commence: Work 400 loops upon the FOUNDATION LOOP, with the half-inch Mesh. First and Second rows—PLAIN NETTING into every Loop with the half-inch Mesh and the darkest wool. Third row—use the lightest wool and the largest Mesh, and Net three Loops into every Loop upon the last row. Fourth and Fifth rows—use the smaller Mesh and the darkest wool, and Net into every Loop upon the last row. Sixth row—use the widest Mesh and the lightest wool, and work a Loop into every Loop upon the last row. Seventh row—use the half-inch Mesh and the darkest wool, and Net three Loops of the last row together. Eighth row—use the half-inch Mesh and the darkest wool, and work a Loop into every Loop upon the last row. Ninth row—as the third row. Tenth and Eleventh rows —as the fourth and fifth rows.

Curtains.—These are generally Netted in Plain Netting, and then ornamented with a pattern Darned upon them; but they can also be worked in any of the fancy Loops given under their own headings, and in that case will not require any Darned Pattern. The number of Loops that form the length of the Curtain will have to be put upon the FOUNDATION LOOP to start with; these, if Netted with a No. 9 Mesh, will measure four Loops to an inch, which will be a guide to the number required. In Netting such large articles as Curtains, the worker, from time to time, will have to tie up the work out of her way, so as to allow of room to move her hands when making the Knots. To do this without interfering with the shape of the Loops, run a tape into a row of the Netting, taking up every Loop, and being very careful to keep in the one row. Tie this tape to the foot as a Stirrup, and work until the length has again to be altered.

Edging.—(1). The Edging shown in Fig. 636 is worked with two Meshes, one a large flat Mesh, and the other a

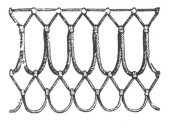

FIG. 636. NETTING—EDGING.

round Mesh; the flat Mesh should be an inch in width, the round, an inch in circumference. Two sizes of cotton are also used, one a coarse Knitting cotton, and the other a fine Crochet cotton. The Edging is worked in Plain

Netting, and the pattern can be repeated to any length, and, therefore, used for the centre of curtains or window blinds, as well as for Edgings. To work: First row—Net in PLAIN NETTING, with the fine cotton and the round Mesh, the length required for the work. Second row— Net in Plain Netting, with the Large Mesh and the coarse cotton, into every Loop in the last row. Third and fourth rows—as the first row. Should the width of the Edging be increased, repeat from the first row.

(2.) This border is worked with a round Mesh of a medium size, and with two different sizes of cotton, one coarse and one fine, Walker and Evans' Knitting cotton Nos. 12 and 30 being the required thicknesses. To work as shown in Fig. 637: First row—work in PLAIN NETTING, and with the fine cotton, the length required for the border. Second and third rows—as the first row.

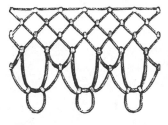

FIG. 637. NETTING—EDGING.

Fourth row—take the coarse cotton, and work the first Loop in Plain Netting; for the next Loop, work it in Plain Netting, but pass the thread twice round the Netting needle; repeat these two loops to the end of the row. Fifth row—Knot the fine cotton into the first Loop on the last row (a small Loop), and work two Loops in Plain Netting into the long Loop in the last row, then one Loop into the small Loop on the last row, and two into the next large Loop. Continue to the end of the row.

FIG. 638. NETTING—EDGING.

(3.) The Edging shown in Fig. 638 is an extremely light and pretty finish to curtains, or other articles that require borders. It is worked with a flat Mesh an inch and a quarter in width, and a round Mesh an inch in circumference, and with Strutt's knitting cotton No. 12. To work: Make a FOUNDATION with single cotton the length required for the Edging. First row—fill the Netting needle with doubled cotton, take the flat Mesh, and Net in PLAIN NETTING into every Loop of the Foundation. Second row—fill the Netting needle with single cotton, and use the round Mesh; Net the first two Loops together, and continue to Net two Loops together to the end of the row. Third row—use the round Mesh and the single cotton, and Net in Plain Netting into every Loop. Fourth row—take the flat Mesh and the doubled cotton, and Net two Loops into every Loop of the preceding row. Fifth row—use the round Mesh and the single cotton, and Net every Loop of the last row separately.

(4.) The Edging given in Fig. 639 is used for curtains and other articles that require borders; but, as it is a pattern that can be repeated indefinitely, it can also be

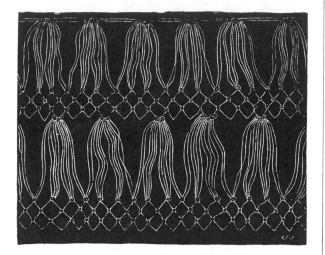

FIG. 639. NETTING—EDGING.

used to make curtains, centres, and other Netting patterns. The Edging should be worked with Strutt's Knitting cotton No. 12, and with two Meshes of unequal size, a flat Mesh an inch in width, and a round Mesh half an inch in circumference. To work: NET the FOUNDATION in single cotton, and with the round Mesh, and make Loops enough to form the length required for the Edging. First row—take the flat Mesh, and fill the needle with doubled cotton; work in PLAIN NETTING, and make three Loops into the first Loop on the Foundation row; then miss the second and third Loops, and Net three Loops into the fourth; repeat to the end of the row, missing two Loops, and making three Loops into every third Loop. Second row—take the round Mesh, and a needle filled with single cotton; Net in Plain Netting every Loop upon the preceding row. Third and Fourth rows—repeat the second row. Fifth row—commence again at the first row.

(5.) *Scalloped.*—A Scalloped Edging is a better border to a shawl or curtain than one made of vandykes, as the half-circles composing the scallops keep their stiffness and shape better than the points of the vandykes. Scallops are all formed in Plain Netting, and can be made either of silk, cotton, or wool, and with any size Mesh or number of Loops to a scallop, the usual number of Loops to each scallop being eight, twelve, or sixteen. The varieties in the scallops are formed by the size of the Meshes used (all requiring two Meshes, and some three) and the number of rows worked. To work for a medium sized scallop: Use the same cotton as the centre of the curtain or shawl is worked in, and three flat Meshes of different sizes, the middle size being the same as used in the centre part of the article. First row—with the largest Mesh work twelve or sixteen Loops into the first Loop of the edge, then miss eight or twelve Loops on the border, and work twelve or sixteen Loops into the ninth or thirteenth Loop; continue to the end of the row, missing a fixed number of Loops between each worked Loop. Second and Third rows—work into every Loop, using the medium-sized Mesh. Fourth and Fifth rows—work into every Loop, using the smallest sized Mesh. This scallop can be enlarged by a greater number of rows worked upon the two last-used Meshes, or made smaller by one row only being worked upon each Mesh.

(6.) *Vandyke.*—A pointed Edging, as shown in Fig. 640, particularly useful for making ornamental borders to d'oyleys, chair backs, and toilet cloths. After the plain Vandyke Edging has been Netted, a pattern should be Darned upon it in DARNED NETTING. To work as shown in Fig. 640: Make one loop upon the FOUNDATION LOOP, Net in PLAIN NETTING two Loops into this first loop, and INCREASE one Loop in each row until there are five Loops in a row. Then Increase at the end of every alternate row, until there are nine Loops in the row, taking particular care that the Increase is always made upon the same side of the work. In the next row, leave unworked four Loops on the side which has not been Increased, and thus form the Vandyke; work the other five (the dotted line in the illustration shows this row), continue the work, and Increase in every alternate row until there are nine Loops again, and then miss the four upon the Vandyked edge as before.

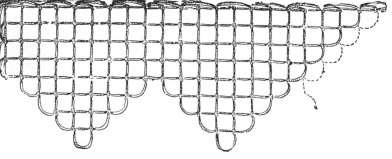

FIG. 640. NETTING—VANDYKE EDGING.

Fichu.—This can be worked either in bright-coloured silks or fine wools, and with a flat Mesh half an inch in width. The Loop is used in Plain Netting; but this can be varied and rendered more ornamental if worked as explained in Fly Netting. To work: Commence with one Loop upon the FOUNDATION LOOP, and INCREASE every row by working two Loops into the last Loop. Continue to do this until the widest part of the Netting is as long as the widest part of the Fichu, and then commence to work a border. For this, two different sized Meshes are required, one round, ½in. in diameter, and one flat, ½in. wide. Net the first and second rows round the sides of the Fichu, but not across the widest part, in PLAIN NETTING. Third row—take a different coloured wool or silk to that used in the Fichu, and the large Mesh; double the wool or silk, and Net it into every Loop of the second row. Fourth and Fifth rows—like the first row. Sixth row—use the large Mesh and the doubled wool, and Net two Loops into every alternate Loop upon the last row. Seventh and eighth rows—like the first row. Ninth row—like the sixth, but work the first double Loop into the second Loop, and not into the first on the row. Tenth and Eleventh rows—as the first row. Twelfth row—carry this row all round the Fichu; use the large flat Mesh and the coloured wool, but single, not double. Net eight Loops into the first Loop on the row, miss two Loops, Net eight Loops into the next Loop, miss two Loops, and repeat to the end of the row. Thirteenth and Fourteenth rows—Plain Netting into every Loop with the wool or silk used in the body of Fichu. Fifteenth row—use the round Mesh and the coloured wool, but single, not double; put the wool twice round the Mesh, miss a Loop, Net six Loops into the corresponding six on the row, put the wool again twice round the Mesh, miss a Loop, and Net six Loops as before into the corresponding Loops upon the row. Sixteenth row—work as in the fifteenth row, but Net the four centre Loops of that, and miss the outside ones, and pass the wool three times round the Mesh. Seventeenth row—as the fifteenth row, but Net the two centre Loops and miss the outside ones, and pass the wool four times round the Mesh.

Fringe (1).—This fringe is all worked in Plain Netting, and can be worked with single Berlin wool and flat Meshes an inch and half an inch in width, or with Crochet cotton of a medium size, and flat Meshes half an inch and a quarter of an inch in width. First, second, and third rows—PLAIN NETTING with the small Mesh into every Loop on the edge of the article. Fourth row—use the large Mesh, and work four Loops into the first Loop of the last row, miss two Loops on the last row, and work four Loops into the fourth Loop; repeat to the end, working four Loops into every third Loop, and miss the ones between. Fifth row—use the small Mesh, and Net into every Loop. Sixth row—use the large Mesh, and work four Loops into the second Loop on the last row, and miss the next two Loops, repeat to the end, work four Loops into every third Loop on the last row. Seventh row—as the fifth. Eighth row—as the sixth.

(2). Work with two Meshes, one half the size of the other, and use the same cotton as that with which the body of the article has been netted. First row—Net in PLAIN NETTING with the small Mesh into every Loop at the edge. Second, Third, and Fourth rows—Plain Netting, with the small Mesh. Fifth row—Plain Netting, with the large Mesh. Sixth row—draw the first Loop through the second, Net the second Loop, first using the small Mesh, and then Net the first; draw the third Loop through the fourth, and Net the fourth and then the third; repeat to the end of the row. Seventh row—use the small Mesh, and Net in Plain Netting. Eighth row—cut a number of 4-inch lengths of cotton, double them, and knot three into every Loop.

Hair-nets.—Net with fine Netting silk and a small round Mesh, work in PLAIN NETTING, and place upon the FOUNDATION LOOP twelve Loops, and Net in Plain Netting backwards and forwards for twelve rows to form a perfect square. Fasten off and pass a Loop through the middle of the square, so that all the edge Loops can be easily worked into, and Net all round the square. INCREASE at every corner by working two Loops into the corner Loop. Work round and round, Increasing in the corner Loops in every second round until the size required for the Hair-net is obtained; then work a round with a quarter-inch Mesh, and into this pass a piece of elastic with which to draw the net together. A circular Hair-net is Netted after the instructions given in CIRCLE.

Hammocks.—These should be very strong, and should, therefore, be made with mattress twine, and with a round Mesh, 3 inches in circumference, and a long, thin, wooden needle, made for Netting up twine, and with notched, and not scalloped, ends. Net thirty Loops, and then work sixty rows. Run a stout cord through the FOUNDATION ROW, and through the last row, and attach hooks to these with which to suspend the Hammock, and draw the edges of each side slightly together, by running a coloured cord up them, and fasten them with that to the top and bottom of the Hammock. Slip a notched bar, 27 inches long, and 1 inch in width, across the upper and lower ends of the Hammock when it is in use. A more ornamental Hammock can be formed by working with a double thread in Fly Netting. To do this, make one thread of twine, and the other of a bright-coloured, coarse worsted; and when the Netting is finished, cut the worsted thread, and fluff it up into a ball round the Knot.

Lawn Tennis Ball Bag.—This is useful for carrying balls about in, and for keeping them together when not in use. To make: Take some fine twine, and a three-quarter inch flat Mesh, and make a small FOUNDATION LOOP, into which work six Loops in PLAIN NETTING; unite them together, as in the directions for a CIRCLE, and continue to INCREASE as there directed for eight to twelve rounds, according to the size required for the bag; then work round after round without any Increase until a bag a foot and a half in length is obtained; cut away the spare twine, and run a piece of strong tape through the top round of the meshes, with which to draw the mouth of the bag together.

Lawn Tennis Net.—The Nets for lawn tennis are made of various dimensions, but all on the same plan, the alteration being in the width and length, which is done by working as in Oblong Netting. Nets are varied in size according to Tennis rules; they are mostly made 2½ feet in width, and 8 or 9 yards in length, and with a 2in.

Loop. To make: Procure good mattress twine, a flat Mesh of an inch in width, and a wooden needle. Commence with one Loop on the FOUNDATION LOOP, and work as directed in OBLONG NETTING; make the Loops with FISHERMAN'S KNOTS, and not in Plain Netting. INCREASE in each row until thirty-two Loops (for a 3-feet net) are in a row, and then Increase upon one end of the row, and DECREASE upon the other to form the straight piece of the net. Measure the length from time to time, and when 8 or 9 yards can be measured from the first Loop to the last Increase, commence to Decrease in every row without any Increase until only one Loop remains. Soak the Net, when finished, in indiarubber solution, or in boiled linseed oil, to render it waterproof.

Mittens.—Work with Meshes No. 3 and No. 6, and fine black or coloured Netting silk. Six or seven skeins of this are required, according to the length of the Mitten. The size given is for a Mitten 12 inches long. Commence by putting upon the FOUNDATION LOOP forty-eight Loops, and work with No. 6 Mesh eight rows, either in PLAIN NETTING or in CROSS NETTING; then, with the smaller Mesh, Net twelve rows in Plain Netting. Continue this Plain Netting with the same mesh for forty-eight rows, or make the same number of rows with two coloured silks in FLY NETTING, cutting one of the silks when the Mitten is finished and fluffing it as a ball round the knots. Work six rows in Plain Netting with the large Mesh, which completes the part of the Mitten up the arm. Unite the ends of the netting, and Net with small Mesh one round, INCREASE on the twelfth Loop and on the fourteenth, but not upon the other Loops (the Increase on these Loops is for the thumb). Net sixteen rounds, Increasing two Loops, to form the thumb, in the two Loops already mentioned every other round; finish off the thumb by Netting, upon the Loops that have been formed by the Increasing, seven to nine rows, according to the length required, Decreasing two Loops in every row, and working the last few rows like Edging No. 636 upon a very fine Mesh. Continue to Net the hand of the Mitten for sixteen plain rows with the small Mesh, and then finish with a SCALLOPED EDGING. Ornament the back part of the hand with tufts of silk matching the silk used in the Fly Netting upon the arm of the Mitten.

Netted or Darned Insertions.—These insertions look very well as stripes between coloured satin for antimacassars or sofa covers. Fig. 641 is worked with Evans' Crochet cotton No 40, and a flat Mesh three-quarters of an inch in width. To work: Net six rows of PLAIN NETTING of the length required for the antimacassar, and starch the Netting slightly. CROCHET the edges of the Netting as follows: One DOUBLE CROCHET into the first Loop, one CHAIN, one Double Crochet into the next Loop, continue to the end, and work both edges in this manner. Then TACK the Netting on to stiff paper, and Crochet along each side of each row of Knots, except the middle row, with one Double Crochet into the first Loop, one Chain and one Double Crochet into the next. Then DARN with fine Knitting cotton the pattern shown in Fig. 641 upon the meshes. Darn in and out five threads for the outside piece of the pattern, Knot two threads

together for the next piece, Knot four threads together for the next piece, and for the middle Knot the two centre

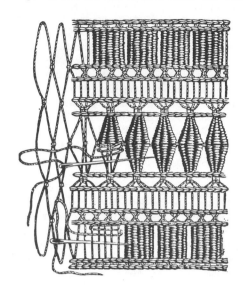

FIG. 641. NETTED AND DARNED INSERTION.

threads of four threads together, and then Darn them; draw the ends together in the Darning, and expand the middle to form the cone shape in the pattern.

To work Fig. 642: This insertion differs but little from the one above, but is not so wide nor so much Darned. Use a half-inch Mesh and Walter and Evans' Crochet cotton No. 40, and Net five rows of PLAIN NETTING the

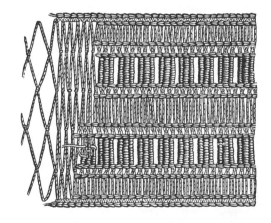

FIG. 642. NETTED AND DARNED INSERTION.

length required. CROCHET the edges of the insertion and in rows upon each side of every row of Knots, in the manner described above. For the Darned part of this pattern, DARN together six threads of the FOUNDATION, and draw these close, to have a clear space between the thick lines so formed. To Darn these six threads together, Darn over and under two threads at a time.

Purses.— Long netted purses for gentlemen's and ladies' use are either made all of one colour of Netting silk, or with contrasting shades. The purses are generally netted in Plain Netting, but single and treble Diamond Netting, or Cross Netting, can be used upon them if wished.

To net a *Gentleman's Purse*, 10 inches in length: Use Mesh No. 13, and five skeins of coarse Netting silk. Work eighty Loops into the FOUNDATION LOOP, and net rows of PLAIN NETTING until the 10 inches required are made. The same purse, if made with fine Netting silk, will require one hundred Loops to commence with. Sew up the sides of the purse, leaving a space for the opening; BUTTONHOLE round this opening with the Netting silk, then TACK it up, and place the purse upon a piece of wood, of a barrel shape, to stretch it; damp the Netting, and leave it on the wood until dry, when take it off, untack the opening, sew up the ends, and add the tassels and the rings. If a piece of wood of the proper size and shape is not procurable, damp and stretch the Netting, and then pass a warm iron over it.

To net a *Lady's Long Purse*, 9 inches in length: Use Mesh No. 10, and five skeins of fine Netting silk, of two different shades. Put ninety Loops upon the FOUNDATION LOOP, and Net in PLAIN NETTING, with the two colours, seven rows of the colour of which there are three skeins, and five rows of the colour of which there are two skeins. Repeat until the length required is obtained. Finish the purse in the same manner as described in the Gentleman's Purse.

To net a *Purse with Beads*: Use Mesh No. 3, and four to five skeins of fine Netting Silk, and the smallest beads procurable. Put ninety Loops upon the FOUNDATION LOOP, and close them up so as to have no seam. Work three rounds in PLAIN NETTING without any beads; in the fourth round put a bead into every third Loop; in the fifth round, a bead upon the loop upon each side of the bead in the last round; and work the sixth round like the first round. Repeat these three rounds for 3½ inches, then make the opening of the purse, by working as rows, and not as rounds, for 2 inches, and continue to put the beads in as before; then return to the rounds, and work 3½ inches as before, and end with three plain, unbeaded rows. Elaborate patterns for beading purses can be made by using the small diaper and sprig patterns that are printed for Berlin wool designs.

Stove Ornaments.—These netted ornaments are extremely light and pretty, and as they wash, will remain good for many years. The centre part is Netted with medium-sized Crochet cotton, the border with Strutt's Knitting cotton No. 12, and the Meshes used are flat, and half an inch and a quarter of an inch in width. To work: Commence the work at the side, and Net in PLAIN NETTING seventy-four Loops upon the FOUNDATION LOOP. First row—work a row of Plain Netting with the small Mesh. Second and following ten rows—Plain Netting with the small Mesh. Thirteenth row—in Plain Netting with the large Mesh. Fourteenth row—Net in Plain Netting with the same Mesh, but net the second Loop before the first, the fourth before the third. Fifteenth row—repeat the fourteenth row, but Net with the small Mesh. Sixteenth to Twenty-seventh rows — work with

the small Mesh in Plain Netting. Twenty-eighth row—repeat from the thirteenth row. Repeat the pattern twelve times, and at the end work twelve plain rows with the small Mesh, and then one plain row with the large Mesh. Commence the border on the Foundation side, and work round three sides of the Stove Ornament as follows: First row—use the small Mesh and the knitting cotton, work a plain Loop into the first six Loops, five LONG LOOPS into the seventh Loop, five Long Loops into the eighth Loop, and repeat from the commencement. Second and third row—use the small Mesh, and Net into every Loop. Fourth row—use the large Mesh, and Net a Loop into every Loop, but Net the second Loop before the first, and the fourth before the third. Fifth row—use the small Mesh, Net twelve Loops into the corresponding twelve Loops on the last row, three Long Loops into the thirteenth Loop, three Long Loops into the fourteenth, and three Long Loops into the fifteenth Loop, and repeat from the commencement. Sixth and seventh rows—use the small Mesh, and Net into every Loop. Eighth row—Net into every Loop with the large Mesh. Ninth row—Net into every Loop with the small Mesh. Having completed the border, starch and pull out the netting, run a tape through the side that has no border, and tie the Ornament with the tape to the register, fill the grate with muslin threads, arrange the netting over them, and finish by laying a few fern leaves upon the netting.

Netting Crochet.—*See* CROCHET NETTING.

Netting Needles.—These Needles are employed in conjunction with MESHES, and vary in length, according to the coarseness and width of the work on which they are used. They are divided at each end, the two points converging together, and the yarn or silk is wound round through these forks, from one end to the other, lengthwise along the Needle. There is a small hole through the latter, below the fork at one end, through which the yarn or silk is threaded to secure it. Netting Needles may be had in steel, wood, ivory, and bone.

Network.—In olden days, Netting, when ornamented with Darning, or when worked quite plainly, was known as Filatorium and Network, and ranked as a Lace. The Network produced by the Egyptians was worked with silk or gold threads, or with extremely fine flax thread, and further ornamented with beautiful patterns darned upon it with many colours, and was far superior to the productions of modern times. From the twelfth to the sixteenth century, Network was largely worked in Europe, and was used for ecclesiastical purposes.

New Lace Appliqué.—A modern work intended to give the appearance of lace laid upon satin. To work: Trace out a bold design of leaves and flowers upon a gaily coloured piece of satin. Lay some open meshed Brussels Net upon this foundation, and attach it to the design by lines of BUTTONHOLES. Work these lines round the design, and use various coloured filoselles, so as to diversify the colouring. When the outline is finished, cut away the Brussels Net where not secured, and finish the leaves and flowers by working veins and centres to them with bright silks. Connect the pattern together with stems and tendrils worked with dark filoselles.

Nœuds.—A French term, signifying bows of ribbon, or other materials, employed in Millinery and Dressmaking.

Noils.—The short wool taken, by combing, from the long staple wool, and employed to give thickness and solidity to wool stuffs, in the weaving.

Normandy Lace.—The Laces made in Normandy are of various descriptions. Of the narrow thread Pillow Laces, the Petit Poussin, Ave Maria, Point de Dieppe and Havre, and Dentelle à la Vierge are well known, as well as the imitation Brussels and Valenciennes; but besides these, there are the Silk Blondes, both black and white, which are manufactured at Caen and Bayeux, and which are similar to the Silk Blondes made at Chantilly and in Spain.

Norman Embroidery.—This is a modern work, founded upon Crewel Work, and consists of working a conventional design in the Crewel Stitch, and then covering over certain parts of that stitch with open and fancy Embroidery Stitches. To work: Select a Crewel Work design of a stiff and regular pattern, and trace this upon Oatmeal Cloth or a coloured material. Fill in all the design with CREWEL STITCH, and work with Crewel wools and with shades that are appropriate. Select various light shades of filoselle silk that harmonise with the colours used in the Crewels, and cover over the latter with light BARS made with the filoselles and with WHEELS, DOTS, HERRINGBONE, TRELLIS, and other Embroidery Stitches. Fill in the centres of the flowers with stamens and knots made with the filoselle, and cross all the stems and sprays supporting the foliage and flowers with Bars, also made with filoselle.

Northampton Lace.—Many descriptions of Pillow Lace are made in Northamptonshire, but none of them are of English invention, they all being copies of Brussels, Lille, and Valenciennes Laces. They are all good imitations, but the two best are the one shown in Fig. 643, of Lille Lace, with a ground that vies, as to its clearness and regularity, with that of foreign manufacture, and the narrow Valenciennes Lace. Much of the lace made in Northamptonshire is called Baby

FIG. 643. NORTHAMPTON LACE.

Lace, as it was at one time made in the narrow widths that were used for children's caps. Baby Lace is now obsolete, but the lace shown in Fig. 643 is still manu-factured, and is frequently called English Lille, as it possesses the beauty of Lille Lace, and imitates its clear ground and small running pattern.

Norwegian Yarn.—This yarn is made of the undyed hair of the Scandinavian lamb, which is very soft, and is especially suitable for the knitting of shawls and other wraps. It is to be had in both white and grey—the natural colours—and is sold by the skein.

Norwich Crape.—A textile composed of a silk warp and a worsted woof, generally of two different colours, or at least, of two shades of one colour. It somewhat resembles Bombazine, but is not twilled, and may be had in all colours.

Noué.—A French term to signify knotted, employed by dressmakers with reference to certain styles of trimming.

Nuns' Cloth.—This material is otherwise called Toille de Nonne, and by Americans, Bunting. It is a woollen dress material, superior to Grenadine in appearance and durability, yet light, is plainly woven, and to be had of every colour, as well as in white, but is chiefly worn in black. It is made in various widths, from 30 inches to 1 yard, and is, with Beige, Carmelite, and the comparatively new dress material, produced especially for mourning wear, called DRAP SANGLIER, a variety of the same description of cloth which is known as "Bunting"; but the latter is of so loose and coarse a texture, that its use is almost entirely restricted to the making of Flags. The name originated in Somersetshire, where the word Bunting was used for Sifting; and this worsted cloth, being of very open make, was employed for the sieves for sifting meal. There are few makes of woollen stuff which can be had in more extensive varieties of quality; the fine and delicately tinted light and white kinds being suitable for evening dresses; the dark, thick, and rough sorts equally satisfactory for ordinary wear, and, being durable, and not liable to creasing, are especially suited for travelling costumes. The Monks of Mount Carmel, being dressed in habits made of undyed wool, and woven after the manner of Nuns' Cloth, Beige, &c., originated the name of Carmelite, in France, for the stuff so called.

Nuns' Work.—Crochet, Knitting, Netting, Cut Work, Drawn Work, Pillow and Hand-made Laces, Satin Embroidery, and Church Embroidery, were at one time all known by this name. From the eleventh to the fifteenth century the best needlework of every kind was produced by the Nuns, who imparted their knowledge to the high born ladies who were educated in their convents, and from this circumstance each variety, besides being distinguished by a particular name, was classed under the general one of Nuns' Work.

Nutria, or Coypou Fur (*Myopotamus Coypus*).—An animal of the genus Rodent, somewhat resembling both the Musquash and the Beaver; it is smaller than the latter, but larger than the former, and inhabits the banks of rivers in Buenos Ayres and Chili, being a kind of water rat. Nutria skins are dressed and dyed as a substitute for sealskin, and are also used, in the manufacture of hats, as a substitute for beaver.

O.

Oatmeal Cloths.—Under this descriptive name there are textiles of Cotton, Linen, and Wool, deriving their designation from having a corrugated face, woven to represent Bannock Cakes. These cloths are thick, soft, and pliant, may be had in all colours, and are 54 inches in width. There are also Fancy Oatmeal Cotton Cloths, woven in diamond designs and stripes, but uncoloured, and measuring only 18 inches wide. Some amongst these varieties are employed as a foundation for Embroidery in Crewels and Silks, a thin quality being used for dress, and a thicker one for upholstery.

Octagon Loop.—A name applied to the loop made in Pillow Lace in BRUSSELS GROUND.

Œillet.—The French term for an Eyelet-hole.

Oilcloth.—A coarse hempen fabric, the fibres of which are saturated with oil; when dry and hard, it is painted with devices in various colours, by means of stencil plates, or blocks cut for the purpose, as in engraving. These cloths are employed for the covering of floors, stairs, &c.

Oiled Leather.—This description of Leather is sometimes called Washed Leather, being only an imitation of CHAMOIS LEATHER. The Leather is dressed with fish oil, and, when partially dried, is washed in a strong alkali, to render it very soft and pliable. It is employed as a lining, particularly for waistcoats and women's petticoats, perforated with small round holes, to obviate its air-tight character; it is also used for riding breeches and trousers, and for gloves.

Oiled Silk.—Silk so prepared by saturation in oil as to be made waterproof. It is used for linings, and likewise for medical and surgical covering of bandages and compresses. It is semi-transparent, and may be had in green and in gold colour.

Oiled Tracing Paper.—This substance is used in Embroidery, and many kinds of variegated needlework, for the purpose of obtaining a correct outline of the design to be worked, without the trouble of drawing the same.

Old English Embroidery.—A modern imitation of Anglo-Saxon embroidery. In this work, Crewels are used instead of gold and silver threads, and fancy Embroidery stitches fill in the design. To work: Use CREWEL STITCH to cover all the outlines of the design, and fill all centres with LACE or COUCHING STITCHES. Work stems and sprays with HERRINGBONE and FEATHER STITCHES.

Old Lace.—A term indifferently used either for Pillow or Needle-point Laces worked before the introduction of machine-made net grounds to Laces.

Oleograph Work.—A modern Embroidery, and a combination of Watteau figures printed in colours on to the material and embroidery. The colours are fast, and the work can be washed. To work: Procure the material, upon which a Medallion with coloured figures is printed Make a frame for the same with lines of CREWEL STITCH, and work a garland of small flowers in SATIN STITCH. and round the frame.

Ombré.—The French term for shaded. Braid Ombré is so called because it is shaded with graduated tints, from light to dark, of one colour.

Onlaid Appliqué.—*See* APPLIQUÉ.

Open Braid.—One of the stitches used in Pillow Lace making, and described under BRAID WORK.

Open Crochet Stitch.—*See* CROCHET.

Open Cross Bar.—The Bars that connect the various parts of Modern Point and Point Lace together are called Open Cross Bars when they cross each other to form that figure. To make: Throw two strands of thread from one edge of lace to the opposite piece, and cover the lines thus made with close BUTTONHOLE until the centre of it is reached. Throw from this place a thread to cross the first at right angles, and cover this with Buttonhole to the centre of the first line; throw a thread from there, so as to be exactly opposite the last one, cover that with Buttonhole to the centre of the first line, and then finish by covering the unworked part of the first line with Buttonhole.

Open Cross Braid.—One of the stitches used in Pillow Lace making, and described under BRAID WORK.

Open Cross Stitch.—*See* CROCHET.

Open Diamonds Stitch.—This is a general term applied to stitches used as Fillings in Modern Point and Point Lace that are worked with close rows of Buttonhole, except where an open space is left, which takes the shape of a die or diamond. Cadiz, Escalier, and Point d'Espagne are all varieties of Open Diamonds, as are the patterns of Fillings shown in Figs. 402 and 403

FIG. 644. OPEN DIAMONDS.

(see page 206). To work in the Open Diamond shown in Fig. 644: Commence with twenty-one close BUTTONHOLES worked across the space to be filled, and work three plain rows. Fourth row—work 9 Buttonhole, miss the space of three, work 9, miss 3, work 9, miss 3, work 15. Fifth row—work 18 Buttonhole, miss 3, work 3, miss 3, work 15, miss 3, work 3, miss 3, work 12. Sixth row—work 15 Buttonhole, miss 3, work 9, miss 3, work 9, miss 3, work 9, miss 3, work 9. Seventh row—work 12 Buttonhole, miss 3, work 15, miss 3, work 3, miss 3, work 24. Eighth row—work 9 Buttonhole, miss 3, repeat three times, and then work 15. Ninth row—work 18 Buttonhole, miss 3, work 3, miss 3, work 15, miss 3, work 3, miss 3, work 12. Tenth row—work 15 Buttonhole *, miss 3, work 9, repeat from * three times. Eleventh row—work 12 Buttonhole, miss 3, work 15, miss 3, work 3, miss 3, work 24. Twelfth row—work 9 Buttonhole *, miss 3, work 9, repeat from * twice, miss 3, work 15. Thirteenth row—work 12 Buttonhole, miss 3, work 15, miss 3, work 3, miss 3, work 24. Fourteenth row—work 15 Buttonhole *, miss 3, work 9, repeat from * three times. Fifteenth row—work 18 Buttonhole, miss 3, work 3, miss 3, work 15, miss 3, work 3, miss 3, work 12. Repeat from the fourth row until the space is filled in.

Open Dice Stitch.—Similar to OPEN DIAMONDS STITCH.

Open Dots.—These are holes made in Pillow Lace, in order to lighten any part of the design that might look too thick and close. To work: Continue to work in CLOTH STITCH until the centre of the lace is reached, there make a TURNING STITCH, and return to the same edge; take up the BOBBINS upon the other side, work to the opposite edge and back again to the hole, the last stitch being a Turning Stitch; now return to the first worked Bobbins, and work right across the lace with them, and continue to work in Cloth Stitch with the whole number of the Bobbins until the place is reached where another open Dot has to be made.

Open English Lace.—A stitch used in Point Lace and Modern Point Lace, similar to POINT D'ANGLETERRE.

middle, slant upwards again with the twisted threads, and sew to the opposite side, and to the band there, and repeat this twisting and sewing to the opposite sides, and to the middle, until the right number of Fibres is obtained. Work the other small leaves in the same way, and with the same number of Bobbins, but hang on seven pairs of Bobbins for the large leaf. To finish the spray: Work the flower in STEM STITCH for the outside petals, and in RAISED WORK for the inside. Work the Shamrock edge in CLOTH and HALF STITCH, the rosettes in STEM STITCH with CUCUMBER PLAITINGS, and the band with OPEN BRAID and CROSS PLAITINGS. For the ground, rule some blue paper in squares, and stitch the various pieces of lace on to this with their right side downwards;

FIG. 645. OPEN FIBRE IN HONITON LACE.

Open Fibre.—These are used in Honiton Lace making to form open centres to various parts of the pattern, and are illustrated in the open work in the centre leaves of Fig. 645. To work the leaves shown in centre spray: Commence at the lowest leaf, hang on five pairs of BOBBINS at the top of the main fibre, and work STEM down it; at the bottom of the leaf, hang on another pair of Bobbins, and work the band round the leaf in CLOTH STITCH, joining the middle fibre to this at the top. Carry the band in Cloth Stitch round one of the adjoining leaves, cut off a pair of Bobbins when the bottom of that leaf is reached, work the Fibre stem upon it, join to the band, and cut off the Bobbins. Work the open inside of the leaf thus: Sew a pair of Bobbins to the band near the top of the leaf, TWIST the threads, slant them downwards, and sew to the

then pin the paper on the Pillow and work along the lines. Hang on four pairs of Bobbins, and work over these lines in Stem Stitch and with a PEARL EDGE, and work in squares. Make all the lines one way first, and at the cross lines make a SEWING, thus: Drop the loop underneath the line to be sewn to, and pass the other through it. When, in the process of making the ground, the lace is reached, plait BEGINNERS' STEM with the Bobbins, after sewing to the lace, down to the next line, in preference to cutting off the Bobbins and re-tying them.

Open Knotting.—*See* MACRAME.

Open Lace.—A name sometimes applied to Netting when ornamented with a Darned Pattern. *See* DARNING ON NETTING.

Open Ladder Stitch.—See *Ladder Stitch* in EMBROIDERY STITCHES.

Open Stitches, Tricot.—*See* CROCHET.

Open Work.—A term employed in Embroidery, Lacemaking, and Fancy Work of all kinds, such as Knitting, Netting, Tatting, Cut Work, Crochet, &c. It simply means that the work is made with interstices between the several portions of close work, or of cut or open material. Much of the Irish White Muslin Embroidery and Madeira Work is called Open Work, and is fully described under BRODERIE ANGLAISE, IRISH WORK, and MADEIRA WORK.

Open Work Stitches.—These are all EMBROIDERY STITCHES, and will be found under that heading.

Opossum Fur.—The Opossum is of the genus *Dydelphys*, and is a marsupial quadruped, of which there are several species. One of these abounds in the United States, another in Texas, and others in California, South America, and Australia. The skins measure 8 inches by 16 inches, some being of a reddish-brown colour on the back, and of a buff colour on the stomach; some grey, but called "blue Opossum," the hair being rather short, thick, and soft. The Opossum of Australia is of this description, but of a particularly rich and warm shade of red-brown and buff. There is also, in America, a long-haired species, the skins of which look handsome when made into capes, tippets, muffs, and trimmings. It is more glossy than the other varieties, although dyed black, but is not so soft to the touch. The skins of all varieties of the Opossum are employed for articles of dress, and for sofa and carriage rugs.

Opus Anglicum, or Opus Anglicanum.—A name given to English needlework produced in the time of the Anglo-Saxons, which was celebrated for its extreme beauty and delicacy of execution, and also for the introduction of a peculiar stitch, said to be invented by the workers. This stitch resembles CHAIN STITCH, but is SPLIT STITCH, and was then, and is now, used to work the faces and hands of figures in CHURCH EMBROIDERY, and in the best kind of Embroidery.

Opus Araneum.—One of the ancient names for SPIDERWORK or DARNED NETTING.

Opus Consutum.—The ancient name for APPLIQUÉ.

Opus Filatorium.—The ancient name for NETTING and DARNED NETTING.

Opus Pectineum.—This was a fabric woven in a hand-loom so as to imitate Embroidery; it was manufactured with the help of an instrument resembling a comb, and from this received its name.

Opus Plumarium.—The old designation for FEATHER STITCH, and for Embroidery chiefly executed in that stitch, and upon thick, and not open, foundations.

Opus Pulvinarium.—The ancient name for Embroidery worked upon open canvas materials with silks and worsted, and with CROSS and TENT STITCH. This kind of Embroidery was also called Cushion Style, from its being used for kneeling mats and cushions. Our modern BERLIN WORK answers to the old Opus Pulvinarium.

Opus Saracenicum.—The ancient name for TAPESTRY.

Opus Seissum.—One of the names given in the olden times to CUT WORK, or lace of that description.

Opus Tiratum.—*See* DRAWN WORK.

Organzine.—This name is applied to the silk of which the warp of the best silk textiles is made, which has been cleaned, spun, doubled, thrown, and considerably twisted, so as to resemble the strand of a rope. It is composed of from two to four strands of raw silk, each thread being separately twisted in a mill, and then two twisted together in an opposite direction to that of each separate strand, which is accomplished by reversing the motion of the machinery, thus forming a thread like a rope. When finished, Organzine is wound on reels, instead of Bobbins, from which it is made into skeins, and sorted for sale. In former times we imported this article from Italy, as the Italians kept the art of "throwing silk" a profound secret; but Mr. John Lombe (of the firm of Thomas and Lombe) privately took a plan of one of their complicated machines, at the risk of his life, and, being a wonderfully ingenious mechanic, mastered all difficulties, and so procured the desired model in the King of Sardinia's dominions, which, on his return home, resulted in the establishment of a similar set of mills in Derby; and "throwing" was commenced in England in the year 1719. Since then, great improvements have been made in the mills, on the cotton "throstle" plan, driven by steam engines; but the old, hand-turned, small machines continue to be employed on the Continent. Thus, we scarcely import any Organzine, but supply ourselves. The name Organzine is French. The material is also known as THROWN SILK.

Oriental Embroidery.—Under this title is classed all the various kinds of Embroidery produced in the East, and which are described under their own headings. The Embroideries that are the most famous are Chinese, Indian, Japanese, Persian, Bulgarian, and Turkish. Oriental Embroideries are all celebrated for the amount of labour bestowed on their execution, the costliness of the materials used about them, and the vigour and boldness of conception and colouring displayed in their design. The East has always been looked upon as the cradle of fine needlework, and the Phrygians and Babylonians as the founders of the art; and for many centuries, during which nothing of any importance in Embroidery was produced in Europe, Africa and Asia continued to manufacture most beautiful articles; but since the introduction in the East of the bright-hued dyes of Europe, and the greater demand for the work, that which has been produced has not displayed either the same good taste or minuteness of execution that distinguishes the needlework of former days.

Oriental Rug Work.—*See* SMYRNA RUG WORK.

Orleans Cloth.—This cloth is composed of a mixture of wool and cotton, and designed for a dress material. It is plain made, the warp being of thin cotton, and the weft of worsted, which are alternately brought to the surface in the weaving. There are some varieties which are made with a silk warp; others are figured, and they may be had both with single and double warps. They are durable in wear, are dyed in all colours, as well as in black, and measure a yard in width. The name is derived from the town in France where the Cloth was first made. The only difference between this Cloth and a Coburg is, that the latter is twilled. The chief seats of the manufacture are at Bradford and Keighley, it having been introduced there in the year 1837.

Ornamental Knot.—*See* KNOTS and MACRAMÉ.

Orphrey.—The broad band, or clavi that adorns the priest's alb, and that was also used in olden days to border the robes of knights. These were always made of the very finest needlework, and the name given to them is considered to be derived from Auriphrygium and Phrygium, by which Embroidery worked with gold and silver thread and wire was called by the Romans, from the fact of the Phrygians being celebrated makers of this kind of needle-work, and most of it being imported from Phrygia. Authorities, however, differ as to the origin of the word, and some consider that it is derived from a gold fringe. The word Orphrey, in some early chronicles, is found as distinguishing this band of needlework when entirely worked with gold and silver threads, and the word Orfrey when silk threads only were used; but in all later works, Orphrey stands for both descriptions of work when placed in the particular position indicated. The bands placed vertically on an altar cloth, reredos, ecclesiastical vest-ment, or hangings, are all called Orphreys. They may be of gold lace, or cloth of gold, embroidery, lace, velvet, satin, silk, or stuff, and sometimes are decorated with jewels and enamels. They vary in width, as well as in material, colour, and character of their adornment. The term Orphrey is in common use with all engaged in ecclesiastical needlework. In olden times it used to be written Orfrais.

> For it full wele,
> With Orfrais laid, was everie dele,
> And purtraid in the rebaninges,
> Of dukes' storeis, and of kings.
>   —CHAUCER'S *Romaunt of the Rose*.

Orris.—A comprehensive term, employed in trade to signify almost every kind of Galloon used in upholstery. In the early part of the last century, it had a more re-stricted application, and denoted certain Laces woven in fancy designs in gold and silver. The name is a corruption of Arras. *See* GALLOONS.

Osnaburg.—A coarse linen textile, made of flax and tow, which originated in the German town in Hanover after which it is called.

Ostrich Feathers.—The Ostrich has exceedingly long and soft plumage, of which there are several varieties in texture and quality, influenced by the climate and food to which the bird has been habituated. Ostrich Feathers are imported from Mogador, Aleppo, Alexandria, and the Cape of Good Hope. The Feathers on the upper part and extremities of the back, wings, and tails are valuable in commerce, being superior in quality and colour to the others; those of the wings being employed for head-dresses. The greyish Feathers of the female are less valuable than those of the male, which are better in colour. They may be obtained dyed in every hue, the art of dyeing having been brought to great perfection, both in this country and in France. The Feathers of the Rhea, or American Ostrich, are imported from Buenos Ayres. They are dyed by the natives, and em-ployed for coverings of the body, as well as the head. The flossy kinds are used in South America and in Europe for military plumes; and the long brown Feathers of the wings are made into brooms and dusting-brushes.

Otter Fur.—The Otter is a native of Europe and America. Its Fur is thick, soft, and glossy, of a grey colour at the base, but tipped with brown. The Otters found in Europe are rather smaller than those of America, which latter are of a dark reddish-brown in winter, and nearly black in summer. The Indian species has a fur of a deep chestnut colour. About 500 skins are annually collected for home use. Those employed by the Russians and the Chinese are obtained from North America. The Sea Otter is a larger and more valuable animal. In China, a fine skin of the Sea Otter is valued at about £40; and older and less beautiful specimens at from £18 to £20 each.

Ouate.—The French name for Wadding, and in common use amongst French dressmakers.

Ourlet.—The French word signifying a HEM.

Outline Embroidery.—An adaptation of Indian and Oriental quilting to modern uses, and a work particularly suitable to the present desire to ornament articles in daily use with needlework. Outline Embroidery is worked upon linen or other washing materials, either with ingrain silks or cottons, or in crewels; but upon cloth and silk materials the work is executed in filoselles. The real Outline Stitches are a double RUN line and CREWEL or STEM STITCH, which is sometimes called POINT DE CABLE and ROPE STITCH, when used for this Embroidery. To Crewel Stitch, such fancy Embroidery Stitches as POINT DE RIZ, POINT DE MARQUE, and POINT LANCÉS can be added at the pleasure of the worker; but these are not real Outline Stitches, and are only introduced with caution, the motive of the work being to produce effect by the contour of an outlined, and not by a filled-in, pattern.

Fig. 646 is intended for a square for counterpane or chair back. To work: Trace a number of these squares all over one large piece of linen, and then surround each square with a border of DRAWN WORK; or work each square on a separate piece of material, and join them together with lace insertions. Draw out the design with the help of tracing paper and cloth, and work in all the outlines with CREWEL STITCH. Put the needle in across the outline line, in a slightly slanting direction; keep the cotton to the right, and draw it up. Put in these slanting stitches up the outline, and work them close together to make a line closely covered with slanting stitches.

The variety is given to the pattern by the number of colours used, by Running some lines and working others in Crewel Stitch, or by using thicker cotton to mark out the bolder lines of the design. Three shades of red are used in Fig. 646, the darkest shade being used to form the centre ornament, the four outside circles, and the two lines at the outside of the square; the second shade to form the conventional sprays that fill in the four circles;

and the lightest shade for the rest of the design. The position of these colours is shown in the illustration by the different shading of the lines. Form the fancy stitch that fills in the curves left by the rounds with a series of square lines covered with POINT DE MARQUE, and work them in the darkest shade of red.

Outline Stitch.—*See* EMBROIDERY STITCHES.

Ouvrage.—The French term for Work.

the dress material, and two of the lining—are stitched together on the inside, leaving a projecting edge. The darts of the bodice, and the seams of the sleeves, from the shoulder to the wrist, are OVER-CAST. Insert the Needle about halfway between the Running and the raw edge, from the far side of the ridge, pointing inwards; and, beginning from the left, work to the right, taking the stitches rather widely apart.

FIG. 646. OUTLINE EMBROIDERY.

Ouvroir Musselman.—*See* ARABIAN EMBROIDERY.

Ovals.—*See* GUIPURE D'ART.

Over-casting.—A method of plain sewing of as slight a character as TACKING. It is employed for the purpose of preventing the ravelling-out of raw edges of material, which have been either Stitched or Run together, such as the seams of skirts and the edges of the sleeves and armholes of a bodice, when the four edges—two of

Over-cast Stitch.—*See* EMBROIDERY STITCHES.

Over-hand Knot.—*See* KNOTS.

Over-sewing.—A method of Plain-sewing, otherwise known as Seaming, or Top-sewing, and executed somewhat after the manner of OVER-CASTING. But the great difference between Over-sewing and Over-casting is that the former is closely and finely executed for the uniting of two selvedges or folds of material, and the latter is very loosely done, and only for the purpose of keeping raw edges from ravelling out. Place the two selvedges side by side, insert the needle at the far side of the seam on the extreme right, and, having drawn it through, re-insert it close to the stitch already made, working from right to left. Extreme regularity in the length and disposition of the stitches should be carefully maintained. If the two pieces to be united have not selvedges, fold each inwards ; and when the Over-sewing has been done, make a small double HEM on the wrong side, to conceal and secure the raw edges. In olden times, this stitch was known by the name of Over-hand.

Oyah Lace.—A lace made in the harems in Turkey, Smyrna, and Rhodes, and sometimes called Point de Turque. It is formed with a Crochet hook and with coloured silks, and is a description of Guipure Lace ; but, as it is made by ladies for their own use, it rarely becomes an article of commerce.

P.

Pad.—A Pad of soft cotton is used in making Raised Needlepoints, such as Rose or Spanish Point. To make : Having outlined the part to be raised, fill in the space between the outline with a number of stitches made with Soft Moravian thread. Be careful to carry these from point to point of the outline at first, and then gradually INCREASE them, and lay them over each other at the part where the Raised Work is to be the highest.

Padding.—Sheets of cotton wadding inserted between other materials and their lining, sewed lightly, sometimes after the manner of quilting, so as to keep it in its right place. It is much employed in uniforms and in riding habits, as likewise to supply deficiencies in the figure, in cases of deformity, or extreme spareness.

Padlettes.—A French term, signifying spangles, or small discs of metal, of gold, silver, or steel, pierced in their centres, by which means they can be attached to dress materials. The name refers to the thin plates or scales, easily separated, in the case of some mineral substances, such as mica.

Pads.—Watered Doubles, or silk ribbons, of extra thickness, made in various colours, plain or striped, in mixed colours, expressly manufactured for use instead of watch-chains. Narrow widths in black are made as guards for eye-glasses.

Paduasoy.—Also known as Poddissoy, Pou-de-soie, and Silk Farandine. A smooth, strong, rich silk, originally manufactured at Padua, and much worn in the eighteenth century.

Paillons.—A French term for tinsel, or small copper plates or leaves, beaten till very thin, and coloured. They are employed in the ornamentation of embroidery and the stuffs for fancy or theatrical costumes. They are also used as foil by jewellers, to improve the colour and brightness of precious stones.

Painted Baden Embroidery.—A modern Embroidery and a combination of water-colour painting and embroidery. The work is executed on canvas materials or upon satin, with Crewels, Berlin wool, or Filoselles. To work : Trace the outline of a group or spray of flowers upon the material, and paint the body of the leaves, and the centres and petals of the flowers, with powdered colours mixed with Chinese white and gum-water. Grind the powdered colour in a muller until quite fine before mixing with the white and gum-water. Work the outlines of leaves and petals in CREWEL STITCH, selecting shades that contrast with the painted parts ; vein the leaves, and outline stems and stalks, with the same stitch. Finish the centres of the flowers with a few FRENCH KNOTS or CROSS STITCHES,

Painters' Canvas.—This is a closely woven material, also called TICKING, to be obtained both in grey and drab colour.

Pall.—This term has two significations — viz., the covering cloth of a coffin, and the mantle or robe worn by the Knights of the Garter when in full costume. It originated in name and in construction as a mantle from the Roman *Pallium*, which was shorter than the trailing *Toga* ; and our Anglo-Saxon ancestors adopted it under the name *Pœll*, when it was made of costly materials and work. The name Pall was subsequently adopted to denote a particular description of cloth, of most valuable character, worn by the nobles ; this has become a manufacture of the past, to which we find many references made by distinguished authors :

> Sometime let gorgeous Tragedy
> In sceptred Pall come sweeping by.
> *Milton.*

In an old Christmas carol, quoted by Hone, in his "Ancient Mysteries," it is mentioned in reference to our Saviour, in His infancy, viz. :

> Neither shall be clothed in purple or in Pall,
> But in fine linen, as are babies all.

Pan.—A French term employed in dressmaking, synonymous with Lappet, or Tab, in English. A flat ribbon-like end of material, or flap, which is sewn to the dress at one end, but is otherwise detached from it, and hangs as a decoration, like the end of a sash.

Panache.—An old French term, still in use, signifying a decorative arrangement of feathers in a helmet, hat, bonnet, or cap. The term is adapted from the French, to the exclusion of any English word, and was sometimes written Pennache.

Panama Canvas.—The old name for Java canvas. A kind of straw material, woven coarsely, after the style of ancient Egyptian cloth. It may be had in yellow, black, and drab, and is stiff and thick in quality. Another kind of this canvas is to be had in all colours of cotton ; and a third, of linen thread, in white only. All these will allow of washing.

Panels.—A term employed in dressmaking to denote certain side trimmings to a skirt, which extend down its whole length, and are attached to it at the side next to the train.

Panes, or Slashings.—Straight vertical cuts made in dresses, designed to open out, and show some under garment of contrasting colour ; or designed for the insertion of a piece of rich material sewn into the Panes, to simulate the exposure to view of an under-dress. When the Panes were real, the material inside was drawn through these openings like puffings. This fashion was of very ancient date. " Tissued Panes " are mentioned by Bishop Hall in his " *Satires*," A.D. 1598, as being then in vogue ; and hose, " paned with yellow, drawn out with blue," are mentioned in " *Kind Hart's Dream*," A.D. 1582. The fashion had its origin a the battle of Nancy, 1477, when the Swiss overthrew the Duke of Burgundy, and recovered their liberty. The Duke's tents were of silk of various colours, as well as of curious Tapestry, and the Swiss soldiers, tearing them to pieces, made themselves doublets of one colour, and caps, breeches, and hose of others, in which gay apparel they returned home. This signal and decisive victory has been more or less extensively commemorated ever since by the wearing of parti-coloured dress. Henry Peacham—who wrote in 1638—says, in his " *Truth of our Times*," that their dress then consisted of " doublets and breeches, drawn out with huge puffs of taffatee or linen, and their stockings (like the knaves of our cards) parti-coloured, of red, yellow, and other colours." These Panes, or Slashings, were subsequently adopted by the Court of France, and from thence came over to our own. Even up to the present time, the Swiss Guards of the Papal Court at Rome may be seen in this quaint style of uniform.

Pannier.—A term used in Dressmaking to signify a description of puffed overskirt, which was the chief feature in the Watteau costumes. The large balloon-like puffings at the back, and on each hip, sprang from the waist, and were trimmed all round at the extremity with a flounce, or frill, or edging of lace. The petticoat-skirt appearing beneath was always of a different material or colour.

Paper Patterns.—These Patterns are employed in Dressmaking, Millinery, Plain Sewing, and Embroidery, and are all, with the exception of the latter, made of tissue paper, in white and in colours. Whole costumes, of which the several parts and trimmings are gummed in their respective places, may be procured, demonstrating the current fashions, for the use of dressmakers and sempstresses, or for private individuals who perform their own needlework, plain or decorated. Patterns for Berlin woolwork, coloured for the assistance of the amateur embroiderer, are executed on thick paper, called Point Paper, and in Germany have long formed an article of extensive commerce with other countries. Not only arabesques and floral designs, but copies of celebrated pictures, in landscape and figures, are comprised in the trade. Good artists are engaged in the designing, and subsequent engraving or etching on copper plates, previously ruled in parallel lines, crossing each other at right angles, in imitation of the threads of an open canvas webbing; the decorative design is executed over this. Then, one colour at a time is laid upon a number of these patterns at once, with great rapidity—one sweep or touch of the square-cut brush sufficing. Thus, every separate colour is laid on. These paper patterns are available for Embroidery on satin, cloth, or any other material, in either Cross or Tent Stitch, by attaching a piece of canvas securely to them, and working on the canvas, withdrawing each thread of the same singly when the Embroidery is finished.

Designs are now very frequently executed in outline upon the canvas, or other material to be worked—at least, a single "repeat," or a specimen of a portion of the same—some part being also completed in needlework.

Paramatta.—A kind of Bombazine, the weft of which is of worsted, and the warp of cotton. It is employed as a dress material for the purpose of mourning (*see* MOURNING MATERIALS). Being of a light quality, and as crape is worn with it, a lining is indispensable for its preservation. For this, black Mull Muslin is to be recommended as the most suitable. Were a lining dispensed with, Paramatta would be found to split wherever the weight of the crape trimmings caused a strain upon it. When it was first introduced, it was composed of a silk warp and worsted weft, on which account it resembled Coburg. The cloth had its origin at Bradford, but the name it bears was derived from a town in New South Wales, on account, in all probability, of the wool of which it was composed, being imported thence. Paramatta measures 42 inches in width.

Parament, Parement. — A cuff sewn upon the outside of a sleeve, as in the coats of the eighteenth, and beginning of the nineteenth, century. The literal meaning of the term is " ornament," and it is applied to decorative additions to certain textiles, or ornamental hangings and furniture of State apartments.

Parchment Lace. — In old wardrobe accounts, this term is often applied to Pillow Laces, irrespective of their make, to distinguish them from the Laces made with the needle. The name is derived from the pattern upon which Pillow Laces are worked.

Parchment, or Vellum.—The skin of the sheep, which has been subjected to a process rendering it suitable for use as a writing material, or for bookbinding. The description known as Vellum is made of the skin of kids, calves, and stillborn lambs. It is much employed for illuminated addresses and mottoes, being further qualified for the reception of water colours, and gilding, by means of a little prepared ox-gall. The ancient and beautifully illuminated Missals were all of Vellum. Drumheads are made of Parchment procured from the skins of goats and wolves. The process by which skins are converted into Parchment is simple, and consists of steeping them in lime and water, stretching them on a frame, working well with hot water, and then applying whiting, drying each application—of which there should be several — in the sun. All grease will thus be removed from the skin. By scraping with a round, sharp knife, which needs skilful use, a fine surface is procured ; and when the skin is dry, it is ready for use. Should it be desired to write upon Parchment or Vellum, rub it lightly with a damp sponge, and, when dry, the ink will hold.

Parfilage.—This work is also called Ravellings, and consists in unpicking materials into which gold and silver threads or wire have been woven. It was an extremely fashionable employment with ladies in England and France during the latter part of the eighteenth century, and was pursued to such an extent in the Court of Marie Antoinette as to have led to many comments upon it by writers of that period. The original object of the work

was to obtain from old and tarnished articles the valuable
threads woven into them, and to sell such threads to the
gold-beaters; but when the ladies who worked at it had
used up all the old materials they could obtain, they
did not scruple to demand from their gentleman friends the
sword-knots, gold braids, gold laces, and bands, that were
often worn as part of the fashionable dress of the day; and
it was said that a courtier who had a reputation to maintain for gallantry and courtesy, was likely to go to an
assembly fully dressed, and to return from it as if he
had fallen among thieves and had by them been deprived
of all his braveries. The work is now obsolete.

Paris Cord.—A rich thick silk, with small fine ribs
running across the width, from selvedge to selvedge, and
deriving its name from Paris, the place of its first manufacture. There are various close imitations of it made in
England, but adulterated with cotton to form the Cord,
which should be of silk. Paris Cord is chiefly employed
for scarves, men's neckties, and waistcoats.

Paris Embroidery.—This is a simple variety of Satin
Stitch, worked upon piqué with fine white cord for washing
articles, and upon coloured rep, silk, or fine cloth, with
filoselles for other materials. The designs are the same
as those used for Crewel Work, but are selected with
small leaves shaped, like those of the olive or jessamine
flowers, with distinct and pointed petals, and circular or
oval-shaped fruit or berries. To work: Trace the outline
of the design upon silk or piqué, use fine white cord for the
piqué, and filoselle of various colours for the silk; split the
filoselle in half before using it. Thread a needle with the
silk, and commence the work at the extreme point of a
leaf or petal. Bring the needle up at the point of the leaf,
and put it into the material in the middle of the outline, at
the right side of the leaf, thus making a slanting SATIN
STITCH; pass it underneath the leaf, and bring it out in
the outline on the left side, exactly opposite the spot it
went in at. To cross the Satin Stitch just formed, put the
needle in at the top of the leaf on the right side, close to
the point of the leaf, and bring it out on the left side of
the point. Make another slanting Satin Stitch, by putting
the needle into the material directly underneath the first-
made one, on the right side of the leaf, bringing it out
on the left, below the stitch there, and crossing it to the
top of the leaf, next the stitch there on the right side,
and out again at the left. Continue making these slanting Satin Stitches and crossing them until the leaf is
filled in. Work the petals in the same manner, and make
FRENCH KNOTS for the stamens of the flowers. Work
the berries and fruit in OVERCAST, and the connecting
stalks, stems, and sprays in ROPE STITCH.

Paris Net.—A description of Net employed in
Millinery.

Paris Silk Stay Laces.—These consist of a flat silk
Braid, the numbers running 1, 2, and 3; the lengths, 6-4,
8-4, 10-4, 12-4, 14-4, 18-4, and 20-4.

Parure.—A French term denoting a set of collar and
cuffs, as well as one of ornaments.

Passant.—The French term denoting a piping without
a cord running through it.

Passé.—The French term signifying the front of a

bonnet or cap. It is likewise applied to gold and silver
Passing.

Passement.—This term is one by which Lace was
known, in conjunction with Braids or Gimps, until the
seventeenth century. The common use of the word is
considered by some to have arisen from the fact that the
first Pillow Laces were little more than Open Braids, and
by others, that the Lace trade was much in the hands of the
makers of Braids and Gimps, who were called Passemen-
tiers. These men did not for many years distinguish the
one work from the other, and they then termed Needle
Laces, Passements à l'Aiguille; Pillow Laces, Passements au Fuseaux; and Laces with indented edges, Passement à Dentelle. The present use of the word Passement
is to denote the pricked pattern, made either of Parchment
or Toile Ciré, upon which both descriptions of Lace are
worked.

Passement à l'Aiguille.—A term applied to Laces
made with the Needle, and not with Bobbins.

Passement au Fuseau.—A term applied to Laces
made upon the Pillow, and not with the Needle.

Passementerie.—The old name for lace-workers,
derived from Passement, the term used to denote Lace,
whether made upon the Pillow or by the Needle. Also a
French term, employed in a collective manner to denote
all kinds of Lace and ribbons, but especially to signify
the lace or gimp trimmings of dresses.

Passe-Passante.—This is merely an old term, signifying the securing of laid gold or other thread with
PASSING, employed in reference to embroidery.

Passé Stitch.—*See* EMBROIDERY STITCHES.

Passing.—A smooth, flattened thread, of either gold
or silver, of uniform size throughout, twisted spirally
round a thread of silk, and used in the same way as silk for
Flat Embroidery, by means of a needle which should be
round, and large in the eye. It can also be used in
Knitting, Netting, and Crochet Work. In the early
and Middle Ages, Passing was much used in the gorgeous
dresses then worn.

Passing Braid.—A description of Braid employed in
Embroidery, made with gold or silver thread, such as used
on military uniforms. It is a description of Bullion Braid.
In Ecclesiastical Embroidery, this Braid is often substituted for stitches to fill in certain parts of the pattern.

Pasting Lace.—A narrow kind of Coach Lace, used to
conceal rows of tacks.

Patching.—Replacing the worn-out portion of any garment, or piece of stuff, by another piece of material. To do
this: Cut the new portion exactly even, to a thread, and
place it on the worn spot, also to a thread, and upon
the right side, taking care to arrange the pattern, if
there be any, so that the patch and the original material
shall exactly correspond. Then TACK it on, to keep it
in its place, and HEM all along the four sides to the
original stuff, having turned in the raw edges. Then
turn the work, cut out the square, and, turning in the
edges of the original material, Hem them round, snip-
ping the patch at the corners, to make the Hem lie
flat and smoothly. The Patch should be nearly an inch
larger each way than the worn part which it has to cover.

If the material be calico or linen, SEW—otherwise called Top-sewing — instead of Hemming it, and well flatten the work afterwards; but it should be Hemmed on the wrong side. Flannel Patches must be HERRINGBONED. Cloth should be finely BUTTONHOLED at the raw edges. In Knitting, to re-heel or re-toe a stocking is sometimes called Patching. *See* KNITTING STOCKINGS.

Patchwork.—This needlework, which consists in sewing pieces of material together to form a flat, unbroken surface, possesses many advantages, as it is not only useful and ornamental, but forms out of odds and ends of silk, satin, or chintz, which would otherwise be thrown away, a handsome piece of work. Its manipulation requires both patience and neatness, and also calls into play both the reasoning and artistic faculties, as the designs chiefly depend for their beauty upon the taste displayed in the arrangement and selection of the shades of colour used to produce them. Patchwork originally only aimed at joining together any kinds of materials in the shapes they happened to have retained, so that, when arranged, a flat surface was produced; but, at the present time, much more is required from the worker, and the pieces used are selected from the same make of material, though of varied colours, and are cut into one or several set shapes and sizes, and put together so as to make a design by fitting into each other, both as to shape and shade, and this design is reproduced over the whole area of the work. The designs so worked out are necessarily geometrical, as it is essential that they should reply to fixed and accurate measurements, and the figures selected are the angles formed by squares, diamonds, and hexagons, in preference to the curved lines formed by circles and ovals, as the joining together of ovals and rounds in perfectly correct patterns is much more difficult to accomplish than when points are fitted into angles, as is done with the first-named figures.

Patchwork, when completed, is used for many purposes, and is made of velvet, satin, silk, leather, cloth, cretonne, twill, and chintz; in fact, of any material sufficiently soft to be cut into set shapes, and to bear a needle through it. Velvet and satin form the handsomest kind of work, and brocaded silks mixed with plain silks the next. Satin and silk are not used together, but velvet can be used with either. Cloth should be used by itself; cretonne, twill, and chintz, together or alone. It is not judicious to use a material that requires washing with one that will keep clean, but this is often done. Satin, silk, and velvet Patchwork is used for cushions, hand-screens, fire-screens, glove and handkerchief cases, and pincushions; cloth Patchwork for carriage rugs, couvrepieds, and poor people's quilts; cretonne, twill, and chintz for couvrepieds, curtains, quilts, and blinds. These larger articles require a greater amount of material than can be collected from private sources, but large silk mercers and linen drapers sell bundles of pieces by the pound. The working out of the design, and the manner of making up the patches, are the same, whatever the material or size of the article, the difference being made in the size of the patches used, they being increased or decreased for the occasion. The great essential is that every piece should be cut with perfect uniformity, and the use of a thin plate of

tin, cut to the size required, is therefore recommended; the other requisites are old envelopes and letters, or other stiff pieces of writing paper, the patches, and sewing silk or cotton matching the patches in colour, with which to sew them together.

The manner of working is as follows: Select the design to be copied and the shades of material, have a piece of tin cut out to correspond with each shape to be used, and lay this upon the silks or satins, and outline round with a pencil. Cut out the shapes larger than the outline, to allow of turning in the raw edges, and divide off the various pieces, keeping together all of one shade and all of one form. Then cut out upon the paper the exact outline of the tin plate, leaving nothing for turnings. TACK the paper and the silk piece together, turning the raw edge of the silk over the paper, and Tacking it down so as to keep it from fraying out while working. Arrange the patches thus made on a table, according to

FIG. 647. APPLIQUÉ PATCHWORK, OTHERWISE CALLED "PUZZLE."

the design and the position each is to occupy as to colour; take up two that are to be close together, turn the silk sides inwards, so as to stitch them together on the wrong side, and then carefully stitch them together so that they accurately join point to point, angle to angle. Continue to sew the pieces together until the size required is obtained, then tear the paper away from the silk, and iron the work upon the wrong side. Line it with twill or some soft, smooth material, and if it is required for a counterpane or couvrepied, wad and quilt the lining; if for a mat, handkerchief case, &c., put a ball fringe round it.

Patchwork Patterns can be made from geometrical figures, and are chiefly copied from old Mosaic or Parqueterie designs; however, the designs can be made as elaborate as the worker likes, and they have been carried to the extent of working coats of arms in their natural colours, and pictures containing large-sized figures. One of these works of art was exhibited lately, and was remarkable, both for the patience and skill displayed in its execution, and the beauty of the colours employed. The following Patchwork Patterns are amongst the best, and can be enlarged or decreased in size as required:

Appliqué, or Puzzle.—The pattern shown in Fig. 647 (page 379) is a useful one for using up odds and ends of material, but a difficult one to adjust. To work: Prepare a number of pieces of cretonne or silk, 4 inches long and 3 inches wide, and slope off one corner of some of these, to form a curve, leaving the rest perfectly square. Cut a few larger pieces, 5 inches long by 3 inches wide, and out of scraps cut some odd-shaped pieces, either of the right length or width. Arrange these various pieces upon a lining, to form the design shown in the illustration; but, instead of stitching two pieces together, as in ordinary Patchwork, lay one over the other, and turn under the edges of the top piece, and RUN it to the bottom. When all are in position, and Run to each other and the lining, work round the edge of every patch with HERRINGBONE STITCHES made with bright-coloured filoselle. The whole beauty of this design depends upon the judicious selection of the colours and patterns of the patches used.

Block.—See *Box.*

Box.—This design is sometimes known as Block Pattern. It is made by arranging diamonds so that three of them form a solid raised block, of which two sides and the top are shown; and this look is given to the flat surface entirely by the arrangement of the diamonds as to colour. To form: Procure a number of pieces of silk of three shades of one colour, such as yellow, deep gold, and chestnut, or pale blue, peacock blue, and indigo blue, and cut out from each shade an equal number of diamonds. These must be made 3 inches in length, 2 inches in width, and 2 inches from corner to corner. Join a chestnut-coloured silk to a deep gold silk, so as to make a straight line between them, the slant of the diamond in each going upward; put the dark colour on the right hand, the lighter upon the left hand. These two diamonds form the sides of the Block. Take the light yellow diamond, and make with it the top of the Block, fit it into the angle formed by the upward slant of the sides, so that it lies across them, the points of its width being upwards, and those of its length horizontal. Make a number of these blocks, shading them all in the same way, and then join them together, thus: On the left side left unattached of the light yellow top, join the under side of a chestnut piece, and to the right side of the yellow top the under side of a deep golden piece. This will produce the effect of a number of successive blocks of wood arranged diagonally across the work. The dark side of these blocks is often made with velvet, and by this arrangement the sections stand out with great boldness.

Canadian.—This particular pattern in Patchwork is one that in Canada is known as Loghouse Quilting. It is a variety made of several coloured ribbons instead of pieces of silk or cretonne, and these ribbons are arranged to give the appearance of different kinds of wood formed into a succession of squares. To work as shown in Fig. 648: Cut out in lining a square of 12 inches, and TACK to it, in its centre, a small square of a plain colour, 1½ inches in size. Procure ribbon three-quarters of an inch wide, and of two shades of every colour used; take the two shades of one colour, and Tack the darkest shade right down one side of the small square, and overlapping three-quarters of an inch beyond at both ends; sew to this, and to the square, a dark piece at the bottom and a light piece at the top, and allow both to overlap beyond the square on the left side for three-quarters of an inch; completely surround the square by filling it in with the light colour for the side not already filled up. Change the ribbons, and again surround the square with two shades of the same colour, putting the darkest underneath the dark part and the lightest against the light part, and arrange their manner of overlapping

FIG. 648. CANADIAN PATCHWORK.

(always allowing three-quarters of an inch extra for the same) according to the design. Seven rows of ribbon are needed to fill the 12-inch square; diversify these as to colour and design, but always make two shades of one colour form a square, and place the darkest of such shades underneath each other. Prepare a large number of these 12-inch squares, and then sew them together as ordinary patches, but so that the light side of one square is next the light side of another, and the dark against the dark, thus giving the look of alternate squares of light and dark colours. Large pieces of work, like counterpanes, should be made with the 12-inch square and the three-quarter inch ribbon; but small pieces, such as cushions, with narrow ribbon and 5-inch squares.

Check.—This design is worked to imitate a chess or draught board, and is one of the easiest patterns, being formed of squares sewn together. To work: Cut out a number of 2-inch squares in pale yellow, and a number of the same size in brown. Sew the brown square to the yellow square, and underneath and above the brown sew a yellow, and underneath and above the yellow square sew a brown one. Continue to join the pieces together in this

CANADIAN OR LOGHOUSE PATCHWORK

MOSAIC PATCHWORK WITH EMBROIDERY

CRAZY PATCHWORK

manner, so that no squares of the same hue are next to each other. Any two colours can be used, or varieties of two colours, but it is advisable not to employ more.

Cloth.—Cloth Patchwork is used for carriage rugs and tablecloths, and can be made extremely effective, either as a bordering to these articles, or as entirely forming them. As cloth is of too thick a substance to allow of turning under the raw edges, each patch has to be bound with either a narrow ribbon or braid before it is sewn into its right position in the work, and as the material is only made plain, or with patterns that would not look well if inserted, bright self-coloured foundations are selected, which are embroidered with designs worked out with silks or narrow braids. To work: Select a large-sized pattern, either of a *Hexagon* or *Mosaic* shape, cut the pieces out in the ordinary way, and Embroider them in SATIN STITCH; bind each round with a braid matching it in colour, and then stitch it into its proper position. No lining is required.

Crazy.—Made with pieces of silk, brocade, and satin, of any shape or size. The colours are selected to contrast with each other; their joins are hidden by lines of Herringbone, Coral, and Feather Stitch, worked in bright-coloured filoselles, and in the centres of pieces of plain satin, or silk, flower sprays in Satin Stitch are embroidered. To work: Cut a piece of Ticking the size of the work, and BASTE down on it all descriptions of three-cornered jagged, and oblong pieces of material. Show no ticking between these pieces, and let the last-laid piece overlap the one preceding it. Secure the pieces to the Ticking, by HERRINGBONE, BUTTONHOLE, and FEATHER STITCH lines worked over their raw edges, and concealing them. Ornament them with CROSS STITCH, TÊTE DE BŒUF, POINT DE RIZ, and ROSETTES, if the patches are small; upon large, plain patches work flower sprays, or single flowers, in coloured silk Embroidery.

Diamonds.—The Diamond (next to the Hexagon) is the most used design in Patchwork, and looks well when made of two materials, such as silk and velvet, or silk and chintz. It is the easiest of all the figures. To work: Cut out a number of Diamonds, 3 inches in length and 2¼ inches in width. Make half of them in dark materials, and half in light; join them together so that they form alternate rows of light and dark colours across the width of the article, or join four pieces of one shade together, so as to make a large Diamond, and sew this to another large Diamond made of four pieces of a contrasting colour to the one placed next it.

Embroidered.—This kind of work is only suitable for small articles, such as cushions, handkerchief cases, and glove cases. It is formed by sewing together squares of different colours, after they have been ornamented with fancy stitches. To work: Cut a number of 3-inch squares in dark velvet and silk or satin, and upon each satin or silk square, work a spray of flowers, or a small wreath, in SATIN STITCH, and in filoselles matching the colours of the flowers; make each spray or wreath of a different kind of flower, and upon a different coloured satin, but care must be taken that the colours of the satins used will blend together. Take the dark velvet squares (these should

be all of one shade), and work a pattern upon each of their sides in lines of CORAL, HERRINGBONE, or CHAIN STITCH, and then join the velvet and satin squares together—a satin and a velvet patch alternately. A simpler pattern in Embroidery is made as follows: Cut out, either in silk or satin, small 2-inch squares of various colours, sew these together, and, when all are secured, work a RAILWAY STITCH in coloured filoselles from each corner of the square to the centre, and a Satin Stitch on each side of it; this, when repeated in every square, will make a pretty design. Another manner of embroidering squares is to make them of Holland and Plush alternately, and to work a line of Herringbone or Coral on two sides of the Holland square, but to leave the velvet plain.

Honeycomb, or Hexagon.—(1). The pattern known by these names is the one commonly used in Patchwork, as it is easily executed, produces many varieties of devices, according to the arrangement of the colours, and is a shape into which most remnants of silk or cretonne may be cut. To make as shown in Fig. 649: Cut out a number of Hexagons

FIG. 649. HONEYCOMB, OR HEXAGON, PATCHWORK.

and make each of their six sides three-quarters of an inch in length. Take a dark-coloured patch, and sew round it six light patches. These should agree in their shade of colour, but need not as to pattern. Into the angles formed on the outside of these light Hexagons sew dark-coloured patches, and continue to work so as to give the appearance of a dark patch surrounded by a set of light patches.

(2). Another variety of the same pattern is made with Hexagons, and arranged to form light-coloured stars upon a dark velvet ground. It is useful when only a few, but good, pieces of brocade or satin are available, and makes handsome sofa cushions or banner screens. The Hexagons are all of the same size, and should be three-quarters of an inch upon each side. To make: Cut out a number of Hexagons in deep maroon velvet or dark peacock-blue velvet, to form the ground; then take the satin scraps, and from them cut out the same sized Hexagons. Pick up one of these, and surround it with six other pieces, arranged as follows: Should the centre piece be pale blue, surround it with old gold; should it be crimson, with yellow-pink; should it be lavender, with purple; should it be yellow, with chestnut. Make a set of these stars, and then reverse the colours, putting the centre colour as the outside colour. Arrange as follows : Sew on two rows of the ground, and for the third row sew on the stars already made, and put one of the ground-coloured Hexagons between each star; for the next two rows, only use the ground-coloured patches, and then recommence the stars. Arrange these to contrast with those first placed, and to come between them, and not directly underneath.

(3). In this variety of the same pattern it is intended to produce the appearance of Raised Work without the stuffing. To work: All the pieces are made of equal-sided Hexagons, three-quarters of an inch to every side. Cut out a number of Hexagons, all in one light colour, and of the same material—these should be either of French grey, maize, or sky blue—then cut out a number of Hexagons in dark maroon velvet, and a few in brocaded silks, either pale blue, green, chocolate, flame colour, or peach. If brocade cannot be procured for these last pieces, work each with a small flower in silks, and in SATIN STITCH. Arrange as follows: Surround each brocaded Hexagon with six dark velvet ones, and make them all up in this way. Then stitch all round these a row of the light silk patches, so that every dark section is separated from its corresponding section with a border of light silk. Finish this pattern with a straight border worked with flowers, and a ball fringe.

Jewel.—The pattern shown in Fig. 650 is intended to give the appearance of large precious stones, set round with smaller ones, and a plain setting. Each of the large squares represents a cut stone with the light falling upon it, and to produce this effect is made either of two shades of blue satin brocade, two of ruby brocade, emerald, or yellow brocade. The small squares are made of any colours, and should be much varied; the long lines, of

FIG. 650. JEWEL PATCHWORK.

plain brown gold satin. To work: Cut out in paper a perfect square, measuring 2 inches each way, run a line across this from the left-hand top point to the right-hand bottom point, and horizontally across its centre. Cut down the diagonal line from the left-hand top corner to the centre of the square; cut across to the right on the horizontal line. The two pieces the square is thus divided into will be the two sizes required for the centres of the

pattern; have them copied in tin, and cut from the smallest piece half the light shades of satin and half the dark shades, and from the larger half the dark shades of satin and half the light shades required. For the straight pieces, cut out lengths of two inches, an inch wide; and for the small squares an inch every way. Join the light satin to the dark, so as to make a perfect square, and put the light colour on the right side of the dark colour for three patches on one line, two patches on the next line, and one patch on the third line of the work, and reverse it for the next three rows; surround a square thus made with the long brown pieces, and fill in the four corners with four little squares; then join on another large square, and surround that on the three sides left open with the straight pieces of brown satin and the small squares.

Kid.—This Patchwork is generally confined to the making of such small articles as pincushions, slippers, or mats, as the Kid generally used for the purpose is cut from old gloves, and, therefore, is not of a large size; but if the pieces can be obtained of sufficient size, cushions, footstools, and other larger articles may be attempted. To work: Select an easy geometric pattern, and cut out from a tin plate a number of Kid patches without allowing for any turnings, sew these together upon the wrong side, without turning any of the Kid under, and iron the work over when finished; then take a narrow cord of gold thread or silk braid, and COUCH this down to the Kid with a silk thread matching it in colour, so that it follows and conceals all the lines of stitches. Where it is not possible to turn the cord or braid, make a hole with a stiletto, and push it through this hole to the back and fasten it off there. If the Kid is stitched together with great neatness, and a very fine needle used, the outline cord will not be required; it is only used to hide the stitches where their size or irregularity would spoil the look of the work.

Leather.—Patchwork made with leather scraps differs in one essential from true Patchwork, as the pieces are glued to a foundation, instead of stitched together, as in the other kinds; but the patterns used, and the manner of cutting out the sections, are the same. The Leather used is morocco, and is procured of bookbinders and leather dressers, and the articles formed are chessboards, folding screens, flower mats, note cases, &c. To work: Having obtained scraps of Leather, fix upon some geometrical pattern that the scraps will most easily lend themselves to make; draw this pattern quite correctly out upon a sheet of millboard, and mark out what coloured scrap is to cover each space. Arrange the scraps on a table in their proper order, make hot some common glue (which is free from impurities and of equal consistency), spread it upon the backs of the Leather, and lay the Leather in its proper place upon the millboard. Work with despatch, but be careful that every point is glued down, and that all the pieces are accurately arranged; then press the millboard in a linen press, and keep it there until the glue has quite dried. The millboard can be covered, upon its wrong side, either with silk or watered paper, pasted down upon it; the edges at the sides should either have narrow ribbon pasted upon them before the

Leather is put on, or they should be gilded with shell-gold when the work is finished. A fringe, made by cutting strips of thin narrow leather into close, ⅛-inch lines, should be used for edging mats and any flat articles that would be improved by such a finish.

Loghouse Quilting.—See *Canadian.*

Lozenge, or Pointed Oblong.—A useful shape for using up small scraps of material, and one that is easily made. The Lozenge is a figure of six sides, and is an oblong with pointed instead of straight ends, the points being in the centre of the width, and formed with two angles. To work: Cut out a number of these figures, make them 3 inches from point to point, 1½ inches across, and 1½ inches for the side lines, and 1 inch for the lines from the point to the side. Sew these together in rows, placing a light Lozenge next a dark one. In the next row, arrange the Lozenges in the same way, so that, when all the patches are arranged, diagonal lines of alternate shades will cross the material.

Mosaic.—(1). The pattern shown in Fig. 651 is formed with squares and acute-angled triangles. It is a good pattern to use for cretonne patches, and for small pieces of silk and satin, the large square being made with pieces of cretonne of flower designs, and the small triangles of various coloured silks. Cut out the squares, and make them 6 inches each way; cut the triangles out, and make their base 6 inches, their height 3 inches. Take a cretonne square, and sew to each of its sides the base of a dark

FIG. 651. MOSAIC PATCHWORK (No. 1).

triangle, and fill in the triangle with three other triangles; turn all their points inwards, and make a perfect square with their bases. Make this kind of square to the four sides of the centre, and fill in the sides of the cross thus made with four large cretonne squares. Join a number of pieces together in this manner, and then sew them to each other, and make a variegated pattern by using various patterned and coloured cretonnes and silks in different sections.

(2). Another variety of Mosaic is composed of three differently cut pieces, viz., squares, parallelograms, and unequal sided hexagons. To work: Cut out the squares in pale yellow silk, and make them 1½ inches in length. Make the parallelograms 2 inches long and 1 inch wide. The two side lines are upright, and of equal lengths, but the left-hand line commences before the right-hand one, and ends before it. The top and bottom lines join these

slants together; cut half the number required in dark brown silk brocade, and half in old gold silk brocade, and make the angles slope different ways in the two colours. Cut the unequal hexagons all from the same silk or brocade, which should either be dark blue, crimson, or black—their two sides are 2 inches long, their width 2 inches, and the four lines that form the angles 1½ inches each; join four parallelograms together at their long sides, the light colour to the left of the dark, and arrange their shades alternately; let their short lines slope upwards, and form angles; join a number of these together in this way before placing them. Take two squares, and fit them into the upper angles made by the parallelograms; and, into the angle made between the two squares, fix the pointed end of the hexagons. To the left of the hexagons sew the dark side of a set of four parallelograms; to the right, the left side of another set; and to the top, fit in the angle made by the second and third pieces of a set of four parallelograms. Repeat the pattern until the size required is made, then join a piece of silk to the top and bottom as a border, and make it straight at one side, and vandyked at the other, so as to fit into the angles of the pattern for the sides; cut some half hexagons, and fit them in, and finish with a plain straight border.

(3). The pattern shown in Fig. 652 is intended to be used in making counterpanes, and other large articles, and should be worked with cretonnes or gaily-coloured chintzes. It is made with squares of two different sizes, and of pointed oblongs. To work: Cut out in tin a square of 6 inches, and form a face 1¾ inches in length at each corner, by cutting away the point of the square.

FIG. 652. MOSAIC PATCHWORK (No. 3).

Choose a flower-patterned chintz, with bunches of flowers, and from this cut the large squares, so that each has a bunch of flowers in the centre. Cut from various coloured chintzes a number of small squares, 1¾ inches in size, and from a coloured chintz of one shade, the pointed oblongs which make 6 inches from point to point, 2½ inches wide, and 3½ inches upon each side; join five of the small squares together, place the lightest-coloured square in the centre, surround it with four of a darker shade, and fit into the four angles that are thus made the points of four of the oblongs, and into the four corners of the outer squares, the angles of four of the large squares, which have been so cut as to join on to the small squares, while their straight sides correspond with the straight sides of the oblong; join the pieces together, so that every large square is surrounded with the ornamental border made by the oblong and small squares.

This pattern can be varied almost indefinitely by altering the colouring, and the material composing the patches; thus, all the large squares can be made of a ground colour, and differently coloured and shaped flowers APPLIQUÉ on to them, and the oblongs may be formed of different shades of one colour, instead of one shade only, while the small squares can be made of velvet or satin, instead of chintz, with the centre square of plain material, and the four outer squares of variegated, or *vice versâ*.

(4). A pretty set pattern, made with three different sized patches, and forming a combination of squares, crosses, and hexagons. To work as shown in Fig. 653: Cut out in black satin a number of perfect squares, 1½ inches in width and length, and some of the same size in yellow satin. Cut out in red silk, lozenge-shaped or pointed oblong patches, each measuring 3 inches from point to point, 1½ inches across, 1½ inches for the long lines, and ¾ inch for the short lines that form the right angle. Take some violet silk, and cut a number of larger Lozenges, 4 inches from point to point, 2 inches across,

FIG. 653. MOSAIC PATCHWORK (NO. 4).

3 inches for the long lines, and 1½ inches for the short lines that form the right angle. Join together five squares as a square cross, one dark square being in the centre, and four light ones round it; take a black square, and join to it four red Lozenges, and sew the points of the Lozenges to each other. Sew the cube thus made to the outside of one of the arms of the cross, so that the centre square is on the same line as the centre of the cross, and fill in the spaces on the sides of the cubes and cross, with the violet Lozenges. Continue the pattern by connecting a cross to a cube, and a cube to a cross, always filling up with the violet Lozenges. The pattern measures across one cube

and a cross 9 inches, and as each design takes four light squares, two dark squares, four red Lozenges, and four violet Lozenges, a brief calculation will give the number of patches required for a given space, to which must be added a few extra of all the sizes, to fill in corners, &c.

Raised.—This is also known as Swiss Patchwork, and is made by stuffing the patches out with wadding, so that they are well puffed up. The shapes selected for the patches should be either good sized hexagons or diamonds, and only one shape should be used, as intricate patterns, made by combining various sized pieces, render the work troublesome. To work: Cut out the hexagons or diamonds, from a tin plate pattern, from pieces of silk or brocade; size of diamonds, 2½ inches upon each side; of hexagons, 1½ inches along each of the six sides; cut the same shapes out in old lining, and make a small slit in the centre of each; sew the lining patches to the silk patches, and join each lined patch together in the pattern selected. When finished, sew a piece of silk, 5 inches wide, all round the work, and ornament it with CORAL, HERRINGBONE, and other fancy Embroidery Stitches; this border need not be lined. Take soft wadding, and push it into every slit made in the lined patches, until they are well puffed out, and quite hard, fill them in thoroughly, and be careful that the corners are not neglected. TACK over the hole made in the lining, to prevent the wadding coming out, and then line the whole of the work, including the straight border, with a piece of old silk, or red or blue twill, or cretonne. A more difficult plan, but one that does not need the extra, or second lining, is as follows: Cut out the shapes, from the tin plate, in silk or brocade, and cut out cretonne or good twill linings to fit them, join these linings to the patches, but leave one side in all of them unsecured. Join the patches together as a row, leaving the open side of them exposed. Into this stuff the wadding, taking care to make each section quite hard and full. Sew the lining up, tack on another row of patches, and stuff them out as before, and continue to sew on row after row, and stuff them, until the size required is made.

Right Angles.—The principle of the pattern shown in Fig. 654 is much the same as that of the Box Pattern, but

FIG. 654. RIGHT ANGLES PATCHWORK.

in this case, the diamonds forming the design are cut away, so as to form a number of right angles. To work:

Procure a number of pieces of silk, three shades of one colour, such as pink, crimson, and maroon, of which the darker shade is brocaded. Cut out a diamond on paper, length 3 inches, width 2 inches, from point to point; out of one side of this cut out a right angle, leaving 1 inch upon each line, and cutting it to the depth of 1 inch, thus making the shape required for the design. Have this cut in tin, and from that cut out an equal number of sections from each coloured silk, and then join them together, according to the pattern; sew together the straight side of a ruby and crimson section with the cut-out edge to the right and left, and fit a pink section into the angle at the top of these two, with its cut-out edge upright. Make up all the pieces in this manner, and then join the figures together. The cut-out edge of the light pink of one figure will fit into the bottom angle of the crimson and maroon colours, and the angles at the sides of these sections will fit into the sides of a fresh row of figures. In making this pattern, care must be taken that the position of the colours is never altered.

Tinted.—A new variety, made with coloured muslin of a stiff description, and of four shades of one tint. The material is cut into hexagons, and embroidered with coloured filoselles and tailor's black twist. The hexagons are arranged to form stars, rosettes, and other devices, all the dark shades of colour being arranged in the centre of the device, and the light colours at the edge. To work: Cut out, on paper, a large eight-pointed star, or other device; then a number of hexagons, 2 inches in diameter. Use four shades of blue, crimson, purple, yellow, green, or other colours, arranging that each ray of the star is worked with a distinct colour. The hexagons cut, fill their centres with a star worked with yellow, white, or a shaded filoselle, and over this star, and across every point of the hexagons, bring a line of black twist, working the ends into the centre of the star. OVERCAST the hexagons together to make the pattern, laying them on it as a guide, and place one hexagon, made of white muslin, as the centre patch. Lay the star, when finished, upon a plain velvet or satin background. The work, when used for a footstool cover, is made with one large star, nearly covering the surface; for small tablecloths, cushions, &c., with a number of more minute devices fastened to a plain ground.

Twist.—This pattern is formed of eight-sided cubes and squares, which are separated from each other by long narrow patches, cut so as to appear to twist, or interlace each other, and twine round the squares and cubes. To work as shown in Fig. 655: Cut a number of squares measuring 1¼ inches each way, and eight-sided cubes measuring 1¼ inches at top, bottom, and side lines, but only three-quarters of an inch across the lines that form the four corners. Make these cubes and squares of pieces of dark-coloured satin and brocade. Cut out, in light silk or satin, the long, narrow stripes, make these half an inch in width, 2 inches in length on one side, and 2¾ inches in length on the other. Cut them so that one side of the width is quite straight, and the other pointed. Take one of the squares, stitch to it, on the left, a long, narrow piece, turn its short, or 2-inch, length to the square, make

it even on its straight width with the bottom line of square, and let the overlap and the point come at the top; to this end, but not to the point, join another long piece in the same way, fit it into the overlap where it is straight, and join its short 2-inch length to the top of the square, allowing the overlap and the point to be to the right hand. Come down the right side of the square, and put a piece

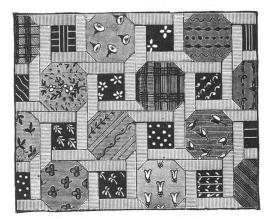

FIG. 655. TWIST PATCHWORK.

on at the bottom of the square; in the same manner join the long pieces to all the squares. Now arrange the cubes as to colour, and join them to the long pieces. The short corners of the cubes will fit into the points of the long pieces, four different cubes will join the four different points, and the straight parts will fit into the straight lines of the long pieces.

Patent Flannels (Welsh and Saxony).—A very fine quality of Flannel, said not to shrink when washed, but not durable. They are much used for infants' clothing.

Patent Knitting.—The old-fashioned name for Brioche Knitting. *See* KNITTING.

Patent Silk Sealskin.—This is a very beautiful textile, in every respect as perfect an imitation of sealskin as could be manufactured. The gloss is very fine, and the softness equally great, and it has the advantage of lightness, by comparison with the real skin. The pile is raised on a double warp of cotton. The material measures 52 inches in width; its wear is said to be very satisfactory, and the cost is estimated at about one-fourth of that of the real skins. Silk Sealskin has been patented by the inventors, and is produced at Newtown, North Wales.

Patterns.—These are required for every description of Ornamental Needlework, and are as diversified as the articles they help to form.

For Berlin Work, and in all Work with Wools upon Open Canvas: Trace the pattern upon point or ruled paper, with squares to represent each stitch, and colour the tracing as each stitch should be coloured when worked. Place this pattern upon the table, and work from it, counting the stitches upon it, and working the same number on the canvas.

For Church Embroidery: Draw out the pattern as a whole upon a large piece of paper, in proper scale, and colour this; then, upon separate pieces of paper, make sections of the pattern of those pieces that are worked in frames by themselves, and afterwards joined together. Trace these sections on linen stretched in Embroidery Frames, and colour them from the large pattern.

For Crewel Work, Satin Embroidery, Tapestry, and all Embroideries upon Thick Materials : Make a small coloured design, trace the outline of this, in its full size, upon oiled tracing linen, transfer this outline to the material with the aid of blue or white carbonised linen, and work out the colours from the small design. When the materials are rough and dark, it is extremely difficult for an amateur to trace a design upon them, but the following plan is the best : Trace the pattern upon oiled tracing linen (not paper), and place underneath it a cream-coloured piece of carbonised linen (not paper), lay the material and pattern upon a piece of glass, and trace the design through with a bone crochet hook. The traced lines will rub off some rough materials on contact, and for these the best plan is, immediately after tracing, to RUN round all the chief outlines with a fine white thread, or to paint them with Chinese white, with which water-colour size has been mixed. The carbonised linen is sold at Frances', in Hanway Street, Oxford Street, London, in several shades of colour.

For Crochet, Knitting, Netting, and Tatting : Make or obtain a small illustration of the article required, with directions of how to work it from row to row; the illustration is not necessary as long as the directions, either printed or written, are obtained, but it facilitates the work, and shows the effect.

For Holbein and Kreuzstich Sticherei Patterns : A want that has been widely felt by many workers in these Embroideries has been met by a French invention of a metal plate, which stamps small spots upon the material to be worked, and so does away with the constant and weari-some counting of thread, or the interposition, on dark and thick stuffs, of canvas, which has to be drawn away when the work is completed. With the help of these stamps, the tracing of patterns upon velvet, plush, or silk, need no longer present the difficulties, nor take the time, it has hitherto done. The French stamp is formed of a piece of thick wood, made of various sizes, from which a number of metal points protrude, these points being placed at even distances from each other. The colour they are to transport to the work is spread out upon a pad, and the stamp put face downwards upon that, and immediately afterwards on to the material, which it marks with even rows of tiny spots, over which Cross Stitch or Holbein Stitch is worked with ease. This stamp could be made less cumbersome if formed of a thin sheet of copper, and the holes punctured in it, and then the colour brushed over them as in Stencilling, or as the small name and figure plates for marking are manipulated. The colours for stamping are powder colours, just diluted with water, and strengthened with a small quantity of gum—but water-colours in cakes would do equally as well. For washing materials, blue is the best; for dark stuffs, Chinese white. The density and stiffness of the colour used for a washing material need not trouble the worker so much as that used over a non-washing; in the first case, the faint blue spots are removed at the first washing, but in the latter they are brushed away with a soft velvet brush, and must, there-fore, only contain sufficient gum to allow of their adhering temporarily. The mixture should be tried on a waste piece of stuff before using, and care taken that it is not very liquid.

For Pillow Lace Making : Prick the outlines of the sprig, or piece of lace, upon thin parchment or Toile Ciré, so that each pricking shall represent one of the holes required in the design, and into which a pin is stuck while the lace is in process of making, in order that a stitch can be formed round the pin, and kept in position by it.

For Point or Needle Laces : Trace the design upon parchment as a whole; take copies of portions of it upon small pieces of parchment, outline these with two prickings close together and a small space between each group, and work the portions of lace with the needle upon these scraps; then join all together.

For White Embroidery, including Work upon Muslin and Net, and Imitation Laces made with Braids : Trace an outline of the pattern upon pink calico, back this with brown paper, lay the white materials over it and work, guided by the lines of the pattern seen through them; or, in the case of the lace, tack the braid straight upon the pattern.

The word Pattern is likewise a term employed to denote a specimen of any material. Strips of these are fastened together, and are in universal use in trade, to show varieties in quality, make, design, and colour, in woven stuffs, braids, &c.; and cards of buttons, and other articles of Haberdashery, are likewise in use.

Pattes.—A term denoting the small straps securing the loose cuffs of an outdoor coat, jacket, or ulster; or designed to close the stand-up collar, by stretching across the opening which, only just meeting, could not be buttoned otherwise; also for drawing in an Ulster at the back, when there is no belt round the waist. It may con-sist of one piece with a button at each end, or of two short straps, each sewed on the article of dress at one end, and buttoned across its fellow by a single button.

Peacock Fingering.—This is also known as Peacock Knitting Wool.

Peacock Ice Silk.—This is a comparatively new description of silk, for the purpose of knitting. It is made in two sizes, twofold and fourfold. The former quality can be employed in the knitting of fine stockings, and is suitable also for Crochet Work. The fourfold quality is very suitable for gloves, shawls, stockings, socks, and scarves. Peacock Ice Silk bears the same relationship to other silks so employed as Eis, or Ice, Wool bears to ordinary wools. It is prepared in a particular manner, and is said not to become chafed in use. It can be had in ½oz. balls, and in almost every hue and shade; and the dyes in which it is produced are very beautiful.

Peacocks' Feathers.—The skin taken from the breast of the Peacock, of which the plumage is blue, with a peculiar shot appearance, is employed for the crowns of women's hats, as well as for collarettes and cuffs. The tips, also, of the beautiful tail feathers, some having an eye-like spot at their several extremities, and others a shining green fringe, extending just round the point on one side, and all the way down on the other, are employed as trimmings for dresses, as well as for hats, fans, screens, and mats. A Peacock's Crest was, in ancient times, employed as one of the decorations of our English Kings; and in China, at the present time, to be awarded the distinction of wearing three Peacocks' Feathers, is a point of ambition amongst all Mandarins.

Pearl.—The loops that decorate the edges of Pillow Lace are called Pearls, or Purls, and are made to any parts of the design that are disconnected in any way from the main body of the work, or upon the Bars forming the ground. These loops are called Right, Left, and Inner, according to the side of the Lace upon which they are made.

To Make a Left Pearl.—Work as in Right Pearl until the thread has to be placed on the pin. Place the pin upon, and not under, the thread, and bring the BOBBIN over it with the left hand; run this loop up to the pinhole, stick the pin, and bring the other Bobbin round the pin from the lower side, moving first to the left. The difference is slight, but, unless attended to, the edge of the left Pearl untwists.

To Make an Inner Pearl.—This Pearl, instead of being worked upon the outside edges of a lace design, is made so as to decorate any hollows left in the centre of lace patterns, such as a hole in the wings of a butterfly or hollow leaf. It is worked during the progress of the lace as follows: Work to the inside edge and TWIST the working pair of Bobbins six times, stick a pin into an inside hole, put the twist round it, and work the lace back with the same pair of Bobbins.

To Make a Right Pearl.—Continue working the Lace until the pinhole that is to form the loop is reached, then turn the Pillow until the edge that was on the left is on the right side. Bring the working pair of BOBBINS across the Lace, and TWIST once before the last stitch; then, without sticking a pin, make a CLOTH STITCH with the pair lying outside, pull this up, Twist the working pair seven times to the left, lift one of these Bobbins in the left hand, take a pin in the right hand, place the pin under the thread, give a twist of the wrist to bring the thread round the pin, run the pin up to the hole it is to be placed in, stick it in, lay down the Bobbin that was held, and pass the other one round from the lower side, Twist once, make a Cloth Stitch, again Twist once, and work back across the lace.

Pearl-edge.—Otherwise written Purl-edge. A narrow kind of thread edging, made to be sewn upon lace, as a finish to the edge; or projecting loops of silk at the sides of ribbons, formed by making some of the threads of the weft protrude beyond the selvedge.

Pearlin.—This is the old name in Scotland, for lace, and was there applied to all descriptions of it. During the seventeenth century it was used in Enactments against the importation of foreign laces into that country, and in all Scotch poems, legends, and histories written during that period. Pearlin and Pearling have the same meaning.

Pearling.—*See* PEARLIN.

Pearl-purl.—A gold cord of twisted wire, resembling a small row of beads strung closely together. It is used for the edging of Bullion Embroidery, is sold by the ounce, and is more costly than plain Bullion. It is too delicate to be drawn through the material to be embroidered, and must be laid on the surface, and stitched down with waxed yellow silk; it requires careful handling.

Pekin.—A French term employed to denote a silk stuff made in alternate stripes of satin and velvet, which vary in width in the different pieces manufactured. Pekin Silk goods may be had in black, and all colours, and are much used as portions of dresses and trimmings. There are also Pekin Gauzes, the Gauze being substituted for the satin stripe.

Pelerine.—This description of cape, or tippet, had its origin in that worn by pilgrims, and which had the addition of a hood—the French word *pélerin* meaning a pilgrim or palmer. As worn by English women, they only just reach the waist at the back, and have long, straight-cut ends in front, which are tied once, without a bow at the waist in front. They are made in silk, muslin, cashmere, and other materials.

Pelisse.—An over-dress for outdoor wear by women, formerly made of cloth, and often trimmed with fur, open all down the front, and fastened with closely-set buttons, the sleeves tight, like those of a coat. The Pelisse of former times resembled in style the modern "princesse polonaise." The form is still used for infants' and children's dress, in merino, cashmere, Nankeen, piqué, &c. The first mention of the Pelisse dates back in English history to the year 1185, when, in the reign of Edward the Confessor, the nobles wore dresses of fur, or skins called "Pelles," from the Latin *pellis*, a skin.

Pelisse Cloth.—A woollen textile, twilled, and made soft, of about seven quarters in width.

Pelote.—A French term, denoting a kind of Moss-fringe, employed for the trimming of dresses.

Pelts, or Peltry.—These terms denote the raw, unprepared, but dried fur-covered skins, which, subsequent to their "dressing," are called Furs.

Peluche.—The French name for PLUSH.

Penelope Canvas.—A description of cotton Canvas made for Berlin Woolwork, in which the strands run in couples, vertically and horizontally, thus forming squares containing four threads each. It is less trying to the eyes of the embroiderer than ordinary canvas, as there is little counting to do; and the squares are large compared with the single threads of the latter.

Penguin Skin.—The skin of the Penguin is used for purposes of women's out-of-door dress.

Peniche Lace.—On the little peninsula of Peniche, lying north of Lisbon, in the Estremadura Province, the lace industry of Portugal is chiefly carried on. In that place, the population being debarred from agricultural pursuits, the men become fishermen and the women are all engaged in the lace trade. The latter begin to acquire the art at four years of age, work all their lives, and, when too old to make elaborate designs, return to the first patterns they made in youth. For the last forty years this lace has become an article of commerce. The implements used are the same as in other kinds of Pillow Lace making, except that the Lace, being made in very wide widths without joins, necessitates a very long Pillow to work upon. The Pillows are made in the form of a cylinder; the women sit with this Pillow across their knees, and with its ends resting upon low stools or in baskets. It is made with a hole at each end to lift it by. The patterns are of card, and dyed saffron, to make them yellow, and look like parchment; they are designed and pricked by women whose trade it is. The Bobbins are of pine wood, Brazil wood, and ivory; a great number are needed, a large piece of lace often requiring eighty to a hundred dozen in use at one time.

The Lace is a coarse Pillow Lace, similar to the white

lace veil of a large size, reduced so that the pattern may be entirely shown. The ground is omitted, as the beauty of the design would not be visible in its present size if filled in. The flowers and leaves are worked thick in CLOTH STITCH, and are surrounded with a FIL DE TRACE or GIMP of a coarser and more shiny thread than they are filled in with. No open lace stitches are worked, the whole beauty of the design resting upon its boldness and the contrast between the fine filmy ground and the thickness of the pattern.

Percaline.—A fine cotton material, employed in ELYSÉE WORK.

Percals.—A fine calico cloth, bearing a French name, yet of Indian origin. It was manufactured in England in 1670, and in France in 1780. That home-made has a small

FIG. 653. PENICHE LACE.

Lace made near Lisbon, but at Peniche both black and white Lace are made, and a greater variety of designs worked than near Lisbon. Some of the patterns resemble Maltese designs, and are geometrical, having no grounds; others are similar to the large flower patterns so well known in Spanish Lace patterns, while another kind have hardly any pattern at all, and are made of a variety of grounds, with a few thick stitches intermixed with the grounds and a gimp thread run in and out, and forming a very simple design. In the thick Spanish Lace designs, the grounds are made of various kinds of Honeycomb and Star, two or three varieties being introduced into one pattern; the favourite varieties being either six or eight pointed Honeycombs of the usual size, or a number of large Honeycombs, each surrounded with a second or double line, filled in with a number of small holes. Fig. 656 is a

printed design, and measures 33 inches in width. It is stiffer, and has more glaze, than the original cloth made in Bengal.

Perewiaska Fur.—The animal producing this Fur is a small rodent mammal, of the genus *Mus*, and is otherwise known as the Russian Musquash. The Fur is employed for muffs, tippets, cuffs, and linings. The skin measures 6 inches by 6 inches.

Perforated Cardboard Work.—This fancy work is of so simple a description that it is generally only made by children, for whom it is peculiarly suitable; but it can be, and is, used for making church book-markers, and when the designs are worked out in many-coloured silks, and are shaded like Berlin Wool patterns, they are rather more difficult of execution. The materials required are perforated white cardboard, skeins of sewing silk, and patterns such as are used for samplers, or small Berlin Woolwork sprays of flowers. The silks, when used by children, are selected of bright colours, but all of one shade; for more difficult work, they are chosen so as to shade into each other. To work: Procure a sheet of cardboard, and count the lines of punctures upon it as rows, to find out how many rows are required for the pattern, one row counting for one stitch. Cut out the cardboard, and in its centre work the selected spray or the letters of a name. Work in CROSS STITCH, and for the letters form those illustrated in MARKING. Line the cardboard with a ribbon matching it in width, to hide the wrong side of the work, and secure this by working a Vandyke border round the edge of the cardboard and through the ribbon; three Cross Stitches to every slant will make a good Vandyke. If the edge of the work is required to be more highly ornamented, after the centre is worked, lay the cardboard upon a piece of glass, and, with a sharp penknife, cut it away to form open crosses round the edge, but leave two rows of board between the real edge and the open edge. Sew on the ribbon, and make the ornamental border inside the cutting, securing the edge with a plain, straight line of Cross Stitches along the rows left at the outside.

Perforated Cards.—These are Cards stamped for the purposes of Decorative Needlework, the designs being punched through them by machinery. At one time very beautiful floral designs used to be pricked in Card, so as to stand out in relief. These Cards were then bound with silk ribbon binding, and sewn together, to form small articles, such as pin-trays, pincushions, &c.

Permanents.—These are cotton cloths, of a light description, similar in texture to Turkey Cambrics; some of them have a slight glaze. They are dyed in a variety of colours, and are much employed for the trimming of dresses, especially Galatea stripes.

Persian.—An inferior description of silk stuff, thin, and designed for linings of women's cloaks, hoods, and articles of infants' dress. It is soft, fine, almost transparent, and not durable: it may be had in all colours, the width running to half a yard. It is extensively made in Persia—whence its name—and is exported to Turkey and Russia.

Persiana.—A silk stuff decorated with large flowers.

Persian Cord.—A slighter kind of dress material than Janus Cord. It is a mixture of cotton and wool, somewhat stiff, and unfinished on one side. It washes well, and is 27 inches in width.

Persian Cross Stitch.—See *Cross Stitch*, BERLIN WORK, and EMBROIDERY STITCHES.

Persian Embroidery.—Persia has given to Europe a large proportion of the art designs that are now so freely employed, not only in our embroideries, but in our textiles, gold, silver, and bronze works. That Embroidery came originally from the East is well known, but few are aware that, in the thirteenth century, Marco Polo, when describing Kerman, or Cashmere, mentions that "the ladies of that country produce such excellent embroidery of silks and stuffs, with figures of beasts, birds, trees, and flowers, that they are marvels to see." Persian Embroidery, from that date down to the present time, has been employed to decorate prayer and other carpets, curtains, shawls, quilts, housings, veils, and fine linen; and whatever has been produced has combined beauty and intricacy of design, variety in colour and workmanship, with skill in its execution. All the descriptions of Embroidery are executed in Persia, as Embroidery with gold and silver threads Couched upon the background, and answering to our Church Embroidery, Embroidery upon Silk or Cotton foundations in Satin Stitch or in Crewel Stitch, Embroidery upon Leather and Velvet, Inlaid Appliqué with coloured cloths combined with Embroidery, Embroidery covering the entire background, and worked in Tent and Cross Stitch, Darned, Netting, Drawn Work, and fine White Embroidery.

The materials used for the foundations to the Embroideries are various. Coarse cotton backgrounds are frequently used, also fine cotton fabrics, the soft silk known as Persian silk, velvet, leather, thin cloth, and wool obtained from goats. The last material is that used in the making of the celebrated Kerman shawls. These shawls are woven by hand, and are made from the under wool of a particular kind of white goat, whose wool attains a peculiar softness from the fine pasturage round Kerman. The pattern known as the Pine, which has been so extensively copied in our Paisley shawls, was used in Persia before the seventeenth century.

Darned Netting.—This is used for veils. The Netting is made with black and white silk threads, and with Diamond Treble Netting, and upon it is worked, with coloured silks, geometrical designs, stars, circles, &c.

Drawn Work.—This is carried, in Persia, to an extent and beauty that has rarely been attained by any European needlewoman. Not only are the borders to pieces of fine linen or muslin drawn out in the familiar squares of European work, but complicated designs are attempted, and the various parts of the material drawn away, so as to form regular patterns. On a piece of muslin in the South Kensington Museum, a Vandyke border is formed by alternately drawing away a section, and forming it into minute squares, each square being Buttonholed over with coloured silks, and leaving a section perfect, and covering that with silk embroidery, while the centre of the muslin is filled with a round of Drawn Work, edged with pots containing flowers, made with many coloured-silks.

Embroidery in Tent and Cross Stitch was at one time used for the wide trousers worn by the ladies of the harems, and though no longer in request, many specimens of it are still to be met with. The foundation is a moderately coarse cotton, which is entirely concealed with patterns worked in Tent Stitch with fine wools and silks of many colours; one thread only of the foundation is covered each time a stitch is made, and the result of such work is so minute that, unless closely inspected, it looks like a finely woven material. The same background is employed when the needlework is done with Cross Stitch, but the appearance of this is slightly coarser, as coarser silks are used, and the stitch is not so minute.

Inlaid Appliqué, or Patchwork, is a most remarkable production. It is chiefly made at Resht, and is used for covers, carpets, and housings. It is Patchwork combined with Embroidery. The colours used are extremely brilliant, and the patches (which are of cloth) are cut so small, and into such intricate patterns, that it is marvellous how they can be joined together. Flowers, birds, and animals are freely used, besides geometric and conventional patterns; the pieces are stitched together, and every seam afterwards concealed with lines of Chain Stitch worked over them in coloured silks. Not content with a single line of Chain Stitch, two or three lines upon each petal of a flower, or feather of a bird, are embroidered, and each line is worked in a different coloured silk, while in many places the entire patch is concealed with embroidery, either of gold thread or silk, worked to

other designs, and then ornamented with wide borders of needlework, and with their centres covered with innumerable detached flower sprays. They are always known by the centre being shaped like the three sides of a square, and the other a protruding curve. In the centre of this elongated side a small round is formed with rich embroidery. This spot marks the place where the holy earth of Kerbela is placed, and which is touched by the forehead of the person who kneels in the marked out square while performing his devotions. No embroidery is too elaborate for these carpets, in which Satin, Crewel, Feather, and Herringbone Stitches are worked in varied shades of many colours

FIG. 657. PERSIAN EMBROIDERY.

make a shaded design. Sometimes, instead of Chain Stitches, lines are made with fine gold thread; these are not laid on flat, but are twisted into very small circles, laid so close together as to form a broad, compact line. Gold and silver foil is used instead of gold or silk; it is cut very narrow, and folded over itself, so as to form zigzag lines, which are then sewn to the foundation, either as lines, or to fill up certain spaces.

Inlaid Appliqué Silk Embroideries.—These have been in use hundreds of years for prayer and other carpets, curtains, and for the covers thrown over State presents. The prayer carpets are generally of a pale coloured silk foundation, elaborately quilted in Vandykes, half circles, and

and gold and silver thread, Couched down in patterns like Basket, Wavy, Diamond, and Raised Couchings. The bath carpets are made of cotton fabrics, or of thin white silk. They are also quilted and embroidered, but are less ornamented than the prayer carpets. The covers used for State presents are worked like the prayer carpets, but are more thickly embroidered with gold and silver thread, after the manner of our Church Embroidery, and, being of a much greater size, have large, handsome borders of pomegranates, their leaves and flowers, birds in full plumage, carnations, tulips the size of life, and other bold designs. The pattern of one of the covers worked in the seventeenth century is shown in Fig. 657, and is selected for illustration as it is one that is handsome in itself and is yet capable of being copied without too much labour. It is made as follows: Trace out the design upon white Persian Silk, stitch the quilted lines, according to pattern, with salmon pink silk. Work the oval in the centre of the flower with pink silk in alternate squares, and leave the other part plain, the petals of the flowers in SATIN STITCH, and in crimson and orange silk. These two shades do not blend into each other, where one ends and the other commences being distinctly marked in the illustration. Use the same crimson and orange silk for the flower buds, put the crimson round the outside, and the orange in the centre, but add some pale yellow for quite the centre. Work the leaves in deep olive green and yellow silk, working the olive green all round the edges of the leaves, and the yellow in the centre. Use the same colours for the calyx of the flowers and buds. Edge every petal of the flowers with a line formed with fine gold thread and crimson silk doubled and run into one needle; stitch with this as an outline, and make the stems and stalks with gold thread and green silk threaded on one needle, and worked as close CREWEL STITCHES.

White Linen Embroidery.—This is worked upon fine linen, and in thick Satin Stitches, with a soft glazy thread. The patterns are remarkable for their extreme delicacy and finish.

Persian Lamb.—Of this animal there are two varieties, the black and the grey-furred. The skins are the most valuable of all Lamb Skins, are beautifully curly and glossy, and are employed for articles both of men's and women's wear. They measure 14 inches by 20 inches, and may be classed amongst the most costly of our furs.

Peruvian Embroidery.—A beautiful embroidery combined with Darned Work, executed in Peru, and used for curtain borders, quilts, towels, and other articles that require washing. The Embroidery, being executed on the linen or silk foundation, is lasting; and, as the patterns used are conventional flowers, or arabesques, the work is artistic, however coarse the material. To work: Trace out a bold flower pattern, like those used for the best Crewel Work, and carefully DARN all the background with POINT MINUSCULE. OUTLINE the pattern with CREWEL STITCH, but only work the veins of the leaves and the centres of the flowers. The materials used are China silks of the softest make, linen, or common towelling. The embroidery is done with raw silk, shiny linen thread, or crewels.

Perwitzky.—The fur of this animal, which is short, is chiefly employed for cloak linings, but it affords little warmth to the wearer.

Petersham Cloth.—This is a very thick, shaggy kind of woollen cloth, of a dark navy blue colour, employed for men's overcoats, and what are called "pilot coats," suitable for seafaring purposes, or for wear in very severe weather.

Petershams, or Belt Ribbons.—A similar description of article to Pads, being of double thickness, watered, of all colours, plain and in patterns. Skirts of dresses are sewn upon them; and they are likewise attached to the backs of bodices, on the inside, at the waist; they are supplied with hooks and eyes, for the purpose of securing them in their right place upon the figure of the wearer.

Petit Coté.—A French term to signify the side piece of a bodice.

Petit Point.—The French name for Tent Stitch. *See* BERLIN WORK.

Petit Poussin.—*See* POUSSIN LACE.

Pheasant.—The plumage of this bird is sufficiently handsome to make it popular for the purposes of millinery, being employed for the crowns of hats, the skins being used entire; also for muffs and collarettes. The wings are likewise used as trimmings for hats.

Phrygian Needlework.—*See* EMBROIDERY.

Picôt.—The French term for a prick, as with a needle, being derived from the verb *picoter*. It is employed in lace-making.

Picots.—These are little Loops or Bobs that ornament Needle-made Laces of all kinds, and that are often introduced into Embroidery. To work: Make a tiny Loop upon the work, and cover it over with a number of BUTTONHOLE STITCHES worked into it, or put the needle into the work, and bring it out so as only to take up a very small piece of the material; wind the thread eight or nine times round the needle, place the left thumb upon it, and draw it out of the material, holding the thread down while doing so. The Loops made upon the needle will be transferred to the end of the thread, and will form a spiral raised Dot upon the work. *See* CROCHET, GUIPURE D'ART, and EMBROIDERY STITCHES.

Piece Goods.—The articles classed under this name include Grey Cotton, Mulls, Jacconets, Shirtings, Madapolams, Printers' Cambrics, Longcloths, Sheetings, Drills, Bobbin Net, &c.

Piecing.—Mending; joining two pieces of stuff together. A method adopted for the repair of sheets when worn in the middle, the thinnest portion being cut out, and the outer sides turned inwards, and sewed together up the middle.

Piercer, or Stiletto.—One of the useful appliances of a workbox, consisting of a small, sharply-pointed instrument of steel, ivory, or mother-of-pearl. It is employed for making holes for Embroidery, the shanks of buttons, eyelet-holes for lacings, and, in a somewhat different form, used by embroiderers in gold, who employ it for laying the Bullion in place, guiding the fine cord round the edges of the work, arranging the pattern, and making holes.

Pile.—The thick, short nap on the right side of velvet, cloth, or corduroy, formed in the first and last-named stuffs by the placing of part of the warp threads over a needle, more or less thick, according to the desired richness of the material. When the needle is withdrawn, it is replaced by a sharp instrument, which cuts through the loops formed. The Pile always lies in one direction.

Pillow.—This is an article required by all lace-makers who employ Bobbins, and from its use has given the name of Pillow Lace to the work manufactured upon it. To the Pillow the parchment pattern is secured, and the Bobbins holding the numerous threads attached while the other articles required in lace-making, such as pincushion, scissors, crochet hook, and pins, are all arranged upon it. The Pillows used are of several kinds; that known as the Round is chiefly used for Devonshire and Honiton Lace, the Flat for Brussels Lace making, the Oblong for Macramé, and the Long for Peniche Lace and other laces which are made in one piece, and whose width is great.

To Make a Flat Pillow: Take two circles of either Holland or twill material, 18 inches across, join them together, but leave a small opening, through which stuff the Pillow out with flock or horsehair; sew up the opening, and then, on the top, where the work is to be done, lay several folds of flannel; cover the Pillow over with a red twill or silk cover, made to take off and on as described in Round Pillow.

To Make a Long Pillow: Make this in the form of a cylinder, half a yard long, and 36 inches round. Make a cover of this size, and stuff it out with horsehair; but instead of filling the ends, make a hole like the entrance to a muff, into which the implements used in the lace-making can be put; sew the flock into the cover, so that these two cavities are kept from filling up, and then place a piece of flannel over the top of the Pillow, and finish with a red twill cover, made to take off and on. These Long Pillows are kept in baskets, or upon low stools, in order that, when transported from place to place, they can be carried without disturbing the work.

To Make an Oblong Pillow: Make a stout Holland bag, 12 inches long by 8 inches wide, and fill this with bran, so that it is perfectly hard; cover it over with a piece of strong blue ticking, of a kind woven for the purpose, with blue lines in it, placed at even distances from each other, and lengthways across the cushion. An oblong straw hassock will answer the purposes of this Cushion if covered with the blue ticking.

To Make a Round Pillow: This is made round like a ball, except on the top, where it is flat. Tie up into a round a quantity of horsehair or flock, and bind this over with list; make the Pillow 36 inches to 38 inches in diameter; over the part that is to form the top, lay a piece of flannel or Bath coating, and then cover over the whole with a Nankeen, or red twill, or silk covering. Make this to take off and on, the best way to manage it being to cut a circle the size of the top of the Pillow, run a straight piece of twill round the circle, of sufficient depth to cover the sides and meet underneath the Pillow, and finish this off with a broad hem, through which pass a string. Put the cover on the Pillow, and draw the string up tightly, to secure the folds of the material, and leave no rucks in which the lace threads might become entangled.

All these Pillows, before they are finished, are covered with three cloths, known as Cover Cloths, which are used to keep the lace clean while in progress; the largest Cover

Cloth, made of fine linen, the size of the Pillow, is laid over the Pillow before the pattern is pinned on, and upon this the lace is worked; it is removed and washed whenever it becomes dirty. The smaller cloths are made of fine linen, in size 18 inches by 12 inches. These are detached from the Pillow and removed at pleasure; one is doubled and laid over the pattern and under the Bobbins (see Fig. 658), and the other folded in the same way upon the opposite side of the Pillow, and so as to keep the finished lace clean. When the Pillow is laid by, take off the cover under the Bobbins, and lay it over the whole work. Fig. 658 shows a Round Pillow dressed with covers, with pattern, Bobbins, and pincushion attached, and the lace in the process of working. (*See* DRESSED PILLOW.) When working the lace, rest the Pillow upon the knees, arrange the Passive Bobbins so that they hang down straight in a fan shape, and keep them in this position, particularly when making curves and turns, as the Passive Bobbins are liable to run to the inner parts of the

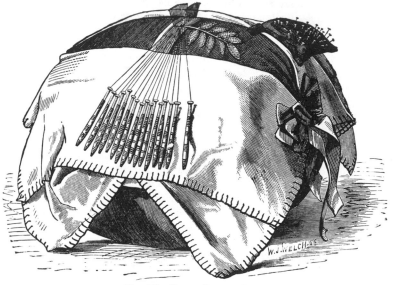

FIG. 658. ROUND PILLOW, DRESSED.

pattern, and leave the edge of the design open and bare. Keep the Working Bobbins at the side of the Pillow, and pin them out of the way of the lace until they are required. The Pillow is turned while the lace is making, if the pattern is more easily worked by so doing.

Pillow Bar.—This is used to connect various detached parts of Pillow Lace together that are made with Bar Grounds. The three kinds of Bar used are the Plain Bar, that forms a straight line from lace to lace; the Guipure Bar, that forms the same straight line, but is worked with threads proceeding from the lace, instead of attached for the purpose; and the Irregular, or Cross-bar, formed by Bars meeting together and starting off at angles to each other. All the Bars are ornamented with a Pearl Edge upon one or both sides.

To Make a Guipure Bar.—Throw out, when making the lace, four pairs of Bobbins from one piece of lace, and work these in CLOTH STITCH, without putting up pins until the lace upon the opposite side is reached. Work in the

MODERN ITALIAN LACES (PILLOW), CHIEFLY MADE ON THE "CAMPAGNA."

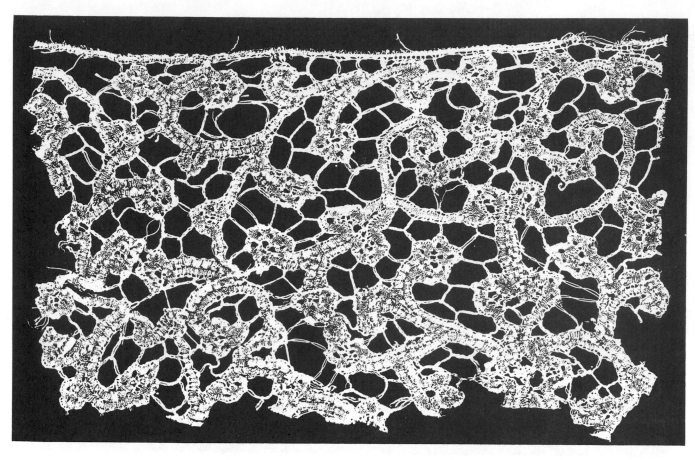

ITALIAN TAPE LACE WITH PLAIN BRIDE GROUND (OLD).

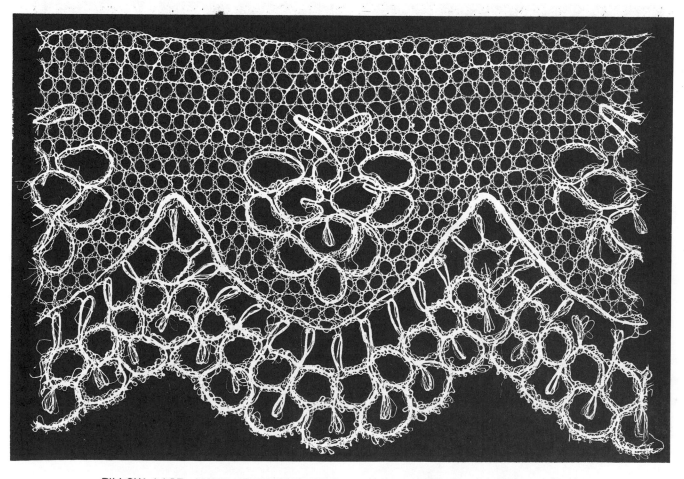

PILLOW LACE, MADE FROM THE FIBRE OF THE ALOE AT ALBISSOLA (OLD).

Bobbins here as part of the pattern. The Bars must be worked from alternate sides, so that the Bobbins taken away to form one Bar are returned by another and used if required, if not, are secured by a loop and cut off.

To Make Irregular or Cross Bar.—Hang on four pairs of Bobbins and work as for Plain Bar with CLOTH STITCH until a place where the Bar is intersected is reached. Here hang on another set of four pairs of Bobbins and leave them alone until the first line is completed. Then work up these and carry the line thus made in a different direction to the first Bar. Several sets of Bobbins can be hung on to the first Bar at intervals, and completed and themselves intersected, if the ground to be filled in will admit of so many Bars being worked.

To Work a Plain Bar with Pearl Edge upon One Side: Take eight pairs of Bobbins and wind the Knots out of the way. Attach them to the lace where the Bar is to be made by drawing up a loop of one pair and passing the rest of the Bobbins through it; draw up tightly and work across in CLOTH STITCH, and back again without setting up a pin; twist six times, take the last Bobbin on the right hand in the left hand, raise it, take a pin in the right hand, twist it once under the thread, and make a loop round the pin; put it in the Pinhole, take up the Bobbin next it, and twist it once round the pin, and work back in Cloth Stitch (having made a PEARL). Return again to the right without putting up a pin on the right, make another Pearl, and repeat until the length of Bar is made and the lace is reached. Draw up a loop with the hook, pass two of these Bobbins through it, tail foremost, draw the loop tight, and cut off two pairs of Bobbins, but not those that made the loop; twist the remaining Bobbins tightly and carry them to the next Bar; make SEWINGS to keep them close where required. Hang on two more pairs of Bobbins at the new Bar, and work as before. A Pearl edge to both sides is made with Right and Left Pearl alternately.

Pillow Fustian.—The most common variety of Fustian. The cord is narrow, and the texture stout. It is chiefly made in Lancashire, and is manufactured in cotton after the manner of velvet. *See* FUSTIAN.

Pillow Lace Wheels.—These are used to fill in round spaces left in the centres of patterns in Honiton and other Pillow Laces. They are described under WHEELS.

Pillow Linens.—These cloths may be had in various qualities. The best Irish are made in widths of 40, 42, 45, and 54 inches. The medium sorts measure 40, 42, and 45 inches in width. *See* LINEN.

Pillow-made Braid Lace.—*See* BRAIDS.

Pilot Cloth.—An indigo blue woollen cloth, used for great coats, and for mariners' clothing. It is thick and twilled, having a nap on one side, and is very strong for wear. Pilot Cloth is sometimes incorrectly called Dreadnought, which should only be applied to the coat itself. Bearskin is a description of Pilot Cloth having a longer nap. It may be had of either 27 inches in width, or 54 inches, and of different descriptions, viz.: in wool-dyed woaded colours, and in unwoaded colours; also in piece-dyed woaded, and piece-dyed unwoaded colours.

Pin.—An appliance used for the temporary attachment of one piece of material to another, before it is basted; and likewise employed for purposes of the toilet. The original Pin was a thorn. Sharpened fish and other bones were also in use before the modern metal Pin was manufactured. The date of the latter in England is doubtful, possibly the thirteenth century. Bristol is credited with being the seat of the manufacture.

Pine, or Pina Cloth.—An expensive textile, made of the fibres of the pine-apple leaf, and manufactured into dress pieces, shawls, scarves, and handkerchiefs, by the natives of the Philippines. It is very delicate and soft in texture, transparent, and usually has a slight tinge of pale yellow. The threads of both warp and weft are each unspun fibres, and only small pieces of cloth can be produced. It is very strong, resembling horsehair cloth, but the best examples are finer than the finest Lawn. Some of the handkerchiefs are beautifully embroidered. This textile is only made at Manilla.

Pine Marten (or Baum) (*Mustela abietum*).—Distinguished from the Stone Marten by some admixture of yellow colour. The skin of this animal is dyed to imitate sable.

Pine Wool.—A description of wool produced from the fibres of the leaves, bark, and comb of the *Pinus Sylvestris*, or Scotch Fir; famous in Norway and Germany; employed for the manufacture of a kind of Stockingette Cloth resembling wool. It is of a light brown wood colour, with an agreeable odour, and is considered invaluable for the use of persons suffering from rheumatism, especially when a few drops of the essence of Pine Oil are applied, upon the wool, to any part especially affected. The Lairitz Pine wool manufactory at Remda, Thuringia, is one of great importance. Flannel, wadding, and woven underclothing of every description are produced there; and are in great repute for their hygienic properties.

Pinking Iron.—A small appliance having a sharp edge, shaped in after an ornamental outline. With this borders of silk, cloth, or leather may be cut, or stamped out with perfect regularity, in a decorative way; the material being laid on a thick block of lead, and the opposite end of the iron struck smartly with a hammer, so as to give a clear sharp cutting at the first application of the instrument.

Pinking, or Pouncing.—A method of decorating dresses, trimmings for furniture, rugs, and shrouds, by means of a sharp stamping instrument. Pieces of the material are cut out by it in scallops, at the edge, and other designs within the border. The stamping is of semicircular, or angular form, and the extreme edge is evenly jagged or notched. The use of the term Pouncing is now nearly, if not quite, obsolete.

Pink Tape, or Red Tape.—This Tape is made of cotton, and numbers 16, 24, 32. It is to be had in very long lengths on reels, and is chiefly employed in Law offices.

Pinna Silk.—This is a description of *byssus* secreted by a mussel of the Mediterranean, of the genus *Lamellibranchiate*. The beard of this mollusc is so abundant, that the Maltese and Sicilians weave stockings, gloves, and other articles of it. In the year 1754, Pope Benedict XV. was presented with a pair of stockings made of the silky material. One species of this mussel—the *Pinna pectinata*—is found in our British Seas.

Pin-rib.—The very delicate lines, either printed or woven, in Muslin Textiles.

Pin Work. — Also known as Crowns, Spines, Thorns, and Fleur Volants. These are stitches used in most Needle-points to lighten the effect of the Cordonnet edgings or of any part in the design that is Raised from the surrounding flat surface. The stitch is formed of Buttonhole, and either shaped as half crescents or long points. To work: Make a small loop into the Buttonhole Edging, run the needle back underneath the edging to where it started from, and BUTTONHOLE closely over the thread; this forms a plain crescent. To form one ornamented with Spines or Thorns, lay the thread as before, and Buttonhole it over as far as the centre, then loop a piece of fine thread into the working thread, hold the two ends of this fine cotton firmly under the left thumb, and continue to Buttonhole with the working thread; then take up the thumb, draw out the fine thread, and leave the Buttonholes that were upon it as a lump or Spine by themselves. Continue to fill up the loop with Buttonholes, until another Spine is desired, when make as before. Spines and Thorns worked by themselves upon the Cordonnet make thus: Make a little loop of thread, and stick a pin in it to keep it tight, and then run the working thread up to the pin and cover the loop with Buttonholes until the CORDONNET is again reached.

Piping.—A border formed on any material of dress or furniture, by means of the introduction into it of a piece of Bobbin, for the purpose of giving an appearance of greater finish, or adding to its strength. To make: Place a piece of Bobbin, or Cotton Cord, along a strip of material—cut on the bias—on the wrong side; leaving a depth of two-thirds of the width of the strip on the side which is to lie uppermost, when placed on the article to be bound. TACK in the Cord lightly, and then lay it on the raw edge of the dress or other article to be thus finished; the Cord side inwards, that is, towards the working, and the raw edges all together outwards, and parallel with each other. STITCH or BACK STITCH all together, keeping close to the Cord. Then turn all the raw edges inwards, and turn in the one outside, over the others, so as to form a HEM, which should then be made.

Piqué.—A French material, made of two cotton threads, one thicker than the other, which are woven and united at certain points, and there make an extra thickness. The pattern is usually of a lozenge shape; the material is strong and durable, and may be had with small printed designs, in white only. It is suitable for children's clothing, and for men's waistcoats. There are coloured and figured varieties, which are made from 30 inches to a yard wide. They are to be had in many qualities, both thin and thick.

Placing.—The term commonly employed in reference to Needlework, meaning the adjustment of the several pieces of any article which have to be sewn together.

Placket.—The opening at the back of a skirt or petticoat, extending from the waist downwards, designed to enlarge the aperture made at the waistband, to allow for passing the skirt over the head and shoulders. HEM the overlapping side, double *Stitch* that underneath, and *Face* the pleat at the extreme end of the Placket-hole, to prevent its being torn downwards. In early times Placket was synonymous with Petticoat, as we find exemplified by a passage in Herrick's Poems:

> If the maides a spinning goe,
> Burn the flax, and fire the toe,
> Scorch their Plackets.

Plaids, or Tartans.—By this name certain textiles in silk, wool, and worsted are alike known. The designs vary in colour, and in the breadths of the lines or bands, which cross each other at right angles, and form squares more or less large. The colours are inserted in the warp, and then a further introduction made in the weft, kept respectively on separate shuttles, and thrown at regular intervals; the colours being woven into the material, and not printed upon it. Tartan, correctly speaking, is the name of the coloured pattern, and Plaid that of the stuff, which is a coarse, strong worsted cloth, as made in Scotland, and worn in the national costume. Plaids are made of finer quality, suitable for ladies' wear, both in dress-pieces and shawls, in England as well as in Scotland. Shepherds' Plaid is a very small check, in black and white only. Plaids can be had in both double and single widths. Woollen and Worsted Tartans are very durable, and each distinct pattern supplies the badge of some clan. Properly speaking, we should call silk stuffs, and Ribbons so checkered Tartan, not Plaid silks and Ribbons.

Plain Edge.—In Pillow Lace, when the outside edges of the parts of a pattern are not decorated with the loops that are known as Pearls, they are finished with what is called a Plain Edge, which is made by working as the last stitch a more open stitch than that used in the other part of the lace. To work: Work across the lace to within one pair of Bobbins at the end. Twist this pair three times to the left with the left hand, take a pin in the right hand, hold both Bobbins in the left hand, stick the pin in front of the twisted threads into a Pinhole on the right, give a pull to draw the twist up, make a stitch with the last pair of Bobbins, and the working pair, putting the second Bobbin over the last but one, the last over the second, and then the last but one over the first Bobbin, and the first over the last Bobbin. Twist both pairs three times to the left, using both hands, pull the twists gently up, and then continue the thicker part of the pattern.

Plain Embroidery.—Also known as Low Embroidery. This term includes all the Embroideries worked in Satin and other stitches upon a flat foundation, whether worked alike upon both sides or in the usual manner, so long as no Raised Work or padding is added.

Plain Flat Couching.—*See* COUCHING.

Plain Knitting.—*See* KNITTING.

Plain Netting.—*See* NETTING.

Plain Sewing.—A term denoting any description of Needlework which is of a merely useful character, in contradistinction to that which is purely decorative. It comprises the following varieties: Hemming in two or three varieties, Sewing (or Seaming), Stitching, Hem-stitching, Running, Whipping, Tacking, Herringboning, Finedrawing, Darning, Overcasting, Buttonholing, Marking, Gathering, Gauging, Felling, Grafting, &c., Slashing, Fringing, Reeving, Quilling, Quilting, Ruching, Honeycombing, Slipstitching, &c.

Plaited Laces.—These are of two descriptions, one being made of silver or gold wire, and sometimes called Wire Lace; and the other being made of fine thread, and called Pillow Guipure. The Plaited Laces made of gold, silver, or silk threads, superseded the Knotted laces and the Reticellas towards the close of the sixteenth century. Italy claims the first invention of these, and much being made at Genoa, it was known as Genoese Lace, but as large quantities were also worked in Spain, and were largely exported thence to other countries, plaited laces also received the name of Point d'Espagne. France, Germany, and England made Plaited Laces, but never rivalled those produced at Genoa and in Spain, in which latter country the manufacture is still continued for ecclesiastical purposes. Plaited Laces are made upon a pillow and with Bobbins; the patterns are geometrical, and open, and have no grounds; for common purposes tinsel is used instead of real gold, and the lace is then used for theatrical purposes.

The thread Plaited Laces of the seventeenth century were first made in the geometrical designs used for the gold lace and for Reticellas, but soon became of much more elaborate design; they were largely employed to trim ruffs and falling collars in the seventeenth century, and only went out of fashion when flowing wigs came in, which hid the collar, and would not allow of a ruff being worn. At the present date the Plaited Laces have revived under the names of Maltese, Yak, or Cluny Laces, and are made at Auvergne, Malta, and in Bedfordshire and Buckinghamshire. These are made with either black or white threads, and with simple geometrical designs.

FIG. 659. PLAITED RIBBON WORK.

Plaited Ribbon Work.—A pretty work, of modern origin, made by plaiting ribbons together to form geometrical and open designs. It is used for sofa cushions,

mantel borders, handkerchief cases, and for any purpose that will admit of its being lined, as part of the effect depends upon the open spaces left between the plaits being filled with silk or satin of a contrasting colour to that of the ribbon. The materials required are wooden or millboard frames, fitting the work, a quantity of narrow silk

FIG. 660. PLAITED RIBBON WORK.

ribbon, rather less than half an inch wide, gold cord, gold coloured filoselle, and some pins.

To work as shown in Fig. 659: Procure a thin wooden frame, or make one with millboard, of the size required, and cut a good many lengths of ribbon an inch longer than the length from side to side of the frame. Pin two of these to the back of the frame close together (*see* Fig. 660), and fasten them to the opposite side; leave an inch space, and pin on two more lengths of ribbon, and

FIG. 661. PLAITED RIBBON WORK.

continue until one side of the frame is thus filled. Commence to fill the other side of the frame in the same manner, but interlace these second ribbons in and out the first ones whenever they cross them, as shown in the illustration. Finish the plait by interlacing into these straight ribbons some ribbons carried diagonally across the frame, as shown in Fig. 661. These cross ribbons are of various lengths, and should be cut as required; the shortest line will be across the corner of the frame, the longest across the centre of the work. Pin them to the back of the frame, and interlace them outside the square formed by the meeting of the straight ribbons, so that they surround it with a diamond. Weave

string is a suitable work for ladies with weak sight, or for anyone who, in the intervals of more engrossing employment, requires rest without being absolutely idle. The work makes good table mats on which to place hot dishes, and as such is shown in Fig. 662; it is also useful to put under ornaments that would otherwise injure the

FIG. 662. PLAITED STRINGWORK.

them over and under the straight ribbons. Run a gold cord down the centre of each plait between the two straight ribbons and over the ribbons forming the diamond, and under those forming the square. Tack the ends of these cords to the ribbon ends, and secure these latter together with a few stitches. Then take the work out of the frame and edge it with a straight line of ribbon. Procure ribbon an inch in width, double it, and sew into it every end of the ribbons forming the plaits, so that a tidy and straight edge is formed. Hide the stitches made in securing the ribbons by working a border of FEATHER STITCH along the edge, upon the right side of the work, which is the side undermost during the working. Make the work up on a coloured satin background, which cut larger than required, and pull up through the openings left by the plaits. Prevent these puffs moving by securing them to their places with a few stitches.

Plaited Stitch.—*See* BERLIN WORK.

Plaited Stringwork.—Amongst the numerous varieties of art needlework now so prevalent, all taxing to the utmost the attention and ingenuity of the worker, it is occasionally a relief to turn to work requiring little thought, and yet when completed of some use. Plaited

polish of the tables they were placed upon, and it is so inoffensive in colour and make when not embroidered,

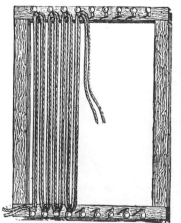

FIG. 663. PLAITED STRINGWORK

that the highest of high art ladies could not find fault with it in its pristine condition.

The materials are, a wooden frame, which can be of rough deal, size and shape depending upon the size mats to be made. Pegs are inserted into the wooden frame at the top and the bottom in the same manner as those used in daisy mat frames, and as shown in Fig. 663. Besides the frame, evenly made packing string, a packing needle, millboard, and silk ribbon, or linen tape are required.

To work: Double the string and wind it up and down the frame on the pegs (*See* Fig. 663), until the pegs are full, then thread the needle with double string, and DARN in and out the upright strands, under two and over two, as shown in Fig. 664. The darning must be done very evenly, and each horizontal line put in at any equal distance between the one above and the one below it; also, the string picked up and the string gone over must be varied in every other line, so as to produce a woven or plaited look in the work. Each line of string, as

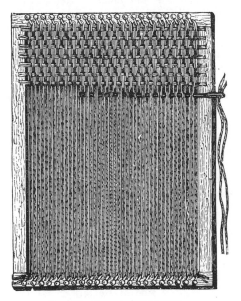

FIG. 664. PLAITED STRINGWORK.

it is Darned across, is not fastened at the commencement or the end, but cut. The whole of the Plaiting being done, paste the back side of the work while in the frame, and leave it to dry. Cut out the shape, whether square or round, in millboard, and cover this underneath with a piece of bright silk, so as to ornament that side. Then cut the plaited strings from the frame, and to the size of the millboard foundation, TACK the edges firmly to the

FIG. 665. PLAITED STRINGWORK.

millboard, and bind them over with silk ribbon or tape matching the lining. The looped edge shown in Fig. 665 is now formed with the double string, and sewn to the edge; it is merely a fine edging, and is enlarged in the design to clearly denote the method of twining the loops one within the other. To finish the mat, plait together in a three-plait nine strands of string, and sew this on so as to conceal the binding ribbon and the stitches round the edge. The plait is shown in Fig. 666.

This mat may be rendered much more attractive by being formed of different materials. Thus coloured braid is used instead of the string, and made to form dice patterns, or one colour used for the upright threads, and the other for the darned lines, which will give the appearance of Couching. Should the foundation be made with-

No. 666. PLAITED STRINGWORK.

out any colour, embroider simple Dots, Stars, or Sprays upon it, before it is pasted or withdrawn from the frame. Work these devices either with filoselle or with single Berlin wool, and introduce the same materials, with the string, in the Plait round the mat, or let them entirely take its place. The looped edge must always be of some stiff material, like string or braid, otherwise it would not retain its shape; but the materials forming all the other parts of the mat can be diversified according to the worker's fancy.

Plaiter and Kilter.—This is a small appliance by which the operation of Plaiting and Kilting may be accomplished with the greatest regularity and ease. The original invention was patented, under the name of the Centennial Plaiter, in 1876; and the little machine can be had in different sizes, so as to suit the finer as well as coarser kinds of Plaiting and Kilting. It has the appearance of a flat box, consisting of two parts, and containing a knife. The first part is a tray, having three compartments, formed by divisions like coarse wooden combs; the second part is a frame of wood, fitted with a number of very narrow flat steel bands, placed across it in close succession, but leaving spaces sufficient for the introduction of the material to be plaited. This frame is fitted into the tray when the work is to be executed. The knife, likewise, consists of two parts, a flat piece of wood and a similar piece of steel, which latter is laid upon it, and affixed by two screws or nuts. The holes in the steel being of some length, it can be made to project beyond the edge of the wood to any extent desired; and, as the knife has a blunt edge, it cannot cut the material to be plaited. The method of working is as follows: Lay the stuff across the steel bands in the frame, and press it in with the knife between them successively. This part of the work being accomplished, lay the flat piece of wood, which forms the cover of the box-like appliance, upon the material, as it remains pressed into the spaces, and turn the whole round, laying the side on which you have been operating downwards into the tray. Then press the folds, which protrude between the steel bars, with a hot iron, passing the latter lightly backwards and forwards, until the folds are rendered sufficiently well defined and permanent. Lastly, turn the frame round into its normal place again in the tray, removing the board (or cover of the box), and now hold the hot iron as near to the other side of the material as may be safe, without touching it. After having been thoroughly heated thus, the material may be removed from its confinement, and the work of plaiting or kilting will be found completed.

Plaitings.—These are Pillow Lace Stitches used as open Fillings for the centres of flowers, the wings of butterflies, or to finish off the centre of a geometrical design. They are used in many descriptions of Guipure Lace, particularly Honiton and Maltese. Plaitings are of various shapes and sizes, and are known as CUCUMBER, CRINKLE, DIAMOND or LONG, and SQUARE.

Crinkle Plaitings.—These Plaitings are used in the centre of flowers, and make Raised Loops in imitation of stamens. They are illustrated in Fig. 486, of Honiton Lace, where they form the centre of the fully-opened poppies. To work: Sew to the PEARL EDGE, two pairs of Bobbins, and PLAIT these together by laying Nos. 1 and 4 of the Bobbins on the outside, and No. 3 in the centre, and, working backwards and forwards across them with No 2, work twelve rows thus, then fasten this Plait back to the Pearl it started from, or to the one next it, with a SEWING. Repeat these Loops until the number of stamens required is complete.

Cucumber Plaitings.—These are illustrated in the upper wings of the Butterfly that forms Fig. 667. Having

FIG. 667. CUCUMBER PLAITINGS.

worked the body, head, and the close wings in CLOTH STITCH, and the outlines of the open wings in Cloth Stitch, with a PEARL EDGE on the outside and a PLAIN EDGE upon the nside, proceed to fill in the lower wings and the Circles with DIAMOND PLAITINGS, and finally work the CUCUMBER PLAITINGS in the upper wings. These are attached to the Plain Edge on one side and the Pearl Edge on the other, as it is less difficult to make SEWINGS to the Plain Edge than to the Pearl Edge; they are all attached to the cross strands in the Cloth Stitch, and it is at first difficult to find out these strands. Prepare nine pairs of Bobbins, stick a pin into each Pearl upon the Pearled side, and hang on a pair of Bobbins at the second Pearl, and twist four times; hang on two pairs of Bobbins at the fifth Pearl, make a stitch with these last, twist twice, stick a pin, make a stitch about the pin, twist four times; then make a Plaiting with the first pair

hung on, and the pair nearest it, leaving the third pair idle. Make the Plaiting thus: Lay down Nos. 1 and 4 Bobbins on the outside of the plait, and well apart, and put No. 3 Bobbin down the centre, then take No. 2 Bobbin in the hand, and pass it backwards and forwards, under and over the other three, changing it from one hand to the other. For the first row, pass 2 over 3 and under 4; for the second row, pass 2 over 4, under 3, and over 1; for the third row, pass 2 under 1, over 3, and under 4. Repeat these last two rows until the Plait is long enough, but after the first two rows, draw 2 quite up, and pull out again with 1 and 4, so as to tighten the twist first made; do not repeat this pulling, and when the Plait is long enough (it requires about twelve rows), twist 2 and 1 together four times, so as to make 1 the outside Bobbin. SEW 1 to the thick wing side of the Butterfly, and pass 2 through it. Hang on two more pairs of Bobbins opposite the next hole, make a stitch, twist twice, stick a pin, make a stitch about it, and twist four times. Then make another Plaiting with the pair left idle in the first Plaiting, and the pair nearest it. For this and the succeeding Plaitings, pass the Bobbin that would be called 2, backwards and forwards, so as to make sixteen rows, then twist four times. Twist the Bobbins that made the last Plaiting four times, and take the third and fourth of those Bobbins, and the first and second of the one in working, and make a stitch with these four, and give 3 and 4 a gentle pull while so doing, but leave 1 and 2 as worked. Stick a pin, twist twice, make a stitch, twist four times. Hang on a pair of Bobbins upon the close wing side of Butterfly, and leave them. Hang on two pairs of Bobbins at the next hole, and make another Plaiting as described above. Hang on the two remaining pairs of Bobbins, make a Plaiting with one, twist the other four times, sew it to the Circle and the end of the wing, twist four times, and by this means bring this pair down, in readiness to make the securing stitch of the last Plaiting. Two more Plaitings will be required to finish the wing; when they are worked, and all the threads sewn to the close wing side of Butterfly, tie up the Bobbins and cut them off. The other wing is worked from its extreme end to the centre, in the same way. Great care is required when working Cucumber Plaitings, especially in handling Bobbin No. 2. A firm hand may be kept upon the other three, but if No. 2 is much pulled, it will throw the Plaiting out of place. The Bobbins must also be handled with great nicety while the securing stitch is made. After the pin is stuck and the stitch made about it, the Plaiting is secure, and may be left. The making of the rest of the Butterfly is described in HALF STITCH.

Diamond, or Long Plaitings.—These are illustrated in the centre of the Daisy shown in Fig. 668, and they are worked after the other parts of the spray have been made. Make the centre circle of the flower in STEM STITCH, round the outside edge, and in CLOTH STITCH, and the outer petals in STEM STITCH. When finished, tie up the Bobbins and cut them off, and commence the Diamond Plaiting. There are four holes in the centre of the four Plaits, and a hole at each commencement of a Plait in the Circle of the Daisy. Stick a pin into one of these last holes, and hang on two pairs of Bobbins, winding the knots out of the way. Connect to the flower by drawing a thread through the nearest hole, and pass one Bobbin from the other pair through it, take out the pin, and stick it into the sewed hole, make a CLOTH STITCH, twist each pair twice, stick a pin in the hole between them. Number the Bobbins 1, 2, 3, 4. Lay down Nos. 1 and 4 on the outside, and some distance apart, and No. 3 in the centre, and take No. 2 in the hand, and pass it backwards and forwards and under and over the other three, in the same way as in CUCUMBER PLAITINGS. Lift 2 with the left hand, 4 with the right, put 2 over 3 and under 4, pass it into the fingers of the right hand, drop 4, bring 2 back over it, lift 3 with the left hand, pass 2 under 3 and into the left hand, drop 3, take 2 over 1, lay it down, and turn 1 over it with the left hand, bring it over 3 and under 4. Every three turns pull 2 gently up to tighten the Plait, and if it is at all drawn in, pull 1 and 4 simultaneously, and this will restore the shape. When the Plait is long enough to reach nearly

FIG. 668. DIAMOND PLAITINGS.

to the centre of the flower, twist both pairs of Bobbins twice; stick a pin between them, and leave them. Hang on two pairs of Bobbins to the detached hole opposite the one first used, and work to the centre with these, as described above. Stick a pin between the two pairs of Bobbins last worked with, make a stitch with the two pairs that lie next one another between the pins, twist each thrice, and carry the respective twists in front of the pins, make a stitch with each outside pair, twist thrice, make a stitch with the two inner pairs, and thus complete the square of holes, twist, stick two pins, and work the two Plaitings that finish the centre. Bring the left-hand Plaiting down to the detached hole opposite it, and after sticking the pin and making the stitch, SEW to the flower, tie up and cut off the Bobbins; finish the other Plaiting in the same way. The spray is finished by working the leaves in CLOTH and HALF STITCH, with PEARL EDGE, and the stem in STEM STITCH, with Plain and Pearl Edge.

Square Plaitings.—The Square Plaiting, or Filling, is shown in the centre of the Camellia in Fig. 669. To work:

Having made the flower, with the exception of the centre, proceed to fill that in. Hang on at the top, and on the right side, a pair of Bobbins into the first Pinhole; miss the next Pinhole, and hang on another pair, and continue to hang on Bobbins in pairs, missing a Pinhole between each, until the space is filled up. Commence to work on the right side, twist the first and second pairs twice, and take these four Bobbins, and Plait them together until a square dot is formed, then twist the two pairs separately twice. Put away the first pair of Bobbins on the right side of the Pillow, and bring into the working the next pair on the left; work with the second pair as described, and continue to the end of the row. For the second row, hang on a fresh pair of Bobbins on the right side, and use them to make the square with the first pair. Work as before, adding another pair on the left side when reached. For the

FIG. 669. SQUARE PLAITINGS.

third row, hang on a fresh pair both at commencement and finish, and work as before. In the next three rows, SEW to the side, and gradually cut off the Bobbins as they were added, so that they are finally reduced to two pairs, which Sew to the bottom edge, tie up, and cut off. Work the rest of the pattern as described in HONITON LACE.

Plait, or Pleat.—A method of arranging frills, borders of lace or muslin, and trimmings of dresses. In ordinary Plaits the folds all lie in one direction; in Box-plaiting they are alternately reversed, two folds facing each other in pairs. When Plaits are sewn in a piece of Muslin or Net, the material should be cut on the straight.

Plaits are also made in Double Box, as well as in Triple and Quadruple form.

Double Box Plaits.—These resemble two single ones of different widths, the smaller set upon the wider, which thus shows at the sides of the upper. First PLAIT the top right-hand half, then the under right-hand half, and lastly, the under right-hand portion in the same way. Place the edges of the upper Plait so as to meet at the back, as for Single Box Plaits, but do not allow the lower one to meet in the centre by as much as it projects beyond the face of the upper one at the sides. Double Box Plaits are necessarily somewhat heavy, and, although they make a handsome trimming, it is not one suitable for all materials alike; nor does it look well for flounces of less than 7 inches in depth. For a skirt of 4 yards, take a strip of 16 yards for Plaiting. According to the thickness of the material and width of the folds, place the under ones farther apart at the back, to economise the quantity. Nothing under 1 inch for the top portion is heavy enough for this style.

Single Box Plaits are rarely more than 1 inch wide, and are never separated by more than their own width. Make them like two Kilt Plaits, turn one to the right, the other to the left, and let the heels of each half of the Plait touch at the back, but not overlap, or it would cause the Plait itself to set sideways. Single Box Plaits take twice the length to be trimmed—*i.e.*, for a skirt 4 yards round take a strip of 8 yards.

Triple and Quadruple Plaits are only occasionally employed, but, when desired, make the top fold 3 inches across, and the underlayers from ½ inch to 1 inch beyond. Place each group very near together—almost, or quite touching. Relieve the extreme heaviness of this trimming (which should be fully 15 inches deep) by cutting out large Vandykes at one edge of the strip, and then Plait them, that the point of each may be in the centre of the flat surface fold, and the narrowest part end at the last edge of that undermost. Arranged in this way, the deepening edge of the Vandyke of course hides the shallower part, which rises upwards inside with every succeeding fold; consequently, a muslin lining, RUN on the wrong side, and then turned over before the Plaiting is begun, will not show; but, if it be desirable to Plait the Vandykes in the reverse way, making the narrowest part of the flounce to come in the middle of each singly, and the long point in a line between each group, it follows that the inside of the material will be shown at every new bend of the folds; in that case, make a facing of its own material, or some of a different colour.

Plastron.—A term adapted from the French (for a breast-plate) to signify a trimming for the front of a dress, of a different material from itself, usually sewn about half-way down the seam on the shoulder, and narrowing as it descends across the chest to the waist. It may end at the waist, or extend to the edge of the skirt, gradually increasing again in width to its termination.

Plis.—The French for the term Folds, as applied to textiles.

Plissés.—The French term for flat plaits, or folds, in making up Crape. These are cut the selvedge-way of the material, lined with muslin, plaited at the top edge, and tacked at the bottom, that they may lie successively side by side, in regular order, while being pressed flat with a hot iron.

Plumes.—A term employed to denote the Ostrich Feathers worn as a head-dress by ladies at Court on special occasions. In the Middle Ages they were worn by men in caps and helmets, under this name; and those used to decorate hearses and catafalques are also thus described.

Plush.—A shaggy, hairy kind of silk, or cotton cloth, used for dress or upholstery. It is sometimes made of camels' or goats' hair. The pile, or nap, is softer and longer than that of velvet, and resembles fur. It is fabricated by means of a single weft of goats' or camels' hair, and double warp; one of the latter supplying the loose pile of woollen thread. Woollen plush made at Banbury is warm and serviceable for upholstery, and is known as Banbury Plush. A mixture of Cotton and Silk Plush, for the trimmings of infants' clothing, such as dresses, cloaks, and hoods, is made at Amiens and Lisle. Black Silk Plush for hats is made of a superior quality at Lyons. Plush is used for small frames and albums. There are also Plush Ribbons, satin backed; and others known as Pomponette Plush Ribbons. Plush Velveteen may likewise be had. Plush is much employed for liveries, and its manufacture dates back at least to the sixteenth century, as we find records of its use up to that time; but how much older it may be we have no data to determine. Counterpoints of Plush are named in the Wardrobe Accounts of James I.

Plush Stitch.—*See* BERLIN WORK.

Plush Velvet.—This is a variety of Plush having a shorter pile. It is made with both a silk and a cotton back. *See* PLUSH.

Ply.—A term signifying a fold, twist, or plait of thread, in any kind of material.

Poil de Chèvre.—This material, otherwise known as Vigogne, is made of the Angora goat's hair, and measures 48 inches in width. *See* VIGOGNE.

Point.—The French word for a Stitch in every description of Needlework, and also very largely used in the names of laces, and to denote the varieties of stitches employed in Guipure d'Art, Embroidery, and Needle Laces. The word Point, when prefixed to a lace, should mean that it is one made with the Needle, and not upon the Pillow; but as it has been applied to many laces that are only made on the Pillow, and to laces that are made either by the hand or on the Pillow, it cannot be looked upon as a perfectly correct indication of the nature of the lace.

Point à Carreaux.—One of the French names for lace made upon the Pillow.

Point à Aiguille.—This name is given to Brussels Lace sprigs that are made by the Needle, and not upon the Pillow. *See also* ENGLISH WHEEL.

Point à la Minute.—*See* EMBROIDERY STITCHES.

Point Alençon.—*See* ALENÇON POINT.

Point Anglaise.—*See* EMBROIDERY STITCHES.

Point Antwerp.—*See* ANTWERP LACE.

Point Appliqué.—A name sometimes applied to Appliqué, and sometimes used to denote lace, whether made upon the Pillow or with the Needle, that is worked in sprays, and then laid upon Machine Net for a ground, instead of the ground being made by the hand or on the Pillow.

Point Bisette.—*See* BISETTE LACE.

Point Brodé.—A term applied to sprigs of pillow Lace, in which the flowers are in relief, and made of Raised Work. Brussels, Honiton, and Duchesse Lace all contain this Raised Work.

Point Campan.—A narrow Pillow Lace, made in France in the early part of the seventeenth century. It was made with fine white thread, and as an edging, and was chiefly used as a border to wider laces.

Point Chemin de Fer.—*See* EMBROIDERY STITCHES.

Point Conté.—The French name for DARNED NETTING.

Point Coupé.—The French Term for CUTWORK LACES.

Point Croisé.—*See* EMBROIDERY STITCHES and GUIPURE D'ART.

Point d'Aiguille.—These are Needle-made Laces, such as Venetian and Spanish Point, Alençon and Argentan Points, and Old Brussels.

Point d'Angleterre.—A Pillow Lace made in Flanders, and smuggled into France by English ships, during the war between Louis XIV. and the Dutch.

Point d'Angleterre Edging.—*See* ANGLETERRE EDGING.

Point d'Argentan.—*See* ARGENTAN POINT.

Point d'Armes.—*See* EMBROIDERY STITCHES.

Point d'Attache.—*See* EMBROIDERY STITCHES.

Point de Biais.—*See* EMBROIDERY STITCHES.

Point de Bruges.—Lace is made at Bruges of two kinds, one being Valenciennes, and the other Point Duchesse, or Guipure de Bruges. The Valenciennes Lace is made on the Pillow, and with a round Net Ground, but as the Bobbins in making this ground are only twisted twice at every Pinhole, instead of four or five times, the lace does not possess the value of the best descriptions of Valenciennes. Point Duchesse is a beautiful lace, similar in workmanship to Honiton Lace, but made with bolder designs and a greater amount of Raised Work. For a full description of this lace *see* DUCHESSE LACE.

Point de Bruxelles.—The French name for BRUSSELS LACE. Also GUIPURE D'ART.

Point de Cable.—*See* EMBROIDERY STITCHES.

Point de Chainette.—*See* EMBROIDERY STITCHES.

Point de Champ.—A term applied to lace made with a Net Pattern or Réseau Ground.

Point de Chant.—A Pillow Lace Ground, also known as Point de Paris. *See* POINT DE PARIS.

Point de Chaudieu.—The French term for Chain Bar, used in Macramé. *See* CHAIN BAR, MACRAMÉ.

Point d'Echelle.—*See* EMBROIDERY STITCHES.

Point de Cone.—*See* CONE, GUIPURE D'ART.

Point de Coté.—*See* EMBROIDERY STITCHES.

Point de Croix.—The French term for CROSS STITCH. *See* BERLIN WORK and EMBROIDERY STITCHES.

Point d'Epine.—*See* EMBROIDERY STITCHES.

Point d'Escalier.—*See* EMBROIDERY STITCHES.

Point d'Espagne.—The French name for Spanish Point.

Point d'Esprit.—*See* GUIPURE D'ART.

Point de Diable.—*See* EMBROIDERY STITCHES.

Point de Dieppe.—*See* DIEPPE POINT.

Point de Feston.—*See* GUIPURE D'ART.

Point de Feuillage.—The French name for the Ridge or Twisted Bar used in Macramé Lace. *See* RIDGE BAR, MACRAMÉ.

Point de Flandre.—One of the names by which Brussels Lace is known. *See* BRUSSELS LACE.

Point de France.—One of the names given to Alençon Point when made in the style of Venetian Point and with the ground formed with Brides Ornées. *See* ALENÇON POINT.

Point de Genes.—*See* GENOA LACE.

Point de Gerbe.—*See* GUIPURE D'ART.

Point de Gibecière.—The French name for the Double or Knotted Bar used in Macramé Lace. *See* DOUBLE BAR, MACRAMÉ,

Point de Gobelin.—*See* GOBELIN STITCH, BERLIN WORK.

Point de Havre.—A narrow make of Valenciennes Lace, much in request during the seventeenth and eighteenth centuries, and resembling the laces made at Dieppe.

Point de Jours.—*See* EMBROIDERY STITCHES.

Point de Marli.—This was a species of tulle or gauze, made upon the Pillow during the seventeenth and eighteenth centuries, and used as a ground for Pillow Laces.

Point de Marque.—*See* EMBROIDERY STITCHES.

Point de Mechlin.—*See* MECHLIN LACE.

Point de Medicis.—The name given in France to the Italian Raised Points, because they were first rendered popular in that country on the arrival there of Catherine de Medicis.

Point de Milan.—*See* MILAN POINT.

Point de Paris.—Also known as POINT DOUBLE. It is a narrow lace made upon the Pillow, and resembles Brussels Lace. It flourished during the seventeenth century and until the great Revolution, and was made in Paris and the surrounding country, and in Normandy.

Point de Paris Ground.—Also known as POINT DE CHANT. A Pillow Lace Ground, and one that is still used when making Black Lace. The design of the ground is that of a hexagon and a triangle alternately, and the effect is extremely good, whether the stitch is used to fill up a large surface, or whether it is only used as a Filling for the centres of flowers and sprigs. To work the insertion shown in Fig. 670: Prick the pattern with two parallel rows of Pinholes, placing the rows the distance apart that is required for the width of the insertion. Hang on twenty-four BOBBINS, numbering them from 1 to 24, in order to distinguish them while working. Separate fourteen from the rest, numbered from 11 to 24, and lay them on the right side, and lay six Bobbins, numbered from 1 to 6 on the left hand, and leave Bobbins marked 7, 8, 9, 10 hanging down in the centre. Put up two pins close together at the edge on the left-hand side of the pattern, leave Bobbins 1 and 2 outside these pins, put up one pin at the top of the next line of stitches on the left side, and leave Bobbin No. 3 against it, put up a pin at the top of the next line of stitches and underneath the last pin, and leave Bobbin No. 4 against it. Put up a pin under the last and at the top of next line, and leave Bobbin No. 5 against it. Five pins are now in position, two stuck into the pattern close together, and three stuck in as headings to three lines. Make a CLOTH STITCH with Bobbins numbered 1, 2, 3, 4, pass 9 over 11 to the left hand, pass 5 over 9 to the left hand, pass 11 over 5 to the right hand, pass 9 over 11 to the left hand, 14 over 11 to left hand, 9 over 14 to the left hand, 11 over 15 to the left hand, 15 over 9 to the right hand, 14 over 15 to the left, 9 over 11 to the right hand, 3 over 9 to the left hand, 11 over 3 to the left hand, 9 over

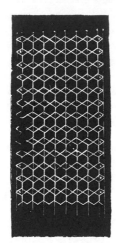

FIG. 670. POINT DE PARIS GROUND.

11 to the left hand, 6 over 9 to the left hand, 11 over 6 to the left hand, 9 over 13 to the left hand, 13 over 11 to the right hand, 6 over 13 to the left hand, 11 over 9 to the left hand, 4 over 11 to the right hand, 9 over 4 to the left hand, 11 over 9 to the right hand; make Cloth Stitch with 1, 2, 9, 11; twist 1 and 2 twice to the left hand, and 9 and 11 twice to the left hand, set up a pin in the small hole at the left hand edge, pass 4 over 2 to the left hand, pass 1 over 2 to the right hand, pass 1 over 2 to the left hand. Leave the thirteen Bobbins on the left-hand side hanging, put up three more pins at the head of the three next lines, and place 12 and 17 at the first pin, 16, 18, and 19 at the next pin, 22 and 25 on the next pin, and 21 and 23 at the outside of the third pin: count these pins from the left hand of the centre; now pass 10 over 7 to the left hand, 8 over 10 to the right hand, 7 over 8 to the left hand, 8 over 17 to the right hand, 12 over 8 to the left hand, 17 over 7 to the left hand, 7 over 12 to the right hand, 8 over 7 to the left hand, 12 over 17 to the left hand, 24 over 8 to the left hand, 7 over 24 to the right hand, 8 over 7 to the left hand, 7 over 16 to the right hand, 16 over 8 to the left hand, 8 over 7

to the right hand, 8 over 16 to the right hand, 18 over 8 to the left hand, 16 over 8 to the left hand, 8 over 16 to the right hand, 7 over 8 to the left hand, 18 over 16 to the left hand, 19 over 7 to the left hand, 8 over 19 to the right hand, 7 over 8 to the left hand, pass 7 over 20 to the left hand, pass 22 over 7 to the left hand, pass 20 over 8 to the left hand, pass 8 over 22 to the right hand, pass 7 over 8 to the left hand, pass 20 over 22 to the left hand, pass 8 over 24 to the right hand, pass 24 over 8 to the left hand, pass 7 over 8 to the right hand, make a Cloth Stitch with 7, 8, 21, and 23. Twist 7 and 8 twice to the left hand, 21 and 23 twice to the left hand; set up a pin in the border just under the former one, leaving the four Bobbins hanging on the right hand of the pin.

Pass 24 over 23 to the right hand, pass 21 over 24 to the left hand, pass 21 over 23 to the left hand. Leave fourteen Bobbins hanging on the right side, and pass 5 over 14 to the left hand, pass 15 over 19 to the right hand, pass 18 over 15 to the left hand, pass 19 over 14 to the left hand, pass 14 over 18 to the right hand, pass 15 over 14 to the left hand, pass 14 over 18 to the left hand, pass 14 over 19 to the right hand, pass 18 over 14 to the left hand, pass 19 over 14 to the left hand, pass 15 over 14 to the left hand, pass 14 over 12 to the right hand, pass 17 over 14 to the left hand, pass 12 over 15 to the left hand, pass 15 over 17 to the right hand, pass 14 over 15 to the left hand, pass 17 over 12 to the left hand, pass 24 over 15 to the left hand, pass 14 over 24 to the right hand, pass 15 over 14 to the right hand, pass 14 over 19 to the right hand, pass 16 over 14 to the left hand, pass 19 over 15 to the left hand, pass 15 over 16 to the right hand, pass 14 over 15 to the left hand, pass 16 over 19 to the left hand.

Having worked once across the pattern, take the numbers off the Bobbins and re-number them straight across from 1 to 24, and repeat the pattern as above. The stitch being worked across the pattern and not straight down, it is a difficult one to acquire, but the manner of working it renders it very suitable for a FILLING if not required for a GROUND. The illustration shows how the Pins are stuck, and how the Bobbins are placed that hang down from the top of the work and remain in that position throughout to form the straight lines, while the others are working across the lace and forming the triangles.

Point d'Or.—*See* EMBROIDERY STITCHES.

Point de Plume.—*See* EMBROIDERY STITCHES.

Point de Pois.—*See* EMBROIDERY STITCHES.

Point de Poste.—*See* EMBROIDERY STITCHES.

Point de Pyramid.—*See* CONE, GUIPURE D'ART.

Point de Ragusa.—*See* RAGUSA LACE.

Point de Repasse.—*See* GUIPURE D'ART.

Point de Reprise.—*See* EMBROIDERY STITCHES and GUIPURE D'ART.

Point de Riz.—*See* EMBROIDERY STITCHES.

Point de Rose.—*See* EMBROIDERY STITCHES.

Point de Sable.—*See* EMBROIDERY STITCHES.

Point de Smyrna.—*See* EMBROIDERY STITCHES.

Point de Tigre.—*See* EMBROIDERY STITCHES.

Point de Toile.—*See* GUIPURE D'ART.

Point de Tricot.—*See* CROCHET.

Point de Tulle. — A name sometimes given to Mignonette Lace.

Point de Valenciennes.—*See* VALENCIENNES LACE.

Point de Venise.—*See* GUIPURE D'ART and VENISE POINT.

in Fig. 672 is a variety, as the ground and the pattern of Hollie Point are worked together in close Buttonhole Stitches; and the other the laces worked in detached pieces and connected together with Bar or Bride Grounds. This division includes the Spanish and Venetian Raised and Flat Points, Caterpillar Point, and some of the early

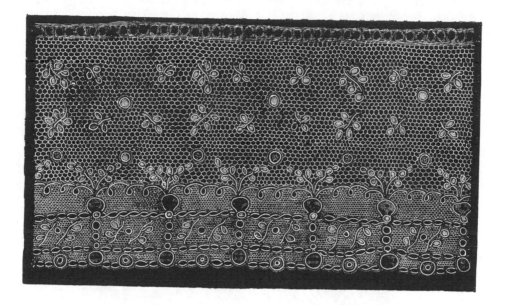

FIG. 671. ALENÇON POINT—RÉSEAU OR NET GROUND.

Point Devise.—This term, which is now only employed to signify perfection in dress or manner, was originally derived from stitches either in Embroidery or Lace, that excelled either for their beauty of arrangement or execution. Point is the French name for stitch, and Devise means well arranged.

Point Double.—*See* POINT DE PARIS.

Point Eventail.—*See* GUIPURE D'ART.

Point Faisceau.—*See* GUIPURE D'ART.

Point Gaze.—A variety of Brussels Lace. The Point Gaze contemporary with Alençon and Argentan lace was a Pillow Lace. The modern Point Gaze, the finest lace now manufactured, is a needle-made lace with Réseau ground.

Point Guipure à Bride.—A term applied generally to Guipure Laces, whose grounds are made with Brides or Bars.

Point Guipure à Réseau.—A term applied generally to Guipure Laces, whose grounds are formed with the Réseau or Net Pattern Ground.

Point Lace.—This name is applied generally to all Needle-made Laces except Cut and Drawn Works, that are made upon Parchment Patterns with varieties of Buttonhole Stitches. The Points are divided into two separate classes, one being for those laces made with the Réseau or Net Patterned Ground, as shown in Fig. 671 of Alençon Point, and including Alençon, Argentan, Old Brussels, and Burano, and of which Hollie Point, shown

Point de France, and is shown in Fig. 673 of Venetian Lace. These laces, though differing so essentially as to design have in common that all are worked with a needle and fine thread, in small sections upon Parchment Patterns, and that each part of the Pattern is surrounded by a line of Buttonholes, either thick and raised, or of

FIG. 672. HOLLIE POINT.

the finest make according to the lace, that the Fillings or centres which these lines surround are made with Buttonholes, formed into devices by working some parts close and others open, and that their grounds if Réseau are made with loose Buttonholes formed into hexagons, and if Bar, by thickly covering a line of thread with Buttonholes.

The art of making Point Lace fell into decay in the eighteenth century, mainly through the dictates of fashion which preferred the light and fine laces produced upon the Pillow to the heavier laces made by the Needle, but also because the Pillow Laces, being worked much more quickly than the Needle, were cheaper to buy; as the fine Points, such as Alençon, Argentan, and Brussels, from the time they took to make, were most expensive and only within the means of the wealthy. For many years Needle made Laces have not been worked for trade purposes, but

this in small sections upon separate pieces of parchment Prick the outline of each separate piece of lace, with two pinholes close together, and make the same number of pinholes upon the inside of the lace as upon the outside. With coarse Mecklenburgh thread, No. 12, outline this pricked pattern with a FIL DE TRACE, thus: Begin from the back of the pattern, bring the needle up in one of the pinholes that are close together, and put it down in its companion hole. Go all round the outline and then tie the two ends of the coarse thread together

FIG. 673. VENETIAN LACE WITH BAR OR BRIDE GROUND.

the art of making them has lately revived, and reproductions of old designs and stitches are now worked by ladies for their own adornment, although the peculiarly fine lace thread used in making old Points cannot any longer be procured.

The manner of working Needle Laces with Réseau Grounds is fully described in ALENÇON POINT and HOLLIE POINT, therefore it does not require recapitulation. For working Points with Bride Grounds, proceed as follows: Make a design of the lace upon Toile Ciré and then copy

at the back of the parchment; fill the needle with No. 7 Mecklenburgh thread and begin again underneath the pattern, pass the needle up through the first hole of two holes and go all round the outline, slipping the thread underneath the little stitches made with the coarse thread. These outline threads are required to keep the lace in position while it is working and to prevent its slipping about: when the piece is finished the coarse thread is cut stitch by stitch underneath the pattern and the work is thus released without its being pulled or disarranged.

Fig. 674 shows a piece of lace worked. Take No. 20 Mecklenburgh thread and commence by filling in one of the leaves of the design. Fasten the thread firmly to the left side of the leaf, pass the needle through the Fil de Trace, which use as a foundation, and work upon it a row of POINT NOUÉ or BUTTONHOLE STITCHES not too close together, and yet so as to fill in well. When one row is finished, fasten the last stitch firmly to the right side and pass the thread back again to the left side of the leaf and make another row of Buttonhole; work each stitch over the laid thread and into the Buttonhole above it. Continue to make rows of close Buttonhole until the open row in the pattern is reached, which work as a row

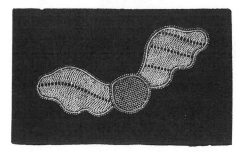

FIG. 674. POINT LACE.

of POINT D'ESPAGNE. Work the second leaf as the first, and the circle in the centre entirely in Point d'Espagne. Having finished the filling in of the design, run round the outside of the leaves and circle with a coarse thread, and Buttonhole this over so as to form a fine CORDONNET or Edge. Ornament the Cordonnet with PICOTS. All the various sections of the design are worked as described above, except that the Fillings are varied, and instead of close Buttonhole and Point d'Espagne, the stitches described below are introduced to give a variety, but not more than four or five different stitches are worked upon one pattern, and close Buttonhole Stitch is always used for thick parts, and in a larger proportion than the others.

The separate pieces of the lace having been taken off,

FIG. 675. ORNAMENTAL BARS.

their patterns are connected together as follows : TACK the various pieces of lace on to the full-sized pattern, and connect them together by working plain BUTTON-HOLE BARS from point to point, or by working the Ornamental Bars shown in Fig. 675, which are ornamented with Picots.

These Point Lace directions are given for the Flat Points; the Raised Points, which are a peculiarity of Spanish and Venetian Points, where they differ from Flat Points, are described under their own headings. They differ from other Points, by being joined together with Cordonnets raised considerably above the rest of the lace, and which are ornamented with FLEURS VOLANTS. The stitches used in their Fillings are the same as are used in the Flat Points; these are as follows :

Picot or Dotted Bars.—To work : Prepare a foundation of loose threads as bars all over the space, work five close BUTTONHOLE STITCHES on to the first Bar, then a loose stitch, pass the needle under the loop and over the thread and draw up quickly. Work five Buttonhole Stitches, and repeat the dot. Another way to work—make four close Buttonhole Stitches, and one loose, put the needle through the loose stitch, wind the thread several times round the needle, hold tightly with the thumb, and draw the needle and twisted thread quickly through to form the Dot.

Point d'Alençon.—Used to fill up narrow spaces. To work : Make a number of HERRINGBONE STITCHES a quarter of an inch apart, and from left to right. To vary it, work a twisted thread over the plain Herringbone Stitches; or, work a thick BUTTONHOLE STITCH on the plain Point d'Alençon.

Point d'Angleterre, or Open English Lace.—To work, as shown in Fig. 676: Fill up the space with single threads

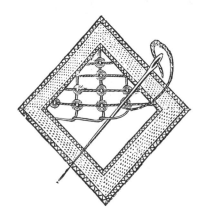

FIG. 676. POINT D'ANGLETERRE.

at an equal and short distance apart and in one direction. Then cross the threads in the opposite direction, and pass the needle over and under the lines alternately. Fasten the last thread well to the edge, and twist over with the needle to where the first lines cross. Work round the cross about six or eight times, and pass the needle over and under to make a spot. Twist again over the thread to the next cross, and repeat as before. Continue this until all the spots are made over the space.

Point d'Anvers.—This is not a real Point Lace Stitch, but is often used to fill up small spaces. To work : Take two single threads down the centre of the space, fasten to the edge of the lace, and DARN a Close Stitch over and under the two threads for a short distance; then make a loop into the lace on either side, Darn again to the same distance, make a loop, and repeat to the end.

Point de Brabançon.—To work : Commence at the left side. First row—work one long and one small BUTTON-HOLE STITCH in succession to the end of the row, and fasten to the lace. Second row—work seven close Buttonhole Stitches into the long and two loose stitches into the small loops. Repeat the rows alternately. *See* Fig. 677.

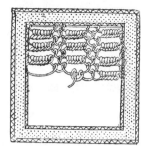

FIG. 677. POINT DE BRABANÇON.

Point de Bruxelles.—This is formed with successive rows of Buttonholes. To work: Commence on the right hand of the space in a corner, and make a loop across the work. Return by making a loose BUTTONHOLE into the

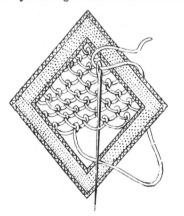

FIG. 678. POINT DE BRUXELLES.

first loop, and so form two loops. For each row, fill every loop of the previous row with a loose Buttonhole. Fig. 678 shows this stitch made as a row from left to right, and Fig. 679, the same stitch worked back from right to left.

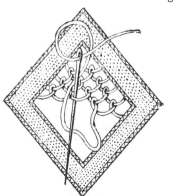

FIG. 679. POINT DE BRUXELLES.

Point de Cordova.—There are two ways of working this Stitch, one like the Point de Reprise of Guipure d'Art (which *see*), the other as follows : Commence by taking three threads across the space, place them nearly close together, then twist the needle twice round the third line, and DARN a spot across all three lines ; twist the needle again over

the thread several times, and work a spot over the three lines. Continue to repeat to the end of the line, then fill in the rest of the space with three threads, over which work spots, putting the latter opposite the ones first made. When this is finished, work the three threads the opposite way to form a square, passing the threads one way over, and the other way under alternately, and between the spots already worked. Then DARN or work a spot on these as previously described.

Point d'Espagne and Point de Bruxelles.—Fig. 680 shows the manner of forming a fancy filling by working

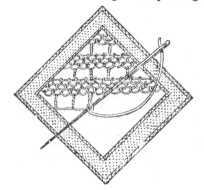

FIG. 680. POINT D'ESPAGNE AND POINT DE BRUXELLES.

these two stitches alternately. To work: Commence at the extreme point of a space, and work three rows of POINT DE BRUXELLES, and then one of POINT D'ESPAGNE. Continue these four rows until the space is filled up.

Point d'Espagne, or Spanish Point.—To work: Commence the first row from left to right, and keep the

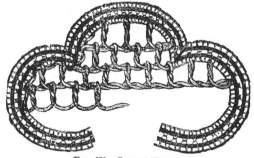

FIG. 681. POINT D'ESPAGNE.

thread turned to the right. Put the needle into the edge

FIG. 682. TREBLE POINT D'ESPAGNE.

of the lace, and bring it out inside the loop made by the thread. Draw it up rather loosely, and pass the needle again under the stitch, fasten to the lace at the end of the row. Second row—return by OVERCASTING into each space, and put the needle once into every stitch to form a twist. Point d'Espagne is worked with the stitches close, or a little way apart (*see* Fig. 681). To work Treble Point d'Espagne: First row—work three close stitches and miss a space alternately. Second row—work three close stitches into the open space, and one long loop below the three close stitches. Repeat as before. *See* Fig. 682.

Point de Fillet.—This stitch makes a good effect as a groundwork. To work: Commence with a loose BUTTON-HOLE STITCH in one corner and fasten to the lace. OVER-CAST two stitches down the lace, and make a Buttonhole

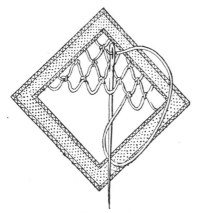

FIG. 683. POINT DE FILLET.

Stitch into the first one, and to make it firm, put the needle first under the knot, over the thread, and under it again. Then continue with the next stitch in the same way. Repeat the rows, and take two stitches down the lace each time. (*See* Fig. 683).

Point de Grecque.—To work: Commence from left

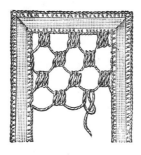

FIG. 684. POINT DE GRECQUE.

to right, and work one loose loop, then three POINT D'ESPAGNE near together; continue the alternate stitches to the end of the space. Repeat the rows in the same way, and always work the three Point d'Espagne into the loose loop. (*See* Fig. 684).

Point de Reprise.—To work: Fill the space with a number of Vandyked lines, at an even distance from and intersecting each other, then into every alternate space formed by the single lines, work a DARNING Stitch over and under the opposite threads to form a triangle. *See* Fig. 685. Figs. 686, 687, 688, and 689, show this stitch

made in various angles, the first threads being arranged either as straight lines or double or single triangles, but

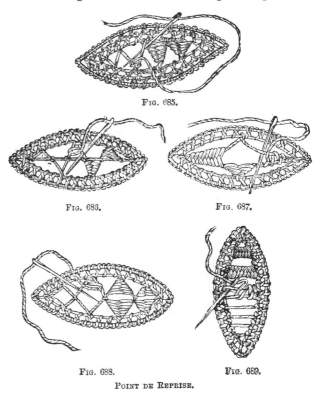

FIG. 685.

FIG. 686.   FIG. 687.

FIG. 688.   FIG. 689.

POINT DE REPRISE.

the varieties are all finished in the manner described above.

Point de Sorrento.—Also known as Sorrento Lace. To work: Make a loose stitch from right to left across the extreme point of a space, and in the return row work two BUTTONHOLE STITCHES into it, and fasten the thread on the right side of the space. Loop back again from left to

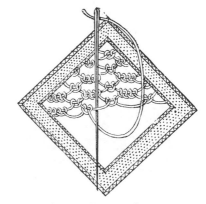

FIG. 690. POINT DE SORRENTO.

right with two loops, one before and one behind the two Buttonholes, and fasten the thread to the left side. Work two Buttonholes into the first space and four into the next, and fasten into the right side. Continue to work a row of loops, and a return row of alternately two and four Buttonholes (*see* Fig. 690) until the space is filled.

Point de Tulle.—A good stitch for the foundation of very fine work. To work: Commence with an open POINT D'ESPAGNE, which work all over the space, then go over a second time, thus—put the needle under the twisted bar in the first line, bring it out and go under the twisted bar in the second line, and alternate this backwards and forwards. When the two lines are finished, work the next two in the same manner, and continue until all the lines are completed.

Point de Valenciennes.—To work: First row—work one long and one short POINT DE BRUXELLES STITCH to the end of the row. Second row—into the long stitch work nine close BUTTONHOLE STITCHES, miss over the short stitch and work nine close Buttonhole Stitches into the next long stitch. Repeat to the end. Third row—work five Buttonhole Stitches in the nine of the last row, and two into the short Buttonhole Stitch. Continue to the end. Fourth row—work two Buttonholes into the five

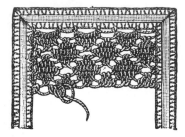

FIG. 691. POINT DE VALENCIENNES.

stitches, and five Buttonholes over the two Buttonhole Stitches, and repeat to the end of the row. Fifth row—work nine Buttonholes over the five stitches, miss over the two Buttonhole Stitches, and work nine Buttonhole over the next five stitches, and repeat. Sixth row—work five Buttonhole into the nine stitches, to the end of the row, two over the single stitch, and repeat. Seventh row—commence like the fourth row, and continue the rows until the space is filled in. *See* Fig. 691.

Point de Venise.—Commence to work from the left to the right, and work one loose BUTTONHOLE STITCH. Into this work four close Buttonhole Stitches, then make a loose stitch and work four close stitches into it. Repeat

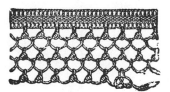

FIG. 692. POINT DE VENISE.

to the end. Second row—work a Buttonhole Stitch into each loop, and fasten the thread at the end into the lace. Repeat these two rows alternately to the end of the space (*see* Fig 692.)

Point Feston.—This stitch is made with Point de Bruxelles Loops secured by being knotted at every loop. First row—make a POINT DE BRUXELLES loop across the

extreme point of the space. Second row—fasten the thread a little lower down than the first loop into the edge of the lace, and make a Point de Bruxelles loop into the first made one, draw it up and then across the Buttonhole that it forms (*see* Fig. 694—Detail A), make a tight Button-

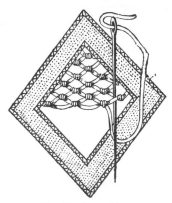

FIG. 693. POINT FESTON.

hole. Work all the rows like the second row. Fig. 693 shows the needle put into the loop of previous row.

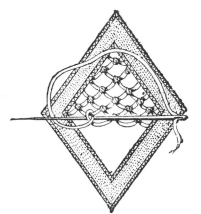

FIG. 694. POINT FESTON—DETAIL A.

Fig. 694—Detail A, the Loop being secured with a Buttonhole across it.

Point Mechlin.—This stitch can only be used to fill in small spaces that require an open stitch. To work as

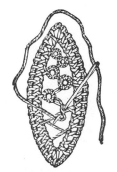

FIG. 695. POINT MECHLIN.

shown in Fig. 695: HERRINGBONE across the space, twist the thread up one of the lines, and where the lines cross each other. Work a small round with BUTTONHOLE STITCHES over the two lines, twist the thread down the next thread and make another round where it crosses the third thread. Continue until rounds are formed over every cross of the Herringbone Stitches.

Point Noué.— This is the close Buttonhole Stitch, which is chiefly used in Point Lace. To work: Fasten the thread to the left of the Filling and work a row of BUTTONHOLE STITCHES to the other side of the work, fasten the thread firmly to the right side, and then return it to the left

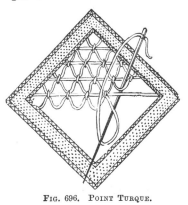

FIG. 696. POINT TURQUE.

and work the second row of Buttonhole over this thread and into every stitch on the last row. When Point Noué is worked with other stitches so as to form devices, the thread from right to left is omitted, and the stitches are worked across the row and back again without any foundation to them, supported by their connection with the preceding row as described above.

Point Turque, or Turkish Stitch.—An easy and useful stitch. To work: First row—make a loop on to the lace, and take the needle through the twist, then through the loop formed by the twist, draw it close and repeat to the end of the row. Second row—take a single thread across from right to left, repeat the first and second row, and always pass the needle under the straight thread as well as into the loops. *See* Fig. 696.

Point Lache.—*See* GUIPURE D'ART.

Point Lancé.—*See* EMBROIDERY STITCHES.

Point Lancé Embroidery.—A modern Embroidery, deriving its name from the frequent use of a particular stitch. It is an extremely easy work, and one that is useful for working borders to tablecloths and curtains. It is made by ornamenting the foundation material with a band of a contrasting colour, and finishing off with Point Lancé and other Embroidery Stitches worked either with filoselles or Berlin wools. To work, as shown in Fig. 697: Select a pale blue or sea-green diagonal cloth, serge, or fine cloth material for the foundation, and a russet red for the band. This band should be 4 inches in width, and can be made either of satin or cloth or braid (ribbon could be used, but is more difficult to work through). Embroider the pattern, shown in the illustration, upon this band before placing it upon the foundation. Work the Star in the centre with a number of long RAILWAY STITCHES, in old gold-coloured filoselles or wool, and COUCH this star down to the material with

FIG. 697. POINT LANCÉ EMBROIDERY.

a light yellow silk, and with stitches arranged to form two circles. For the long lines upon each side of the star, lay down double strands of filoselle or wool of the same colour as used on the star, Couch them down with yellow silk, and finish off with three small Railway Stitches at each of their ends. Having worked all the band, lay it down upon the foundation material, 4 inches from the edge, and tack it round all the sides. Fasten by RUNNING it upon each side, but do not turn any edge under. Take filoselles, or wool of two shades of russet red, one darker and one lighter than the strip, and lay these along the edge of the strip, the darker inside and the lighter outside. Couch these down with silk matching them in shade. Work the fan-shaped sprays upon the foundation with a pale blue or sea-green colour, and in POINT LANCÉ; the little stars beyond them in Point Lancé and in the two shades of yellow, and the Vandyke line in DOUBLE FEATHER STITCH.

Point Mexico.—See EMBROIDERY STITCHES.

Point Mignonette.—See MIGNONETTE LACE.

Point Minuscule.—See EMBROIDERY STITCHES.

Point Moscow.—See RUSSIAN LACE.

Point Natté.—See EMBROIDERY STITCHES.

Point Natté Embroidery.—This work is of modern origin, and is a kind of inlaid Appliqué, being formed with bright pieces of satin laid as a design upon a dark foundation, and their edges surrounded with braid, while their centres are covered over with Point Natté Stitches worked in filoselles of various colours. To work: Select a conventionalised flower design, such as is used in high art Crewel Work as a border to curtains or tablecloths, trace this out upon dark cloth or serge, cut out the various sections of the pattern that form the petals of the flowers, and the leaves, buds, or seed vessels in satin, choosing satin that matches the shade of the leaf or flower required; lay these pieces of satin down upon the foundation in their proper position, and TACK them on; then take a fine gold-coloured braid or cord, and lay it on the edge of the satin, to conceal the tacking threads. RUN or COUCH this to the foundation, thread a needle with filoselle slightly darker than the colour of the satin, and work over all the various pieces with POINT NATTÉ STITCHES, or with HERRINGBONE or LADDER STITCH where the first would not look well, make all the stems and tendrils with CREWEL STITCH, and with single SATIN STITCHES form rays upon the foundation where such ornaments would improve the edges of the Satin Flowers.

Point Neige.—See CROCHET.

Point Noné.—See EMBROIDERY STITCHES.

Point Noué. — See EMBROIDERY STITCHES, and POINT LACE.

Point Ondulé.—A French name for the Double Bar used in Macramé Lace. See MACRAMÉ, DOUBLE BAR.

Point Paper.—This kind of paper is employed for the purpose of forming and colouring designs for Berlin or Tapestry work. It is marked out in squares of minute size, and artists, engaged at high salaries, sketch outlines, and fill them in with colours. From these paintings on Point Paper, engravings and etchings on Copper are made. See PAPER PATTERNS.

Point Passé.—See EMBROIDERY STITCHES.

Point Perlé.—See EMBROIDERY STITCHES.

Point Plat.—A term applied to lace sprigs and flowers that are made upon a Pillow separately from their grounds.

Of these, Brussels Application Lace, Duchesse Lace, and Honiton Application are the best known.

Point Plumetis.—The French name for FEATHER STITCH. See EMBROIDERY STITCHES.

Point Rosette.—See EMBROIDERY STITCHES.

Point Raccroc.—See RACCROC STITCH.

Point Pusse.—See EMBROIDERY STITCHES.

Point Sans Evers.—See EMBROIDERY STITCHES.

Point Serré.—See GUIPURE D'ART.

Point Tiellage.—See GUIPURE D'ART.

Point Tiré.—The French name for DRAWN WORK.

Point Tresse.—Up to the sixteenth century a lace was occasionally made from human hair, and probably originated in the custom, during the barbarous ages, of forming the beards and hairs of the vanquished into fringes wherewith to adorn the mantles of the conquerors. That worked in the sixteenth century was made upon the Pillow, and woven simply for ornament, and was sometimes used to form a foundation, or pad, over which a lady's real hair was carried. Lace made with grey and white hair was valuable, not only for its rarity, but on account of the silvery gloss produced by using that coloured hair. A remnant of this lacemaking survived until our own times as a foundation for wigs, the hair which formed them being plaited together upon a Pillow, after the manner of making a Lace Ground. For work of a thicker description with hair, see HAIR WORK.

Point Turc.—See EMBROIDERY STITCHES.

Polecat, or Fitch Fur (*Mustela Putorius*).—The Polecat is of the Ermine or Weasel tribe, and its Fur is employed for general purposes of women's dress. The ground of the fur is a rich yellow, while the upper portion is a jet black. This fur has the advantage of being very durable; but the odour is disagreeable, and difficult of discharge. It is more in request in America than in this country. The skins measure 10 inches by 21 inches, and vary much in quality and price.

Polish Rabbit Fur (*Lepus Cuniculus*).—A white Fur, imported in large quantities into this country. It is much employed for the lining of women's cloaks, being one of the best and cheapest for that purpose.

Polygon Work.—Made with plaited ribbons, or braids, in the form of open-centred hexagons. The ribbons when plaited are laid upon velvet or satin foundations that show through the open work. The foundation should contrast with the colour of the ribbons. Thus, brown or grey ribbons are laid upon blue satin, rose-coloured ribbons upon black velvet, gold ribbons on brown velvet. To work: Trace a pattern of a number of hexagons side by side, and underneath each other, paste the pattern on to cardboard, cut long lengths of ribbon, and plait them, guided by the pattern; double the strips of ribbon, and pin the doubled pieces on to the top of a hexagon and down one of the sides, then interlace the side strips with the top ones, each going over and under alternately. The lengths of ribbon are not cut, but turned when they reach a side, or the open centre, and worked back.

Pompadour Patterns.—The distinctive characteristic of the small floral designs so named is the combination of pink with blue in the colouring. All the tints are of very delicate hues, and shades of the same. The style is named after the famous Madame de Pompadour, who appears to have been the first patroness of such a combination of colours in her costumes.

Pompon.—A French term used to signify a fluffy ball of silk or wool, worn in the front, at the top of a soldier's shako, and adopted as a trimming for bonnets and hats.

Poplin.—A kind of Rep made of silk and wool, or silk and worsted, having a fine cord on the surface, and produced in several varieties, brocaded, watered, and plain. There are three classes of Poplin—the single, the double, and the Terry. The difference between the first two kinds consists in the thickness respectively of their warps. The last-named, or third-class, is richly corded, and resembles a Terry velvet, excepting that it is alike on both sides. The single and double are alike figured, the design being thrown up in the brocade. Tartans are likewise produced in Poplins, of which the colours are durable, being woven of silks already dyed, and, like all other varieties of this material, are alike on both sides, rendering it a less expensive dress material than the comparative costliness would seem to promise. All these varieties are produced in every Poplin manufactory in Dublin, the seat of the industry, where upwards of six hundred looms are in constant work, yet each firm is distinguished by the special attention given to a particular characteristic of the stuff, the design, colouring, or material itself. The loom employed is the Jacquard. There are four large manufactories for producing Poplins in Dublin, two of which employ some 500 men and women. Magnificent Court dresses and hangings are produced in Poplin, the patterns being woven in gold and silver, on white, blue, and pink grounds, with flowers. Poplins of very good quality are manufactured at Norwich, for the most part plain and black. The French material known as such is inferior to both the British manufactures, the weft employed being of cotton, or partially so, instead of fine wool, and the silk of the warp very scanty by comparison. The material is, therefore, very sensitive to moisture, and liable to cockle, and receive stains, and is greatly inferior in this respect to the Irish, which never draws up in puckers from exposure to the rain or damp. The reason for this is easily explained. The wool employed is that fine kind of woollen thread known as "Jenappe," which is carefully selected, and dyed previously to its use, and having thus shrunk to the utmost degree of which it is capable, is rendered indifferent to moisture. Then the silk warp, which is of exceedingly fine quality, is so woven as to cover the woollen threads completely, both wrong and right side of the textile. The original invention of Poplin is claimed by Avignon, once a Papal See, on which account it was called "Papeline," in compliment to the reigning Pope, at which time (the fifteenth century) this rich material was produced to supply the gorgeous ecclesiastical vestments and hangings in use. The industry was introduced into Dublin by French immigrants, refugees, at the time of the Edict of Nantes, who settled in that part of the Irish capital called "The Liberties." The La Touche family established the first organised manufactory there, which commenced operations in 1693. The beautiful Terry Poplins that compose the draperies of Dublin Castle, Windsor Castle, Marlborough House, Osborne, and Blenheim, were produced by Dublin firms. Tabinet is a variety of the same description of textile as Poplin, and is employed for upholstery.

Portuguese Lace.—The laces made in Portugal are, with the exception of that made at Peniche, similar to those worked in Spain. In the olden days, Point Lace in no way differing from the Spanish Needle Points was worked, and at the present time the same kinds of Pillow Laces are made in both countries. *See* SPANISH LACE.

Pouce.—A French term for a measure of length, employed in trade. It is equivalent to an inch, or the first joint of the thumb. The literal meaning is thumb.

Pouf.—The French term denoting a Puffing of any material, as a style of trimming and ornamenting a dress, or other article of wear. *See* PUFFING.

Poult de Soie.—A description of corded silk dress material, measuring 26 inches in width. It is of a rich, thick quality, and may be had in every colour.

Pounce.—This is the gum of the juniper tree when reduced to a finely pulverised state. Besides other uses, it is employed to prepare material for embroidery when the tracing of outlines is requisite. A substitute is obtained in finely powdered pipeclay, which may be slightly darkened, if desired, by the addition of a little charcoal.

Pouncing.—The method of Pouncing is as follows: Rub the Pounce over a piece of paper on which the pattern has been drawn, secure it firmly on the cloth, silk, or velvet, to be embroidered, and prick the pattern through to the material beneath it, so as to deposit the Pounce upon it. Paint the outline with drawing liquid, which may be had in any colour. There are various preparations made; those of gum and white lead should be avoided, on account of the rough character of the surface, and the tendency to peel off, which injures the material employed in working the design. When tracing designs for Embroidery upon dark and raised materials, outline the design upon a piece of strong cartridge paper, then prick with a pin, or No. 6 needles, along every line of the outline, which for the purpose should be laid upon a roll of flannel, or other soft cushion, and make a number of clear round holes, an eighth of an inch, or less, apart. Lay the pricked pattern upon the material, flatten it well down, and keep it in position with heavy weights. Fill a small bag, made of coarse muslin, with white French chalk, or pipeclay, and rub the chalk through the pinholes until every one be filled with it. Raise up the cartridge paper very carefully, not to disturb the dots of chalk upon the material. Take a paint brush, and fill it with white paint (water colour) and gum or water size, and paint the lines upon the material that are indicated by the dots of chalk. When Pouncing through two light materials, use charcoal instead of white chalk, and brush this on with a drawing stump.

Poussin Lace.—Also known as Petit Poussin. This

is a narrow lace resembling Valenciennes, and is made at Dieppe, Havre, and other towns in Normandy. It was used to trim collars and caps, and, being easily made, was sold at a very cheap rate. The name Poussin, which means a chicken, is given to this lace to denote its delicacy.

Preserving Gold and Silver Lace.—This lace, when laid by for any length of time, will become dim and tarnished. If the gold be worn away, the whole surface must be re-gilt; but if not, restore in the following manner: Warm a small quantity of spirits of wine, and apply it to the lace with the help of a fine sable brush; be careful to omit no part of the gold, and to rub the spirit well into all the hollows and thick places.

Prickers.—These are used in Pillow Lace making to prick the holes in the Parchment Pattern that receive the pins, and keep the lace in position while in progress. The Prickers are simply fine needles, either put into a handle, or held in the hand.

Princettas.—This is an all-wool worsted material, which comes under the denomination of a Stuff. It is a description of Lasting, or Serge de Berry, and, like these, can be had of an inferior quality, composed of a union of wool and cotton.

Printed Blinds.—Similar to glazed Chintz, usually printed to look like Venetian blinds, but also to be had in various designs and colours. The widths run from 36 to 38 inches, 40 inches, 42 inches, and so on, by 2 inches, to 80 or 100 inches.

Prints.—Calico, Cambric, and Muslin stuffs, so called because printed with designs in colours. The art was commenced in England in 1676, but is of very ancient origin in India, and the Egyptians also practised it by the use of mordants. Lancashire is the chief seat of the manufacture in England. Lilac and pink are usually the fastest colours, but good washing prints can now be obtained in every colour. All the nap is singed off the surface of the calico before printing; it is then bleached and smoothed, and the designs, engraved on copper cylinders, are printed upon them. In cleansing them, chemical powders and dry soaps should be avoided. Vast quantities of Printed Cotton goods are exported yearly to all parts of the world. Amongst these there is a large proportion manufactured with colours and designs especially adapted to suit the taste of the native populations of certain parts of the African Continent, and also of India, which never appear in the English market. The printing of cotton or linen cloths is of very remote antiquity. Strabo (B.C. 327) mentions that finely-flowered Cottons or Chintzes were seen by the Greeks in India on the occasion of an expedition under Alexander. That the ancient Egyptians practised the art of dyeing is recorded by Pliny; Homer speaks of the variegated linen cloths of Sidon; and Herodotus of those produced in the Caucasus, which were dyed in durable colours. This last historical statement dates back beyond 400 B.C.

Pro Patria Tape.—A fine Linen Tape, of a similar make to Dutch Tape, the numbers running from 11 to 151.

Prunello (derived from the French *Prunelle*).—A thin woollen, or mixed Stuff, formerly used for scholastic black gowns, and now for shoes for elderly women. It is a kind of Lasting, a coarse variety of which is called, by the French, "Satin Laine."

Prussian Bindings.—These are designed for the binding of mantles, dressing-gowns, and waterproofs, and sometimes for flannels, in lieu of Italian Ferrets and Statute Galloons. They consist of a silk face and cotton back, having a diagonal twill, and are sold by the gross of four pieces, each containing 36 yards.

Ptarmigan (*Tetrao Mutus*).—A bird of the Grouse family. It is almost entirely white in the winter. The skin is employed for the making of women's hats, collarettes, and muffs.

Puckering.—A term used in reference to Needlework, both plain and decorative. It signifies the drawing-in of one side of two pieces of material tighter than the other, in reference to plain sewing; and in the execution of embroidery, it denotes a drawing of the surface of the material in and out, so as to make it uneven, by the irregularity with which the embroidery threads are drawn —some loose, some tight. It may also arise from using too coarse a thread for the closeness of the material to be embroidered.

Puffings.—Bands of any material, cut either straight or on the bias, and gathered on both sides; used as headings to flounces, round the sleeves, or down them. In olden times they were much in fashion for the dress of both men and women. The method of making these, like everything else, depends on the current fashion. At one time Puffs are made on the cross of materials, and at another, even those that are transparent, are invariably cut on the straight; and this from the length, not width, way of the stuff. The proportion, however, is the same, for both Tarlatan net and Tulle require as much again as the space they are to cover—*i.e.*, a skirt 4 yards needs a strip of 8 yards for the Puff. Grenadine and silk gauze, being slightly more substantial, do not need quite as much; and for thick, opaque fabrics, half as much again as the foundation is sufficient. When skirts are much gored it is impossible to make a group of Puffs; but you may divide every two with a ruche, or other device, to admit of cutting the Puffs asunder, so as to lessen the length for the upper ones. If all were made at once, by a series of Runnings on one width of stuff, the top Puffs on a gored skirt—which is, of course, narrower as it goes upwards— would be by so much the fuller than the Puffs nearer the Hem, and the effect would be very clumsy, as the trimming should be lighter above than below. Run crossway Puffs straight along a creased mark, and TACK the thread, when drawn up, lightly down to the foundation. Fold the skirt into four, and put a pin at each quarter; fold the strip into four, and do the same. Run a thread from pin to pin, fixing one on the Puff, to one on the skirt, at each division. Then, while spread over the corner of a table, far enough in to distend a quarter at a time, pull up the drawing thread, twist it round the pin, equalise the fulness with a needle, and secure it with pins every few inches. Every quarter being so arranged, turn the skirt inside out, and RUN along on the inside, to sew the Puff to the dress, which is seen through. This saves much fingering, as the left hand underneath need scarcely touch the dress. A long straw needle is the best for all trimmings made of clear tissues.

Puffs that seem to hang over at the bottom are called " falling *bouillionées.*" Crease them down on the wrong side, and make a RUNNING a little way in, while still creased, so as to take up the material double. Sew each succeeding row, made on one piece, to the skirt by Running the inside of the Puff, to the right side of the dress, the creased edge lying upwards. The topmost Puff may have the edge turned down. Make a Running, so as to gather it up into a little frill heading. Puffs on the straight, not meant to hang downwards, as above, may not show the gathering thread; Crease them on the inside, and WHIP them scantily over.

Stout woollens and silks may be gathered up better, and are more durable, if a small cotton cord be run in the crease.

Upright Puffs are never much in use as skirt trimmings when gored dresses are in vogue, as the upper portions of them would project more than the lower. They do not look well unless fully as much again be gathered as the height they are to reach. Mark the portion of the skirt to be covered into spaces, by placing a pin at each division. Make the Runnings on the length of the material, secure the top of each Running to one of the pins, and draw the thread even with the skirt, twisting the loose end round a pin, opposite that of the top. As every two or three are so far arranged, distribute the fulness along the thread with tolerable equality, but more towards the lower part. Make a Running down the lines, and then continue the rest. Close the openings of the Puff at the bottom, by using the width in little plaits in the middle of the Puff; and draw the tops upwards, chiefly in the centre, and sew them there. Make a series of semicircles thus; presuming that no other trimming surmount them. If tiny Puffs be used for entire plastrons, from throat to feet, make them on one piece of material, and that on the selvedge-way; as widthway or crossway would show so many joins. When making them of such great length, cut off the quantity, and BASTE a line at every third or quarter, and also on the lining, or dress to be covered; then make the Runnings, ending them at every Basting, and fix them, division by division, beginning at the top one.

Puff Netting.—*See* NETTING.

Punto à Groppo.—Italian name for KNOTTED LACES.

Punto à Maglia.—Italian for DARNED NETTING.

Punto à Relievo.—The Italian name for VENICE RAISED POINT LACE.

Punto d'Aere.—Italian for RETICELLA LACES.

Punto di Milano.—Italian for MILAN POINT.

Punto di Venezia.—Italian for VENICE POINT.

Punto Gotico.—A lace made in Rome during the sixteenth century, and resembling the Italian, Venetian, and Spanish Points. The patterns are all geometrical, and resemble the designs used in Gothic Architecture. But few specimens of this lace are to be met with at the present time, as though not the oldest description of lace, Punto Gotico is nearly so. The specimens remaining are all of a coarse make, and are worked entirely in close BUTTONHOLE over threads, and connected by BRIDES ORNÉES.

Punto in Aria.—Italian for flat VENETIAN POINT.

Punto Serrato.—The Italian name for the close Stitch used in Needle Points, and known as BUTTONHOLE or POINT NONÉ.

Punto Tagliato.—The Italian name for CUTWORK.

Punto Tirato.—The Italian name for DRAWN WORK.

Purdah.—An Indian cotton cloth, having blue and white stripes, used for curtains.

Purl.—For Pillow Lace making, *see* PEARL. For Knitting and Tatting, *see* KNITTING AND TATTING.

Purse Moulds.—There are two kinds of these moulds, which are made of ivory and wood; one is called a "Moule Turc," and has small brass pins fixed round the edges of the largest circumference; the other is formed for making a purse *en feston*, which is shaped like a thimble perforated with a double row of holes, like a band, round the open end, a little removed from the rim. Through these perforations the needle is passed, to secure the Purse to the Mould where the work is commenced.

Purse Silk or Twist.—A thick-twisted sewing silk, used with a needle in Embroidery, or with a Crochet needle in Purse making. It is also worked with an ordinary large needle, when the Purse is a short one, made on a thimble-shaped wooden frame, to be fitted with a clasp.

Purse Stretcher.—This small appliance is useful for drawing the several stitches made in Crochet, Knitting, and Netting long Purses, into their exact relative positions, and tightening each knot into a uniform rate of firmness. The Stretcher could easily be home-made, as it consists of two small pieces of wood round on the outside and flat inside, just like a split pencil. Long screws are introduced through apertures at either end of these pieces of wood, and the latter, being inserted into the Purse (before it is sewn up at the ends), it is stretched by means of the screws.

Pushmina Cloth.—A beautiful material made of Vicuna wool, produced in India. It is plain-made, exceedingly soft, and in grey and buff colours. It is to be had by the yard, and likewise in the dress, ready prepared for making up, and embroidered in silk.

Pushum.—The downy substance which grows only close to the skin of the Thibetan goat, below the long hair, of which the wool for shawls consists.

Putto.—The cloth made of camels' hair, which is inferior in quality to that called Pushum, or Shawl Wool (which *see*). It is employed by the natives for the making of their long coats called Chogas, which are decorated with braidings in silk. Putto is softer in quality than those resembling our Kerseymere cloths.

Puy.—The department of Haute Loire, and particularly the town of Le Puy, has been one of the most important lace centres since the fifteenth century, and the industry is still carried on, though it does not flourish as in the latter part of the eighteenth century, when the workers in the department numbered 70,000. The first laces made were a kind of coarse Darned Netting, to these succeeded an imitation of most of the Flanders Laces which obtained a large market both in England and Spain beside their own country. Latterly the manufacture has included Blonde Laces, Silk Guipures, and Brussels Application.

Pyrenean Wool.—A very fine description of woollen yarn, finer than the Shetland wool used for making crochet shawls. It does not wash well, and is sold by the pound weight.

Q.

Quadrille Paper.—This is paper marked out in squares, for the purpose of painting Embroidery Designs. It is also known as POINT PAPER.

Quality Binding, or Carpet Binding.—A kind of tape made of worsted, used in Scotland for binding the borders of carpets. This is the best description of Binding for carpets, but inferior kinds may be had of a union of cotton with worsted. *See* CARPET BINDINGS.

Queen Stitch.—*See* EMBROIDERY STITCH.

Quille Work.—An Embroidery executed by the Nuns in Canada, with split Porcupine quills, and fully described under CANADIAN EMBROIDERY.

Quillings.—Small round plaits made in lace, tulle, or ribbon, lightly sewn down, with an occasional back stitch, the edge of the trimming remaining in open flute-like folds. They are generally made for the frills at the neck and wrists of bodices, and the fronts of caps and bonnets. Quillings are distinguished from Kiltings by their roundness at the open or outer edge, the latter being ironed down in flat folds. Blond Quillings are sold highly sized and finished. There are also Mechlins made of silk, which are soft and unfinished; "Lisse Quillings" are also to be had. The Bobbin Quillings are a description of plain net lace, made of cotton of various widths. Ruffs and Frills are best made of Brussels Quillings, which have an extra twist round the mesh.

The name was probably given to this description of plaiting because of its round Goffer-like form, just sufficiently large to admit a goose or turkey quill. Plain Quilling is only used in the lightest materials, such as net, tulle, blond, &c., and principally for tuckers. It is made up either single or double, according to the thickness required. Make small single BOX PLAITS at one edge, each rather overlapping the next at the back, and wrapping over the whole width of the plait, if the Quilling be very thick. Hold the right side towards you, and the Quilling downwards, the plaiting being done at the upper edge. Use a long straw needle, and work it in and out as every plait is formed, but do not draw the needle and cotton out of the Quilling; as the needle fills, pass the plaits over the eye, on to the cotton, until the cotton itself be occupied by the plaits. It is bad Quilling which is done by withdrawing the needle, and giving a BACK STITCH to secure the plaits.

There is another description of Quilling, called SHELL QUILLING, which is one of the most effective of trimmings, when made of the same stuff as the dress; and which is specially useful in cases where a second colour is introduced; as the stuff to be Quilled is then lined with it, instead of being merely hemmed at the edges.

Shells are never pretty if made too large; 2 inches is the best width, but the make may be as narrow as desired. Shell Quilling is available also for crêpe or gauze, but the strips must then be cut double the width that is required, and be folded over on each side, so that the edges may overlap down the middle, where it is Tacked, while the (then double) material is being plaited. Stitch three little plaits in the middle of the strip, all one on the top of the other, and the edge of each barely showing beyond the one above it. Commence the next group of three, so that the edge of its first plait shall be as far from the edge of the last plait of the last group, as half the width is of the band which is being plaited. When the length is plaited up, catch the two corners of the top plait of each group together backwards, and sew them to the middle. Done thus, every shell touches, but the shells may be spaced, which takes less material, and marks the kind of trimming better than when close, if a contrasting lining be used to it. The spacing, however, between the edges of the top plait of the last group, and the bottom plait of the new group, must never exceed the width of the strip which is being worked upon.

Quillings, as sold in shops, may be had of two kinds, "Blond Quillings" and "Bobbin Quillings." Both are made up in a similar way, but the former are made of silk, and highly sized and finished; the Mechlins, however, though of silk, are perfectly soft and unfinished. They are equally designed for ruffles and frills for dresses, and may be had of various widths. The Bobbin Quillings are of a plain net lace, made of cotton; they may be had in various widths, and are employed for caps, dresses, and underclothing. Those of Brussels Net are of superior quality, having an additional twist round the Mesh.

Quilting.—This term is employed to denote Runnings made in any materials threefold in thickness, *i.e.,* the outer and right side textile, a soft one next under it, and a lining; the Runnings being made diagonally, so as to form a pattern of diamonds, squares, or octagons, while serving to attach the three materials securely together. If a design of any description be made in tissue paper, and temporarily Tacked upon the right side of the coverlet, or other article to be Quilted, the Runnings may vary the design from the ordinary Plain Crossings. A piece of flannel is the best middle layer between the satin, silk, or piqué, and the lining. Quilting is usually employed for coverlets, silk slippers, linings of work boxes and baskets, and the hoods, bonnets, and bibs of infants. It may also be effected by sewing down, and covering with a button, the intersections of the tacking threads, previously made with long stitches, which form the connected points of the diamonds or squares. The tackings should, of course, be very lightly taken, and in the silk or satin only, not all through, and very carefully removed when the buttons are sewn on, or stars worked in their stead.

The diamond-shaped checkers produced in Quilting were anciently called "Gamboised." When Petticoats are to be Quilted, the Runnings should be well indented and the satin or silk set up puffily. To accomplish this, use the best and thickest wadding, split it open, lay the satin over the unglazed side, and stitch through the two, without having any lining behind the cotton wool. Common slips are generally Quilted through the lining of Silesia at the same time as the padding and outside; but, it must be remembered, that half the effect of thickness and lightness is thereby lost. The shiny side of the wadding is quite enough to protect the inner hairs from catching the feeding teeth of any machine, and no hand-quilting comes up to machine work. Mantles, opera cloaks, and babies' cloaks that are wadded for warmth, should not be so puffy as petticoats, or they would set clumsily; therefore thin muslin is put behind the wadding, and the sheets of this may be of the poorer unbleached quality. When Quilting is used more for appearance than warmth, as in lining Paramatta, Cashmere mantles, &c., it is done on Domett, without any cotton wool between it and the silken fabric. Sewing machines have their own Quilting gauges; but in hand-working, fold the material directly on the cross, at its longest part, iron it down, and then fold and iron—by the aid of a paper-strip cut the right width—each side of the centre, until all oblique lines from right to left, and left to right of it, be defined. Then cross them in a contrary direction with others made in the same way. Pressed lines can be more quickly followed than a strip of paper held under the thumb of the left hand, with one edge of it on the running last made, and the other serving as a needle guide.

(2). Ornamental Quilting, although practised in Europe, has never attained to the minuteness and beauty of design that distinguish Oriental Quilting. The patience and skill of an Asiatic worker are fully displayed upon the designs that are worked out with these stitched lines, scenes of the chase, battles, and ships in full sail being executed by them with the most marvellous minuteness. These pictorial scenes are worked by the natives of India, but the Persians are not behind that nation in this art, although they display it more by working elaborate geometrical designs or conventionalised flowers as backgrounds to their embroideries than as a separate needlework. A large amount of Quilting was executed in England and on the Continent during the seventeenth and following centuries, some specimens of which are still to be met with, and which are evidently copies of Oriental Quilting, but the art at present is now only practised for useful purposes, and has ceased to be considered an ornamental work, although anyone who is acquainted with good quilting would set such an idea on one side. The Run line backgrounds, so frequently seen in high art Crewel Work, are intended to imitate Oriental Quilting, and their designs are frequently taken from old Persian prayer carpets and covers of ceremony.

Quilts or Counterpanes.—These are made of cotton of various sizes, according to the dimensions of the bed to be covered, from $2\frac{1}{4}$, $2\frac{1}{2}$, $2\frac{3}{4}$, to 3 yards in length. They are always of threefold thickness. Coloured Quilts and Fancy Linen Bed Coverlets are also to be had. Squares of embroidered linen still exist in old country houses, having emblems of the Four Evangelists worked at the corners, both large and small. In Dr. Daniel Rock's *Textile Fabrics*, we read that "At Durham, in 1446, in the dormitory of the Priory, was a Quilt *cum iiij. Or Evangelistes in corneriis.*" "Hospital" or "Scripture Quilts"

are made of Patchwork on certain squares, in which texts of Scripture are either written with marking ink or embroidered.

Quilts of Paper are much used for charitable purposes, as the material they are made of is very insusceptible to atmospheric influences, and promotes warmth by retaining heat. To make: Cut up a number of pieces of chintz, old silk, or any remnants, into four-inch squares, and join two of these together, as if making a bag. Join up three sides of this bag, then stuff it thickly with odds and ends of paper, shred into fine pieces, and sew the fourth side up. Having made a number of squares, sew them together, as in PATCHWORK, joining them, if possible, so as to form a design of contrasting colours and materials.

Quoifure.—A French term, denoting a head-dress. To be "*bien Coiffée*" means that a woman's head is becomingly and thoroughly well dressed. In former times, a Quoif was a plain and closely-fitting head-dress, worn alike by both sexes. The modern spelling is "Coiffure."

R.

Rabbit Fur (*Lepus cuniculus*).—The Fur of the common wild Rabbit is of a greyish-brown colour, and the tail is brown above and white underneath. There are also Fancy Rabbits, some of which are of a pure white, those having the handsomest skins being of a tortoise-shell colour—white, brown, and yellow. The chief use to which Rabbit Fur is applied is the making of felt hats; but the skins with the fur are dressed in many ways, so as to resemble various others of a more costly description. So-called Ermine, and Miniver, are made of the white rabbit skins, the tails being those of the real Ermine, and the spots of dark fur sewn upon the latter being of the Weasel or "Gris." In the reign of Henry VIII. Rabbit Fur was greatly esteemed, and worn by the nobility. Those dyed of a dark colour are "French lustred," and look well when employed for articles of women's dress and for trimmings. They measure about 10 inches by 18 inches.

Raccoon Fur (*Procyon tolor*).—The fur of this animal is grey, and diversified with gold colour and dark markings. The tails are bushy and variegated. They are employed both for dress and for rugs. The whole fur is thick and deep, and there is an under-growth of a soft woolly character, greyish in colour. In the year 1793 the fur was adopted as a distinctive decoration by the Jacobins. The skins measure about 10in. by 18in.

Raccroc Stitch.—Also known as Point de Raccroc and as Rucroc. This is a stitch used by the lace makers of Brussels and Calvados to join together Réseau lace grounds made upon the pillow in narrow stripes. This joining is made by using the very finest thread, and uniting the meshes together with it by Overcasting them in such a manner that the loops of two pieces fit into each other as if of one thread. It is done by experienced lace makers so cleverly that the join cannot be detected by the naked eye.

Radsimir, or Radzimir Silk.—This is a very rich description of silk textile, especially designed for Mourning, and otherwise known as " Queen's " Silk, her Majesty having always patronised it. It is a kind of silk serge, and the name is synonymous with the French "*Ras de St. Maur,*" by which a silk dress material was designated in the last century, when it was much in fashion. Radsimir Silk measures about 32 inches in width.

Ragusa Guipure.—*See* ROMAN WORK.

Ragusa Lace.—The lace made at Ragusa formed an important article of commerce during the latter part of the sixteenth and earlier part of the seventeenth century. It consisted of two kinds, one a Needle Point, and the other a Gimp Lace. The Needle Point was extremely costly, and was much appreciated both in Greece and Italy. It resembled Venice Point, and was frequently sold as Point de Venise. Its manufacture ceased when heavy needle points gave place to the lighter Alençon and Argentan makes and the cheaper Pillow Laces. Ragusa Gimp Lace seems of very early origin, patterns of it being published as far back as 1557; and the manufacture of it has not entirely died out, the peasants still making a Gimp Lace and using some of the sixteenth century designs. The Gimp Lace is made either with gold, silver, or silk threads; these are sewn together until they form a flat braid about a quarter of an inch in width, with the outer thread twisted into numerous loops to make an ornamental edging. The braid thus made is sewn down in designs and connected together with Corded Bars, but is rarely filled in with lace stitches.

Rag Work.—An easy and suitable employment for invalids and children, who, with little expense, can make rugs or bedroom strips by this means at a nominal cost. To work: Collect together all the pieces of cloth, serge, list, flannel, chintz, or cotton procurable, and sort the pieces as to colour; tear all of them into strips half an inch in width, and sew these together at their narrow ends; wind them into balls, and keep the different colours or shades of one colour apart. Take the largest pair of wooden knitting needles procurable, CAST ON twenty-four stitches, and KNIT in PLAIN KNITTING with the rags a strip the length or width required for the carpet or rug, using the shades of one colour upon the same strip. Make a number of these strips, and join them together, so that the colours contrast, and then line them with a strong sacking or canvas, The rags, instead of being knitted together, can be woven; in that case the thick materials are cut half an inch in width, the thin three-quarters of an inch. Join, and make up into 1lb. balls, which send to a weaver with instructions to weave as strips of contrasting colours. Seven balls will make five yards of carpet of narrow width, and the cost of weaving will be from 10d. to 1s. the yard. No lining will be required for the woven articles. Silk pieces make good rugs. Ribbons and pieces of brocade can be mixed with the plain silks; they are cut into half-inch strips. They are knitted together with coarse knitting needles, lined with sacking, and bordered with imitation fur or stamped leather. With attention to the selection and disposal of the colours used, these silk rugs can be made very orna-

mental. They can be woven, like the thicker materials, it taking three 1lb. balls to make a good rug.

Another Kind.—Cut the cloth or silk rags into strips 3 inches long, and half an inch to an inch in width, according to their texture. KNIT these together, using soft twine as a foundation, thus: CAST ON 30 stitches with the twine, and KNIT a row. For the next row, Knit 1, put the strip of cloth across the knitting between the first and second stitch, knit the second stitch, and put the end of cloth back to the side where its other half is; knit the third stitch, put the strip of cloth across the work, and repeat. Work to the end of the row and knit back without inserting any strips. Work these two rows to the end, always inserting the cloth in every other row, and leaving its ends on one side only of the knitting.

Railway Stitch.—*See* BERLIN WORK, EMBROIDERY STITCHES, and CROCHET.

Raiment.—A generic and comprehensive term to denote Clothing of every description, both of men and women. It is a contraction of Arrayment.

Raised Crewel Work.—This work in no way resembles Crewel Work, except that the wools used in it are Crewel Wools. It consists in making flowers raised from the surface of the foundation with a number of loops, and forming buds and leaves for the same with raised Satin Stitches. As the work will not bear washing, it should be made upon cloth, satin, sheeting, or serge. To work: Trace the design upon the material, and select one in which the flowers are single petalled and round in shape. Take crewel wools matching the shades of the flower, and thread four strands of the same shade together. Work from the centre of the flower to the outside. Bring the needle up from the back of the work to the front, and put it down again quite close to the place it emerged from; leave about a quarter of an inch of crewel wool upon the front of the material, and fasten the work securely at the back to prevent the loop so formed from pulling out or becoming absorbed into the next stitch. Work loops in this manner until the design is filled in, altering the colour of the wools to suit the light and dark parts of the flower, For the stems, work them in ordinary CREWEL STITCH; for the leaves and buds, lay down a foundation of lines in SATIN STITCH until they are well raised from the background, and cover this padding with other Satin Stitches arranged as to the colour of the leaf or the bud, and following its shape.

Raised Cross Stitch.—*See* CROCHET.

Raised Double Stitch.—*See* CROCHET.

Raised Embroidery.—A handsome kind of Embroidery, but difficult to execute, consisting of working raised flowers upon a flat foundation. Two different methods are employed. In the first (the one shown in Fig. 698), the working is upon a thick material, such as cloth or rep silk, or with Satin Stitches laid over wadding to make the pattern. In the second, upon Penelope canvas, the design is formed with loops of Plush Stitch, which are afterwards cut and fluffed up, so as to imitate velvet, while the canvas is covered over with Cross or Tent Stitch, and forms the background. To work (as shown in Fig. 698): The materials required are

BURANO LACE (RARE).

RAISED VENETIAN LACE (RARE).

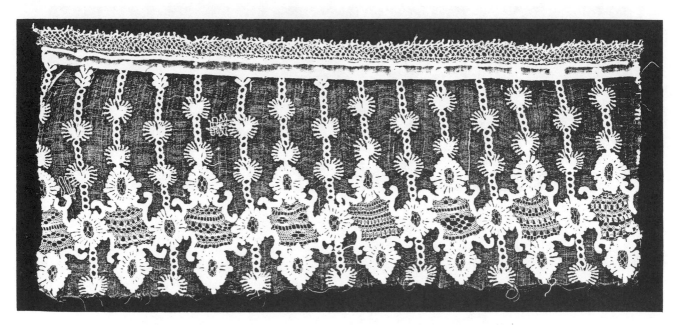

FINE ENGLISH EMBROIDERY, FINISHED WITH LACE STITCHES AND "BABY LACE."
WORKED IN THE 18th CENTURY.

RAISED EMBROIDERY ON MUSLIN.

DETAIL A.

DETAIL C.

DETAIL B.

DETAIL D.

FIG. 698. RAISED EMBROIDERY.

cotton wool, white embroidery cotton, filoselles, Zephyr wool, or Arrasene wool, the latter producing by far the best effect. The wools must be in shades of the natural colours of the flowers and leaves, and such as would be selected for Berlin wool work. To work: Trace the outline of the design upon cloth or rep silk, back this with brown holland, and frame it in an EMBROIDERY FRAME; work the raised parts of the pattern first. Take a piece of cotton wool the size of the Rose without its outer leaves, and half an inch thick, and fasten this lump to the canvas by a Cross Stitch of embroidery cotton, as shown in Fig. 698, Detail A; then, with the same embroidery cotton, Overcast the whole with regular stitches, as shown in Detail B, where half the stitches are made; then re-cross the lump, as shown in Detail C, with long Cross Stitches, also made with embroidery cotton. Take the wool or Arrasene, and with that make the Satin Stitches that are shown in Detail D. In this Detail use the darkest-coloured wool, and work the Satin Stitches so that they overlap and culminate towards the centre; then proceed to make the petals that finish the centre of the Rose. Make them all with Satin Stitch; work the inner ones first, with wools shading gradually from dark to light, and make the Satin Stitches so that they take the shape of the petals. By commencing from the centre the outer leaves will be the parts most raised, and a kind of hollow will be formed in the centre. Work the turned back petals in flat Satin Stitches, and mix light-coloured filoselle with the wool used in making them. Having made the Rose, proceed to make the Aster, which is not so raised as the Rose: Take a piece of wadding, and fasten it down with a Cross Stitch to the material, and then work a number of Satin Stitches in embroidery cotton from the centre to the outside of the wadding; then with the wool or Arrasene form the petals. Make the outside ones first with the darkest shade, and work to the centre, making three rows of petals, each in a different shade of wool. Fill in the centre with a number of French Knots made with filoselle. To form the Rosebud: Tack down and Overcast a small ball of wadding; work the centre of the bud first, and the green calyx last. Form the rest of the flowers and all the leaves with long Satin Stitches, and with different shades of colour, but do not wad them. When working small sprays of Raised Embroidery for pincushions, handkerchief cases, &c., in which the design is small, make a padding with Satin Stitches of embroidery cotton, and then cover this padding with filoselles instead of wools, as wadding covered with wool would be too coarse for such fine Embroidery.

Raised Embroidery with Plush Stitch. — In this description of the work a number of flat Meshes, gauge 18 in breadth and gauge 11 in thickness, or steel Meshes with edges that will cut, are required; also wool or filoselle, and Berlin canvas, or white silk canvas. To work: Select a coloured Berlin pattern, and keep it by the side of the work for reference. Count the stitches on the pattern and canvas, and outline these upon the canvas, then place it in an Embroidery Frame. Work all the leaves of the design in Tent Stitch, shading them as in Berlin Work should the canvas be fine; if it is coarse, work the leaves in Cross Stitch, and ground the work in Cross Stitch. When using silk canvas it is not necessary to ground the work, but when the embroidery is finished this description of canvas must be lined with coloured silk. The raised flowers are first worked. A number of Meshes are required for these, as when once covered with stitches they are not withdrawn until the flower is complete. Thread a number of wool needles with the colours

required in the flower, take a Mesh in the left hand, and lay it on the pattern at the bottom of a flower, so that its edge touches the line of canvas to be filled, and its length extends to the end of that line. Take up a needle filled with the colour used for the first stitch at the bottom of the flower, put it in at the back, and bring it out in the front of the work under the Mesh, cross it over the Mesh, and put it into the canvas two threads above, and on the right of where it came out, as if making a Tent Stitch; then cross this stitch as if making a Cross Stitch, not over the Mesh this time, but slipped behind it. Work the next stitch in the same way, but should it be of a different shade of colour to the one last worked, do not fasten off the first thread, but keep it at the back of the work out of the way, but ready to make another stitch when required. Work a whole row of stitches over the Meshes, using the shades of wool as wanted, and when these require fastening off be careful that they are well secured. Take a fresh Mesh for the next row, and work all the rows that make the flower without removing any of the Meshes. Finish by gumming the back of the raised flower with gum arabic, and remove the Meshes when this is perfectly dry. The steel Meshes will cut the wool as they are withdrawn; when using the wooden ones, cut the loops with a sharp pair of scissors. Shape these loops with the scissors so as to form a hollow for the centre of the flower, when such a hollow is necessary, then comb out the wool with a fine tooth comb, until it resembles velvet pile. The French plan of working Raised Embroidery is to miss a thread of canvas between each stitch, and work over only one thread instead of working over two threads of canvas, and leaving no threads between the stitches. Also, *see* Embroidery on the Stamp.

Raised Loop Stitch.—*See* Crochet.

Raised Open Stitch.—*See* Crochet.

Raised Patchwork.—*See* Patchwork.

Raised Point.—These are Spanish and Venetian Points, and are described under those headings.

Raised Satin Stitch.—*See* Satin Stitch, Embroidery Stitches.

Raised Spot Stitch.—*See* Crochet.

Raised Stitch.—*See* Berlin Work.

Raised Treble Crochet.—*See* Crochet.

Raised Work.—This is the distinguishing mark of Honiton Lace and Point Duchesse, and consists of a Raised Edge worked down one side of the leaves, flowers, and stems of a spray or Honiton sprig. It is illustrated in Fig. 699, and worked as follows: Commence at the end of the stem, and wind the Knots out of the way; when the middle leaf is reached, change the side for the pins, and continue the Stem Stitch up the lower side of the leaf until the last pin but one is stuck. Take the Passive pair of Bobbins that lie next the pins, lay back over the work, and do a row of Stem Stitch without them. At the last pin hang on four pairs of Bobbins, letting them lie by the side of the pair put up; make the stitch about the pin, and do a row of Stem Stitch with the Bobbins worked with before; come back to the edge, turn the Pillow quite round, so that the Bobbins lie down the leaf facing the worker. Take out all the pins but the last three, and work straight across in CLOTH STITCH. Do the last stitch with the pair put up, tie this pair once, and work back with it. Work in Cloth Stitch with PLAIN EDGE at one side, and SEWINGS to the cross strands of the stem at the other side of the leaf, until the leaf narrows, where cut off four pairs of Bobbins in separate rows, and make a ROPE SEWING down the stem. When the leaf worked in HALF STITCH is reached, straighten the Bobbins, work

FIG. 600. RAISED WORK.

Stem Stitch up the upper side, hang on three pairs of Bobbins at the top, and work down in Half Stitch, making the Raised Work as described in the previous leaf. Cut off three pairs of Bobbins in separate rows where the leaf narrows, cross the stalk of the leaves, and carry Stem Stitch up the lower side of the third leaf; hang on three pairs, and work as in the second leaf; at the end tie the Bobbins up in the last Sewed pair, and cut off.

Raleigh Bars.—These are used in Modern Point. To work: Commence at the corner of the lace, and throw across a number of loose Loops, so as to fill up the space with irregular lines to make a foundation. Work four or five close BUTTONHOLE STITCHES to the centre of the first Loop. Make a DOT or PICOT, and work the same number of close Buttonhole Stitches to finish the Loop. Cover every Loop in the same way until all are worked.

Rampoor-Chuddah. — This is the name of a fine twilled Indian woollen cloth, used as a shawl, as well as a dress material. The name Chuddah signifies a Shawl, being made of very fine wool, which is exceedingly warm and soft. Rampoor-Chuddah may be had in different shades of red and white, and in grey and dove colour. Rampoor is the name of a large State and town in Rohilkhand, North Western Provinces of India.

Ras de St. Maur.—A kind of serge silk textile. In the last century it was much used for mourning. It is known in the present day as RADSIMIR.

Rash.—This is an inferior description of silk stuff, or a combination of silk and cotton.

Ras Terre.—A French term in use amongst dress-makers, signifying that the skirt of a dress just touches the ground at the back, when fastened on by the wearer.

Rateen.—One of the class called Stuffs, chiefly employed as a lining material. It is thick, quilled, and woven on a loom with four treadles—like serges. Some Rateens are dressed and prepared like cloths; others are left simply in the hair, while a third description has the hair or nap frizzed. Rateen was originally of Spanish manufacture. The name Rateen is likewise employed in commerce in a generic sense for a certain class of coarse woollen stuffs—such as Baize, Drugget, and Frieze, to which it bears a great resemblance—and which are classed as Rateens.

Rattinet.—A description of woollen cloth, of a thinner substance than RATEEN. It is of French manufacture.

Ravel.—To draw, fray out, or untwist the weft threads of ribbon, silk, or linen, so as to produce a fringe from the threads of the woof. This method is much employed in trimmings, for the edges of d'oyleys, towels, &c., but it necessitates the Overcasting of the raw edge, where the threads of the fringe commence. Fine thread, or sewing silk should be used, and the stitches should be made very regularly, at a little distance from the edge, as accidental ravelling would spoil the article. The Ravelling of ribbon ends may be more or less prevented by cutting them on the bias, or rounding them. Flannels, and all woollen materials of a loose make, should be bound; but Broadcloth may be cut, and left with a raw edge. Buttonholes, in every description of textile— the latter included—need to be secured from Ravelling by means of Buttonhole Stitching.

The term is employed by Shakespeare, where Macbeth speaks of—

. . . Sleep, that knits up the ravelled sleeve of care.

Milton likewise adopts it—

Till, by their own perplexities involved,
They ravel more, still less resolved.

Ravellings.—*See* PARFILAGE.

Ravensduck.—A description of canvas or sail-cloth.

Raw-edge.—The edge of any textile which is not finished by a selvedge, and may, therefore, ravel out, if not either Bound, Hemmed, Overcast, or confined by Buttonhole Stitching.

Raw Silk.—Reeled silk before it is spun or woven, of which there are three kinds, the "Floss," "Organzine," and "Tram." The filaments of Floss are broken, and comparatively short; those of Organzine are fine, and twisted; those of Tram are inferior in quality, and are less twisted. The character of Raw Silk may be tested by its weight, although this appears to be a somewhat uncertain standard of merit; for as silk, when wound off the cocoons on reels, has to be detached by immersion in warm water, it absorbs a considerable quantity of moisture; and it is quite possible that an inferior kind may sometimes obtain a greater fictitious weight than that of a better quality. There is another method of deception in reference to Raw Silk—by means of the use of certain vegetable decoctions.

Rayure Bayadeur.—This is a French-named textile, manufactured for a dress material; it is made of silk and cotton, and striped horizontally. Its price varies according to the quality of the stuffs, and it measures 24 inches in width.

Reaving, or Reeving.—This term is synonymous with un-weaving, or dis-uniting the threads of any textile, such as unravelling knitting, or stockingette cloth, or drawing apart the threads of any kind of cloth.

Red Tape.—This is also known as Pink Tape, and is much employed in Law Offices for tying briefs and papers, and in the Haberdashery department in trade, for tying up sets of cambric handkerchiefs, &c. It is made of cotton, and can be had in different numbers, viz., 16, 24, and 32, cut in any length desired, or sold in long lengths, and on reels.

Reef Knot.—*See* KNOTS.

Reel.—A roller of wood, turning in a frame, for winding thread; also one of the appliances of a workbox, made of ivory or pearl, having metal stems, on which to wind silk; and, thirdly, the wooden article on which sewing cotton is sold, when not made up in balls. A manufacturing cotton

mechanics, and, more recently, for seaside costumes for women, for children's dresses, and for shirts. When employed for the latter it is more usually called Galatea, or Marine Stripes. The material is of a more durable quality than Prints, the pattern consisting of blue and white stripes of equal width.

Regency Point.—This is one of the Bedfordshire Laces. It was much made in that county during the first part of the present century, and therefore named after the Regent. The lace (*see* Fig. 700) is made upon the Pillow in narrow width, and is of a more complicated pattern than the ordinary Bedfordshire Laces, being made with Cloth Stitch and a Gimp for the thick parts of the designs, with Cucumber Plaitings and other open stitches for the Fillings, and with a Honeycomb or Net Pattern ground similar to Brussels ground. It is no longer manufactured in Bedfordshire.

Re-heel.—*See* KNITTING STOCKINGS.

Re-knee.—*See* KNITTING STOCKINGS.

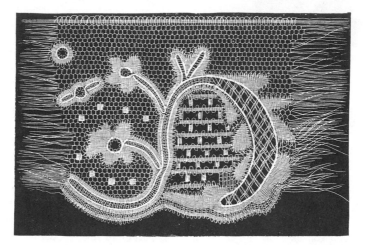

FIG. 700.   REGENCY POINT.

or linen Reel is 54 inches in circuit, a worsted Reel 30 inches. "Reeling Yarn" of any description, means to make it into skeins by winding it round the appliance used in manufactories for that purpose, or thence on to "spools." In Ireland, all Reels are called "Spools," and in the North of England they are very commonly designated "Bobbins."

Reel Cotton.—Sewing cotton which is not made up in balls (otherwise called "sewing cotton"), and sold in lengths of from 25 to 1000 yards. In the best class, known as "six-cords," there is an extensive variety of makes, the most saleable lengths containing respectively 200, 300, and 400 yards. Reel Cotton in colours may be had in many shades. For sewing machines, a Reel has been recently brought out, for which it is especially adapted as to shape and size. The numbers run, almost without exception, from 1 to 100; but it is unnecessary to keep Nos. 14, 18, 22, 26, or 28. *See* COTTONS FOR SEWING.

Re-foot.—*See* KNITTING STOCKINGS.

Regatta Stripes.—By this designation a calico cloth is known, which is extensively employed by sailors and

Relief Satiné.—The French term for Raised Satin Stitch. See *Satin Stitch*, EMBROIDERY STITCHES.

Relief Work.—This is used in Honiton Lace, and is fully described under that heading.

Remnants.—A term applied in trade to odd lengths of dress stuffs, ribbons, linen, cotton, and woollen cloths, left unsold from the original pieces, and which are disposed of at a cheaper rate for children's clothing, patchwork, and other purposes. The uses to which the needlewoman may apply almost the smallest remains of material after making any article are very numerous. Strips of woollen stuff may be cut sufficiently narrow to be knitted with large needles (of wood, bone, or gutta-percha), and made into coarse rugs, suitable for the use of the poor.

Remnants of cloth may be used in Appliqué Work; cloth, flannel, and all woollen stuffs, every cotton, silk, satin, all descriptions of velvet, and of ribbon, can be used in Patchwork for cushions, quilts, and window blinds, the latter being of silk (as being semi-transparent), and the colours selected so as to represent diamond-shaped panes of stained glass.

Renaissance Braid Work.—This is also known as Renaissance Lace, and is really only Modern Point Lace, worked with a very Open Braid, and with only one stitch as a Filling, instead of several. To work as shown in Fig. 701: Trace out the design upon pink calico, and Tack the Braid to it, placing the Braid that forms the Vandykes over the one forming the curves; OVERCAST round all the edges of the Braid, and sew the curves and Vandyke points (where the Braid has to be turned in) securely down. Connect the two upper straight lines of Braid together,

FIG. 701. RENAISSANCE BRAID WORK.

either with a thick strand of lace cotton, passed alternately backwards and forwards between the two Braids, or with the stitch shown in Fig. 702, Detail A, which work thus: Take a line from one Braid to the other, and CORD this back to the Loop it started from on the outer edge of the lowest line of Braid; work three lines on one side of the first line and three on the other. Cord them all, and start them all from the same Loop; first fasten them into the top Braid and into separate Loops. Miss a space of a quarter of an inch on the lower Braid, and work the stitch

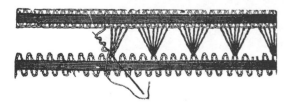

FIG. 702. RENAISSANCE BRAID WORK—DETAIL A.

as before. Work BUTTONHOLE BARS ornamented with PICOTS and eight-armed WHEELS between the Braids upon the lower part of the pattern, and in the thick parts of the lace work the following stitch: Make two BUTTONHOLES, miss the space of two, and work two more. Repeat to the end of the row. In the return row work two Buttonholes into every Loop, and a Loop under the Buttonholes of the previous row. Repeat these two rows to the end of the space; finish the edge of the lace with a bought lace edging.

Renaissance Embroidery.—This term is so general, that any descriptions of Lace or Embroidery worked from old designs are indifferently called by the name. The best known Renaissance Embroidery is an Appliqué. Designs formed with quaint figures of animals, hunters, &c., are traced upon coloured materials, cut out, transferred to a flat background of velvet or silk, and outlined with coloured silk cords, a process fully described under the heading of APPLIQUÉ.

Renaissance Guipure.—*See* GUIPURE RENAISSANCE.

Renaissance Lace. — *See* RENAISSANCE BRAID WORK.

Renaissance Work.—This work is formed with large, heavily-made braids, arranged in geometrical forms, and kept in those positions with plain or ornamental Buttonhole Bars. To work: Draw out, upon pink calico, a bold lace design, and back this with brown paper; take some of Haythorne's coarsely woven linen braid, three-quarters of an inch in width, made with a plain edge, and Tack this down upon the calico with ordinary cotton. Turn in all the edges and points of the braid where required to form the design, and sew them down with lace cotton; then connect the various parts of the braid together with BUTTONHOLE BARS and WHEELS. Make one or more PICOTS upon each Bar, and use the Wheels to fill in the centres of the design, instead of working any lace stitches. When the work is finished, cut the tacking threads at the back of the pattern, and pull them out, which will release the lace from the calico without stretching it.

Rent.—A term synonymous with tear, and applied to any textile that is accidentally torn.

Renter.—A technical term employed by Tapestry workers, derived from one of the French names applied to this class of artists. To *Renter* is to work new warp in a piece of damaged Tapestry, upon which to restore or supply again the original design.

Rep, Repp, or Reps.—Of this textile there are three descriptions, those composed of silk, those of silk and wool, and those of wool only, and which measure from 30 inches to 32 inches in width. It has a thick cord, and has much resemblance to Poplin. Silk Rep is chiefly made at Lyons; its width is 27 inches; but Curtain Rep averages 1½ yards in width. Silk Rep is used for dresses and waistcoats, and also for ecclesiastical vestments and hangings. The quality made for upholstery is composed of wool only. The ribs of all Reps run across the width. There are figured kinds, measuring 53 inches wide.

Reprises Perdue.—The French term for Fine Drawing, which is a description of Darning applied to Broadcloth, and other varieties of thick woollen stuffs. *See* FINE DRAWING.

Rep Stitch.—*See* BERLIN WORK.

Réseau.—Identical with Rezel, Rezeul. This is the Net-patterned or Honeycomb ground of lace, made either with the needle or with Bobbins, and called Réseau to distinguish it from the Bar or Bride Ground, made in irregular lines across the lace, and so joined together. The Réseau ground connects the lace pattern together by filling in every space with fine meshes, made with great exactness, either with the needle—first making a Buttonhole, and then, by successive stitches, forming that into a hexagon—or by the Bobbins being twisted round each other and round a pin a certain number of times. These grounds are extremely laborious to execute, and occupy so much time in making that the lace, when finished, can only be sold at very high prices; and since machine nets have been manufactured they have fallen into disuse, except for special orders, the lace being made and then APPLIQUÉ on to machine net, instead of the ground being also made. To make a Réseau Ground, *see* GROUND.

Réseau Malins.—*See* MECHLIN GROUND.

Réseau Rosacé.—The name given to the Réseau Lace ground worked in ARGENTAN LACE.

Genoa Stitch. In the first-made Reticellas the patterns are chiefly formed by these stiff lines, which are ornamented at set intervals with Picots; but later specimens of the work show more variety of execution and more solid patterns. Fig. 703 is one of this description, and is a copy from a piece of lace found in a convent at Milan. The making of Reticella has been revived, and will be found fully described under GREEK POINT.

Return Rope.—*See* SEWINGS.

Revers.—A French term, adopted by dressmakers in lieu of an English word, and signifying the turned back corner of the basque, or lappel of a bodice, or the robing of a dress skirt, so placed to show the lining, and producing

FIG. 703. RETICELLA, OR GREEK POINTS.

Restore Lace.—*See* LACE, *Mend* and *Restore*.

Retaper.—A French term, signifying to "make up" a bonnet or hat. It is chiefly employed by milliners.

Reticella.—The Reticellas, or Greek Points, are considered the first Needle-made Laces; they succeeded the Cutworks, and have somewhat the same appearance. They flourished from the end of the fifteenth century to the beginning of the seventeenth century, and were used for altar cloths, Church vestments, and the starched trimmings to ruffs, their stiff and geometrical patterns being peculiarly adapted for the purposes for which they were designed. This Lace is produced by lines of thread being thrown across a space, so as to form a pattern, and afterwards connected, either with Overcast, Buttonhole, or

thereby a decorative variety in colour and form. In such cases, the linings are of some suitably contrasting colour, and may be of silk, satin, velvet, plush, brocade, &c. The tails of uniform tunics and coats, and the facings, are sometimes thus turned back, and are, in these cases, of a differently coloured cloth.

Reversed.—*See* KNITTING.

Reversible Linings.—These Linings are of linen, having a white or a grey side, and decorated with a small pattern in black, the other side having a plain black face. They are especially made for lining black dresses, the black side being laid on the wrong side of the dress material, and the white, or grey figured side, outwards. They are made a yard wide.

Reversibles.—Cloths having the back of a different colour from the face, and sometimes having a check pattern, the right side, or face, being of some uni-colour. They are used for men's coats.

Révolte des Passemens.—This poem is so frequently quoted to fix the date of various laces, that a short glance at its theme will help our readers to understand why it is so universally referred to. When the Minister Colbert introduced the manufacture of Alençon Lace into France, he compelled the most skilful of the workers of other laces to labour at the Royal manufactory, and thus produced a revolt amongst them, which was terminated by a compromise. Shortly afterwards, in 1661, an Enactment against the luxury of dress was passed, and this was seized upon for the theme of a poem, in which the Laces, fearing that they would become extinct if no longer used as an article of dress, take example from their makers, and determine to revolt. They assemble in battle array, and all make speeches; but as soon as they are opposed they run away. Every lace that was of any importance in the year 1661 is mentioned in this poem, and its value and beauty shadowed forth in the speech it makes, thus enabling the lace collector to fix upon the date and worth of various laces; hence the value at the present time of a poem that was merely written to amuse the circle surrounding Madame de Sevigné.

Rezel.—*See* RÉSEAU.

Rhea Feathers.—The Rhea is the Ostrich of South America; its plumage is imported from Buenos Ayres, and is not only valuable for women's head-dresses, but the flossy kinds are used for military plumes in Europe, as well as in South America; while the long brown feathers of the wings are made into brooms and dusting brushes. The feathers of the Rhea, made up for wear by the *plumassiers*, are called by them "Vultures'" feathers. *See* OSTRICH.

Rhodes Lace.—The islands in the Grecian Sea have been celebrated for their laces since the art was known, Crete, Cyprus, and Rhodes, besides producing CUT WORK, RETICELLA, or GUIPURE, and GOLD NET WORKS, were celebrated for their coloured SILK LACES, or GIMPS. At the present date, two descriptions of lace are made at Rhodes: a fine white silk guipure Lace, of Oriental design, worked with a tambour needle, and a coloured silk lace, sometimes called RIBBON LACE. In this, upon a gauze foundation, floral and conventional flower designs are embroidered in coloured silks. The floral designs are varied with pyramidal and geometrical patterns, but the embroidery is alike on both. It consists of thick borders of silver thread, pattern outlined with raised cords, flowers shaded on every petal, silver thread round every petal, or part of pattern, and the design, by the labour and number of stitches lavished upon it, made to stand out in high relief from the ground.

Ribbed.—A term signifying woven or knitted so as to make the textile have a barred appearance, the surface presenting alternate ridges and hollows. Stockings so made have a double degree of elasticity, and fit more closely than others. *See* KNITTING.

Ribbed Stitch.—*See* CROCHET and KNITTING.

Ribbed Velveteen.—*See* VELVETEEN.

Ribbon, or Riband.—Strips of silk, satin, gauze, and velvet, sometimes having a selvedge edge on both sides, and designed as trimmings to dresses, caps, and bonnets, for the use of recruiting sergeants, and other purposes. They are to be had in a variety of widths and colours, and with or without patterns. Satin Ribbons may be obtained of stout quality, having a different colour on one side to the other, and equally perfect on both. Ribbons are woven much after the method of weaving cloth; and, in the "engine looms," from eight to twenty-eight may be woven simultaneously. The French Ribbons, chiefly made at Lyons, are of the best quality; but our own manufacturers, especially those at Coventry, have reached a high degree of excellence. Ribbons are classed as the Satin, Sarcenet, Lutestring, Gauze, Velvet, Fancy, Pads, and Chinas—the latter a common kind of Satin Ribbon, used for rosettes and book markers—and may be had in any colour. The Gauze are but little worn at present. Lutestrings are a kind of Gros de Naples, which may be had in various widths, with a corded pearl and four edges. The Sarcenets have plain edges. Velvet Ribbons of silk in the common kinds are cut in strips from the piece, and have no selvedge, the edges being only gummed; the superior kinds are woven in strips; their widths run in even numbers (no odd ones) up to 50, and then to 200, 250, and 300; the lengths ought to be 18 yards, but, always proving short in measure, have to be joined.

Ribbons are usually woven in pieces of 36 yards each, the best kinds being those made of Italian silk, and the inferior, of the Chinese and Bengal. There is often a considerable amount of cotton mixed with the silk used in the making of Ribbons, and a meretricious glaze is given to them to produce a silky appearance. Fancy Ribbons may be had in combinations of velvet, satin, and silk stripes, and likewise brocaded in all colours.

Pieces of Satin Ribbon contain 36 yards, those of Sarcenet, 18 yards only. French Ribbons generally have more substance in them than those of our own manufacture.

Cotton-made Ribbon Velvets are cut in strips from piece velvets, and the edges, having no selvedge, are sized, to prevent ravelling. They are made in lengths of 12 yards, the numbers running from 1 to 40. They are also produced in a variety of colours besides black, and the widths run from 1 inch, 1½ inches, and 2 inches, up to 10 inches, then in even numbers up to 20 inches, and then to 24 inches, 30 inches, and 40 inches. The lengths (of 12 yards nominally) run short in Cotton Ribbon Velvets, as in the inferior kinds of Silk Ribbon Velvets. Ribbons designed for waistbelts are called Petershams; and Watered Doubles, which are made in various colours and patterns, are called Pads. Some of the French Brocaded varieties, which are produced in several colours, and in floral designs, are as rich looking as hand embroideries. Coventry is the chief seat of the industry in England, and the art has been brought to such perfection, that landscapes, portraits, and pictorial representations are produced there rivalling those of the Lyons Ribbon Weavers. By a peculiar style of management in the process of dyeing, "clouding" is produced in Ribbons.

Doubles, Ferrets, and Galloons are all varieties of Ribbons. Ferrets are coarse and narrow in width, and are shot with cotton. According to Planché, "it is not until the sixteenth century that Ribbons, in the present sense, are seen and heard of; and only in the seventeenth that they acquired that hold on public favour which has lasted to the present day." As a trimming for a dress, Ribbon is mentioned by Chaucer in his *Romaunt of the Rose*:

> . . . . Full well
> With Orfraies laid everie dell,
> And purtraied, in the Ribaninges,
> Of dukes' stories, and of kings.

Ribbon Embroidery.—*See* CHINA RIBBON EMBROIDERY.

Ribbon Lace.—*See* RHODES LACE.

Ribbon Wire.—A narrow cotton Ribbon, or Tape, into which three or four wires are woven, and which is sold in packets containing twelve pieces, of as many yards each, eighteen of 18 yards, or six of 24 yards. But, as in the case of other varieties, Ribbon Wire is usually deficient in measure. It is employed in the millinery trade.

Rice Embroidery.—This is a white Embroidery upon washing materials, in which the principal stitch used is Point de Riz, or Rice Stitch. The work need not be confined to washing materials or to embroidery cotton, but looks well when made upon silk, diagonal cloth, or serge foundations, and with filoselles or coloured crewels. To work as shown in Fig. 704: Trace the outline upon the

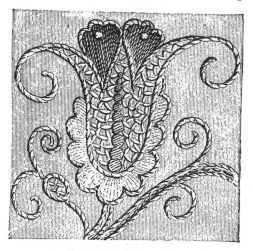

FIG. 704. RICE EMBROIDERY.

design, and work the centre of the flower in POINT DE RIZ STITCH, which scatter carelessly over the surface; fill in the calyx of the flower with AU PASSÉ, or flat SATIN STITCH, and in the same stitch work the two upright petals. Work round the flower in POINT DE CABLE, so as to outline every part, and also work with it the stems and tendrils; make the dots in the centre of the flower in OVERCAST.

Rice Stitch.—This Stitch resembles Rice, or Crumbs, loosely scattered over a flat surface. To make: Bring the needle up from the back, and put it down in a slant, one-eighth of an inch from where it came up. Scatter these stitches over the surface to be covered. *See* EMBROIDERY STITCHES.

Richelieu Guipure.—This is work of a modern date, and differs but little from Roman, Strasbourg, and Venetian Embroidery. It is founded upon the ancient Point Coupé, or Cutwork, which was one of the first laces, and was extensively used in conjunction with Linen Embroidery, on the Continent and in England, from the fourteenth to the sixteenth centuries, when it was superseded by Reticella Lace. The modern Richelieu Guipure differs from the old Cutwork in being worked in more open patterns, and separated by Bars formed of threads Buttonholed over. In the old work, the linen foundations were cut, and Buttonholed over wherever bars were required, and the patterns were closer and more solid, almost entirely covered with needlework, and required greater patience and skill in their execution.

For many varieties of trimmings, and for washing materials Richelieu Guipure is well adapted, for, as long as the foundation is selected of good strong stuff, there is no reason why the Embroidery should not be as lasting as the old Point Coupé, specimens of which, worked in the fifteenth century, are still to be seen. To work as shown in Fig. 705: Select cream white, pure white, or écru coloured linen, or cotton foundation, upon which trace the outline of the pattern, and indicate the lines for the Bars. Back this foundation with brown paper should it not be stiff; but this is not generally necessary. Then RUN all the outlines with a double line of thread or silk, using a colour matching the material; Run the second line of thread the sixteenth of an inch above the first, and work the Bars during the process of Running. These make thus: Throw two threads across the space the Bar is to cover, catch them well into the edges of the pattern, and then BUTTONHOLE them thickly over, and make a PICOT in the centre Bar. Then carefully Buttonhole over every outline with the same coloured silk or thread; always turn the edge of the Buttonhole to the side of the material that is to be afterwards cut away. Great nicety is required to keep so many lines of Buttonhole all of the same width and thickness, and the second running of each line will here prove very useful, as, if the needle be always put in just beyond it, the width of each line will be the same. The thickness will depend upon the perfect regularity of distance with which each stitch is taken after the preceding one. This Embroidery can be done with any coloured washing silks or washing threads. The usual practice is to match the colour of the foundation, but red, blue, and black silks make pretty borders to écru or drab-coloured linens.

If the work is intended for a trimming to a mantel board, as shown in Fig. 705, one edge of it will be made straight where it is sewn on, and the other scalloped. This scalloped edge must be ornamented with Picots, like those made upon the bars. Having finished all the Buttonholing, proceed to cut away the foundation material from under the Bars. Use sharp and small scissors, and cut very slowly from underneath the Bars, and not over them. The Bars are much stronger and neater when made during the progress of Running than if worked when the material is cut away (as is sometimes recommended), but the cutting out of the superfluous stuff is rendered much more troublesome by their presence.

ROMAN WORK.

RICHELIEU GUIPURE.

VENETIAN EMBROIDERY,

RUN LACE.

IMITATION BRUSSELS.

This work requires a background to throw it in relief, although it can be worked as an edging to tablecloths, and will then not require one. A coloured cloth is the most suitable one for mantel borders, but satin or velvet look rich when Richelieu Guipure is used for cushions or banner screens.

Rick Rack Work.—Made with crinkled white and very narrow braid, and Point Lace stitches, worked with fine crochet cotton. Rick Rack Work is very strong, and will bear constant washing; it is used for trimming children's underlinen. To work: Buy a hank of narrow crinkled braid, and sew five rows of it together in the shape of a diamond; commence this diamond at the left-hand lower side, and bend the braid backwards and forwards in lines of 1½ inches in width. The fifth row of braid will form the top right-hand side of the diamond;

six shades of one coloured wool, and rings 1 inch in diameter. Cover the rings with the wool thus: Cut the skeins of wool, thread a wool needle, and BUTTONHOLE over a curtain ring with the wool until it is quite covered, and a wool ring formed. Prepare a number of curtain rings in this way; make them of the shades of wool, so that each shade will make a circle of rings; but as the circle will enlarge towards the outside, there must be more rings covered with the colours selected for the outside shades than for those that form the centre. Sew the rings together with silks for a mat. Commence with one ring, round this sew six rings, which sew to the centre ring and each other, and round the second circle sew twelve rings for a third circle, and eighteen rings for a fourth circle. For a basket: Make the base as for a mat, and for the sides turn the first row of rings so that they stand upright

FIG. 705. RICHELIEU GUIPURE.

carry this down to form the first and bottom row of the next diamond, and make a number of connected diamonds in this manner for the length required. SEW the bottom points of the diamonds on to tape, and fill in between them with POINT DE BRUXELLES, worked coarsely with the crochet cotton.

Ridge.—A term employed to denote a raised line, like that produced by Gathers when drawn together by means of a drawing thread. Also, the furrow produced by Over-sewing selvedges, or seams in linen or calico. It is likewise demonstrated in a certain style of knitting, and weaving, by which the article is rendered very elastic; and by the raised nap on corduroy, which is produced in parallel lines across the cloth. *See also* KNITTING.

Ring Work.—An easy work used for forming mats and baskets, and made with small brass curtain rings, single Berlin wools, and beads. To work: Select five or

upon the last circle of the base, and do not increase in that row, but increase in all the succeeding rows, and sew together, so that they rise upwards in circles. Having sewn the rings together, fill in their centres with WHEELS made with coloured beads. Thread enough beads to cross one ring, and fasten it to the ring on the wrong side. Cross it with a second line of beads, and interlace with the first in the centre; fill in the sides with diagonal lines of beads taken across the centre from side to side. Rings can be covered with CROCHET instead of BUTTONHOLE if preferred. The rest of the work is executed in the same way.

Ripon Lace.—A lace manufactory was at one time carried on at Ripon, and twenty years ago coarse lace was still made there; but the trade has completely died out, and only the tradition of it now remains.

Ripping.—A term used in needlework to signify the

cutting of the stitches made to connect two parts of a garment or other article together; or the drawing out of the Sewing Threads.

Robe.—The French term for a woman's gown or dress. *Robe de chambre* signifies a dressing gown, but at times the name *Saut de lit* is substituted for it. There are also Robes of State worn by sovereigns, peers, and peeresses, judges, sheriffs, and mayors; and the term Robing is used in reference to the putting on of their Vestments by the clergy. The Fur Rugs used in sleighs are called Buffalo Robes.

Robing.—A description of flounce-like trimming which is attached to the front of a dress, skirt, or infant's frock. In the latter the robings extend from the shoulders, and in skirts from the waist to the lower edge of the skirt, gradually diverging as they extend lower down, to represent a false outer skirt, like a polonaise over an inner petticoat. When Robings are made of crape, they must be taken from the selvedge; because, when dresses have long unbroken lines in length or circumference, the width across from the two selvedges would not be sufficient to enable the dressmaker to dispense with joinings, which would be unsightly, both in Plastrons and Robings. To make: Cut the Crape Robing, when it reaches its full length at the lower end of the skirt, diagonally; and cut the fresh piece which is to be joined to it in the same way—first laying it upon the part of the Robing already sewn on the skirt— to measure the slant in which the cuttings should be made, so as the better to match them; thus, a good mitred corner will be produced. A Crape Robing should be lined, turned in about half an inch in depth, and slightly Herringboned to the muslin lining. Then lay the trimming on the skirt, pin it in its place, and turn the skirt inside out, laying the Robing on your hand. With the points of the left-hand fingers you can feel the edge of the Crape, and you can then RUN the lining of the trimming and the skirt of the dress together, so as to show no stitches taken through the Crape.

Rococo Embroidery.—This is of two descriptions, one formed with China ribbons sewn to satin or velvet foundations, and which is fully described under CHINA RIBBON

FIG. 706. ROCOCO EMBROIDERY.

EMBROIDERY, and the other, a variety of Roman Work, and shown in Fig. 706. This latter description of Rococo Embroidery is used for table borders, fire screens, and cushion

covers, and is made with écru linen foundations, ornamented with filoselles. To work: Draw out the pattern upon écru batiste or linen; select a filoselle of a bright and contrasting shade to the batiste, and split a thread of it into four threads. Thread a needle with one of these, and BUTTONHOLE the outline of the pattern over with even and rather wide rows of close Buttonholes, taking care to turn all the outer edges of the rows so that they are always to the outside of any section of the pattern. When the whole design is thus worked, take a sharp-pointed pair of scissors and cut away the batiste not inclosed by the lines of Buttonhole, and consequently not required. The pattern, by this cutting away of the batiste, will assume the appearance of Open Work. Line the batiste with a coloured Persian Silk before using it.

Rolling.—Also known as HALF HITCH. A peculiar twist given to the thread when bound upon the Bobbins used in Pillow Lace, by which the thread, when the Bobbins are hanging downwards, is prevented from unwinding. It is done as follows: Wind the thread upon the Bobbins; hold the latter in the left hand, with the palm upwards, and the thread in the right hand, the middle finger of the left hand upon the tightened thread; with a turn of the wrist bring the thread round the finger; transfer the loop formed by this twist to the Bobbin thus: gently pull with the right hand while the loop is put by the left finger over the head of the Bobbin. The thread can be shortened at any time thus: lift up this loop, wind up the thread, and then put the loop back; or it can be lengthened by tightening the loop and turning the Bobbin round to the left at the same time.

Roll Towellings.—These are described under LINEN. They may be had in crash, crape, diaper, fancy stripe, Forfar, grey twill, huckaback, and loom twill, and vary in width from 14 inches to 18 inches.

FIG. 707. ROMAN WORK.

Roman Work.—Also known as Ragusa Guipure, Strasbourg Embroidery, and Venetian Embroidery, and differing but slightly from Richelieu Guipure. It is made with washing materials, and is very durable, as, from the nature of the materials used, it neither fades nor comes to pieces by wear. To work as shown in Fig. 707: Draw out the design upon écru-coloured linen or batiste, and RUN the outlines over with thread of écru colour. Take machine silk or Pearsall's washing silk matching the écru in colour, and work over the outlines of the pattern with close and even rows of BUTTONHOLE. Turn the outside edge of these Buttonhole rows so that they always outline the edge of the various parts of the pattern, and follow its curves, a result that, in a complicated one, will require care. Connect together the various outlines of the pattern with CORDED BARS, or BUTTONHOLE BARS, and work WHEELS in any large spaces left between these parts. Having finished the work, take a sharp-pointed pair of scissors, and cut away the écru linen wherever the outer edge of the Buttonhole lines are, so that the pattern only is left connected together by the Bars and Wheels, which must be carefully avoided in the cutting away. These Bars and Wheels can be made after the pattern is cut out, but they are made more easily, and fit their spaces better, when worked before that process. Line the work with a bright-coloured silk or velvet, and use for cushions or banner screens.

Rond Bosse.—A term applied, in old needlework accounts, to denote that the Embroidery is raised up from the background it is upon, either by a padding, or by a number of stitches placed one over the other.

Rond Point.—Sometimes applied to laces that are made with work in relief, like Spanish and Venetian Rose Point, Point Duchesse, and some of the most elaborate of Honiton Laces.

Rone.—*See* GUIPURE D'ART.

Rope Sewing.—*See* SEWINGS.

Rope Stitch.—*See* EMBROIDERY STITCHES.

Rose Point.—*See* SPANISH and VENETIAN LACES.

Rosette.—A collection of bows of narrow ribbon, so arranged as to form a circle, and to resemble, in some degree, the form of a rose or dahlia. These little loops of ribbon are attached to a foundation of stiff, coarse Muslin or Buckram, cut in circular form, which can be sewn upon a dress, an infant's hat or cap; or used as wedding favours, attached to the breast of a man's coat.

Rouleau.—A French term denoting a large Piping, or rolled trimming, sometimes used as a decorative covering for the heading round a Flounce, or any such kind of Hem. The common way of making one is as follows: Take a strip of material cut on the bias (or diagonally), of 2 inches or upwards in width, lay a strip, or even roll of lambswool or wadding along it, fold the former over it, and run it down at the back. To conceal the stitches it would be better still to adopt the following method: TACK a piece of cord, and a length of wadding or lambswool, to the end of the strip of bias covering. Fold the latter together, leaving the lambswool outside, and the cord lying inside the fold of material. When the running is done, pull the cord, and, as it draws the lambswool or wadding inwards, it will turn the covering fold of material inside out at the same time—that is to say, the right side

will be turned out, ready for laying on the dress. The raw edges and stitches will thus be neatly turned in.

Round.—This term is applied, in CROCHET, KNITTING, and NETTING, to the stitches in those works which complete one circle.

Round Cotton Laces. — These laces are made of bleached cotton cord, having metal tags at each end. The numbers run 0, 1, 2, and the lengths 8-4, 10-4, and 12-4. *See* LACES.

Row.—A term applied, in CROCHET, KNITTING, and NETTING, to the stitches or loops that begin at one end of a straight piece of work and end at the other.

Royal Cashmere.—A light cloth made for summer coating. It is both fine and narrow, and is composed of Saxon wool in worsted weft. *See* CASHMERE.

Ruche.—A French term, employed in needlework to denote a particular style of decorative arrangement of material, both in dressmaking and millinery—a kind of quilling; a plaited, or goffered strip of ribbon, net, lace, or other material, applied to a bodice, skirt, or head-dress. Of these Ruchings there are four descriptions, viz., the Feather, Twisted, and Gathered Ruches, and that which is known by two designations—the Fluted, or *Ruche à la Vieille* (*see* Fig. 708). This latter is used as a dress trimming, and resembles a single Box-plaited Flounce. To produce the desired effect, make a number of small Box-plaits, leaving the respective distances between each Plait and an equal amount of the Plaiting at the top and bottom of the Ruching loose beyond the respective stitchings, so as to form a sort of Frilling above and

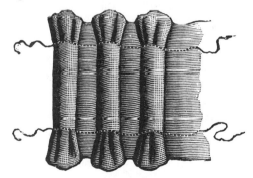

FIG. 708. RUCHE À LA VIEILLE.

below; bind both the edges of the material. A half-inch is the common width of each Plait, and this is the best size for Tarlatan, Muslin, and thin materials; but for Silk the Ruche flutings should measure from ½ inch to 1 inch. In Tarlatan or Grenadine, turn the edge down, so as just to be past where the stitches confining the plaits will be made; or snip out the raw edges in small points, TACK several strips together, and cut through all at once. Silk needs a book muslin lining as wide as the Ruche when made, including the headings, but no wider, as the silk alone folds over the edges of the muslin, to the depth required for the headings, which should never be more or less than the width of the fluting employed at the same time. The same proportion must be maintained as that, in length and spacing, for Box plaits.

A Twisted Ruche is sometimes made on the straight,

but, for a separate trimming, looks best when on the bias. To make: Turn down the edges, and fold one of them in Plaits of about three-quarters of an inch in width, and let all respectively touch each other. Then make up the other edge in the same way, only turning the plaits in the opposite direction. This will give them a twist in the middle. Plissé Flounces may be stitched at about 1½ inches or 2 inches from the top, and the edge plaited to the opposite side, thus giving a kind of heading to the Flounces, and a spiral effect resembling a separate Twisted Ruche.

A Feather Ruche is produced by fringing-out silk, which must be unravelled the width way, or across the stuff, but not along the selvedge line, as the fringe would thus be too poor. Snip the depth the fringe is to be apart at every 2 inches, for, if further than that, the threads are not drawn nearly so fast, and, when the feathering is wide, the silk is liable to knot. These Ruches on the straight need to be fuller than crossway ones, and quite treble its own length must be allowed in estimating the quantity required for a given space.

A single Gathered Ruche is not often employed, as it is confined to crossway strips never more than 2 inches wide, pinked out at both edges, and gathered over a cord down the centre. The amount of fulness is not great, and is always the same; and whatever material is used, when cut on the cross for the Ruche, will be gathered up into the width of the material before it was cut. Cut an 18-inch material on the cross, and gather this piece, and it will be the correct fulness to place on an 18-inch space.

Ruck.—A very inelegant term as applied to the materials of women's dress, or needlework in general. It signifies the awkward and undesirable wrinkles, or unsightly folds of a small size, by which any material may become creased. Wrinkles or Rucks are produced either through bad cutting-out in the first instance, or through equally bad sewing.

Rucroc.—*See* RACROC.

Ruff.—An article of dress worn round the throat, and, in olden times, equally by men as by women. Some were made of muslin, of great width, either with a plainly hemmed edge, or bordered with lace, and much stiffened and goffered. These Ruffs may be seen in portraits by the Dutch masters. In the present day, very small Ruffs of muslin, tulle, or lace are worn, and by women only. Some few years ago, Ruffs of fur and of swansdown were used, instead of Boas, by children, and were tied round the throat by ribbon strings. They were adopted for the sake of economy.

Ruffle.—A frill worn round the wrist, made of silk, muslin, Cambric, or lace, or a combination of any of these materials. In the time of the Tudors they were much worn, both by men and women, and were called Handruffs. Strutt names them as being entered in an Inventory of Henry VIII.'s own wardrobe, where they are described as being made of "quilted black silks, ruffed at the hand, with strawberry leaves and flowers of gold, embroidered with black silk." Some were turned back over the arm; and in Elizabeth's time embroidered Ruffles were worn, bordered with rich lace. They appear in the portraits of Queen Katharine Parr, and in those of Mary and Elizabeth, by Holbein: and worn afterwards, in combination with armour, they looked exceedingly well, and softened the hardness of the lines. In the last century they were also in fashion, worn with velvet, red cloth, silk, satin, and embroidered coats by men, and an arrangement of lace round the neck and down the shirt front. Ruffles are still adopted by women for certain styles of evening costumes.

Rug.—A description of coarse, nappy, woollen carpet, covering only a portion of the floor, or used in a carriage. Rugs are not only produced in looms, but hand-made, by knitting, crochet, or ordinary needles. Woollen cloths, produced in great varieties of design and combinations of colours, are manufactured for travelling wraps and sofa coverings. Very beautiful floor Rugs are produced in the East—in Turkey, India, and Persia more especially.

Rumchunder Silks.—These are, as the name shows, Indian silk stuffs. They are manufactured in many varieties—plain, twilled, satin-faced, crape, and in double-warp weaving. The prices of these several kinds vary considerably, and they measure from 32 inches to 36 inches in width. They are all very beautiful in quality and make, and are of white and cream colour.

Run and Fell.—This is a description of needlework which comes under the denomination of Plain Sewing. It is a method sometimes adopted in lieu of Over-sewing, and employed in making seams, either in underlinen, or in the skirts and sleeves of dresses. To make a Fell: RUN two pieces of material together, having placed the raw edge of the piece nearest to the worker a little below that of the outer piece. Then open out the two now united, turn over the outer edge, and fold over both edges together. Then HEM them down, making the Hem as flat as possible.

Run Lace.—During the eighteenth century this description of lace was made in Northamptonshire, and appears to have been copied from foreign designs, probably from those of Lille. The lace ground, which is a Réseau Honeycomb, like Brussels Ground, was made upon the Pillow, and the design embroidered or run upon it afterwards with the needle, the thick parts being darned, and outlined with a thick thread or gimp. RUN LACE is now worked in Ireland upon a machine-made net; the pattern is placed under the net, and transferred, in outline, to the net, by lines RUN with a silky linen thread.

Runners.—The name by which the Bobbins that work across a pattern in Pillow Lace making are known.

Running.—A term used in needlework to denote the passing of a needle and thread in and out of the material to be sewn, at regular intervals, taking much smaller stitches than when Tacking (*see* Fig. 709), Runnings being made for permanent, and Tackings only for temporary use. Tucks in dresses and underclothing are always made by Running, which is also the stitch employed for making Gathers. The breadths of

FIG. 709. RUNNING.

skirts are also Run together; the needles employed should be long and slender. When one breadth is gored, and the adjoining one is not, the former should be held next to the worker. If the Running were effected by means of a sewing machine, the gored breadth must be placed on the machine, and the straight one laid uppermost.

Running String. — This term may be employed instead of "drawing string," as it denotes the ribbon, tape, braid, or Bobbin, which is passed through a Hem, or double Running, by means of a bodkin. Running Strings are much employed for infants' and children's clothing, and for articles of women's underlinen; also in infants' hoods and bonnets, when the Running threads are drawn to pucker the material.

Russell. — A woollen cloth, first manufactured at Norwich. It resembles baize, but with knots over the surface. It was at one time known as "Brighton Nap." In the time of Henry VIII., certain Acts were passed for the protection of the manufacture of what were called Russells — a kind of worsted stuff, hot-pressed, or calendered, to give it the lustrous appearance of satin. Some mention of it was again made in the last century, when it was described as a sort of twilled Lasting, or a stout variety of Calimancoes, chiefly employed for petticoats and waistcoats. Subsequently, this textile was improved in character, and manufactured with a design as a dress material. It is now merged in the cloth called RUSSELL CORD.

Russell Cord. — A kind of corded Rep, employed for making summer coats, scholastic gowns, lawyers' bags, &c. It is a mixture of cotton and wool, the cord being of cotton; and it washes well. There are several kinds of Cords: Janus Cord is entirely of wool, as also is Persian Cord, both of which are used for women's dresses, the former being usually made in black, for mourning wear.

Russet. — A coarse kind of woollen homespun cloth, formerly worn by country people. It is otherwise called "Russeting," the colour being either grey, or of a reddish-brown hue, such as would be produced by a mixture of paint — two parts being red, and one part each of yellow and blue. From the resemblance in colour between this material, and a certain Devonshire apple, the latter derived its name of Russet. Peacham alludes to the costume of the peasantry in 1658:

Most of them wear Russet, and have their shoes well nailed.

Grey Russet is mentioned as

The ordinary garb of country folks.

Shakespeare adopts the term when he speaks of:

The morn in Russet mantle clad.

and Dryden likewise, in the passage:

Our summer such a Russet livery wears.

Russia Braids. — These are made respectively in two materials — Mohair and Silk. The former consist of two cords woven together, cut into short lengths, and sold by the gross pieces. The wide are in 36 yard lengths, and four pieces go to the gross. The numbers run from 0 to 8, and they may be had in colours and black. The silk is a Braid of similar make and designed for Embroidery Work,

such as that on smoking caps. It is sold in skeins, six to the gross, each skein being supposed to contain 24 yards; but, when silk is dear, the skeins — while priced equally high — are reduced in quantity to 16 or 18 yards. It can be bought by the yard. *See* BRAID.

Russia Crash. — A coarse linen or hempen textile, derived from Russia, or made of Russian hemp. The width varies from 16 to 22 inches. It is very durable, the threads being rough and coarse in quality. It is sometimes employed as a foundation for Crewel Embroidery, and much for jack towels. It is sold unbleached, and is of a greyish brown colour.

Russia Duck. — This is a description of strong, coarse, linen Jean, made for trouserings, and having its origin in Russia; see also RAVENSDUCK, which seems to be very similar, if not altogether identical, to it. Both cloths so called have been manufactured at Dundee, and the adjoining districts, of superior workmanship, and equal in material.

Russia Leather. — Russia Leather may be recognised at once by its agreeable odour, if not by its colour. The leather is first steeped in an alkaline lye, and tanned with the cheapest bark in the country. It is then fulled, tanned a second time with birch bark, and dyed red, with the aromatic sanders-wood, or else of a drab colour. Afterwards it is rubbed over with the empyreumatic oil of the birch, and stamped, as a rule, with a small cross-barred pattern. A certain roughness is produced on the face, by pressure with an iron implement. This Leather is valuable on account of its being proof against the mould by which other kinds of Leather are injured, and against all attacks of insects. It is employed by boot and shoemakers, for travelling and other bags, for the binding of books, for straps, and many other articles; and shavings of it are valuable for use in the preservation of furs, and any materials liable to destruction by moth. Genuine Russia Leather may usually be known by dark, blackish looking spots, which are not regarded as blemishes.

Russia Musquash (*Fiber zibethicus*). — This animal is also known as the PEREWIASKA.

Russian Diaper. — This is a description of Diaper having a double diamond pattern of a larger size than that of the fine Irish kinds. *See* DIAPER.

Russian Embroidery. — This Embroidery is worked either upon hollands and washing materials, as trimming

FIG. 710. RUSSIAN EMBROIDERY.

to children's dresses, or upon cloth or other dark foundations, for table borders, mantel borders, and cushions, in all Embroidery Stitches, made long, or diamond shape. When used for trimmings, it is worked upon bands of material in designs like that shown in Fig. 710, and the stitches are executed with ingrain cottons, Pearsall's washing silks, or Pyrenean wools. If both sides of the Embroidery are to be shown, work in Holbein Stitch and Point Sans Evers; if only one, in Point Russe. To work the Embroidery upon one side: Trace out the design upon holland, batiste, or écru-coloured linen, and work over all the outlines with POINT RUSSE STITCH, thus: Bring the needle up from the back of the work at the end of a line, and put it down at the other end of the line. Bring it out again at the end of the next line farthest away from the first made one, and put it down again close to the end of the first stitch. To work upon both sides, see HOLBEIN EMBROIDERY. The design shown in Fig. 710 is made with a line of stitches resembling battlements for the centre, and vandyke or diamonds as an edging. It is worked

line three times, in different shades of colour. Work the cross in the centre with two shades of filoselle, make the four small CROSS STITCHES with the lightest shade, the outline and centre cross with the darkest. When the work is finished, cut the canvas threads near the work, and pull them away singly, thus leaving the stitches upon the cloth. A brown cloth, with the work done with three shades of chestnut wool, and two of gold-coloured filoselle looks well, also an olive green cloth with peacock blue shades of wool, or a pale blue cloth with maroon wools shading to red silk or cinnamon-coloured silks.

Russian Lace.—This lace, although known on the Continent for many years, has never been much imported into England, and it was not until the International Exhibition of 1874, and the present, by the Duchess of Edinburgh, to the South Kensington Museum, of a collection of Russian Laces, that attention was drawn to its production. From these two sources we find that lace-

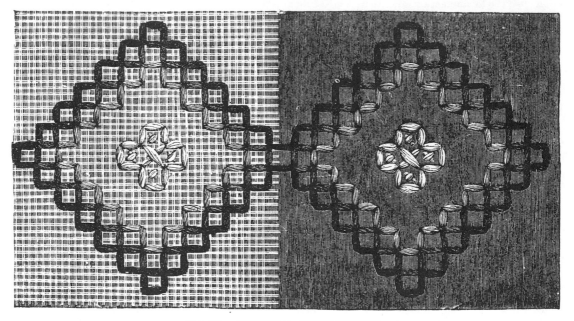

FIG. 711. RUSSIAN EMBROIDERY.

entirely as described above, except that the three stitches forming the ornament to the battlements are made with SATIN STITCHES.

To work Fig. 711: This is intended for a table border, and is worked upon cloth, with canvas, and with Berlin wools and filoselle. Carefully frame some coarse Penelope canvas, and the cloth, in an EMBROIDERY FRAME. Take the darkest shade of wool, and work the outside line of the design, in POINT RUSSE, over three squares of the canvas, and in horizontal and upright lines alternately. Repeat with the next shade of wool for the second line, and with the lightest shade of wool for the third line. To work without a frame: STITCH the canvas and material together, and work in POINT DE CARREAU thus: Run a line, in a diagonal direction, up one side of the diamond, with the wool under four horizontal strands and over four upright strands alternately. Turn back and work down the line, filling up the spaces left uncovered. Repeat this

making is of very ancient origin in Russia, and that many of the designs still used are the same as made in early times; while the peculiarity and quaintness displayed in their execution is traceable, not to European influence, but to the ancient Oriental character of the Russian nation.

In the Cutworks and Drawn Works this influence is particularly detected, the threads that are retained being covered over, like those of Persian, Turkish, and Algerian Embroidery, with coloured silks, such as deep reds, bright yellows, dull coloured blues and greens, and with gold or silver threads interwrought with the design, and the linen left between the patterns in the Drawn Work embroidered with Satin and other stitches, in flower and geometrical designs worked with coloured silks. Bands of coloured silk brocades are frequently let into the lace, and are ornamented with embroidery, that produced at Jeletz being of animals with parti-coloured legs, two white, two blue, with red bodies in outline, and spots embroidered upon the body, in red, yellow, green, and bronze silks.

Darned Netting is also made in Russia. In some cases the meshes are made with silk or linen threads, and the darning executed in coloured silks; in others, the meshes are made of fine gold or silver wire, and the darning in silk.

Peter the Great protected the manufacture of Pillow Lace at Novgorod, and the lace made there was also made at Torjok; it is a kind of Tape, or Braid Lace, and is still manufactured in Russia. The pattern in it is outlined with Plain Braid, made with Cloth Stitch and Plain Edge, and the only variety to this outline consists in forming Hole Braid, also with a plain edge; but the peculiarity of the work consists of a Plaiting, or a single line of coloured silk thread, being worked in the centre of the braid, and following all the contours and turns. The Fillings are simple crossed threads, Plaitings, or Wheels, while the ground is either Plain Bars, or Réseau of Valenciennes pattern. The lace is executed with a small number of Bobbins, and is worked loosely and carelessly.

With the exception of the Cut, Drawn, and Darned Works, Russia has not produced any Needlepoints until the present century, when a lady founded a school at Moscow, under the patronage of the Czarevna, for the making of old Venice Point. This lace has been most successfully copied, and much of it is sold under the name of Point de Moscow. The stitches are all faithfully copied from old laces, also the Picots, or Brides Ornées, and Fleurs Volants. The thread used is fine, and of English make.

Russian Stitch.—*See* CROCHET.

Russian Tapestry.—A material woven from hemp, designed for window curtains, having a decorative design, and a border of fringe. It is a durable article, and may be procured in various widths. The hemp of which it is made is said to be prepared with seal oil, and has a certain unpleasant odour in consequence; but this soon passes off on exposure to the air.

Russian Tapestry Work.—This is a strong and effective work, particularly suitable for ladies who have not much time to devote to fancy needlework. It is made with Russian Tapestry, woven as a border with two coloured threads, one forming a conventional design upon the other, which appears as a background to the pattern. The work consists in either outlining this conventional design, or filling it entirely in with coloured crewels. The Embroidery is done according to the design, and the colours chosen so as to contrast (without being too glaring) with the material threads. The best colours to use are two shades of peacock blue, two of ruby reds, two of olive greens, and two of old gold colours. The manner of working is as follows: Work the centre of the pattern on the material in outline, and in CREWEL STITCH, outline each separate piece of it in that stitch with a line of dark and light blue crewels, or fill it entirely in with the light blue crewels in CREWEL STITCH, and outline it with the dark shade. Work with the reds, greens, and yellows over detached pieces of the pattern in the same

way. For the border upon each side of the pattern, make vandyked lines with CROSS STITCH of the darkest shades of the colours, or work STARS and WHEELS with all the colours used in the centre.

S.

Sable (*Mustela zibellina*).—The fur of the Sable, an animal of the Weasel tribe, is one of the most beautiful and valuable of those imported to this country. The animal is a native of Siberia, although it is often called the Russian Sable. The fur is very dark and lustrous, and of great depth, and is in its highest perfection in winter. When prepared ready for making up, the skins measure 6 inches by 14 inches, and the best kinds are valued at from £6 to £20 a-piece. Although about 25,000 or 30,000 are annually collected in the Russian territories, only a small quantity, comparatively, are imported to this country. Other furs are known as " Sables " besides the real Siberian—viz., the Hudson's Bay, which is the *Mustela Canadensis*; the Baum, or Pine Marten (*M. Abietum*); the Sable of North America (*M. leucopus*); that of Tartary (*M. Sibirica*); of Japan (*M. melanopus*); and the Stone Marten (*M. Saxorum*), otherwise known as the French dyed Marten. The Hudson's Bay species ranks next in repute and value to the real Siberian; but all the varieties enumerated are inferior to it. In the reign of Henry VIII., no person under the rank of an Earl was permitted to wear the genuine Siberian Sable. Some brushes used by artists for painting are made from the tail of this animal.

Sabrina Work.—This work, which is a variety of Appliqué, first came into notice some fourteen years ago, and, though Crewel Work superseded it for some time, it has again become popular, and is capable of much artistic effect. It consists in cutting out, either from coloured velvets, velveteen, satin, silk, cloth, serge, or washing materials, whole or single petals of flowers, leaves, or conventionalised flower patterns, and affixing these pieces to coloured cloths or white linen backgrounds, with wide apart Buttonhole Stitches; while such parts of the design that are too small to allow of being cut out are worked, with Chain or Crewel Stitch, upon the material used as the background.

The work is used for quilts, table, mantel, and curtain borders, also for cushions and slippers, but looks better upon the first-mentioned large articles than upon the small ones. The whole beauty of it depends upon the selection of suitable patterns and appropriate colours, the execution being of the simplest description; but, with a judicious use of harmonies and slight contrasts together, good effects can be obtained without much labour. Gold-coloured backgrounds, with a pattern made with brown and yellow flowers and russet and green leaves; soft-coloured backgrounds,with designs in the same colour, but of several shades all darker than the background; blues shading to yellow, upon dark green backgrounds; pale blue background, with creamy white and pink designs; deep blue twill, with designs in shades of red cloth; dark grey oatmeal background, with either blue or red twill designs, will all be suitable combinations. To work: Select an outline crewel design composed of small leaves, fruit, or flowers, with tendrils, and, if it is an ironing design, and to be worked upon cloth, iron it off upon the material; or trace it out upon linen or oatmeal cloth, should it be required to wash. Cut out the various shapes of the pattern in cardboard, and lay these pieces down upon the colours that are to form the design. Cut these pieces out very carefully with sharp scissors, as upon their accuracy the neatness of the work depends. Prepare a number of pieces, and, though retaining the colour originally assigned to each, vary the shade of that colour where such a change would give more

cut out each flower and leaf separately, and many designs will allow the punches used by artificial flower makers to be employed instead of scissors for preparing the pieces. These punches are bought of the required shape, and are used as follows: Obtain a piece of lead, and upon it lay the material, in four or six layers, according to its thickness. Hold the punch in the left hand, over the material, strike it sharply down with a wooden mallet, and it will cut through the folds with the blow.

The design shown in Fig. 712 is intended as a mantelpiece or curtain border, and is a conventional flower pattern, taken from an Italian design of the seventeenth century.

FIG. 712. SABRINA WORK.

diversity to the design. For the leaves, choose dark yellow greens in preference to very light or blue green shades, but make them as varied in tint as possible. TACK the pieces down upon the foundation in their places, being guided by the traced design, and then BUTTONHOLE round each piece with wide apart stitches, and with Pearsall's washing silks or ingrain cotton, and in the colour that matches the piece so secured. Work the stems and connecting stalks, or tendrils of the design, with the same silks, and in CHAIN STITCH, and ornament the centres of the flowers with FRENCH KNOTS, or with SATIN STITCH.

When working a table border or quilt, it is tedious to

It can be worked, either with satin or velvet, upon cloth or satin sheeting, or with cloth upon grey oatmeal cloth. It is shown worked out in silk upon cloth. The colours should be varied according to the materials used, the ones described being only a guide. Select a medium shade of art blue cloth as foundation, cut out the lighter scrolls in a soft cinnamon shade of red silk, the darker scrolls in a deep rich red silk, the round flowers in light yellow pink silk; make the carnation of a deep shade of the same yellow pink, the leaves close to it in dark olive green, and the three balls in the same colour as the carnation. Work the connecting stems in CHAIN STITCH, and the small rounds in SATIN STITCH, and surround each piece of silk with wide apart Buttonhole lines of silk matching it in shade.

Sac (Sack, or Sacque).—An old term, still in use, denoting a superfluous, but decorative, piece of a dress material, fastened to the shoulders at the back of the gown in wide, loose plaits, and descending to the ground, of such a length as to form a train. The gown itself is always complete without this appendage. Amongst others, Pepys speaks of a Sac, writing on 2nd March, 1669: "My wife this day put on first her French gown, called a Sac, which becomes her very well." It was introduced from France in the time of Charles II., died out, and was revived again *temp.* George I. Sir Walter Scott likewise alludes to it in the *Tapestried Chamber*: "An old woman, whose dress was an old-fashioned gown, which ladies call a Sacque—that is, a sort of robe, completely loose in the body, but gathered into broad plaits upon the neck and shoulders."

Sackcloth.—Large, coarse sheeting, employed for the wrapping up of bales, and the making of bags or sacks. In former times this term was used to denote a coarse haircloth, which was worn in token of penitence, mourning, or self-mortification.

Sacking.—A coarse description of flaxen or hempen textile, employed for bagging, and likewise for the bottoms of bedsteads. The manufacture is carried on chiefly in Ireland and at Dundee. Sacking is also known as "Burlap" and "Coffee-bagging." Cheap door mats and hearthrugs are made of Sacking, or Burlap, by embroidering in CROSS STITCH with coloured wool, as on Java Canvas. Leave a border outside the embroidery of two or three inches in depth, then ravel out a fringe, and make a second fringe of the wool drawn through the Sacking, which is to fall over that made of the Sacking. Lastly, sew the Rug upon some firm foundation, such as a piece of old Brussels carpet.

Saddle Cloths.—These are easily made, and are very useful presents to people who keep carriages. To make: Procure a piece of fine cloth—either dark blue, brown, or maroon, according to the colour of the carriage. Cut it 2 feet wide, and 7 to 8 inches long, curve it slightly inwards, to shape it to the horse's neck on one side, and round it at the ends, so that it is a little larger at the back than in the front. On the outside of this cloth, half an inch from the edge, trace a braiding pattern of 1 inch in width. Choose the pattern known as the Greek key, or one of small running scrolls; stitch firmly down to this the narrowest white or black silk braid procurable. Trace the monogram of the owner, in letters not more than 1½ inches long, upon the right-hand corner, at the back of the saddle cloth, above the braiding. Either COUCH down gold thread to cover their outlines, or work thickly over in SATIN STITCH, and in silk matching the braid. Should two Saddle Cloths be necessary, arrange one monogram on the right-hand side of the first one, and the other monogram on the left-hand side of the second one. Coronets or crests are sometimes worked instead of a monogram. The cloth must be lined with buckram

and stout black linen before it is completed; but this is better done at a saddler's than at home.

St. Andrew's Stitch.—*See* EMBROIDERY STITCHES.

Sam Cloth.—The ancient term for Sampler.

Sammal.—A woollen material employed in Ecclesiastical Embroidery.

Sampler.—Samplers, or, as they were first called, Sam Cloths, first came into use during the sixteenth century, on account of the great scarcity and high price of Lace pattern books; therefore, all the earliest laces, such as Cut Works, Drawn Threads, Reticellas, &c., were copied upon Sam Cloths by those who were not sufficiently rich to buy the pattern books, with the combined purpose of obtaining the design, and exhibiting the proficiency of the worker. At a later date, when lace was not so much made, and designs of all kinds were more abundant, Samplers were still worked, no longer with the object of perpetuating a pattern, but to exhibit the skill of the embroiderer; and no young lady's education, during the seventeenth and eighteenth centuries, was considered complete until she had embroidered in silks and gold thread a Sampler with a bordering of Drawn Work, and a centre filled with representations of animals, flowers, and trees, accompanied by verses appropriate to the undertaking. These Samplers were looked upon as such proofs of skill that they were preserved with much care, and many of those worked in the earlier part of the seventeenth century are still in a good state of preservation. Amongst the numbers exhibited, in 1881, at the Ancient Needlework Exhibition, the verses upon one worked in 1780 are quaint. They run as follows:

> Elizabeth Hide is my name,
> And with my needle I work the same,
> That all the world may plainly see
> How kind my parents have been to me.

To Make a Sampler: Take some Mosaic Canvas, of the finest make, and woven so that each thread is at an equal distance apart. Cut this 18 inches wide and 20 inches long, and measure off a border all round of 4 inches. For the border, half an inch from the edge, draw out threads in a pattern to the depth of half an inch, and work over these with coloured silk; then work a conventional scroll pattern, in shades of several colours, and in TENT STITCH, to fill up the remaining 3 inches of the border. Divide the centre of the Sampler into three sections. In the top section work a figure design. (In the old Samplers this was generally a sacred subject, such as Adam and Eve before the Tree of Knowledge.) In the centre section work an Alphabet in capital letters, and in the bottom an appropriate verse, the name of the worker, and the date.

(2) An oblong square of canvas, more or less coarse, upon which marking with a needle in Cross Stitch or otherwise is learned. Common canvas usually measures from 18 inches to 20 inches in width. In this case, cut off a piece of about 4 inches deep from one selvedge to the other. Then cut the remainder along the selvedge into three equal parts, so that each strip will be about 6 inches

in width. These strips must each be cut across into four parts, and this will make a dozen Samplers, 8 inches long and 6 inches wide respectively. This size will contain all the letters, large and small, besides numerals. As the raw edges of the canvas have to be turned in and sewn down by Hem Stitching, lay the fold down exactly to a thread; draw a thread or two under the hem, on each side respectively, and sew the end of the turn. To make the Hem Stitch, pass the needle under two threads and draw it, the point directed towards the worker. Then insert the needle back again, across the same thread, and out through the edge of the Hem. *See* MARKING.

Samples.—Trade patterns of every description of textile, arranged in graduated shades of colour, and attached to large cards, at one end of each little piece. They are all cut in oblong parallelograms—that is to say, the length is double that of the width of each. In this manner ribbon and men's cloths are frequently offered to the purchasers for sale, as are likewise samples of lace and frilling, ready plaited or quilled. Buttons, also, of a fancy description, short lengths of trimmings in braids, gimps and beads, and fringes of all kinds, are arranged on cards, sufficient being supplied of the goods having large patterns to show the whole design without any "repeat." Silks and woollen cloths are more generally made up into packages, and labelled with the name, price, and width of the material, and the name of either the manufacturer or of the firm where the goods are to be purchased. These Samples are sometimes disposed of for the making of Patchwork Quilts, or given away in charity for the same or a somewhat similar purpose.

Sanitary Clothing.—By this name under garments of pure undyed wool have been patented by Dr. Gustav Jaegar, of Stuttgart, also outer clothing and bedding; woollen stuffs being substituted for linen or calico sheets and pillow-cases; animal fibre being exclusively employed. *See* UNDERLINEN.

Sarcenet.—A name derived from Saracennet, given to indicate the Oriental origin of a thin kind of silk stuff, of a character superior, yet otherwise similar, to Persian, first used in this country in the thirteenth century. It can be obtained either plain or twilled, and in several colours, and is used for linings, being fine and very soft. The Silk Stuff known in the olden times as "Sendall" was said by Thynne, in his *Animadversions on Speght's Chaucer*, to be "A thynne stuffe lyke Sarcenett, and of a raw kynde of sylke or Sarcenet; but coarser and narrower than the Sarcenett now ys, as myselfe can remember." The scholastic dress, or costume of the doctor of physic, was described by Chaucer as being

	. . . . lined with Taffata and Sendal.

Sarcenet Ribbons.—Ribbons of this description are much like piece Sarcenet of a superior quality, with plain edges. They are comparatively cheap, and suitable for caps.

Saree.—A cotton stuff, of Indian manufacture, worn by the natives as a wrapping garment; also the name of a long scarf of silk, or gauze, used in the same country.

Sashes.—A woven silk scarf, of thick and heavy quality, manufactured expressly for the use of officers, and finished with long fringe. Broad silk ribbons, worn as waist belts, by women, and children of both sexes, are also called Sashes. Those worn by officers in uniform are of a very handsome and peculiar make, and rich quality, being of thick woven silk, and having a deep fringe at each end. These military scarves are worn over one shoulder, and knotted at the waist under the other.

Satara.—A ribbed cloth, brightly dressed, lustred, and hot pressed.

Sateen.—A cotton textile, of satin make, glossy, thick, and strong, resembling Jean. It is chiefly employed for the making of stays, and sometimes for dresses and boots, and can be procured in black and white, and in various colours. It is twilled, and is superior to Jeans. There are not only Sateens of uni-colour, but figured varieties, in many combinations of colour, employed for women's gowns. The width measures from 27 inches to 1 yard.

Satin.—A silk twill, of very glossy appearance on the face, and dull at the back. Very usually seven out of every eight threads of the warp are visible; whereas, in other silk stuffs, each half of the warp is raised alternately. Its brilliancy is further augmented by dressing, it being rolled on hot cylinders. Some Satins are figured and brocaded, and amongst the best examples are those made in Spitalfields. A good quality Satin wears exceedingly well; the width runs from 18 inches to 22 inches. The lustre of Satin is produced by the irregular method in which the respective threads of the warp and weft are taken in connection with each other. Satin cannot be cleaned or dyed satisfactorily, as it is liable to become frayed. Strutt makes an allusion to it in an account of *Revels at Court, temp.* Henry VIII., when its usual colour was red. Dekker likewise speaks of it in Gull's *Hornbook*, 1609, as the dress material of the higher classes: "Though you find much Satin there, yet you shall likewise find many citizen's sons." Satinette is a thinner and cheaper description of the same stuff, but equally durable, and may be had in black and colours as a dress material. Its brilliancy is produced in the process of manufacture, without dress, or other artificial means.

Satin is of Chinese origin, the flowered kinds—those manufactured and imported into this country — being celebrated. It is also made at Lyons and Florence. Amongst other varieties may be mentioned the Indian Cuttanee Satin, which is a fine thick cotton-backed Satin, produced in stripes. There are three varieties of mixtures in colour — two each, in each variety. It is 27 inches in width, and is chiefly employed for upholstery, but is sometimes used by ladies for tea-gowns. There are also Satin Damasks, Satin de Lyons, Satin Foulards, Satin Merveilleux, Satin Sheeting, Satin Beige, Satin Sultan, and Satinette. These are all Silk textiles. There are others of mixed materials—such as the Satin de Bruges, which is a combination of silk and wool, made for upholstery. Sateen, which is a cotton stuff of Satin make; Satin striped Canvas, the former being of silk, and the Canvas of thread. Satin de Laine, composed of wool;

Satin Sultan, which has a mixture of wool with the silk, and is employed for mantles; and Satinet, an American cloth of Satin and wool.

Cyprus Satin is often mentioned in old inventories and account books, as, for instance, those of the Church-wardens of Leverton, near Boston, Lincolnshire, dated 1528: "For a yard of green sattyn of Sypryse, viijd.," which was probably employed in the repair of the Vestments. Also, in an inventory of the goods belonging to the Abbey of Peterborough, in 1539, it is said: "On Vestment of red, coarse Satten of Cyprus, with harts and knots." Satin proper was first introduced into this country from China. It represents the "Samite" of ancient times, which was frequently embroidered or interwoven with gold or silver threads:

> And in over-gilt Samite
> Y-clad she was by great délite.
> CHAUCER's *Romaunt of the Rose.*

It is likewise spoken of by Tennyson:

> An arm
> Rose up from out the bosom of the lake
> Clothed in white Samite.

Satin Cloth.—A French woollen material of Satin make, having a smooth face. It is employed for women's dresses, is produced in most colours, and is of stout quality and durable. The width measures from about 27 inches to 30 inches. It is otherwise known by its French name of SATIN DE LAINE.

Satin Damask.—A very costly silk material, varying in price according to the weight of silk, and the richness and elaboration of the design. In some examples it is enriched with gold threads, and may be procured of an exceedingly costly quality, having velvet flowers. The width varies from 28 inches to 32 inches.

Satin de Bruges.—This is a cloth of Satin make, having a smooth face. It is composed of a combination of silk and wool, and is designed for purposes of upholstery.

Satin de Laine.—A French textile of Satin make, but composed entirely of wool, and otherwise known as SATIN CLOTH. It is manufactured at Roubaix.

Satin de Lyons.—This description of rich silk has a gros grain back in lieu of a twill. *See* SATIN.

Satin Embroidery.—*See* EMBROIDERY IN SATIN STITCH.

Satinet.—An American cloth of mixed materials, both cheap and durable, and used by the labouring classes in that country as fustian and velveteen corduroy are employed in England. The warp of Satinet is of cotton, and the "filling-in" is composed mostly of the short, waste threads of woollen manufacture, combined with a sufficient quantity of long wool to permit of its being spun. It is woven in a peculiar way, so as to bring up the wool to the surface of the stuff; and is then heavily felted, so that the cotton should be entirely concealed.

Satin Foulards.—These are silk stuffs printed in various designs and colours, and measure from 24 inches to 25 inches in width.

Satin Lisse.—A French dress material made of cotton, but having a Satin-like lustre. It is lighter in substance than an English Sateen, and is twilled. For slight mourning it is very suitable, made up as a summer costume; and the small designs, floral and otherwise, with which it is covered, are pretty and elegant. It is produced in varieties of black, white, and violet or grey.

Satin Merveilleux.—This is a description of twilled Satin textile, of an exceedingly soft and pliable character, and having but little gloss. It is sold in different qualities, all of which measure 24 inches in width.

Satin Sheeting.—One of the "waste silk" materials, of Satin make on the face, and twilled cotton at the back, the chief substance of the material being of cotton. It is made in different degrees of fineness, runs to 54 inches in width, and is employed for purposes of embroidery, fancy, dress, and upholstery. Satin Sheeting is thicker in substance, coarser in the weaving, and less glossy, than the ordinary "cotton-backed Satin." It can be obtained in most beautiful shades of every colour, both new and old, and is made 22 inches in width. The Diapered Satin Sheeting is a comparatively new textile.

Satin Stitch.—*See* BERLIN WORK and EMBROIDERY STITCHES.

Satin-striped Canvas.—This is a fancy variety of Embroidery Canvas, having alternate stripes of Satin and plain thick Canvas, somewhat resembling the Java make. The Satin stripe has a horizontal cording, as the weft of flax runs through the silk stripe.

Satin Sultan.—A textile somewhat resembling Bengaline in the method of its manufacture, but having a Satin face. It is designed for mantles, measures 24 inches in width, and varies considerably in quality and price.

Satin Turk.—A peculiar description of silk textile made at Amiens; it is very durable, and is suitable as a dress material, being soft, not liable to much creasing, and less thick and stiff than Satin. It is also used for evening shoes, and waistcoats, and is about 27 inches in width.

Satin Veiné.—A French term, sometimes applied to the veins of leaves, or the tendrils of sprays worked in Embroidery and with Satin Stitch.

Saut de Lit.—One of the French terms employed to denote a dressing-gown, the extra covering put on immediately on rising from bed, and worn in the bedroom until the costume suitable for the breakfast-room be put on.

Saxon Embroidery.—The Anglo-Saxon ladies were celebrated for their outline Embroidery upon fine linen or silk before their Church needlework excited the envy of Pope Adrian IV. This outline work was formed of the richest material, and was remarkable as much for the delicacy of its workmanship as for the pure and symbolical character of its designs, which were chiefly taken from the emblems used by the early Christians to represent our Saviour, the Trinity, and the Unity of the Godhead. Thus, the Gammadion, the Triangle, and the Circle occur in this work, either combined or forming separate geometrical patterns, used for the wide borders upon priests' vestments or upon altar linen. The outlines and all the chief parts of the design are executed upon the surface of the material, and are made by laying down gold or silver threads, or thick silk threads, and Couching them to their places by a stitch brought from the back of the work on one side of the thread, and put down into the material on the other, and so securing it into its position. A few light stitches are worked directly on to the material as a finish to the chief lines, but they are always made subordinate to the Couched lines, to which much variety and richness are given by the use of the best and most varied materials. Fig. 713 is a specimen of Saxon Embroidery, taken from a quilt now in the South Kensington

FIG. 713. SAXON EMBROIDERY.

Museum. The subject is not ecclesiastical, as the quilt was not intended for Church uses, but it gives a fair idea of the manner in which this Embroidery was worked, and is a pattern that can be easily copied. To work: Trace the design upon fine linen (but only the outline) or white Surah silk, which back with holland. Put the material into an EMBROIDERY FRAME, COUCH gold thread round the outlines, and work the stitches that form the fillings to the leaves and flowers. These consist of Lines crossing each other diagonally and caught down with a stitch, and CROSS STITCH and DOUBLE STARS. Work the diagonal lines in green silk, lay them down on the material, and

secure them with a stitch made with red silk. Work the Cross Stitches in red silk, and the double Stars with red and green silk. Take a dark olive-green silk cord, and Couch this along every outline, sewing it to the material with a silk matching it in colour.

Saxony.—Cloth or flannel made of wool of the Merino sheep pastured on the loamy soil of Saxony, which is peculiarly favourable for the rearing of fine animals. Wool from the same breed pastured in Spain is much harsher in quality. The cloth is made in the West of England, and the flannel chiefly at Saddleworth, near Halifax. *See* FLANNEL.

Saxony Lace.—The making of Pillow Lace in Saxony dates from the sixteenth century, the art having been introduced from Flanders. Old authorities consider that it was introduced into Germany by Barbara Uttermann, the wife of a master miner at Annaberg, who founded a school for lace-making at that place in 1561; but modern writers look upon the religious emigrants as the probable sources of the industry, though all agree that during the life of Barbara Uttermann (1514 to 1575) lace-making became known in Germany, and continued to be a source of profit to that nation until the eighteenth century. Lace-making has much declined since that period, though lace still forms an article of manufacture. The best that is made resembles old Brussels, and obtains a good price; but the greatest sale is confined to a coarse Guipure Lace, known as Eternelle and Plaited Lace; and as it is one that any amateur with a little patience can make, the details are here given.

The materials required are a pillow and stand, lace patterns, bobbins, pins, thread, scissors, and Knitting needle; the bobbins and pillow differ from those used in Honiton Lace-making.

The pillow is oblong, the cover or bag for which make of twill 28 inches long and 8 inches wide. RUN this piece of material together, then make a wide HEM at the sides, to hold tape as a drawer. Draw up one side, but do not pull the material up close together; leave a round of 7 inches, into which TACK a piece of cardboard covered with twill. Fill up the cover with horsehair, bran, or wool, draw the second side together with the tape, and insert the cardboard to match the side first made. The white Cover Cloths for protecting the Lace are made like ordinary Cover Cloths. Cut a piece of strong linen 4½ inches wide, and long enough to go round the Cushion, and sew this round the Cover in the centre, to serve as a support to the lace and the pattern. The Cushion is not held upon the knee, but is fixed into a stand, which is from 28 inches to 30 inches high, so as to be within reach of a worker when sitting down. Make the stand either as an ordinary table with four legs, of a size just to hold the cushion, and elongate the four legs or supports above the table part to secure the Cushion between them; or make a table with two legs or supports like crutches, and secure these two upright pieces of wood into a strong foundation, while the fork or crutch of the upper part holds up the Cushion. The lace patterns are pricked out upon either Toile Ciré or Parchment, and do not differ from other Pillow Lace patterns. The Bobbins are

4½ inches long, and, after the thread is wound upon them, a thin metal shield is secured over it, to prevent its soiling when held in the hand. Ordinary large Bobbins can be used, but the sort sold expressly are the best. A great number are required. The pins are of brass, and finer than ordinary pins. No. 30 thread is used to commence upon, Nos. 50 and 60 being used for making ordinary lace, and No. 200 for fine lace. A Knitting needle is required to fasten the threads to when commencing the Lace, instead of tying the threads into a Knot, and pinning this Knot to the Cushion, as in Honiton Lace.

Before commencing to make any pattern, it is necessary to learn how the Bobbins are secured, increased, and decreased, and the manner of making the stitches. To adjust the Bobbins: Arrange the Cushion on the stand, and secure the pattern by pinning it down. Run the Knitting needle in across the Cushion where the pattern commences, push it into the material on the right side of the pattern, but leave it free on the left side. Take up each Bobbin separately, and fasten it to the Knitting needle thus: Hold the end of the thread in the right hand in front of the needle, with the left hand put the Bobbin under the needle, round it, and under the thread in the front, to form a secured loop; draw this up, and make another loop in the same way with the same Bobbin. Put on the required number of Bobbins in this manner.

To Cut off Threads.—Threads that have broken, and have been replaced by new ones, or threads no longer required in the pattern, are done away with as follows: Where they occur in Cloth Stitch or other parts of the Lace, tie them in a WEAVER'S KNOT, and pin them out of the way on the Cushion until some inches of the

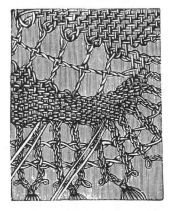

FIG. 714. SAXONY LACE—TO CUT OFF THREADS.

Lace beyond them have been made, then cut them away close to the Lace. Fig. 714 shows threads arranged for cutting away from Cloth Stitch. Where the threads are no longer required in the border of a pattern, they are formed into a little bunch thus: Take one thread and bind it well round the rest, then pull its end through the binding to secure it. Cut off the threads close, so that only a small bunch is made not larger than an ordinary PICOT. The bunches shown in Fig. 714 are purposely enlarged, in order that the manner of making them may be understood.

To Increase the Bobbins.—Bobbins are frequently added while the Lace is in progress, either for the purpose of increasing the Lace or when threads have been broken; they are adjusted as follows: Tie two threads together with a WEAVER'S KNOT, and hang these threads (which are

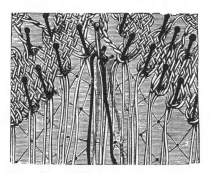

FIG 715. SAXONY LACE—TO INCREASE THE BOBBINS.

coloured black in Fig. 715) over the pin which is placed in the hole nearest the part to be increased. Work in these new threads as they are reached in the proper course of the lace-making. Should the threads be added at the thick part of a pattern where Cloth Stitch is worked, after they have been woven in with the others the Knot that joins their ends together may be cut away; but should they be required in the ground or open parts of the Lace, this Knot must be retained.

The chief STITCHES are worked as follows:

Cloth Stitch, or Plain Dotting.—This Stitch is used

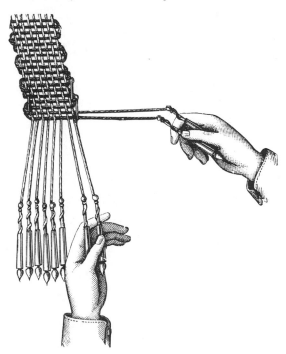

FIG. 716. SAXONY LACE—CLOTH STITCH OR PLAIN DOTTING.

for all the thick parts of the Lace, and closely resembles the ordinary Cloth Stitch of other laces. For the narrow piece, shown in Fig. 716, use ten Bobbins, of which allow eight to hang down the Pillow, using the other two to interlace in and out of the stationary threads. Hold two of the Hangers in the left hand, and take the Worker Bobbins in the right hand; put up a pin at the end of the Lace, twist the two workers together twice (see Fig. 716) so as to make an edge, leave one behind the pin, pass the other over the first Hanger in the left hand and under the second; take up the next two Hangers, and pass the Worker over and under them, and so continue until the other edge is reached. Then take the second Working Bobbin, and reverse the passing over and under until it reaches the other edge; here twist it together with the first Bobbin, stick in a pin at the edge, and then work them back. Keep the Hanging Bobbins in the left hand, so that the long lines down the Lace are evenly stretched.

Crossing.—A movement frequently resorted to when making this Lace, and worked as follows: Take up two Bobbins that lie close together, and move the one on the left hand over the right hand, and the one on the right hand under the left hand. A Crossing is shown in the Double Twist, Fig. 721.

Half Stitch, or Net Device.—This open Lattice Stitch is used for all the lighter parts of the design and is more difficult than Cloth Stitch, as the threads, while making it, are crossed. To work as shown in Fig. 717: Fasten on

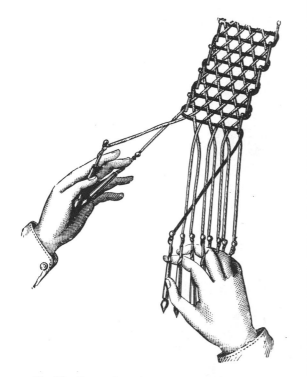

FIG. 717. SAXONY LACE—HALF STITCH OR NET DEVICE.

ten Bobbins, and use nine as Hanging or Passive Bobbins, and one as a Worker to form the Lace. Cross the Hangers one over the other, letting the left-hand Bobbins cross under the right-hand Bobbins (the left hand in the

illustration shows how the crossing is managed). Keep all the Hanging Bobbins in the hand. Stick a pin at the edge of the Lace, and pass the Worker Bobbin under and over each Bobbin, as in Cloth Stitch, until it reaches the other end. Do not draw it up close, but allow space for the crossing to show. Stick a pin in at the other edge, cross the Hanging Bobbins as before, and work back.

Lozenge.—Threads twisted together so as to form a thick and pointed diamond shape are much used in coarse Guipure Saxony Lace, and are called Lozenges. They are made generally with four Bobbins, as follows: Tie four Bobbins together, then hold three in the left hand but apart, as shown in Fig. 718, and take the fourth Bobbin in the right hand and pass it over, under, and over the three held down. This will bring it out upon the left side.

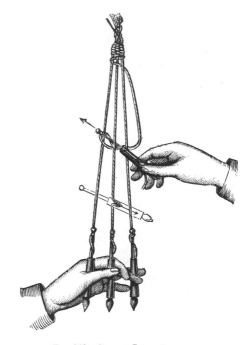

FIG. 718. SAXONY LACE—LOZENGE.

To return it, pass it under, over, and under the three held Bobbins (as shown by the white arrow in the engraving). Repeat these two lines until the length of the Lozenge is made. A small Lozenge takes twelve rows, a large one twenty, but no certain number of lines can be given, as all depends upon the thickness of the thread used. When the Lozenge is made, Knot the threads together, and proceed to make another if required.

Pin-sticking.—This is a movement that is required in all kinds of Pillow Lace making, and is used to form the design and to keep the various parts that are worked even and in their proper positions. The holes into which the Pins are put are all pricked upon the pattern. When one of these is reached, hold the Bobbins firmly in the left hand, take up a Pin in the right hand, and stick it firmly into its hole, keeping the threads in their right places on each side of the Pin. The manner of doing this is shown in Fig. 719.

Plaitings.—These are sometimes used to form the ground of the Lace. To make: Take four Bobbins and Plait them together until a pinhole is reached, divide them

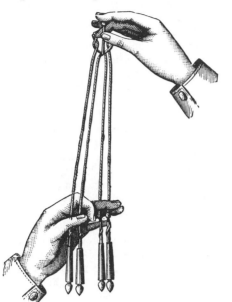

FIG. 719. SAXONY LACE—PIN STICKING.

at that place, and take two Bobbins from the Plait upon the other side of the pinhole. Cross the threads, and continue to Plait to the next pinhole; here divide the

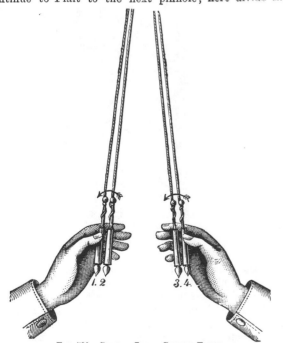

FIG. 720. SAXONY LACE—SIMPLE TWIST.

Bobbins, leave two and take up two, and continue the Plait to another pinhole, where divide again; work up the threads left at the pinholes in the same way.

Twists.—The Twists are of two kinds, Simple and Double, and are worked as follows: To form a *Simple Twist* as shown in Fig. 720. In the illustration the Bobbins that make the Twist are numbered from 1 to 4. Hold 1 and 2 in the left hand, 3 and 4 in the right hand. Simultaneously pass 2 over 1 with the left hand, and 4 over 3 with the right hand. The arrows in the engraving point in the direction of the Twist, which is not shown accom-

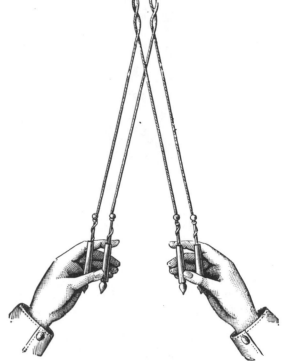

FIG. 721. SAXONY LACE—DOUBLE TWIST AND CROSSING.

plished, but with the Bobbins ready to make it; but the Twist made is shown in Fig. 721 in the first turn of the Double Twist. To form a *Double Twist*, the movement described in Simple Twist is repeated, and then the Bobbin marked 1 is moved over 2, and Bobbin marked 3 over Bobbin marked 4. Fig. 721 not only shows the Double Twist, but the manner of making a Crossing, the Bobbins being crossed after they are twisted.

Turn.—When the edge of the Lace is reached, or the thread turned in a contrary direction to that in which it started.

Wheels.—Form these by taking two Bobbins from the Lace wherever the upper lines of the Wheel are drawn. TWIST each couple together four times, then work the centre round of the Wheel in CLOTH STITCH; divide off the Bobbins into pairs again, Twist them four times, and work up into the lace where the lower lines of the Wheel end.

PATTERNS.—To work the Pattern shown in Fig. 722: Prick the pinholes where shown in the upper part, and hang fourteen Bobbins on to the Knitting needle. For the first row (indicated by two pinholes), commence on the left-hand side of the pattern. DOUBLE TWIST four of the eight left-hand Bobbins, and stick a pin in the right-hand hole; tie up two left-hand Bobbins, and take up, in addition to them, two right-hand Bobbins, SINGLE TWIST, CROSS, Single Twist, Cross, and stick a pin in the last hole of the second row (the one with three holes), tie up two left-

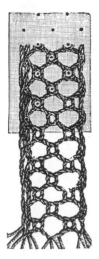

FIG. 722. SAXONY LACE.

hand Bobbins, take up the last two right-hand Bobbins in addition. Double Twist, Cross, Single Twist, Cross, tie up the two right-hand Bobbins, and take up, in addition, two left-hand Bobbins. Single Twist underneath the last pin, Cross, Single Twist, Cross. For the second row, commence on the left-hand side, take up ten Bobbins, Double Twist, Cross, stick a pin in the middle hole of the second row, Double Twist, Cross, tie up two left-hand Bobbins, take up

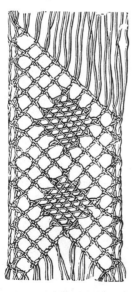

FIG. 723. SAXONY LACE.

two additional right-hand Bobbins, and repeat the work as before, stick a pin in the last hole of the third row. Work the double border with six outside Bobbins, and stick a pin in the last hole of the fourth row. For the third row, commence at the left-hand side row, take twelve Bobbins, work for three times as already described in the second row.

Stick a pin for the first pin in the first hole of the third row, and work the double border with six outside Bobbins. For the fourth row, commence at the left-hand side, take up all the Bobbins, work with the first four left-hand Bobbins the single border; repeat the work of the first row three times, and finish with the double border. Repeat for the rest.

The Pattern shown in Fig. 723 is simply made with Twists and Half Stitch. To work: Prick the design so that a pinhole is made in every open space. Work with Lace cotton No. 50, and hang on twenty-eight Bobbins. Commence at the left hand, make the double border with six Bobbins, and work the holes with DOUBLE TWISTS and CROSSINGS in the slant shown in the Pattern. For the second row, commence again at the left-hand side, and work the border and the holes until the diamond is reached, which work in the HALF STITCH or NET DEVICE. The threads arranged for working the diamond are shown at the bottom part of the engraving.

To work Fig. 724: Prick the Pattern with eight holes, hang on twenty Bobbins, and use lace thread No. 50. For the first row, form the left-hand border with six Bobbins, tie up four left-hand Bobbins, take the other two, and with two right-hand Bobbins TURN, CROSS, stick a pin, Turn, Cross again, tie up two left-hand Bobbins, take up two right-hand Bobbins, and repeat Turning, Crossing, and Pin-setting as before. Repeat alternately

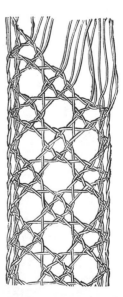

FIG. 724. SAXONY LACE.

until the first mesh of the first row is finished. For the second mesh, tie up two left-hand Bobbins, after having turned and crossed the last time in the first row, take up two right-hand Bobbins, Turn, Cross, stick a pin, as in the first row, tie up two right-hand Bobbins, take up two left-hand Bobbins, and repeat Turning, Crossing, and stick a pin, then tie up all these four Bobbins, and work with the four adjoining right-hand Bobbins, tie up two right-hand Bobbins, take up two left-hand Bobbins, and repeat. Turn and Cross to commence the third mesh, work this like the first, and finally work the right-hand border line. The second row contains the same meshes, only differently arranged, and is worked accordingly.

In the design given in Fig. 725, the pricked pattern of which is shown in Fig. 726, Detail A, the stitches used are Cloth Stitch, Half Stitch, or Net Device, the diamond-shaped hole, explained in Fig. 723, and the mesh shown in Fig. 724. Work with forty Bobbins, and with No. 40 thread. In the pricked pattern, the letter *a* shows where the Bobbins divide to work the slanting Cloth Stitch, the letters *d* and *c* give the side points of the diamond, and *b* the bottom point. Inside the large diamond at *b*, the square meshes shown in Fig. 725 are made; there are nine

Embroidery to signify a border of material, or work cut out after the pattern of a scallop shell's edge. It is more suitable for washing materials than a Vandyke border, the points of the latter being more easily frayed out. Sometimes a scallop edge is "pinked out," especially in silk, or in glazed calico; but in white stuffs it should be worked closely in BUTTONHOLE STITCH.

Scarves. —These are more or less long, straight, and comparatively narrow lengths of material designed for wear round the throat or the waist, or across one or both shoulders. They are generally made of a silk material, or else of lace; but also sometimes of woollen stuff, either woven or knitted. They may be had in every shade of

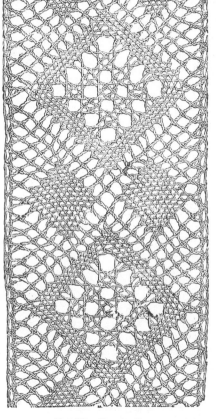

FIG. 725. SAXONY LACE.

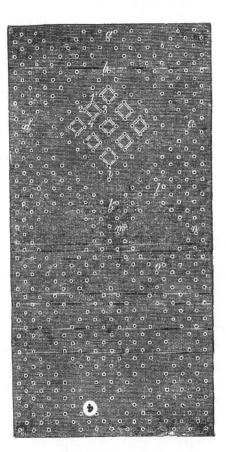

FIG. 726. SAXONY LACE—DETAIL A.

of these, and they end at the letter *t*; and the points where the threads commence to make each separate one are indicated by the numerals 1, 2, 3, and 4. The small diamond upon each side of the large one is worked with Half Stitch, and is marked as to its points by the letters *l, m, n, o.* The border to the insertion is formed with six threads, like the borders already described. When an edging is made to Saxony Lace, form it with four threads, and plait together, carrying it along as a scalloped line; ornament this plait with the ordinary PICOTS or Loops that adorn the edges of other Pillow Laces.

Scallop Edge. — A term used in Dressmaking and

colour, in Tartan patterns, with brocaded, embroidered, or fringed ends. The Roman Silk Scarves, striped across the width, in combinations of various colours, are very handsome, and so are the embroidered Indian and Algerian.

Schleswig Pillow Lace.—Cutwork appears to have been made in Denmark from a very early period, and is still one of the occupations of Danish ladies. White Pillow Lace making was introduced into that country in the sixteenth century, when a manufactory was founded at Schleswig, and protected by heavy duties levied upon foreign laces. The early productions of Schleswig are a mixture of Flemish and Scandinavian designs, ornamented with the Stitches or Fillings that are usually found in Italian Laces, and are distinguished from Flemish Laces, to which they bear a great resemblance, by being worked in a very solid manner, and containing none of the lighter Plaitings or light parts of Brussels Lace. Much of it is still to be met with in English collections, having probably found its way there during the reign of Queen Anne, in the suite of her consort, Prince George of Denmark. The modern laces made in Denmark are copies from Lille and Saxony Laces, and are of a much lighter design than those of an earlier date; but the industry has not flourished since the commencement of the present century, except in the working of Tonder Lace, which is described under its own heading.

Scisseau.—The French word for SCISSORS.

Scissors.—Of this most essential appliance of a work-box there are great varieties in shape, size, and quality. They are classed respectively under the following description: The cast steel polished Shot Scissors, having shanks and bows of iron; Sheer Steel Scissors, comprising those in ordinary use, of which the blades only are hardened; and Lined Blades, which are made in large sizes, and almost entirely of iron, a strip of steel only being welded along the edge of the blades. Besides these, there are fancy varieties, the bow and shanks being leather-covered, or of gold or silver; Nail Scissors, having a file on each blade; Grape Scissors, with a groove on one blade, into which the other fits; Lamp Scissors, having a bend, bayonet-shaped, and other kinds, one of which, known as Buttonhole Scissors, is an important article in the workbox, and has a sharply-cut gap in the blades, for the purpose of accurately cutting a hole of certain invariable dimensions. Scissors are capable of much decoration by means of blueing, gilding, and studs of gold, as also by rich filigree work in the shanks, and embossed figures. The handles are some-times made of mother-o'-pearl; but this plan is never satisfactory, as the cement loosens very quickly. The seat of the cutlery industry is at Sheffield. In Wilson's "*Rig Veda*" we find a passage which implies the use of Scissors, by the Ayrians, several centuries before Christ.

Sclavonic Embroidery. — Similar to RUSSIAN EM-BROIDERY.

Scotch Cambric.—A cotton textile, incorrectly called Cambric, fine in quality, rather starchy finished, and unglazed. Cotton Cambric is to be had of two kinds, that designed for dresses, either white or printed, and that to be used as French Cambric; the former is made in Lancashire, the latter at Glasgow. One variety is made of a mixture of cotton and flax, and is designed for handkerchiefs. Scotch cotton-made Cambric is employed for women's dresses. *See* CAMBRIC.

Scotch Fingering.—A loose worsted yarn, much used for the knitting of stockings, cuffs, scarves, gaiters, and other articles. It is dyed in bright colours, and is sold by the spindle of six pounds.

Scrim.—This is a description of canvas, manufactured in several qualities. That especially for the use of paper-hangers is made of Hemp and Jute. The Jute would dis-solve if placed in water. The best quality is made entirely of Flax. Scrim is likewise used by gardeners for covering fruit trees. It measures from 36 to 40 inches in width. *See* CANVAS.

Seal (*Phoca*).—Of this animal there are many varieties. They are natives of the western coasts of Scotland and Ireland, the shores of Labrador, Newfoundland, and Greenland. Some kinds supply leather (tanned and enamelled with black varnish) for women's shoes; others a beautiful fur, thick, soft, and glossy. The coarse hairs are removed, and the fur shaved, and dyed either a golden colour, or, more usually, a dark Vandyke brown, when it resembles a fine velvet. Medium-sized skins measure about 20 inches by 40 inches; when made into jackets, or used as trimmings, the fur should be turned in the cutting out, so as to lie upwards.

Sealskin Cloth.—The yarn used for this kind of cloth is the finest kind of Mohair, and the shade given in the dyeing is exactly similar to that of the real fur. It is manufactured in Yorkshire, and employed for women's outdoor jackets. This cloth must not be confounded with that called SILK SEALSKIN.

Seam.—A term used to denote the line of Over-sewing which connects the edges of two pieces of material together. The term is of Saxon derivation, and has always been retained in the English language.

Seaming.—A certain method adopted in Plain Sewing for uniting two pieces of material together, either by Over-sewing the selvedges, or by turning down two raw edges, the needle being passed through the folded edges very straight. When there is no selvedge, make a FELL on the wrong side; and, in the case of a gored skirt, either of a dress or under garment, hold the gored side with the raw edge next to the left-hand thumb, and take great care that, being cut on the bias, it does not become drawn or puckered.

In Over-sewing the seams of underclothing, place the two edges of material very evenly together, and keep them in position by means of pins inserted at regular distances. Hold the work very straight between the forefinger and thumb—not round the former, as in Hemming—and beware of slanting the needle, or the seam will become puckered. If one side of the material have a selvedge, and the other be cut on the cross (or diagonally), or have a raw edge, hold the latter nearest to you, under the thumb, as it will thus run less chance of being stretched.

Seaming Lace.—This term, with that of Spacing Lace, is continually mentioned in old Wardrobe Accounts of the sixteenth and seventeenth centuries, and does not intimate a particular kind of lace, but lace used for a certain purpose. It was the custom in those times to set apart the best and finest linen for such State occasions as births, deaths, or marriages, and the table linen and bed furniture so set apart were adorned with lace let in as an insertion wherever a seam in the linen appeared, and frequently where no seam was really needed. The lace chiefly used for this purpose was Cut Work, as, being made of linen, it accorded best with the rest of the article; but in England, Hollie Point was frequently substituted for Cut Work; and upon the Continent, the least costly of the various native productions. There is still preserved a sheet ornamented with Cut Work that was once in the possession of Shakespeare, and large quantities of linen adorned with Cut Work are constantly met with in Swedish or Danish families of consideration.

Seam Stitch.—*See* KNITTING.

Seamstress.—A term employed to denote a woman who seams or sews; a needlewoman whose department in her particular art is to perform Plain Sewing, as distinguished from dress or mantle making, and from decorative Embroidery.

Sea Otter Fur.—The Sea Otter (*Enhydra Marina*) is a species of the genus *Lutra*. It yields the most costly of all furs, the colour of which is a silver-grey, tipped with black; the fur is splendidly thick, soft, and shining, and exceedingly velvet-like to the touch. The Sea Otter is larger than the species frequenting rivers, and is found in the North Pacific, from Kamschatka to the Yellow Sea on the Asiatic coast, and from Alaska to California on the American coast. Only about a tenth part of the skins taken are exported to this country. The Russians, Japanese and Chinese, prize the fur greatly, and it is one of the most costly in the English market. *See* OTTER.

Seating.—A textile made of hair, of satin make, designed for upholstering purposes, such as the seats and backs of chairs, sofas, and cushions. *See* HAIR CLOTH.

Seed Embroidery.—A work practised in Germany, but not much known in England. It is formed by making flowers and buds with various seeds, and connecting these together with stems and stalks of Chenille, and working the leaves in Chenille. The seeds used for the work are those of the Indian corn, pumpkin, and cucumber, for large flowers, and canary and aster for the small. These seeds are pierced at each end with a carpet needle, and attached by these holes to the material. To work: Select a Crewel Work design of single flowers, such as daisies, sunflowers, or marigolds, and seeds that match the size of the petals, also Chenilles of various shades of green, and sewing and purse silk matching the flowers. Trace the design upon white or pale coloured blue satin, back it with holland, and frame it in an EMBROIDERY FRAME. Pierce the seeds at the top and bottom, and sew them to their places, either as flat petals, when lay them flat upon the satin, and secure with a stitch, made in sewing silk, at each of their ends; or as raised petals, when place them upright upon the satin, sew them together, and then down to the material. Having placed the seeds, work the centres of the flowers in FRENCH KNOTS with the purse silk, and the stems, stalks, and leaves in the green Chenille and in SATIN STITCH. The Embroidery is used for sachets, hand bags, and fire-screens. Necklaces and bracelets are made of melon or pumpkin seeds, by threading them upon fine silk, and forming them into balls, chains, tassels, and other devices.

Seerhand Muslin.—This is a description of cotton fabric somewhat resembling Nainsook and Mull, being a kind of intermediate quality as compared to them. It is particularly adapted for a dress material, as it preserves its clearness after being washed.

Self-Coloured.—A term employed in reference to textiles, to signify that the dye is of one colour only, and other-wise indicated by the term uni-coloured. It is sometimes employed to signify, either that the stuff is of its natural colour, in the raw material, or that it has not been dyed since it left the loom.

Selvedge.—The firmly finished edge of any textile, so manufactured as to preclude the ravelling out of the weft. It is sometimes spelt Selvage. The excellence of the make of the cloth is shown by the even quality of the Selvedge. In flannels it is grey, pink, or violet-coloured, and varies in depth. Black silks likewise have coloured Selvedges. In "The Boke of Curtasye," of the fourteenth century, we find it mentioned:

> The over nape schall dowbulle be layde
> To the utter side the *selvage* brade.

Semé.—A French term denoting "sewn," and having reference to the small dot-like patterns (as distinguished from "Running" ones) embroidered on any textile; otherwise called Powderings.

Semes.—An ancient term applied to Embroidery that is worked as if it was thrown or cast upon the background in detached sprays and bunches, instead of being designed in a connected pattern. The word is derived from the French *semer*, "to sow, or sprinkle."

Serge.—A loosely woven, very durable, twilled material, of which there are several varieties, distinguished by some additional name; the warp is of worsted, and the woof of wool. It is dyed in every colour, besides being sold in white and black. Serges may be had in either silk or wool. Some of those made of the latter material are smooth on both sides of the cloth, others are only smooth on one side and woolly on the other, while varieties are manufactured rough and woolly on both sides. All these kinds of Serge are employed for women's dress, and the stoutest in quality for purposes of upholstery. Amongst the most serviceable, as well as the warmest kind, is that manufactured, under Government auspices, solely for the use of the Royal Navy; but this can only be obtained by favour, for private use, from the captain of some man-of-war, who may chance to have more in stock than is required for immediate use amongst his crew. It is dyed in a more permanent way than that sold in the shops, and is very much warmer and heavier. Ordinary Serge is made like Sateen, one side being woolly and the other smooth, the longest wool being used for the warp, which is more twisted than the woof. There are a great many varieties of cloth known as Serge—viz., French Flannel Serge, composed of long wool, and somewhat of the appearance of Indian Cashmere; the Serge de Berri, is a French-made, woollen stuff, produced in the province of which it bears the name; Serge Cloth is smooth on one side and rough on the other; Witney Serges are hairy throughout; Silk Serge is employed in the making of costly mantles; Serge Ribbon Sashes are soft, tie easily, do not crease, and may be washed; and Pompadour Flannel Serges, so designated on account of the small floral designs with which they are decorated; they are 29 inches in width. Serge varies in width in its several varieties of make and material. The coarse and heavy kinds, employed for upholstery, are of double width, whether of wool or silk; that of the ordinary woollen dress Serges runs from about 30 inches to a yard; Silk Serges are narrower. One variety of the last-named is used by tailors for the lining of coats. Though the twill is fine, it is of stout make, and can be had both in black and colours.

Serge de Berri.—This is a French woollen textile, employed as a dress material, and is produced in the province of which it bears the name. *See* SERGE.

Setting-in Gathers.—A phrase employed in reference to Plain Sewing, to perform which proceed as follows: Halve and quarter the band, and the material to be gathered, placing a small pin at each spot where these divisions are to be indicated, which is at the same time to secure the band and the full portion of material together. Hold the work so as to keep the left thumb on the junction of the Gathers and the band. As the latter is double, insert the raw edge of the former between the two sides of the band. Take up one ridge only of the gathering with the needle at a time, and proceed with great regularity, so as to form what will have the appearance of a neat Hemming Stitch. When the back of the band has to be secured to the gathers, endeavour to work as neatly as before, so as not to draw them awry, nor to show through any stitches taken at the back on the front or right side. Before commencing to sew in the Gathers, they must be stroked into their respective places in very even succession. *See* STROKING.

Setting-up Lace.—This is only required when Raised Pillow Lace flowers are made, and consists of sewing the raised petals to their right positions, and then stiffening them so as to stand upright. To work: Wash the hands in warm water, then shake the lace out upon a piece of tissue paper; take the finest possible needle, and, with lace thread, adjust the petals by sewing them down; make a small knot in the thread, fasten down lightly to the lace any back petals, running the thread from one petal to the other at the back of the lace; fasten inner petals by curving them inwards, or irregularly, according to design, and sew on to the lace any loose butterflies or other portions that have been made separately. To fasten off the thread, make a loop, and pass the needle through it, then draw it up, and cut the thread close. To finish or stiffen the flowers: Boil a quarter of an ounce of rice in a pint of water, and when cold strain it, and with a camel-hair brush paint over with it the inside of the parts in relief. When making a bold curve in the Raised Work, dip an ivory knitting needle into the rice water, and apply that to the lace; only damp the lace with the mixture, never make it wet.

Sew and Fell.—The process of Felling is effected by Running and Felling, and Sewing and Felling. To do the latter, fold one of the raw edges of the cloth on the wrong side, over the other raw edge; and thus form a Hem, after the manner of RUNNING and FELLING.

Sewing.—A comprehensive term, signifying stitchery of all plain kinds performed with a needle, by which means garments, or articles of upholstery, are made and mended. The word Working is frequently employed to signify Sewing, although one of general application to every kind of manual and intellectual labour. The word Stitching may be used, like Sewing, as a generic term, to

denote any description of work with a needle. In Wilson's *Rig Veda*, II., p. 288, we find the words: "May she sew the work with a needle that is not capable of being cut or broken . . . of which the stitches will endure." *Sivan* is the term for the verb to sew, or sewing. Twenty-two centuries ago the Buddhists wore made, or sewn, dresses, in lieu of mere wrappings.

In Pillow Lace making, what are called Sewings are frequently required, either to join on fresh Bobbins to the pattern at certain places, or to secure one part of the lace to another. Sewings are called Plain Rope and Return Rope, and in Lace instructions, the word "Sew" is generally given as an abbreviation.

To make a *Plain Sewing*: Stick a pin into the pinhole above the one where the Sewing is to be made, to keep the work firm. Insert a crochet hook into the vacant pinhole, and under the twisted strand of the lace, draw one of the working threads through in a loop, pass the second working Bobbin through this loop, tail foremost, and pull the loop down. Take out the pin put in to secure the lace, and put it into the pinhole, and continue the work. Sewing with a Needle Pin: This is done where there are a long series of Sewings to be made, and when the securing pin of the lace upon the cushion is likely to interfere with their making. Stick a securing pin into the hole below the pinhole to be sewn to, so that there will be a vacant hole, lay one of the working threads across this space, and hold the Bobbin in the left hand. Insert the Needle Pin into the lowest strand, and insinuate the thread underneath it, which is done by holding the thread tightly down with the forefinger. Directly it is held, slacken the thread, bring the Needle Pin over, keep the thread under the point, then give a little sharp flick, and the thread will come through in a loop; draw this loop farther through, and hold it with the Needle Pin, and put the next Bobbin through it. Take out the securing pin, put it into the pinhole, and continue the lace.

Return Rope.—The same as Rope Sewing.

Rope Sewing.—To make: Lift all the Bobbins but one pair; pass this pair round the others. Sew to the next hole, pass the pair round again, sew to the next hole from the last Sewing, and continue until the spot is reached for the work to re-commence.

Sewing Cotton.—Cotton thread, which may be had on reels of 25 to 1000 yards in measure. The latter are much in requisition. The better class are known as "six cords," of which there is a large variety of makes, glazed and unglazed, the most saleable lengths running from 200 to 300 and 400 yards. Reel as well as Ball Sewing Cotton can be had in every variety of colour, and the ingrain marking cotton in red and blue.

Sewing Machines.—Appliances by which needlework may be executed more rapidly, and with greater regularity than by hand. The first invented and introduced into England was that by Elias Howe, a mechanic, of Massachusetts, in 1841. It was then employed for staymaking only; the needle imitated the action of the hand, and passed entirely through the material. The second kind of machine was of French invention, and made a Chain Stitch. Amongst those of the greatest repute, besides that invented by Howe, the following should be named—viz., Wheeler and Wilson's Silent Automatic Tension Machine, Wilcox and Gibbs' Automatic Machine, Grover and Baker's, Singer's, Thomas's, the Florence, and the Wanzer. There are several varieties of these Machines, including those producing Lock Stitch or Chain Stitch, and those respectively worked by hand or by treadle, and by one or both feet. The hand-worked Machine is naturally more portable than that which has a treadle. Amongst the latest improvements in Sewing Machines, that distinguished as the "Vertical Feed" should be named, which will sew elastic materials of many thicknesses, which needs no basting, and which will not pucker one side of the material sewn. Another is the White Sewing Machine, which does not need an ordinary needle, and has a self-setting description of needle, and self-threading shuttle of its own.

Sewing Silks.—Of silk thread employed for plain or Fancy Needlework there are three classes—viz., that for Plain Sewing, that for Knitting, and the third for Embroidery. Amongst those used for Plain Sewing there are the following: The China Silk, which is very fine, and of a pure white, and is much used by glove-makers; a coarser kind, of two or three-cord twist, employed in staymaking. The Light Dyes, or coloured Sewing Silks, may be had in all shades, and fine in quality, and are sold in skeins of from fifty to eighty in the ounce, and also on small reels; those sold in skeins are the cheapest. Machine Silks are sold by the gross, and by their weight on reels, the latter containing from 30 to 200 yards. These are to be had both in black and in colours. Floss Silk, or Soie Platte, is to be had in raven-black, China, and all colours; it is sold twisted into hanks, and used for darning silk stockings. Filoselle, otherwise called Spun Silk, or Bourre de Soie, is the portion of ravelled silk thrown aside in the filature of the cocoons, which is carded and spun like cotton. This is employed both for Plain Sewing, in the darning of stockings and silk vests, and likewise for Embroidery. Tailors' Twist, a coarse silk thread, of which a number together are wound on reels, each bearing two ounces, the numbers running from 1 to 8; also to be had in small reels containing a single thread of 12 yards. They are in many shades of colour. For Knitting there are many varieties, amongst which is the Ice Silk, which may be had of both two and four-fold strands, and is produced in very beautiful shades of several colours. Crochet Silk, or Soie Mi-serré, which is only half tightened in the twisting, as its name denotes. It is flexible, glossy, and peculiarly suited to Crochet work. Purse, or Netting Twist, which may be had of various sizes and qualities, and designed especially for purse-making, although likewise employed for the purposes of Embroidery. The principal kinds of Silk employed for Fancy Work and Embroidery are the white Dacca Silk, or Soie Ovale, and Mitorse Silk. The former is sold in large skeins, varying in degrees of fineness, and employed in flat Embroideries, and likewise in some kinds of Raised Work. It is also used in working on fine canvas, and can be had in a variety of colours. It will bear sub-division of the strands when too coarse for the work required, and is

sold done up into knotted skeins. The latter, Mitorse Silk, which is only half twisted, somewhat resembles Floss Silk, but is of a superior quality, and is more suitable for purposes of Embroidery. Also what is called Three Cord, is closely twisted silk, resembling Bullion, and likewise used for Embroidery. Sewing Silks are sold on cards, reels, and skeins, singly, or by the ounce; that for machine use on larger reels than the other kinds, and in longer lengths.

Shadow Stitch.—*See* HALF STITCH.

Shalloons.—A loosely woven worsted stuff, thin, short-napped, and twilled, used by tailors for coat linings, and also for dresses. It is woven from Lincolnshire and Yorkshire Long Staple Wool, of the finest qualities, twilled on both sides, and mostly dyed red. It is the staple manufacture of Halifax, whence upwards of 10,000 pieces are annually exported to Turkey and the Levant. It is made in various colours, and the width varies from 32 inches to 36 inches. This stuff was originally manufactured at Châlons, whence the name is derived. There is a very fine variety called "Cubica."

In blue *Shalloon* shall Hannibal be clad.—DEAN SWIFT.

Shantung Pongee Silk.—This is a soft, undyed, and undressed Chinese washing silk, and much resembles the Indian goods of the same character, but is somewhat duller in colour. The various qualities are uniformly of 19 inches in width, and differ respectively in price very considerably for the piece of 20 yards. Shantung is the name of the province in which the silk is manufactured. It is much employed in this country as a dress material.

Shap-faced.—A term employed to denote that the plush or velvet cloth is faced with the short ends of waste silk, the back of the material being of cotton.

Sharps.—A description of needles in common use among sempstresses for ordinary Plain Sewing. *See* NEEDLES.

Shawl Materials.—These are a mixture of silk and wool, the silk being thrown to the top; the patterns are copied from the Oriental damassé designs. These materials are employed for the partial making and trimming of dresses, and measure from 23 inches to 24 inches in width, the prices varying very considerably. Real shawls made of goat's hair, thick and warm in make and quality, are also sold for cutting up into dresses and mantles.

Sheep's Wool.—The peculiar substance called wool is, in a great degree, the product of cultivation. It is produced, not only on sheep, but on the Llama, and the Thibet and Angora goat. The coat produced on all other animals can only be described either as fur or hair. All the varieties of the sheep owe their origin to the Argali, which has a coat of wool next to the skin, supplemented by a longer growth of hair. In the States of Barbary, the South of Italy, Sicily, and Portugal, the wool of a once remarkably fine wool-bearing breed of sheep has greatly deteriorated through neglect. In Spain it was produced in high perfection when the product was carefully cultivated. Sheep's wool takes a year in completing its full growth, after which the animal changes its coat, which, if not sheared, will fall off *en masse*, leaving a short crop of the new soft wool in its place. That which is shorn from the living animal is called "Fleece," and that which is pulled off by the fellmonger after death is called "Pelt," which is very inferior to the former, and will not take a good dye, being harsher and weaker, and is generally too short to be worked without an admixture of longer wools. It is also known as "Skin Wool," and is commonly used for flannels, serges, and such kinds of stuff as need little, if any, milling. The manufacturers classify sheep's wool into two kinds—the long, or "combing" wool, and the short, or "clothing" wool. The former varies in length from 3 to 8 or 10 inches; the latter from 3 to 4 inches. Of this clothing wool all cloth is made, its shortness rendering it fit for carding (effected with a comb of fine short teeth) and spinning into yarn, and for the subsequent felting. The long, or "combing" wool, is prepared on a comb with long steel teeth; it is combed out straight, opening the fibres like flax, either by hand or machinery. This is made into crape, poplin, bombazines, carpets, and the finer sorts of worsted goods. These two classes of wool are likewise described as the long, or short "stapled" wool, and by this term the separate locks into which the wool is naturally divided are designated, each of which comprises a certain number of fibres or curly hairs. The longer kinds of the fleece (or superior) wool are employed for hosiery yarns, or for hand-yarn for the warps of serges, and other cloths, which have a warp of "combed" and a woof of "carded" wool. In the fleece of a single English sheep there are some eight or ten varieties in degrees of fineness, known respectively by different names, and applicable for the manufacture of various textiles. Thus the wool is sorted with much care. Its softness is of equal importance to its fineness, and in this silky characteristic that of the English sheep is inferior to the Indian, or to the Peruvian and Chilian Llama. No Merino sheep, however fine, yields so soft a wool as the Indian, of which Cashmeres are made. Not only the breed of the sheep, but the district in which they are reared, influences the quality. The counties of Leicestershire and Lincolnshire, and the districts of Teeswater and Dartmoor, produce a greater length of "combing" wool than elsewhere, the staple being sometimes a foot in length. Dorsetshire, Herefordshire, and the South Downs produce our short-stapled variety, and those grown on the Cheviot Hills give a wool of considerable softness, though not otherwise of the first quality.

Sheep's wool in its natural state is of a white, grey, or brownish-black colour. Of the latter coarse cloths are made, undyed. The white is selected for dyeing in bright colours. The soft wool of lambs is extensively employed in the manufacture of hats, on account of its felting quality. That of dead lambs, having less of the felting properties, is used for hosiery and soft flannels, and is called "skin-lambswool." The lambs of certain breeds of sheep, natives of the North of Europe, have such fine skins that they are dressed as furs, are very costly, and held in much esteem as articles of wear, or for trimmings of outdoor apparel, by wealthy Russians and others.

Our Australian wools are very fine, the Spanish Merino sheep having been imported there. The staple is long and the quality soft, and it is excellent for combing and spinning. The Shetland Islands also produce a breed of sheep bearing remarkably fine and delicate wool. (See SHETLAND WOOL.) Saxon wool, much employed in this country, is of a very superior quality, and is produced by the Spanish Merino breed, introduced by the late King of Saxony. This Spanish variety of wool is considered the finest in Europe, and is of remote Eastern origin, introduced into Italy, and thence, by the Romans, into Spain. Comparatively little of this wool is now employed in England, the Australian and Saxon sufficiently supplementing our own breeds. *See* WOOLLEN CLOTHS.

Sheetings.—Stout cloths made of different widths for bed linen—both plain and twilled, bleached and unbleached—and constituting one of those manufactures classified under the name "Piece Goods." They are made in Wigans, Croydons, and double warps, from 2 to 3 yards wide. Those of linen are named Scotch and Barnsley bleached, loom Dowlas, and loom Scotch, the widths of which are known distinctively by the number of inches they measure. Also the Irish, union Irish, which is mixed with cotton; Lancashire linen, union Lancashire, Russia, and imitation Russia. The respective widths of these run from $\frac{7}{8}$ths to $1\frac{1}{4}$ths. The strongest coarse Sheeting is the Russia, which may be had of various widths, from an ell to $2\frac{1}{2}$ yards. Bolton Sheeting, otherwise called Workhouse Sheeting, is of calico, and is sold in pairs of sheets. They should each measure from $2\frac{1}{4}$ yards to 3 yards for ordinary beds. The width for a single bed is about 66 inches, that for a double one from 78 inches to 3 yards.

Shell Couching.—*See* COUCHING.

Shetland Point Lace.—A work known in Italy as Trina de Lana, where it is used much more than in England. It is a Needle-made Lace, composed of Shetland wool instead of fine Lace cotton, and therefore of sufficiently coarse texture to form babies' shawls, quilts, or scarves, and other objects that require to be both light and warm yet ornamental. The Lace is made either with white or black Shetland wool, from designs selected from old Flat Needle-made Points, which are enlarged, and then worked out by being formed of some of the simplest of the many Point Lace stitches. The cordonnet of the Buttonholed outline of flat Points is replaced by a line of Chain Stitch, which serves as a stay to the stitches that fill in the design. To work as shown in Fig. 727: Enlarge the design to twice its size, then trace out outlines of the parts that are to be filled in upon blue wrapping paper, from which remove any stiffness by crumpling it up and smoothing it out flat. Take the Shetland wool, thread a darning needle with it, and surround the pattern with a line of CHAIN STITCH. Let this Chain Stitch be quite distinct from the blue paper, and perfectly connected stitch to stitch. Then connect these lines of stitches together for the ground of the Lace by filling in the open spaces between the design with CORDED BARS, which occasionally vary with WHEELS. Fill in the design with lines of plain BUTTONHOLES, or with POINT DE BRUXELLES, LATTICE, or POINT DE GRECQUE. Form the FOOTING of the Lace with a line of Chain Stitch, the outer edge with the same Chain Stitch line, and enrich with POINT DE VENISE edging and Wheels, ornamented with PICOTS. Shetland

Point Lace looks particularly well when worked over a baby's shawl and edged with the pattern shown in Fig. 727; the design for the centre of the shawl should be detached sprigs, joined by Corded Bars.

Shetland Wool.—As sold in the shops, this is a yarn much employed for the knitting of shawls, and the weaving of stockings of the finest quality. The yarn is exceedingly soft, and has only two threads. It is to be had in oleander (a new pink), white, black, slate, brown, azurine, scarlet, violet, buff, coral, purple, partridge, gas blues and greens, and ingrain, and is sold by the pound or ounce. Wool of this kind is not produced in England proper. It is thicker than Pyrenean wool, and softer than both it and the Andalusian, not being so tightly twisted. It is employed for the knitting of shawls, hoods, jackets, and shoes for infants. The sheep producing it are of small size, and run

piece of narrow cardboard, and put it into a little bag, which pin down to the Pillow out of the way of the Bobbins. To avoid constant shifting when working very narrow lace, prick two pieces of PASSEMENT at the same time with the same design, and fasten them on to the Pillow so that no break intervenes, or prick as long a pattern as the Pillow will allow, taking care that the ends will correspond, and allow of the design being continued.

Ship Ladder Stitch.—See *Ladder Stitch*, EMBROIDERY STITCHES.

Shirred.—A word employed by Americans, derived by them from the old German *Schirren*, and employed to signify an irregular GAUGING. Shirrings are close Runnings, or cords, inserted between two pieces of cloth, as the lines of indiarubber in Shirred Braces or Garters, or the drawing and puckering up any material. See French

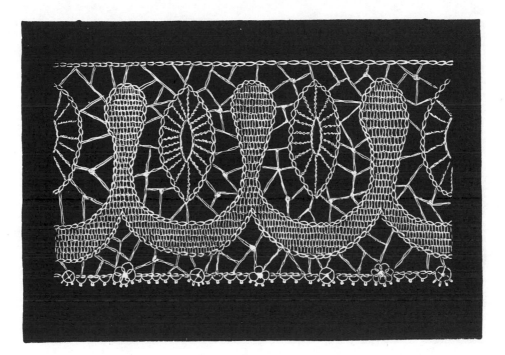

FIG. 727. SHETLAND POINT LACE.

wild all the year over the hills until—the ground being covered with snow—they descend to the seashore and feed on weed. The staple of these sheep is longer than that of the Merino, and their skins are much employed as Furs. The breed goes by the name of Beaver Sheep, and the wool produced is of various colours—viz., black, brown, grey, and white.

Shifting Pillow Lace.—The pattern upon which Pillow Lace is worked rarely exceeds a few inches in length; therefore, when working a lace edging or insertion, the lace, while in progress, has constantly to be taken off the pillow and re-adjusted on to the pattern. To shift: Work the lace to the edge of the pattern, take up all the pins, but leave those in the last part of the work still sticking into the lace, and then stick these into the top part of the pattern, so that the working can be continued at the proper place. Roll up the finished lace on to a

term *Coulissé*; also Reeve, borrowed from the nautical term to "Reef" a sail, to gather up in small folds.

Shirt.—A man's linen or calico under-garment, the name having reference to its being of a "short" length. It was worn in Saxon times by both sexes, of the same form, and by the same name. Under the Normans, the nobility wore them embroidered. In the fourteenth century, Silk Shirts were worn by some, and also those of fine Holland and Cambric. Shirts decorated with either embroidery or gold, silver, or silk, were prohibited by a Sumptuary Law, in the reign of Henry VIII., to all persons under the rank of knighthood. Mr. David Anderson, damask manufacturer, of Deanside Brae, made a shirt entirely in the loom, without any kind of needlework, and sent it to Dr. Cupar, as a specimen for the Hunterian Museum, Glasgow. The neck, wristbands, and shoulder-straps were of double cloth, and neatly stitched; the buttonholes properly worked with the appropriate stitch, the buttons sewn on, the gussets inserted, and a ruffle added. On the breast the Glasgow arms were woven, and the motto, " Let Glasgow flourish," beneath which were the words: " Woven and presented by David Anderson." See *Shirt*, under CUTTING OUT.

Shirtings.—These are otherwise called Fancy Cotton Shirtings, and consist of cotton cloths manufactured after the same manner as Ginghams, only that they bear somewhat of a resemblance to flannel in the looseness and fluffiness of the threads. Shirtings are classified in the trade as one of those manufactures denominated " Piece Goods," and are made in pieces of 36 yards in length, and from 36 inches to 45 inches in width. Pretty and serviceable dresses are sometimes made of the same description of cotton cloth, which has been sized and glazed. They may be had in stripes and fancy designs in various colours,

mantles of Queen Elizabeth is described by Paul Heutzner (1602) as being of " bluish silk, Shot with silver threads." In the present day, there are not only Shot Silk Stuffs but Shot Alpacas, and mixtures of two different materials employed for women's gowns. Shakespeare alludes to this description of weaving in a Silk Stuff:

The tailor make thy doublet of changeable Taffeta, for thy mind is a very opal.—*Twelfth Night.*

Shuttle.—An appliance made of wood, used in the process of weaving for shooting the thread of the woof, which is wound upon it, between the threads of the warp. Also *see* TATTING.

Sicilian Embroidery.—An effective and easy work, formed with muslin, thin cambric, and braid, and used for trimmings to washing dresses, or for teacloths and ornamental linen. The work is sometimes called Spanish

FIG. 728. SICILIAN EMBROIDERY.

chiefly in pink, blue, and violet. Women's cuffs and collars are made largely in these Shirting Cloths. There are also ZEPHYR SHIRTINGS.

Shoddy.—Cloth made either of the flue and fluff thrown off from other woollen stuffs in the process of weaving, mixed with long hair from new wool; or else of old garments torn into fibres, or cut up into small pieces, and re-spun. It differs from what is known as " Mungo " in being of an inferior quality, and producing a coarse kind of cloth.

Shot Stuffs.—Textiles of various materials, made to change in colour according to the different positions in which they are viewed, and therefore of the lights and shades upon them. This is effected by a particular method adopted in the weaving, and the intermixture of a weft and warp respectively of different colours. In the sixteenth century they were called " Chaungeantries," and were mixtures of silk, "sailtrie," or linen yarn. One of the

Embroidery, and is intended to imitate Embroidery upon muslin; but as no stitches, with the exception of Buttonhole, are worked, it is much more quickly formed than true Embroidery. It consists in tracing out a modern Point Lace design, and Tacking muslin, and then thin cambric, over the design, the outlines of which are marked out with a thick braid, known as Spanish Braid. Both the materials are retained in those parts of the work that are intended as the pattern parts, but the cambric is cut away beyond the braid from the ground, and only the muslin left, while the raw edges of the cambric are concealed by the braid being sewn down to the muslin foundation. Wheels, Eyeletholes, and Ladder Stitch are worked when open spaces lighten the design, and then both materials are cut from underneath these stitches, and the raw edges Buttonholed round, while the edge of the pattern is formed with scalloped or straight lines of Buttonhole. To work as shown in Fig. 728: This pattern is reduced in size, and can be made larger if required. Two widths of braid are used in it, either white or écru-coloured, and muslin and cambric matching the braids in tint. Trace out the design upon stiff paper, and fill in the parts forming the pattern with black ink, so that they may be visible through the materials that cover them, or TACK down the muslin and cambric upon brown paper, and trace the design upon the cambric when it is secured. Take the narrower braid, and sew it along the top of the pattern, to form the FOOTING. Stitch it down securely upon both sides, then Tack the wider braid on to the design with a tacking thread, and when in position OVERCAST it to the material upon the side where both cambric and muslin are to be retained. Cut the round holes for the WHEELS, and make them, drawing the Braid round the circle thus formed, and cut away both materials and make the LADDER STITCH where indicated; BUTTONHOLE the edge of the materials over in those places. Cut away the cambric underneath the other edge of the broad braid, and Overcast the braid to the muslin. The edge of the pattern is made with both materials; Buttonhole in small scallops round the extreme edge, and ornament this place with PICOTS; then form the wide scallops with a line of Buttonhole, turn its outer edge to the interior of the design, and cut the cambric away beyond these scallops, leaving only the muslin.

Sicilienne.—A description of fine Poplin, made of silk and wool, and especially employed for the making of mantles. It may be had from 24 inches to 56 inches in width.

Sienna Point.—One of the names by which DARNED NETTING is known in Italy.

Silesia.—A fine brown Holland, originally made in the German province of Silesia, and now produced in England. For roller window blinds it is glazed, and may be had in various widths, from 28 inches to 90 inches.

Silk.—The fine, glossy, soft thread spun by the *Bombyx mori*, or silkworm, so as to form a pale yellow or amber-coloured receptacle, called a cocoon, within which the caterpillar, in its chrysalis form, lies during its transformation into a butterfly. It is the strongest and most durable, as well as the most beautiful, of all fibres for the manufacture of textiles. Our chief supplies are derived from China, India, Italy, and the Levant. An attempt has likewise been made to produce silk in Australia, and, so far as it has been procured, it is of a rich and superior kind; the breed of silkworms discovered of late years in Switzerland has been imported to that colony, as it is free from the disease so long contributing to deteriorate the cocoons. The use of raw silk for spinning and weaving dates back —so far as records of the Chinese Empire exist to demonstrate—to some 2700 years before Christ, when the Empress See-ling-Shee herself unravelled the fibres of the cocoons, and was the first to weave it into a web. The derivation of silk from the cocoons of the silkworm, and the manner in which the material was produced, remained a secret with the Chinese until the time of Justinian, A.D. 555, and it was at this time that the two Persian monks—who were

Christian missionaries—became acquainted with the use of the silkworms, learned the art of working the fibres into textiles, and, at the desire of the Emperor, contrived to secrete some of the eggs of the caterpillars in a hollow cane, and brought them to Constantinople in safety. It is to these two missionaries that we are indebted for the introduction into Europe of all the various breeds of the insect, which, in course of time, became naturalised in various parts of the Continent. Alexander the Great was the first to introduce both the silk and a knowledge of its use, in the West. For 200 years after the age of Pliny, the employment of silk stuffs as dress materials was confined to women.

Silk Boot Laces.—These laces are to be had both flat and round. The former kind are produced in lengths respectively of 6-4 and 8-4, and are sold in boxes containing one gross each. The latter, otherwise called "Aiguilette," are round, are not twisted, but woven, and have tags. These are also sold in boxes of one gross each, the lengths being the same as those of the flat kind.

Silk Braid.—This Braid is also called Russia Silk Braid. It is employed for purposes of Embroidery, and is used for men's smoking caps, slippers, &c. It can be had in very bright colours, and consists of two cords woven together; it is sold in skeins, six to the gross. Each skein should measure 24 yards in length, but they are rarely found to contain more than 16 or 18 yards.

Silk Canvas, or Berlin.—This description of canvas is of a very even and delicate make, and is especially designed to obviate the necessity of grounding designs in Embroidery; the silks usually employed for its manufacture are Chenille and Floss. It is to be had in most colours, the white, black, claret, and primrose being most in vogue. Different qualities are sold. It is made in widths varying from ½ inch to 1½ yards. The threads are formed of fine silk wound round a cotton fibre. *See* CANVAS.

Silk Cotton.—The silken fibres enveloping the seeds of a tree of the genus *Bombax*, which is a native of Asia, Africa, and America. These fibres are smooth and elastic, but too short to be eligible for spinning, and are especially employed for the stuffing of cushions. Silk Cotton is imported into this country from the East Indies, under the name of "Mockmain." The Silk Cotton is enclosed within the capsules containing the seed, which is embedded in it.

Silk Damask.—A silk woven stuff manufactured after the peculiar method originated at Damascus, whence the name. The Flemings introduced the art of producing designs of every description in the process of weaving the cloth into this country in the sixteenth century. At that time Silk Damask was very costly, and dresses made of it were only worn upon State occasions by women of high position; it is now superseded as a dress material by what is called Broché Silk, having a design thrown upon the face in satin. As a material for purposes of upholstery, hangings, curtains, furniture coverings, &c., Silk Damask is as much employed as ever. It is very thick and rich in appearance, and is the costliest of all stuffs used for these purposes. It can be had in every description of colour and shade of the same. The chief seat of the industry is at Lyons, where it is produced by means of the " Jacquard Loom."

Silk Dress Laces.—These consist of narrow silk braids, dyed in various colours, and chiefly employed for evening dresses. They are made in lengths of 5-4 and 6-4, and may be purchased singly or by the gross.

Silk Embroidery.—*See* EMBROIDERY.

Silk Embroidery on Net.—Worked with écru net, coloured silks, and gold or silver cord. To work: Select a flower design écru lace. BUTTONHOLE round the outlines with coloured silks, and COUCH a line of gold cord inside the Buttonholes. Fill in the pattern with POINT DE BRUXELLES and other POINT LACE stitches, worked in coloured silks.

Silk Imperial Braid.—A very narrow woven fancy Braid, having a kind of Pearl edge. It is made in all varieties of colour, and also of mixed colours, such as green and gold. It is sold by the skein, and is employed for purposes of Embroidery.

Silk Longcloth.—A fine twilled material, manufactured for the underclothing of both men and women.

Silk Mantle Cords.—These Cords may be had in various colours and sizes, are heavy made in quality, and very much in use. The numbers are 1, 1½, 2, 2½, 3, and 4; 1, 2, and 3, are the numbers chiefly in request. There are four pieces to the gross, of 36 yards each.

Silk Sealskin.—This is a very beautiful patent textile, composed of Tussar Silk, made in imitation of Sealskin Fur, and designed for mantles, jackets, hats, waistcoats, and trimmings, and sold at one-fourth the price of the real fur. It measures 52 inches in width, and is a costly material dyed brown or golden colour. In making it up, the nap should be turned so as to lie upwards, to produce the lights and shades upon it, after the manner in which the real skin of the seal is always worn.

Silk Serge.—A stout twilled silk textile, of fine make, and employed for the lining of men's coats. It is to be had in various colours, as well as in black. The ordinary width of this material measures 24 inches.

Silk Spray Embroidery.—A variety of Embroidery with Satin Stitch, and one that is used to ornament dress trimmings with, as it is capable of being transferred from one background to another. The work consists in embroidering, upon fine lawn or holland, a spray of flowers, in silk or filoselle, in their natural tints, cutting away the holland round the spray, and arranging that upon net, silk, or velvet, as it is required. To work: Trace upon holland or lawn sprays of flowers from designs intended for Embroidery, with SATIN STITCH, and frame in an EMBROIDERY FRAME. Work the leaves of the design in Satin Stitch, from the centre vein of the leaf to the edge, and use a light and dark green on the two sides; work the centre vein of the leaf in a darker shade of green to that used in the other part, and surround the leaf with an outline worked in BUTTONHOLE STITCH, to raise it slightly above the Satin Stitch centre. Work the Buttonholes as short stitches, and not too close together; make all the leaves thus, only varying the shades of green used in them. For the flowers, slightly pad them with wool,

and then work them in long Satin Stitches from their centre to their edge with Floss silk, in shades of colour matching the natural hue of the flowers. Surround the flowers, like the leaves, with a Buttonhole Edge, and fill in their centres with FRENCH KNOTS. Work the stalks that connect the flowers and leaves together with double rows of CHAIN STITCH. Before removing the work from the Frame, make some strong starch, and spread it over the back, and when that is dry, cut out the sprays from the holland, carefully cutting round the Buttonhole edgings of leaves and flowers. TACK, with fine stitches, these sprays on to the material they are intended to ornament. The sprays are also worked with crewels instead of silks, or with crewels mixed with filoselles, and when this is done the Embroidery is formed of large bold flowers, such as sunflowers, pæonies, and carnations, and is used for curtain and table borders, or to scatter over a quilt.

Silk Stuffs.—Silk yarn is woven into a great variety of textiles in England and elsewhere, which may be referred to under their respective headings; as well as in thread more or less twisted, for the purpose of sewing and of embroidery. Prior to the sixth century, all silk stuffs were brought to Europe from Bokhara by the former inhabitants of those parts—the "Seres"—from which its Latin name, *serica*, was derived. The variety of textiles made of the fibres of the silkworms' cocoons is very extensive, and varies with the several countries in which they are produced, whether India, China, Japan, Turkey, Great Britain, France, or Italy, in each of which nationalities the varieties are also many and beautiful. Some are dyed in ingrain colours, so that they may be washed with impunity. Some are watered, others brocaded, woven with a pile, forming either velvet or plush, or produced with a combination of velvet and plain silk, or velvet and satin. There are Watered Silks, Moirés, Satins, Satinettes, Satin Turks, Taffetas, Gauzes, Persians, Stockingette Silks; Poplins, which are combined with wool; and corded Silk Cloths, unmixed with any other substance—as the Paris Cords. Besides these, there are ribbons of every variety and quality, and Silk Canvas for purposes of Embroidery. In the Middle Ages, the manufacture of Silk Stuffs made great progress in Europe. The trade spread from Italy to France and Spain, where it was introduced at an early period by the Moors; and we read that some Silk Textiles were purchased for our Henry II. The manufacture of these stuffs in England dates from the time of the immigration of the French refugees, at the revocation of the Edict of Nantes, when a manufactory was established at Spitalfields; and the introduction of the throwing machine, by Sir Thomas Lombe, completely established the industry in this country. The first silk manufactory at Derby was opened by him in the year 1717; but silk stockings were first produced in England in the time of Queen Elizabeth, for whose use they were specially made.

In the selection of a black silk, it should be tested by holding it up to the light, and looking through it, so that the evenness of the rib may be seen. It should then be crushed together in the hand, and suddenly released, when it should spring out as quickly, leaving no crease. This spring is called the *verve*, of which poor silk stuffs have little or none; and those adulterated with jute are also deficient in this characteristic. Pure silk does not stiffen when wetted, and the black dye should have a slight tinge of green when the light is seen through it. Stiff silks do not wear well, as they cannot be pure; the softer the texture, the purer the silk, Another mode of testing the quality is to ravel out the weft.

Silk Tassels.—These may be had in several varieties, both of quality, make, colour, and size. Some are of Chenille, others of twisted silk, the upper portion, where the several strands are confined together, being made on a foundation of wood turned for the purpose, round which the silk is wound. There are also loosely made Tassels attached to a heading of knotted silk, or band of gimp, and Silk Tassels made for purses, some of purse, others of plain sewing silks. *See* TASSELS.

Silk Warp.—A mixed material of silk and wool combined. It is exceedingly fine and delicate in texture, has a grey ground, rayed with scarlet or black stripes, of either two or three threads in width, and is manufactured in widths of 32 inches. Silk Warp is made for shirting of a superior description, for use in hot climates.

Silk-woven Elastic Cloth. — *See* STOCKINGETTE CLOTH and ELASTIC CLOTH.

Silver Lace.—*See* GOLD LACE.

Single Crochet.—*See* CROCHET.

Single Diamonds.—*See* MACRAMÉ.

Skein.—A term signifying a length of any kind of yarn, whether of silk, wool, linen, thread, or cotton, wound off a hank, doubled and knotted. Skeins weigh either an ounce or half an ounce, with the exception of sewing silk and Berlin lambswool, which are lighter. Braid may also be purchased made up in skeins.

Skirt.—A term signifying the lower part of a gown, from the waist downwards. Skirts may be worn double, a short "over-skirt" reaching half-way over the long one beneath it.

Skirt Braids.—These are made of Alpaca and Mohair, and are cut into lengths of sufficient quantity for a dress, and tied up for sale in knots. The numbers so cut are 29, 41, and 53, in the "super" and "extra" heavy sorts. The lengths vary from 4 to 5 yards, but gross pieces may also be procured.

Skirting.—Strong thick woollen, worsted, cotton, or mixed fabrics, woven of certain dimensions, so as to be suitable in length and width for women's underskirts, and to preclude the necessity of making gores and seams. Amongst the several varieties there are Felt Skirtings in dark grey and heather, 72 inches in width. Prairie Skirting is a comparatively new material, as is also Striped Skirting, made of silk and wool combined, with cross-over stripes, and in wide widths. Besides these, other varieties might be enumerated, the number of which is always augmenting with each successive season.

Skirt Linings.—These are of various materials, selected to suit the dress for which they are designed. Instead of following the usual plan adopted in reference to the lining of a bodice, cut out the skirt first, and TACK it upon the lining. For black velveteen, Silesia, striped or checked, is the best suited; for a pale-coloured silk, the Silesia should be of plain white; for dark stuffs and quilted petticoats figured Silesias are preferable. In this case, make a facing of alpaca to cover the lining at the lower part of the skirt, of half a foot or rather more in depth. Owing to a spring, as well as the stiffness in alpaca, it is to be recommended for use in the same way round the extreme edge of long dresses and trains, 10 inches in depth, more especially, because the dress is less likely to roll the wrong side upwards when the wearer turns round; besides that, a light-coloured lining becomes so quickly soiled when sweeping the ground. The lining of a heavy poplin or woollen dress should be restricted to a mere facing of about 10 or 12 inches in depth. When there are trimmings or flounces, extend the lining upwards as high as the top of the trimming, but so that all the stitches shall be concealed underneath them. If the skirt be gored, cut the lining to fit the gores exactly, as otherwise the skirt will set stiffly over the triangular plaits that will have to be made. As a rule, alpaca and Silesia are the principal materials in use for Skirt Linings, more especially the former. When the breadths of a dress have been cut out, pin the raw sides of each flatly together at the bottom, and fold the skirt in half on a table, so as to expose half of the front and half of the back breadth, the hem being towards you. Then lay the lining muslin, with one selvedge, up the folded edge of the skirt front, the torn part of the muslin being at the hem, and slope off the right-hand corner of the muslin even with the dress. Measure the depth of the facing, placing pins at the upper part to mark it; and cut off by them. Next lay the piece so cut on the top of the remainder of the muslin, in exactly the same position, and it will be found that the hollowed-out upper part of the first gives very nearly the proper curve for the lower part of the second. The two pieces, when joined by the selvedges in front, will extend nearly half round the skirt. The rest is taken, piece by piece, in the same way; the selvedges are always joined together although they lie very slantingly after the first, where the skirt front was straight. When the middle of the back width is reached, allow about 1 inch for joinings, and cut off what is not wanted in a line with the folded skirt, so that the centre join there will set upright, like the front. But, owing to the increase of slope as the muslin nears the back, the join will neither be exactly on the straight nor on the cross of the muslin. If alpaca be used, the joins must be opened and pressed flat before the lining is sewn into the skirt. The material employed for mourning called Paramatta should have a lining of black mull muslin.

Skunk Fur.—The skunk (*Mephitis Americana*), an animal allied to the polecat, is a native of British America, and its fur, which is exported by the Hudson's Bay Company, is of a dark brown colour, rather long in the hair, and rough, with two yellowish white stripes running from the head to the tail. Skunk fur is warm and handsome; but the strong and disagreeable odour attached to it forms the great obstacle to its general adoption as an article of dress; those who wear it should expose it as much as possible to the outer air.

Slanting Gobelin.—*See* BERLIN WORK.

Slanting Hole Braid.—*See* Braids.

Slanting Stitch.—*See* Crochet.

Slashes, or Panes.—A term used by tailors and dressmakers to signify a vertical cutting in any article of dress, intended to expose to view some other garment worn beneath it, of a contrasting colour. Sometimes the latter is only an artificially produced effect, pieces of stuff of a different material being sewn under the Slashings. Sir Walter Scott speaks of "a gray jerkin, with scarlet cuffs and slashed sleeves." These Slashes are otherwise called "Panes." Coryat, author of *Crudities*, writing in the year 1611, observes: "The Switzers wear no coates, but Doublets, and hose of Panes, intermingled with red and yellow, and some with blew, trimmed with long puffes to yellow and blew Sarcenet rising up between the Panes."

Sleeves.—The portion of any garment which covers the arms, in whole or in part. In Sleeves, as in shoes, boots, and head-dresses, the most ridiculous freaks of fashion have been exhibited. We read that William the Conqueror brought over extravagant styles in dress, as exemplified more especially in the Sleeves of the dresses, which increased to absurdity in the reign of William Rufus. They were then widened at the wrists, and hung down beyond the hands, as far as to the knees, like those of the Chinese. These were succeeded, under the Plantagenets, by some of more natural proportions; but "Bag Sleeves," large and ungainly, were introduced under Henry VI., and Slashed and Laced ones followed these. In the reign of Henry VII. they were separate articles of dress, worn as ornaments, by the knights and others, and could be put on and taken off at pleasure. They were of enormous dimensions, opening almost up to the shoulder on the inside, and cut and embroidered, in deep tongue-like scallops, of nearly a foot in length. The fact that Sleeves were often separate from the rest of the dress, explains the facility afforded for the giving and receiving of a Sleeve, as a love token between a Knight and his Mistress, which was worn thenceforth in his helmet. Puffed and Tied Sleeves, called the "Virago Sleeve," and those tight in the arm, and increasing in width to the shoulder, there rising high above it, were in vogue in *temp.* Queen Elizabeth, and afterwards of James I. and of Charles II. Under Cromwell, large turned-up square cuffs to close straightly-cut Sleeves were universal. Within our own times, the varieties worn have been considerable, including those filled out at the top of the arm with wadded circular cushions; and the *Jigôt*. They are nowadays sometimes so short as to extend only 2 inches or 3 inches in depth, from the junction with them of the bodice armhole; others are long, and confined to the wrist with a band. There are some that are opened as far as from the inner bend of the elbow, and depend widely from the joint on the outside. Some are cut closely to fit the arm, others are puffed at the shoulder and elbows, or at the shoulder only. They are plain-cut or gauged, and trimmed according to the current fashion of the time. But whatever that fashion may be, more length must be allowed in the sleeve at the shoulder—above the arm—by 2 inches than underneath the arm; the upper or outer part of the sleeve must be cut in a convex

circular form, the inside concave, and an inch allowed everywhere for turning in the raw edges. When the sleeve is to be sewn into the armhole high up on the shoulder, make the rounding at the top large. Many of those now in fashion are cut on the bias, and, to make them thus, fold the material over to the necessary dimensions indicated by the pattern, and lay the latter with the straight part of the outside seam on the straight fold, and so cut out the sleeve. Then join the sides on the inside of the arm, and extend the outer seam from the elbow to the wrist only. Should the Sleeves be tightly-fitting, make three very small plaits at the point of the elbow, on the outer side, before regulating the cutting and adjustment of the wrist. Cut the inner (or under) part of the sleeve a little narrower from the top to just below the elbow. Stitch the sleeves all the way down the outer and inner seams. A method much adopted by dressmakers is to place the right sides of the material together, and the right sides of the lining together also, then to stitch them all at once, and turn them right side out, which is the means of concealing the stitches and raw edges. When the sleeve is to be sewn into the armhole, place the point at the extreme length of the sleeve, about 1½ inches below the shoulder seam of the bodice.

Slips.—These are plain skirts, made for the purpose of wearing under thin dress materials, such as Grenadine, Muslin, Net, and delicate Zephyrs. Sometimes they are of white, but more frequently of coloured silk, to show through the outer skirt.

Slip Stitch.—*See* Crochet, Guipure d'Art, and Knitting.

Slot.—An inelegant term, employed in the Eastern counties of England to denote a casing formed either by a double Running, or by a Hem, for the reception of a ribbon or tape, to be used as a Running-string, for drawing the article into small gathers, or to close the opening of a bag.

Small Dots.—In Needle-made Laces small dots are often made over a net-patterned ground, to enrich it, or to edge parts of the design. The Dots made in Alençon grounds are distinguished by being formed of Buttonhole centres, and surrounded by a tiny raised cord, edged with horsehair; but form ordinary dots either with rounds of Buttonhole or with Overcast, or twist the thread five times round the needle, and then pull the needle through; the twists will remain upon the work as a small raised knob.

Smock.—An old English name for shift, or chemise. The term is now obsolete in refined society, excepting in the use of quotations from old writers, by whom it was employed. The word shift, used in the sense of a woman's inner garment, has also fallen into disuse, and the French term *chemise* adopted in its place.

Smock Linen.—The linen of which our peasants' Smock Frocks are made, which is a strong, even, green linen, employed also for articles designed for embroidery.

Smyrna Rug Work.—Also known as Oriental Rug Work, or Knitting. The patterns used for this work are printed upon Point Paper, and coloured in the same manner as Berlin wool patterns; but the work is Knitting, and similar to RAG WORK. The materials required are the thick wools known as Smyrna Wools, a grooved mesh to wind the wool on and cut it, Knitting needles No. 13, Smyrna Cotton, or Netting Cotton, and a Pattern. To work: Wind wool matching the colours used in the pattern on the mesh, and cut it into pieces by running the scissors up the grooved line. Cast on from thirty to forty stitches on the needle, and KNIT the first row plain. For the second row—* Knit 1, pick up a strand of wool matching the first stitch on the pattern, and lay it across the knitting, between the first and second stitch, Knit 1, pass the end of the wool at the back of the work round the last knitted stitch, and to the front of the work, where its other half is; repeat from * to the end of the row, and repeat the first and second rows alternately to the end of the work. All the ends of wool will lie on the outside side of the Knitting, the inside will only show the loops of wool; but, as each loop answers to one stitch of the pattern, the making of the same correctly is rendered easy. The two ends of a piece of wool should be of the same length; this is managed by pulling them together. When the strip is finished, turn it flat side downwards, and, with a large pair of scissors, clip the ends even. Large pieces of work are made in strips, sewn together, and finished with border strips attached to them. Rugs, small carpets, and mats, are made with Smyrna Rug Work.

Smyrna Work, Imitation.—*See* IMITATION SMYRNA WORK.

Snowflake.—A term employed to denote a particular method of weaving woollen cloths, by which process small knots are thrown upon the face, as in Knickerbocker Cloths, which have the appearance, when white, or light in colour, of a sprinkling of snow. *See* KNICKERBOCKERS.

Socks.—These woven or knitted articles of wear belong to the class of goods called "Hosiery." They are short stockings, such as worn by men, instead of stockings. In Mediæval times they were made of Fustian; and such we find were worn by Edward IV. And it would seem, that in those early times they were employed as extras, to be worn over long stockings. Elizabeth of York (1502) was charged "For ij yerdes of white fustyan, for Queen, xiij^d." Also, "To Thomas Humberston, hosyer, for the cloth & making of vij. payre sokkes for the Queene's grace, at vj. the payere."—*Privy Purse Expenses of Elizabeth of York.*

Amongst our modern varieties of Socks, there are those of silk—including the description known as spun silk—produced in a great variety of colours besides white and black. In cotton, white unbleached, and in colours; with fancy patterns stripes, "Heather," and combinations of two colours; in Worsted, white, black, and coloured; in lambswool, white, black, and coloured; in Shetland, lambswool and yarn, mixed; in Angola and Vigonia, white, black, and coloured; in Fleecy, having a smooth face and a thick warm nap inside; in Gauze, remarkably thin, and suitable for wear under silk; made of cotton and worsted. Men's Hose are to be had in various sizes, known respectively as Boys', Youths', Men's, Slender-men's, Men's Out-size, Gouty Hose, and Fishermen's Hose. The best sorts have a double thickness of woven material at the heels and toes, and while in both knitting and weaving many varieties of

make are to be had, Socks are always knit or woven after a more elastic pattern at the top, for about 2 inches in depth, to render them more tightly-fitting round the leg. *See also* KNITTING STOCKINGS.

Soie Mi-serré.—This kind of sewing silk is also known as crochet silk, and its French name denotes that the twist is but half tightened, *mi'* being a contraction of *à moitié serré,* or "half tightened or drawn." It is a coarse kind of the silk twist known as Cordonnet, differing in the method of twisting. It is more glossy than the sorts employed for netting and for purse making, on account of the comparative looseness of its make, and is, on the same account, more suitable for Crochet work, being very soft and flexible.

Soie Platte.—The French name for floss silk. It is thicker than the Decca silk, or Soie Ovale, and is employed for all descriptions of tapestry work, for adding lustre to certain portions, such as designs of gems. It is also used in grounding embroideries on canvas. English floss silk is superior to the French, and is made in several degrees of fineness, so that it can be adapted to the canvas selected, whether coarse or fine; it may be had in any colour and shade desired.

Solomon's Bar.—*See* MACRAMÉ.

Solomon's Knot.—*See* MACRAMÉ.

Sorrento Edging.—Used in Modern Point Lace. To work: Make a BUTTONHOLE STITCH the eighth of an inch long, and secure it with a tight Buttonhole Stitch upon it. Then make another Buttonhole half the length of the first, and secure that. Continue alternately to the end of the row.

Sorrento Lace.—Used in modern Point Lace. To make: Work successive rows of SORRENTO EDGING, and make the short BUTTONHOLE STITCHES fall always above

FIG. 729. SORRENTO LACE.

the longer ones. To vary the stitch as shown in Fig. 729: First row—commence at a corner, and work from right to left, and make a loose Buttonhole Stitch. Second row—work two loose Buttonhole Stitches, then one into the braid, and fasten off. Third row—take the thread back to the left side, and draw tight, and fasten to the braid, cover with six Buttonholes. Fourth row—Work loose Buttonhole Stitches into the first loop, but not over the straight thread. Return with two Buttonhole Stitches into every loop. Repeat from the third row.

Another way, and as shown in Fig. 730: Commence at the point of the lace, and take a single thread across from right to left. Second row—work one BUTTONHOLE STITCH over the straight thread, and fasten to the braid. Third row—twist the needle in and out every loop, draw tight, and fasten to the braid. Fourth row—work a Buttonhole

Stitch into every loop, and take up the single thread with it. Fifth row—twist the thread back, and fasten to the braid; then commence again, and work the same as the second row, and continue the rows until the space is filled.

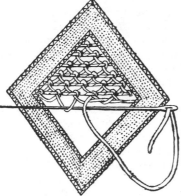

FIG. 730. SORRENTO LACE.

Soutache Braids. — These are very narrow silk braids, varying a little in their several widths, and having an open-work centre. They are produced in many colours, and employed for embroidery and the braiding of mantles, dresses, &c., and are likewise known as RUSSIAN BRAIDS.

Spaced Braid.—This Braid is made in various patterns in imitation of lace stitches. The spaces or divisions into which the two patterns are severally woven are alternately thick, or close and narrow, and comparatively wide and open. The form consists merely of a little plain band connecting the open pearl-edged and lace-like braid. This latter space measures about half an inch in length, and the connecting and very narrow band about a third of an inch. Spaced Braid is made of cotton, and employed for the embroidery of white articles of wear, or other use.

Spaced Braid Work.—A variety of Modern Point Lace, but made without fancy stitches, and with braids outlined with cord. The peculiarity of the work consists in the braids that are used being woven not as a plain and straight surface, or one continually repeated design, but in an irregular manner imitating various lace stitches. Thus, in one space the threads will be closely woven, and give the look of Buttonhole worked closely together, while in another the braid will appear like a number of loose and open loops such as are used in Sorrento Lace Stitch. The effect of the work depends upon the judicious adjustment of these thick and open parts of the braid, so that they carry out the idea of the pattern. To work: Select a design such as is used in MODERN POINT when worked with fancy stitches. Trace this out upon pink calico, and back the calico with brown paper; TACK the braid to the design, so that its thick and close parts should principally form the connecting stems or parts of the design, and its light and more open braid the flowers and more ornamental parts; OVERCAST the braid securely down with fine lace thread as in Modern Point, and work BARS to connect the various parts. Make the Bars of BUTTONHOLE lines ornamented with PICOTS. Fill in any centre spaces in the pattern that the braid leaves exposed with WHEELS. Then take a fine lace cord, and Overcast it on the braid, so that it follows every curve made, and place it on the outer edge of the braid, not the inner edge. Put the cord on carefully, and rather tight, but not so as to draw the braid up. Finish the work with a line of plain braid, to form a FOOTING by which to sew the lace on the material, and for the other edge, sew on the looped edging used as a finish to Modern Point Lace.

Spacing Lace.—*See* SEAMING LACE.

Spangles (called in French *Pailettes*).—These are usually small tin plates, silvered or gilded, having a perforation in the centre. Some are flat, and others concave in form, and vary much in price. Flat Spangles are extensively used in theatrical and fancy costumes.

Spanish Embroidery.—A modern work, and closely resembling Darning on Muslin. The Embroidery is executed for washing purposes upon mull muslin with darning cotton, and for dress trimmings upon black or coloured net with filoselles. It is easily executed, and merely consists of filling in the pattern with lines of Herringbone Stitches; but it looks well for children's aprons when worked upon white materials, and for ball trimmings when made upon coloured nets. To work: Select or draw a pattern composed of leaves and tendrils arranged as continuous sprays, and one in which the leaves are narrow, and with pointed terminations, such as flags and carnations, or where the leaves used are grape or ivy leaves. Trace this upon pink calico, back it with brown paper, and TACK the muslin to the pattern. Commence to work from the extreme point of a leaf, and carry a line of close and even HERRINGBONE STITCHES from the point to the base of the leaf. Work from every point to the base in this manner until that leaf is filled in, and work all the rest in the same way. Then, to form the veins of the leaves, HEM STITCH down the centre of each, over the Herringboning, to the point or points, giving a separate line of stitches for each point. Work the stems, stalks, and tendrils that complete the pattern by doubling the filoselle or darning cotton, and going over them with a RUN line. Unpick the material from the work, and make the right side that which is not worked on, the stitches showing through the thin foundation. *See* SICILIAN EMBROIDERY for another kind of Spanish Embroidery.

Spanish Guipure.—One of the names given to SPANISH LACE; also to HONITON, IRISH, or POINT CROCHET.

Spanish Lace.—Lace was made in Spain from the fifteenth century, the earlier kinds of it, such as Cut Works, Laces, and gold and silver lace, being all manufactured there; but the Spanish Laces that have become the most celebrated are the gold and silver laces known as Point d'Espagne, the Blonde Laces, and the Spanish or Rose Points. The laces of Spain, with the exception of Point d'Espagne, were not so widely known on the Continent as those made in Italy, Flanders, and France, until the dissolution of the Spanish religious houses in 1830, as the finer laces were not used in that country as articles of daily wear, and all the magnificent Needle-made fine laces were absorbed for the adornment of the churches. When the vast hoards possessed by each religious establishment were brought to light, it was perceived that Venetian and Italian Points were rivalled by those made in Spain, from the earliest part of the seventeenth century down to the eighteenth. Point d'Espagne was made as far back as the middle of the fifteenth century, and the best and earliest workers are believed to have been Jews, as, after their expulsion from Spain, in 1492, the lace produced was not so good. However, in the seventeenth century it enjoyed a very high reputation, and was extensively used, not only in its own country, but in France and Italy. The earliest banner of the Inquisition, still in existence at Valladolid, is trimmed with Point d'Espagne, and that lace is still made in small quantities. Point d'Espagne is made

Spanish Point, or Spanish Guipure à Bride, or Rose Point, is a Needle Lace, in the making of which infinite variety and patience is displayed. In design and execution it is so similar to the Venetian Points that the best judges cannot always distinguish between the two, although there are some slight differences. This resemblance can be

FIG. 731. SPANISH OR ROSE POINT.

with gold and silver threads, upon which a pattern is embroidered in coloured silks.

Silk Blonde Laces are made in Catalonia, and particularly in Barcelona. They are either white or black

accounted for by the lace being made, in both countries, almost exclusively by the members of religious houses, who were transferred, at the will of their Superior, from one country to the other. The Spaniards and Italians both believe themselves to be the original inventors of Needle Point. The Italians claim it as coming to them through the Greeks who took refuge in Italy from religious

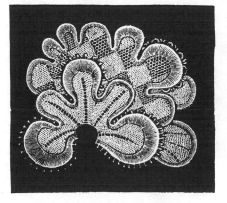

FIG. 732. SPANISH POINT—DETAIL.

FIG. 733. SPANISH POINT—DETAIL.

blondes, and the patterns are of thick heavy work, upon light Réseau Grounds. The mantillas worn by the Spanish ladies are the chief articles of manufacture, the black blonde mantilla being used for afternoon wear, and the white blonde for evening or State occasions.

persecutions in their own land. The Spaniards assert that they learnt it from the Moors of Granada and Seville. Some of the Spanish Points are not raised, but are formed with a pattern worked out in Buttonhole Stitches, which is joined together with a fine Bride Ground. These were worked just when the lace was declining, and only differ in design from other Point Laces, the stitches and manner of workmanship being the same. The Raised Spanish Points, with those of Venice, are distinguished by the thick Cordonnet that surrounds the outline of the design and the principal parts of the interior, and also by the Brides connecting the parts being ornamented with Couronnes rather than Picots, and more elaborate than those used in the Venetian Points.

The piece of lace shown in Fig. 731 is a piece of Rose Raised Point that belonged to Queen Elizabeth, and one which exhibits the beauty of this lace, and is also capable of being copied. To make: Trace the pattern with white paint upon dark green linen, or Toile Ciré, which TACK to stiff paper, and keep at hand to stitch the pieces of lace to as worked. Then trace, upon separate pieces of Toile Ciré, portions of the de-

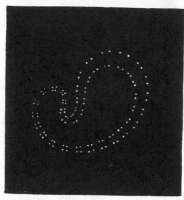

FIG. 734. SPANISH POINT—OUTLINE.

sign of a size such as are shown in Figs. 732 and 733. Trace the outlines only of these, and prick with pinholes placed at stated intervals, as shown in Fig. 734 (which is the crescent-shaped flower) as follows: Tack the Toile Ciré on to a double fold of green linen, take a needle and prick out the outline with two holes close together, then a space, and then two holes. Follow the outline of the thick raised part of the pattern in this manner, and make as many holes upon the inside line as upon the outside. Rub a little white paint into the holes to see them better. Make the FIL DE TRACE (see Fig. 735, which is of the stalk connecting the flower shown in Fig. 732, and the crescent) round these holes with Mecklenburgh thread, No. 12. Secure it to the back, and bring it up to the front of the pattern in the first of the small holes, and put it down

FIG. 735. SPANISH POINT—FIL DE TRACE.

again to the back in the second, so that it makes a small stitch upon the right side of the pattern. Tie the cotton together at the back, and then take No. 7 Mecklenburgh thread and run it round the outline and through the small stitches made with the coarse thread. The pattern is now prepared for the stitches to fill in between the raised CORDONNET. These are made of BUTTONHOLE, and in the varieties of that stitch already described in POINT LACE. The ones shown in Fig. 731 can be copied from that pattern, or any others inserted that the worker may prefer, as long as not more than six or seven different stitches are used over one piece of lace, and that the chief part of the filling in is done with close and even rows of Buttonhole. Having worked the inside of the detached piece of lace, proceed to surround it with a flat or raised Cordonnet, or sew it to another piece of

FIG. 736. SPANISH POINT—DETAIL.

lace, and join them together by working the Cordonnet over them. In the pattern of lace given in Fig. 731, the inside pieces are all worked separately, and joined to the outside by the heavy Cordonnets that appear surrounding the centres: thus, work the two wings and small circle outside the pine-shaped crescent, on the right side of the lace, on one piece of Toile Ciré, and the crescent centre on another; take them both off the Toile Ciré, and lay them upon the large pattern, run in the filling for the raised part, and join the two together with the Buttonhole that covers it. Work the large Rose at the top of the pattern, and shown in Fig. 736, in pieces, and put together. Commence with the five centre leaves, work in plain But-

FIG. 737. SPANISH POINT—DETAIL.

tonhole with a row of open stitches down the centre of each leaf, which make by missing three stitches in the centre of every row. Sew these pieces together, and make a small padded crescent to fit their centre. Work the two small leaves of the five forming the outside with Buttonhole, leaving three stitches in every row, as shown in the pattern, so that an open Diamond is formed; repeat this stitch in the half of the leaves on each side of the smallest leaves, and then work the other entirely in thick Buttonhole, except for the open square in the centre. Work the middle leaf in one piece, but alter the stitches where shown in the illustration. Join these various parts together with a raised Cordonnet, which trim with FLEURS VOLANTS. In the spray, shown in Fig. 737, use the same fillings as those used in the outer leaves of the Rose; work the narrow raised Cordonnet before taking the lace off the Toile Ciré. Work the thick raised Cordonnet when the piece is attached to the one nearest it in the design. For the crescent in the centre: Wind soft Moravian cotton round a pencil, and when the pad thus made is thick enough slip it off, and catch it lightly together; lay it down in its place, and Buttonhole it thickly over, and then trim it with SPINES. Work two BUTTONHOLE BARS in the centre of it, and trim with Spines; work these at the back of the crescent after it is taken off the Toile Ciré, and before it is placed in its right position. The other separate parts of the pattern are worked in a similar manner to those already described. For the raised Cordonnets surrounding each flat part proceed as follows: For the narrow and only slightly raised lines, run soft Moravian thread along their outlines and in their centre, and then Buttonhole this thread carefully over; for the highly raised parts, make a pad of Moravian thread, as shown in Fig. 738. Take the

FIG. 738. SPANISH POINT—RAISED CORDONNET.

stitches from point to point of the outline until there are sufficient to raise it well above the surface, and then increase the pad at the inside of the Cordonnet, and at the centre, so that these parts are well raised above the outside and the ends. Then cover the whole pad with an even row of Buttonhole Stitches, as shown partly worked in Fig. 738. Work now the lace-like edge that trims the Cordonnet. These are made of loops resembling Couronnes and Spines, and are known as Fleurs Volants or Pinworks. Much of the beauty of the lace depends upon these lace-like edges, and no labour should be spared to bring them to perfection. For the Couronnes: Make a loop upon the edge of the lace, return the thread from the spot it started from, and work Buttonholes over these two threads with PICOTS to trim the outer edge of the Buttonhole line. For the Spines: Make a tiny loop, and pin it

out upon the Toile Ciré, in a straight line from the edge of the lace, take the thread up to the pin and cover it and the loop with a line of Buttonholes until the edge is again reached. Make Bars ornamented with Picots where required, and where shown in Fig. 738, to keep the lace together, and when the lace is quite finished, rub over every raised part with a small ivory AFICOT, so as to polish and smooth the threads.

Spanish Lace—Imitation.—A lace made in imitation of the hand-made and raised Spanish Points. It is formed of fine linen, fine linen cord, and lace cotton, and is worked as follows: Trace out the design shown in Fig. 739 upon

FIG. 739. SPANISH LACE—IMITATION.

white or écru-coloured linen, and back this with brown paper for a foundation. Commence the work by forming the ground. Work this over the linen, but be careful that no stitch of the ground takes up the linen beneath it. Make the ground with one of the lace stitches used in hand-made Point Lace, and described under that heading. The one shown in the illustration is POINT DE VENISE, but POINT DE FILLET or POINT DE TULLE can be used equally well. The ground finished, lay along the stems of the pattern and round every outline of leaf or flower a fine white cord. Tack the cord down so as to keep it in position, and BUTTONHOLE it down upon the linen with fine lace thread either of white or écru colour. Every stitch of the Buttonhole must take in the linen material as well as the lace ground. Finally unpick the work from the brown paper, turn it, and cut away the linen from the back of the ground along the lines of Buttonholes, and only retain the material where it is surrounded with Buttonhole and forms the thick parts of the pattern.

Spider Couching.—*See* COUCHING.

Spider Stitch.—*See* GUIPURE D'ART.

Spider Wheel.—*See* CATHERINE WHEEL.

Spindle.—One of the attachments or appliances belonging to a sewing machine. It is also an apparatus used for making thread and yarn. It consists of a round stick of turned wood like a broomstick, tapering at the ends. The distaff was stuck into the spinster's waist-belt, and at the other end the flax, cotton, or wool was wound, and from this she drew a few strands at a time, and attached them to the spindle, which was set revolving by striking it frequently, and so both twisting the thread and winding it into a ball. The spindle in modern machine-spinning forms a part of a complicated apparatus. The spindle and distaff were for many ages the only appliances used for the making of thread. The simple method of turning the spindle by striking it was superseded by the adoption of a wheel and band, which appliance was called a "one-thread wheel." This has long been employed in India, and in Europe also for making cotton, flax, and wool; but various kinds of wheels are found to be necessary for the spinning of different sorts of yarn. *See* SPINNING WHEELS.

Spines.—These are also called Pinworks, and are used to trim the raised Cordonnets that surround Spanish and Venetian Point Lace, and also other kinds of Point Lace. The Spines are long straight points that stick out from the edge of the Cordonnet. To work: Secure the thread into the CORDONNET, then make a tiny loop one-sixteenth of an inch and pin this out from the lace by sticking a pin into it and drawing it out with the pin straight from the lace. Run the thread up to the pin and put it round it, then BUTTONHOLE over the loop and the last thread until the lace is again reached. Another way: Secure the thread into the Cordonnet, then twist it six or eight times round the needle, and draw the needle through; push the loops thus made on the thread up to the lace edge, and secure them.

Spinning.—A method by which the fibres of plants and the hair of animals were formed from short and entangled filaments into long and secure threads strong enough not to break when woven together, and of a continuous thickness. This art dates from the first efforts of civilisation, but no record of its invention is preserved. Reference is made to it in the Divine writings by Moses, proving, at the smallest computation, that it existed some 1500 years before Christ. Amongst the Ancient Greeks the invention was ascribed to Minerva. From the very earliest ages it was the duty of women to prepare these threads, and either weave them into garments or sell them for the same purpose; and it is curious to notice that the spindle and distaff represented upon Egyptian monuments as being then in use, is still met with in some of the remotest parts of Scotland, although these ancient implements were much modified and improved before hand Spinning succumbed to modern machinery. The art of Spinning consists in drawing out from a bundle of wet yarn, hemp, or wool, a number of small threads and twisting them together, so that they form an unbroken and continuous line of firmly-twisted material. This was first effected only by the spindle, which was twirled round in the hand and even thrown in the air, while the threads were pulled out of it by the hand and twisted together by the action of the spindle. An improvement was made to this by winding the thread as spun upon the distaff, a long thin piece of wood.

The spinning wheel succeeded to the spindle and distaff, which was driven by the foot, and left the hands of the spinner at liberty to guide the flax, which she drew towards her, having previously wetted from the spindle, which was mounted on the wheel, and which twisted the thread by a treadle.

The distaff was introduced into England in the fifteenth century, by an Italian. It was superseded by a spinning wheel, invented at Nuremburg, in 1530; then by the spinning-jenny, invented by Hargreaves, a Lancashire cotton spinner, in 1764, and by means of which the spinster could make eight threads at once. Fifteen years later, the mule jenny replaced it, by which no less than eighty threads could be simultaneously produced, instead of one only, as in the primitive use of the distaff. In the process of Spinning by means of the mule jenny the several threads are opened, cleansed, twisted, and then wound off upon reels.

Spinning Wheels.—These appliances have long been adopted for the purpose of turning the spindle, round which the yarn is wound, instead of the ancient method of striking it perpetually, to keep it in motion. What was designated a "one thread wheel," was first invented; and has long been employed in India, as well as for cotton, flax, and wool spinning in Europe. Various descriptions of yarn require different kinds of wheels for their respective spinning. That for flax is turned by a treadle, moved by the foot; a catgut cording passes round in a groove in the rim of the wheel, over the pulley of the spindle on which the thread is wound. The wheel for cotton and wool spinning is of a different kind from that for flax. The spindle is made of iron, placed horizontally upon the extremity of a wooden frame, supported on legs. Upon this there stands a wheel, round which, and the spindle likewise, a band passes. Worsted is spun more after the manner of Flax. Spinning wheels were universally employed on the Continent of Europe and in this country until the year 1764, when a wonderful series of mechanical inventions were adopted by all the weaving manufactories, and left the pretty spinning wheels of the olden times to decorate the cottages of the peasantry, and supply the artists with a charming object, to break the hard straight lines in his sketch. *See* SPINNING, &c.

Spinster.—One who spins, an occupation followed by women from times of the remotest antiquity, and in all civilised nations. Thus the work so designated became a sort of characteristic of the sex; and as unmarried women used in some parts to spin the yarn of all the linen required for their *trousseaux*, and for their household—when they should commence their own housekeeping—they were given the name of Spinster, which came in course of time to denote a single woman.

Split Stitch.—*See* EMBROIDERY STITCHES.

Spools.—A word employed to signify reels, but more in use in Ireland than in England. They are made in wood stained black, brown, or red, of many different sizes; and some may now be had of gigantic dimensions, respectively containing, it is said, cotton, which unwound, would reach a mile in length. There is a hole—the Spool running lengthwise through the centre—to allow of their being fixed on a pin, upon which they can turn round, so as to give out the thread as required. Spools, or Reels are to be had of bone, ivory, and mother-o'-pearl, as well as of wood; and some are made like a succession of Spools made in one piece, the divisions being of use for the purpose of keeping the different colours of sewing silk respectively apart.

Spot Stitch.—*See* Crochet, page 125.

Spotted Knitting.—*See* Knitting.

Spotted Lace or Net.—A cotton textile, chiefly used for veils, or women's caps. Formerly the spots were worked upon the Net with a needle and thread, but now by machine. Some kinds are spotted with chenille, and others with beads, but these being heavy are apt to tear the Net. It is an inexpensive material.

Sprigs.—A term employed by Pillow Lace makers to denote detached pieces of lace, which are afterwards appliqué on to net foundations, or joined together so as to make a compact material. Sprigs are made in Honiton Lace, Brussels Lace, and Duchesse Lace, and need not be formed of flower sprays, but of some detached and small design.

Spun Silk.—This silk is very commonly called by two French names, *i.e.*, Filoselle and Bourre de Soie. It consists of that part of ravelled silk thrown on one side in the filature of the cocoons, which is subsequently carded, and then spun. The yarn has rather a rough and cotton-like appearance, but is very suitable for socks and stockings, being warm and durable. Handkerchiefs, shawls, and scarves, as well as a great variety of dress silks, are made of it, especially of Indian manufacture; and the peasants of Lombardy also employ it extensively for their home-made articles of dress. Spun Silk, or Filoselle may be had in white and black, in common, and in ingrain colours; and can be purchased retail, by the skein, or the pound. It may also be had in 1 ounce balls, for knitting and mending.

Square Crochet.—*See* Crochet, page 126.

Square Netting.—*See* Netting.

Square Plaitings.—*See* Plaitings.

Squirrel Fur (*Scuivus vulgaris*).—There are seven varieties of this Fur, which are prepared for the making of muffs, tippets, cuffs, linings, and trimmings, and consist respectively of the Black Russian, the Blue Siberian, the Razan-Siberian, Indian striped, English, American, and Flying Squirrels. These are all employed in their natural colours, which, according to the several varieties of the animal, are respectively grey, white, black, red, and of a bluish hue; the latter is the most highly valued, and is known as the *Petit Gris*. This description is obtained from Siberia. Inferior kinds are often dyed. Our chief supply of these skins is derived from Russia. They are light, warm, and durable. The tails of the animals are made into boas, and the hair is also extensively employed for artists' painting brushes. The fur on the common squirrel's stomach is of a yellowish white, while that on the back is grey, the latter being the most in esteem. The skins, when prepared for making up into articles of wear, measure 4 inches by 8 inches in size.

Squirrel Lock.—The fur known by this name is that portion of the grey squirrels' fur that grows under the animal's body on the belly. It is of a yellowish white colour, and, being cut out with a bordering of the grey fur of the back, it has a pretty variegated appearance when made up. It is lighter in weight than the grey fur on the back, which should be remembered when purchasing a cloak lined with it. It measures 10 inches by 3 inches in size.

Stamped Plush.—This variety of Plush is manufactured in strips of about 4 or 5 inches in width, for borders to curtains and other articles of upholstery. It is also employed for purposes of Embroidery, and is to be had in various colours. *See* Plush.

Stamped Utrecht Velvet.—A textile similar to the plain kinds of this name, excepting in the designs stamped upon it. It is employed for furniture decorations, and also for purposes of Embroidery. *See* Velvet.

Stamped Velvet.—There are two kinds of Velvet which have the effect of being stamped, although only one of them has a pattern produced by stamping. This latter, or real Stamped Velvet, which is of comparatively inferior quality, has a silk face and a cotton back. It is woven with a silk pile, and, by means of heated stamping irons, formed into various designs; it is so pressed as to make the portions between those that are raised appear as if of satin make. The superior Velvet, known as Velvet Broché, has a design in silk pile, woven into the web, and not stamped. Stamped Velvet is employed for the making of dress bodices and trimmings.

Stamped Velveteen.—A material used for Embroidery, and likewise employed for women's dress. It is 27 inches in width. *See* Velveteen.

Stamped Velvet Work.—A modern Embroidery that is both effective and easy, and which has arisen from the use in the present day of stamped velvet for furniture trimmings. The Embroidery consists of giving a certain prominence to the pattern stamped upon the velvet by outlining its edges with gold or silver thread or filoselle, and filling in some of the chief parts with Satin Stitch worked with filoselle. To work: Select a velvet of a deep ruby, olive green, peacock blue, or salmon shade, with a pattern stamped upon it that is bold and geometrical. Take some Japanese gold thread and lay it down along the outer lines of the pattern. Couch this thread to the material with silk matching it in colour, bring the silk up from the back of the work, put it over the gold thread and back into the velvet, so that it makes a short stitch over the thread, and thus secures it. Work round all the principal outlines with the gold thread, but fill in minor lines with filoselle of a contrasting shade to the velvet, and with Crewel Stitch. Having finished the outline, take two light-coloured filoselles, one a shade lighter than the velvet, and the other a shade darker, and with these cover with SATIN STITCH the extreme centre of a stamped flower or geometrical design, using the filoselles alternately. The stamped pattern should not be too much filled in with stitches, as if they are overdone the work will look heavy. Stamped Velvet Work is used for cushions, handkerchief and glove cases.

Stamping.—This is a method adopted for producing a pattern on cotton, silk, or woollen stuffs, having a stiff raised pile on the face. It is effected by hot irons pressed on the material by a machine. There are stamped velvets used for dresses and trimmings made of a combination of silk and cotton, and there are stamped woollen stuffs, having a pile—such as the Utrecht velvets, employed for purposes of upholstery.

Star.—*See* BERLIN WORK, GUIPURE D'ART, and MACRAMÉ.

Star Braid.—A kind of Braid designed for Fancy Embroidery, made in blue and red, and having a white star. It is 1½ inches in width, and these stars are woven at successive intervals of an inch apart. It is very smoothly woven, and is much employed for covers of chair backs, strips being united together in suitable lengths in Crochet Work. An arrangement of narrow white cotton Braid is also made so as to form an openwork trimming. It is folded into the form of conventional stars, which are sewn in position in their centres; sometimes a smaller Star is worked in embroidery cotton, white or coloured. It is sold by the yard in shops, for the trimming of children's dresses; and a narrower make of the same sort of trimming is produced for edgings.

Star Ground.—This is a lace ground, made with a needle, and one that is often used to connect sprays of lace made on the Pillow. To work, as shown in Fig. 740:

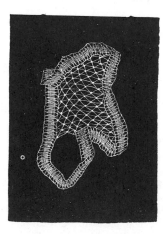

FIG. 740. STAR GROUND.

TACK the sprays to be connected on to coloured paper, right side uppermost, which back with brown paper, use Lace thread No. 9, and a fine, long, and pointless needle. Commence on the left hand, at the space of one pinhole down the side of the work. Make a BUTTONHOLE STITCH

at the distance of one-eighth of an inch from the commencement, and fasten it into the lace; then make a second Buttonhole Stitch, close to the first, thus: Put the needle up through the lace from behind, and bring it down under the thread. Repeat these two stitches one-eighth of an inch apart, and so on to the end of the row. Work down the side to the next pinhole, carry the thread from that pinhole across to the pinhole on the opposite side, fasten it there, work down to the next pinhole, and then repeat two stitches in each loop of the last row, working over the stretched thread, and so securing it.

Star Netting.—*See* NETTING.

Statute Galloons.—These are narrow cotton or silk ribbons, employed for the binding of flannels. They are made in five widths, known respectively as the twopenny, fourpenny, sixpenny, eightpenny, and tenpenny, the first named three being those most in request. They are sold in four pieces of 36 yards each to the gross.

Stay Bindings.—These Bindings are of twilled cotton, and may be had in white, grey, drab, black, blue, red, and buff colour. They are sold by the gross in lengths of 12-12, 8-18, or 6-24; and the widths run ⅜, ½, and ⅝ inch; or from No. 10 up to 30.

Stay Cord.—This Cord is to be had made of cotton and of linen, for the purpose of lacing stays, and it is sold either by the gross yards, or sufficient for a single pair.

Stay Hooks.—These Hooks are more or less employed for the purpose of keeping the petticoats or the skirt of a gown in its proper place, the band or yoke of any or all of these being passed under the Hook, and so held down securely, or else a hole is worked in them through which the Hook passes. They are sewn on the busk of the stays, the point turned downwards, and may be had plated, of white metal, brass, or japanned, measuring about an inch in length. Stay Hooks should only be employed to keep the skirt of the gown in its right place, as all the underskirts should be worn beneath, that is, inside the Stays.

Stay Laces.—These are otherwise called Stay-cord, and are made of both cotton and linen; and silk Staylaces, made of a flat braid, are also to be had. The first are sold by the gross yards, and also in small lengths, and are always supplied with the Stays in the shops, and by the makers. The latter, known as Paris Silk Stay Laces, are likewise sold with the best kinds of Stays. The numbers are 1, 2, and 3; the lengths 6-4, 8-4, 10-4, 12-4, 14-4, 16-4, and 20-4.

Stays.—These are otherwise known as Corsets, which latter name has been adopted from the French. They consists of a low bodice, without sleeves or shoulder-straps, made of either jean, satin, or coutille, which latter is a French material of slighter make than jean. They are more or less supplied with casings, to contain either strips of whalebone or steel, which are placed in various directions, according to the discretion of the several makers, the better to keep the garment from wrinkles, so as to form both a support to the wearer, and a firm foundation on which to fit the bodice of a gown. Some Stays are made to open not only at the back and front, but at the hips and bosom.

They may be had in white, black, red, blue, and grey colours; and sometimes consisting of one colour, are stitched and embroidered with another. They are laced at the back and fastened in front by means of two steel busks, one provided with metal buttons and the other with metal loops. Some of these busks, which have quite superseded the old whalebone and wooden ones, formerly in use when Stays were only open at the back, are of equal width throughout; but others are widened below the waist into what is called a Spoonbill. Steel busks are to be had for sewing under the narrow double busks of the Stays to preserve them from being broken when the wearer may stoop, which is of frequent occurrence when she is a stoutly-built person. There are no less than 300 different makes of Stays, which are given out to private houses to be made by the great manufacturers. French Corsets are largely imported into this country.

Stay Tape.—This is more properly called STAY BINDING.

Stem Stitch.—This stitch is largely used to form the stems, tendrils, curves, and raised parts in Honiton and other Pillow Lace making. There are three kinds of Stem Stitch—Beginner's Stem, Buckle Stem, and Stem Stitch proper.

To work *Beginner's Stem:* This stitch is used to form the stalks of leaves, or to carry the Bobbins at the back of the lace from one part to another. Divide the Bobbins into three and plait them together in a three plait, until the length required is made.

To work *Buckle Stem:* Buckle Stem differs from Stem Stitch by being worked with a Plain Edge upon both sides, and a row of open work down its centre, instead of being quite thick and solid; it is used for working the main stem of a spray of flowers, where that stem is to be rather broad. Hang on eight pairs of Bobbins where the main stem commences, four pairs for Hangers and four pairs for Workers. For the first row: Work from left to right into the middle, that is, across two Hanging pairs of Bobbins; Twist the Workers once, and also the next pair (which will now become the fourth Working pair, make a stitch, Twist both pairs once again—the Twists make the centre holes). Continue to work across to the other side with the first pair, make a Plain Edge with them, bring them back into the middle, Twist once, and leave them. Take up the fourth working pair, work to the left edge, back into the middle, and Twist once. There are now two pairs of Workers in the middle and both twisted, make a stitch with these pairs, Twist once, then again work to the edges and back into the middle.

Stem Stitch.—This stitch is not only used for Stem, but it forms the circles inside flowers, and frequently the Raised Work at the side of leaves, and in other parts of the pattern. The little trefoil shown in Fig. 741 is formed entirely of Stem Stitch, and will therefore, if made, enable the worker to thoroughly master this stitch. To work: Hang on six pairs of Bobbins at the end of the stem (four or five pairs are used if the stem is to be very fine, but ordinary stems are made with six pairs). Prick the pinholes that form the Plain Edge upon one side of the Stem; it

is on the stitch at the other edge that the variation is made, the rest of the work being simply CLOTH STITCH and PLAIN EDGE. Give three TWISTS to the outside pair, and put them on one side; with the next pair work across in Cloth Stitch until the last pair is reached, then make a stitch and a half or TURNING STITCH, as follows: Work a Cloth Stitch, give each pair one twist to the left, put the middle left hand Bobbin over the middle right hand Bobbin, lift the two pairs with each hand, and give them a little pull to make the inner edge firm; put aside the inner pair and work back with the other to the pins, where make the Plain Edge with the pair which have been first put aside. Stem Stitch must always be more or less of a curve, and the pinholes on the outside, so that it is sometimes necessary to turn the Plain Edge from the right to the left hand in the course of the work, but the Turning Stitch never varies. The innermost Bobbin works backwards and forwards, but the second one of the pair at this part remains stationary. In working round sharp curves slant the pins outwards and run one

FIG. 741. TREFOIL IN STEM STITCH.

down to its head here and there; three or four upright pins will hold the lace steady except where the Stem is almost straight, then a greater number of upright pins are required. Knots are passed away in Stem Stitch, and extra threads cut away six rows after they are discontinued. When the circle round the inside of the flower shown in Fig. 741 is worked, the work will come across the Stem, and there a SEWING must be made before the Plain Edge; then make the Plain Edge Stitch, and continue the work as before round the first petal, there make another Sewing, but slightly different to the one first made. In the first place it was made with the inner pair of Bobbins, but on this occasion the Turning Stitch is dispensed with work straight across, sew to the nearest pinhole but to the outside edge instead of the strand across, work straight back, and continue Stem Stitch round the middle petal. At the end of the middle petal make a Sewing like the last, but at the end of the third where the work is finished off, make two Sewings. Then tie the threads inside the last pair, tie up two or three more pairs, and cut off quite close. Also *see* EMBROIDERY STITCHES.

Stephanie Lace.—A modern lace, worked by hand, in imitation of Venetian Point. It was exhibited at the Lace Exhibition at Brussels in 1880, and called by that name after the Princess Stephanie. It is worked as detailed in SPANISH and VENETIAN POINTS.

Stiletto.—A small sharply-pointed instrument, otherwise called a PIERCER forming one of the necessary appliances of a workbox. It is like a very small dagger or *Stylus*, only round instead of flat in the blade, and graduated to a point. Stilettoes may be had entirely of silver, steel, bone, mother-o'-pearl, or ivory, or else mounted in silver if of mother-o'-pearl, or mounted in the latter if of steel. The best are of steel. It is employed for making eyeletholes in dressmaking, staymaking, Embroidery, and for other purposes, and with the advantage of the preservation from tearing of the material, to which a cutting of the tissue would render it liable.

Stirrup.—*See* NETTING.

Stitchery.—The art of Needlework, for which Stitchery is a synonymous term; it is of Anglo-Saxon origin.

Stitches.—Under this term all the various ways of putting a needle into a material, or forming a solid fabric out of thin threads of linen, silk, or wool, are described; and the word is used not only to denote the manner by which one fabric is connected to another, or embellished by another, but by which thin threads are joined together, so as to make a material more or less solid. The ornamental stitches formed by the sewing needle for the purposes of Embroidery comprise all kinds of Embroidery with wools, silks, or crewels, upon solid foundations, Berlin Work upon open canvas, and all Needlemade laces. The same term is used to designate the various modes by which articles of clothing or upholstery are made and mended, by means of needles of various descriptions, and silk, woollen, flax, cotton, hair, gold or silver thread, either worked by hand or in a machine. The various stitches, together with the modes of their application, are fully described under their several heads.

Stitching.—This is one of the varieties in Plain Sewing, and is a method by which two pieces of material are very firmly sewn together. To work in this style: RUN two pieces of cloth together, and turn them so as to leave the raw edges inside, and out of sight. Then commence to

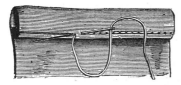

FIG. 742. STITCHING.

make a kind of double Running, but only taking one stitch at a time. When one has been taken, and the needle drawn out, replace it in the spot where it was previously inserted, bringing it out beyond the spot where it was last drawn out. Thus there will be a line of stitches respectively touching one another (Fig. 742), and no spaces left between

them as in Running. The Stitching should be made at a little distance, within the edge formed, at the union of the two pieces of cloth; and they should be of uniform length, and the horizontal line of perfect evenness. This description of work may be executed with a Sewing Machine.

Stockingette Cloth.—This textile is otherwise known as Jersey, or Elastic Cloth, varying respectively in their widths, though differing little otherwise. Elastic Cloth measures 24 inches in width, Jersey Cloth 30 inches, and Stockingette may be had up to 2 yards in width.

Stockings.—Elastic coverings for the feet and legs, extending upwards above the knee, and woven in a loom, knitted by hand, or made in a stocking machine. In the early Anglo-Saxon and Mediæval times they were not elastic, but simply cut out of some woven textile which was embroidered or plain, of costly silk, woollen, fustian, or cotton cloth, according to the condition in life of the wearer. Previously to the time of Henry VIII. knitted silk stockings were unknown in England. According to Stowe, the King himself "did wear only cloath hose, or hose cut out of ell broad taffaty; or that by great chance there came a pair of Spanish silke-stockings from Spaine." The same writer notes that Sir Thomas Gresham gave the King "a great present" in a "payre of long Spanish silk stockings," from which country they were originally introduced. According to the same authority, Queen Elizabeth's "silk woman, Mistress Mountague," presented her with "a payre of blacke knit silk stockings for a new year's gift." It appears that these so well pleased the Queen that she told her "silk woman" she would "henceforth wear no more Cloth Stockings." Stocking knitting was thenceforth practised in this country and elsewhere; but the stocking loom was invented by William Lee, of Woodborough, near Nottingham, in 1589, when the Queen was in her decline. Her successor, King James, did not patronise the art, and thus Lee established his manufactory at Rouen, under the patronage of Henri IV. and his Minister Sully. But he was proscribed under the excuse of his being a Protestant, through the means taken by the jealous inhabitants of that manufacturing city, and had to conceal himself in Paris. Some of his workmen, however, escaped to England, and planted the first stocking manufactories in the counties of Leicester, Nottingham, and Derby.

For the production of "ribbed stockings" we are indebted to Jedidiah Strutt, 1758; and to Arkwright for the spinning machine for the manufacture of cotton stockings. The method of stocking-weaving is an art distinctly differing from that of cloth-weaving. In the former, instead of two threads, viz., the warp and the woof, the whole fabric consists of one continuous thread, formed into a series of loops in successive rows, those of each row being drawn respectively through their several predecessors. The yarn of which this peculiar cloth is woven is also spun after a different method from that of other yarn, as two rows are united to form one thread, which is called "double-spun twist." Very numerous varieties are manufactured, both in make, patterns, combinations of material and of colour, quality in every description of material, and of size, both in knitted and in woven Stockings. Of silk hose there are the fine silk and spun silk, plain, embroidered, open-worked, and with clocks (or clox) in white, black, colours, and mixtures of colours, and also silk with cotton feet, or cotton tops from half way up the calf of the leg. In those of spun silk, partially cotton feet and tops may likewise be had. There are Shetland Stockings, which are peculiarly soft and fine; others of Angola and Vigonia, in colours white and black; of lambswool, also, in colours, white and black; of merino; in ditto of gauze (a combination of cotton and worsted) which are exceedingly thin and worn under silk; of Lisle thread, in white, black, and all colours, and likewise of commoner thread; of worsted, grey, black, and speckled; and of unbleached cotton, of various degrees of fineness, some being very fine and having silk clocks, the best descriptions being known as "Balbriggan"; and of fleecy, having a smooth face and a thick nap inside, very warm, and suitable for invalids. They are all made in a variety of sizes, viz., infants', children's, girls', maids', slender women's (a size which may be worn by persons of tall stature and full proportions, who have small feet), women's full size, and women's large or "out-size." Stocking-knitting frames for handwork are much employed; and there are likewise small Stocking-knitting machines for home use, if required. *See* Socks, and also Knitting Stockings.

Stocking Yarn.—This is Cotton thread, and is spun softer and looser than either Mule or Water Twist. Two threads are afterwards doubled together, and then slightly twisted round each other.

Stone Marten (*Mustela saxorum*).—This fur is much esteemed throughout Europe. The fur underneath the body is of a bluish white, the top hairs being of a dark brown. The throat is usually of a pure white, by which it is distinguished. The French excel in dyeing this fur, on which account it is called French Sable. It is also dyed in this country, the excellent qualities of the skin adapting it to a great variety of purposes. *See* Sable.

Straight Holes.—These are made in Pillow Lace, and are described in Braids under the heading of *Hole Braid.*

Strand Ground.—This ground is used to connect sprays of Honiton Lace, and is formed of irregular Bars made on the Pillow, and with two Bobbins. To work: Tack the sprays, right side downwards, on to blue paper, and commence the ground. Sew a pair of Bobbins on to one edge of a spray, Twist these Bobbins until they form a rope, and carry them across to a piece of lace opposite to the one they started from. Sew them to this lace, Twist the threads, carry them down to where a new bar is to be made, Sew them to the lace, Twist them until they form a bar of the necessary length, and attach them to a piece of lace on the opposite side. Make the Bars irregular, and when they cross one another in the grounding, Sew them together, and when starting them from the lace edges always twist them down to a fresh point of departure instead of cutting them off, as, being at the back of the work, the twisted threads will not show.

Strap Work.—Darned and Netted Laces were anciently known by this name.

Strasbourg Work.—*See* Roman Work.

Straw Braids or Plaits.—These are made after various methods, and of many qualities of straw, according to the country or soil in which the wheat or grass is grown, and the national fancy of the several countries where the industry is carried on. Its chief seat in England is Bedfordshire. There are two sorts of straw, known respectively as the Red Lammas, and the White Chittein, which are grown in the Midland and Southern counties, and are produced best in a light but rich soil. There are Plaits also, made at Luton, and elsewhere, of Rye-straw, grown in the Orkney Islands, and fabricated in imitation of the Tuscan.

The principal plait made in this country is called the Dunstable, which is made of two split straws, of which the insides are placed together so as only to show the outside of each in the plaiting. Straw-plaiting is an industry carried on by women and children in their own private homes, after the manner of the Devonshire Lace-making. The edges of the several plaits are laid successively over that of the next in order, and coiled round and round, thus forming a ridge, and as our straw is strong and thick in quality, the hats, bonnets, and other articles, such as baskets and chair-seats, are of a heavier description than any made of foreign straw.

Straw Braids are made in very long lengths, and are sewn together by means of long thin Needles, called Straws. The straw is split when used in Embroidery on silk or velvet, the latter is found most suitable; when for introduction into worsted work for carriage bags or baskets. Rushes are likewise used for men's and women's hats and bonnets, and also for baskets. There are several kinds of straw in use for such purposes. Of our own straw manufactures immense cargoes are exported to all parts of the world, some of the whole straw, some split, and of both superior and of inferior quality, the plaits or made-up articles of the latter being of very trifling cost. There are large importations of articles made of Straw Plaits, and interlacings from Swiss manufactories, and much, also, from Japan, and the south of France, of a very delicate character, dyed in a variety of colours. Very pretty cabinets, boxes, and cardcases, as well as many other articles of use, are decorated with a covering of coloured Straw-work, much resembling Mosaic work. In the Cantons of Argau, Fribourg, and Appenzell, the manufacture of Straw Plaits for hat making, and fancy kinds of Plaits, some round as well as flat, together with tassels and flowers and other trimmings, have been brought to great perfection. In Appenzell the embroidered straw bonnets are very handsome. The industry is of a peculiar and creditable description in Fribourg; but, perhaps, that of Argau may still rank as the first in Switzerland, as it did at the time of our English Exhibition in 1851. Taking a comprehensive view of the industry of all nations in Straw Plaiting, that of Leghorn and the various districts of Tuscany may be regarded as holding the first place in order of merit in the manufacture of bonnets.

Those of Leghorn are plaited in one piece; the Tuscan are made flat—without any twist forming a ridge, after the English method—and sewn together successively. These two Italian kinds excel all others both in beauty and durability, and in the variety of designs executed. The straw is of a beautiful buff colour, being the stalks of a very fine and peculiar description of wheat. There is a delicate Straw Plait produced in Brazil for hat and bonnet making, formed of a species of grass, which is very light in weight, and all made in one piece, like that of Leghorn.

The origin of Straw Plaiting is of somewhat recent date in England, only going back about one hundred and thirty, or forty years, but it has now reached a high state of perfection. The industry is also carried on with considerable success in Germany and Lombardy.

Straw Cotton.—This is a wiry kind of thread, starched and stiff, produced chiefly in the neighbourhoods of Dunstable and Luton. The numbers run from 10 to 100, and the cotton is exclusively made for use in the manufacture of straw goods. It is but little sold in the retail trade.

Straw Embroidery.—This work is used for ball dress trimmings, or to ornament an entire net dress. It consists in tacking upon black Brussels silk net, or yellow coloured net, leaves, flowers, corn, butterflies, &c., that are stamped out of straw, and connecting these with thick lines made of yellow filoselle. The leaves are stamped in eight different shapes, of which three are shown in Fig. 743,

FIG. 743. STRAW EMBROIDERY.

and the flowers and butterflies can also be bought in different sizes. These straw leaves, &c., are bought at Messrs. Barnards, or Catts. To work: Trace out upon white linen a Running pattern of leaves, flowers, &c., back this with brown paper, and TACK on to it a strip of black or coloured net. Take some filoselle, matching the straw leaves in colour, divide it in half, and RUN with it, or work in ROPE STITCH, all the stems and tendrils in the pattern. Then slightly gum the straw leaves and flowers to their places, and afterwards stitch them into their positions with a few stitches down their centres, made with fine silk.

Straws.—These are needles of a particular description, employed in hat and bonnet making. They are long and slight, as compared with those commonly used in Plain Sewing and Embroidery. *See* NEEDLES.

Streak Stitch.—In hand-made laces the veins of leaves or flowers are made with an open line, that is sometimes designated Streak Stitch. It is formed thus: Trace the shape of the leaf or flower, and draw a line down its centre with a pencil, fill in the leaf with close BUTTONHOLE STITCHES, but when the pencil line is reached in each line of Buttonhole, miss over three stitches before working the next Buttonhole. This will leave an open line down the leaf, and give the appearance of a vein. It is also another name for the CLOTH STITCH used in Pillow Laces.

Strengthening.—*See* KNITTING.

Stretch Needlework.—*See* EMBROIDERY.

String Netting.—This particular kind of work is made to cover glass bottles or other perishable articles that are often used, the network formed by the string protecting the more fragile object that it covers. To work, as shown in Fig. 744: Procure some fine but good twine, and a

FIG 744. STRING NETTING.

carpet needle, through which the twine can be threaded. Take the bottle and tie a piece of twine tightly round its neck close to the stopper; carry it down the side of the bottle, and tie it round the bottom of the bottle, then up the opposite side, and round the neck again, and down to the bottom. Thread the twine, and work from the bottom of the bottle to the neck. Make a row of close BUTTONHOLE STITCHES over the loop to commence with, and then work rows of loose Buttonholes, with a return thread, back to where each row commenced, round and round the bottle, so that they enclose it in a tightly-fitting case, until the neck is reached. OVERCAST the loops of string round the neck, and plait up a piece of string to hold the bottle by.

String Rugs.—These are made from odds and ends of coarse Berlin or fleecy wool, which are either knitted up with string or worked into coarse canvas in loops. *To Work with String*: Take the largest pair of bone knitting needles, balls of strong twine, and balls made of the various lengths of wool, tied together so as to make a long length. CAST ON thirty-six stitches of twine, and KNIT a row in PLAIN KNITTING. In the next row put the needle through the stitch to be knitted, then wind the wool (having first secured its end) three times round two fingers of the left hand, pass the needle round these threads, and Knit them with the stitch. Repeat for every stitch. Knit the next row plain, and repeat the plain and looped row until the length required for the rug is obtained. Work as many strips as will make the width of the rug, sew them together, and line with coarse sacking.

To make upon Canvas: Select strong and firmly woven sacking, and cover the whole of it with a number of tufts of wool. Cut the wool up into lengths of 4 inches; take three of these lengths, double them, and fold them together. Make a hole in the canvas with a large stiletto, push the ends of the wool through this hole, and tie them all together in a knot at the back of the canvas. Continue to insert these loops, and secure them until the canvas is quite filled up, then line it with a piece of sacking. Also *see* IMITATION SMYRNA WORK.

Stroking.—A term of Saxon origin, used, in reference to Needlework, to denote the disposing of small gathers formed in linen or calico, in regular order and close succession respectively. It is effected by drawing the point of a blunt needle from the top of each gather, where it is

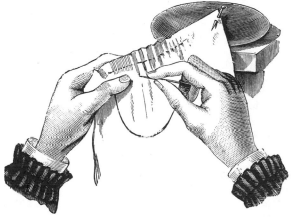

FIG. 745. STROKING.

attached to a band or yoke downwards, after the manner indicated in Fig. 745, which shows the process as adopted in the case of a Running. To make: Draw up the fulness on the Running thread, and secure it round a pin to the left, and with the needle or a pin stroke down the several gathers, placing the thumb of the left hand upon each successively, and proceeding from left to right. *See* SETTING-IN GATHERS.

Stuffs.—This term is one of general significance, and may be applied to any woven textile, whether of gold, silver, cotton, hair, thread, silk, or wool, but it more especially denotes those of worsted, made of long or "combing wool," such as Callimancoes, Camlets, Florenteens, Lutestrings, Merinoes, Moreens, Plaids, Shalloons, Tammies, &c. Stuffs are distinguished from other woollen cloths by the absence of any nap or pile, and having little or no tendency to shrink nor curl when damp, nor to felt in the process of weaving. They are woven either plain or twilled, with spots or designs of various kinds, but in all the thread is laid bare, the superfluous fibres of hair being singed off by means of a red-hot

iron. After the process of weaving and singeing, they are tightly rolled, soaked in hot water, and boiled, then scoured, stocked, or milled, and the moisture pressed out between rollers. They are then passed through a mordant and dyed. To dry them, they are rolled round iron cylinders filled with steam, and, lastly, placed in Bramah's hydraulic presses.

Style Cashmere.—A name which originated from Cross and Tent Stitch, being largely used in Persia in Embroideries upon open canvas materials. It is sometimes applied to Berlin woolwork.

Sunn.—The fibre of the *Crotalaria juncea*, grown in various parts of Hindostan. The strongest, whitest, and most durable species of Sunn is produced at Comercolly. Although called the "Indian Hemp," it is a perfectly different plant from the *Cannabis sativa*, from which Hemp is obtained. Under the name of "Sane" it is named in many Sanscrit books, but by that of "Sunn" it is known in most parts of India. It is probably the earliest of the distinctly mentioned fibres of that country, and in the Hindoo *Institutes of Menu* it is stated that the sacrificial thread of the Rajpoot is ordered to be made of Sunn, cotton being reserved for the Brahmins. It is much cultivated throughout the whole of India, and is employed for sacking, cordage, &c. It is also largely imported to this country.

Surah Silk.—A fine soft twilled silk stuff, employed for dresses, and especially for those of brides and young ladies. It is distinguished from a foulard by its greater softness and flexibility, which preserves it from creasing; and it has no dressing or glaze, like the former. It is to be had in silver-grey and white, and in various light colours of a delicate tint, and measures 26 inches in width. It bears an Indian name, and is probably of Indian origin, but is imported from France, where it is manufactured.

Swansdown.—The breast of the Wild Swan, composed of exceedingly fine soft fluffy white feathers, like down. The bird abounds in Iceland, Lapland, and in the eastern parts of Europe and Asia. The Swanskins imported to this country are employed for tippets, boas, ruffs, muffs, and trimmings for opera cloaks and infants' dress. The skins measure 10 inches, by 24 inches, and are imported into England from Dantzic and the Baltic.

Swanskin, or Swansdown Calico.—A description of calico stuff, one side of which is fluffy, the fibres being pulled to the surface and forming a nap, and somewhat resembling Swansdown feathers. It is much used for underclothing, especially by labourers and persons suffering from rheumatism, for which latter, as cotton holds moisture, it is not as suitable as any woollen textile. It is tightly and closely woven, similar to "Cricketing," but of a commoner description of quality, and may be had both white and unbleached. In America it is sometimes employed in lieu of flannel. There is also a cloth called Swanskin, a very thick and closely-woven textile made of wool, and much employed by sailors and labourers; it is likewise used by laundresses for ironing cloths.

Swedish Drawn Work.—*See* Tonder Lace.

Swedish Pillow Lace.—The nuns at Wadstena are believed to have been the founders of lace-making in Sweden, and claim to have been taught the art by their founderess, St. Bridget, who died in 1335, but they more probably learnt it from Spanish and Italian nuns during the first part of the sixteenth century. The Wadstena Lace has attained great celebrity in Sweden, and until the suppression of the monasteries, the nuns retained the secret of making it. It was made with gold and silver threads netted or knitted together at first, and finally plaited together. Cutwork and Darned Netting were also made in Sweden from a very early date, and the first, under the title of Hölesom, is still worked by Swedish ladies, who adorn their linen and their houses with it; but the gold-plaited laces have quite disappeared, and the only Pillow Lace now made in Sweden consists of a coarse Torchon Lace resembling the Torchon makes of lace in Bedfordshire, Buckinghamshire, and Germany, made by peasants in the neighbourhood of the convent of Wadstena, and being of no value is only used in Sweden for common purposes.

Swedish Work.—A kind of weaving much practised in Sweden, and useful for making braids of various colours, string straps, and narrow ribbon borders. It is worked in

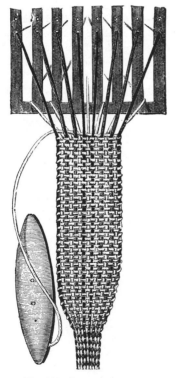

Fig. 746. Swedish Work.

a small frame, shaped like a comb, and with two sets of threads to form the woof, while the warp is made by a thread wound upon a very thin shuttle, passed backwards and forwards, and in and out of the stationary threads. To work as shown in Fig. 746: Choose two colours of silk thread; for the upper threads let it be red, for the lower white. Wind eight red threads separately up into balls, and pass their ends through the holes made for them in the upper part of the frame. Wind up seven white threads separately in balls, and pass their ends through the gaps in the comb at the lowest part. Tie the red and white threads together in the front of the frame, and pull them out long enough to use. Arrange a lead cushion at the back of the frame, and to this attach the red and white threads securely, pin them down exactly one thread over the other, and at a distance of a foot from the frame, with all the threads perfectly stretched. To keep the red threads divided from the white, put a wooden knitting needle between them on the cushion and a small wedge of wood, a little nearer the comb. Upon a very thin Shuttle wind the warp thread, which make either of black silk or of a deep blue, or of any colour according to fancy. Attach this to the knot that joins all the threads together, and hold in the left hand; pass it for the first row underneath the red threads, between them and the white; and for the second row, bring it to the front of the work, over a red thread, under a white, over a red thread, under a white, and by so doing bring the white threads forward; for the third row pass the Shuttle through the threads, dividing the red from the white, and so again bringing the red uppermost. Repeat the first and second row to the end of the work. As the threads become used up, alter the frame, push it as far back as it will go first, and afterwards unwind more threads from the balls at the back, being careful always to secure these tightly. First fasten the braid as it is made to the waist, to prevent the trouble of holding it, and then wind it up out of the way. The edge of the braid will be made quite secure, as there being more threads in the upper than the lower line, the warp thread will always twine round a red one at each side.

Fig. 747 is woven in the same manner as Fig. 746, but the threads arranged for the upper and under threads

Fig. 747. Swedish Work.

of the woof are the same as to colour. When the work is finished, Darn the long lines into the braid, passing over five rows and under two. Make these Darned lines of various shades of contrasting colours.

In Fig. 748 the upper holes in the frame are used, as well as the set through which the threads are passed, as in Fig. 746, and these double lines of upper threads are worked up in the weaving as follows: In the return, or second row, pass the Shuttle over two threads, one from

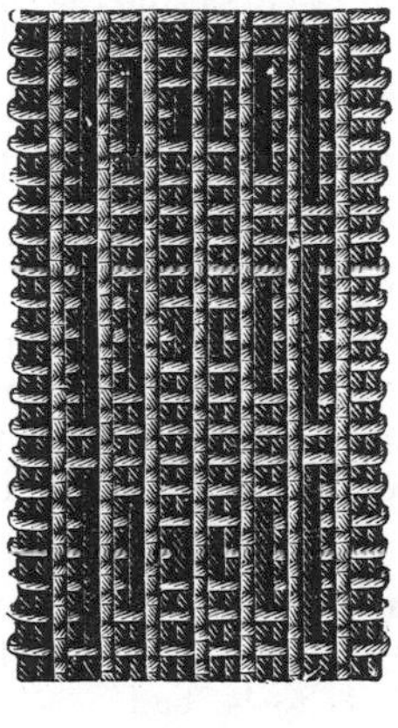

FIG. 748. SWEDISH WORK.

the upper line and one from the double line, then bring up one thread from the lowest line, and put the Shuttle under that, and then over two threads of the upper lines, as before. Darn in the long dark lines when the braid is made.

Swiss Cambric.—This is a cotton material, manufactured at Zurich and St. Gall for a long period before muslins (of which Swiss Cambric is one of the varieties), was produced in England; but, when made in our looms, we obtained a great advantage over the weavers in Switzerland, owing to our inventions in the art, which were subsequently adopted by them. Swiss Cambric is only to be had in white; it is a description of Victoria Lawn, and is chiefly employed for frillings, flounces of petticoats and dresses, and also for infants' wear. It measures about 1 yard in width. *See* MUSLIN.

Swiss Darning.—The method of reproducing Stocking-web by means of a darning needle and a thread of yarn worked double. *See* DARN.

Swiss Embroidery.—This Embroidery is the same as is known as Broderie Anglaise, Irish Work, and Madeira Work. It consists of working upon fine linen or thin muslin patterns in Satin Stitch and other Embroidery Stitches with white Embroidery cotton. During the first half of the present century the peasants of Switzerland were celebrated for the beauty and delicacy of the work they produced, but since white Embroidery has been made by machinery, the Swiss Embroidery has obtained but little sale, and the work is dying out as a trade manufacture. For a description of the work *see* BRODERIE ANGLAISE.

Swiss Lace.—Lace was manufactured in Switzerland during the sixteenth century, and some curious pattern books, printed during that time for the use of Swiss lacemakers, are still in the possession of the Antiquarian

Society at Zurich. These patterns are only of narrow Plaited Pillow Laces or of Knotted Thread Laces, and, although Cutworks and Darned Netting were also made, Swiss Laces obtained no celebrity until the revocation of the Edict of Nantes filled Switzerland with Protestant refugees, many of whom were lacemakers, and who established at Nuremberg a lace manufactory, and smuggled the lace there made into France. The lace was an imitation of Brussels Pillow Lace, which was considered quite equal to the real; also of Point d'Espagne Wire Lace, made with gold or silver threads, and Lille Lace. The manufactory continued to flourish until the end of the last century, but since then the lacemakers have not been able to compete with cheaper manufactures, and the trade has disappeared.

Swiss Lace—Imitation.—This is a machine-made textile, employed in upholstery for window curtains, wall paper preservers, behind washstands, and for short blinds. The chief seat of the industry is Neufchâtel, but imitations of it are produced at Nottingham, made of coarse cotton. Some new kinds have been produced in broad stripes, alternately coloured with designs, and white of the ordinary open-work description. The Swiss Lace produced at Nottingham is very inexpensive, and varies in width; it may be had to suit the largest windows.

Swiss Muslin.—Muslin was manufactured at St. Gall and Zurich long prior to the production of the textile in England. It is a coarse description of buke or book muslin, much used for curtains, made with raised loose work in various patterns, and also plain. It measures from about 30 inches to a yard in width.

Swiss Patchwork.—*See* RAISED PATCHWORK.

T.

Tabaret.—A stout satin-striped silk, employed for furniture hangings, and much resembling Tabbinet, but is superior to it in quality. It has broad alternate stripes of satin and watered material, differing from each other respectively in colour; blue, crimson, or green satin stripes are often successively divided by cream-coloured Tabby ones. *See* TABBY.

Tabbinet.—A name for poplin of rich character, the warp being of silk, the weft of wool, and so called because the surface is "tabbied" or watered. Sometimes a pattern is introduced into it. It is chiefly used for window curtains and other upholstery purposes. It is a more delicate description of textile than what is called Tabby, and was at one time very extensively manufactured in Ireland. One variety is woven in diaper patterns.

Tabby.—A coarse kind of Taffeta, thick, glossy, and watered by pressure between the rollers of a cylinder, and the application of heat and an acidulous liquor. It is manufactured after the manner of Taffeta, but is thicker and stronger. The name is derived from the verb "to Tabby," or to wave or water. The beautiful description of silk called *Moiré* is a Tabby; and worsted stuffs, such as moreen, are likewise Tabbies.

Table Linen.—Tablecloths, table napkins, tray ditto, damask slips, damask d'oyleys, and five o'clock teacloths are all included under this denomination. Tablecloths may be had of various dimensions, and either in single or double damask. They may be had from 2 yards square, or 2 yards by 2½ yards, or else of 2½ yards by 3, 3½, 4, 4½, 5, 5½, up to 8 yards in length, so as to dine from six to twenty persons; also, in due proportions, up to 10 yards in length. Tablecloths may also be had of 3 yards square in double damask, advancing half a yard up to 10 yards; also the same, in a finer quality, may be had of 3½ yards square, or manufactured expressly in any dimensions required. There are also altar cloths, and other linen, made expressly for ecclesiastical purposes. Damask slips to match any of the Tablecloths named may be had of 22 inches in width, up to 27 inches. Five-o'-clock tea-cloths, with d'oyleys to match them, are made in white damask with coloured borders, and checked in crossbars of ingrain colours; also in drab, and in coffee colour. Dinner napkins are to be had in single and double damask, of three-quarters of a yard square, also of three-quarters of a yard by seven-eighths, also of seven-eighths by 1 yard. Damask d'oyleys are manufactured in a round, oval, or square form. Tray cloths, of 1½ yards square, and 1 yard by 1¼ yards. Servants' hall and kitchen Tablecloths may be had both in diaper and damask, of either 1¼ yards in width, or of 2 yards. Men servants' thumb waiting napkins may be had 18 inches square; pastry napkins, 22 inches square; fish napkins, 22 inches square; and breakfast napkins, of damask, double damask, and with a small spot pattern, of several dimensions. All these are produced in the best Irish linen manufactories, and the sizes are generally about the same as those produced in England. There are also bleached Barnsley and Scotch diaper cloths.

Tablier.—The French term to signify an apron, or protective covering for the front of a dress; it is tied or buttoned round the waist, and sometimes extends upwards over the front of the bodice.. *See* EN TABLIER.

Tabs.—A term denoting the square-cut loosely hanging border-trimming of a bodice or skirt, and consisting of a succession of regularly recurring cuts of an inch, or 2 or 3 inches in depth, the three raw edges of each pendant square of material being bound round, usually with a piece of the same material, cut on the bias. Tabs are sometimes made on flounces. In making a Battlemented trimming, Tabs are first made, and then every second Tab is cut out, leaving the appearance of architectural battlements. Also loops of ribbon, or of strong twilled and striped tape attached to the fronts and backs of boots at the top, with which they are pulled on the foot are called Tabs. They are likewise made of leather, and nailed on carriage window sashes, for the purpose of raising, or letting them down, and to the lids of desks for the same purpose.

Tacking.—A term synonymous with Basting, and employed in needlework to designate small stitches taken through two pieces of material, at wide and regular intervals. It is most securely effected by working from left to right, and designed to keep the two portions of stuff in place, preparatory to their being permanently sewn together. Paper patterns directing the cutting out of a garment, or for embroidery, are thus Tacked or "Basted" on; but simple Running from right to left suits best for this purpose. An inferior kind of thread is sufficiently good for the purpose of Tacking, as the use made of it is only temporary. To Tack an article of wear or other use: Lay the dress (for instance) on the table, and the lining upon it, and take up a small piece, through both materials, with the needle, of about one-eighth of an inch at a time, each stitch at about an inch apart, successively, and work from left to right, as above directed.

Taffeta, or Taffety.—A thin glossy silk, of a wavy lustre, the watering process being of the same nature as that for Tabby. It is to be had in all colours, some plain others striped with silk, gold, and silver, and likewise chequered and flowered, the different kinds being distinguished by the names of the localities where they are made, such as the English, Lyons, Tours, Florence, and China Taffetas. The latter is made in various descriptions, and used for apparel, amongst which there is one that is so pliant, as well as thick, that it shows no creases after pressure, and will also bear washing. Our own Taffeta was used in the sixteenth century for costly articles of dress, and in the next century for pages, and for doublets. In Stubbes's *Anatomy of Abuses*, published in 1583, he speaks of all persons dressing alike, indiscriminately, in "silks, velvets, satens, damaskes, taffeties, and suche like, notwithstanding that they be both base by birthe, meane by estate, and servile by calling; and this I count a greate confusion, and a general disorder; God be merciful unto us!" He adds that the ladies wore "taffatie of ten, twenty, or forty shillynges a yard." These were of silk, and those worn by pages early in the seventeenth century were also of a thin description. Our modern home-made Taffeta is of a stout thick make, and usually black. Long silk gloves, extending up towards the elbow, are of this description of material. Taffeta was first imported into England in the fourteenth century. There were also several English made varieties produced, such as the Armesin-Taffeta, the Ell-broad Taffeta, and the Tuft-Taffeties, having a raised pile, and of different widths. Besides these, foreign varieties were imported, such as the Alamode and Lustring black Lyons Taffetas, and others from Avignon, Florence, and Spain, each respectively known by the places where they were manufactured. According to *Chambers's Cyclopœdia* (1741), these stuffs were to be had in every colour, and every kind of design, some being striped with gold or silver. The sort described by Ben Jonson (1610) was very delicate in texture:

> . . . . My shirts
> I'll have of Taffeta-Sarsnet, soft and light
> As cobwebs.
>
> —*The Alchemist.*

We also find an allusion to this stuff made by Shake-speare :

> Beauties no richer than rich Taffata ;

and again—

> Taffata phrases, silken terms precise,
> Three-pil'd hyperboles.
> —*Love's Labour Lost.*

An imitation of Taffeta was made in the sixteenth century, composed of linen. According to Planché, silk Taffeta was called Tafta in Brittany.

Taille.—A French term denoting the waist or figure.

Tailors' Buttonholes.—These Buttonholes are made after the ordinary method adopted in Plain Sewing, but precede the usual work by laying a piece of fine black cord all round the hole, exactly at its raw edge, and there BASTE or OVERCAST, to keep it in the right position while the Buttonhole Stitch is performed over it. *See* BUTTON-HOLE STITCH and the accompanying illustration, Fig. 749.

thread, but leaving a loop at every stitch, instead of drawing it tight. Continue so doing through every loop, round and round, till the hole be filled.

Another variety of this stitch will be seen in Fig. 751,

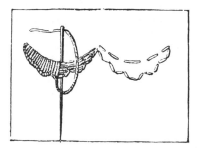

FIG. 751. DECORATIVE BUTTONHOLE STITCH.

as applied to decorative trimmings. The chain, or linked portion of the stitch is made round the outer

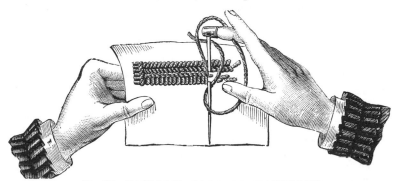

FIG. 749. TAILORS' COAT BUTTONHOLES.

There are two other varieties of Buttonhole Stitch besides Tailors' Buttonholing; one is the Open Button-hole Stitch, which is employed to fill in a hole in a

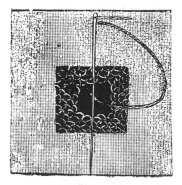

FIG. 750. OPEN BUTTONHOLE STITCH.

tight glove, when there is no piece of kid of the same colour which can be used as a patch. *See* Fig. 750.

To produce this kind of Network, which resembles in appearance a piece of chain armour, insert the needle at the edge of the hole, passing it in downwards, and point-ing towards yourself, through the loop formed by the

edge of any article of wear, or other use, so as to form a secure border outside the raw edge, whether of cambric muslin or of flannel. It is also employed to produce small designs on the material, irrespective of any use but that of decoration.

To work the decorative Buttonhole Stitch : Make several runnings within the outer and inner outlines, to be covered, as indicated in the illustration, so as to make a thickness over which to work, and then insert the needle at the outer edge of the inner outline (traced in Embroidery cotton) and passing it straight down at the back, bring it out again outside the outer outline through the loop formed by the thread. If it be intended to form an edging for the border of any article, finish the Embroidery Work before the cutting away of the straight raw edge of the material, but not very close to the work.

Tailors' Twist.—A coarse silk thread, made of several threads twisted together, wound on reels, of 2 ounces in weight each. The numbers used by tailors run from 1 to 8. There are also small reels containing a single thread of 12 yards, equivalent to 1 yard of twelve threads. By this arrangement dealers can keep a larger supply of shades at a smaller cost.

Take in.—*See* KNITTING.

Tambour Cotton.—This is a description of sewing cotton, suitable—as the name indicates—for embroidering the Tambour muslins, and is likewise employed by tailors for the purpose of Basting. It is to be had in skeins, sold in half bundles of 5 pound each. The numbers are 12, 14, 16, 18, 20, 24, 30, 36, and 40. It is also sold in balls of a variety of sizes.

Tambour Lace.—This Lace, chiefly worked in Ireland, where it is known as Limerick Lace, but also at Islington, Coggleshall, and Nottingham. The lace known as Tambour only differs from Tambour Work by the ground that it is made upon, which in the lace is either of black or white Nottingham Net. Since machinery has produced Tambour Lace, the making of the real lace has declined.

Tambour Muslin.—This is a muslin embroidered by hand on a small frame, called a Tambour—a name adopted for it in consequence of the resemblance formed to a Tambourine, when the muslin is stretched over it. Tambour Muslins are of open make, and clear and semi-transparent in texture. The designs produced on them are various, some being in spots, some in small sprigs, and others in long running patterns like delicate wreaths. It may be executed by means of a sewing machine, the work being composed of Chain Stitch. In former times, evening dresses were made of this muslin, but now curtains only. The widths run from 27 inches, to 30 inches, and the muslin is sold in lengths of 12 yards.

Tambour Needles.—These Needles resemble those employed for Crochet Work, and known also as Shepherds' Hooks. They are, however, smaller, and invariably of steel, and are very commonly made of the length of a medium-sized sewing needle. A small handle of suitable size is sold with it, into which it is securely fixed by means of a small thumb screw, and can be released at pleasure, should it be broken. This handle, which is made of ivory, bone, or wood, is hollow, and the opposite end can be unscrewed to supply a receptacle for a small stock of needles.

Tambour Stitch.—*See* CROCHET, page 126.

Tambour Work.—This Embroidery is of Eastern origin, and was worked in China, Persia, India, and Turkey, long before it became known in England, and up to the present date it is still largely employed in the East, and the work there executed is much appreciated from the beautiful colours employed and the labour expended upon it. Until the middle of the last century, Tambour Work, except in Turkey and the Levant, was not known in Europe, but at that time it was introduced into Saxony and Switzerland, where it was worked only upon white muslin and cambric with white thread, and used to ornament dresses, curtains, caps, borders, and all varieties of white trimmings. The peasants of these countries soon excelled in the Embroidery, and their Tambour Work was not only eagerly bought on the continent but large quantities of it were shipped to the East, whence the work originally came. In England, Tambour Work (the name of which is derived from the French, and means a drum, in allusion to the shape of the frame used), or Tambouring, upon white materials with white thread, became an article

of manufacture sixty years ago, and gave employment to the poorer classes in Middlesex, Nottingham, and Ireland, but since the introduction of machinery, and the facility with which the stitch is executed by its means, to make it by hand is no longer profitable. For many years English and Continental workers only embroidered in this work upon crêpe, muslin, and fine cambric, it being considered indispensable that the left hand manipulating under the material to form the Tambour Stitch must be visible to correctly form the design, but when this was found unnecessary, the embroideries with gold thread and many coloured silks upon fine cloth, and other thick materials, were produced, and were successful. Since Chain Stitch has taken the place of Tambour Stitch, the left hand is released, and the material if solid, does not require framing, which is a great saving of time, as the Embroidery is done much more quickly when held in the hand than when stretched in a Frame.

The materials required are Frames, netting silks of all colours, gold thread, known as Passing, white Embroidery cotton, and muslin, cambric, crêpe, cloth, satin or serge.

The old *Tambour Frames* consist of two hoops shaped like the top of a drum, and made either of iron or wood. These hoops are covered with velvet, and fit closely one into the other. The material is stretched upon the smaller hoop, which is then fitted into the larger, and the work thus held cannot become slack. The round hoops are no longer used, except for fine muslin or crêpe, which would tear if lashed to the tapes of an ordinary square Embroidery Frame. For all other materials the ordinary Embroidery Frame is used, and the material attached to it in the usual method.

The real Tambour Stitch, which is now superseded by Chain Stitch, is made as follows : A Tambour needle, which resembles a Crochet needle but not quite so hooked at the tip, is used. Frame the material, and attach the thread to the under side. Put the Tambour needle with the right hand through to the back of the frame at the commencement of one of the traced lines. Hold the thread in the left hand under the line, catch hold of the thread with the hook, and bring it through to the front of the work as a loop. Only allow enough thread to come through to make the loop, which retain on the hook. Put the hook again through the material to the back of the frame, one-tenth of an inch beyond the first puncture. Let it take up the thread there, and pull it up as a loop to the front, and let the first made loop slide over the second and down upon the traced line. With a little practice the stitches can be made with marvellous rapidity. The only things to observe is that the loops follow the outline of the design, are the same distance apart, and that the thread making them is always evenly stretched.

Chain Stitch, used at present in Tambour Work, is the ordinary Chain Stitch described in EMBROIDERY STITCHES.

To Work upon Crêpe : Trace the design, frame it in a Tambour Frame, outline the pattern with CHAIN STITCH worked in gold thread, and then mark out this with an inner Chain Stitch line, made with coloured netting silk.

To Work upon Muslin, Cambric, and Net: Trace the design upon the material, frame it in a Tambour Frame, and then work in CHAIN STITCH with Embroidery cotton.

FIG. 752. TAMBOUR WORK.

Select this cotton so that it is coarser than the threads of the material, as if of the same texture it becomes absorbed and does not stand out sufficiently.

To Work upon Thick Materials: Trace the design upon the material, which either frame in an Embroidery Frame or hold in the hand. Work over in CHAIN STITCH every outline of leaf, flower, or petal with netting silk of a colour matching its shade, and to fill in, work a straight line of Chain Stitch down the centre of the leaf or petal, and then lines of Chain Stitch from the outline to the centre. For the stalks, work two or three rows of Chain Stitch, according to their thickness. Geometrical patterns will only require their outlines indicated by two lines of Chain Stitch worked close together. These lines should be of two shades of one colour, the darkest outside, or the outside line of gold or silver thread, and the inside of a bright silk.

To work Fig. 752: This is worked upon dark navy blue cloth, with three shades of ruby coloured netting silk and one of pale blue. Trace the design, and outline all the chief parts of it, such as the rosette and the flowers, with CHAIN STITCH in the darkest shade of ruby. For the scrolls and tendrils, outline them in the second shade of ruby, and in Chain Stitch. Then work a second Chain Stitch line inside the first in the lightest shade of ruby. Work the POINT LANCÉ STITCHES in the darkest shade of ruby, also the filled-in SATIN STITCH, and make the FRENCH KNOTS and the little edging stitches with the pale blue silk.

Tamis.—A worsted cloth, manufactured expressly for straining sauces. It is sold at oil shops.

Tammies.—These stuffs are composed of a union of cotton and worsted, the warp being like Buntings, made of worsted; yet, unlike the latter, they are plain, highly glazed, and chiefly used for upholstery. They are a kind of Scotch Camlet, and are otherwise called "Durants." They are twilled, with single warps, and are usually coarser than twilled Bombazets, and may be had in most colours. Their width varies from 32 inches, to 72 inches, and are mostly used for women's petticoats, curtains, and for window blinds.

Tape Lace.—The Braid and Tape Laces, or Guipures of the seventeenth and eighteenth centuries comprise most of the coarse Pillow Laces made in Italy, Spain, and Flanders, and are endless in variety of design and ground, although all retain the leading characteristics of the design appearing to consist of plain or ornamental braids or tapes arranged to form patterns, and connected together with either Bride or Réseau Grounds. The earliest Tape Laces are made with Bride Ground and simple Cloth Stitch, but gradually these were superseded by very elaborate designs, worked as part of the braid-like patterns, and connected by open meshed grounds. The stitches used in Tape Laces are given in BRAID WORK, and the manner of working the lace in GUIPURE LACE.

Tape Measures.—These Tapes are employed in trade, as well as for home use, for the measurement of dress and upholstery materials of all kinds. They are painted, and marked with figures and lines to indicate measurements from a quarter of an inch to 36 inches in length. Those in general use are wound up in small circular brass or boxwood boxes, by means of a little projecting handle or nut. They may also be had in coloured ribbon, with a case made in ivory, mother-o'-pearl, bone, or of some shell, having like those before named a pin running through the centre, on which it is wound.

Tapes.—Narrow bands of linen or cotton, employed as strings. They are of various makes, and are known as Star; India (or Chinese), which is of superior strength, and may be had either soft or sized, and cut in any lengths, and sold in large quantities, the numbers running from 00 to 12; the Imperial, a firmly made superior article, in numbers from 11 to 151; Dutch, of good, fine quality of linen, numbered as the Imperial; Frame, a stout half-bleached linen, and also made with a mixture of cotton; Filletings, a very heavy unbleached Holland, Nos. 3¼ to 10, and sold in various lengths; Stay, which is striped and narrow, employed by tailors to bind buttonholes and selvedges; Pink, made of cotton, numbers 16, 24, and 32,

Greece it was introduced into the Roman Empire. By Latin writers it is called Tapes or Tapete—a word derived from the Greek, and signifying an outer covering of any kind; from this its present name comes. After the break-up of the power of Rome, the making of Tapestry seems to have been discontinued in Europe until the time of the Holy Wars, when the Crusaders found it still practised and used by the Saracens. The manufacture was re-established by them in Europe, and the work for some time was known as Opus Saracenium, or Saracenic, and the maker called Saracens. Up to the sixteenth century Tapestry was worked either by the hand upon close cord-like canvas, and was really embroidery with coloured worsteds, silks, and gold thread, or was made in a loom in a manner that was neither true weaving, nor embroidery, but a combination of both, it being formed with a warp of cords stretched in a frame and worked over with short threads of coloured worsteds, threaded upon

FIG. 753. TAPESTRY.

cut in any length, or to be had very long on reels, it is used in law offices, and known as Red Tape; Pro Patria, a fine linen of similar make to Dutch, and of the same numbers. Bobbin Tape is made in cotton and linen, either round or flat, the sizes running in uneven numbers from 5 to 21, inclusive. The Indian Tape is twilled, and rather stiff. The Dutch plain, and does not easily knot; but it is less durable than the former. Tapes are loom-woven, after the manner of ribbons; many improvements having in recent years been invented in the machinery employed. Tapes are named by Chaucer:

> The Tapes of hire white Volupere,
> Were or the same suit of hire colere.
> *The Miller's Tale.*

Tapestry.—The making of Tapestry originated in the East, whence it spread to Egypt, and was there largely practised, and by the Egyptians taught to the Israelites. The art was known to the Greeks in the time of Homer, who makes frequent mention of it in his *Iliad*, and from

needles which filled in the design, without the cross threads or weft of true weaving. This manner of working Tapestry is alluded to in the Old Testament, in the verse, "I have woven my bed with cords."

From the time of its introduction into Europe until its final decay, Tapestry formed a very important item in the expenditure of the wealthy, it being used to hang round the walls of palaces and churches, and to lay down as coverings to the floors upon State occasions, when it took the place of the ordinary rush-strewn floor. Every monastery possessed a loom, and the work was reckoned among the accomplishments of the monks, who decorated the sanctuary with hangings, and worked altar-cloths and coverings. The first manufactories of any size established on the Continent were at Arras, in Flanders, Antwerp, Brussels, Liège, and other cities; but the work produced at Arras soon became so famous that the name of that town superseded the name of the work it executed, and for many years Tapestry, wherever made, was known as Arras. Thus, Canon Rock mentions that the Tapestry hangings given to the choir of Canterbury Cathedral by Prior Goldston (1595), though probably made by the monks of that establishment, are spoken of in the description of them as Arras Work. France soon entered the field in rivalry of Flanders, Henry IV. founding in 1606, the celebrated manufactory of Gobelin, which was re-modelled by the Minister Colbert, in the time of Louis XIV., and then became celebrated as a royal manufactory, and one that exists in the present day. The name Gobelin comes from the first artist who set up his looms in Paris, and who was a native of Flanders. His property known as the Hôtel de Gobelins, was purchased by the Crown. The first Tapestry manufactory was established in this country in 1509, by one William Sheldon. This he worked with the co-operation of a master Tapestry maker, Robert Hicks, at Barcheston, in Warwickshire. The second attempt to

A species of the same description of manufacture is called Moquette Tapestry, and is of recent date. It is of wool, designed to imitate the genuine Tapestry, and much resembling Utrecht Velvet. The fine kinds are employed for table-cloths, and the thick for carpets. It has a long close pile, and is chiefly woven in floral devices.

Tapestry worked by the needle, as illustrated in Fig. 753, differs but slightly from Embroidery. The stitches are made to lie close together, so that no portion of the foundation is visible, and each stitch is worked over only one cord of the foundation. The Stitches are Tent and Satin Stitch, with the outlines of the design followed by a gold thread, Couched to the surface. The labour of working large pieces for hangings by this method is great, particularly as every design is shaded and worked with colours matching the natural tints of the objects

FIG. 754. TAPESTRY.

establish the industry on a large scale in England was made at Mortlake, Surrey, about a hundred years later, by Francis Crane, at whose death the manufactory was closed, after having enjoyed the patronage of James I., Charles I., and Charles II. The work was assisted by foreign artists and workmen, and a small manufactory was instituted at Soho, London, as also others at Fulham and Exeter. The manufacture then ceased in this country, until re-established by Her Majesty the Queen, at Wind-sor, where it now is carried on, with great success, from designs executed by good artists, and particularly from those of the late E. M. Ward, R.A. It is under the patronage of H.R.H. the Princess Louise, Marchioness of Lorne.

represented. The designs are drawn upon the canvas, but the colouring of them is left to the taste of the worker.

Fig. 754 represents Tapestry made upon a loom. The work that is generally recognised as true Tapestry was made either with an upright or with a horizontal frame. When using the latter, the pattern was placed beneath the cords, and the worker executed it upon the wrong side This make is the one revived at Windsor, and is executed as follows: A double warp of strong white thread is stretched and worked with treadles. Upon a roller beneath the warp, but close to it is the coloured pattern. The worker takes a reel of coarse crewel wool, depresses one of the warp line of threads, runs the wool into the space where the colour is required, and brings it out again. He then by a movement of the treadle, brings the depressed warp line above the one first uppermost, and returns his colour through the intermediate space. The threads as worked, are pushed tightly together with a carding instrument, and all the ends of wool are left upon the surface of the work. In this process the worker never sees the right side of the Tapestry until it is taken out of the frame. With the high frame, although the worker cannot see what he is doing while manipulating the threads, he can pass to the back of the frame and there inspect it if required.

Tapestry Cloth.—This material is a description of Rep made in linen, and unbleached; it measures 28 inches in width, and is employed as a foundation for painting in the style of Tapestry.

Tapestry Stitch.—*See* EMBROIDERY STITCHES.

Tape Work.—A modern work, and one that is generally combined with Crochet or Tatting. It consists of forming rosettes with broad or binding tape, and uniting these rosettes with Crochet or Tatting as antimacassars, mats, or other drawing-room ornaments. The materials required are soft untwilled Tape, known as Chinese or Binding

FIG. 755. TAPE WORK.

Tape, the width depending upon the size of the rosette to be made; the widths most used are half an inch to an inch: Crochet cotton, and Tatting cotton of medium sizes.

To work the rosette shown in Fig. 755: Take a piece of Chinese Tape 1 inch in width; cut it to a length of 13 inches, fold it in half-quarters, eighths, and sixteenths, so that sixteen lines are formed down its width. Crease these well to render them visible; sew the two ends

together neatly with RUNNING and FELLING, and take a thread and run it in as a Vandyke line, as shown in Fig. 756, Detail A, from the bottom to the top of the tape, so that each point is upon one of the sixteen lines. Draw the tape together by means of this line, but not quite close, and fasten off the thread securely. Take a Crochet hook and Arden's Crochet cotton (No. 16), and finish off the rosette with Crochet. For the outside, pull out the points, and commence to work at the bottom of one of them. Make 4 CHAIN, †, a PICOT (made with 5 Chain drawn together by putting the hook back into the

FIG. 756. TAPE WORK—DETAIL A.

first made of the five), 1 Chain, 1 TREBLE, into the place where the Crochet commenced, 3 Chain, 1 Treble into the top part of the point, *, 1 Chain, a Picot, 1 Chain; repeat from * twice; 1 Treble into the top of the Treble first worked on the point to make the crossbar; 1 Treble into the point side by side with the first Treble, 3 Chain, 1 Treble into the hollow or lower part of the point, 1 Chain, and repeat from † until the circle is complete; then fasten the first 3 Chain to the last, and tie and cut off the cotton. For the centre: Work 1 DOUBLE CROCHET and 1 Chain between every centre point, catching the Double Crochet into the top of the point.

To make an *Antimacassar*: Work thirty-six of these rosettes and join them by the following small Crochet rosette: Make a CHAIN of 10 stitches, which join up, and work 16 DOUBLE CROCHET into it. Second round —1 Chain and 1 Treble into every second stitch on the first round. Third round—1 TREBLE *, 1 Chain, 1 PICOT; repeat twice from *, 1 Treble into the same stitch as the first Treble, 6 Chain; repeat from the commencement, and work this over every Treble in the second round.

Rosettes can be made entirely of tape. They are cut and sewn up, and run with a Vandyke line as previously described, but are drawn together quite in the centre. Unite them by sewing together at the points, and use the following small Tatted Circle to fill in spaces left between the uniting points. To work the Tatted Circle: Make a loop, work 4 DOUBLE, 1 PURL, *, 1 Double, 1 Purl; repeat from * four times, 5 Double; draw the loop up as an oval and work a second, but in this omit the first Purl and join the work to the last Purl on the first row instead; repeat until eight ovals are made. The number of ovals will depend upon the size of the cotton used and can be varied. Join the Rosettes to the Tatted Circles at their Purls.

Another Description of Tape Work is made by simply joining Vandyke braid to form insertions, like the one shown in Fig. 757. To work: Take Vandyke braid of a narrow width, and sew three of the points close together upon one side of it, and sew together the next three points upon the opposite side. Continue to sew these points together alternately at each side until the length of the insertion is obtained. Make three lengths of tape in this way, and then join them. For the edge,

FIG. 757. TAPE WORK.

work in Crochet 3 CHAIN, 1 SINGLE, join to the point nearest to the one commenced at; then 4 Chain over the hollow, 1 Single, join to the points; repeat from the commencement, and work both sides alike. This last kind of Tape Work, when executed with narrow braid instead of tape, is known as Mignardise Crochet, and is described under that heading in Crochet.

Tape Lace Work.—In this work the solid parts are made with narrow tape, drawn up into scallops or points, as previously described, and the open parts with Lace Stitches. To work: Take fine braid, a quarter of an inch in width, either white or coloured; cut off 12 inches, which sew up and run as described before, and make twelve points upon both sides. Draw these only slightly together, and sufficient to form an open rosette. Take Lace cotton, and fill in the centre of this rosette with a series of rounds in POINT DE BRUXELLES. Connect each Point de Bruxelles in the first row to a point of the rosette; work into the loops of the first row for the second; and work three to four rows, gradually lessening the size of the loops, so as to draw to a centre. Enclose this rosette with straight lines of tape. Make these by Running the Vandyke lines upon the tape as before, and drawing them up, but leave as long straight lines. Sew these to the rosettes at the top and bottom, and the rosettes together in the centre of the work; fill in all spaces left between the tapes with ENGLISH WHEELS and ORNAMENTAL BARS.

Tapisserie.—The French term for Tapestry, and for any description of hangings, the word *Tapis* denoting a carpet. *See* TAPESTRY.

Tapisserie d' Auxerre.—This Embroidery consists of working with Berlin single wool, in Satin Stitches, upon net. It is used to form antimacassars, or to stretch upon a frame in front of fire grates. The designs are chiefly of stars, circles, diamonds, and other geometrical figures. To work: Select a rather open and stiff hexagonal net, either of black or white; divide this off into squares before commencing the work, so that the designs may be evenly embroidered. Take a black or white thread, so as to contrast with the net, and run it into one row of the net. Miss thirty meshes, and run in another line, and repeat until the net is marked out with horizontal lines of thread,

then run lines across the horizontal ones to form perfect squares upon the net. Mark out upon paper the outline of the diamond or cross to be worked, and see that it fits into one or several squares, hold this under the net, and make SATIN STITCHES upon the net with single Berlin wool, to fill in the figure, move the paper pattern, and work in the design until all the squares are full, varying the colours of the wool. Finish off by drawing out the threads from the net that made the squares.

Tarlatan.—A thin, gauze-like muslin, much stiffened, and so called from the chief centre of the manufacture, Tarare, in France. It may be had in various colours, and is much used for evening dresses. It was originally an Indian manufacture, which was copied in Europe. The width of Tarlatan is very considerable, measuring from 1½ yards to 2 yards in width.

Tartan.—A term denoting the chequered pattern peculiar to the Scotch national costume, the varieties in the colours, combinations of the same, and the dimensions of the squares in each pattern, distinguishing one Clan from another. There are also Fancy Tartans, which, together with those of Scotch origin, are produced in silk and stuff dress materials, woollen shawls, handkerchiefs, ribbons, stockings, and socks. Tartan woollen stuffs were introduced from Normandy in the eleventh century, and are commonly called Plaids, the material and the chequered patterns and combinations of colours being usually confounded together under the name Plaid. Before the sixteenth century there is no record of the *Tartan* being the distinctive costume of the Scottish Clans, as it was common to many nations besides. Their *Brechan*, or Plaid, consists of 12 or 13 yards of narrow chequered woollen cloth, wrapped round the body, brought over one or both shoulders, and crossed at the back, the ends hanging to the knees. Its use in Scotland, as such, was prohibited by Act of Parliament in 1747, and the Grey Shepherds' Mauds were manufactured instead; the Act was repealed in 1782. *See* FANCY CHECKS and PLAIDS.

Tassel.—Tassels are used as a finish to embroidered cushions. To make: Take some of the silks or wools used in the embroidery, selecting the greatest number from the shade chiefly used in the work. Wind these round a piece of cardboard, 3 or 4 inches wide, and, when enough has been wound to make a thick Tassel, push the whole off the card. Thread a wool needle with some silk, twist this round the wound wool, half an inch from the top, secure it with a stitch, push the needle up through the top of the Tassel, and fasten the Tassel on to the material with it, and then cut the ends of wool apart that are at the bottom. There are also Tassels which are machine-made, pendent tufts of silk, wool, cotton, thread, or gold and silver cord, sometimes attached to the end of cords, or to a gimp or braid heading, following one another in a row. They are sold separately, or as a trimming, by the yard; they may be had in every colour and combination of colours, to suit any article of dress or upholstery, and are made in Chenille, fine silk thread, and silk twist. The worsted sorts are chiefly used for furniture decorations, but are also manufactured in fine qualities for dress.

Blind Tassels are made of unbleached thread, as well as of worsted in white, scarlet, green, and other colours.

Tassel Stitch.—*See* EMBROIDERY STITCHES.

Tatted Lace.—*See* TATTING.

Tatting.—The precise date of the first introduction of Tatting cannot be determined, as, for many years, it did not take any prominent position in the arts of the day, but it has been practised for more than a hundred years, and is a reproduction of the Ragusa Gimp Laces and Knotted Laces of the sixteenth century, of which Knot Work was the first imitation. Knot Work is made over a cord, with the cotton forming it wound upon a netting needle, but in Tatting the stitches are made over a thread, and the thread wound upon a Shuttle small enough to allow of its being passed easily backwards and forwards over and under the thread it is forming the stitches upon.

The English name of Tatting, taken from the word Tatters, indicates the fragile piece-meal nature of the work, as does the French name of Frivolité; but however fragile and lace-like in appearance, it is exceedingly strong, and capable of bearing much rough usage. Unlike Crochet and Knitting, where each stitch is slightly dependent on its neighbour, and one becoming unfastened endangers the rest, the stitches of Tatting are isolated as far as their strength goes, being composed of knots and remaining separate knots, and are very difficult to undo when once formed. The work consists of so few stitches that it is extremely simple, and requires neither thought nor fixed attention when once the nature of the stitch has been mastered, a glance, or the feel of it passing through the fingers, being sufficient for an experienced Tatter. It also has the advantage of being very portable, and can be worked at for a few minutes and put down again without becoming disarranged, which is an impossibility with many descriptions of lace.

For many years Tatting was made as a succession of Knots over a loop of its own thread, which was then drawn up and the stitches on it formed into an oval by being drawn together. These ovals had the appearance of Buttonholes, and were only connected by the little piece of plain thread that was missed after one oval was made and before the next loop was formed. To connect them at all tightly a needle and thread were used, and they were sewn together at their widest part. Two great improvements to Tatting have been made within the last fifteen years; first, the introduction of the lace loops known as Picots, and called Purls in Tatting, which trim the edges of real lace and add much to its lightness; and secondly, the use of a second thread or Shuttle, which enables straight lines and scallops to be worked, as well as the original ovals. The Purls worked round the edge of the ovals and straight lines serve to soften their thick look, and they also are used to connect the various parts, the thread being drawn through a Purl and secured with a knot (where a join is to be made), while the lace is in progress, instead of having recourse to a needle and thread. The second thread or Shuttle enables the Tatter to execute elaborate designs that were quite

impossible when only one thread was used. The two threads are tied together, and the first is used to form a loop and make an oval, while on the second the first thread forms the stitches, and leaves them upon it without drawing it up; it is then in a position to make a loop and work an oval if required, and to continue forming stitches upon the second thread whenever the pattern so directs, thus making the work twice as ornamental, and enabling large and wide designs to be formed.

There are two ways of working with the double threads, the one most used is made by winding the first thread upon the Shuttle and securing it to that, while the second thread is either left attached to the skein or wound upon the second Shuttle and remains passive, all the stitches being formed upon it with the first thread, which forms loops of itself, and covers them, to make ovals where required. In the second plan, invented by Mrs. Mee, the working thread is not detached from the skein, and so joins in it are obviated—and these must be frequent when it is wound upon a small Shuttle and detached from the skein. In this second plan, the second thread attached to the skein is placed above the one wound upon the Shuttle, when both are held in the left hand, and is put round the fingers of that hand to form a loop upon which the knots are formed by the Shuttle thread. As the knots are really made from the loop, the waste all comes from that thread. When an oval has to be made, as the loop will not draw up, a crochet needle is used to draw the foundation thread up as a loop close to the last piece of completed lace, and the Shuttle being put through this loop, as in an ordinary join, forms the stitches into an oval.

The Stitch or Knot of Tatting is formed with two movements—sometimes only one of these movements is made—and the stitch so made is known as Half Stitch, but the Whole or Double Stitch is the one almost universally used. It is very simple, but depends upon the position of the hands. Hold the shuttle horizontally in the right hand, between the first finger and thumb, and rather backwards, and let the thread fall from it from the inner part of the right side; pass the other end of the thread, after making the loop (when only one thread is used) over the left hand. Slip the Shuttle under the loop thread, which let pass between it and the first finger of the right hand and back between it and the thumb, and bring it quickly out between the first and second fingers of the left hand. Drop the loop from the last fingers of the left hand, but retain that finger and thumb upon it, give a slight jerk, so as to make the twist just formed transfer itself from the Shuttle thread to the loop, which it should be a part of; put back the left fingers into the loop and stretch it out, and draw the knot up close to the thumb while the Shuttle thread is tightened with the right hand. Bring the Shuttle back over the left hand with its thread hanging downwards, and pass the loop under the Shuttle between the thumb and Shuttle, and back between the first finger and Shuttle, drop the loop, jerk, and draw up as before; when enough stitches have been formed, draw the loop up so that they form an oval. The difficulties of the beginner consists in keeping the thread falling from the Shuttle in its right place, making the knot upon the right thread, giving the proper jerk, turning the stitches to the outside of the oval, and leaving too much or too little space between the drawn up ovals. The fingers at first also seem to be always in the way, and the Purls made too small; but, after a little practice, all these difficulties disappear, and there are no others to contend with.

The STITCHES and TERMS used in TATTING are as follows:—

Double Stitch.—This stitch is the one most used in Tatting. It is made with two loops or knots, and requires two movements of the Shuttle. The first part of the stitch, when used without the second part, is called Half, or Single Stitch. To work: Make a loop of the thread as shown in Fig 758, letter *a*, hold its join between the first finger and thumb of the left hand and the loop over all the fingers; let the unattached end of the thread fall

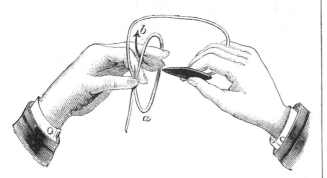

FIG. 758. TATTING, DOUBLE STITCH—FIRST PART.

downwards, and the end attached to the Shuttle arrange upwards (*see* Fig. 758, letter *b*), and let it pass over the knuckles of the left hand, so as to be out of the way of the loop and not interfere with the Shuttle while making the knot. Hold the Shuttle flat between the thumb and first finger of the right hand, and let the end of the thread come from the inner part of the side that is towards the fingers of the right hand; let it pass under the first two, but over and caught by the little finger. Put the Shuttle into the loop (as shown by the arrow in Fig. 758), between the first and second fingers of the left hand, and while pushing the Shuttle out towards the

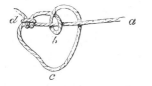

FIG. 759. TATTING, DOUBLE STITCH—FIRST KNOT.

left hand; let the loop thread pass over the Shuttle and between it and the first finger of the right hand; then bring the Shuttle back towards the right hand, and let the loop thread pass back under the Shuttle, between it and the thumb. Do not take the right thumb and the first finger off the Shuttle during this movement, only raise

them to allow of the passage of the loop thread. Draw the last three fingers of the left hand out of the loop, but keep the first finger and thumb still on the join; pull the thread attached to the Shuttle tight with a jerk, and by so doing let the Half Stitch or Knot just made be formed of the loop and held by the Shuttle thread (*see* Fig. 759, where *a* is the Shuttle thread, *b* the stitch made but not tightened, *c* the loop, and *d* a completed stitch). Draw the stitch tight by putting the left-hand fingers back into the loop and extending them. Keep the knot thus made close to the thumb of the left hand, and complete the Double thus: The thread attached to the Shuttle will now be hanging downwards, and not over the left hand. Keep the thumb and the first finger on the loop, and the other fingers in the loop as before. Hold the Shuttle as before, but rather forward (*see* Fig. 760), but put it over the left hand and

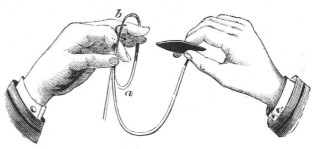

FIG. 760. TATTING, DOUBLE STITCH—SECOND PART.

beyond the loop; push it backwards into the loop *a* (as shown by the arrow *b* in Fig. 760), between the first and second finger of the left hand, and let the loop thread pass under the Shuttle, between it and the right-hand thumb, and then back to the left over the Shuttle, between it and the first finger. Never lose hold of the Shuttle during this movement, only raise the fingers to allow of the loop passing under them. Take the left-hand fingers out of the loop as before, retaining hold with the thumb and first finger; pull the Shuttle thread with a jerk, so that the knot formed is

FIG. 761. TATTING, DOUBLE STITCH—SECOND KNOT.

made of the loop thread, and runs upon the Shuttle thread (*see* Fig. 761, in which *a* is the Shuttle thread, *c* is the new knot tightened, *d* the loop, *b* the first half of the knot tightened, and *e* a completed stitch). Put the fingers of the left hand into the loop again, and draw the knot tight by extending them; hold the stitches down as made, and keep them close together. The error likely to be made in the stitch is that the knot is formed of the Shuttle thread, and not of the loop. This is detected in two ways—first, from the look of the stitch made; and secondly, the loop will not pull up or open out, but remains firm. The loop thread when the stitches are properly made can be drawn up quite close by being pulled, or can be enlarged to any size. A Double Stitch can be made upon a straight piece of thread, instead of a loop, if the thread is held in the left hand between the thumb and forefinger, and caught round the third finger.

English Stitch.—A name sometimes given to the second half of *Double Stitch*

French Stitch.—A name sometimes given to *Half Stitch.*

Half Stitch.—This stitch is also known as Single. It is not so much used in Tatting as the Double, but it is occasionally required. It is the first part of the DOUBLE, and is worked thus: Make a loop with the thread, which hold at its join between the thumb and first finger of the left hand, and let the loop pass round all the fingers. Pass the end of the thread attached to the Shuttle over the left hand out of the way of the loop. Hold the Shuttle flat between the thumb and first finger of the right hand, and let the thread proceed from it from the inner part of the outside of the Shuttle, that is, towards the fingers of the right hand. Let the thread pass underneath the hand until it reaches the little finger; bring it out here, and let that finger tighten, or loosen it at pleasure. Put the Shuttle into the loop between the first and second fingers of the left hand, and while pushing the Shuttle towards that hand, let the loop thread pass over the Shuttle and between it and the first finger of the right hand. Then bring the Shuttle back towards the right hand, and let the loop thread pass back between the Shuttle and the right thumb. Keep hold of the Shuttle, and only raise the thumb and finger so that the thread may pass beneath them. Draw the left hand fingers out of the loop, but keep hold of it with the thumb and first finger. Pull the thread attached to the Shuttle tight with a jerk, and by so doing, let the knot formed by the movements be made of the loop thread, and see that it runs upon the Shuttle thread. Tighten this by putting the left hand fingers again into the loop, and extending them. The loop that is formed is shown in Fig. 758, *a* being the tight Shuttle thread, *c* the loose loop, *b* the knot made and not drawn tight. The position of the hands to commence the stitch is shown in Fig. 759.

Join.—There are two ways of joining Tatting, both of which are frequently required in the same pattern. In one, the Purls are used to attach circles and ovals, and in the other, straight lines of Tatting are made with the aid of a second thread between the ovals and circles formed with the first thread.

To Join with the Purls: Make a loop, and upon it form stitches until the PURL upon an already finished piece of Tatting is reached, to which the piece in progress is to be attached. Take the Tatting pin, or an ordinary pin or Crochet hook, pass it through the Purl, and with it pull the loop through the Purl, where it is beyond the stitches, taking care that the loop thread is not twisted as it passes through. Draw it through until it will admit of the Shuttle, and pass the Shuttle through it and then

straighten out the loop thread again. If the loop thread has been twisted when put through the Purl, the stitches will not run upon it and cannot be drawn up. If it has been correctly drawn through, the stitches will run upon the loop in the ordinary manner.

To Join with Two Threads: When two threads are used, sometimes both are wound upon Shuttles, at others only the first, or working thread, is attached to a Shuttle, and the second left attached to the reel. It is immaterial which course is pursued, but, in the explanation, the "first thread" indicates the one that does the work, and is wound upon a Shuttle; and the "second thread" the one used to make the lines that join the pattern made with ovals and circles, without the necessity of breaking the thread. To work: Knot the two threads together, make a loop with the first thread, and work upon it with the first thread. Draw it up, and continue to work ovals or circles with the first thread, until the desired number is finished. Draw this up tight, pick up the second thread, hold it between the thumb and first finger of the left hand with the work already made, and keep it as a straight line by catching it down with the third finger. Open the first and second fingers with the thread extended between them, wide enough for the Shuttle to pass, and work a stitch with the first thread in the usual way. Drop the second thread, as the loop is dropped while making the stitch, and give the first thread the customary jerk, so that the knot is formed of the straight thread. Work stitches until the length of the line required is completed; then drop the second thread, and continue the pattern with the first.

Josephine Knot.—This Knot is used in Tatting as an ornament to break the line of a straight piece of thread when the work is done with one thread only. It is made as follows: Make a loop, and upon it work five to seven HALF STITCHES, according to the thickness of the thread used; commence to draw the loop up, but before it is quite drawn up, put the Shuttle through it, then draw it quite close, and a lump or thick knot will be formed.

Loop.—All the Tatting that is made with the help of one thread only is formed upon a loop. After the required number of stitches are made the loop is drawn together, and an oval or circle thus formed. To work: Make a loop over the left hand, hold the join between the first finger and thumb, and let the end of the thread attached to the Shuttle be upwards, and pass it over the left hand out of the way of the loop. Make the required number of stitches, then drop the loop, and hold the stitches lightly and firmly in the left hand, and gradually draw the loop together by pulling the thread attached to the Shuttle. Pull this until the first and last stitch upon the loop meet.

Picot.—A name sometimes applied to denote a *Purl.*

Pin and Ring.—The instrument shown in Fig. 762 is used in Tatting for two purposes, one to draw loops of cotton up with so as to connect various parts of the design, and the other to work the Purl with. The ring is put round the little finger of the right hand, so that the pin can be used without moving the ring. This instrument is not a necessity to Tatting, an ordinary black-headed pin answering as well.

FIG. 762. TATTING PIN AND RING.

Purl.—The Purls in Tatting are sometimes called loops, which rather confuses the worker between them and the loop upon which the circles and ovals in Tatting are made. Purls are the small loops that stand out from the edge of any part of the design and trim it, giving to it the appearance of the Picots made in Needle Laces; they are also used to pass the thread through when two parts of a pattern have to be joined. They are made in two ways, of which the following is the easier: Make a stitch, and allow one-eighth of an inch of thread on both the loop and the Shuttle thread before commencing the next stitch, when the stitches are drawn close by the loop being pulled up, the piece of Shuttle thread between them will stand out beyond them as a small loop. When making a number of Purls, always divide them with a stitch, and be careful to leave the same length of thread for each Purl.

Another way: Take a knitting needle or big pin, according to the size required for the Purl, make a stitch, then pass the thread round the needle and make another stitch close up to the needle. When the knitting needle is withdrawn, the thread that went round it forms the Purl. This plan is more tedious than the one first given, but the Purls made by it are sure to be of the same size.

Shuttle.—The Shuttle is the instrument used in Tatting to wind the cotton upon. It is shown in Fig. 763, and is made of three pieces, either of bone, ivory, mother-o'-pearl, or tortoiseshell. Of the three pieces, two are oval, flat on the inside, and convex on the outer, and these are

FIG. 763. TATTING SHUTTLE.

joined together with a small short thick piece of ivory, through which a hole is bored. The Shuttle can be obtained of three sizes: No. 1 is used for very fine Tatting, No. 2 for the ordinary description of work, and No. 3 for coarse.

In selecting a Shuttle, see that the two brass pins that keep it together do not protrude upon the outside, as they are then apt to entangle the thread while working, and prevent the stitches being easily made. Also take care that the points are close. To fill the Shuttle: Pass the end of the thread through the hole bored in the centrepiece of the Shuttle, and then secure it by a knot; wind the cotton upon the Shuttle by passing it alternately through the two ends, but do not put too much cotton on at once, or the points will gape open at the ends.

Single Tatting.—See HALF STITCH.

Stitches.—The number of Stitches in Tatting are very limited. They comprise Double Stitch, Half Stitch or Single Tatting, Josephine Knot, and Purl.

Tatting with Two Shuttles.—Tatting with Two Threads or Shuttles is a modern invention, and one that has done much to render the work like real lace. Before it was invented all the Tatting that could be done had to be made upon a loop of the only thread used, and then drawn up. This produced any amount of circles and ovals, but as these were only connected with a line of plain thread, the designs they formed were poor, and mainly consisted of Stars, Trefoils, and Rosettes, worked separately, and joined together at the Purls. By the introduction of a second thread, scalloped and straight lines

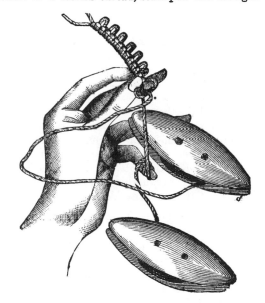

FIG. 764. TATTING WITH TWO SHUTTLES.

can be worked between the ovals and circles, and this is an immense improvement to the work, as the designs are intricate and much more serviceable, and the wearisome joining of separate pieces is greatly avoided. To work with two Shuttles: Wind thread upon both Shuttles, which latter should be of different colours, to distinguish between them. Knot the two threads together, and hold both between the finger and thumb of the left hand. Make a loop, and work with the first Shuttle, as in ordinary Tatting for ovals and circles, but when a straight line between these is shown in the pattern take up the second thread and catch it round the little finger of the left-hand to keep it out in a straight line from the thumb (*see* Fig. 764). Then with the first Shuttle or thread make the usual stitches, using the second thread instead of a loop, and dropping it, so that the knot is formed of it, and stretching it out again over the hand, so that the knot is tightened. Work upon the straight thread the number of stitches required, and leave them without drawing them up as a loop, but draw them together by pulling the shuttle thread. Then to make ovals, drop the second thread, and work only with the first, but be careful to commence the oval close to the stitches upon the second thread, so that no space is left between the stitches. Continue to work upon the second thread when any straight parts of the pattern are required, and tie it up and fasten it off when no longer wanted. It is not necessary to attach this thread to a second Shuttle, as it makes no stitches; it is quite sufficient to leave it fastened to the reel. Fig. 764 shows a straight line, ornamented with Purls made with the two threads as follows: Tie the two threads together, and hold both in the left hand between the thumb and first finger; wind the thread from the second Shuttle round the little finger, and open the hand out; then make 1 DOUBLE, 1 PURL, alternately, upon the straight thread. The illustration shows a Purl just made, and the first Half of the Double.

Another Way to work with two Shuttles: Tie the two threads together, and wind up upon the Shuttles, but let one of the Shuttle threads be still attached to the skein. In working, always use this as the foundation thread, and keep it stretched across the fingers of the left hand, or as a loop, so that as the knots are really formed upon the foundation thread the thread used most is from the skein. As the foundation thread will not allow of being drawn up like an ordinary loop when making an oval, draw the stitches together with the help of the pin, and form a small loop, as in *Join*, through which pass the Shuttle. By using this plan of working, the knots formed by joining lengths of thread are avoided.

The following selection of TATTING PATTERNS will be found useful:

Diamond.—The Diamond shown in Fig. 765 is used, when worked with coarse cotton, to make pincushion covers, or parts of an antimacassar, and when worked with fine cotton, for caps or trimmings. For coarse work, use Walter and Evans' Crochet cotton, No. 1; for fine Tatting, cotton No. 40. Use two Shuttles, and work the four corners of the diamond singly. First corner—Make a loop, work upon it 7 DOUBLE, 1 PURL, 1 Double, 1 Purl 1 Double, 1 Purl, 1 Double, 6 Double, draw the loop up, and make another close to it, on which work 6 Double, fastened to the last Purl of first loop; 4 Double, 1 Purl, 2 Double, 1 Purl, 2 Double, 6 Double, draw the loop up, and make another loop close to it, and upon that work 6 Double, fastened on the last Purl of preceding loop; 4 Double, 1 Purl, 1 Double, 1 Purl, 8 Double. Take up the second Shuttle, fasten the thread to the end of the thread at the first loop, throw the thread of the first Shuttle over the fingers of the left hand, and work with the first thread

upon the second thread. Work 5 Double, and then a circle made with the first thread only, make a loop upon which work 8 Double, fastened on the last Purl of the last of the loops worked close together; 5 Double, 1 Purl, 5 Double, 1 Purl, 4 Double, 1 Purl, 6 Double, draw the loop up, and so make the circle, then work over the thread of the second Shuttle 5 Double, 1 Purl, 1 Double, 1 Purl, 3 Double, 1 Purl, 1 Double, 1 Purl, 5 Double; make a loop with the first thread, and upon it work with the first thread a circle thus, 6 Double, 1 Purl, 4 Double, 1 Purl, 5 Double, 1 Purl, 5 Double, fasten to the first Purl made on the loop made first of the three together; 8 Double, draw the circle up and work upon the second thread with the first, 5 Double, fasten the thread so as to form a circle with the stitches worked on the second thread, and then cut off. The engraving shows the three little loops made first at the extreme point of the corner, and the two circles fastened to these, and upon each side of the large loop which is made gradually upon the second thread. Work the four corners as described, and then the centre of the

FIG. 765. DIAMOND TATTING.

design. This consists of four leaves, which touch each other at their base. To work a leaf: Make a loop, 3 Double, 1 Purl, 2 Double, 1 Purl, 1 Double, 1 Purl, 1 Double, 1 Purl, 2 Double, 1 Purl, 3 Double, and draw up. Work all the leaves thus, and join them as worked to the first Purl made upon the preceding leaf, omitting that Purl in the newly made leaf. Work the oval circles which connect the corners to the centre as follows: Fasten the thread to the Purl of a corner, make a loop, work 7 Double, 1 Purl, 8 Double, fasten the thread into a Purl of another corner opposite to the one on the first corner, work 8 Double, 1 Purl, 7 Double, and draw up the loop, fasten the thread through the same Purl of the first corner that it was first fastened to, carry it on to the next Purl of the same corner, and fasten it to that, then work an oval circle as before, and continue until the 4 oval circles on that side are made, then fasten the thread on the two cross Purls of the centre pattern, and work 4 oval circles on the other side of the corner, connecting a new or third corner with them to the design. Work the 8 oval circles still remaining as described, connecting the last or fourth corner into the design with them. When the diamond is completed, draw two threads on each side of each corner pattern, along the lines made at the top and bottom of the oval circles, to strengthen the lines there made, and so that they stand out boldly.

D'Oyley.—The pattern shown in Fig. 766 can be used for a D'Oyley if worked with fine Tatting cotton (No. 60) and the smallest Shuttle; or for an antimacassar when

the work thus: For the twelfth and fourteenth ovals— Make a loop, work 1 Double, 1 Purl, 9 Double, 1 Purl, 9 Double, 1 Purl, 1 Double. For the sixteenth and eighteenth ovals—Make a loop, work 3 Double, 1 Purl, * 1 Double, 1 Purl, repeat from * thirteen times, 3 Double. Work the twentieth and twenty-second ovals like the twelfth and fourteenth, and in the twenty-first oval join in the middle Purl to the thirteenth, fifteenth, seventeenth, and nineteenth ovals, and repeat from the first oval. Repeat until

FIG. 766. TATTED D'OYLEY.

worked with Crochet cotton. A fourth part of the round is shown, and the Tatting is made with one thread and in four pieces, which are joined with a needle and thread and finished with Ornamental Wheels inserted into the centres of the Tatted Circles. To work: Commence in the centre of the D'Oyley, and work the eleven little ovals that are close together first, these are all made alike and the work reversed between each. First oval—Make a loop, upon which work 1 DOUBLE, 1 PURL, 6 Double, 1 Purl, 6 Double, 1 Purl, 1 Double; draw the loop up, reverse the work, make a second loop, and work as before; join every alternate oval in the first and last Purl, omitting those Purls in the making of the new ovals. When the tenth oval is reached, work to the centre Purl, and then join on to the eighth and sixth, fourth and second ovals. Proceed with the work after the eleven ovals are made with the same kind of ovals, reversing them as before, but increase the size of those ovals that come to the outside of

eight patterns or points are made, then take a piece of stiff paper, cut it out in a circle the size of a D'Oyley, lay the Tatting upon it, join the first and last oval and any ovals that touch in the engraving and have not been joined in the work, and gather together as a centre two ovals from each pattern, which connect and draw up by an Ornamental WHEEL made with a needle and thread. Leave the Tatting on the paper and add the fresh work to it as made. The next round will consist of the double scallops that connects the first part of the work to the stars. This scallop is more clearly defined in the engraving in the lower scallops beneath the stars than in the upper ones, as it is there not drawn up so much, both rounds being alike. Commence by working the oval under the one which is attached to the large outside oval at the right of the pattern for the oval; make a loop, work 1 Double, 1 Purl, 6 Double, 1 Purl, 6 Double, 1 Purl, 1 Double, and draw up; go on working and reversing the ovals, and join the three inside ovals; continue until sixteen small ovals are made, join the sixteenth oval to the fourteenth, twelfth, tenth, and eighth ovals, and when working the eighteenth and twentieth ovals join them in the centre, Purl to the sixth and fourth ovals respectively. Join the twenty-second and twenty-fourth ovals together at the middle Purl, and join the twenty-sixth and twenty-eighth ovals with a long Purl to the middle Purl of the two highest of the large Purls in the centre of an outside oval on the last round (*see* Fig. 766). Join the thirtieth oval to the last four inside ovals, and repeat the pattern until all the scallops are made, and then fasten off. The third round is composed of Stars; these are worked separately and joined to the last Round and to each other as the Purls that touch are made. Make each Star with twenty-four ovals; work these alternately for the outside oval. Make a loop, work 1 Double, 1 Purl, 8 Double, 1 Purl, 8 Double, 1 Purl, 1 Double, draw the loop up. For the inside oval: Make a loop, work 1 Double, 1 Purl, 7 Double, 1 Purl, 7 Double, 1 Purl, 1 Double. Join every alternate oval in the first and last Purl, omitting that Purl at the join on the new oval; when the twelve inside ovals are made, draw the centre Purls on them together into a Circle, and make an Ornamental Wheel with a needle and thread inside the Circle. Work the last round of the Tatting as a double scallop, and like the second round, except that in each oval make 8 Double instead of 6 Double, so as to make the ovals larger.

Edging.—(Block Pattern.) Work in Arden's No. 18 Crochet cotton for a three-quarter inch border. The pattern is done with two threads, and it is important that when the first or shuttle one is used, its first stitch is made quite up to the last stitch formed with the under thread, and, when the latter is taken over the fingers for working the first stitch is made close to the root of the loop made with the shuttle cotton. Commence on the second, or under thread; put this round the fingers, and on it make 5 DOUBLE, 1 PURL, 5 Double, 1 Purl, 4 Double. Drop the under thread, †, make a loop with the shuttle thread, and on it work 5 Double, join to the first Purl upon the under thread, 5 Double, 1 Purl, 5 Double, 1 Purl, 5 Double, draw up the loop, take up the under thread, and work 4 Double on it. Drop it, make a loop with the shuttle thread, and work 5 Double: join to the last Purl of first loop, *, 2 Double, 1 Purl, repeat from * seven times, work 5 Double. Draw the loop up, make a third loop like the second one, and close to it, and join it to the last Purl on the second loop. Take up the under thread, work 4 Double, drop it, and with the shuttle thread make the fourth loop, thus: 5 Double, join to the last Purl on the third loop, 5 Double, 1 Purl, 5 Double, 1 Purl, 5 Double, draw the loop up. Put the under thread round the fingers, work 4 Double, join to the Purl last made on the under thread before the first loop was commenced, and, still using the same thread work 5 Double, join to the last Purl on the fourth loop, work 5 Double, 1 Purl, 5 Double, 1 Purl, 4 Double. Drop the under cotton, and commence with the shuttle thread to repeat the pattern from †; but after the second group of 5 Double, join to the Purl in the middle of fourth loop, instead of making a Purl.

(2). Work the edging illustrated in Fig. 767 with Walter and Evans's Tatting cotton No. 40, or Crochet cotton, No. 20. Two threads are required, and the work is made in two pieces, the first consisting of the ovals and connecting line, the second of the single oval and line forming the border. To work the Ovals: Tie the two

FIG. 767. TATTING—EDGING (NO. 2).

threads together, *, make a loop upon the shuttle thread, and upon it work 8 DOUBLE, 1 PURL, 4 Double, 1 Purl, 4 Double. Draw this up, and close to it make another loop, upon which work 4 Double; join to the last Purl on the first oval, 4 Double, 1 Purl, 2 Double, 1 Purl, 4 Double, 1 Purl, 4 Double. Draw up, and work close to the 2 ovals a third. Make a loop, work 4 Double, join to the last Purl on the second oval, 4 Double, 1 Purl, 8 Double. Draw this oval up, and tighten all the ovals; then pick up the under or second thread, and upon it work 10 Double. Drop the second thread, and work the three lower ovals with the first thread. In the first oval make a loop, work 8 Double, 1 Purl, 1 Double, 1 Purl, 3 Double, 1 Purl, 4 Double; draw up. Work the second oval, make a loop, work 4 Double, join to the last Purl on the preceding oval, 5 Double, 1 Purl, 5 Double, 1 Purl, 4 Double. Draw up, and work the third oval. Make a loop, work 4 Double, join to the last Purl on the second oval, 3 Double, 1 Purl, 1 Double, 1 Purl, 8 Double. Draw up all the ovals close together, and work on the second thread 10 Doubles. Then repeat the pattern from *, but, instead of the first Purl upon the first oval, join the work to the last Purl upon the third oval. Do this also when the first oval of the bottom set of ovals is reached. For the border: Tie two threads together, and work the single oval with the first thread, the connecting line with the two threads. For the oval make a loop, and on it work 6 Double, join the oval to the Purl left upon the last oval of the three bottom ovals, work 4 Double, join the oval to the Purl left upon the first oval of the next group of three, work 6 Double. Draw up and pick up the under thread, upon which work 8 Double, and connect to the top Purl on the second oval of the group of three, work 8 Double, drop the second thread, and work the single oval with the shuttle thread. Repeat the border from the commencement. Sew the edging to the material by attaching the border line to it.

(3) Work the Edging shown in Fig. 768 with Walter and Evans' Tatting cotton, No. 40, or Crochet cotton, No 20. It is made with two threads, the three ovals being formed on the first thread, and the line connecting them

with both the threads. To work: Tie the two threads together, and for the first Oval make a loop with the thread on the Shuttle and work on it 4 DOUBLE, 1 PURL, 4 Double, 1 Purl, 4 Double, 1 Purl, 4 Double; draw up tight, and work the next oval quite close to the first. Make a loop, work 4 Double, join to the last Purl upon the first oval, work 9 Double, 1 Purl, 4 Double; draw up. Work the the third oval like the first, but omit the first Purl, and join to the second oval instead. Draw the three ovals well together, and tie the two threads together; turn the ovals downwards, and upon the under or second thread work 4

FIG. 768. TATTING—EDGING (NO. 3).

Double, join to the last Purl on the third oval; work 1 Purl, 4 Double, 1 Purl, 8 Double. Turn the work, and repeat the three ovals made with the shuttle thread, join the first to the straight line by passing the thread round the straight line after the first 4 Double is worked, and omit the Purl there. Then work 4 Double and join to the third loop of the first group of ovals, work the rest of the first oval and the others as already described, and repeat the ovals and the connecting line to the end of the Edging. Sew the Edging on to the material with the help of the Purls upon the connecting line.

(4) *Pointed.*—This Edging is useful for trimming ladies' underclothing. It is worked with two threads, and is made by working five ovals divided from each other with curved lines, which are joined in the centre, while the ovals are arranged in a pyramidal form, two upon each side and one as a point. Each group of five ovals is connected by a straight line of stitches. To work: Use Walter and Evans' Crochet cotton, No. 10, and the medium-sized Shuttle. Knot the two threads together, and work upon the second thread, *, 12 DOUBLE, 1 PURL, 3 Double, *, then make a loop with the first thread and work an oval of 4 Double, 1 Purl, 2 Double, then 1 Purl and 1 Double five times, 6 Double (make the Purls of a good size); draw the loop up, pick up the second thread, and work on it 3 Double, 1 Purl, 3 Double; drop the second thread, and make an oval like the last, but join it to the last Purl upon the first oval, instead of making the first Purl; draw the oval up and take up the second thread, upon this work 3 Double, drop the second thread and make the third oval like the second, but work 1 Double, 1 Purl, seven instead of five times; draw it up, and work 3 Double upon the second thread. Work the fourth oval like the second, then 3 Double upon the second thread, join to the Purl last made upon the second thread and work 3 Double. Make the fifth oval like the second oval, work 3 Double upon the second thread, and join to the first oval made on it; then work 9 Double, 1 Purl, 3 Double; repeat the pattern from *, but in making the second point join the fourth and fifth ovals of the last point to the centre Purl of the first and second new ovals, and omit those Purls in them.

(5) *Scalloped.*—The Scalloped Edging in Fig. 769 is represented with only one Scallop formed, and without the Crochet line that completes the Edging, and that is worked to sew the Edging to a foundation. The work is so represented, as it shows the Tatting more clearly, and as the Scallop is frequently joined to an insertion, the Crochet line would then be superfluous. To work: Use Walter and Evans' Boar's Head cotton, No. 14. Commence with the ring in the centre; make a LOOP, work 1

FIG. 769. TATTING—SCALLOPED EDGING (NO. 5).

Double, 1 Purl, * 2 Double, 1 Purl, repeat from * ten times, 1 Double, draw the loop up, and Twist the thread into the first Purl on the ring. To make the outside edge: Leave half an inch of cotton, and then work the oval; make a loop, work 5 Double, 1 Purl, * 1 Double, 1 Purl, repeat from * four times, 5 Double, draw the loop up, leave the same length of cotton as before, and join it to the next Purl on the centre ring and repeat the oval. Make six ovals, joining each to the one preceding it, and to the Purl on the centre ring.

(6) *Simple Double Thread.* — Work with Arden's Crochet cotton, No. 18, and with two threads. Tie the two threads together, make a loop with the first or shuttle thread, work 5 Double, 1 Purl, 6 Double, 1 Purl, 5 Double, draw the loop up, and turn it upside down under the left finger and thumb, then upon the under or second thread close to the loop, work 5 Double, 1 Purl, 5 Double, × turn the work upright and with the shuttle thread make a loop, work 5 Double, join to the last Purl on the first loop, *, work 2 Double, 1 Purl, repeat from * seven times, work 5 Double, draw the loop up, and close to it, upon the under thread work 5 Double, 1 Purl, 5 Double; make a loop with the shuttle thread and work 5 Double, join to the last Purl of the last loop, work 6 Double, 1 Purl, draw the loop up, and on the under thread work 5 Double, 1 Purl, 5 Double. Repeat the pattern from ×. Work a CROCHET CHAIN as a foundation to this Edging.

(7) *Simple Single Thread.* — Work with Arden's cotton No. 18, or with Walter and Evans' No. 50, and with one thread. × Make a loop, upon it work 5 DOUBLE, 1 PURL, *, 2 Double, 1 Purl, repeat from * five times, work 5 Double. Draw the loop up; turn the loop upside down, and place it under the finger and thumb, make a loop one-eighth of an inch beyond the first one, and on it work 5 Double, 1 Purl, 5 Double, and draw up. Reverse the work, make a loop one-eighth of an inch from the last made, and repeat the first loop, joining it to the last Purl on the second loop after the first 5 Double instead of working the Purl. Repeat the pattern from ×. Connect the smaller row of loops with a CROCHET CHAIN,

which take from Purl to Purl, and keep these at equal distances apart. Use this Chain as the foundation to the Edging.

(8) See *Lappet.*

Ground Work.—The design shown in Fig. 770 is intended to be used when Tatting in large pieces, such as veils, caps, scarves, and other articles where a ground resembling net is required. The design, if used for a veil, should be worked either in cotton No. 100, or in the finest black machine silk; if for large articles, in stouter silk or thread. To work: Cut out upon a sheet of paper, the shape of the article to be made, and Tat backwards and forwards in rows, regulating the length of the rows by the paper pattern. Commence at the widest part of the material.

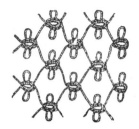

FIG. 770. TATTING—GROUND WORK.

First row, first oval—Make a loop, work 3 DOUBLE, 1 PURL, 3 Double, 1 Purl, 3 Double, 1 Purl, 3 Double, draw up, leave half an inch of cotton, then repeat the oval; work to the end of the row in this manner, being careful always to leave the same length of thread between each oval. Second row—Make a loop and commence an oval, join the second Purl of the oval in progress to the centre of the half inch of cotton left between the ovals in the first row, and finish the oval. Continue these rows of ovals until the article is finished, and where any extra breadth is required, make the threads between the ovals longer; where a slight contracting is needed, make the threads between them shorter.

Insertions. — The patterns given for these Tatting Insertions are chiefly used for trimming underclothing. They can either be sewn to a Tatted Edging when finished, or can be turned into an Edging by a line of Crochet in Chain Stitch being worked along one of their edges, to which it is attached by the Purls at the edge of the design.

(1) To work Fig. 771: In this pattern, only one thread is used. For a coarse Insertion, such as is shown,

FIG. 771. TATTING—INSERTION (No. 1).

use Walter and Evans' Crochet cotton, No. 10; for a finer make, Tatting cotton, No. 30. To work the first oval—

Make a loop, work upon it 5 DOUBLE, 1 PURL, *, 1 Double, 1 Purl, repeat from * four times, 5 Double, draw the loop up, leave a quarter of an inch of cotton, reverse the work, and make the second oval as the first. For the third oval—Repeat the directions, but join the new oval to the first one after the first 5 Double. For the fourth oval—Repeat the directions, but join it to the second oval after the first 5 Double of the new oval is made. Repeat for the whole length.

(2) The pattern shown in Fig. 772 is in two pieces, and worked with Walter and Evans' Crochet cotton, No. 10; two threads are required. To work: Fill the Shuttle with the first thread, make a loop with it, and on it work for the first circle 10 DOUBLE, 1 PURL, 10 Double. Draw the loop up, put the second thread round the left hand, and work upon it with the first thread, 8 Double, 1 Purl, 8 Double. Second oval: Make a loop, work 10 Double, join to the Purl of the first oval, 10 Double: draw the loop up, repeat from the commencement until the length required is made, then re-commence to make the other side of the Insertion. First oval—Make

FIG. 772. TATTING—INSERTION (No. 2).

a loop with the first thread, 10 Double, join to the Purl which connects the first and second ovals of the first piece, work 10 Double, draw the loop up. Take up the second thread, and upon it work with the first thread 8 Double, 1 Purl, 8 Double. Second oval—Make a loop, work 10 Double, join to the same Purl as the first oval was joined to, work 10 Double, and draw the loop up. Repeat the work from the commencement, and join the next two ovals to the Purl which connects the third and fourth ovals worked on the first piece. Repeat until the right length is made. and then make the outside lines. Crochet 7 CHAIN, 1 DOUBLE CROCHET, into the Purl upon the second thread, 7 Chain, 1 Double Crochet into the next Purl upon the second thread, and repeat for both lines.

(3) To work Fig. 773: Use Walter and Evans' Crochet cotton No. 50, and use two threads. Work the insertion in two pieces. Commence by tying the two threads together, and work with the cotton in the right hand over that in the left hand. Commence with the first thread, working upon the second and without a loop, 1 PLAIN, 1 PURL, (turn the Purl downwards), 1 Plain, 6 DOUBLE, 1 Purl, *, 6 Double, 1 Purl, 1 Plain. Turn these stitches all downwards from the first, 6 Double, then turn the work so as to bring the upper edge downwards, and work 6 Double, which fasten on to the last Purl

turned downwards with the right hand thread, thus forming an upward loop. Turn the work downwards,

FIG. 773. TATTING—INSERTION (No. 3).

draw the thread in the right hand underneath the one in the left hand, and work 6 Double, 1 Purl, 6 Double, turned upwards. Fasten these stitches to the first down-

Lappet.—In working the designs shown in Fig. 774, where is given the size of the Lappet, use Tatting cotton No. 50 and two Shuttles or threads. ' The Lappet is worked in four pieces and joined. The pieces consist of the large and small Rosette that make the centre, the insertion surrounding them and the edging round the insertion. To work: Commence with the largest Rosette. Wind the cotton upon two Shuttles and knot the two ends together with the first thread. Make a loop, and work upon it 10 DOUBLE, 1 long PURL, 10 Double; draw up the loop and turn it downwards, *; close to it work upon the second thread with the first thread the scallop that connects the six centre loops of the Rosette together, make the scallop with 8 Double, 1 Purl, 8 Double. Turn the work, and close to the scallop work a loop as already described, but join this

FIG. 774. TATTING—LAPPET (No. 1).

ward Purl. The first part of border is now completed; turn it downwards, and work 8 Double, 1 Purl, 8 Double, 1 Purl, 1 Plain. Turn the work downwards, and work 6 Double, which fasten on to the last Purl, turned up. Repeat the work from *, and continue until the first piece is made the length required. Then work the second piece, and fasten it to the first at the Purls between the 8 Doubles, which are repeated twice in every pattern.

(4) See *Lappets* Nos. 1 and 2.

loop to the first one made, instead of making a Purl in it. Repeat from * four times, so as to make five with the first loop, six loops and five scallops. Then work another scallop and fasten both the ends of the thread on to the second thread over which the first scallop was worked, where the scallop joins the first loop. The inner round of the rosette completed, work the outside round. Commence where the first round left off and work upon the second thread with the first thread, * 6 Double, 1

Purl, 5 Double; fasten to the Purl of the scallop on the first round, and then continue with 5 Double, 1 Purl, 6 Double; fasten to the thread between two scallops of the preceding round. Repeat from * five times. For the small Rosette, work like the first round of the large Rosette.

The Insertion.—This is worked in two pieces; the half which touches the edging is worked first, and as follows: Unite the two Shuttles by knotting the threads, *, work with the first thread, make a loop, and upon it work 8 Double, 1 long Purl, 8 Double, draw the loop up, turn it downwards, and close to it and upon the second thread with the first, make a scallop with 6 Double, 1 Purl, 6 Double. Turn the work, and close to the scallop work a loop, but fasten this second loop to the first one instead of making a Purl upon it. Turn the work, make another scallop, and repeat from * fifteen times, but make the two scallops at the lowest part of the Lappet (where shown in the illustration) longer than the others with 8 Double instead of 6. After working the last scallop, fasten the threads to the first loop of the Insertion, and cut them off. Work the second half of the Insertion like the first part, but join the loops to those made in the first half and omit the Purls. Work the scallops with 5 Double, 1 Purl, 5 Double, as they are smaller than the ones first made.

For the Edging.—Tie the two threads together, make a loop with the first thread and work upon it 8 Double, 1 Purl, 1 Double, draw the loop up; turn the work, make another loop, work upon it 2 Double, *, 1 Purl, 1 Double; repeat from * eight times; work 2 double, draw up; fasten this loop to the preceding one, so that both loops meet. Turn the work, and work over the second thread with the first thread 9 Double to form the scallop between the loops; repeat from * to the end of the Edging.

Make up the Lappet as follows: Tack the different pieces in their right positions on to a piece of stiff paper, join the Rosettes together, and to the Purls upon the inner scallops by passing a thread alternately through a Purl upon the Rosette and upon the scallop, and Cord this thread, so as to make it strong enough. Tack the outer Purls of the Insertion to the part of the Lappet, where it is connected with the muslin, and then Buttonhole the edge of the muslin over, taking up the Purls in their positions with the Buttonholes. Work the long line that connects the Insertion with the Edging with two threads, make Doubles upon the second thread with the first, and connect the Purls upon the outer edge of the Insertion, and the Purls of the inner loop of the Edging to the straight line of Doubles. Work 7 Double between each Purl, and connect the Purls of Edging and Insertion, except at the extreme point of the Lappet, there work 6 Double, and connect a Purl from the Edging, *, 6 Double, and connect the two Purls, 6 Double, and connect a Purl from the Edging; repeat from * twice, and then continue to connect the two Purls as at first.

(2) Work the Lappet illustrated in Fig. 775 with Tatting cotton, No. 100 for fine trimmings, No. 50 for caps or cravat ends, and No. 20 for coarse work. It is worked with two threads or Shuttles, and in three pieces—

the graduated ovals inclosing the centre of the design, the edging, and the centre. To work the Ovals: Commence with the smallest, which is at the top of the Lappet. Make a loop, and on it work 3 Double, 1 Purl, 7 Double, 1 Purl, 7 Double, 1 Purl, 3 Double. Draw the loop up, and then close to it work a second oval with 3 Double, join the oval on to the last Purl of the one preceding it, work 8 Double, 1 Purl, 8 Double, 1 Purl, 3 Double. Draw the loop up, miss one-fifth of an inch on the thread, and work a third oval, thus: Make a loop, work 4 Double, fasten to the preceding oval, work 9 Double, 1 Purl, 9 Double, 1 Purl, 4 Double. Repeat this third oval four times, but in the fourth oval work 10 Double instead of 9; in the fifth, 11 Double instead of 9; and in the sixth, 12 Double instead

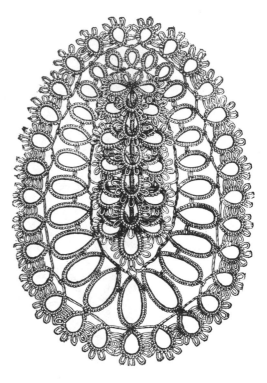

FIG. 775. TATTING—LAPPET (No. 2)

of 9. Work the seventh oval like the sixth. Slightly increase the distance between each oval as they become larger. Eighth oval—Work 5 Double, join to the preceding oval, work 13 Double, 1 Purl, 13 Double, 1 Purl, 5 Double. Ninth oval—As eighth, but work 14 Double instead of 13 Double. Tenth oval—Work 6 Double, join to the preceding oval, work 15 Double, 1 Purl, 15 Double, 1 Purl, 6 Double. Eleventh and twelfth ovals—As tenth, but work 16 Double in them, instead of 15 Double. Thirteenth oval—Work 6 Double, join to the preceding circle, work 17 Double, 1 Purl, 17 Double, 1 Purl, 6 Double. Repeat these ovals backwards from the twelfth to the second, and then join the first and the twenty-fifth oval.

Form the Edging with a row of small graduated circles joined to the outer Purl of the ovals. Fasten the thread to the first oval, make a loop, and work on it 3 DOUBLE, 1 PURL, * 2 Double, 1 Purl, repeat from * five times, work 1 Purl, 3 Double (make the Purls rather long), draw the loop up, and fasten on the thread to the top Purl of next oval. Work the second circle like the first, but omit the first Purl, and fasten the circle to the last Purl on the first circle. Third circle—Work like the second. Fourth and Fifth circles—Like the second, but work the fourth with 4 Double instead of 3 Double, and the fifth with 5 Double instead of 3 Double. Sixth to ninth circle—Work 5 Double, join to the preceding circle, *, work 2 Double, 1 Purl, repeat from * six times, work 5 Double. Tenth to fourteenth circle— 5 Double, join to the preceding circle, *, work 2 Double, 1 Purl, repeat from * seven times, work 5 Double. Fifteenth circle—Work 5 Double, join to the preceding circle, *, work 2 Double, 1 Purl, repeat from * eight times, work 5 Double. Work the circles backwards from the fourteenth to the second for the other side of the Lappet, and fasten the twenty-ninth circle to the first, and the Purls of the scallops to the circles during the working, as shown in the illustration.

The Centre is composed of six pieces, each piece containing five circles of three different sizes. For the first and smallest set of circles—Make a loop, work 5 DOUBLE, 1 PURL, *, 3 Double, 1 Purl, repeat from * five times, work 5 Double. Draw up this circle, and make two others like it, omitting the first Purl in them, and joining them at that place to the preceding circle. Fasten the thread to the first circle, so as to join the three circles close together, and work two little circles close to this join. Make these of 6 Double, 1 Purl, 6 Double. Leave an interval of thread, and commence the second set of five circles. Work this like the first. For the third set work as before, but enlarge the three biggest circles composing it with an extra Purl and 2 Double, and enlarge the two small circles with an extra 2 Double upon each side of the Purl. For the fourth, fifth, and sixth sets of circles work as before, but enlarge each of them every time with an extra Purl and 2 Double, worked to the three largest circles, and an extra 2 Double worked upon each side of the Purl in the two smallest circles. Arrange these pieces so that they overlap each other, as shown in Fig. 775. BUTTONHOLE over the thread upon which they were worked, so as to make it firm, and give a stitch here and there to keep the circles in their right places. Then CORD a thread over the thread upon which the ovals are made, and connect this to the outer Purls upon the centre pattern and to the Purl made in every one of the small circles.

Medallion.—(1) The round shown in Fig. 776 is one much used in Tatting, as with it several articles can be formed; thus, if worked with coarse Crochet cotton No. 12 and a large Shuttle, it will make medallions for Antimacassars, while if worked with fine cotton it forms pincushion covers and mats. To work for a pincushion: Use Walter and Evans' Boar's Head cotton, No. 14, and a small Shuttle. Make the eighteen outside ovals and the small dots before the six ovals forming the centre. First dot —Make a loop, work 2 DOUBLE, * 1 PURL, 2 Double,

repeat from * twice; draw the loop up and turn this dot down under the left thumb. First oval—Make a loop, work 4 Double, *, Purl, 2 Double; repeat from * four times, work 2 Double, and draw close. Reverse the work. Second dot—Make a loop, work 2 Double, join to the last Purl of the previous dot, work 2 Double, *, 1 Purl, 2 Double; repeat from * once and draw close. Second oval—Make a

FIG. 776. TATTING—MEDALLION (No. 1).

loop, work 4 Double, join to the last Purl of the oval, work 2 Double, *, 1 Purl, 2 Double; repeat from * three times, work 2 Double, draw close and reverse the work. Repeat the second dot and the second oval until eighteen dots and ovals are formed, then break off, but leave an end of cotton. To work the centre, First oval—Make a loop, work 8 Double, join to the Purl of the first dot, work 8 Double, and draw up. Work six ovals like the instructions, and join an oval to every third dot. When they are made, fasten off, and then attach the two threads together, so as to join the medallion. An ordinary sized pincushion will require nine of these medallions.

When making a pincushion of the Tatted medallions, the centre, as a variety, can be a Crochet instead of a Tatted medallion. The Crochet medallion shown in Fig. 777 is suitable. To work: Use the same cotton that

FIG. 777. CROCHET MEDALLION TO INSERT INTO TATTING.

is employed in the Tatting. First round—Begin in the centre and make an 8 CHAIN, which join as a round; into this round work 16 DOUBLE CROCHET. Second round—Work 1 Double Crochet, 10 Chain, turn, work a Slip Stitch in each of the 10 Chain. Work round the the stem thus made in Double Crochet, working three stitches in one to turn the point, miss one stitch upon the preceding row, work 2 Double Crochet, and repeat from * seven times, so as to form the eight raised petals. Third round—Work at the back of the last round behind the petals, make a petal between each of those on the last row, 1 Double Crochet at the back of each, and cut off the cotton when the round is finished. Fourth round— Work 2 Double Crochet at the point of each petal, and 5 Chain between each point. Fifth round—*, Work 2 Treble over the first 2 Double Crochet, 5 Chain, 2 Double Crochet in the centre of the last 5 Chain, and 5 Chain; repeat from * to the end of the round. Sixth round—1 Double Crochet in the centre of the last 5 Chain, *, 5 Chain, 1 Treble in the centre of the next 5 Chain, 5 Chain, 1 Slip Stitch in the top of the Treble Stitch, 6 Chain, 1 Slip Stitch in the same place, 5 Chain, another Slip Stitch in the same place, 5 Chain, 1 Double Crochet in the centre of the next 5 Chain, repeat from * 15 times so as to make 16 points.

(2) The small medallion shown in Fig. 778 can be enlarged by using coarse cotton, or worked with fine cotton of the size given in the previous one. It is used to fill up spaces left by larger medallions when making pincushions and antimacassars. Two threads or Shuttles are required to make the design. To work: Commence with the thread from the first Shuttle and make 9 Double

FIG. 778. TATTING—MEDALLION (No. 2).

with it upon the thread from the second Shuttle; then take the first thread and work three ovals with it close together for each oval; make a loop, work 7 Double, 1 Purl, 7 Double, and draw up. Pick up the second thread and work over it with the first thread, 9 Double, join to the thread before the first 9 Double, and repeat from the commencement. Work eight points and join the first oval of each point to the last oval of the preceding point.

(3) The small medallion shown in Fig. 779 is particularly useful for joining large pieces of work or

FIG. 779. TATTING—MEDALLION (No. 3).

medallions. It is worked with Walter and Evans' Boar's Head cotton, No. 14, and with one Shuttle. To

work: Commence with the single oval on the right side of the figure, make a loop, *, work 2 Double, 1 Purl, and repeat from * eight times; draw up the loop, and work another oval in the same way; leave very little cotton between the two ovals and join them in the first and last Purl Stitches. Leave a quarter of an inch of cotton and work another oval, join it to the last made in the fourth Purl Stitch of each oval, work a fourth oval, and join it to the preceding oval; in the first Purl Stitch work a fifth oval as the last, knot the cotton into the middle of the thread left between the second and third ovals, and leave the cotton so that the next oval will be exactly opposite the second oval; work the last oval, and join it to the preceding one in the fourth Purl, and to the first oval in the last Purl; then fasten off.

(4) The design shown in Fig. 780 is a simple double oval, and is used for the same purpose as the last pattern. It should be worked in the same cotton as the other part of the article it is intended to join. First oval—Make a

FIG. 780. TATTING—MEDALLION (No. 4).

loop, work 4 Double, 1 Purl, * 2, Double, 1 Purl; repeat from * nine times, work 4 Double, draw up the loop close, and commence the second oval, which completes the figure. Join to the rest of the work at the centre Purl of both ovals.

Tatting and Tapework Mat.—Small mats are very useful for drawing room purposes. They can be made entirely of medallions, such as are shown in Fig. 776, joined, or with Rosettes of Tatting and Rosettes of Tapework. To form the Tatting Rosette: Use shuttle No. 3, and fine Tatting cotton, No. 60 or 80. The Rosette is made of large and small ovals, the large ones form the outside of the Rosette, and the small are turned towards the centre part. Make a loop and work 5 Double, 1 Purl, 5 Double for the small oval; draw up and turn the oval down under the left thumb. For the large oval miss one-eighth of an inch of thread, make a loop, work 5 Double, 1 Purl, *, 1 Double, 1 Purl; repeat from * six times, work 6 Double, join the oval up, and reverse the work. Miss one-eighth of an inch of thread and work the small oval as before; then repeat the large oval, but instead of working the first Purl, join to the last Purl of the first made large oval. Work twelve large and twelve small ovals, then fasten off and make the centre, thus: Make a loop, work 1 Double, join on to the Purl in the first small oval, 1 Double, join to the Purl in the second oval, and continue to work a Double and join until all the small ovals are joined on; then draw the loop up and tie the thread firmly before cutting it off. Make ten Rosettes for a small mat, twelve or fourteen for larger mats. To make up the small mat, join nine Rosettes, leave seven of the large ovals in a Rosette free, join the eighth to the eighth of another Rosette, and the twelfth to a Rosette upon the opposite side. Take tape three-quarters of an inch wide and make a Rosette with it, as shown in TAPEWORK, make 8 Tape Rosettes, join them together and to the Tatted Rosettes between Purls 8 and 12. Then take the Tatted Rosette that is left and put it into the circle left inside the Tape Work and join it to it.

Tatting Combined with Crochet and Lace Stitches.—The description of Tatting shown in Fig. 781 is used for trimmings, and is worked with a Crochet Edging, and with Tatted Circles joined with Lace Stitches, worked upon the thread left between the Tatted Circles. Work with Tatting cotton No. 50. Commence the work with the circles. Make a loop, upon which work 13 DOUBLE; draw the loop up, miss two-thirds of an inch of thread and make a second circle like the first, and repeat for the length required for the row, always leaving the same sized piece of thread between the circles. Fasten a second row

FIG. 781. TATTING—CROCHET AND LACE.

of circles to the first row, thus: Work a circle as before on the thread one-third of an inch from the first row, miss the same distance after the circle is worked, and fasten the thread to the second circle on the preceding row and repeat to the end. To fasten the thread to the already made circles, draw it through them to form a loop, and put it through the loop thus made. Make the third row of circles like the second, one-third of an inch of thread between the new circles and the ones on the second row. Finish the centre part of the Tatting with a line of thread without circles, fasten this to each circle, leaving two-thirds of an inch between each.

To work the Edging: Fasten the thread to the first row of the circles in the centre of the thread, miss a tiny bit of thread, and work the small Josephine Knot thus: Make a loop, work 5 SINGLE upon it, and draw the loop up quite tight, putting the thread downwards between the loop. Leave a tiny bit of thread and work a circle, make a loop, work 3 DOUBLE, 1 PURL, 2 Double, and 5 Purl, divided by 2 Double, 2 Double, 1 Purl, 3 Double, draw up; miss a tiny bit of thread and work another Josephine Knot,

then miss the same amount of thread; make a small loop and upon it work 8 Double, then turn, and make a loop, upon which work 3 Double, 9 Purl, divided by 2 Double, 3 Double; draw up this loop, and join it to the last made small loop. Break off the cotton, connect it with the other side of the small loop to the centre part of the thread left in the first row, and repeat the edging from *, only omitting the second Purl of the first circle, and joining it to the last Purl on the preceding circle, as shown in the illustration. Make the upper edging of CROCHET. First row—Connect the cotton to the centre part of the thread left in the third row of the centre with a DOUBLE CROCHET, *, work 5 CHAIN and 1 Double Crochet into the centre part of the thread between the next two circles; repeat to the end of the row. Second row—1 TREBLE into every other Chain in the first row.

To work the Lace Stitches: TACK the work upon a piece of stiff paper, and upon each side of the thread left between the circles work POINT DE GRECQUE, each stitch an equal distance apart. Work the same stitch along the two edging lines.

To Wash Coarse Tatting.—Put it in a saucepan with a lather of soap and cold water, and leave it until the water boils; then rinse it, and, if it looks yellow, pass it through blue water; when nearly dry, pull it out and iron it, placing a handkerchief between it and the iron.

To Wash Fine Tatting.—Take an ordinary wine bottle and sew several folds of flannel upon it. To this flannel TACK the Tatting, taking care to stretch out the design so as to keep it in its right positions. Make a lather with curd soap and thoroughly rub this into the Tatting; then put the bottle into a saucepan and boil it. Rinse the soap well away from it, and when it is nearly dry, untack it from the flannel, stretch it out, and lay a handkerchief over it, and then iron it. Open out all the Purls with a Pin.

Tatting.—A description of stout matting of Indian manufacture, is employed for doorways, and kept wet. The native name for this textile is *Tattie*, whence our word Tatting is derived.

Tatting Shuttle.—This kind of appliance resembles somewhat a Netting Needle in the mode of its employment, and reception of the cotton or cord; but instead of a long narrow and pointed form, it is of a flattish, and of rather an oval shape, a little pointed at the ends. It consists of two sides, united in the centre by a piece of the same material, whether of ivory, bone, or wood. The thread is wound round this central part of the Shuttle.

Taunton.—A description of broadcloth, so called from the town in Somersetshire where it was originally manufactured.

Tent Stitch.—A stitch employed in Tapestry Work and in fine Embroideries. It is produced by crossing over one strand of canvas in a diagonal direction, sloped from right to left, and resembles the first half taken in Cross Stitch. When beads are sewn upon canvas this stitch is employed. *See* BERLIN WORK and EMBROIDERY STITCHES.

Terry Velvet.—A textile made entirely of silk, and having fine ribs or cords on the best side. Inferior kinds are made with a cotton back. Chiefly used for trimmings, particularly for children's garments; and can be had in most colours. It is not to be recommended in black. Although called velvet, it has not the nap or pile, that is a distinguishing characteristic of such a textile. When employed as a trimming, it is cut on the bias. The width of the material is about 27 inches.

Tête de Bœuf.—*See* EMBROIDERY STITCHES.

Tête de Mores.—A very narrow Guipure Lace made in the sixteenth century, but now obsolete.

Textile.—A generic term, signifying any stuff manufactured in a loom, of whatever material, produced by weaving the products of the animal, or vegetable worlds, into cloth, webs, or any other make of fabric, for clothing, upholstery, or other use. Textiles may be produced in wool, hair, fur, silk, cotton, flax, hemp, mallow, the filaments of leaves and barks, and the coating of pods and tree-wool; also a fine silk thread, the chief manufacture of which is carried on at Palermo, spun by, and procured from, the *Pinna marina*, a large mussel, found on the coast of Italy. The Textile made of this silk was known by the name of Bygsus by the ancients. A kind of vegetable silk is procured from the Paper-Mulberry tree of Japan, and a strong cloth from Hop-stalks in Sweden; Nets and Fringes from mulberry fibres in Louisiana, as also fine cloth from the same tree in Otaheiti. In France a cloth is made from the fibres of the pine-apple, and one from the stalks of nettles. In Yorkshire, as elsewhere in England, a fine firm russet-coloured cloth is produced from the cotton-grasses. Textiles are also made of very fine gold and silver wire.

Thibet Cloth.—A stuff made of coarse goat's hair. Also a fine description of woollen cloth, used for making women's dresses; it is a kind of Camlet.

Thickset.—This is a description of fustian, employed for men's dress, of the working class. Like velveret, it is a kind of cotton velvet.

Thimble.—An appliance fitted as a guard to the top of the right-hand middle finger, and for the purpose of pressing a needle through any material to be sewn. The name is derived from the Scotch *Thummel*, from *Thumb-bell*, a bell-shaped shield, originally worn on the thumb; the practice is still maintained among sailors. The Dutch have the credit of the invention; and in 1695 one John Lofting came over from Holland, and established a manufactory of Thimbles at Islington. They are of two forms, the closed, or ordinary bell-shaped, and the open, such as employed by tailors and upholsterers. They are made in gold, silver, plated steel, brass, celluloid, bone, ebony, ivory, steel, brass-topped, &c., and are pitted with little cells to receive the blunt end of the needle. Thimbles are made in various sizes; and all common sorts are sold by the gross, but may be purchased singly. Gold thimbles are sometimes set round with turquoises and other gems. Those made of ebony, ivory, and celluloid are very suitable for embroidery and lace work. The former are known by the name of "Nuns' Thimbles." Those of brass and steel are used by tailors and upholsterers, and by the working class in general. In England Thimbles are made by means of moulds, and then of a stamping and punching machine. In the fourteenth century our Thimbles were made of leather, and in the present day a leather band worn round the hand, and having a thicker part for the hollow of the palm, is employed by shoemakers. Thimbles were called Fingerlings so long as they were made of leather; and when, in the fourteenth century, they were superseded by metal, the name Thimble was adopted. There are two allusions made to Thimbles by Shakespear—one in *King John* and another in the *Taming of the Shrew*. In the former we read—

> Your ladies and pale visag'd maids,
> Like amazons, come tripping after drums;
> Their thimbles into armed gauntlets change,
> Their needles into lances.
>
> —*King John.*

> And that I'll prove upon thee,
> Though thy little finger be armed in a Thimble.
>
> —*Taming of the Shrew.*

Thorn Stitch.—*See* EMBROIDERY STITCHES.

Thorns.—Used in Needlepoints to decorate the Cordonnets and raised parts of the lace. *See* SPINES.

Thread.—This is a comprehensive term denoting the finest description of manufactured fibre, or filaments, of whatever material it may be composed, for the purpose of needlework. In the manufacture of it several strands are doubled and twisted in a frame, the yarn being moistened with a paste of starch, which has been passed over flannel, to absorb the superfluous moisture. The yarns are then brought together by rollers, slightly compressed, and twisted together; and the thread is made up in hanks, skeins, balls, or wound on reels. Silk twist is made up in hard round bars, of about 5 or 6 inches in length. Thread is, however, a term which is distinctively applied to Flax; thus, Thread or Lisle thread stockings, or gloves, are only made of fine Linen Thread. Fine gold and silver wire, flattened, or cotton, silk, wool, and worsted yarns prepared for needlework are all called Thread in trade. A yard measure of cotton Sewing Thread contains 54 inches; of the real Linen Thread, 90 inches; of Worsted, 35 inches. Silk Sewing Thread is usually twisted in lengths of from 50 to 100 feet, with hand reels, somewhat similar to those employed in rope making. The manufacture of white Sewing Thread, known as Ounce Thread—to distinguish it from different kinds of coloured and white Thread then made in Aberdeen and Dundee—was begun about 1750, having been introduced into this country from Holland in 1725, and carried on for a long time privately in the family of a lady, who first learned the secret, and began the trade. This Ounce Thread had been originally called Nuns' Thread or Sisters' Thread, so designated because it was spun by the Nuns of Flanders and Italy. The earliest mention of Thread is in connection with Paris, Cologne, Bruges,

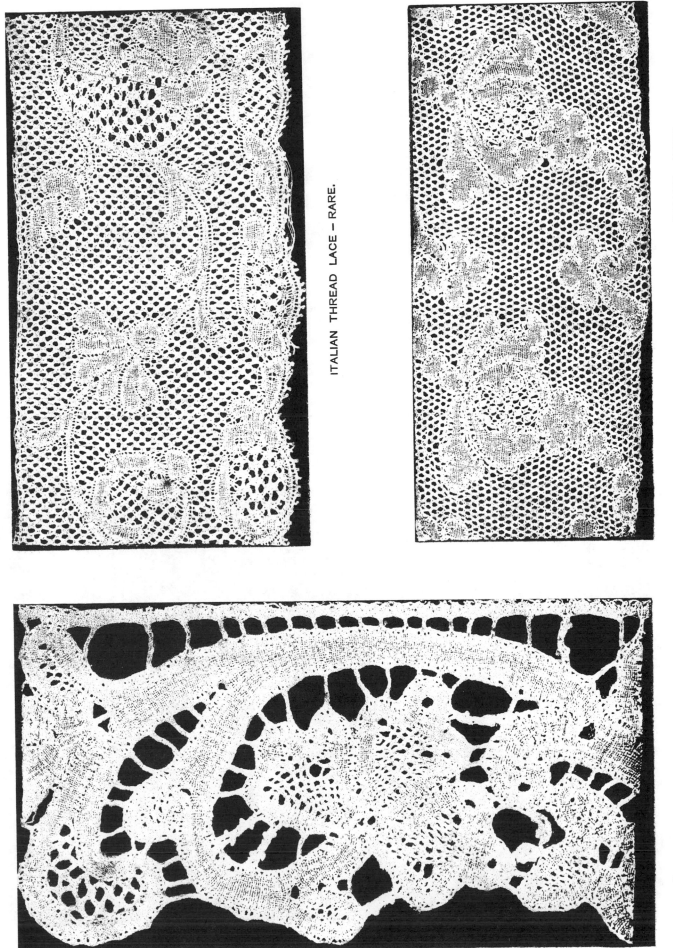

ITALIAN THREAD LACE – RARE.

ITALIAN THREAD LACE, WIRE GROUND – RARE.

ITALIAN PILLOW BRAID LACE.

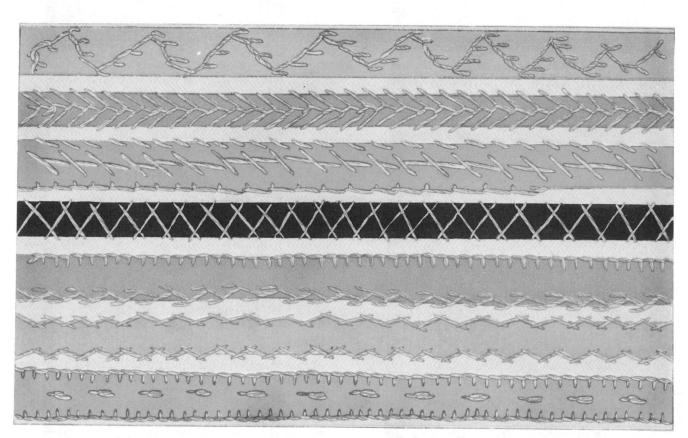

TICKING WORK

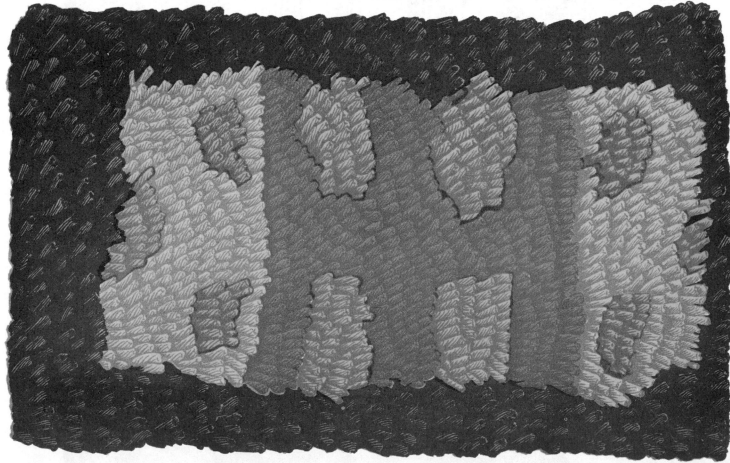

RUG WORK OR SMYRNA KNITTING

and Lisle, in the fifteenth century, and subsequently in the seventeenth century at Coventry. At the present day the largest quantity is made in Scotland.

When flax is spun for weaving, it is termed Yarn, and when two of these strands are twisted together for sewing, it is called Sewing Thread or Twist. Amongst the various makes are the strong Stitching Thread; the much-twisted Wire Thread, used by bonnet-makers; the Shrewsbury, in various colours, and sold in pound papers, for strong coarse work; the Scotch, in all colours and thicknesses, and the Lace Thread. Ordinary Linen Thread, is to be had unbleached, black, and drab, and in soft satin finish. It is sold by the dozen pounds, done up in half-ounce knots, and also in small skeins; when sold in small quantities, it should be by the number of skeins. Carpet Thread is a heavy-made three-cord, and may be had in unbleached, black, drab, yellow, red, brown, and green; in soft and satin finish. Flourishing Thread is used for repairing table linen, and for this purpose the most useful sizes are 4, 5, and 6. It is also used for Embroidery on linen and flannel, not only on account of its flossy appearance, but as it does not shrink when washed.

Thread Canvas.—This textile is manufactured from hemp, and is woven in the usual sizes and widths. A fine description made of flax is also to be procured.

Threader.—*See* NEEDLE-THREADER.

Thread Lace.—Also known as Dentelle de Fil. The term is applied indifferently to all laces made with flax thread to distinguish them from laces made with gold and silver or cotton threads, whether of the Pillow or Needle. Laces made with flax are much superior to those of cotton, as the latter stiffens and becomes thick when cleaned, while the former always retains its flexibility and clearness. Much of the beauty of the lace depends upon the fineness of the thread employed in its make, and the supremacy of the laces of Flanders over those of France was partly owing to the flax grown in Brabant being of superior quality. This was steeped in the River Lys, whose waters were unusually clear, and then spun in a dark and damp cellar, the thread breaking if exposed either to warmth or light. Mechlin, Lille, and Brussels Lace are all made of this flax thread, and frequently costs £240 a pound, while the thread used for Honiton Lace, until a recent period, was obtained from Antwerp at a high price.

Three Cord.—*See* BRAID or TWIST.

Thrown Silk.—Raw hanks of silk, consisting of two or more strands, tossed and swung to and fro in the process of being doubled, twisted, and reeled; and so transformed from roughly assorted hanks, as imported into this country, into a suitable condition for the use of the weaver. Thrown Silk is otherwise known as Organzine. Those employed in throwing the raw silk are called Throwsters. When thrown, the strands are twisted in a contrary direction to that in which the strands, or singles, are twisted.

Thrums.—The waste fringe-like ends of thread, cut off by weavers from the cloth in process of weaving, or the fringed edge of the material. It also signifies a thick nap on a woven textile. A description of hat was worn in the time of Queen Elizabeth having a long pile-like shaggy fur, which was called a "silk thrummed hat," and to it allusion is made by Quarles:

> Are we born to thrum caps or pick straw?

Likewise we find the word and its signification employed in connection with it in *Midsummer Night's Dream*:

> Come, sisters, come;
> Cut thread, and thrum.

Ticking.—A strong material made both in linen and cotton, for the purpose of making mattresses, feather beds, pillows, and bolsters; and is usually woven in stripes of blue and white, or pink and white. It is also used for window and door blinds, and for this purpose can be procured in other stripes of fancy colour. Ticking is of Jean make, or basket-woven. It measures from about 32 inches to a yard wide. When employed in making feather or down pillows the cloth sack should be well rubbed with beeswax on the wrong side, after the sewing up of one end and the two sides, before being filled with the feathers. Ticking is much used as a foundation for Silk Embroidery, as the lines or stripes in the cloth render the work easy, and contribute to the formation of the various designs. *See* TICKING WORK.

Ticking Work.—A modern Embroidery worked in imitation of the bright and elaborate embroideries executed in Arabia, Persia, and Turkey, and one which reproduces the gorgeous colouring for which they are celebrated, without the same amount of labour being expended. The work is intended to be bright and therefore is formed of bright colours, but these are selected with a due regard to their contrasts, and care is taken that they are such as would be found in Eastern embroideries, and not those obtained from aniline dyes, such as gas green, mauve, magenta, and startling blues. The work is used for summer carriage rugs, garden chairs, banner screens, couvrepieds, parasol covers, and such small articles as mats, bags, and cushions, and it is made with ordinary blue and white Ticking, or white and grey Ticking, or with French Ticking, which is woven with bright lines of red and orange colours, instead of being only of subdued tints. Besides the Ticking, which is used as a foundation, bright coloured ribbons, braids, and ribbon velvet, varying from half an inch to an inch in width, are required; also narrow gold braids and purse silk of many colours. For very narrow work, such as is required for needlecases and other small articles, what is known as Breton ribbon and China ribbon are used, as these are woven in quarter inch widths. The braids or ribbons are sewn down at intervals upon the Ticking, following the lines woven in it, so as to allow of the foundation appearing between them; they are then secured either with narrow gold braid stitched down to each edge, or they are edged with lines of stitches worked in the purse silks, and finished off in the centre with Embroidery Stitches. The Ticking left exposed is also embellished with Embroidery Stitches, and there is no limit to the variety of stitches or colour that can be blended together in one piece of work. Black velvet and dark velvets add considerably to the effect by their use, as do the gold braids and gold twist, but odd lengths of

FIG. 782. TICKING WORK (No. 1).

ribbon and braid will make very good patterns of Ticking Work.

Fig. 782 shows the general effect of a number of lines of Ticking covered with fancy stitches, and Figs. 783 and 784

(1) To work Fig. 782, Select a grey and white Ticking, and to cover up the grey lines sew on a dark blue

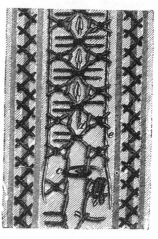

FIG. 783. TICKING WORK (No. 2).

velvet strip, then a maroon or ruby velvet strip, a dark green ribbon or braid, a scarlet braid, a bronze braid, a

FIG. 784. TICKING WORK (No. 3).

give some of the combinations of stitches that can be worked upon one or several pieces of silk or braid.

blue braid and a scarlet braid, edge each of these upon both sides with a narrow silk braid of an old gold colour (not yellow). Work upon the velvet strips in old gold silk with FRENCH KNOTS, and work SATIN STITCH made as a cross. Work a line of HERRINGBONE STITCH in pale blue silk upon the white lines of Ticking between the velvets, which repeat between the green and scarlet braid, and the blue and scarlet braid; work the eight pointed stars in scarlet black silk, and make the black silk stars upon the scarlet and braid.

(2) To work Fig. 783 : This pattern is worked upon Ticking woven in narrow lines; the centre part made upon a coloured braid an inch and a half in width, and the side lines over the Ticking lines. Work the side lines in scarlet silk and in HERRINGBONE STITCH, and for the centre commence at the line marked *a* in the illustration. Make two long BUTTONHOLE STITCHES, one-eighth of an inch apart, and then two more of the same length, with a loose loop between, at the distance of half an inch from the first two. Repeat these two Buttonholes down one side, and then upon the other side, and make the long loops always opposite each other. Fasten the thread off securely, and commence again at the spot marked *b*. OVERCAST the two Buttonholes at that place together, and then run the needle under the work to *c*, where Over-

(4) To work Fig. 785 : This is a variety of Ticking Work into which Chain Stitch is introduced, and is worked with three shades of one colour. Make the dark narrow lines of gold or black braid of the narrowest width Work vandyke lines between them, which unite in the centre with a CROSS STITCH with the darkest colour; work the scroll in CHAIN STITCH in the lightest colour, and the outer line of the pine-shaped patterns in the darkest colour. Fill their centres with FRENCH KNOTS, which make in the medium colour; make the three stitches together with SATIN STITCH, in a colour matching the Chain Stitch.

(5) The design shown in Fig. 786 is intended to be worked over Ticking woven with the ordinary sized

FIG. 786. TICKING WORK (No. 5.)

narrow lines. To work: Lay down upon the blue lines

FIG. 785. TICKING WORK (No. 4).

cast the two long loops (one from each side) together. Then make the two lines upon each side of this centre spot with SATIN STITCH, and work the two Buttonholes together above the *c*. Repeat to the end of the row. Take a different coloured silk or thread, and work in the centre of the pattern a line of TÊTE DE BŒUF STITCHES, putting one stitch into each vacant spot, as shown by the letter *d*. With the same coloured silk, RUN the outer lines of the pattern marked *e*, and secure these lines by passing them through the two Buttonhole Stitches. Use three coloured silks for this design, two in the centre pattern and one for the Herringbone.

(3) To work Fig. 784 : This is worked either upon bright French ticking or upon broad ribbon of a bright colour. The scroll designs upon each side of the centre match each other in colour; work them in POINT RUSSE and FRENCH KNOTS. Work the scroll in bronze silk, and the wreath in gold coloured silk. For the centre, which is upon the white part of the Ticking, make the vandyke lines edging it in blue, red, and green, the sprays in red, and the rosette, and diamond, in deep ruby, with pale blue lines as centres.

in the Ticking, black, scarlet, green, blue, and golden brown braids alternately, and over these work Stars and FRENCH KNOTS with yellow filoselle. Work a double vandyke line in filoselle of shades matching the braids over the white lines in the Ticking; make each line of vandyke with one CHAIN STITCH, as shown in the illustration.

(6) The design given in Fig. 787 is an Embroidery pattern that is used to work over the brightly woven lines of French Ticking. To work: Trace the outline upon

FIG. 787. TICKING WORK (No. 6).

a band of orange or red colour, and work with brown filoselle and in POINT RUSSE. Use only one coloured filoselle for each strip of Embroidery, but change that colour in every strip.

(7) Fig. 788 is an Embroidery pattern worked out with fine braid and Embroidery Stitches, and is used to cover the broad lines of the brightly woven French Ticking. To work: Trace the design and STITCH over the chief outlines the very narrowest black braid. Between the lines of braid in the long ovals make FRENCH KNOTS in filoselle, and between the lines of braid surrounding the circle make a double curved line of CHAIN STITCHES in filoselle. Work the centre flower in SATIN STITCH and French Knots, and in natural colours. Work the wreath passing over the long ovals and the lines forming diamonds in their centres in filoselle contrasting in shade to the Ticking, and fasten down each point of the diamond with a CROSS STITCH of black filoselle.

Tied Work.—A work not much practised in England, and introduced from the Continent, where it is used to make fringes to Crochet and Knitting, or for white and dark materials, according to the fringe being made with white cotton, or black or coloured worsteds and silks. The implements required for the work are long narrow frames made with broad pieces of wood placed from 3 to 6 inches apart, a Netting Mesh and needle, and skeins of silk, worsted, or cotton. The frames used for Tied Work require a row of brass hooks fastened along the inner edge of the upper piece, and the outer edge of the lower piece of wood; these hooks are placed half an inch apart and arranged upon the upper and lower wood so as to be opposite to each other. To work: NET with a half inch Mesh five rows of Netting the length required for the fringe. In the fifth row wind the thread twice round the Mesh to make those loops double the length of the other rows. Sew the knots of the first row of Netting on to a piece of narrow black or white braid, opening them out so that the loops are properly stretched. Fasten this piece of braid with drawing pins to the top of the frame quite at the edge, and see that each knot is above and between the row of hooks upon the lower edge of the top part of the frame, and fasten the row of hooks into the second row of knots, and fasten the last row of knots (those belonging to the long loops) over the hooks on the bottom part of the frame, thus leaving the Netting rows well stretched and tight between the two parts of the frame. Take a skein of silk or worsted, cut it once across, divide the strands so as to obtain a tolerable thickness (too many will make the fringe heavy, too few poor, so that no exact number of strands can be given, as the number depends upon the material used). Fasten one end of these strands tightly to the first top hook, carry the skein down to the hook on the lower part of the frame, beyond the one underneath the top hook, twist it backwards round this, and take it up to the top again, miss a hook, and pass it over the next one; bring it down to the bottom again, miss a hook, and twist it backwards round the next hook. Repeat for the length of the frame and there secure the skein to prevent that part of it wound round the hooks from slipping, and so that the work can be continued. Take a second skein and repeat the winding, using up the hooks not covered the first time. Thread a darning needle with a piece of worsted or silk, and make with it a good knot under the first hook on the top line. Draw together both sides of the skein that went over the hook with this

FIG. 788. TICKING WORK (No. 7).

knot, and wind the thread several times round, so as to make a good knot, and secure it into the Netting Knot. Run the needle and thread to the Netting Knot on the second netting row, and make a knot there of the skeins that cross at that place, run the thread diagonally down to the Netting Knot on the third row, beyond the one first secured on the second row, and make a knot there with the two skeins that cross at that place. Repeat these knots, always working up and down the netting rows diagonally, and carefully securing each knot made with the threaded needle to the knot beneath it belonging to the Netting. When the work is finished, cut the worsted knots made on the second, third, and fourth rows, but be careful not to cut the netted foundation. Cut the first, second, and third rows of knots both above and below them, and fluff up the little balls of wool thus left in the same way as in DAISY MATS; for the fourth row leave only the already cut piece above the fourth knot; cut the worsted secured to the hooks on the lower part of the frame, so as to make tassels as a finish. Any length of this Tied Work can be made, as long as the new strands or skeins are always added at the lower hooks, where, as that part forms the tassels, the join will not interfere with the strength of the fringe.

Tiffany.—A thin description of semi-transparent silk textile, resembling gauze. It is of French manufacture.

Tiffeny.—A description of muslin, of open make, and a pale écru colour. It is of double width, and is employed for Needle Embroidery.

Tinsel.—A term used to signify a thin and loosely-woven material, formed partly or entirely of gold and silver threads, and introduced into embroidery, but chiefly employed for theatrical purposes. The dress of the harlequin is composed entirely of tinsel. We find allusions to this bright and sparkling material in some of our classical authors. Tinsel can be purchased in thin sheets for application to Net, Gauze, and Velvet, or for the wrappers of bonbons and crackers. The use of Tinsel was limited in the reign of Henry VIII. to certain ranks amongst the nobility, and, according to a Sumptuary Law, "No man under the State of an erle were in his apparel of his body or horse, any cloth of gold or silver, or tinceld satin."

Tinsel Embroidery.—This is worked upon net, tulle, and thin muslin materials, and is an imitation of the Turkish Embroideries with gold thread upon crêpe. The patterns are in outline, and consist of geometrical or arabesque designs, which should be simple, and with lines rather wide apart. To work: Trace the design upon pink calico, which back with brown paper, and upon this TACK the net. Take the very narrowest tinsel, thread it on to a wool needle, and work it backwards and forwards along the outlines. Put it in below a line, and bring it out above it in a slanting direction to the right, slant it again, and put it in below the line, and press it down with the thumb, so that it rather overlays itself, and forms the line as a series of VANDYKE STITCHES. Work in floss silk and in SATIN STITCH such parts of the pattern that are too small for the tinsel lines. Tinsel can be used instead of gold thread in embroideries upon velvet, brocade, and silk, but, as it soon tarnishes, the latter is the best to employ for good work.

Tinted Patchwork.—*See* PATCHWORK.

Tippet, or Cape.—An article of dress, worn alike by men and women. It is circular in form, and covers the shoulders, extending from around the throat to below the shoulders, and sometimes to the waist, and even longer. Tippets are usually made of the same material as the coat or dress, or else of fur. Those of Fur are much worn by women, especially of the upper classes, and by coachmen and footmen, over their out-of-door livery great-coats. Sometimes several cloth capes are worn with ulsters, especially by coachmen.

Tissues.—A comprehensive term, including all textiles composed of threads interlaced by means of a shuttle. But there is also one particular fabric especially so designated. It is a species of cloth, woven either with gold and silver strands, or else with some of varied colours. It may be made of silk, and shot with gold and silver. We find entries in the household bills of Henry VIII. of both descriptions of this material—"broad and narrow silver Tissue," and "crimson Tissue;" for in olden times it was the distinctive name of a particular textile. Ben Jonson speaks of a—

> Cloth of bodkin, or Tissue;

and, earlier still, Chaucer makes allusion to it in "Troilus and Cressida":

> His helm to hewen was in twenty places
> That by tissue hong, his back behind.

Milton and Dryden both mention it. The latter describes its character as—

> A robe of tissue, stiff with golden wire.

Tobines.—A stout, twilled silk textile, much resembling Florentine, employed for women's dresses. It is to be had in all colours, and is very durable.

Toe.—*See* KNITTING STOCKINGS.

Toile.—A French term, signifying linen cloth. It is also the name given in France to distinguish the pattern in lace from the ground. The pattern is so called from its flat, linen-like appearance.

Toile Cirée.—The French name for oil-cloth or oil-silk.

Toile Colbert.— This is a loosely woven canvas material, identical with that employed in the Turkish and Algerian Embroideries imported to this country, and sold in the fancy-work shops. It is an inferior description of material. It is made in widths varying from 18in. to 54in., and can be had in white, cream, grey, and gold. *See* AIDA CANVAS. The same make of web is to be procured both in woollen and in cotton cloth. *See* BASKET CLOTH and CONNAUGHT.

Toile d'Alsace.—This is a description of linen cloth made for a dress material, and closely resembling that known as Toile de Vichy. It is imported from France.

Toile d'Araigner.—This is a beautiful open-work French dress material, produced in a variety of colours. It is composed of wool, and measures 46in. in width. In make it is an open cross-bar, with a strong, diamond-shaped netting over it, holding all together.

Toile Damascene.—The French name for Embroidery

executed upon damask, or honeycomb canvas, similar to towelling embroidery.

Toile de Religeuse.—This cloth is otherwise known as *Toile de Nonne,* or Nun's Cloth.

Toile de Vichy.—A linen cloth, usually produced in stripes of two colours—blue and white, or pink and white—like striped grass. It is employed as a summer dress material, and is to be had in ready-made costumes, as well as by the yard. It is a French material, and measures 1 yard in width.

Toile Satinée.—This material is of a cotton-like foulard. It is soft, and is produced in all colours, and printed in a great variety of patterns. It measures about 30 inches in width. Toile Satinée may also be had in plain colours.

Toilet Covers.—These small cloths, made for the covering of dressing-tables, are usually manufactured of marcella, or picqué. They are also to be had in damask, of various dimensions, finished with common fringe, and also by the better kinds of fringe, which are knotted (*see* TOILET FRINGES.) These Covers may be bought by the yard also if desired.

Toilet Fringes.—These are of various descriptions—the "bullion," "scarlet and white loop," "bobbin-loop," "open," "plain," "black and white head," and "star," all made of white cotton, and sold in pieces containing 36 yards each. As indicated by their name, they are used to trim toilet covers. The widths of these fringes vary from three-quarters of an inch to 2 inches.

Toilinette.—A cloth composed of silk, cotton, and woollen yarn, the warp being of the former two combined, and the weft of the latter. It is employed for making waistcoats for men, and is a kind of German quilting.

Tonder Lace.—This is lace worked in Tonder and in North Schleswig, and is of two kinds, one being made upon the Pillow and of native design, although freely copied from Italian, Flemish, and Scandinavian patterns. These Tonder Laces are heavy and solid in appearance, and require a close inspection before the beauty of their workmanship can be discovered; and they are almost entirely free from the plaited and braided parts that add so much to the effect of other laces. The second description of lace made at Tonder, and known as Tonder Muslin, is Drawn Work, similar to Broderie de Nancy. In this lace, Needlepoints and Pillow Laces are imitated with the greatest accuracy, by the threads of the material being drawn out, re-united, and divided so as to follow all the intricacies of a flower or arabesque design. No lace stitches, such as are known as Fillings, are added, and no Embroidery Stitches, as are found in Indian Work and Dresden Point, but a raised or thin Cordonnet frequently marks out the outline of the chief parts of the patterns.

Tongue Shaped.—A term used by dressmakers in reference to the decoration of border trimming, by means of cutting out in that form.

Torchon Ground.—This stitch is used either for a Pillow Lace Ground, or to fill in the centres of flowers instead of the Plaitings in many varieties of lace. Being rather large, it requires a certain amount of space, and the real

beauty of the design consists in its regularity. Therefore, great attention should be paid to the pricking of the parchment pattern. To work Fig. 789: Obtain some Point paper, such as is used for tracing out Berlin patterns upon, put a piece of parchment underneath it, and folds of flannel. Sketch out the groundwork of the design with a fine tracing pen upon the Point paper, guided by the lines in making the points of the diamonds, and prick the five holes each diamond requires through to the parchment with a large pin. Put the parchment pattern on to the Pillow, and hang on two pairs of Bobbins at *a,* two pairs at *b,* make a CLOTH STITCH with the two pairs at *a.* TWIST each pair three times, and put up a pin between them. Leave them and take up the two pairs at *b;* make a Cloth Stitch with them, and TWIST each pair three times; put up a pair of Bobbins between them, make a Cloth Stitch with the four centre Bobbins, Twist each pair three times, put in a pin between the two pairs, and make a Cloth Stitch close up to the pin to inclose it. Take the centre pair to the right, and make a Cloth Stitch with the pair next to them on the right. Twist each pair three times, put up a pin, and leave them. Take the pair of centre Bobbins to the left, and make a Cloth Stitch with the pair to the left, Twist each pair three times, and put up a pin between them. Take the

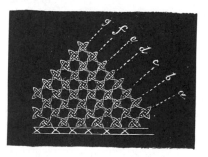

FIG. 789. TORCHON GROUND.

four centre Bobbins and make a Cloth Stitch.* Put up two pairs of Bobbins at *c,* make a Cloth Stitch, Twist each pair three times, put up a pin between them, take the nearest pair of Bobbins from the last diamond marked *b,* make a Cloth Stitch with one of the pairs from *c,* Twist each pair three times, and set up a pin between them. Repeat from * for the point not marked with a letter in the illustration. Take up the four centre Bobbins of *c,* make a Cloth Stitch, and Twist each pair thrice, and put up a pin between them; inclose the pin with a Cloth Stitch, take up the pair of *c* Bobbins nearest the pair of *b* Bobbins, and work a Cloth Stitch. Twist each pair three times, and put up a pin between them, and inclose the pin with a Cloth Stitch. Take the other pair of *c* Bobbins nearest to the unmarked Bobbins, make a Cloth Stitch, Twist each pair three times, and put up a pin between them, which inclose with a Cloth Stitch. Repeat for *d, e, f,* and *g* points. This ground can be worked either with fine or coarse thread, and the three twists given to the Bobbins can be altered to one or two twists, according to the thread used. The rest of the pattern is not altered.

Torchon Lace.—A simple thread lace that was at one time known as Beggars' Lace, and at another as Gueuse Lace. It is worked upon a Pillow and resembles Saxony Lace, the patterns being of the simplest, and formed with a loose thick thread, while the ground is a coarse Réseau ground. This lace was made in the seventeenth century, and from that time has been largely used on the Continent for common purposes. It is still worked on the Continent and in England, but much of the cheap Torchon Lace now sold is made by machinery.

Torjok Lace.—*See* RUSSIAN LACE.

Tournure.—The French term employed to denote the general outline and appearance of a person or costume. It is also used to signify a Bustle, or arrangement of

lengths; linen diaper and damask, to supply a thinner and softer kind of towel; linen having borders in blue or red, and decorated with designs and fringes; Turkish Bath Towelling, with or without a long nap; cotton towels in honeycomb pattern, with coloured striped borders, cotton diapers, Russian, and other kinds. For kitchen use there is the Linen Crash for roller towels; and Russia Crash, coarse and very durable, the widths running from 16 inches to 22 inches; and the White Loom Towelling for best kitchen use. Forfar Towels are coarse, heavy, and of unbleached flax, of 32 inches to 75 inches in width, and suitable for rough kitchen service. Dowlas Towelling, half bleached, with round threads like Russia Crash, but not so coarse, runs from 25 inches to

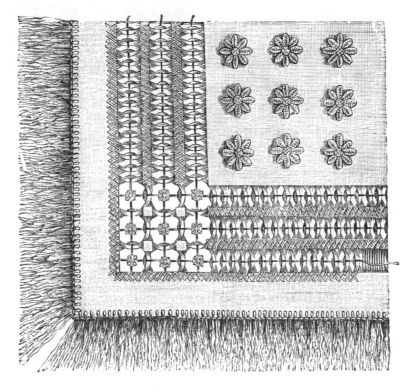

FIG. 790. TOWELLING EMBROIDERY.

puffed out crinoline, or wire, worn for the purpose of distending the back of a skirt, from the waist, and extending more or less downwards, according to the current fashion.

Tow.—This is a preparation of the fibres of flax. After the latter have been "hackled," they are divided into two sorts; the short and coarse are called Tow, and the long and fine make, Line Tow; which latter is prepared and spun on machines like cotton.

Towelling.—Every description of cloth designed for towels, whether of linen or cotton, sold singly or by the yard, is called by this name. For bed-room use there is Huckaback—the medium quality to be had at one shilling a yard—manufactured in linen, cotton, or a mixture of both, and may be cut from the piece or sold in towel

30 inches in width. In the accounts of Henry VIII.'s wardrobe expenses there is a mention made of "certeyne pieces of diaper for table cloths and towelles," as also still earlier in those of Edward IV. Ailesham, in Lincolnshire, was celebrated for fine linen napery as far back as the fourteenth century. Both Towelling, Glass and Tea Cloths, as well as Linen Damask, are employed for the purposes of Embroidery. Glass Cloths having red and blue stripes are especially so used.

Towelling Embroidery.—A modern work so named from the foundation being of thick materials, such as Java Canvas, Honeycomb, and white or stone coloured linens, such as could be used for Towels. The work consists of making handsome borders of Drawn Work, and ornamenting the plain squares left between the drawn threads and the centre of the material with Stars made with Satin Stitch and lines of Herringbone, Chain, or Feather Stitches worked either in filoselle, single Berlin wool, double crewels, or ingrain cottons. The embroidery is used for table-cloths, antimacassars, toilet cloths, bed pockets, mats, and for the ornamental towel so frequently suspended in front of the useful towels in a bedroom. To work, as shown in Fig. 790: Select a rather strong and coarse linen material, cut it to the size required, including a space of two inches for the fringe. At the end of this space make a line of wide apart BUTTONHOLE STITCHES. Leave an inch of material, and draw out threads beyond it to the depth of half an inch, leave a quarter of an inch of material, and draw out another half inch of threads, leave a quarter of an inch of material and draw out another half inch of threads. Draw out the threads in this manner along the four sides of the material; at each corner the only threads left will be those belonging to the undrawn parts of the material. Great care must be taken in cutting the threads, particularly at the corners, as a wrong cut of the scissors will spoil the whole work. Protect the corners at their edges with a close and narrow line of Buttonhole, worked with fine cotton, so as not to show in the design. Take a bright coloured filoselle or wool, and work a line of CROSS STITCH with it round the outer edge of the drawn threads, and fill in the spaces left between them with the same lines of Cross Stitches. Take a piece of fine Crochet cotton and make with it the pattern formed of the threads left in the material where the rest have been drawn away. Fasten the Crochet cotton securely at one of the corners, carry it across the first open space, divide in half the few threads between this and the next open space, take the last half upon the needle, and twist them over the first half, draw up the needle and cotton, and repeat to the end of that corner. When the threads are reached that are close together, divide them off into sets of eight threads, and take the last four first upon the needle, and twist them over the first four. Repeat until every space of drawn threads is worked over. Work small WHEELS over the open squares left at the corners. Fill in the centre of the design with stars made with coloured filoselle. Finish by drawing out the threads to form a fringe.

Fig. 791 is a pattern in Holbein Stitch used to em-

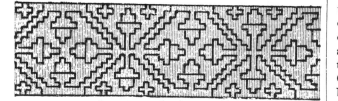

FIG. 791. TOWELLING EMBROIDERY.

broider the centres of Towelling Embroidery. To work: Trace out the design upon fine linen, or count the threads during the progress of the work in coarse materials. Use fine purse silk or Pearsall's washing silk, and work entirely in HOLBEIN STITCH.

When working Towelling Embroidery for nightgown cases omit the Drawn thread border and the fringe, and work a border with single Cross Stitches close together before commencing a pattern. The simplest design is to cover the centre with six pointed stars, made in a wool of a bright shade, and to connect these together with long lines of SATIN STITCH worked in a darker shade of wool.

Tracery.—Honiton Pillow Lace making is often enriched with Tracery, which is a kind of raised work, formed over a background of Cloth and Half Stitch. Its use gives to the patterns a very handsome effect, but, of course, increases the difficulty of the work. In Fig. 792

FIG. 792. TRACERY.

this Tracery is illustrated, and the butterfly is worked as follows: Commence at the tail, hang on eight pairs of Bobbins and two Gimp Bobbins, work in CLOTH STITCH, crossing the gimps at the narrow part, and tie and cut them off when the head is finished. Add two more pairs of Bobbins and work each of the antennæ with five pairs, finish the tips with two SEWINGS, then tie and cut off. Hang on five pairs of Bobbins at the small ring on the lower wing of the butterfly, work round it, join where it touches, then work down the body, add another pair of Bobbins, and work STEM STITCH round the inside edge of the lower wing. Sew to the body for the first three rows, work round the wing to the body again, sew once, and carry the Tracery round the oval in the upper wing, then round the inner edge of the wing to the spot where it is joined to the lower one. Sew as the Tracery is crossed and hang on four more pairs of Bobbins, so as to have five upon each side for the CUCUMBER PLAITINGS, which are made as follows: Work a row of Stem on each side, and when the working pairs come into the middle again, make a Cucumber Plaiting; when finished, turn Bobbin No. 2 back over the Pillow and keep it there with a pin. Work the Stem rows with Bobbins No. 3 and 4, so that the Cucumber Plaiting will not pull when Bobbins No. 1 and 2 are again used. Make four of these plaitings, joining the little ring to the edge as passed. Cut off five pairs of Bobbins and bring the remaining ones back in a VANDYKE tracery, then tie and cut off. Fasten on ten pairs of Bobbins for the Cucumber Plaitings in the upper wing, which work, and then fill up the rest of the space with two Vandyke Traceries, that cross each other, or with LONG PLAITINGS. Having finished the wings, work the background. Hang on eight pairs of Bobbins to the upper end of the large wing of the butterfly, and work in HALF STITCH; sew to each side, and add a pair of Bobbins to each Sewing for six turns. As there will be most holes on the lower side of the wing, occasionally sew twice into the same hole on the upper side. Cut off three or four pairs of Bobbins as the narrowing down the body proceeds, then turn and fill in the lower wing, adding Bobbins as required, and sew securely before cutting off. Hang on five pairs of Bobbins near the head, and work the open edge with PEARLS.

Cross Tracery.—The two arms of the Cross are commenced at the same time from different sides, are brought down to meet in the middle and are carried once more to the side. Two Twists have, therefore, to be attended to. In doing a cross it is always best to put a pin into the middle hole so as to mark it, and when working over a large space to Twist thrice instead of twice. The number of Bobbins used is altered to the space to be filled. To work a Cross Tracing over ten passive pairs of Bobbins without counting those that form the outside edge: First row—Work 1 CLOTH STITCH, TWIST (which means Twist the Workers twice, the Passive pairs on each side once), work 8, Twist, work 1. Second row—Work 2, Twist, work 6, Twist, work 2. Third row—Work 3, Twist, work 4, Twist, work 3. Fourth row—Work 4, Twist, work 2, Twist, work 4. Fifth row—Work 5, Twist, stick a pin, work 5. Sixth row—Work 4, Twist, work 2, Twist, work 4. Seventh row—Work 3, Twist, work 4, Twist, work 3. Eighth row—Work 2, Twist, work 6, Twist, work 2. Ninth row—Work 1, Twist, work 8, Twist, work 1.

Vandyke Tracery.—This Tracery is worked much in the same way as Cross Tracery, and forms a zig-zag device on the open parts of leaves and other spaces. It is illustrated in the lower wings of the Butterfly (Fig. 792). It is not marked out with pins, but formed with Twists, and unless great attention is paid to it, will not work out satisfactorily. The Working Bobbins in it are Twisted twice as they pass to and fro, and the Passive Bobbins on each side of the strand thus formed, once. The pattern is made by varying the place of the Twist. To make a Vandyke Tracery across ten Passive Pairs of Bobbins without counting those that form the outside edge which are worked as usual. First row—Begin from the inner side, work 2 CLOTH STITCHES, TWIST (which means Twist the workers twice, the passive pair on each side of the workers once), work 8. Second row—Work 7, Twist, work 3. Third row—Work 4, Twist, work 6. Fourth row—Work 5, Twist, work 5. Fifth row—Work 6, Twist, work 4. Sixth row—Work 3, Twist, work 7. Seventh row—Work 8, Twist, work 2. The point of the Vandyke is now reached. Eighth row—Work 3, Twist, work 7. Ninth row—Work 6, Twist, work 4, Tenth row—Work 5, Twist, work 5. Eleventh row—Work 4, Twist, work 6. Twelfth row—Work 7, Twist, work 3. Another point having thus been made, repeat the Tracery from the first row.

Tram.—A kind of doubled silk yarn of inferior raw silk, in which two or more thicknesses have been slightly twisted together. It is wound, cleaned, doubled, and thrown so as to twist in one direction only. Tram is employed for the weft or cross-threads of Gros de Naples velvets, flowered silk stuffs, and the best varieties of silk goods in general. Tram is also known by the name of Shute.

Transfer Embroidery.—In old needlework it frequently happens that the material upon which the embroidery is placed, and which forms its ground, becomes soiled and worn out, while the embroidery itself is still fresh and good. To transfer Embroidery: Trace the outline of the pattern upon the new material, which frame in an EMBROIDERY FRAME. Procure narrow silk cords, dyed exactly to match the colours used in the embroidery, or use gold cord, edge the Embroidery by stitching a line of cord down to it, then paste tissue paper at the back of the old material, and when that is perfectly dry, cut out the embroidery, leaving but the sixteenth of an inch of material beyond it. Lay the Embroidery upon the traced outlines in the Frame and pin it well down, and stitch it down in its proper lines with fine waxed silk, securing the little edging of old material to the new. Take a second cord like the first, and COUCH this upon the outline, so as to hide the small edging of old material. Work upon the new material tendrils, sprays, rays, and other pieces of the embroidery that could not be transferred. Some people prefer to put the two cords on after the Embroidery is laid upon the new material, but the first method is the best.

Transfer Lace.—Laces made with detached sprays, such as Brussels, Honiton, and Point Duchesse, and laid upon net foundations, are easily transferred to new grounds. To transfer: Carefully unpick the tacking stitches that secure the lace to the net, make a design of the lace upon calico, and back this with brown paper, lay the sprigs of lace face downwards upon the pattern, and keep them in place with a few light tacking stitches. Then lay over them some of the finest and best Brussels cream coloured net, and tack this to the margin of the pattern. Thread a needle with the finest cream lace thread, and OVERCAST round the outline of every part of the lace, and thus secure it to the net. Unpick the lace very carefully from the pattern.

Travail au Metier.—*See* FRAME WORK.

Treble Crochet.—*See* CROCHET.

Treble Diamonds.—*See* MACRAMÉ LACE.

Treble Star.—*See* MACRAMÉ LACE.

Treble Stitch.—*See* CROCHET.

Trefoils.—These are much used as edgings in Honiton Lace, and are made in various ways. To work the Close Trefoil shown in Fig. 793: Prick the pattern and hang on six pairs of Bobbins. Commence at the upper part of the left hand lower leaf of the first Trefoil, and work down it in HALF STITCH, make a PEARL EDGE to the point of contact with the next pattern of Trefoil, turn the Pillow, and work the other half of the leaf in CLOTH STITCH, SEWING every row in the middle except the first, which is secured by taking up the Runners or Working pair of Bobbins, that lie idle at the pins. Work the middle leaf

FIG. 793. TREFOILS—CLOSE.

of the pattern like the first leaf, but make the Cloth Stitch before the Half Stitch and put a Pearl Edge to both sides, and lastly, work the third leaf; work the lower side first in Cloth Stitch, and put a Pearl Edge to the upper part. The number of Pinholes in the centre of the leaves is not so great as those upon the outside, a false Pinhole is, therefore, made at the top. Work STEM STITCH with an open edge upon one side to the next pattern, and then repeat the three leaves.

To work the open Trefoil shown in Fig. 794: Prick the

the bottom of each petal on the outside edge, where the work turns. Work round the centre petal entirely with Pearl Edge on one side and Plain upon the other, and Sew twice to the inner circle. For the third petal work until seven Pearls have been made on the outer edge, and then work both edges Plain, and where the Pearls leave off TWIST the outside pair of Bobbins three times before making the first stitch. As the leaf narrows, cut off a pair of Bobbins and connect to the leaf at the nearest place, and when the inner circle is reached, Sew to it, and then make a ROPE SEWING down it to the next leaf; here disentangle the Bobbins and commence on the leaf. Hang on two pairs of Bobbins in addition if the leaf is worked in Half Stitch; three pairs if in Cloth Stitch. Work down the leaf, connect to the nearest petal of the Trefoil at the point of contact, and at the bottom of the leaf cut off two or three pairs of Bobbins. Make Stem Stitch for two pinholes, and repeat from the beginning; the only difference being that in the following Trefoils, at the third petal, Sew twice to the Trefoil preceding it. If the Trefoil Edge is to be repeated beyond the four Trefoils given, move the Bobbins thus: Turn the flap of the COVER CLOTH over them, pin the doubled cloth tightly upon each side and to the pillow, so that the threads are a little slack, take out all the pins from the finished lace, but leave those at the last part still in the lace. Detach the cloth containing the Bobbins from the lower end of the pattern and fasten it down again at the

FIG. 794. TREFOILS—OPEN.

pattern and hang on ten pairs of Bobbins at the end of the first leaf, work it in CLOTH STITCH with an open edge upon each side; when it is complete cut off four pairs of Bobbins and commence the Trefoil at the inner circle. Work this in STEM STITCH, Sew as the circle is crossed, and commence the first petal of the Trefoil; work this in Cloth Stitch, hang on two pairs of Bobbins in successive rows, and make false Pinholes where required. The edge will be an open or PLAIN EDGE until the point where the first Trefoil touches the next is passed, at which place work the outer edge as a right-hand PEARL. Work a PEARL EDGE on one side and a plain upon the other to the end of the first petal, when Sew twice to the inner circle. Make plain and not pearl the lowest hole at

upper end, pin the last made Trefoil and leaf down on the first one of the pattern, putting the pins in half way; undo the Bobbins and continue the work.

Another description of Open Trefoil, and one used for the sprigs in Lace, and not for the edging, is illustrated in STEM STITCH.

Treille.—One of the names by which the Réseau Grounds of Pillow and Needle Laces are distinguished from the Toile or pattern they surround. The value of many laces is decided by the thickness or fineness of the thread used in the Treille, and the number of Twists given to the Bobbins when making it.

Trellis Work.—An Embroidery of recent date, resembling Strasbourg Embroidery or Roman Work, by being cut away from its background, but made with coloured instead of plain materials. It is intended to represent a climbing plant trailing over trellis work, and for this reason only plants that climb can be used, such as honeysuckles, passion flowers, roses. The materials required are American gold cloth, Sateens of green shades and whole colours, and coloured cretonnes of flower patterns, and filoselles. The Trellis is made with the gold cloth, the leaves and sprays of the design with the green sateen, and the flowers and buds with the cretonne, while the whole is finished with Embroidery worked with the filoselles. The work is used for summer fire screens or for mantel boards or cushions. To work: Frame two pieces of strong linen one over the other in an EMBROIDERY FRAME. Trace the design through upon this, and retain the design to cut the leaves and flowers from. Cut out long strips of gold cloth half an inch wide and lay these over the linen in diagonal lines, to form an open diamond-pattern Trellis Work. BASTE the cloth to the linen to keep it in position, but take the basting stitches right over the cloth from side to side, so as not to prick it with a needle. Cut out the leaves and stems from the sateen cloth, varying their shades of colour as much as the material will allow. Place the leaves, &c., upon the linen, and keep them in their right positions by pasting them down, as in Cretonne Work (APPLIQUÉ, BRODERIE PERSE). Cut the flowers and the buds from the chintz, and paste them to the linen. Bring the leaves and flowers over the Trellis Work, and give them the appearance of twining about it. Leave the work stretched in the frame until the paste is dry, then take it out, and, with filoselle silk matching the tints of the leaves and flowers, BUTTONHOLE round their edges, to secure them to the linen foundation. Mark out the veins of the leaves with CREWEL STITCH, and the centres of the flowers with FRENCH KNOTS, and heighten the colouring of the flowers by adding in SATIN STITCH some lines of light filoselle. Buttonhole round the edges of the Trellis Work with Buttonhole Stitch in two shades of old gold, so that one side of the lines is darker than the other. When the Embroidery is finished, cut away the linen from the back where it has not been connected to the pattern by being caught by the Buttonholes.

Tresse.—A French term for Braid.

Tricotage.—A French term for Knitting.

Tricot Stitch.—*See* CROCHET.

Triellis d'Allemagne.—One of the names given to Netting, but generally meaning the head nets made in Germany in this work.

Trimmings.—A term of general application to ready-made decorations, varying in material, form, and method of manufacture. Those in Muslin are made in Edgings, Flounces, Insertions, and Scollops. They are made in pieces of from 24 yards, to 36 yards, and in short lengths; but may be bought by the yard. Quillings and Ruches of ribbon, net, and tarlatan, Plaitings of any material for dresses, fringes, spangles, beads, gimps, and braids of every colour, or mixture of colours, in

cotton, silk, and worsted, and every description of lace, are all to be included under the term Trimmings. They may also be had in strips of fur of all kinds, and in arrangements of flowers and feathers.

Trina de Lana.—*See* SHETLAND POINT LACE.

Trolle Kant.—An old Flemish lace no longer manufactured, but of great beauty. The flower or Toilé of the lace was usually made with Cloth Stitch, which was completely surrounded with a raised thread, while the grounds used were Trolly, Plaited, and Net, all being frequently employed upon the same piece of lace. The name of this lace has been corrupted into Trolly and given to a coarse English lace.

Trolly Laces.—These are Pillow Laces, made in Normandy, in Flanders, and in Buckinghamshire, and Devonshire. The distinguishing feature of these laces is their ground, which is an imitation of the Antwerp Trolly Net or Point de Paris Ground, and is made with twists, while the pattern is outlined with a thick thread like that used in the old Flemish Laces, and known as Trolle Kant. The lace is still made in Buckinghamshire, Northampton, and Devonshire, but like other pillow laces has declined since the introduction of machine made imitations.

Trouserings.—This is a term of general significance, denoting a great variety of cloths, specially made for the use which the name indicates, such as varieties of broadcloth, tartans, drills, &c.

Tucks.—These are parallel folds of material, lying either horizontally, or perpendicularly on any article of dress, of whatever material, either for shortening a garment, or for the purpose of ornamentation. These folds, or Tucks, are sometimes graduated, when several of them follow each other successively; and at other times they are made of respectively differing sizes. When about to make them, first measure the cloth accurately, to ascertain how many Tucks of a given size may be made. Fold it from selvedge to selvedge, and press the fold sufficiently firmly so as to form a crease, following a single thread to ensure perfect straightness. Turn down the folded portion to the depth desired, and then make a very close and delicate RUNNING along the double inner fold. Do not take more than three stitches at a time on the needle, when Running. When many Tucks are to be made parallel with each other, as in the case of infants' clothing, shirts, and underlinen in general, make the measurements by means of a piece of cardboard, cut exactly of the right width, and correct any unevenness in the folding before making the Runnings.

When Tucks are to be made in crape, the difficulty of the needlewoman is increased, and the method of making them is somewhat more complicated, as they require to be lined, and the material itself proves troublesome of management. The size of Tucks in crape varies from 2 inches in width to the depth of what are worn on a widow's skirt. Formerly they were made, like those of other materials, simply doubled in an ordinary fold of itself only; now they are lined. Employ mull-muslin for a good and new crape, but if the latter be of poor quality, or a piece that has been re-calendered, use book-muslin. For wear on a gored skirt, cut the crape from the straight way, across from selvedge to selvedge, not on the bias, as for an old-fashioned "all round" skirt. Then proceed to join the front and side gores of the skirt together. Lay it on the table with the hem towards you, and the roll of crape across it, with the selvedge to the hem. Then pin it down flat, cut off the pieces that come lower than the skirt, at the edge of the last gores, so that the crape may be the same distance from the hem at the sides, as in the middle of the front gore, and allow half an inch for the Running and Turning up with the muslin; and when completed, let the Tuck be quite 1 inch above the hem, as it so quickly frays out, if permitted to touch the ground. When the extreme edge is cut into the right shape, take the yard measure and place pins as far up the crape, measuring from the edge first cut, as the trimming is to be, allowing an additional quarter of an inch for Running it on the dress; then cut off by this pin guide. After this, treat the train in the same way, using the curvature just left by hollowing the top of the front Tuck for the middle of the back breadth, to economise the slope, if it be a long train. By laying on the trimming in this way, there will be a join at each side of the train, but it does not show at that point in gored or demi-trains, and it is a very great improvement to avoid making conspicuous joins, or triangular overlapping plaits, so as to make a straight flounce follow a bend.

Crape is sold in 23 inches, 42 inches, and 60 inches widths, therefore it is very easy to judge which will be most advantageous for dividing into one, two, or three Tucks, according to the degree of mourning demanded. When crape trimmings are taken from the straight way of the stuff, so are the muslin linings; and if the crape be cut crosswise, so must be the muslin. Proper unglazed cotton, called crape cotton, must be used in the making of mourning, as glacé thread would be perceptible on dull black stuffs. In Running the crape and muslin edges together on the wrong side, a quarter of an inch in, hold the former towards you, and do not pull against the muslin. Neither should project beyond the other. Draw the cotton fairly, but not tightly; and set the stitches tolerably closely. Then, when the two are turned right side out, for the seam to be between them, draw the muslin up about a quarter of an inch beyond the crape, so that the extreme edge of the Tuck shall be really double crape for a quarter of an inch. This, and the inner turning, uses up the half inch which was mentioned in reference to the cutting. TACK the upper edge of the crape a quarter of an inch in on the muslin with white cotton, in stitches of the same length in front as behind; as those at the back will serve as a mark for running the Tuck upon the skirt afterwards. A white Basting ought to be previously Run on the foundation, at the height the trimming should reach; the least irregularity in the arrangement of these Tucks is apparent, when devoid of any heading, and to attempt it while working on the inside of a Tuck, on a gored skirt, without an accurate white cotton line on both, would prove a great mistake. This plain mounting is most suitable for deep mourning, but otherwise cording, or

one-eighth of an inch fold standing upwards may head the Tucks; and then this cord or fold can be put on the skirt first, and be used as the guide line for sewing on the Tuck, instead of a Running of white cotton.

Fancy folds and rouleaux may sometimes serve as a suitable finish to Tucks, and by some are made in one with them. But it is better to make them separately, and to lay them on the raw edge of the flounce. Take care in this case to match the rouleau, and the flounce or Tuck, in the diagonal slope of the crape and the grain of the two pieces. If that of the Tuck slope from right to left, and that of the trimming the contrary way, the effect will be very bad.

Tulle.—A fine Silk Net, manufactured in the Jacquard looms, and which is a wide description of the material called blonde, which is employed for quillings. It is a silk bobbin-net, the manufacture of which in this country commenced at Nottingham. It originated in France, where it was called after the town in which it was first produced, Point de Tulle. A variety of the same delicate textile is known as Tulle Bruxelles. Tulle may be had in black and white, and in every colour, and is about a yard wide. It is employed for veils, bonnets, and dress trimmings, and is made both with spots of different dimensions, and varying in closeness one to the other; and also plain.

Tulle Embroidery.—This is a very simple kind of Embroidery, worked with floss silks upon fine black or white Tulle, and used for trimmings to ball dresses and other light fabrics. To work: Select an easy outline Crewel Work or Embroidery pattern, trace this out upon pink calico and TACK the Tulle on to the calico. Thread a fine darning needle with floss silk and RUN this along so as to trace the pattern out with a run line. DARN the floss silk into the Tulle to fill in any parts of the design that are thick, and work two to three Run lines close together to make stalks or any prominent lines. To work as shown in Fig. 795: Work upon black tulle, and with

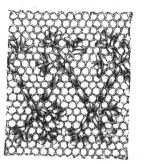

FIG. 795. TULLE EMBROIDERY.

crimson floss silk. RUN the floss silk diagonally across the tulle, to form the chief lines of the pattern, and work the rest with short SATIN STITCHES.

To work Fig. 796: Use white tulle and blue filoselle. Twist the filoselle several times in and out the tulle to form the diamonds, and work the centre of the device by darning the filoselle into the tulle.

To work Fig. 797: Trace the design upon a piece of pink calico, lay the black tulle material upon it, and work over the traced lines with SATIN STITCH, using a bright floss silk of a yellow shade.

FIG. 796. TULLE EMBROIDERY.

Tunisian Crochet.—One of the names given to Tricot. *See* CROCHET.

FIG. 797. TULLE EMBROIDERY.

Tunisian Work.—A modern embroidery, that consists of working in SATIN STITCH, and with embroidery silks, detached sprays of flowers, or birds, horses, and other animals. These embroideries are cut out, and then Appliqué to a velvet, satin, or plush foundation. A line of gold cord, or silk cord, is COUCHED round the outlines, to hide the stitches that attach the embroidery to the foundations. *See* APPLIQUÉ and EMBROIDERY.

Tunisian Crochet. — One of the names given to Tricot. *See* CROCHET.

Turgaux.—The French term for fluted plaitings. *Turgaux d'Orgue* signify wide flutings, resembling the pipes of an organ, whence its name.

Turkey Red.—A cotton cambric, of a bright scarlet colour of indelible dye, made both twilled and plain. It was originally imported from Turkey, whence its name. The art of dyeing this red was practised in the Middle Ages in the East; in the course of the last century it was introduced into France by Greek dyers, and imported thence by Frenchmen, who founded the first manufactory in this country. It is now made in Glasgow and in Lancashire, and is much employed for trimmings and linings, the colour being proof against any amount of washing.

The method of dyeing this cloth is as follows: The bleached yarn is soaked in oil, then dipped in carbonate of soda, and exposed to the action of the air and of steam in a hot room. It is then passed through a solution of nut-galls and a red mordant successively, and is thus ready for dyeing. To effect this it is boiled for two or three hours in a vessel containing madder-root, or *munjeet*, and, lastly, it is boiled in a solution of soap.

Turkey Red Handkerchiefs.—These can be had already hemmed, in sizes measuring from 18 inches by 18 inches to 28 inches by 28 inches; the price varying to a considerable extent, according to their quality.

Turkish Embroidery.—The Turks, although not so celebrated as the Persians, East Indians, and Japanese for their needlework, have the same true appreciation of design, and fondness for brilliant colouring harmoniously blended, as other Asiatic nations. Their braiding with

gold thread upon cloth is as well-known as the Indian Braiding, as is also their Patchwork or Appliqué Work done with cloth or silk; and besides these they are known for their embroideries with silk and gold thread upon thin gauze-like materials. At the present time attention has been peculiarly directed to this particular class of their work, vast quantities of it having been exported to England and France. This work is done upon Toile Colbert, a thin open canvas material far inferior in value to the elaborate Embroidery of which it forms the background, but in Turkey labour is cheap, and the price of materials considerable, so the workers who earn a scanty living have to obtain the least expensive. The patterns for Turkish Work are all arabesque or of conventionalised flower designs, the silks used are known as raw silks dyed with vegetable dyes, and gold thread or tinsel. The stitches differ from those employed in ordinary European embroideries by being worked very much at the fancy of the worker as to place and uniformity. The stitches most used are Rope Stitch most elaborately twisted, Satin Stitch made with short stitches, Point de Riz, Cross Stitch, Tent Stitch, Herringbone worked so closely that no ground appears between the stitches; also lines of thread thrown across the space and covered with Tent Stitch, while threads are drawn out in a design and Overcast over so as to form small open squares as the centre to a flower or pine-shaped arabesque. The silks used in the two stitches that make a Cross Stitch are frequently of different colours, and the stitches themselves are rarely worked in straight rows, but oblique or following the curves of the pattern, sometimes half of them will start from one side of the piece of the design being worked, and slant to the centre, to be met by others slanting in an opposite direction, these latter being executed in a different kind of stitch to those first made; in fact, there is no rule to the filling in of any of the designs, beyond the employment in the colouring of large quantities of dull yellow and a kind of cinnamon red, with smaller proportions of blue, green, and orange. The borderings to most of the Embroidery upon Canvas are made with Drawn Work, whose threads are Overcast or Buttonholed over with silks of different shades, and are never left visible. The best way to make up this Embroidery for use (the ground being generally dirty and coarse) is to cut out the design from the background, arrange it upon Stamped plush or brocaded silk, slightly OVERCAST the edges to those materials, and cover the Overcasting and the raw edge with a line of gold thread, COUCHED down. Very handsome tablecovers, mantel-boards, and cushions, can thus be obtained without much additional labour.

Turkish Embroidery upon Cloth.—This is executed in a variety of colours, and with gold thread, and floss or raw silk. To work as shown in Fig. 798, which is the half of a tablecloth or coverlet: Cut the centre of the pattern, shown by the horizontal lines, out of a fine carmine red cloth, embroider with SATIN STITCH the arabesque design upon it with pale green silk and black silk, arranged as shown in the illustration, and then outline every part of the Embroidery with two lines of gold thread, which COUCH down upon the material with gold silk. Make the background of the outer part of the tablecloth of fine black cloth, and conceal the join by working it over with pale green silk, and outlining that with gold thread. Embroider the scroll upon the black cloth with bright red, blue, and green, outlining every part with gold

FIG. 798. TURKISH EMBROIDERY.

thread. For the border either cut out the ovals from light red cloth and Couch them on to the background with gold thread, or work them in ROPE STITCH and outline them with yellow silk cord; make the lines enclosing them like those in the centre.

The Turks also embroider with gold thread upon gauze and crape, and also with gold threads upon morocco, and in this latter work they frequently insert gold coins, and execute the minutest designs without spoiling the delicate thread they use.

Turkish Lace.—The lace made in Turkey is limited to one description, and is not made for the market, but in the harems, for the use of the ladies of the harem. It is a species of Tambour and Crochet Work, made with a needle and with silk of various colours. It is called Oyah Lace.

Turkish Towels.—These are cotton cloths, having a long nap, cut or uncut. Some are all white, some unbleached, and others are bordered with ingrain red stripes, with stripes across from selvedge to selvedge, or cross-bars throughout. They have fringes at each end. Turkish Towelling may also be had by the yard, and has latterly been employed for women's bathing dresses, &c. *See* TOWELLINGS.

Turned Row.—*See* KNITTING.

Turn Heel.—*See* KNITTING STOCKINGS.

Turnhout Lace.—The lace made in this place is Mechlin Lace.

Turning Scallops.—In Pillow Laces it frequently happens that the pattern is formed of open petals or scallops that are wider upon their outside curve than upon

their inner. This form of the pattern necessitates more pinholes being pricked upon the outer curve than upon the inner, and in order to keep the threads working backwards and forwards across the lace, and thus forming it, secured at each curve, it is necessary that false pinholes shall be arranged upon the inner curve so as to keep the outer and inner edges level with each other.

To Turn a Scallop: Work across to the inside, TWIST thrice and stick a pin, but instead of completing the edge, work back with the same pair of Bobbins, and when the inside is again reached take out the pin and re-stick it in the same hole, then finish the plain inside edge with the idle pair. Repeat until the scallop has been rounded.

To Turn a Scallop in Stem Stitch: Use six pair of Bobbins. In making these scallops the last two holes of the scallop belong equally to the scallop upon each side. Work round the first scallop until these holes are reached, stick a pin in the first and complete the plain edge, then lay back by the pins the outside pair. Work across, and as the pins are again reached twist the Hanging or Passive pair of Bobbins lying next them thrice, and make the PLAIN EDGE with these, but do not twist the Worker or Runner pair which is left at the pins, work across, SEW to the inner part of the design, turn the pillow, work back to the pins where the untwisted pair is lying, do not touch the pins, but work across and back with this pair, and when the pins are again reached take out the second one, Sew to the hole, re-stick the pin, and work another row of STEM STITCH. All this is done without Twisting, the work having arrived at the second scallop, here twist the outside pair, and stick a pin, and finish the Plain Edge with the pair put away.

Turning Stitch.—*See* TURN STITCH.

Turn Stitch.—Also known as Turning Stitch, and used in Honiton and other Pillow Laces at the end of a row. It is made with a Cloth Stitch and a half Cloth Stitch as follows: Work a CLOTH STITCH, give each pair of Bobbins one TWIST to the left, put the middle left hand Bobbin over the middle right; lift the two pairs with each hand, and give them a little pull.

Turn Stitch.—*See* KNITTING.

Turquoise Silk.—This silk is likewise known as Gros de Suez. It is a description of material made for bonnets and trimmings, which measures from 18 inches to 22 inches in width.

Tuscan Straw Work.—Finely plaited straw of wheat, having a delicate and slender stalk, and golden hue; growing in Tuscany, and manufactured into circular "flats," for hat and bonnet, mat and basket making, in the neighbourhoods of Florence, Pisa, and Sienna. The "tress" is sometimes formed of seven or nine straws, but generally of thirteen; and, being tied at one end, it is plaited by hand, till a length of about 20 yards is made. The hat when completed is made of but one piece.

Tussore Silks.—These are of Indian manufacture, and are all "wild" and raw silks, plain made, and without any cord or woven patterns, although some are stamped or printed in England from Indian blocks. They are sold by the piece of 9½ yards, are 34 inches in width, and vary much in price. They are produced by the larvæ of the *Antheræa mylitta* of Linnæus, while the cultivated silk fibres come from the *Bombyx mori*. These silks in their unbleached state are of a darkish shade of fawn colour, unlike the golden and white hues of that produced by the mulberry-fed worms. The particular characteristic of the Tussar silk fibre is that it is flat, while that spun by the *Bombyx mori* is round. The silk textile made from the former is strong, yet light in wear, soft to the touch, very suitable for summer costumes, and will bear both cleaning and washing. The silks of this description are respectively known by a variety of names; that previously given is the French application, but the native names are Tussar, Tussah, and Tasar; it is the most important of the wild silks of India.

Tweed.—A woollen cloth woven of short lengths of wool, and lightly felted and milled, the yarn being dyed before it is woven. It is soft, flexible, and durable, being unmixed with either shoddy or cotton. Tweed of the finest quality is made of Saxony and Australian wools, while the common sorts are of the Danish and South American sheep. It is manufactured at Selkirk, Hawick, and Jedburgh, in the neighbourhood of the Tweed—whence its name. There is also a variety, produced by a very peculiar method of manufacture, called the Harris Tweed, having its origin in the island after which it is called. It is a homespun material in diagonal weaving, undyed, and of a kind of warm sand colour. Others of older date are distinguished by the names Cheviot, Glengarry (which is mottled), Scotch, and Waterproof Tweeds; they may be had either checked or plain, and their average widths run to about 48 inches. In former times they were known as Tweel. The Donegal Tweeds are exceedingly thick and warm, being of pure wool, undyed, and also to be had in all colours. *See* TWILL.

Twill, or Tweed.—A term descriptive of a certain process of weaving—*i.e.*, passing the weft thread across diagonally, so forming small ribs, the weft going over one and under two warp threads alternately, or else over one and under three or more, which method is reversed on its return. The thread is generally doubled one way. In plain weaving it would pass over one and under the next in succession. All stuffs, whether of silk, woollen, or cotton, are stronger when of this make.

Twist.—This term is used when one Bobbin has to be turned over another, and a twist together thus given to the threads. In Pillow Lace directions, the worker is constantly told to Twist once, twice, or three times, as the case may be. To make a Twist: Lift the pair of Bobbins in the hand, and hold them loosely, Twist them over each other with a rapid motion of the forefinger and thumb, and then give them a pull.

A description of cotton yarn made in several varieties, and also of sewing silk, is known as Twist, such as Purse Twist and Tailors' Twist, also Gold and Silver Twist, employed for purposes of Embroidery. The Silk Sewing Twist is sold in balls, hanks, and reels, in all colours. Of the cotton-yarn Twist there are three kinds—

viz., the Green, Mule, and Water, of which the numbers run from 20 to 100.

Twisted Bar.—*See* MACRAMÉ LACE.

Twisted Chain.—A name by which the Ridge or Twisted Bar in Macramé is sometimes called; it is also used instead of Rope Stitch. *See* EMBROIDERY STITCHES, and RIDGE BAR, MACRAMÉ.

Twisted Net.—The ordinary kind is of cotton, which was machine-made early in the present century, and before that by hand. It is composed of three threads; one passing from right to left, another proceeding the opposite way, while the third winds about them both, in a serpentine course, intertwisting so as to form regular openings, which in the best qualities appear rather elongated in the direction of the selvedge. The common kinds are used as linings and foundation. The Brussels is the best, and may be had for dresses in widths of 2 yards. The meshes in this quality are extra twisted. Fancy sprigs and spotted patterns may be had in net, from 18 inches to 36 inches wide.

Twist Stitch.—*See* EMBROIDERY STITCHES.

Tying Bobbins.—When making Pillow Lace, the Bobbins used are first tied together in pairs, and then knotted together in greater or smaller numbers, according to the width of the lace and the Bobbins required to make it. When any part of the lace is finished, and the Bobbins have to be cut off, the Bobbins are first secured together by a movement known as Tying-up. Take the two outside Bobbins, turn their tails to one another, and tie them by passing one over, one under, the opposite thread, and draw through. Do this twice; take two other Bobbins and repeat, and then cut away the Bobbins that are not required.

U.

Ulster.—A loose overcoat, worn by men and women the breadths of which are cut straight, and confined at the waist by a belt of the same material. Sometimes Ulsters are made of thick tweed; a double-faced cloth of unicolour, and a plaid inside; or of other warm woollen cloth; and also of alpaca of different colours, for summer wear. Ulsters are well-furnished with pockets, and sometimes have either a hood or cape of the same stuff.

Umbrella.—An appliance made to give shelter to the person when exposed to the rain, and for which a variety of textiles are expressly made, and rendered waterproof. Amongst these are certain twilled, or plainly-woven silk stuffs, to be had in several colours; also in alpaca, gingham, Orleans cloth, and dyed calico. There are many varieties in the construction of umbrella frames, as also in the sticks and handles; and the ribs may be either of whalebone or metal. Umbrellas were employed by the Anglo-Saxons, an illustration of which may be seen in Harleian MSS., in which a figure wearing some description of hat, a cloak, tight-sleeved tunic, and boots to the ankle, is followed by a bare-headed attendant, who holds over him an Umbrella, or Sunshade, having a handle with a joint, the stick slanting obliquely from the centre. But the use of this appliance is of far more remote antiquity. The Chinese have employed it from time immemorial, and there, as in various Oriental countries, it is used as an article of State rather than a mere shelter from the sun. Illustrations of those in use in the ancient metropolis of Persia (Persepolis) may be seen on the ruined wall. Umbrellas are also represented on the ruins of Nineveh (1,200 years before Christ). Dr. Layard states that, "on the later bas-reliefs, a long piece of embroidered linen or silk, falling from one side like a curtain, appears to screen the King completely from the sun." He also observes, in reference to the Ninevitish illustrations, that "the Parasol was reserved exclusively for the Monarch, and is never represented as borne over any other persons." In Eastern lands they were and are very handsome; composed of silk, and decorated with an openwork border, with tassels, and a flower on the top of the stick. In ancient Greece and Rome they were also employed as a mark of distinction, as well as a shelter from the sun; but they were not of so decorative a character, being made of leather or skin.

On occasions, however, when the Veil could not be spread over the roof of the Amphitheatre, women, and effeminate men used to shield themselves from the sun by these rude Umbrellas, or *Umbraculum* of the period. Amongst the ancient Greeks, the Dayshade, or *Skiadeion* was employed at a certain Festival (the Panathenia) by the Athenian maidens, held over them by the daughters of the aliens.

In later times, they have been in use all over Europe, and much employed in ecclesiastical processions, and in the Regalia of the Pope. The State Umbrella of the native Princes of India continues to be employed, the handle of which is of gold or silver, and the silk cover splendidly decorated and embroidered with gold and silver thread. Only in the last century was its use adapted to shield the person from the inclemency of the weather. The first man who made a practice of carrying one was Jonas Hanway, and in the *Statistical Account of Glasgow*, by Dr. Cleland, it is said that about the year 1781-2 Mr. John Jamieson, surgeon, brought with him, on his return from Paris, an Umbrella, which was the [first seen in the city, and attracted universal attention. When first introduced into England as a protection from the rain, their use by men was regarded as very effeminate.

Those first made in England were exceedingly coarse and heavy, and by no means a decorative article of use. They were covered with oilsilks, and were not easily opened when wet; the frames were made of rattan canes, split and dried. Afterwards whalebone replaced them, and a ring attached to a narrow ribbon was employed to draw the folds together. We find a mention of the article in one of Ben Jonson's comedies, in 1616, and in Beaumont and Fletcher's *Rule a Wife and have a Wife* (1640):

> Are you at ease? Now is your heart at rest?
> Now you have got a shadow—an umbrella,
> To keep the scorching world's opinion
> From your fair credit. . . .

When selecting a silk Umbrella, it is as well to hold it up to the light and look through it, to judge of the evenness of the grain and the shade of the black dye, which in the best black silks will have a greenish hue

when the light is seen through. When wet, they should not be placed near the fire, and neither shut up nor stretched open, but left to hang in loose folds in some dry place. A silk case drawn over them when travelling is a good protection against injury, but the continual drawing on and off of a case will rub and wear out the folds. Large oiled cotton yellow Umbrellas are still in use amongst the Italian peasantry, and enormous specimens, of a bright red colour, are employed as tents to cover fruit, flower stalls, &c., in the streets of Continental towns, and have a very picturesque effect.

Umritzur Cashmere.— A peculiar manufacture of Cashmere, having a kind of zigzag chevron pattern, produced in the weaving, instead of a twill. It is made in every variety of Indian colour, and is exceedingly soft and warm. It is 26 inches wide, and is sold in pieces of about 9 yards each.

Unbleached Thread Tassels.—These are employed, amongst others, for Window Blind Tassels. *See* TASSELS.

Underlinen.—This is a comprehensive term, applied to almost every article worn beneath the external garments, by day or at night, both of men and women. Underlinen is made of a variety of materials, although the several articles of wear come under the general denomination of Underlinen. These may be made of silk, stockingette, spun silk, lawn, cambric, merino, flannel, longcloth, pine wool, elastic cotton cloth, &c. The several articles of Underclothing, such as shirts, chemises, drawers, nightdresses for men and women, "combination" garments, square-cut and high petticoat bodices, knickerbockers, white petticoats, and infants' clothing—comprising the barrow, petticoat, shirt, and stays—are all described under CUTTING OUT; as also FRILLS and LININGS, for all measurements and placing. In the great ready-made Underlinen manufactories, where the several articles are all hand-made, the cloth, of whatever quality, is folded in immense blocks, in appropriate lengths and widths, of which a certain thickness is laid on a long table to be cut out *en masse*. In the centre of this table there is a hollow space, occupied by a steam-propelled circular tape saw, without teeth, like the blade of a knife, which turns rapidly round, and the folded cloth—sufficient for some three hundred or upwards of shirts, or other articles—is pressed against it, and turned according to the outline pencilled on the top layer of cloth, when the whole is cut sharply through; the pieces taken out of the neck and other places are cut into cuffs and collars. The plain sewing is then executed by hand, and with such extreme cleanliness, that it is not washed, but passes at once into the hands of the ironers. The several smoothing irons are heated by gas, introduced into the hollow of each through a tube and lighted. Thus, greater expedition in the work is obtained.

There is a new description of Underlinen, made on the system of Professor Gustav Jaeger, M.D., of Stuttgart, and patented by the Messrs. Benger, in this country, America, and most of the kingdoms of Europe. The material is pure wool, woven after the method of stockingette cloth, and designed to clothe the body from the throat to the extremities, including the feet. The shirts and chemises can be had separately from the drawers: but "combinations" are also produced. This description of Underlinen is called the "Normal" wool Underclothing. In substance it is light, fine, and smooth, and is made both for summer and winter wear.

The Underlinen of the institution called the "Rational Dress Society" forms a portion of what is called the "Hygienic Wearing Apparel," and the new improvements which this Society is endeavouring to introduce, in lieu of the ever-changing fashions, are patronised by the National Health Society. Amongst other changes in the style of outward apparel, this Rational Dress Society advocates and produces stays without whalebones, under-petticoats and skirts divided in the form of leggings, called dual, or divided skirts; and stockings, manufactured like gloves, or digitated, which is very clumsy, and not likely to meet with favour. There is also an extensive manufacture of ready-made Pine-wool Underclothing. *See* PINE WOOL; also *see* CUTTING OUT.

Undyed Cloths.—These woollen cloths are produced both for trouserings and suitings, in greys, drabs, and buffs, of various shades.

Undyed Stockingette Cloth.—This description of elastic cloth may be had in single, double, and treble width. *See* STOCKINGETTE CLOTH.

Union Cord.—A round white cord, made for stay-laces, of firm quality, being composed of both linen and cotton thread. The combination of the two substances is supposed to improve the quality of the cord, the cotton supplying a degree of pliability and softness, and the linen thread the requisite firmness and strength.

Union Cord Braid.—This kind of Braid consists of two or more cords, woven together, of Mohair or worsted, also called Russia Braid. It may be had in black or in colours; the numbers run 0 to 8. It is cut into short lengths, and sold by the gross pieces, each gross containing four pieces. The wider lengths measure 36 yards.

Union Diaper.—This cloth is made of a combination of linen and cotton thread; but, in the method of weaving, and the small diamond-shaped designs, of two or three varieties, it in all respects resembles linen diaper.

Unions.—Stout materials composed of a mixture of linen and cotton, much dressed and stiffened, and chiefly used for linings and window blinds. There are imitations made of cotton. The width is regulated by inches, and the sizes required to fit the various widths of window frames are always to be had. In procuring Union Cloths for window blinds, it is advisable to purchase inferior kinds, well glazed, as they do not bear washing satisfactorily, and when soiled should be replaced by new ones.

Unwinding Bobbins.—All workers of Pillow Lace, until they become thoroughly acquainted with the art, will experience great trouble with their Bobbins, either in keeping them disentangled and straight down the Pillow, or in keeping them the same length, which requires continual unwinding and settling.

To Unwind a Bobbin so that the thread hanging from it is to be longer: Tighten it, and slowly turn the Bobbin to the left; if the thread will then unwind nothing more

is needed, but should it not do so, raise the Half Hitch of thread that keeps the Bobbin thread secure, lift this off over the head of the Bobbin, unwind the length required, and then make the Half Hitch again.

To Shorten or Wind up the Thread: Lift the Bobbin with the left hand, hold it horizontally, raise the Half Hitch with a pin, and keep it raised until sufficient thread is wound up, when drop it over again into its old position.

Upholstery.—A term by which every description of textile employed in the making and covering of furniture is designated. Varieties of silk, velvet, horse-hair, reps, chintz, leather, cloth, moreen, Utrecht velvet, cretonnes, muslin, dimity, and cotton, are all included under the name of Upholstery Cloths or Stuffs.

Upholstery Cotton.—A coarse description of sewing cotton, made in scarlet, crimson, blue, green, yellow, drab, and brown, to suit the colours of furniture coverings and curtains.

Utrecht Velvet.—A very strong and thick material, composed of worsted, but of velvet make, having a raised deep pile, and sometimes a cotton back. It may be had in all colours, and is used by upholsterers and coach-builders. It derives its name from the town in Holland to which it owes its origin. There is an imitation made, which is woven in wool, and is called Banbury Plush.

V.

Valenciennes Lace.—The beauty of this Pillow Lace and its solidity has earned for it the name of "belles et eternelle Valenciennes," and a fame extending from 1650 to the present time. The first manufacture of Valenciennes was in the city of that name, which, though originally one of the towns of Hainault, had been transferred by treaty to France. When first the lace was made, it had to contend for public favour with the beautiful Needle-points of Italy, and those of Alençon and Brussels; but Louis XIV. encouraged its growth, and it soon attained celebrity as a lace useful for ordinary occasions and for all descriptions of trimmings, being especially used for the ruffles then so much worn. It attained its greatest celebrity between the years 1720 and 1780, and, in Valenciennes alone, 14,000 workers were employed in its manufacture, while in the surrounding villages it was also made. The number of these workers, however, declined, and during the French Revolution the ones that remained were dispersed, fleeing to Belgium from their persecutors, and giving a trade to that nation, which it has made most flourishing. In Belgium there are six centres for Valenciennes lace making—Alost, Ypres, Bruges, Ghent, Menin, and Courtrai, and the work produced has individual marks by which it can be separately known. The distinguishing characteristics of this lace are that it is a flat lace, with ground and pattern worked simultaneously with the same thread, and no different kind of thread introduced to outline the pattern or to work any part of it. It is worked in one piece, and by one person, unlike Brussels Lace, which passes through many hands.

In the manufacture of this lace, so much depends upon the whole fabric being made by the same person, that it always commands a higher price when this can be certified; and in the old days, when the manufactory was carried on in Valenciennes, the difference between lace worked in the town and lace worked out of the town could be detected, although made by the same person. This difference arose from the peculiarly damp climate of Valenciennes, which was favourable to the smooth passing backwards and forwards of the Bobbins, and the lace being there formed in underground rooms. From these circumstances, the lace made in the town was known as Vraie Valenciennes, and commanded a much higher price than that made in the surrounding villages and in Flanders, which was known as Fausse Valenciennes, and Bâtarde. The flax employed was of the finest quality, but in the oldest specimens it has a slightly reddish tinge,

instead of being close, were formed of hexagon and octagon meshes, and what is known as the Dotted style introduced, in which the design is small, and is thrown as powderings over the ground, instead of taking up the greater part of the work. This style has been somewhat altered in the laces lately made at Ypres, through the exertions of Felix Brunfaut, who has designed connected patterns and bouquets of flowers far superior to those worked during the Dotted period; but Valenciennes Lace of the present day cannot compete in its graceful arrangements of pattern, evenness of work, and variety of ground, with the old Vraie Valenciennes. In each town where it is worked the ground is made differently; in Alost the ground is square-meshed, and is made by the Bobbins being twisted five times, which adds to the solidity of the lace, although the patterns from this town are inferior. In Ypres the ground is square-meshed, the

Fig. 799. VALENCIENNES—OLD.

while the number of Bobbins used (300 being required for a piece 2 inches in width, and 12,000 being often in use together), and the labour required in forming the lace, made it most expensive, a yard of a flounce, or a pair of broad ruffles, frequently taking a year to execute, although the work was continued for fourteen hours of the day.

The earliest patterns of Valenciennes are of great beauty; they consist of conventionalised scrolls and flower designs, made in thick Cloth Stitch, so that it resembles the finest cambric, upon grounds varied in several ways in one piece; sometimes these grounds resemble minute circles, surrounded by another circle, and pierced with numerous pinholes; at others they are formed of small squares, each containing five pinholes; while some patterns have twisted and plaited grounds of great beauty. Fig. 799 represents an old Renaissance pattern. These Flemish designs were gradually changed, and the patterns became much simpler, while the grounds,

Bobbins twisted four times, and the lace made of the widest and most expensive kind. In Ghent the ground is square-meshed, and the Bobbins only twisted two and a half times; the lace is there made only in narrow widths, but is of good quality. In Courtrai and Menin the grounds are square, and twisted three and a half times; the lace produced is among the cheapest manufactured. In Bruges the grounds are circular, and the Bobbin twisted three times; this lace is the one most imported into England.

The Valenciennes Lace which is now manufactured is not nearly so elaborate as that of earlier date, and the narrow widths are quite within the power of an amateur to make. To work as shown in Fig. 800: In this design the manner of pricking the pattern is shown as a continuation of the lace. The pattern requires 130 Bobbins, five of which form the Engrelure, and the rest the ground and the thick part, or pattern. The ground is formed of

Twists, and is the same as used in some of the Mechlin Laces. To work the ground, which is shown enlarged in Fig. 801: For each mesh four Bobbins are required. Hang on two Bobbins at each pinhole, at the top of the pattern, and seven at the FOOTING. Work the Footing by twisting four of the Bobbins together, leave two, which carry

divide them. Cross, and repeat from *. The illustration shows the manner of working the ground in diagonal lines. Work in CLOTH STITCH for the thick parts of the design, and hang on extra Bobbins, which cut off when no longer required, and run through as shown, where possible. To work Fig. 802: This narrow edging is very simple; it is

FIG. 800. VALENCIENNES LACE EDGING—MODERN.

through the three other Bobbins belonging to the Footing, and which remain hanging straight down through the length of the work. TWIST the two Bobbins taken from the

worked with the ground already explained, and with Cloth Stitch and a PEARL EDGE. The pricked pattern is shown in Fig. 803, Detail A. Use fine Lace thread, No. 300, and forty-four Bobbins, six of which are required for the

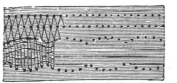

FIG. 803. VALENCIENNES LACE EDGING—DETAIL A.

double Footing. To work: Make the ground with three Twists to each pair of Bobbins, cross, and set up a pin; work the thick part in Cloth Stitch, Twist two Bobbins

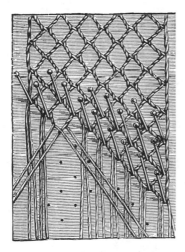

FIG. 801. VALENCIENNES TWISTED GROUND.

three times, take the two Bobbins from the next , Twist them three times, divide them, cross, set n, leave one right-hand and one left-hand Bobbin

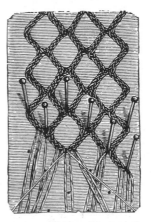

FIG. 804. VALENCIENNES PLAITED GROUND.

FIG. 802. VALENCIENNES LACE EDGING.

at the pinhole. *Twist one right and one left-hand Bobbin together thrice to the next pinhole, here stick a pin, Twist the two Bobbins from the right-hand down to this pin,

for the edge to it on the inner side, and use four Bobbins for the outside Twist.

To Work a Valenciennes Plaited Ground: The ground shown in Fig. 804 is one of the original Valenciennes

Grounds, and is more difficult to execute than the simple Twist; it is, however, much more durable. To work: Eight Bobbins are required for each mesh; PLAIT four of these together down on the left side to a Pinhole, and four on the right, set up a pin, and cross a pair of threads as shown in the illustration; take two of the original Bobbins, and two from the other side, and plait them together.

Valentia.—A mixed material, having a cotton warp, or a cotton and silk warp, for the silk pattern, and a worsted weft of British wool. Valentias are produced at Spitalfields, and many are showy in appearance. They are manufactured for waistcoats, and are very similar to TOILINETTES.

Vandyke Albisola Point.—An Italian Lace, worked in the sixteenth century, but now obsolete.

Vandyke Couching.—See COUCHING.

Vandykes. — This term is descriptive of a particular pointed form cut as a decorative border to collars and other portions of wearing apparel, and to the trimmings of dress skirts and bodices. It may be described as the form called chevron. The style owes its name to the great painter, who immortalised it in his portraits, and it may be seen in those of Charles I., and men of his time.

Vandyke Stitch.—See EMBROIDERY STITCHES.

Vandyke Tracing.—See TRACERY.

Vegetable Lace.—This is a product of Jamaica, obtained from the *Lagetta lintearia*, or Lace-bark tree, which grows in the most inaccessible rocky parts of the island. The inner bark consists of numerous concentric layers of fibres, interlacing in every direction, forming delicate meshes. By lateral stretching it is made to represent the finest lace manufactured. It is said that Charles II. received as a present a cravat, frill, and pair of ruffles, made of this material, from the Governor of that island; and up to the present time it is employed for bonnets, collars, and other articles of apparel, by the natives. It is much worn for evening attire by the Creole women, by whom it is studded with the brilliant fire beetles, or *Cucujos*, the effect produced being very beautiful.

Veils. — These articles, chiefly worn with hats and bonnets, for the protection of the face, may be had of lace, net, spotted net, gauze, tulle, and crape. They may be purchased ready-made, cut, woven, or pillow-made, in shapes, or purchased by the yard. The gauze material sold for Veils for country, travelling, or sea-side wear, may be had in blue, brown, grey, green, and black. Large white muslin and coloured cotton Veils may still be seen at Genoa. In Spain they are made of lace, in large squares, covering the head, and lying over the shoulders. In Lima the Veils cover one eye. Brides wear them of great size, made of white lace, and covering them, from the crown of the head to the knees. The widths of gauze for Veiling measure from half a yard to three-quarters in width; some being worn so long, especially in very cold countries, as to take 2 yards of material. The ordinary size would take three-quarters of a yard. Spotted net is about half a yard in width, and, for an ordinary Veil, three-quarters of a yard would be sufficient. Eastern Veils are worn very large, covering the forehead, and bound round the mouth.

Vellum.—The skins of calves, kids, and lambs, prepared for the purposes of engrossing, bookbinding, and illumination. Vellum is a superior kind of parchment. For the method of preparing Vellum, see PARCHMENT, which, as well as Vellum, is employed in the process of making certain Laces and Embroideries.

Velluto.—A description of Velvet Cloth, with a fast pile and colour. It measures from 24 inches to 27 inches in width, and is produced in various colours.

Velours.—The French term signifying Velvet, derived from the Latin *Villosus*, "shaggy." Amongst our old writers, and in the entries made in lists of Royal wardrobes, we find the terms *Velure* and *Valures*; as well as *Vallonettes*, mentioned by Chaucer. It also denotes a special description of furniture, carpet velvet, or plush, partly of linen, and partly of double cotton warps and mohair yarn wefts, manufactured in Prussia.

Velours Venitien.—A magnificent new material, made of silk, having large bouquets of *Chéné* velvet "printed" or embossed upon the silk ground. It is only suitable for the trains of Court dresses. It measures about 36 inches in width.

Velouté.—The French name for a description of Velvet Lace employed as a trimming.

Velveret.—An inferior sort of Velvet, employed for trimmings, the web of which is of cotton, and the pile of silk. The cotton makes it stiff; and when black, its inferiority to velvet, as in Thickset, is especially remarkable, as it does not keep its colour equally well. It is not to be recommended for a dress or jacket material, owing to its stiffness, and tendency to crease; besides which, the cotton which forms a part of its substance does not retain the blackness of the dye.

Velvet.—A closely-woven silk stuff, having a very thick, short pile, or nap, on the right side, formed by putting a portion of the warp threads over a needle, more or less thick, so as to regulate the quality of the Velvet, and, when the needle is removed, by passing a sharp steel instrument through the long opening it has left, to cut all the loops that had been formed. This nap always lies in one direction, and thus it must only be brushed that way, and that with either a piece of Velvet or cloth. The finest qualities of this material are made at Genoa and Lyons. When required for the purpose of trimmings, it should be cut diagonally. There are inferior sorts made with a cotton back. Others consist of a mixture throughout of silk and cotton, called Velveteen, of which there are many qualities, and which may be had in all colours, and also brocaded. There are also Cotton Velvets, produced in various colours, and having small chintz patterns. According to Planché, in his *History of British Costume*, Velvet, under the Latin name of *Villosa*, or the French *Villuse*, is stuff mentioned during the thirteenth century. Shakespeare, in the *Taming of the Shrew*, and *à propos* of a saddle, speaks of

One girt, six times pieced, and a woman's cruppe of Velure.

And in *Henry IV.*,

I have removed Falstaff's horse, and he frets like a gummed velvet.

Also in *Measure for Measure*, the First Gentleman replies to Lucio :

> An thou the velvet; thou art good velvet.
> Thou'rt a three-piled piece, I warrant thee.
> I had as lief be a list of an English Kersey,
> As be piled, as thou art piled, of a French velvet.

The large northern cities of Italy (especially Genoa) were the first to excel in the manufacture of Velvet. The French followed in acquiring a great proficiency in this branch of silk-weaving, and, at the revocation of the Edict of Nantes, the French silk weavers introduced the art into this country, and established it at Spitalfields.

Velvet Cloth.—A plain cloth with a gloss, employed in Ecclesiastical Embroidery.

Velvet Cloths.—These are beautifully soft and warm descriptions of cloth, suitable for ladies' jackets. They may be had both checked and striped, as well as in plain uniform colours.

Velveteen.—A description of fustian, made of twilled cotton, and having a raised pile, and of finer cotton and better finish than the latter. It is made in claret, blue, green, and violet. Rain drops do not spot it, but the heat of a fire is injurious to the dye. It is a thick, heavy material, useful for winter dresses, children's clothing women's outdoor jackets, and men's coats.

Velvet Flowers.—These, as well as the leaves, are cut by means of a punch for purposes of Appliqué Embroidery, when the stems can be worked in gold bullion. When to be thus employed, paste a piece of thin paper at the back of the velvet before it is cut out into the desired forms, and cut through both, otherwise the edges will become frayed. Flower-making, including those of Velvet for wear on bonnets, and the trimmings of evening dresses, is an art which has latterly been brought to great perfection.

Velvet Ribbons.—Of these there are many varieties, the plain, black, and coloured, plain Terry, figured, and embossed plush, and Tartan, both fancy and original checks. *See* RIBBONS.

Velvet Work.—From the nature of this material but few Embroidery Stitches can be executed upon it. It is, however, largely used in Church Embroideries as a background for altar cloths and hangings. The chief parts of the Embroidery are then worked upon linen stretched in a frame and transferred to the velvet when finished, and only tendrils, small scrolls, and tiny rounds worked as a finish to the Embroidery upon the velvet. For this description of work *see* CHURCH EMBROIDERY.

Another Way : The second kind of Velvet Work is made with embossed velvet, and is very effective and easy. It consists of outlining with gold thread the embossed flowers and arabesques, and filling in the centre of such parts with Satin Stitch worked in coloured filoselles. To work; Select a deep and rich toned piece of embossed velvet, and COUCH along every outline of the embossing two threads of Japanese gold thread. Then take two shades of green filoselle, and vein any of the leaves of the design with CREWEL STITCH and a pale shade of filoselle of the same colour as the velvet, and fill in the centres of any flowers or geometrical figures with long SATIN STITCHES.

Another Way : Frame the velvet, and back it with holland. Trace out the design to be worked on the velvet with the help of white chalk, and work it over with floss silk. Bring the floss silk up from the back of the material, and put it down again to the back, making a long SATIN STITCH. Make as few stitches as the pattern will allow of, as, from the nature of the material, they are difficult to work; ornament parts of the work with gold or silver thread, or silk cords, Couched down with silks matching them in shade.

Another Way : This is really Velvet Appliqué, and consists in cutting out of various coloured pieces of velvet, leaves, flowers, and scroll work, and attaching them to silk or satin backgrounds. To work: Back the pieces of velvet with brown holland, which paste evenly on them; lay a paper design of the right size over these pieces, and carefully cut them to the right shapes. Frame the satin or silk background, after having backed it with linen, and arrange the pieces of velvet upon it as they should be laid. First TACK them slightly down to the foundation with tacking threads, to judge of their effect, and, when that is decided, OVERCAST each piece carefully to the foundation. To conceal these Overcast Stitches, COUCH down upon them, either two lines of gold thread, or one of silk cord and one of gold thread, and work stalks and tendrils upon the background in SATIN STITCH; finish off the centres of the flowers with FRENCH KNOTS.

Venetian Bar.—This is used in modern Point Lace. To work Fig. 805: Work the first row from right to left

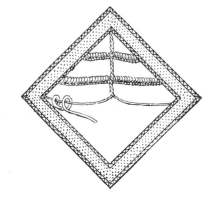

FIG. 805. VENETIAN BAR.

in SORRENTO BAR. Second row—work a number of close BUTTONHOLE STITCHES on the lines thrown across the space. Third row—work from right to left like the

FIG. 806. VENETIAN BAR.

first row, and return with Buttonhole Stitch as before. Continue these two lines to the end of the space. For

Fig. 806: Take the thread from left to right across the space, and work over it in BUTTONHOLE STITCHES. Work a number of these bars, a little distance apart, until the space is filled.

Venetian Carpets.—These are manufactured both in England and Scotland. They are composed of a worsted warp, traversed by a woollen weft, and arranged in stripes of different colours, the shoot being invisible, in consequence of its very dark colour. By a peculiar interchange of the two threads, the production of the design on both sides of the stuff is accomplished. The pattern is necessarily a simple "diced" one, and the carpets are durable as well as thick, and suitable for bedrooms and nurseries.

Venetian Embroidery.—This is work resembling

parts of the design that are intended to imitate light and open flowers and leaves with WHEELS, POINT DE BRUXELLES, HERRINGBONE, POINT DE GRECQUE, and other POINT LACE STITCHES, and vein the heavier leaves with lines of ROPE STITCH. Having finished the whole of the Embroidery, carefully cut away the linen that is not secured by the Buttonhole lines from underneath the Buttonhole Bars, and the Lace Stitches. Use a very sharp and small pair of scissors, and cut with the utmost care.

Another Way: In this second description of Venetian Embroidery, the work is formed upon Brussels net, and is an imitation of lace. To work: Trace a lace design of some arabesque and running pattern upon pink calico, which back with brown paper. Then TACK net over it, and,

FIG. 807. VENETIAN EMBROIDERY.

Roman Work and Strasbourg Embroidery, but is lighter than either in effect, on account of the introduction of Lace Stitches in some of the parts where the material is cut away. The work is done upon strong linens, hollands, and batiste, and is used for furniture trimmings, such as mantel and table borders, banner screens, and curtain borders. To work as shown in Fig. 807: Trace the outlines of the pattern upon écru-coloured linen, and RUN these outlines with thread, both on their scalloped and plain side. Work them over with BUTTONHOLE lines, made of silk matching the linen in colour, and while doing so connect the various parts with plain Buttonhole Bars. Be careful that the lines of Buttonhole always turn their edges as shown in the illustration, as, should they be made otherwise, they will not secure the design when the material is cut away. Take some fine écru silk, and fill in the

with a needle and fine thread, RUN the outlines of the design on the net. Work these over with lines of BUTTONHOLES, made with various coloured floss silks or filoselles, and work a scalloped Buttonhole edging. Cut the net away from the outside of the edging, and work in the centres of flowers or other centres to the outlines with a few long SATIN STITCHES. Use more than one shade of colour on each piece of lace, but let them blend together, and only use the soft shades of yellow, pink, blue, salmon, and green, and no dark or vivid colours.

Venetian Guipure.—One of the names given to Venetian Point, the word Guipure originally meaning lace made either of silk or thread upon parchment. *See* VENETIAN LACE.

Venetian Lace.—The Venetians dispute with the Spaniards the invention of Needle-made laces, considering that they obtained the rudiments of the art from the Saracens settled in Sicily before the Spaniards became acquainted with it. It is difficult to decide which nation has the superior claim, particularly as lace was in early times almost exclusively made in convents, and the nuns were not always of the same nationality as the people amongst whom they lived; but there seems to be no doubt that both Needle and Pillow Laces were made in Italy in the fifteenth century, although they attained their greatest renown during the sixteenth and seventeenth centuries, being then used at most of the Continental Courts, and rivalling for many years the productions of Flanders.

The laces made in Venice during the sixteenth and seventeenth centuries included Reticellas (Punto à Reticella), Cutwork (Punto Tagliato), Flat Venetian Point (Punto in Aria), Raised Venetian Point (Punto à Fogliami), Macramè (Punto à Groppo), Darned Netting (Punto à Maglia), Drawn Work (Punto Tirato), and Burano, or Argentella Point, a grounded Venetian Lace. Of these numerous kinds, the flat and raised Venetian Points were not worked before 1600, but they gradually superseded the others, and, though very costly, became the universal decoration of dress for all occasions, besides being largely used for ecclesiastical purposes; and it was not until the middle of the seventeenth century that their fame at all declined. In 1654, Colbert prohibited the importation of the Venetian Laces into France, in order that the lace manufactories he had founded in Alençon and Argentan might be protected; and these same laces, although at first only intended to imitate Venetian Points, developed into something lighter and finer, and soon became the fashion. The fine Needle-points made at Brussels also shared in this change of taste, and were worn by the nobles of the Italian and French Courts in preference to the heavier Venice Points. Under these adverse circumstances, the making of Venetian Points was discontinued, and at present the manufacture is quite extinct.

The Venetian flat Needle-points made when the lace was declining are difficult to distinguish from the Spanish flat Points, but their patterns are generally lighter and finer. They are connected with Brides that do not run straight from one part of the pattern to another, but are irregular, and broken up into several short Bars, each of which is trimmed with two plain Picots, and not with Couronnes. The Venice Raised Points are extremely rich ard varied as to their designs, which are either arabesque or conventionalised scrolls and flowers. They are sometimes worked in coloured silks, such as purple, yellow, and cream. They are distinguished by their Bride grounds, highly raised Cordonnets, solid stalks, and chief parts being worked in high relief, surrounded by Fleurs Volants, sometimes three rows deep; while many lace stitches, known as Fillings, are introduced into the various parts of the pattern, so that the effect of the lace is less solid and heavy, and more running, than the Raised Spanish Points. To work these Needlepoints: Draw the pattern upon detached pieces of parchment, outline with a FIL DE TRACE, and OVERCAST with BUTTONHOLE STITCHES, either padded or flat; to make the raised or flat Cordonnet,

trim this with PICOTS, and fill with fancy stitches the spaces surrounded by the Cordonnets; TACK each separate piece when finished to a tracing of the whole design, and secure by BRIDES ORNÉES; make the raised work separately, and then attach to the flat parts. For the detailed manner of making the lace, *see* SPANISH LACES.

The grounded Venetian Lace known as Burano, or Argentella Point, was made long after the disappearance of the Venetian Raised and flat Points. It resembled both Brussels and Alençon Laces, but was distinguished from them by its extreme flatness, and absence of all raised parts, the lines of Buttonhole that surrounded the Fillings being as flat as those stitches, and the designs consisting chiefly of powderings, either shaped as circles, ovals, or small sprays thrown upon the net-patterned ground. By many critics Burano Point is considered superior to Needle-made Brussels Lace, from the whiteness of its thread and the great delicacy of its designs. It was made in Burano at the beginning of the present century, and the manufacture has now revived.

Imitation Venice Points.—An imitation of the celebrated Venice raised and flat Points has lately been worked by ladies with much success. The design is all drawn upon one piece of linen, and the raised outlines made by working over a linen cord. The rest of the lace follows the old manner of making. To work as shown in Fig. 808: Trace the design upon Toile Ciré or thin Parchment, obtain some of Catt's fine linen cord, and slightly TACK this to the Toile Ciré, marking out with it all the outlines of the thick parts of the lace. Take fine Mecklenburgh thread, No 20, and fill in the parts surrounded with the cord, chiefly in rows of thick BUTTONHOLE STITCHES, but also with POINT DE BRABANÇON and POINT DE GRECQUE (*see* POINT LACE). In the process of the work, make the Bars that connect the detached parts of the pattern with BUTTONHOLE BARS, ornamented with PICOTS, SPINES, and COURONNES. Cover the cord over with even rows of Buttonholes with the same fine thread, and ornament the raised CORDONNET thus made with Picots. Make the edge of the lace with a cord covered with Buttonholes, and with loops covered over with Buttonholes and trimmed with Picots.

Venetian Long Stitch Embroidery.—This is an old-fashioned description of Worsted Work, in which the design is worked with coloured worsteds or crewels upon open canvas, such as Toile Colbert, or upon net, or white silk canvas, the ground being left exposed. To work: Select an arabesque or geometrical Worsted Work pattern, containing several colours, but with little shading. Frame the canvas or net in an EMBROIDERY FRAME, to keep it well stretched, and work the design upon it in LONG STITCH. Let each Long Stitch pass over four, five, six, eight, or ten squares of the material one way, but only cover one square the other way (a square being two warp and two woof threads); arrange the length of these stitches according to the space one shade of colour has to cover, and make their greatest length either across the width of the material or perpendicular, according to the shading required. In shading the designs, use the old-fashioned colours, and not those obtained from aniline dyes.

Venetians.—A heavy kind of tape or braid, resembling double Londons. They are employed more especially for Venetians blinds, whence the name. The colours are ingrained, and the widths run half an inch, 1¼ inches, and 1½ inches. Another kind of braid or tape is made for Venetian blinds—thread webs, in white, unbleached blue, and green; sold in lengths of from 18, 24, to 36 yards, the widths running from 1 inch to 1½ inches.

Venetian Stitch.—A term sometimes applied to close rows of Buttonholes as Fillings in Needle-point Laces, as this particular stitch is the one most used in Venetian Points. To work: Fasten the thread to the right side of the place to be filled in, and take it across to

Venice Point.—*See* VENETIAN LACES.

Vest.—A generic term, signifying a garment, but adopted to denote a special article of wear, as in the case of the word Vestment. A Vest now means a waistcoat, or a closely-fitting elastic article of underclothing, worn by both sexes, with or without long sleeves, and with either a high or low neck. They are worn inside a shirt or chemise, and are to be had in spun silk, merino, lambswool, cotton, or gauze, the latter of silk, or a union of silk and cotton, or silk and wool. These latter may be worn all the year round, and do not shrink when washed. Cotton vests are to be had both bleached and unbleached, and are strong and thick. Vests may be had both hand-made and machine-made; the trade in the former is extensively carried on by Scotchwomen, who knit them at a reasonable charge.

FIG. 808. VENETIAN POINT—IMITATION.

the left; cover it with a line of close and even BUTTON-HOLES, and secure to the right side; fasten the thread again to the left side, and work it over with Buttonholes, working each new stitch into the rib of the stitch above it in the first line. Repeat the second line until the space is filled.

Venezuelan Drawn Work.—The lace that is made at Venezuela is remarkable for its beauty. It resembles the Oriental Drawn Thread Work and the Italian and Swedish Drawn Works. The work is executed upon cambric or linen, and the threads are drawn away and divided, as shown in Drawn Work, but instead of being Overcast or Buttonholed over with plain linen thread, fine purse silks of various shades of colour are used, as in the Oriental Embroideries. *See* DRAWN WORK.

Vests, as well as other undergarments, may be had woven of the Norwegian Pine Wool in its natural colour; this material is strongly to be recommended for persons exposed to a damp or very changeable climate, as it contains very curative properties in cases of rheumatism, a strong essential oil being procured from the bark of this pine for application to affected parts.

Vêtement.—The French term signifying a garment.

Victoria Crape.—A comparatively new description of crape, composed entirely of cotton. It is made in different widths, from 1 to 2 yards, like ordinary crape. In appearance it is like silk crape, and is very inexpensive; but it is not economical to the purchaser, as it does not wear at all well.

Victoria Frilling.—This is a description of cotton

cambric Frilling, produced at Coventry, for the purpose of trimming bed and under-linen. Its distinctive characteristic consists in the fact that the drawing cord is woven into the fabric, which is an advantage in every respect. Victoria Frilling may be had in three different widths for bed linen, viz., of 2 inches, 2½ inches and 3 inches. It is also made, for the trimming of underlinen, as narrow as half an inch. It is a patent manufacture.

Victoria Lawn.—This is a description of muslin, semi-transparent, and employed as a lining for skirts of dresses. It is rather stiff, and may be had in black and white, and is also used for frillings, and for petticoats worn under clear muslin dresses. It was at one time employed for evening dresses.

Vicuna Cloth.—This beautiful cloth is made from the wool of the vicuna, which is a species of the llama of Peru and Chili. It is employed as a dress material, is very soft in texture, and is produced in neutral colours. It measures 29 inches in width.

Vienna Cross Stitch. — See *Persian Cross Stitch*, EMBROIDERY STITCHES.

Vigogne.—A delicate all-wool textile, twilled, and produced in neutral colours—greys, lavenders, and steel—as well as black. The widths run from 45 inches to 48 inches, according to the quality; the commoner kinds have a small *Armure* pattern woven in them. Vigogne is the French name for the wool of the Peruvian sheep, or for a woollen stuff of the finest Spanish wool. It is very suitable as a summer dress material, for which it is designed.

Volant.—The French term denoting either a flounce or a frill, both of which are descriptions of dress trimmings.

Vraie Réseau.—This term indicates that the Network ground to either Needlepoint or Pillow Laces has been either worked with a Needle, or with Bobbins. Before the introduction of machine-made net, all the grounds of lace were worked in this way, but since then the lace flowers or pattern has been Appliqué on to the machine net, except when especial orders for the Vraie Réseau, or real ground is given, as the costliness of the thread used, and the time the real ground takes to manufacture, more than trebles the price of the lace. Two of the Vraie Réseau Grounds a e shown enlarged in VALENCIENNES LACE, but there are a great many varieties both of the plaited and twisted net patterns, besides the DAME JOAN, TROLLY, TORCHON, STAR, POINT DE PARIS, and ITALIAN, all of which are described under their own headings. The term Vraie Réseau is often given exclusively to the ground used in Brussels Lace, but in reality all the lace grounds made without the assistance of machinery are Vraie Réseau.

W.

Wadding.—Wadding, as sold in the shops, is carded cotton wool; bleached, unbleached, slate-coloured, and black, cut into sheets of various sizes, and sold by the gross; but it is also manufactured in lengths of 12 yards for quilting. It is placed between the outer material and the lining of any garment; if not quilted, it is necessary to attach it to the linings, or it is apt to form into lumps. It has latterly been regarded as preferable to flannel or domett for shrouds, for which the bleached Wadding is employed. The French name for Wadding is *Ouate*, which was that originally given to the downy tufts found in the pods of the plant called *Apocynum*, imported from Egypt and Asia Minor. To make Wadding, a lap or fleece, prepared by the carding machine, is applied to tissue paper by means of a coat of size, which is made by boiling the cuttings of hareskins, and adding alum to the gelatinous solutions. When two laps of cotton are glued with their faces together, they form the most downy kind of Wadding.

Waistcoatings.—These are fancy textiles made of worsted and cotton, or worsted only, or of silk in which there is a pattern, worked in the loom, different coloured yarns being employed. The name by which these cloths are known explains the use to which they are applied. Huddersfield is the chief seat of the industry.

Wamsutta Calicoes—Various descriptions of cloth made at New Bedford, Massachusetts, and known as Wamsuttas. One of them is a double warp cotton sheeting, which may be had in Manchester, where there is a depôt. The Wamsutta Mills produce some 12,000 miles of sheeting and shirting, or 20,000,000 square yards of cotton cloth, every year; they were opened in the year 1846, and the annual consumption of cotton is about 19,000 bales. The cotton chiefly employed is what is called in the markets "benders," because raised within the bends of the Mississippi river, where the rich soil produces a peculiarly strong-fibred variety. The strength of these yarns is tested by a machine, eighty threads together being steadily stretched by means of a screw, to prove their endurance, until they part, and the breaking weight is indicated on a dial. Thus, according to the results of this daily test, the yarn produced in these mills is claimed to be 20 per cent. stronger than the standard for "super extra" wearing yarns, according to the tables laid down in English books; and every piece of cloth is examined by a committee of inspectors before it is allowed to leave the mills. Not only are bleached and brown sheetings and shirtings, both heavy and fine, produced at Wamsutta, but also muslin and cambric muslin, for underclothing.

Warnerized Textiles.—These medicated stuffs are produced of every description of material made, in silk, wool, cotton, linen, and leather, by means of a process rendering them water, mildew, and moth-repellent. By the same method, which appears to be a great improvement on ordinary waterproofing, ready-made articles of wear, and of household use, are likewise treated by the "Warnerizing Company."

Warp.—This term is employed by weavers to denote the threads that run longitudinally from end to end of a textile and are crossed by the weft, otherwise called the woof. The Warp passes through the treadles and reed, and the Weft, otherwise called the Woof, which is wound round the shuttle, crosses it.

Warp Stitch.—*See* EMBROIDERY STITCHES.

Washing Lace.—*See* LACE.

Wash-leather.—An imitation of chamois leather, made of split sheep's skins, from which gloves and linings for waistcoats, bodices, and petticoats are produced. The skins go through a process of oiling and aluming, and, when thoroughly prepared for use, may be washed until worn out, without losing their buff colour. Wash-leather is formed into regimental belts, and into gloves for both sexes; it is employed for household purposes, such as the cleaning of plate and of brasses. It also goes by the name of Buff Leather.

Watered.—This term, as applied to any kind of textile, signifies that a wavy pattern has been impressed upon it, which has not been woven into its texture. The method of producing it is, to place two pieces of material together lengthwise in triangular folds, and to pass them between two cylindrical metal rollers; into the hollow within one of the latter a heated iron is introduced. Thus, as the two pieces of stuff will not exactly coincide in their respective positions with the rollers, one portion will be subjected to a greater degree of pressure than another, resulting in the wave-like pattern desired. As only one side needs to be waved, pasteboards are placed between each second fold, so that, when hot-pressed, the side next the pasteboard comes out glazed throughout, while the opposite side is watered or waved.

Watered Linings.—These cloths may be had both in linen or cotton, in cream, slate, and dove colour, and are chiefly employed for the lining of men's coats. The width is 38 inches. *See* LININGS.

Watered Twist.—Cotton thread, manufactured for the weaving of calicoes by means of water mills. It is spun hard, and is much twisted. Arkwright's water mill was the first ever erected. He set up the works at Cromford, Derbyshire, employing the Derwent as the water power. The kind of machines employed used to be called "water-spinning" machines, and thus the name of the cloth produced was Water Twist, but had no reference to the process called "watering."

Watered Woollen Cloths.—These are new materials, produced at Bradford, for women's dresses. They are soft and undressed, and are to be had in black. For the method of watering, *see* WATERED.

Waterproofed Fabrics.—An extensive variety of textiles rendered impervious to moisture without thereby being injured in their texture or colour. They may be had in thick and thin woollen cloths; in silk, alpaca, and in what is called "Macintosh;" but the latter, being air tight, as well as waterproof, is a very unwholesome article for wear, and is only suitable for hot water bottles, air cushions, water beds, &c.

Waterproofed Zephyr Tweed.—This is a very light material, employed for summer wear, and rendered waterproof. It measures 55 inches in width, and is suitable for wear as a dust cloak, as well as in rain. It can be had in different shades of drab and grey.

Wavy Couching.—*See* COUCHING.

Weaver's Knot.—*See* KNOTS.

Weaving.—The method by which the web of every kind of textile is produced, and of which there are many varieties. Plain Weaving signifies that the warp and weft intersect each other in regular order, crossing at right angles, and producing a simple web of uniform face and construction. Tweeling, that every thread of the weft passes under one and over two or more threads of the weft. Twilled silk yarn is called Satin, twilled cotton is fustian, or jean, and twilled wool is Kerseymere, or serge. This tweeling may be executed on both sides of the material, as in shalloon; and this method of weaving may be so diversified, by various dispositions of the loom, as to produce stripes and decorative designs, such as those exhibited in damask, diaper, and dimity. Pile Weaving is the method by which velvets are produced, a third series of short threads being employed, besides those of the warp and weft, and introduced between the two latter, being doubled under the weft so as to form loops. These are afterwards cut to form the "pile," and, when uncut, they present an appearance like Terry Velvet. When pile weaving is adopted in the production of cotton cloth, the result may be seen in fustians, corduroys, &c. Figure Weaving is another and beautiful method of Weaving, by which designs—either of different materials, or colours—are introduced in the warp or weft. To effect this, the threads are so disposed as that certain colours shall be concealed, whilst others are drawn to the front, and they must change places from time to time, according to the necessity for their re-introduction, in carrying out and completing the design. In producing stripes, a variety of dissimilar threads may be arranged in the warping, and so left without change; or the threads of the warp and those of the weft may be of different colours respectively, which will produce that changeable hue on the cloth which is known by the term "shot." The Jacquard loom is the most perfect kind of "draw-loom" yet produced to carry out Figure Weaving in its most beautiful and intricate varieties; and damasks in silk, linen, cotton, and wool are now wholly manufactured by it. Stockingette, or Elastic Cloth Weaving, is another form of the art, which is very distinct from those branches already named. Instead of a foundation consisting of two threads—the warp and weft—there is but one continuous thread employed for the whole web. This single thread is formed into a perpetually successive series of loops, and the loops of one row are drawn through those of its predecessor. Stockingette Cloth is produced in imitation of knitting; and, besides the large looms in which it is manufactured wholesale, there are hand-worked machines, in which small articles may be woven—such as stockings, scarves, and vests. Ribbons are woven in the same way as ordinary cloth.

The power-loom, which succeeded the hand-loom, was invented by the Rev. Dr. Edmund Cartwright, in 1757. Horrocks' loom was afterwards produced, and Monteith's in 1798; and the "Jacquard," invented in 1752, has been greatly improved in England since the time it was first introduced. Hand Weaving is now confined to cloth produced in gaols by the felons. Weaving is an art of the most remote antiquity, and of Eastern origin. In this country it can be traced back to the Anglo-Saxons and early Britons. In London, the weavers formed one of the most ancient of the Guilds, and were called the *Telarii.* The domestic title, "wife," is derived from the verb "to weave," as she was distinguished so much in olden times by her labours with the distaff. The Saxon for weave was *wefan,* and the German is *weben,* whence, in the same way, *weih*—a woman, one who works at the distaff and makes a web—is derived. King Alfred, when speaking in his will of his descendants, distinguishes the sexes as those respectively of the "spindle side" and the "spear side"; and this idea may be seen exemplified on many graves in Germany, which are severally distinguished by the effigies of spears and spindles. In reference to Queen Anne, Dryden speaks of "a distaff on the throne." This adoption of the name "wife" from the art of weaving is a natural sequence to that of giving the name "spinster" to an unmarried woman—the girl is supposed to spin the yarn for her future clothing, which she is to wear woven into webs for garments, as a wife.

Webbing.—This is a strong, thick tape, woven in a peculiar way, usually striped in blue and white, or pink and white, and may be had from 2 to 3 inches in width. It is made of hemp thread, and designed for the support of sofa squabs, and bedding, being nailed to the wooden framework at both ends and sides, and interlaced successively in and out, at regular distances apart. It is also employed for the stands of butlers' trays and trunks, for trunk lid supports and trunk trays; and also for girths, &c. The various kinds are known as Manchester, and Holland, black or red, and stay tapes. The term "Webbing" is also used to signify Warp as prepared for the weaver.

Webbing (Elastic).—A preparation of indiarubber inclosed in silk, mohair, or cotton. Their respective widths are given according to the number of cords—from one to sixteen, or upwards. The narrow single cords are to be had in two lengths of 72 yards to the gross; the wider makes are in four pieces, containing 36 yards each, and are generally sold by the gross. These goods should not be kept in air-tight parcels, or they will lose their elasticity. Webbings are produced of appropriate dimensions for belts, the sides of boots, known as "spring sides," and narrow frilled cotton ones, employed for underlinen.

Weeds.—The description of mourning attire which is distinctively that of a widow. With this exception, the term is obsolete as regards general use; though it may be found in Spenser's *Faërie Queene,* in Milton's *L'Allegro;* and in Shakespeare, employed in its original sense, as denoting a dress or garment:

> The snake throws her enamelled skin,—
> Weed wide enough to wrap a fairy in.

The word "weed" is derived from the Anglo-Saxon *woed*—*i.e.,* "clothing."

Weft.—The yarns or threads running across the length of the cloth—that is, from selvedge to selvedge, in a web. The Weft is also known by the name of Woof, and is wound round the shuttles during the process of weaving, while the Warp is extended in many successive threads, and passes through the treadles and reed.

Weldbores.—This is a description of woollen cloth manufactured at Bradford, Yorkshire.

Welsh Flannels.—Welsh-made flannels are of a bluish shade, and have a broad grey selvedge on both sides. They somewhat resemble the Lancashire Flannels, and measure from 30 inches to nearly 36 inches in width. There are also Patent Welsh Flannels, which are very fine, and of superior texture, but not very durable, and are made for infants' clothing. Wales is the country where Flannel was originally made. Much is still produced, by hand labour, from the fleeces of the flocks on the native mountains, and this is of peculiar quality and finish; but the most extensive manufacture of Flannels, not only in England, but in the whole world, is in Lancashire, especially in the neighbourhood and town of Rochdale, where the greatest variety of widths, finish, and substance is produced, in the thin gauze, medium, thick, double raised, and Swanskin.

Welted.—This term signifies the ribbing of any material, by the insertion of wadding between it and the lining, and Run in parallel lines. It is of the same nature as Quilting, only that the Runnings do not cross each other so as to make a diamond pattern. Stays are Welted to stiffen them, in places where whalebones would be objectionable; black petticoats are sometimes Welted, to make them stand out, after the style of hoops.

Welting.—See *Ribbing* in KNITTING.

Welts.—These are the rounds of Ribbing worked in Stocking Knitting as the commencement to a stocking, and are intended to keep the top of that article from rolling up.

Whalebone.—This bone is taken from the upper jaw of the whale, and is utilised for umbrella frames; it is also very extensively employed by staymakers and dressmakers. For the use of the former, it is cut into suitable lengths, the widths varying between three-sixteenths and 1¼ inches. It is sold by the pound. For the use of dressmakers it is also prepared, neatly cut into lengths, and sold by the gross sets, or in small quantities. The price of Whalebone fluctuates much, being dependent on the success of the whalers. Steels, cut in lengths, and sold in calico covers, have greatly superseded the use of Whalebone, both for the stay and dressmaking trades. About 1¾ tons of the bone are produced in the mouth of one whale of 16 feet long, the ordinary value of which is about £160 per ton. This bone forms a kind of fringe, or strainer, in the mouth of the Baleen whale, acting as a net to retain the small fish, on which the creature preys, which, when his jaws are open, are washed in and out. This bone takes the place of teeth, and consists of numerous parallel *laminæ,* descending perpendicularly from the palate. In a whale of 60 feet long, the largest piece of Baleen would be 12 feet in length. To prepare Whalebone for use, immerse it for twelve hours in boiling water, before which it will be found too hard for the purposes of manufacture.

Wheatear Stitch.—*See* EMBROIDERY STITCHES.

Wheeler Tapestry.—An embroidery executed in New York, and which takes its name from the inventor. It is a hand-made Tapestry upon silk stuffs, woven in colours, and especially for the embroidery. The designs are of still life, pastoral scenes, Cupids with garlands of flowers, &c., and these are produced upon the material by DARNED LINES executed in coloured embroidery silks, and so carefully and closely done, that they are quite flat upon the surface, and yet start out from their backgrounds. Wheeler Tapestry is not worked in England. Its principal stitch is the Darned Line; but thick embroidery stitches are sometimes worked, to bring into prominence some especial portion of the design.

Wheeling.—A description of yarn used for charitable purposes. It may be had in all colours.

Wheels.—These are required in all descriptions of ornamental needlework, and in Pillow and Needle Laces. They are made in a variety of forms, from the simple

FIG. 809. WHEEL.

Wheel formed of Corded Bars, to the most elaborate device. To work Wheels used in Needle-made Laces and Embroidery, and as shown in Fig. 809: This design

FIG. 810. WHEEL—DETAIL.

illustrates a Wheel wherein the centre of the material is retained. Trace a circle upon the material, and RUN threads round the tracing to the thickness of a quarter of

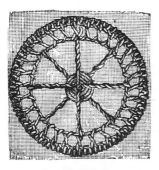

FIG. 811. WHEEL.

an inch. BUTTONHOLE over these threads with a close and even line of Buttonholes, as shown in Fig. 810, Detail, and turn the Buttonhole edge to the outside.

Work a line of POINT DE VENISE as an edging to the Buttonholes.

To work the Wheel shown in Fig. 811: This Wheel is chiefly used in Embroideries and in Point Lace. Outline the circle, Run a thread round it, and BUTTONHOLE over the thread with close Buttonholes, turning the edge of the

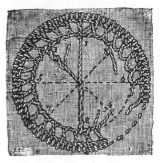

FIG. 812. WHEEL—DETAIL.

Buttonholes to the inside. Work upon that edge a row of loose POINT DE BRUXELLES into every other Buttonhole. Run a thread into these loops, to draw them together into a circle, and make BARS across the open space left in the centre of Wheel. Commence at 1 in Fig. 812, Detail, and cross to 2, CORD the line to the centre of the

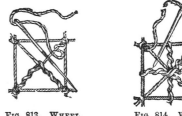

FIG. 813. WHEEL.   FIG. 814. WHEEL.

Wheel, then take the thread to 3, and Cord back, and so follow all the numerals, always Cording the thread back to the centre. When the lines are all made, fill the centre of the Wheel up by passing the thread over and under the threads for five rounds, and then finish by Cording the thread up 1, which has been left uncorded in order to bring it back.

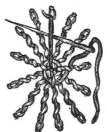

FIG. 815. WHEEL.

To Work an Open Wheel: This Wheel is formed with Corded Bars, which are many or few according to the size of the space to be filled.

Fig. 813 shows a Wheel worked with four Bars, Fig. 814 a Wheel worked with eight Bars, and Fig. 815 one worked with thirteen Bars. They are all worked alike. Fasten the thread to the corner of the space, and take it across to the opposite corner. CORD it back to the centre, and carry it to the angle on the other side. Cord it back to the centre, and take it to the last angle, Cord back, and fill up the rest of the space with the same kind of lines, always returning to the centre; fill that in with rounds of thread worked over and under the lines, and where these are sufficient, Cord the thread up the first line that was made.

To work Fig. 816: This open Wheel is much more elaborate than the others, and is chiefly used in fine Embroidery or Lace Work. Run a line of thread round the space, and cover it with a close row of BUTTONHOLES. Turn the edges to the inside, make a tiny loop in the centre of the Wheel, which cover with a round of Buttonholes, and TACK this down with tacing threads to keep it steady; work a round of open Buttonholes with six loops, and continue to work in rounds with close Buttonholes where the spokes of the Wheel come, and loose Buttonholes to divide them. Finish the spaces between the spokes with a Vandyked CORDED BAR, but take the spokes in lessening rows of close Buttonhole down to the edge of the Wheel. Finish by taking the tacking thread out of the centre, and cutting the material away underneath, if there is any.

FIG. 816. WHEEL.

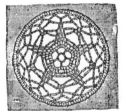

FIG. 817. WHEEL.

To work Fig. 817: This Wheel is of the same kind as the last. Enclose the circle with a round of BUTTONHOLE, and then make POINT DE BRUXELLES loops round; work a second round of Point de Bruxelles, and gradually thicken with closer stitches where the spokes come; then work three rows of close Buttonhole, and finish with a circle of six Buttonhole Stitches.

To Make a Pillow Lace Wheel.—Prick a pattern with holes, eighteen holes to the inch, and a quarter of an inch wide. Hang on twelve pairs of Bobbins, work in the pins right and left six times, take the four centre Bobbins and TWIST the pair to the left three times. Take the pair to the left and work it to the left-hand pin, and Twist the pair now nearest the centre pair three times, put up a pin in the centre between the two pairs of twisted Bobbins, make a CLOTH STITCH to enclose the pin, and Twist the two pairs three times, leave them, take up the pair of Bobbins behind the left-hand pin, work in the pin, and work across to the pair of centre Bobbins nearest the left hand, Twist the working pair three times, make a CLOTH STITCH, Twist each pair three times, and carry back the pair nearest the left hand to the left-hand pin, putting a pin between the two pairs to the left. Take up the right-hand Bobbins behind the right-hand pin and work in the pin; bring the Worker Bobbins to the pair of centre Bobbins nearest the right-hand pin, Twist the workers three times, and make a Cloth Stitch with the right-hand centre pair, Twist each pair three times, and take back the pair nearest the right hand to the right-hand pin; having put a pin between the twisted Bobbins in the centre, take up the four centre Bobbins, make a Cloth Stitch, and Twist each pair three times, put up a pin between the twisted pairs. The pins will be in the form of a small diamond, and the design will form a Star with an open hole in the centre and six small ones round it.

Wheel Stitch.—*See* EMBROIDERY STITCHES.

Whipcord Couching.—Similar to Wavy Couching. *See* COUCHING.

Whipping.—A term used in needlework, denoting a method of drawing up a piece of frilling of any fine material into gathers, by means of sewing loosely over a delicately rolled edge of the same. To work: Hold the cambric with the wrong side towards you, and insert the needle at the back of the proposed roll, not through, but just below it. Secure firmly the end of the thread there, at the extreme right. Then hold the cambric in the left hand, close to where the roll should begin; and damping the thumb, roll the material over towards you, very closely and finely, first passing the thumb upwards, and then downwards. As soon as space is made for the setting of two or three stitches, make them, inserting the needle at the back as before, and at very regular distances apart; the thread should be drawn a little at first, to test its capability for running easily, when required as a drawing string, and then drawn a little from time to time. The second part of the work is to adjust the frilling in equal proportions to the article for which it is intended. To do this, it is essential that the cambric frill be "halved and quartered," and even divided into smaller spaces; pins are inserted to mark the several measurements. The article to be trimmed must be marked with pins in the same way, and when ready for the drawing of the string, place each centre, and each quarter, one against the other, the Frilling next to you; secure them to each other by means of pins, one being now sufficient at each division of the material, the corresponding pin may be removed. The article and its trimming will thus be equally divided, and there will be no greater fulness in one quarter than in another. This done, adjust the Whipping evenly in each compartment, and secure the needle end of the loose drawing thread temporarily, by twisting it round the top and end of a pin several times. Then hold the two pieces of pinned material between the thumb and forefinger of the left hand; keeping the work very flat, lying along the finger. Take up every Whip, or portion of the roll, between the stitches, in sewing the two parts together, and insert the needle in a slanting direction that the thread may exactly lie in the folds of the Whipping.

White Embroidery.—*See* EMBROIDERY.

White Wolf Skins (*Canis oxidentalis*).—The fur of wolf skins is very thick, warm, and durable, the tail bushy and handsome; but the skin of the white wolf of northern latitudes is the most valuable, and rarest of any of the varieties known. The hair is long, and tipped with a darker colour. Wolf skins are made into carriage and sofa rugs, and mats for the hearth, &c.

Whittles.—These consist of a description of fringed Shawls, or Squares, to cover the shoulders. They are now made in colours, but were originally white. The Anglo-Saxon was *Hwitle*, denoting a "white cloak."

Whole Stitch.—A name sometimes applied to the Cloth Stitch of Pillow Lace. *See* CLOTH STITCH.

Widen.—*See* KNITTING.

Widow's Lawn.—This material can only be procured in certain shops, and for Widows' Weeds. It is a linen muslin, very clear, and even in make, 52 inches in width.

Widows' Weeds.—This is a comprehensive term, denoting the whole mourning apparel of a widow, of which, the broad flat fold of crape, extending backwards over the top of the bonnet, and falling straight down the back; the peculiarly shaped muslin cap, with very long broad muslin strings, which are never tied; and the broad muslin cuffs, thinner in the centre than at the two borders, form the most remarkable features. The custom for widows to wear a peculiar style of cap is of Roman origin, and the wearing of their "weeds" was compulsory for a period of ten months. See the *Epistles of Seneca*, 65. The term "Weeds" was used in the Middle Ages to signify an entire dress. In such a sense it is employed in Ritson's *Ancient Popular Poetry*, in which the cloak, or complete suit, is denoted by it, viz.:

> He cast on him his Royal weed;

and, again, in reference to Ecclesiastical vestments:

> His cope, and scapelary,
> And all his other weed.

The poet Spenser speaks of "lowly shepherds' Weeds"; and Milton of "Palmers' Weeds." Also, as a badge of sorrow, he says:

> In a mourning weed, with
> Ashes upon her head, and tears
> Abundantly flowing, &c.

Width.—A term employed in dressmaking synonymously with that of Breadth, meaning the several lengths of material employed in making a skirt, which—according to the fashion of the day—is composed of a certain number, gored or otherwise. The term Breadth is more generally in use.

Wigans.—These consist of a description of calico so named after the place of its manufacture. In quality they are soft, warm, and finished; but are stout and heavy, and are employed for many purposes. They are made for sheetings, amongst other purposes, and measure from 2 to 3 yards in width.

Wild Rose Border.—The design shown in Fig. 818 is one made in Honiton Lace. To work: Commence at the flower, and work the centre round of that in STEM STITCH, with five pairs of Bobbins, Sewing each row to the edge of the round. Make the petals alternately in CLOTH and HALF STITCH, with eight pairs of Bobbins and a GIMP. Work down the flower stem to the knot of the next pattern with six pairs of Bobbins and in Stem Stitch, make the knot and work in Stem Stitch to the leaves. Make the small leaf touching the flower first, carry Stem up the side and return, making Cloth Stitch with eight pairs of Bobbins, connect to the flower with a SEWING. Work the large leaf on the opposite side in the same way, and with ten pairs of Bobbins. Cut off four pairs when they reach the leaf stem, and work in Stem Stitch to the last leaf, cut off a pair, and take the Stem Stitch down the middle of that leaf; here hang on two pairs of Bobbins, turn the pillow, and work down one side in Cloth Stitch, RAISED WORK and PEARL EDGE. At the bottom of the leaf cross the leaf stem, cut off a pair of Bobbins, turn the Pillow, and work the other half of the leaf in Half Stitch and PLAIN EDGE. Cut off a pair of Bobbins at the tip, and work the centre fibre of the leaf touching the last made one, and when the bottom of it is reached, turn the Pillow, work down one side in Half Stitch and Plain Edge, turn the pillow, and work the other in Cloth Stitch and Pearl Edge. When finished, work the stalk in Stem Stitch to the next flower with six pairs of Bobbins, then cut off the Bobbins.

FIG. 818. WILD ROSE BORDER.

In working the stalks, make the Pearls to the inner side, and not to the outer, as shown in the illustration, as they would be lost when the lace is sewn to a foundation. Fasten on six pairs of Bobbins, and work the two lower leaves in Cloth Stitch, with Pearls upon the edge towards the flowers, and connect them at the tips; and, lastly, work the four middle leaves with Raised Work, and join each to the main stalk, and work them in pairs. Work the centre of the Rose in CUCUMBER PLAITINGS.

Wilton Carpets.—Carpets of this description are rather expensive, in consequence of the large amount of material demanded, and the slow process of the weaving. Nearly 3,000 threads of yarn are employed on a web of linen only 27 inches wide. Wilton Carpets much resemble Brussels in the manner of manufacture, the surface yarn being worked on a linen web, the designs raised entirely from the warp, and the yarn carried over wires, more or less fine, which, when withdrawn, leave a series of loops. These wires are sharp, and cut through them in their removal, leaving a velvet pile. In the manufacture of Brussels carpets the wires are round, and are not designed to cut the pile, but to leave the loops intact, after the style of Terry velvet. The original seat of the industry was at Axminster, Devonshire, but the manufacture is now principally carried on at Wilton, near Salisbury. Inferior imitations are made in Yorkshire, and also in Scotland.

Wimple.—An article of Mediæval dress, now only retained in conventual houses by the Nuns. It is a neckcloth, which is sometimes drawn across the chin, as well as up the sides of the face and temples, meeting the band which tightly covers the forehead, passing straight across it just above the eyebrows. It is made of linen, but formerly was sometimes made of silk. Wimples may be seen on monumental effigies of many of our early Queens, abbesses, nuns, and great ladies.

In Chaucer's *Romaunt of the Rose*, this ancient, and still existing article of dress is mentioned, viz.:

Wering a vaile instead of wimple,
As nounes don in their abbey.

Winseys.—These are made of two descriptions—all wool, and of wool and calico. They are very durable, and are used by the poorer class of people. There is a quantity of oil in the common qualities, accompanied by a disagreeable odour.

Wire Ground.—This ground is sometimes used in Brussels Lace; it is made of silk, with its net-patterned meshes partly raised and arched, and is worked separately from the design, which is sewn on to it when completed.

Wire Ribbon.—A narrow cotton ribbon or tape, used for the purposes of millinery, into which three or four fine wires are woven. It is sold in packets, which respectively contain twelve pieces of 12 yards each, eight of 18, or six of 24 yards.

Witch Stitch.—*See* EMBROIDERY STITCHES.

Wool.—This is the soft curled or crisped species of hair or fur of which the coat or fleece of the sheep consists. It is also to be found on other animals. There are two classes of wool, the short and the long stapled; the short, not exceeding 4 inches, keeps the name of wool; the long, which measures from 6 to 10 inches, is prepared for weaving in a different manner, and is combed and made into worsted stuffs. The longest length of staple obtained has been 20 inches. The long-stapled wool sheep of England are of four breeds: those of Dishley in Leicestershire, Lincolnshire, of Teeswater, and Dartmoor, those of Lincolnshire sometimes growing wool a foot in length. The average weight of these fleeces is reckoned from 8 to 10 pounds. Our short-stapled sheep are those of Dorsetshire, Herefordshire, and the Southdowns. The manufacture of woollen cloth is commenced by cleaning the wool, which is a long process of boiling, &c. It is then dyed, sprinkled over with olive oil, and beaten with rods. It then passes through a scribbling engine, to separate the fibres into light flakes, called "laps," thence through the carding engine; after that through the slubbing or roving machine, to make the wool into the soft, loose thread, which is subsequently spun into yarn and made into cloth. Milling and fulling then follow, by which a length of 40 yards, and 100 inches in width, would be reduced to the proper thickness of ordinary superfine cloth, by shrinking it to some 30 yards long and 60 inches wide.

The manufacture of woollen cloths by the ancient Britons is demonstrated by their presence in the tumuli or barrows already opened; and it is a matter of historical record, that not its use alone, but its manufacture, is connected with the names of the highest ladies in the land. In the spinning of wool, King Alfred's mother was distinguished for her skill; and Edward I., while he wisely arranged to "settle his sons at schole," set his daughters to "wollwerke." In the reign of Edward III. the export of wool from England was made a felony, and the exportation of the woollen yarn forbidden under a penalty of forfeiture.

Woollen-backed Satin.—A very serviceable make of Satin, chiefly employed for jackets and mantles, and which, owing to the mixture of wool with the silk, does not form creases in its wear. It is 24 inches in width.

Woollen Cord.—This is one of the varieties of corduroy. It has a warp of cotton and a weft of wool, and is cut after the same manner as cotton cord—another description of the same class of textile—but the face is wholly woollen, whence its name. It is suitable for men's riding breeches or trousers, and is both warm and strong.

Woollen Matelassé.—This description of cloth is manufactured exactly after the manner of silk Matelassé, and is chiefly employed for the making of mantles, being a thick material, of handsome appearance, and satisfactory in wear. It has much the appearance of being quilted in the form of leaves, flowers, and other devices. The width measures from about 1½ yards to 2 yards.

Woollen Textiles.—These are spun from the soft, curly, short-stapled woollen yarn, crossed and roughed in spinning, which varies in length from 3 inches to 4 inches, and is the only kind employed for making cloth. The term cloth, like stuff, has a general significance, and is applied to textiles composed of every kind of material, but is of more particular application to goods made from short-stapled wool. Amongst those made from it are broadcloth, kerseymere, pelisse cloths, frieze bearskin, Bath coating, duffil, tweed, hodden grey, plush, flannel (of many descriptions), domett, baize blanketing, and PINE WOOL (which *see*).

Woollen Yarn.—All wool which has not passed through the process of combing, whether by hand or machinery, is distinguished by this name. Lambswool fingering is sent out by the manufacturers in ½ pounds, consisting of eight skeins, of 1 ounce weight each; but the correctness of the weight cannot be relied upon. They are from two to ten-fold, are supplied in 3-pound, 6-pound, and 12-pound packages. The fleecy wools are produced in a great variety of colours. Lambswool yarn of a superior quality may be had in white, grey, drab, and other colours, in 3-pound, 6-pound, and 12-pound parcels, the numbers running from 0½ to 4. Smaller quantities may be purchased. Berlin lambswools are dyed in every description of colour; the numbers run from 0½ to 4. They are supplied in parcels of 3 pounds, 6 pounds, and 12 pounds, and may be had of single and double thickness, and by weight or skein, according to the requirements of the purchaser. There is also the Leviathan wool, which is composed of many strands, and is full and soft, and designed for Embroidery on canvas of considerable coarseness; the Lady Betty wool, in black, white, and scarlet, sold by weight or skein; the Eider Yarn, which is peculiarly delicate and glossy, and employed for hand-made shawls and scarves; the Andalusian, a tightly-twisted wool, about the thickness of single Berlin; the Shetland wool, which is finer than the latter; the Pyrenean, which is of a still finer description; and Zephyr wool, which is remarkably thin and fine. Wool mendings, sometimes incorrectly called Angola, consist of a mixture of wool and cotton, and may be had in small skeins, or on cards or reels, in many shades of colour. *See* Wool.

Wool Needles.—These are short and thick, with blunt points, and long eyes, like those of darning needles. They are sometimes called Tapestry Needles. *See* Needles.

Wool Velours.—A description of very soft, thick, and close-grained flannel, having much nap, and employed for making dressing jackets and French peignoirs, and peasants' or maidservants' short, loose, square-cut jackets, having pockets on each side. It is made in many colours and patterns, and chiefly striped like Ribbon-grass.

Woolwork Flowers.—These are flowers made by winding wool round wire foundations, so that they stand erect, and can be used as detached bouquets, or placed simply round the borders of mats. The flowers that are suitable are convolvulus, poppy, Marguerite daisy, geranium, and lily of the valley. The materials required are netting Meshes, from half an inch to 1½ inches in width; pieces of thin wood, round in shape, 2 inches in diameter, with a small hole in the centre, and with scalloped edges; the same thin pieces of wood shaped as squares of 2¼ inches; very fine cap wire, and single Berlin wool matching the colouring of the flowers.

To Work a Convolvulus: Take a round-shaped piece of wood, and in every scallop round its edge lay down a line of fine wire, bringing all the ends of the wire to the back of the wood, through the centre hole, where twist them together and cut off. Thread a wool needle with white wool, fasten the wool in the hole in the centre of the wood, and pass it round and round in circles between the wires and the wood; as each wire is reached make a stitch over it to enclose it, then carry the wool along to the next wire and make a stitch over that, and so continue to work round after round, each one slightly larger than the other, until half the rosette is covered. Fasten off the white wool, and continue the work with pale blue wool instead, which carry up nearly to the edge of the rosette; cut the wires at the back, close to the edge, and turn these pieces so as to secure them into the edge of the flower, which will assume a trumpet shape as soon as released. Curve the edge of the convolvulus over, make very short stamens, by covering wire with yellow wool, which insert into the flower centre, and then wind green wool round the ends of wire left in the centre of the flower to form the stalk.

To Work a Daisy: Take a netting Mesh three-quarters of an inch wide, some white wool and fine wire; wind the wool round the Mesh and secure it with the wire (as described for making the poppy) forty-eight times, then take the wool off the Mesh (the wire this time will form the bottom of the petals). To form the top, tie together with a little knot every loop in sets of three. Take a round piece of brown velvet, the size of the centre of a Marguerite, which line with buckram, and work a number of French Knots upon it with yellow filoselle; sew round this the bottom or wired part of the petals, and arrange so that it is twice encircled with the wire, and so that the petals from each round come alternately.

To Work a Geranium: The petals of this flower are so small that it does not require a wooden foundation. Take a piece of fine wire, and bend it into a heart shape without the indent in the centre, half an inch in length. Fasten a doubled piece of wool up the centre of this, and work over this foundation with soft shades of rose colour wool. Thread a wool needle, fasten it to the top of the petal, pass it in between the doubled wool and over the wire on the right side, in and out through the doubled wool, and over the wire on the left side; continue this form of plaiting until the wire is entirely concealed with a close and thick line of stitches. Make five petals in this manner, join them by twisting the ends of the wire together, and cover that by winding green wool round the end. A primrose is made in the same manner as a geranium, but with the petals more indented in the centre, and with pale lemon-coloured wool.

To Work a Lily of the Valley: Make the petals with a wire outline, pointed in the centre and wide in the middle; work them over with white wool, as described in the geranium, turn their edges over, and make up four of them as a flower. Arrange them along a stalk to form a lily spray, and make small round buds of twisted white wool for the top part of the spray.

To Make the Leaves: These are all made upon wire, like the geranium, the only alteration being in the shape the wire is bent into.

To Make the Stamens: Cover straight pieces of wire with yellow wool, and turn the end of the wire round to thicken the top part.

To Work a Poppy: Take a netting Mesh, 1½ inches in width, some deep scarlet wool, also some fine wire, and cover with red silk. Wind the wire upon two small pieces of wood or cardboard, to keep it from getting entangled, and leave a piece of it in the centre, double it, and leave 2 inches of it hanging, and also 2 inches of the scarlet wool, which wind once loosely round the Mesh over one of the wires (which open out again) at the edge of the Mesh; lay the other wire over the wool where it has gone over the first wire, and thus secure it. Wind the wool loosely round the Mesh again, this time over the second wire, and lay the first wire over the wool. Wind the wool twenty times round the Mesh, each time securing it with the wires alternately over and under it; then take it off the mesh. The part where the twisted wires are will be the top of the petal; run a wire through the other end of the petal, and draw the loops there up quite tightly with it, then bring the piece of doubled wire down to the bottom of the petal and the piece beyond the loops on the other side, and twist them both in to the bottom part. Make four of these petals, and either put into the centre of them the dried head of a small poppy, or make a knob of green wool on the top of a piece of wire and put that in.

To Work a Rose: Take a piece of thin wood, 2¼ inches square, make a hole in it in the centre, and one at each edge; through these pass fine wires, which lay across the centre, and make quite tight. Take wool of the right shade of rose colour, and, commencing at the centre, wind it carefully round and round under the crossed wires, but never attached to them; keep them flat and evenly laid by holding them down with the left thumb. When sufficient rounds have been made, thread the wool on to a fine darning needle, and draw it through the centre of the petal, from the outside edge at one part to the opposite outside edge, so as to secure the rounds of wool, and to make the cleft in the centre of the rose leaf; then take the petal off the woodwork by undoing the wires. A finished petal is shown

Fig. 819. Woolwork Flowers—Rose Petal.

in Fig. 819. Make a dozen petals in this way, six of which should be large, and the others rather small. Make the centre of the rose with loops of yellow thread, run a wire through them, tie them up tight a quarter of an inch from the wire: cut them off a little beyond the tie, and comb the wool out beyond the tie, to make it fluffy. Sew the petals to the centre, and wind green wool round as a stalk.

The best way of making up Woolwork Flowers is to KNIT a quantity of moss with various shades of green wool, bake it in an oven, unravel it, put it round a centre of black velvet, and insert the flowers into the moss. When an urn stand has to be made, by Buttonholing with dark wool over rounds of window cord a thicker centre to the mat is made than by knitting.

Worcesters.—These are woollen cloths, named after the place where they had their origin, as far back, at least,

as the fourteenth century. It appears that Worcester cloth was considered so excellent, that its use was prohibited to the Monks by a Chapter of the Benedictine Order, held in 1422. Bath was equally famous for the cloth manufactured there, by the Monks of Bath Abbey, from the middle of the fourteenth century.

Work.—A generic and very comprehensive term, often applied to the accomplishments of the needle, whether of Plain Sewing or of Embroidery.

Taylor thus speaks of Queen Katharine of Arragon:—

> Although a Queen, yet she her days did pass
> In working with the needle curiously.
>> *The Needle's Excellency.*

> * * * My soul grows sad with troubles;
> Sing, and disperse 'em, if thou can'st: leave working.
>> *Henry VIII.*, Act 3.

> * * * I'll have the work ta'en out,
> And give't Iago.   *Othello.*

> Work Tibet, work Annot, work Margerie.
> Sew Tibet, knit Annot, spin Margerie.
> Let us see who will win the victory.

NICHOLAS UDALIS, "Work Girls' Song," in *Royster Doyster.*

Workhouse Sheeting.—This is a coarse twilled and unbleached cloth, employed for sheeting, and likewise for bedroom curtains, embroidered with Turkey red, and worked in crewels. It is very much utilised for purposes of embroidery, and is of the ordinary width for sheeting.

Work over Cord.—A term sometimes used in Church Embroidery to denote basket, whipcord, and other couchings that are made over laid threads.

Worsted.—A class of yarn, well twisted and spun, of long staple wool, varying in length from 3 inches to 10 inches, which, after being cleansed, is combed, to lay the fibres parallel before it is spun, and afterwards wound on reels, and twisted into hanks. The wool was originally thus treated and prepared at Worsted, in Norfolk, whence its name, the manufacture having received a great impetus through Edward III. and his Queen, Philippa of Hainault, who introduced a great number of woollen manufacturers from the Netherlands, who settled at Norwich, York, Kendal, Manchester, and Halifax; although it was first established in England in the reign of Henry I., when some Dutchmen, escaping from an inundation, came over and settled at Norwich. In the reign of Queen Elizabeth, a fresh immigration of Flemings took place, who likewise settled at Norwich, and also at Colchester and Sandwich, bringing with them great improvements. Textiles called "Stuffs" are, properly speaking, those composed of Worsted, although frequently used as a comprehensive term applied to all fabrics alike. The principal stuffs made of this fine, long-fibred wool, include moreen, lasting, Denmark satins, rateen, merino, damask, bombazet, tammies, callimanco, shalloon, cubica, serge, plaid, camlet, mousseline de laine, challis, shawls, carpets, crapes, poplins, and hosiery. These are stiffer and more rough than woollen-made fabrics. Cotton warps are often introduced into them, which impair their durability; but, when combined with silk, as in poplins and bombazines, it is otherwise. The term Worsted Stuffs applies equally to those made of combed wool, combining cotton or silk, which are not "fulled" (like woollen cloth), as to those entirely of Worsted. The manufacture of Worsted stuffs, although very ancient, has only reached its present state of excellence within the last fifty years. According to tradition, we owe the invention of the wool-comb to St. Blaise, and the anniversary of his canonisation (3rd Feb.) used for centuries to be kept as a gala day at Bradford. The Flemish refugees who escaped from the tyranny of the Duke of Alva (1570), settling in Yorkshire, made Halifax for many years the seat of the Worsted industry, which became famous for its damasks, lastings, and other such goods. The first spinning machinery was set up at Bradford, in 1790, in a private house, and, five years later, the first manufactory was built. In the year 1834, the union of a cotton warp with Worsted was made, and in 1836 the wool of the Peruvian alpaca was introduced; and, at about the same time, that of mohair of goats' hair of Asia Minor. *See* WOOL.

Worsted Bindings.—These are employed by upholsterers and saddlers, produced in a variety of colours, and can be procured in various lengths to the gross: 6-18, 9-16, or 6-24. The several widths have been designated "double London," "shoe," "double shoe," "extra quality."

Worsted Braids.—These Braids vary in width and make, are employed as dress trimmings, and produced in various colours, though chiefly in black. The numbers run 53, 57, 61, 65, 69, 73, 77, 81, 85, 89, 93, 97, 101. They are sold in 36-yard lengths, four pieces to the gross, or a shorter piece if desired. Many Braids that are called mohair or alpaca are really of Worsted. There are also Waved Worsted Braids, sold in knots, containing from 4 to 5 yards each. The numbers run 13, 17, and 21, and the Braid is sold by the gross pieces. It is employed for the trimming of children's dresses. Skirt Braids, said to be of mohair and alpaca, and called Russia Braids, are, many of them, made of Worsted. They consist of two cords woven together, cut into short lengths, and sold by the gross pieces. The wider ones are in 36-yard lengths, four pieces to the gross. The numbers run from 0 to 8, and the Braid may be had in black or colours.

Worsted Damasks.—These are thick cloths, to be had in many varieties of excellence, for the purposes of upholstery. They are produced in all colours, and the widths are suitable for curtains, &c. The chief seat of the industry is at Halifax.

Worsted Fringes.—These are made in very extensive varieties of length and pattern. They run generally from 2½ inches to 4 inches in depth, and the several varieties are classified under three descriptions—viz., Plain-head, Plain-head and Bullion, and Gymp-head. They may be had in all colours and degrees of richness. There are also Worsted Fringes, designed for dress, which are called Fancy Fringes, and are made of Worsted

or silk, from half an inch in width to 2 or 3 inches. Worsted tassels, if required for dress or furniture, may be had to match any of these fringes.

Worsted Work.—This needlework, once known as Opus Pulvinarium, then as Cushion Style, and Worsted Work, is now generally entitled Berlin Work, a name given to it when coloured patterns and Berlin Wools were first used in its manufacture. The origin of Worsted Work is very ancient, it being undoubtedly known and practised in the East before its introduction into Europe from Egypt; but it is difficult to trace an account of it, from the practice of ancient writers classing all descriptions of needlework under one heading, until the latter end of the thirteenth century, when the various methods of Embroidery were distinguished and classed with great accuracy, and what was then known as Cushion Style was especially mentioned as being used for kneeling mats, cushions, and curtains in cathedrals, and occasionally upon sacred vestments, as can still be seen on the narrow hem of the Sion Cope (date 1225), now in the South Kensington Museum. Like all other works of Art during the Middle Ages, it was chiefly practised in convents and nunneries, and used for the adornment of sacred objects; but as the nuns were the only instructors in those days, noble ladies were sent to them to learn to work as well as to read, and beguiled many tedious hours by adorning their homes with specimens of their skill. Worsted Work, distinguished from Embroidery by being made upon a foundation of loosely woven canvas, that requires to be thoroughly covered instead of being worked upon materials that can be left visible, was in favour after the Reformation, and much of it, worked by Anne Boleyn, and Mary Queen of Scots and her ladies, is still in existence. In the time of Queen Anne and Queen Mary, silk Embroideries and Crewel Work were more fashionable; but in the reign of George III., much Worsted Work was done, that executed by the Duchess of York for Oatlands Park being particularly noticeable, from the designs, colouring, and workmanship, being her own. The Linwood Exhibition of Worsted Work, during the earlier part of the present century, consisting of sixty-four full-length pieces, deserves notice, as these were all executed by one lady (Miss Linwood), who copied the designs from oil paintings, upon a canvas, known as Tammy, and worked them out in Worsteds that were especially dyed to suit the required shades.

When it is remembered that, before the year, 1804 all designs for Worsted Work had to be drawn by hand, and coloured according to the taste of the worker, and that the Worsteds used were harsher and coarser than those now employed, some idea of the labour of the work then, as compared with what it is at present, can be gathered. It was to remedy this that a printer at Berlin produced a series of designs, copied from pictures, and printed upon Point paper so that each stitch was plainly visible; these were coloured by hand with due regard to the real colouring of the pictures they represented, and afterwards worked out in Tent Stitch upon very fine canvas with fine Worsteds and Silks. Shortly afterwards, a large and coarser canvas began to be substituted for the fine, and

Cross Stitch instead of Tent Stitch; and finally, the Worsteds were superseded by Berlin Wool, and the good patterns by large unwieldy flower or impossible animal designs, which, coupled with their execution in the brightest colours producible, was the death blow to Worsted Work from an artistic point of view. For the last twenty years, and since the public mind has become more alive to the beauty and fitness of needlework for decorative purposes, these abominations have been justly discarded; but they must not be confounded with the work itself, which, when executed in fine stitches upon fine canvas, in soft and harmonious colouring and correct designs, is as capable of embodying an artist's idea as other needlework mediums. The design shown in Fig. 820

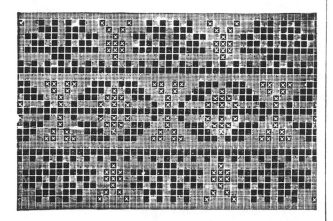

FIG. 820. WORSTED WORK.

is an arabesque pattern, worked with three shades of Berlin Wool, the darkest of which is shown by the dark squares, the next by the squares filled with crosses, and the lightest by the check pattern squares. To work: Fill in the dark squares with CROSS STITCH and with deep ruby-coloured wool, the check squares with pale olive green wool, and the squares filled with crosses with pale blue filoselle. For manner of working, *see* BERLIN WORK.

Worsted Yarns.—There are many varieties in these yarns, such as Worsted, for carpet mending, which is very coarse, and may be had in many bright colours, and which is sold in paper bags, wound in balls; the bags contain from 3 to 6 pounds each. Also Hank Worsted, for knitting stockings, dyed in various colours—white, black, speckled, grey, scarlet, &c.—and sold by the half-dozen or dozen pounds, made up in $\frac{1}{2}$-pound skeins. Also Fingering Worsted, sent out in $\frac{1}{2}$ pounds by the manufacturers, comprising eight skeins of 1 ounce weight each. It may be bought in small quantities in retail shops. Also Scotch Fingering, which is a loosely spun yarn, produced in very bright colours, and sold by the spindle of 6 pounds. Scotch Fingering is much employed for the knitting of children's gaiters, stockings, scarves, and mittens. Ordinary Fingering Worsted is sent out by the manufacturers in $\frac{1}{2}$ pounds, or eight skeins, each skein being considered an ounce in weight. There are also

Worsted balls, sold for the purpose of mending. These can be had in black and white, speckled and grey, made up in balls of 3, 4, or 6 "drams" each, and sold in bags containing 3 pounds, 6 pounds, or 12 pounds weight of yarn.

Wristbands.—These form an important part of a shirt, and the method of making them should, therefore, be known. Although some portion of the garment may be of calico, the breast, collar, and cuffs, or wristbands, must always be of linen. They must consist of three pieces of material, two of linen, and one of thin calico. To work: Cut the wristbands by a thread, the selvedge way of the linen, lay all the triple thickness together, and as the calico must be placed between the other two, lay it outside them, and the two pieces of linen together, when commencing to work. RUN all neatly together on the wrong side, and then turn over one of the linen sides, so that the running and raw edges shall be turned in. Press the edge to make it lie flat, and then draw a thread in the linen, on the side farthest from the ridge made by the portions folded over on the inside. Compare the band with that of another shirt, to regulate the measurement for the drawing of the thread, as the Hemstitching should always be made at a certain depth from the edge. TACK the opposite side and the two ends, to secure them in their right positions, and then stitch the band where the thread has been drawn. The ends of the band will have to be treated in the same way—a thread drawn and a stitching made. The shape of these wristbands, as well as of collars, changes continually, thus a pattern should be obtained, and if the corners have to be rounded, or any new slopings be required, they must be so cut before the first Tacking is made. Great care will be needed where any curve has to be made, as no thread can be drawn in such a case. The method of making a shirt collar is precisely the same as of making a cuff; and while the exact form must depend on the current fashion, these general directions apply to all.

Y.

Yak Crochet.—*See* CROCHET.

Yak Lace.—This is a coarse Pillow Lace, made in Buckinghamshire and Northampton, in imitation of Maltese Silk Guipure. The material used is obtained from the fine wool of the Yak. The patterns are all simple, and are copied from the geometric designs of real Maltese Lace. They are connected with plaited Guipure Bars, ornamented with Purls, that form part of the pattern, being worked with the same threads, and at the same time. The thick parts of the design are worked in Cloth Stitch and Plaitings.

Yak Lace has been most successfully imitated in Crochet (*see* Fig. 821); it is there worked in Maltese thread, and in black, white, or écru colours, according to taste. To work the pattern given, *see* CROCHET directions.

Besides the Yak Lace made with Crochet, an imitation of it is formed with the needle upon a foundation of coarse grenadine, which is afterwards cut away; the work closely resembles the lace made upon the pillow. It can be used for dress and furniture trimmings, though it will not wash. The materials required are strong and rather coarse black, coloured, or white grenadine or tarlatan, Mohair yarn matching the grenadine in colour, strips of cartridge paper, and prepared linen, such as is known as carbonised linen. To work as shown in Fig. 822: Trace the design, which can be taken from the finished scallop on the left-hand side of the illustration, upon the carbonised linen, back the pattern with calico, and lay the grenadine over it, which TACK down quite evenly upon it. Take the cartridge paper, and from it cut out the straight line that forms the FOOTING, the leaves surrounding the scallop, and the scallop. Lay the scallop four, and for the Footing two. DARN each of these lines in and out of the short threads, taking up one and leaving the next, as in ordinary Darning, and where a BAR has to be made to connect the leaves to each other or to the Footing, or the scallops to the centre star, make it as a CORDED BAR with the thread as it is working; as joins of all kinds must be avoided wherever possible, and fresh threads taken in in the darning. Cord the long lines in the Footing, like the Bars, but the other long lines will not require this unless the thread used is very thin. Work the stars in the centre of the pattern so that they are connected to the leaves and the scallops. Make them in GENOA STITCH thus: Carry along their length four lines of thread, and then DARN over them thickly, drawing the stitches in tight at the points of the star, and loosening them in the centre. Make a loop of thread, for the scalloped edge, which secure

FIG. 821.   YAK LACE—IMITATED IN CROCHET.

these bits of paper down upon the grenadine, and stitch them down to it by a securing line in their centres. (They are used to keep the stitches worked over them from taking up the grenadine, where it has to be cut away). Now commence to work. Take an Embroidery needle with a blunt point, thread the Mohair upon it, and work in all the short up and down lines in the lace first, which form the foundation for the long lines. Run a thread across a space, and let it take up two strands of the grenadine beyond the cartridge paper, bring it to the other side, and let it take up two strands of the grenadine there; work backwards and forwards in this way, leaving only one strand of grenadine between each stitch, until the space is filled in; then return over the lines with a second thread, and CORD every one. This Run foundation is shown in the right-hand leaves of the illustration. Take a good long thread and work in the long lines. For the leaves there will be five long lines required, for

into one of the short lines on the scallop, miss the next short line, and make a second loop into the third; continue to the end of the pattern, and make the loops larger at the broad part of the scallop than at the narrow. Cord this line of loops, and run a plain thread through them, which also Cord. Having finished the work, cut away the tacking threads, and so release the lace from the pattern; then carefully cut away the grenadine from the back of the stitches, and leave them without any support.

Yard.—A measure of length employed for every description of textile or material for personal wear, upholstery, &c., or for needlework. One yard equals 3 feet, or 36 inches, and is the standard of British and American measurement. The cloth yard in old English times was of the length of the arrows employed both in battle and for the chase. A Statute of 5 & 6 Edward VI. enacted that the measure of cloth should contain, to every yard, "one inch containing the breadth of a man's thumb," or 37 inches. This "thumb measure" still obtains in the trade. Goods for export are measured by the "short stitch," or 35 inches and the thumb—that is, the bare yard; while goods for the home market are measured by "long stitch"—or the yard of 36 inches and the "thumb"—that is, what is designated "good measure."

Yarn.—This term signifies thread spun from fibres of any description, whether of flax, hemp, cotton, silk, or wool.

Yarn Measure.—A hank of worsted yarn is generally estimated in England at 560 yards, or seven "leas," of 80 yards each. Linen yarn is estimated by the number of "leas" or "cuts," each of 3 yards, contained in 1 pound weight. In Scotland, it is estimated by the number of rounds in the spindle, or 48 "leas." Thus, No. 48 in

at the back of the shoulders, or forming a sort of stomacher at the front of the skirt. This rule holds good for those made of crape likewise, which must be so folded as that there shall be no seam made. Woven Yokes may now be purchased in all colours, made of cotton, and at very low prices, for petticoat skirts. Yokes such as employed in dress are copied from those made of wood, and worn on the shoulders by those who carry pails of either water or milk.

Yokohama Crape.—This is a very fine, close make of Crape, otherwise known as Canton Crape, employed especially for mantle-making, but also for the trimming of dresses. It is made in two widths, measuring respectively 25 inches and 2 yards. There is much more substance in it than in ordinary Crape, and it is not transparent like the latter. The Yokohama is the costliest of all descriptions of Crape, and the most durable in wear.

FIG. 822. YAK LACE IMITATION.

England, is called 1 pound yarn in Scotland. One hank of cotton yarn is 840 yards, and a spindle of 18 hanks is 15,120 yards.

Yaws.—A vulgar term denoting the thin places in cloth.

Yokes.—These are headings, or shaped bands, into which plaitings or gatherings of garments are sewn, and which are so cut as to fit either the shoulders or the hips, and from which the rest of the bodice, nightdress, dressing gown, or the skirt, is to depend. The Yoke of a shirt or nightdress is sometimes called a neck-piece, and is always made of double material, like that of a skirt. Of whatever the cloth may consist, one rule applies to all Yokes—viz., that the straight way of the stuff should be placed at the centre of the Yoke, whether that centre be

Yorkshire Flannels.—These Flannels have a plain selvedge, and are superior to those made in Lancashire. They are made in the natural colour of the wool, so that they are improved in appearance by washing, contrary to the ordinary rule.

Youghal Lace.—The lace made at Youghal is the best of all the Irish Lace, and is called IRISH POINT. It is a copy of ITALIAN POINT LACE, the old Lace being carefully copied, and new Stitches invented. The making of Irish Point is an industry carried on in the convent schools of New Ross, Kenmare, Waterford, Kinsale, Killarney and Clonakilty, but that produced at Youghal is acknowledged to be the best.

Ypres Lace.—The lace made at Ypres is Valenciennes Lace. *See* VALENCIENNES LACE.

Z.

Zante Lace.—This lace is similar to the Greek Reticellas. It is still to be purchased in the Ionian Isles, but the manufacture of it has long been discontinued.

Zephyr Cloth.—A fine, thin, finely spun woollen cloth, made in Belgium, thinner than tweed, and employed for women's gowns. Shawls, also, are made of this material, the wool being fine, and loosely woven, and very light in weight. It can be dyed in very brilliant colours, and resembles a Kerseymere.

Zephyr Ginghams, or Prints.—These are pretty delicate textiles, resembling a cotton batiste, designed for summer wear, and produced in pale but fast colours, which bear washing. They are to be had in pink and blue, and measure from 30 inches to 1 yard in width. They are also to be had spotted with Plush woven into the cloth, in two or three contrasting colours.

Zephyr Merino Yarn.—The term employed by the woolstaplers of Germany to signify what is usually called German, or Berlin.

Zephyr Shirting.—This is a kind of gauze flannel, having a silk warp. It is manufactured for use in hot climates, and is a superior description of cloth. The groundwork is grey, showing the threads of white silk, and there is a pattern formed of narrow stripes, either of black or of pink, running the lengthway of the stuff. Zephyr Shirting measures 32 inches in width.

Zulu Cloth.—A closely-woven cloth, twill-made, designed for Crewel Embroidery or Outline Work, the closeness of the weaving facilitating the drawing of the designs.

SUPPLEMENT

TO THE

DICTIONARY OF NEEDLEWORK

CONSISTING OF

—— A Series of Plates ——

OF

ORNAMENTAL AND USEFUL ARTICLES

MADE OR DECORATED

BY

NEEDLEWORK.

AN INDEX OF THE SUBJECTS ILLUSTRATED IN THIS SUPPLEMENT
APPEARS AT THE END OF THIS VOLUME (PAGES 691-697).

Plate I.

531

No. 1. Beaded Lace.

The lace is imitation black Spanish; the beads, black jet. Run and Back Stitch the beads to the lace with black sewing silk.

No. 2. Ornamental Towel.

This Towel is intended to hang in front of the towels in use. The design is executed upon coarse linen with ingrain scarlet and blue cotton, and in Cross Stitch. The border is made with one row of Cross Stitch, one of Drawn Work, and the rest coarse insertion and edging lace.

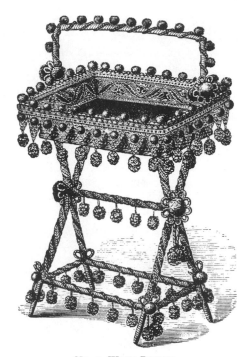

No. 3. WORK BASKET.

Foundation, wicker; legs and handle covered with ball fringe; interior embroidery, crewel work on diagonal cloth; exterior, diagonal cloth cut in vandykes, BUTTONHOLED round, and ornamented with coloured balls.

No. 4. FERN PRESSER.

Made with five strips of strong millboard, tied together with ribbon. The outside strips are covered with perforated cardboard, and worked with coloured silks in CROSS STITCH. Size, 7 inches by 5 inches.

No. 5. BOX PINCUSHION.

Foundation, a round box, the lid of which is stuffed, covered with satin, and trimmed with a vandyked vallance of white cricketing flannel, embroidered in CREWEL STITCH with coloured silks. Full ruchings of ribbon hide the lower part of the box.

No. 6. APPLIQUÉ BORDER.

Foundation of silk; centre of the design, dark plush embroidered in SATIN STITCH; work the rest out in piece satin of various shades of one colour, and attach to the foundation with BUTTONHOLE or COUCHING.

Plate III. 533

No. 7. Work Bag.

Foundation, perforated cardboard or ticking, lining of satin; trimming, a ruche of ribbon. Embroidery executed in chenille, and worked in vandykes, Cross Stitches, and Lines. Colours, shades of greens.

No. 8. Border.

Worked on ecru canvas, with crewels and filoselle, in Cross and Long Stitches. Work the Long Stitches in chocolate crewels, fillings inside flowers in crimson, and leaves in alternate dark blue and green crewels; the rest in fawn-coloured filoselle.

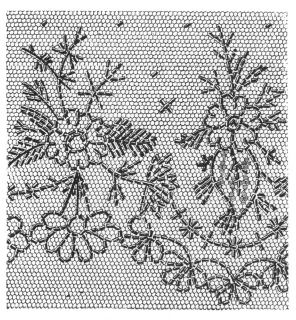

No. 9. Beaded Net.

Pattern worked out in Back Stitch, with jet beads on black net, with opal beads on white net.

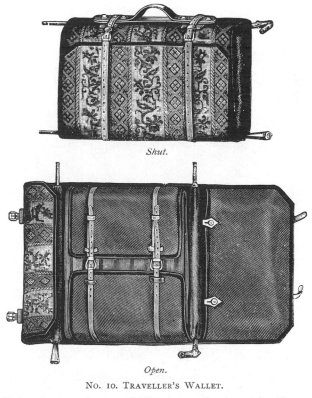

Shut.

Open.

No. 10. Traveller's Wallet.

Made of strong brown sailcloth, the outside decorated with an embroidered canvas cover. The pockets, &c., are shown in the open Wallet, the securing straps and embroidery in the shut Wallet. Size of cover, 48 inches by 25 inches. Embroidery worked in Cross Stitch, with coloured linen thread, in three broad stripes, with coloured linen borders laid on and secured by narrow braids between the work.

Plate IV.

No. 11. CROSS STITCH ON LINEN.

Worked in ingrain cotton—the black squares in chocolate brown, the light squares in scarlet.

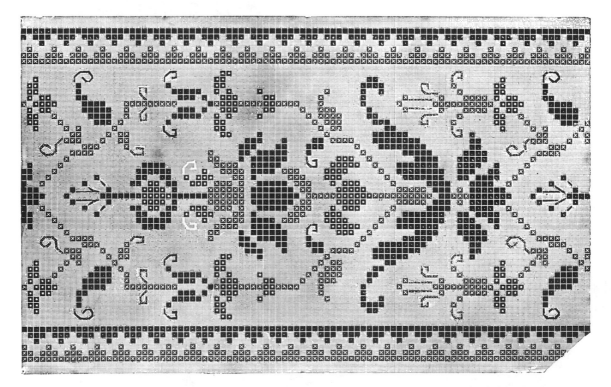

No. 12. CROSS STITCH ON CLOTH.

Worked in three shades of blue crewels, on maroon cloth. The black squares show the darkest shade, the cross squares the second, and the dotted squares the lightest. The Run lines are worked on the cloth, after the Berlin canvas foundation has been drawn out.

Plate V. 535

No. 13. Pannier Basket.

Foundation, wicker; bags of dark-brown satin; embroidery, Bulgarian; ruching and bows of coloured ribbons.

No. 14. Flower Basket.

Foundation, wicker; ornamentation, Macrame lace and silk cords and tassels.

No. 15. Raised Embroidery.

Foundation of rep silk; leaves and flowers cut out in velvet and plush materials, with beads to form centres. Stitches used: Rope Stitch for stems and for cord; Satin Stitch for veining leaves and butterflies, and Chain Stitch for sprays.

No. 16. Key Basket.

Foundation, wicker; ornaments, Beadwork on brown plush—gold beads only are used. Ornamental balls, of shades of yellow-brown silks.

No. 17. Lady's Companion.

Made of a long strip of oatmeal cloth, lined with satin, and folded together as shown. Length of strip, 12 inches; width, 5 inches. Embroidery worked in Satin Stitch with coloured filoselles. Brown cord as a finish.

NO. 18. DESIGN FOR BRACKET, &C.

Worked upon Berlin canvas, with grounding filled in with BASKET STITCH, or upon
Russian canvas, and the foundation left plain. Pattern worked with shades of
Leek embroidery silks in SATIN STITCH ; Flowers surrounded with a fine silk
cord, matching the palest shade used in working them. Colours for centre
flower, three shades of maroon, with plaited and FEATHER STITCH centre in
old gold silk. Star in shades of yellow-pink, conventional fleur-de-lys in three
shades of sky blue. Leaves in olive-green and red-browns ; Stem in olive-green.
Border, a maroon satin ribbon, worked with old gold DOTS. The same design
repeated can be used for Footstool or Small Table.

NO. 19. EGG COSY.

Foundation of old gold satin, on which
are laid narrow strips of scarlet German
canvas, attached with double lines of
BUTTONHOLE. Work on the satin
a flower design, with coloured filoselles in CREWEL STITCH ; work the
canvas in CROSS STITCH, with yellow
filoselle.

NO. 20. WORK BASKET.

The foundation is wicker ; the lining, navy blue plush ;
the embroidery executed upon pale blue cashmere,
with purse silks in shades of crimson and olive green.
Stitches used in rosettes and leaves, SATIN and
FRENCH KNOTS ; in battlements and vandykes,
POINT DE RUSSE.

Plate VII. 537

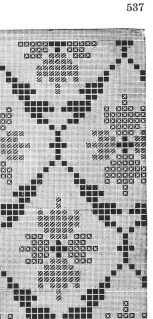

NO. 21. CHURCH CARPET IN CROSS STITCH.

Worked on large Berlin canvas, in Church colours, with Berlin wools, the black squares in black wool, the cross squares in crimson, the lined squares in white silk, and the foundation in dark blue or purple wool.

NO. 22. FOOTSTOOL OF PERFORATED CLOTH.

The Stitch used is CROSS STITCH. Work the black squares in chocolate wool, the cross squares in crimson silk, the lined squares in gold thread, and the foundation in pale grey silk.

NO. 23. WASTE PAPER OR WORK BASKET.

Foundation of wicker. Embroidery executed on two shades of stamped Velvet—either two shades of cinnamon or two of brown. Outline the design in gold thread, fill up in SATIN STITCH with shaded filoselles, and work round each vandyke with a thick line of BUTTONHOLE STITCH.

NO. 24. HAND BAG.

The Bag is made of blue satin, the flap of blue plush, the handles of blue ribbon. Length of bag, 14 inches; width, 8 inches.

NO. 25. TASSEL COVER.

Executed in fine blue and white cloth, and finished with fringe and tassels. The edges of the cloths are secured with BUTTONHOLE. A SATIN STITCH spray is worked in blue silk on the white cloth, and a WHEEL in the same silk on the blue cloth.

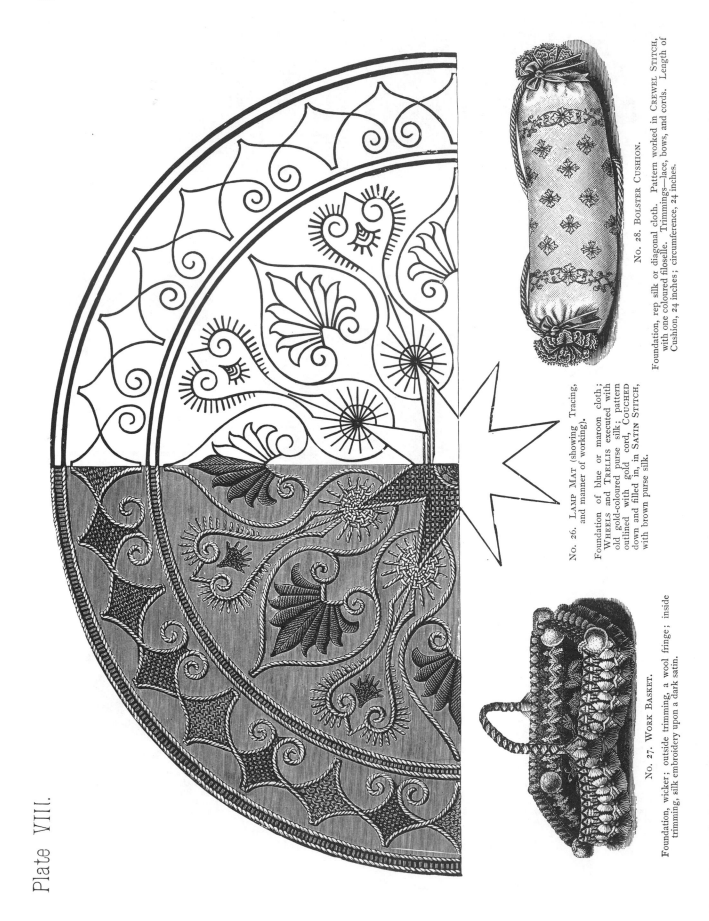

Plate VIII.

No. 26. LAMP MAT (showing Tracing, and manner of working).

Foundation of blue or maroon cloth; WHEELS and TRELLIS executed with old gold-coloured purse silk; pattern outlined with gold cord, COUCHED down and filled in, in SATIN STITCH, with brown purse silk.

No. 28. BOLSTER CUSHION.

Foundation, rep silk or diagonal cloth. Pattern worked in CREWEL STITCH, with one coloured filoselle. Trimmings—lace, bows, and cords. Length of Cushion, 24 inches; circumference, 24 inches.

No. 27. WORK BASKET.

Foundation, wicker; outside trimming, a wool fringe; inside trimming, silk embroidery upon a dark satin.

Plate IX.

539

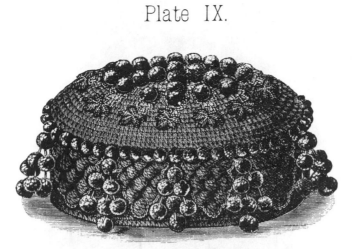

No. 29. STRAW WORK BASKET.

Foundation, straw, covered over with rows of CROSS STITCH, worked in single Berlin wool; ornament to lid, pompons of wool and velvet leaves; ornament to base, a wide edging of HOLLOW SPOT CROCHET, worked in single Berlin wool, and pompon tassels.

No. 30. SQUARE IN GUIPURE D'ART FOR CHAIR BACK.

Foundation, a netted square; stitches used, POINT DE TOILE, POINT DE FESTON, POINT DE VENISE, RONE, and GUIPURE EN RELIEF.

No. 31. Monogram in Church Embroidery.

Used for ornamenting blotting book, sachet, or cushion. Letters worked with two shades of purse silk, and in Satin Stitch, outlined with gold thread Couched down; coronet worked with old gold and brown purse silks; jewels, with crimson and green purse silks; outlines, gold thread, Couched down.

No. 32. Stool, with Patchwork Cover.

Foundation, wicker; materials for patch-work, dark velvets and light satins, the latter embroidered with silk in Satin Stitch flowers.

No. 33. Wall Pocket.

Foundation, cardboard, covered with brocaded silk; flowers executed in Chenille embroidery, and finished with a satin bow. A silk cord and a second bow completes the pocket.

Plate XI.   541

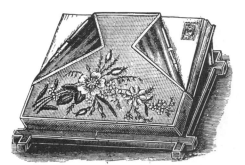

NO. 34. POSTCARD CASE.

Foundation of cover, white silk canvas; spray of flowers worked in ARRASENE EMBROIDERY.

NO. 35. HANDKERCHIEF CASE.

Foundation of satin, with corners finished by ribbon bows; centre square, BEADED NET EMBROIDERY, edged with a wide frill of lace.

NO. 36. KNITTING BAG.

Made with three oval-shaped pieces of rep silk, lined with cashmere of the same colour. Length of pieces, 11 inches; width at widest part, 5 inches. Flower design worked in SATIN STITCH EMBROIDERY.

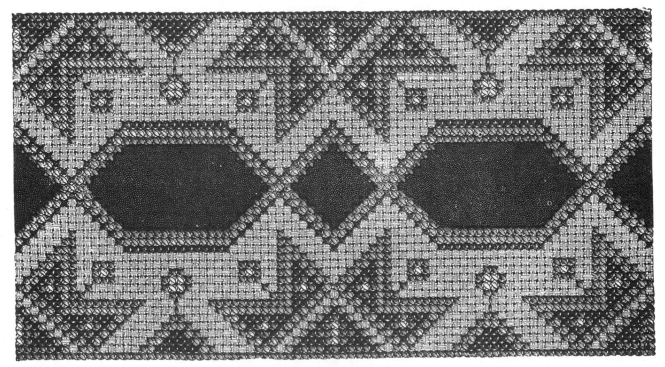

NO. 37. BORDER FOR TABLE CLOTH.

Foundation, Java canvas; dark centre, navy blue ribbon velvet, cut to pattern. Design worked in crewel wool, and in CROSS STITCH—the three darkest colours, shades of crimson; two lightest colours, sky blues.

Plate XII.

NO. 38. CUSHION IN BROCADE EMBROIDERY.

The design is stamped on the material; the fillings are worked with filoselles, in fancy stitches, and gold cord and silk cord COUCHED down round every outline. Size of Cushion, a square of 20 inches.

NO. 39. CHAIR BACK.

The centre and corners are of flowered silk, the border of plush, and the edging of coloured CRETE LACE. Length, 24 inches; width, 18 inches.

NO. 40. LAMP MAT.

Foundation, cloth; bands, of satin ribbon, embroidered with RUSSIAN EMBROIDERY; detached flowers, &c., worked in SATIN STITCH and CORAL STITCH.

Plate XIII.

543

NO. 41. WASTE PAPER BASKET.

Foundation, wicker; embroidery, stamped plush, outlined with silk cords.

NO. 42. CLOTH PENWIPER.

Foundation, dark blue cloth; feather-shaped ornaments, white plush, and soldiers' scarlet cloth. Ornaments decorated with spangles, beads, and CORAL STITCH, and attached to foundation with BUTTONHOLE STITCH. Leaf that hides the points of ornaments, a small brooch.

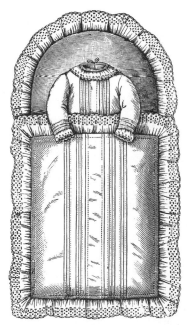

NO. 43. DOLL'S PILLOW.

These Pillows are imitations of the ones used in Switzerland for carrying young babies. The Pillow is stuffed, and placed in a white lawn case, trimmed with frillings of embroidery. An apron of the same material is buttoned over the lower part, and keeps the doll secure.

NO. 44. LINEN EMBROIDERY BORDER FOR SIDEBOARD CLOTH.

Foundation, coarse linen. Design executed with ingrain scarlet cotton, in CROSS STITCH.

Plate XIV.

NO. 45. DRAWN WORK AND LINEN EMBROIDERY BORDER TO TEA CLOTH.

Foundation, coarse linen; thick embroidery worked with linen thread in SATIN STITCH; open pattern and edging in DRAWN WORK.

NO. 46. SAXONY PILLOW LACE EDGING.

Worked with No. 50 thread, with CLOTH STITCH, HALF STITCH, and PLAITINGS.

Plate XV.

545

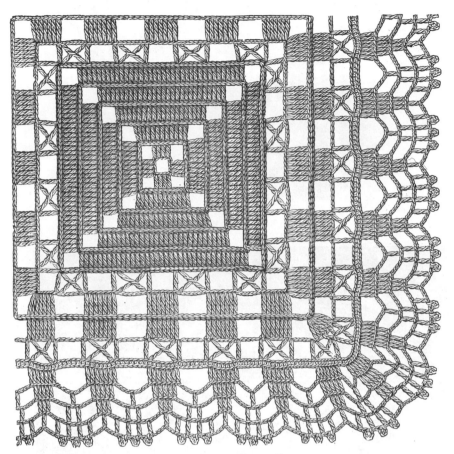

NO. 47. CROCHET CHEESE CLOTH.

Commence in the centre of cloth with 12 CHAIN, which join together; work 4 TREBLE and 8 CHAIN alternately, to form the centre square; work CHAIN, TREBLE, CROSS TREBLE, a TREBLE LONG, as indicated in pattern.

NO. 48. ORNAMENTAL MEAT SAFE, FOR TABLE USE.

The Safe is used to place over meat in the summer, when it is exposed for any length of time. Foundation, an ordinary wire cover, over which is arranged bands of red worsted braid, embroidered with RUSSIAN EMBROIDERY. The border is a broad strip of Russian canvas, worked in CROSS STITCH, with three shades of ingrain scarlet cotton.

NO. 49. WORK BASKET.

Foundation of wicker; trimming, wool pompons and wide Vandyked band of fancy cloth. A broad silk cord is COUCHED round the edges of the Vandykes, and the centre spaces of the cloth ornamented with CORAL STITCH.

546

No. 52. WALL PINCUSHION.

Foundation of stiff cardboard. Centre
Pincushion stuffed with wadding,
covered with navy blue silk, and
outlined with a cord of rose-
coloured purse silk. Feathers
worked in SATIN STITCH, with
navy blue purse silk.

No. 51. SERMON CASE IN CHURCH EMBROIDERY.

The IHS letters are worked in BASKET STITCH, and transferred to the silk foundation.
The emblems of the Four Evangelists are worked in OUTLINE STITCH on the silk
foundation; the dove, flowers, and leaves in SATIN STITCH. The silk foundation
is APPLIQUÉ to velvet; and the securing stitches are hidden with lines of thick
cord, COUCHED down.

Plate XVI.

No. 50. CROSS IN CHURCH EMBROIDERY
FOR STOLE.

Centre worked over padded cardboard, in SATIN
STITCH, with yellow purse silk, upon the material used for the Stole. The outline is a
thick gold cord, COUCHED to material with
fine yellow silk.

Plate. XVII.

547

No. 53. TOE OF SLIPPER WORKED IN
SILK EMBROIDERY.

Foundation of silk. Embroidery worked
with coloured filoselles, in SATIN
STITCH, ROPE STITCH, and FRENCH
KNOTS.

NO. 54. HAND BAG.

Foundation of cardboard; lining of plush. Embroidery worked upon white silk canvas, with Arrasene wools. Narrow ribbon, crossed with loops
of Arrasene, forms the centre bands, and a quilled
ribbon the edging.

NO. 55. FAN BEDROOM POCKET.

Foundation, Japanese Fan; lining and pocket, of cretonne or
figured sateen, trimmed with coloured worsted lace; ribbons
matching the colour of the lace.

NO. 56. WALL WATCHSTAND ORNA-
MENTED WITH APPLIQUÉ.

Foundation of millboard, covered with olive
green silk. Design cut out of dark
green plush, APPLIQUÉ to silk, and
finished with a pale blue silk cord
COUCHED round outlines An ornamental brass hook holds up the watch.

Plate XVIII.

No. 57. Roman Work Mantel Border.

Foundation, ecru linen, embroidered with ecru linen thread in Buttonhole Stitch and Buttonhole Bars, ornamented with Picots. Material cut away behind the bars.

No. 58. Lace and Embroidered Curtain.

Foundation, a bought muslin and lace Curtain. Embroidery executed in Satin Stitch, with Arrasene or coloured filoselles, on the plain squares and strips of muslin.

Plate XIX. 549

NO. 59. CANE CHAIR.

Stuffed seat of Chair covered with velvet brocade, and worked in BROCADE EMBROIDERY.

NO. 60. AMERICAN CHAIR.

The coarse canvas covering of Chair is ornamented with CREWEL WORK, executed with double crewel wools.

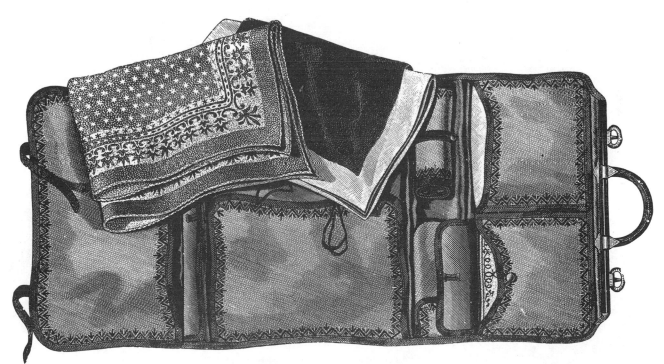

NO. 61. TRAVELLING CASE FOR WRAPS AND BED LINEN.

Foundation of strong leather; lining of brown holland, ornamented with embroidery stitches worked in ingrain scarlet cotton. The pockets are made large enough to hold sheets, pillow cases, rugs, and night gear. The small rolls contain brushes and combs, and washing appliances. The Case is fastened together, when rolled up, with railway rug straps.

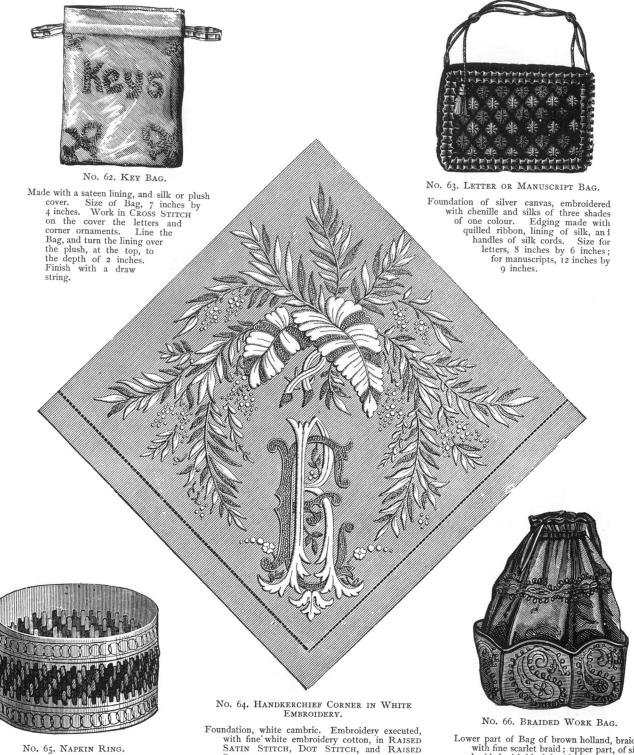

NO. 62. KEY BAG.

Made with a sateen lining, and silk or plush cover. Size of Bag, 7 inches by 4 inches. Work in CROSS STITCH on the cover the letters and corner ornaments. Line the Bag, and turn the lining over the plush, at the top, to the depth of 2 inches. Finish with a draw string.

NO. 63. LETTER OR MANUSCRIPT BAG.

Foundation of silver canvas, embroidered with chenille and silks of three shades of one colour. Edging made with quilled ribbon, lining of silk, and handles of silk cords. Size for letters, 8 inches by 6 inches; for manuscripts, 12 inches by 9 inches.

NO. 65. NAPKIN RING.

Foundation of silver canvas. Embroidery worked in LONG STITCH, with single Berlin wool of two shades of crimson or old gold.

NO. 64. HANDKERCHIEF CORNER IN WHITE EMBROIDERY.

Foundation, white cambric. Embroidery executed, with fine white embroidery cotton, in RAISED SATIN STITCH, DOT STITCH, and RAISED OVERCAST.

NO. 66. BRAIDED WORK BAG.

Lower part of Bag of brown holland, braided with fine scarlet braid; upper part, of silk, braided with black braid. Bottom of Bag, or foundation, a round of cardboard, 9 inches in diameter, to which both the brown holland outer covering and lining are attached. Between each scallop the holland is stitched to the silk lining, and forms pockets.

Plate XXI.

No. 68. Detail of Hanging Basket.

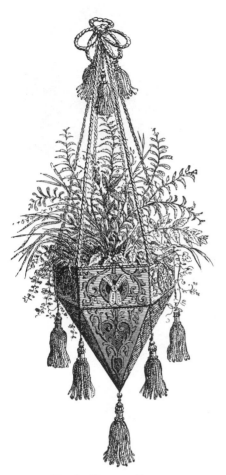

No. 67. Hanging Basket.

No. 69. Detail of Hanging Basket.

No. 70. Owl Pincushion.

Size of Pincushion, a square of 4 inches. Materials, white cricketing flannel and two glass eyes, for the owl; plush, satin, and silk cord for the Cushion. Cut out two squares of cardboard, cover with plush; arrange the owl's head on a brown velvet oval, and sew to card board. Make a Cushion with wadding, cover it with satin, sew it between the two squares, and hide the stitches with the silk cord.

Foundation of millboard. APPLIQUÉ embroidery shown in No. 68 and No. 69 half its natural size. Three shades of satin material are required for the appliqué, the middle shade being used for the foundation colour, the darkest and lightest for the design. The white centre ornament is cut out of white, or amber velvet. The design is COUCHED to the foundation with thick silk cords. Ornamental cords and tassels finish the Basket. A tin liner holds the water, or earth, if real plants are arranged in it; but dried grasses and imitation fern leaves are usually employed.

NO. 71. BOX JEWEL CASE.

Foundation, a bon-bon box. The lid is raised with wadding, and covered with chestnut-coloured satin, an embroidered square of BULGARIAN EMBROIDERY, edged with lace, being laid over the satin. A puffing of the satin conceals the lower part of Box; a row of thread lace and lines of silk cord finishes the ornamentation. The inside of the Jewel Box is lined with quilted satin.

NO. 72. COVER FOR INFANT'S BASKET.

The Cover is made by joining together, alternately, squares of GUIPURE D'ART and Mummy cloth. The latter is finished by OUTLINE EMBROI-DERY, in two shades of filoselles.

NO. 73. TREE PENWIPER.

Foundation, rounds of scarlet and black cloth, forming Penwiper. Tree made of ten chicken's feathers, fastened to fine wires that form its stem, and that are hidden by brown wool being wound round them. Figure, a dressed wooden doll.

NO. 74. PORTFOLIO FOR DRAWING-ROOM.

Foundation, of black bamboo, lined with rep silk. Ornament, a double vallance of cloth, with vandyked edges. The upper vallance is of crimson cloth, and is ornamented with PICOTS in blue filoselle, FRENCH KNOTS in gold filoselle, and green stars in RAILWAY STITCH. The under vallance is ornamented with large FRENCH KNOTS, made of gold filoselle.

NO. 75. WORK BASKET.

Foundation, black cane picked out with gold. Sides and lid filled in with Java canvas, embroidered in coloured SILK EMBROI-DERY. Colours used, those of the natural leaves and flowers.

Plate XXIII. 553

No. 76. Detail of Oblong Antimacassar.

No. 77. Oblong Antimacassar.

Foundation of grey Toile Colbert. Dragon border worked in Cross Stitch, in black and red purse silk. Drawn Work is used for centre of Antimacassar, and as a bordering. Grey thread lace is sewn on as an edging. Pattern shown in working size in No. 76.

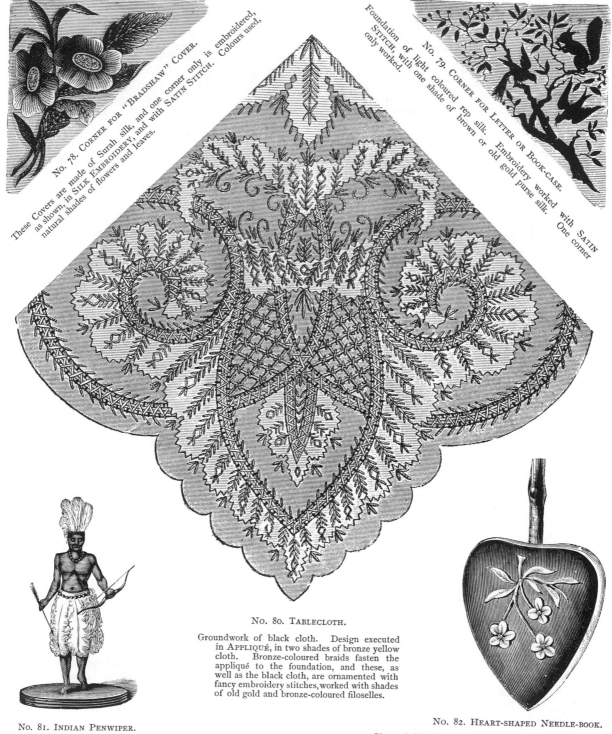

No. 78. Corner for "Bradshaw" Cover.

These Covers are made of Surah silk, and one corner only is embroidered, as shown, in Silk Embroidery, and with Satin Stitch. Colours used, natural shades of flowers and leaves.

No. 79. Corner for Letter or Book-case.

Foundation of light coloured rep silk. Embroidery worked with Satin Stitch, with one shade of brown or old gold purse silk. One corner only worked.

No. 80. Tablecloth.

Groundwork of black cloth. Design executed in Appliqué, in two shades of bronze yellow cloth. Bronze-coloured braids fasten the appliqué to the foundation, and these, as well as the black cloth, are ornamented with fancy embroidery stitches, worked with shades of old gold and bronze-coloured filoselles.

No. 81. Indian Penwiper.

Figure made of cork, strengthened with wire, and covered with fine black cloth. Head ornaments and dress made of white chicken's feathers; bow and arrow, of wire, covered with purse silk; Penwiper, of black and scarlet ovals of cloth and silk.

No. 82. Heart-shaped Needle-book.

Size of Needle-book, one-third larger than woodcut. Handle of bamboo. Case made of two pieces of cardboard, and covered with blue satin, embroidered with Silk Embroidery. Line and quilt the inside of the two pieces; also cut out, in the same shape, two pieces of white flannel, and sew the four pieces together at the point of the fan. Secure the top part of Needle-case with a button and buttonhole.

Plate XXV.

555

No. 83. Detail of Teacloth.

No. 84. Teacloth.

Foundation, ecru linen.   Embroidery executed in Back Stitch, with ingrain fine scarlet cotton.   Full size of cup and saucer shown in No. 83.

Plate XXVI.

NO. 86. HAND SCREEN.

NO. 85. CACHE POT.

Foundation, black wicker. Lining, of coloured velvet or silk. Ornament, MACRAMÉ LACE.

NO. 87. WATCH STAND.

Foundation of wicker, lined with dark green velvet. Ornament, SILK EMBROIDERY, worked in SATIN STITCH, with shades of pale blue filoselle.

NO. 88. DETAIL OF HAND SCREEN.

Framework of black cane. Embroidery executed, on white silk canvas, in SATIN and RAILWAY STITCH; flowers in shades of forget-me-not blues; leaves in dull greens, lightened by veinings of light green. Pale blue silk cords, ending in tassels of the same shade, are wound round the framework.

Plate XXVII.

557

NO. 89. MODERN POINT LACE FOR DRESS
TRIMMINGS.

Plain braid and Honiton braid, of écru colours, are
required, and lace cotton of the same shade. The
only stitches are WHEELS and BARS.

NO. 90. CIGAR CASE.

Foundation of satin or kid. Flowers worked in SILK
EMBROIDERY, in natural colours. Centre, white velvet, APPLIQUÉ to satin, and COUCHED down with
lines of silk cord. Pattern filled in with FRENCH
KNOTS, worked with dark purse silk.

NO. 91. EMBROIDERED BAND FOR
TEA GOWN.

Foundation, pale blue cashmere. Embroidery worked with crewel wools
of a deeper blue shade, in SATIN
and FEATHER STITCHES, with
BACK STITCH in white silk in the
centre of the curved line.

NO. 92. MODERN POINT LACE BORDER FOR HANDKERCHIEF.

One width of fine lace braid, and lace cotton, required. Stitches used, POINT DE BRUXELLES,
POINT DE VENISE, POINT DE SORRENTO, POINT DE FILLET, and WHEELS. Foundation made with twisted BARS.

No. 93. Imitation Japanese Embroidery for Glove Sachet.

Foundation of black satin. Flowers and leaves worked in Satin
Stitch and French Knot, and with purse silk. Colour
of flowers, old gold; of leaves and stem, shades
of bronze brown.

No. 94. Necktie End.

Foundation, Toile Colbert. Flowers worked in filoselles matching their natural colours. Feather Stitch border in red silk.
Stitches used, Feather, Satin, Railway, and Crewel. A lace braid, ornamented with Wheels, finishes the Necktie.

Plate XXIX.

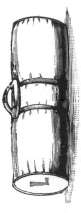

No. 95. Umbrella Case.

Made of brown holland, bound with mohair braid, and ornamented with BRAIDING. Size of bottom strip of holland: 34 inches long, 5 inches wide at the top, and 4 inches wide at the bottom. Cut handle out of this strip. Size of top strip of holland: 28 inches long, 6 inches wide at the top, and 5 inches wide at the bottom. Embroider this strip, bind it to the bottom strip, and arrange draw strings at the top and bottom to hold in the Umbrella.

No. 96. Purse Bag.

Foundation, 1 yard of 2¼-inch wide brown plush. Fold this the long way, and sew together, leaving an opening for the hand. Line the Bag with sateen; ornament with pompons, rings, and a ribbon bow.

No. 97. Bolster Case for Railway Wraps.

Made of brown holland, bound with blue braid. Strip of holland, 23 inches long, 36 inches in circumference. Rounds at each end, 10 inches in diameter. A railway strap keeps the Case tight.

No. 98. Glove Box Cover (Full Size).

Foundation, fine cloth or strong satin. Leaves, flowers, and bird, raised with wadding before embroidered. The bird is worked, in CHAIN STITCH, with shades of brown purse silk; the flowers in SATIN STITCH, with crimson and white purse silk; the leaves, in the same stitch, and in shades of olive greens. CHAIN STITCH, FEATHER STITCH, ROPE STITCH, SATIN and FRENCH KNOTS, are used for the flat embroidery.

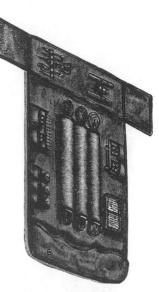

NO. 99. QUEEN ANNE HAND BAG.

Width of Bag, 16 inches; length, 18 inches. Outer cover of plush, lining of pale satin. Silk cord and pompons for ornaments. A yard of each material required, and 3 yards of cord.

NO. 100. GIRL'S CHATELAINE.

The pocket is of blue linen, sewn to a small apron of red twill, on which the name is embroidered in CREWEL STITCH. Blue cords suspend the needle-book, pincushion and scissors, and a blue linen band fastens all to the waist.

NO. 101. HOUSEWIFE.

Foundation, Java canvas, lined with coloured flannel. A piece of stiff muslin is placed between the two materials. The pockets are made with flannel; also the cross-pieces to hold the implements. Size of Housewife, 16 inches long by 8 inches wide. The case is bound with ribbon, and rolled up and secured by a button and buttonhole when not in use.

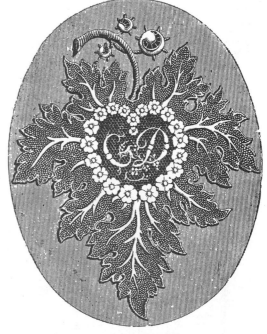

NO. 102. FOOT WARMER.

The Figure shows front flap of a bag Foot Warmer, ornamented with Appliqué. Size of flap, 15 inches long by 13 inches wide. Foundation material, black cloth. Head of roebuck, ecru coloured satin, either painted in oils or embroidered with silks. Oval round head, light grey cloth; framing, dark grey cloth; scroll work, ecru satin. All the appliqué is surrounded with a silk cord of old gold shade, and the embroidery stitches executed with the same coloured purse silk.

NO. 103. CORNER FOR HANDKERCHIEF.

Foundation of cambric, embroidered with white embroidery cotton, in DOT STITCH, SATIN, ROPE and WHEEL, in White Embroidery.

Plate XXXI.

561

NO. 104. ORIENTAL EMBROIDERY FOR CHAIR BACKS.

Foundation of Mummy cloth. Centres of patterns filled in with CROSS STITCH, worked with oriental silks. Gold thread COUCHED round patterns to form the outline, and silver tinsel used for the SATIN STITCH covered spaces.

NO. 105. BAND OF TOILE COLBERT FOR DRESS TRIMMING.

Foundation, Toile Colbert. Embroidery executed with single Berlin wool. Lengths of wool are laid across and down material, and are secured with SATIN STITCH, FEATHER STITCH, and VANDYKES.

NO. 106. WALLACHIAN APRON.

Foundation, black serge or bège. Embroidery executed in double crewels. Stitches used, LONG, BATTLEMENTED, and VANDYKE. Colours: black to outline the large diamonds; two shades of blue and two of brown for the centres; two shades of olive green and two of old gold for the wide bordering.

NO. 107. DETAIL OF WORK BASKET.

Foundation of wicker. Lining of coarse diaper linen, with pattern picked out with SATIN STITCH; work with blue or scarlet ingrain cotton as shown in detail in No. 107.

NO. 108. WORK BASKET.

NO. 109. "JULIETTE," IN CUNEIFORM LETTERS, FOR HANDKERCHIEF.

Foundation of cambric. Embroidery executed in SATIN STITCH, with white embroidery cotton.

NO. 110. "MARY," IN CUNEIFORM LETTERS.

Worked as No. 109.

NO. 111. DETAIL OF FOOTSTOOL.

Foundation, a horsehair Cushion, covered with black satin that is gathered into a knot in the centre of each side. Top of Footstool, alternate squares of dark and light oatmeal cloth, embroidered with filoselles or single Berlin wool, in FEATHER STITCH and COUCHING, as shown in detail in No. 111.

NO. 112. FOOTSTOOL OR CUSHION.

Plate XXXIII.

563

NO. 113. NARROW VALLANCE FOR BOOKSHELVES.

Foundation, invisible green cloth; thick cord made with old gold worsted cord; embroidery stitches,
FEATHER, RAILWAY, and STAR, worked in three shades of purple, with crewel wools.

NO. 114. CHILD'S SLIPPER.

Foundation, garnet cloth. Embroidery executed with garnet-coloured filoselle a
shade da:ker than the cloth. Stitches
used, POINT RUSSE for the flower sprays,
and SATIN for the bird. A single flower
spray is taken along the back part of the
slipper to complete the embroidery.

NO. 115. LAMP SHADE.

Foundation of cardboard; ovals of white muslin, embroidered in SILK EMBROIDERY.

NO. 116. FOOTSTOOL.

Foundation of wood, covered at the sides with
cloth, across the top with PERFORATED
CLOTH. Work the latter in CROSS STITCH,
with single Berlin wools.

NO. 117. BABY'S BIB.

Foundation, white piqué, embroidered in
WHITE EMBROIDERY; edging of the
same.

NO. 118. TENNIS SHOE POCKET.

Made of brown holland, braided
with fine red braid. A leather
band fastens the Pocket round
the waist, and a shoe is placed
in each division of the bag.

NO. 120. KEY BASKET.

Foundation of wicker. Bands across of maroon plush,
braided with a twisted silk cord of mixed old gold
and brown colours. The design is given in detail in
No. 121. Vandyke the edges of the bands, and sew
down these points to the Basket, covering the stitches
with a line of cord,

NO. 119. SATCHEL FOR PRAYER
BOOKS.

Materials used, black satin and ruby
silk; cut these to cover the
prayer book, with an overlapping
flap, and cut two side pieces.
Stitch these together, the ruby
silk as the lining. Embroider
the initials of owner on the flap,
and fasten loops and bows, of
black and ruby-coloured ribbons,
as a finish to the Satchel.

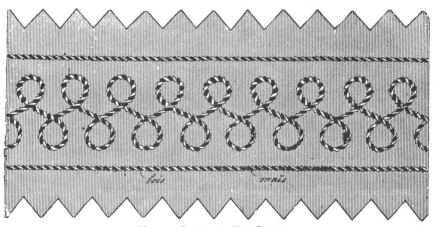

NO. 121. DETAIL OF KEY BASKET.

Plate XXXV.

565

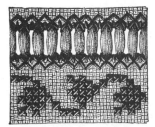

No. 122. Embroidered D'Oyley Border.

Foundation, well-woven linen; Border of Drawn Work, with Cross Stitch pattern, worked with crewel wools, above the Border.

No. 123. Border for Dressing Gown.

Foundation, white cambric, on which is laid Honiton lace braid. Herringbone, Satin Stitch, and Chain Stitch embroidery, in white cotton, finish the Border.

No. 124. Tablecloth.

Centre of grey cloth. Bordering of navy blue cloth. The joining stitches are concealed with a narrow braid of pale blue laid over them. Embroidery executed in single Berlin wool or undivided filoselles. Stitches employed, Couching, Satin, Double Cross, Feather, and French Knots.

No. 125. Embroidered Button.

Foundation of silk, laid over a flat button. Embroidery in filoselles of natural shades, in Satin Stitch.

No. 126. Embroidered Button.

A large flat Button forms the foundation; this is covered with velvet, and worked with a star made with Railway Stitch, and of old gold-coloured filoselle.

Plate XXXVI.

No. 127. Lamp Mat.

Foundation, maroon coloured cloth. Design executed with fancy braid, appliqué, and narrow silk and gold cords.   To work: Arrange pieces of dark maroon coloured plush and cream coloured plush on the parts worked in Appliqué, and Couch round their outlines with gold cord. Stitch on the fancy braid, and couch down on each side of it silk cord.

Plate XXXVII.

567

No. 128. Linen and Crochet D'Oyley.

Foundation, a good piece of Irish linen. A square piece is cut out of this in its centre, and the edges carefully HEMMED. To fill in this open space, use a fine CROCHET HOOK and fine crochet cotton. For the first row, work 1 TREBLE, 2 CHAIN, alternately, and fasten off; for the middle, make the rounds separately, and attach them together with the loops. Work 16 SINGLE CROCHET into a small loop; make a loop of 3 CHAIN, and attach it to the centre round; work 5 chain, and attach to one of the outside rows of TREBLES 5 chain, and attach to the centre round. Repeat the 3 chain and the long loop, working the latter either into the outside line of Trebles, or into another set of rounds, as shown on the Design. For the edging, HEM the linen, and work beyond it a row of 3 treble and 2 chain.

No. 129. Richelieu Guipure Trimming for Mantel Border.

Foundation, Toilé Colbert. Embroidery, in OVERCAST, raised SATIN STITCH, and ornamental BARS. To work: Trace the design upon the foundation, and work the bars that join it together and the TWISTED BARS that ornament the centres of the pattern. Where the broad lines are shown, work in raised Satin Stitch; for the rest of the outline, in OVERCAST. Finish the edging with a bought lace edge.

NO. 130. NEEDLE CASE.

Make the Needle Case foundation with visiting cards, covered with olive green satin, with an embroidered centre of white silk. Work the embroidery with coloured filoselles, as shown in Detail *A*, and in SATIN STITCH. Scarlet flannel, cut into leaves, and finished with a vandyke edge, forms the Needle Book, and a bodkin attached to a narrow green ribbon is used to fasten the Case together.

NO. 131. DETAIL *A* OF NEEDLE CASE.

NO. 132. ORIENTAL EMBROIDERY FOR CHAIR COVER.

The foundation of the Chair Cover is crimson plush, which is cut to size, and finished with silk cords and tassels. The embroidery shown in Detail *A* is worked upon coarse Indian muslin, with Oriental silks and gold tinsel. The parts printed dark are worked with navy blue silk, and the centres of the ornaments with crimson silk; the lines of tinsel are printed nearly white. The stitches used for the centres are RUNNINGS. To work: Take one line across the work, another perpendicularly, and two diagonally, from right to left, and from left to right. The outline is HEM STITCH, with CREWEL and SATIN STITCHES where shown in the Detail. The embroidery when completed is BUTTONHOLED to the plush foundation.

NO. 133. DETAIL *A* OF ORIENTAL EMBROIDERY.

Plate XXXIX.   569

NO. 134. EMBROIDERED BORDER FOR CHILDREN'S
FLANNEL UNDERGARMENTS.

The embroidery is executed on red flannel, with white silk.
Stitches used : DOUBLE CORAL, HERRINGBONE, RAIL-
WAY, BUTTONHOLE, and SATIN.

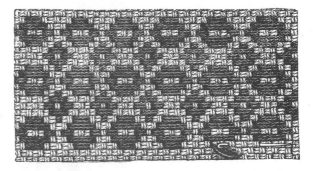

NO. 135. EMBROIDERED GALLOON BRAID FOR CHILDREN'S
DRESS TRIMMINGS.

The Galloon Braid is either scarlet or blue, and the embroidery
is worked in SATIN STITCH, with crewel wool of a darker
shade, but of the same colour as the braid.

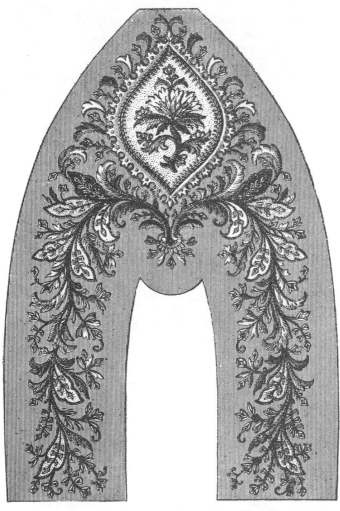

NO. 136. SLIPPERS WORKED WITH APPLIQUÉ AND SILK EMBROIDERY.

Material for foundation, thin scarlet coloured felt. Centre ornament of Slipper and light leaves, APPLIQUÉ of fine white
cricketing flannel ; shaded leaves, Appliqué of dark blue flannel. Embroidery worked in SATIN STITCH and
BUTTONHOLE, in shades of blue Oriental silks. To work : Lay the Appliqués on the felt, and secure them
with Buttonhole and couched lines of braid. Work the centres with filoselles, in natural shades, in Satin Stitch,
and the rest of the work in Satin Stitch.

Plate XL.

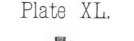

No. 137. Detail *A* of Pincushion (No. 139).

No. 138. Wall Tidy.

Made with plush and coloured embroidery. Cut out two pieces of plush, one for the back, and the second for the pocket, to shape. Sew the back to a foundation of cardboard, and line the plush pocket with cashmere. Make up the pocket, and finish by sewing round it the coloured embroidery, which is bought ready embroidered.

No. 139. Pincushion.

Foundation of Cushion, two shades of blue cloth, and satin ribbon matching the lightest shade. To work : Make a round Cushion with a linen cover; cut out the size of the top in dark blue cloth, and a long strip, 2in. wide, in the lighter cloth; vandyke this strip into eleven vandykes, and tack it round the edge of the dark material. Embroider with Oriental silks; work the centre flower (a cornflower) in Raised Satin Stitch, finishing the calyx with cross lines of a darker shade of blue. Work the stem and tendrils in Crewel Stitch with old gold coloured silk. Embroider the vandykes with sprays in Coral Stitch and old gold silk, and the buds with Raised Satin Stitch and two shades of blue silk. Before adjusting the embroidery to the Cushion, surround the base of the latter with two full pleatings of satin ribbon.

No. 140. Knitting Bag.

Foundation of watered silk, embroidered with wild roses, worked in Crewel Stitch with coloured filoselles. To work : Cut out two pieces of silk in the shape given; sew them together where the bow of ribbon is, and round the bottom, but leave the sides open. Embroider the roses with crewel stitch, line the Bag, put a silk cord round it, and finish with a ribbon bow. The Bag is carried, by the arm being passed through the side openings.

Plate XLI.

571

NO. 141. GLOVE CASE.

NO. 142. HAND BAG.

Worked upon white silk, in a Japanese design, with Oriental silks of three shades of blue and two shades of crimson. To work: Sketch the design on the background, and work it in SATIN STITCH and HEM STITCH; outline the whole pattern, and work the tendrils and sprays with a cord COUCHED to the surface. Make this cord, as shown, with two strands of silk; Overcast with a different coloured silk. Work with crimson silk in the centres of pattern, and with the blue shades for the borders, sprays, and tendrils.

Made with two different coloured silks—navy blue for the outside of the Bag, and crimson for the lining—and a cord matching the two colours. To work: Cut out the shape in the navy blue silk and crimson, join at the seams, and embroider the first-named with a spray of mountain ash leaves and berries, worked in CREWEL STITCH, and with filoselles. Make up the Bag, and cover the seams with the silk cord.

NO. 143. WALL BASKET.

Made of stiff cardboard, quilted blue satin, dark blue silk, embroidered with filoselles and broad silk cord. To work: Cut out the shape in cardboard, and sew the two pieces together; line the inside with quilted satin. Work the design, in CREWEL STITCH, on the silk, in natural colours, sew it to the front of the Basket, and finish with the silk cord.

NO. 144. SHOE BAG.

Made of brown holland, fine scarlet washing braid, and scarlet worsted braid. To work: Cut the back and pocket out of brown holland, BRAID them with the fine braid, sew together, and hide the edges with box-pleated worsted braid.

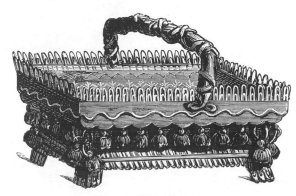

NO. 145. WORK BASKET.

Foundation of wicker, with trimmings of purple cloth, purple worsted tassels, and fine white braid. To work: BRAID the cloth that forms the lining with the fine white braid. For the outside, cut the cloth in scallops, PLAIT the braid together, and sew it on as a curved line; sew on the tassels, and wind the plaited braid round the handles.

NO. 146. THE LUCKY BRACKET.

Made with a large horseshoe, a triangular wooden Bracket, plush, lace, and ribbon. To make: Cover the Bracket with the plush, and trim it with the lace. Bore two holes through the points of the horseshoe, and paint it in oil colours with a flower design. Screw the shoe to the Bracket, and suspend to the wall with ribbon, which pass through the nail holes in the top of the horseshoe to secure it.

NO. 147. DETAIL OF COUVREPIED.

NO. 148. CARDINAL'S HAT FLOWER BASKET.

Made of a low cake tin, strong cardboard, Turkey red twill, worsted cords, and picture wire. To make: Solder four small rings to the top of the cake tin; cover the tin with Turkey red twill; make a wide hat brim of cardboard, cover that with Turkey twill, and secure it to the top of the cake tin. Form the cardinal's lappets with worsted cord; make them each 2 feet long, and finish with small balls of scarlet wool, connected together with CROCHET CHAIN STITCH. Hang up the Hat with the picture wire, run through the small rings.

NO. 149. KNITTING NEEDLE CASE.

Formed of dark blue kid-chamois leather and blue ribbon. Cut a piece of kid, 11 inches by 9 inches, fold it in half, and round off the edges; unfold the kid, line it with chamois leather, and bind it round with narrow ribbon. Make the divisions for the needles with narrow ribbon, and embroider the numerals on them. Fold over the flaps, roll up the Case, and tie it round with ribbon.

NO. 150. COUVREPIED.

Made of five strips of scarlet blanket flannel, joined together with open CROCHET, worked with maroon-coloured wool. Flower design on strips, shown in detail at No. 147, worked, with double crewels, in RAILWAY and FEATHER STITCHES, in natural colours.

NO. 151. BANNER-FRONTED BRACKET.

The ledge of the Bracket is of wood, covered with plush or cloth, and finished with a cord and bow of ribbon. From the back of the ledge falls the banner, on which is embroidered the initials of the owner's name, and a small spray of flowers, worked in SATIN STITCH, and in natural shades of colour.

Plate XLIII.   573

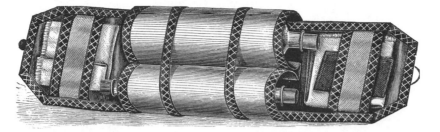

No. 152. Travelling Case for Medicines.

Made of Toile ciré, flannel, and red braid. Cut the Toile ciré in the form of a square cross. Line this cross with flannel, and bind it with worsted braid, which ornament with HERRINGBONE STITCH. Turn the top and bottom limb of the cross over the centre part, and sew them down. These form the two Cases for the bottles, which should be of a size to fit them tightly. Make loops of braid across the side arms, to hold lint and plaister, and finish with two bands of braid across the bottle pockets, and with a loop and buttonhole to secure the side flaps, which turn up over the bottles.

No. 153. Drawing-room Tablecloth.

Foundation of crimson felt or fine blue cloth, on which are stitched yellow silk braid, or gold braid, to form the straight lines of the design and the vandyked lines of the centre. The dark pieces of the centre are APPLIQUÉ of blue or crimson plush. To work: COUCH thick cord round the outlines of the whole pattern, and ornament the design with HERRINGBONE, SATIN, FEATHER, and RAILWAY STITCHES. Work with FRENCH KNOTS and POINT DE POIS where indicated; use several shades, but only one colour, of Oriental silks, for the stitches.

Plate XLIV.

No. 154. Bamboo Key Rack.

The Rack is bought at a basket maker's, and the centre part filled with SATIN STITCH embroidery, worked in natural shades of colour, upon white or black satin.

No. 155. Detail *A* of Bamboo Key Rack.

This Detail shows an enlarged pattern of the work on Key Rack. To work: Use three shades of crimson for the rose and rose buds, three shades of yellow for the carnation, shades of yellow and purple for the pansies, and blue for the nemophila.

No. 156. White Embroidery for Table Linen.

The foundation is of fine damask. The embroidery is executed, in SATIN STITCH and RAISED SATIN STITCH, with linen thread.

Plate XLV.

575

No. 157. Renaissance Embroidery for a Small Cosey.

Foundation material, an olive green cashmere, on which are Appliqué rounds of deep green plush and half-circles of a lighter shade of plush. Embroidery in Satin, Overcast, Buttonhole, Point de Pois, Coral, Point Lancé, and Cord Stitch. To work: Buttonhole round the outlines of the design with dark green purse silk, and fill in the centres with the above stitches, which work with sky blue, old gold, and deep maroon colour purse silks.

NO. 158. PATCHWORK CUSHION—CENTRE.

Worked with squares of grey and crimson silk, and embroidered with old gold and crimson filoselle. To
work : OVERCAST the squares together, and COUCH a
fine gold cord round them. Work the stars at each
corner with SATIN and RAILWAY STITCHES, partly
in old gold filoselle, and partly in crimson filoselle.

NO. 159. PATCHWORK CUSHION—BORDER.

For the Border, use the same coloured filoselles and silk as for
the Centre, but cut the latter into strips, not squares, and
embroider these lines as shown in the design.

NO. 160. BAG FOR HOLDING SILKS AND FILOSELLES.

Foundation of Bag, blue rep silk, lined with Persian silk, and finished with a cord. Embroidery in HERRINGBONE,
SATIN, ROPE, and FRENCH KNOTS. To work : Trace the outline, and fill the centres, with very close Herringbone,
worked with crimson Oriental silk ; surround the outline with ROPE STITCH, worked in the same coloured silk.
Work the initials and the rest of the embroidery in dark blue silks, and with Satin Stitch and French Knots.

NO. 161. SHOULDER CUSHION.

Size : 24in. in length, 22in. in circumference. Made of grey Java
canvas, embroidered with red and gold filoselle, and ornamented with DRAWN WORK. To make : Cut the canvas
on the cross, draw out 28 threads for the Drawn Work,
and leave 28 threads for the stripes between the Drawn
work. Plait the drawn threads together in the centre, and
work in CROSS STITCH on the stripes.

NO. 162. NEEDLE CASE.

Formed of a square of Java canvas, lined with blue silk,
bound with blue ribbon, and worked in CROSS
STITCH with blue filoselle. For the needles, cut
four squares of scarlet flannel, work them round
with BUTTONHOLE STITCH, and sew inside the
Case.

Plate XLVII.   577

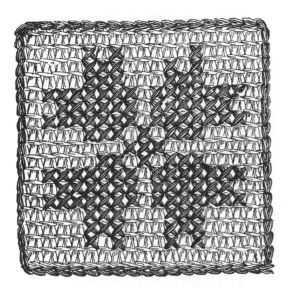

No. 163. SQUARE FOR COUVREPIED.

The Square is worked in IDIOT STITCH, with single Berlin wool, and when finished is ornamented with CROSS STITCHES, worked with single Berlin wool of a darker shade. To work: Make a CHAIN of 20 stitches, and work in Idiot Stitch until a Square is made. Embroider as shown. A number of such Squares are required for the Couvrepied. They are made of two colours, such as crimson and black, blue and green, or yellow and black.

No. 164. BORDER FOR TEACLOTH.

The material used for the Cloth is German canvas, ornamented with DRAWN WORK and CROSS STITCH, worked with ingrain red cotton. To work the Drawn Work: Draw out the threads in squares, as shown on the design, and OVERCAST each line separately. Overcast the edges of the Drawn Work, and work the pattern in Cross Stitch.

No. 165. ROUMANIAN EMBROIDERY.

The foundation is scarlet or bright blue or black cashmere. The pattern is cut out in pale blue or pale green cashmere, tacked to the foundation, and BUTTONHOLED round with silk of the same colour as the pattern. Fancy stitches, such as RAILWAY, CHAIN, and SATIN, finish the ornamentation.

No. 166. RIC RACK EMBROIDERY INSERTION FOR CHILDREN'S DRESSES.

White crochet cotton and white Mignardise braid are required. To work: Form the braid into vandyked lines, with connecting lines of CHAIN STITCH in the centre. Between the vandyked lines of braid, work 1 TREBLE CROCHET, and 5 CHAIN, to form a loop, five times into one point as shown, and connect the work with the lines of plain braid that form the edgings, with Chain Stitch.

NO. 167. FURNITURE LACE FOR MANTEL OR TABLE BORDER.

Materials required : Ecru braid of two widths, and ecru-coloured thread. The braid should be that woven with a picot edge. To work : Tack the braid to a foundation in vandyke lines, OVERCAST it well together at the points, and make the BARS and ornamental WHEELS. Untack the braid from the foundation, and use the lace as an edging.

NO. 168. DRUM WORK-BASKET.   NO. 169. CROSS STITCH PATTERN FOR DRUM WORK-BASKET.

Foundation of Basket, a round of millboard 5 inches in width, and a handle of the same, 8 inches long, and 2½ inches wide. The lining is of dark purple or blue Surah silk, and is sewn to the millboard, and gathered with draw strings at each side. To work : Cut out the size of the millboard in Java canvas, embroider the wide strip with the pattern shown in detail in No. 169, and take the edging of the pattern only to work on the handle. Work in CROSS STITCH, and with coloured filoselles. Bind the Java canvas to the millboard with ribbon, and make up the ribbon bows, and place them at the ends of the handle. Use a handsome silk cord for the draw strings.

Plate XLIX.

579

NO. 170. HANDKERCHIEF SACHET.

Made of a Liberty's Oriental handkerchief, lined with Surah silk, and trimmed with ribbon. To make: Cut the handkerchief to shape, line it, and bind it with ribbon. Embroider the design with SATIN STITCH, make ruches and bows of ribbon, and sew them on to the Sachet.

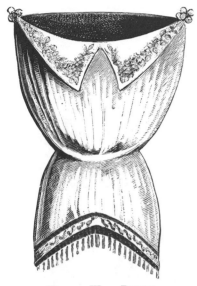

NO. 171. WALL POCKET.

Foundation, a stiff cardboard back, covered with plain velvet, 12 inches square, with the lower corners rounded off. For the Bag, take a piece of satin or brocaded silk, 20 inches wide and 24 inches long, and ornament one edge with a strip of BULGARIAN EMBROIDERY and a ball fringe. Cut the upper edge of the satin down the centre for 5 inches, turn the two points over, stiffen them with buckram, and trim with Bulgarian embroidery. Make up the Pocket by gathering the satin 6 inches from the bottom edge, and sewing it to the lower edge of the cardboard. Line the satin, sew it to the cardboard back, and finish with ribbon bows.

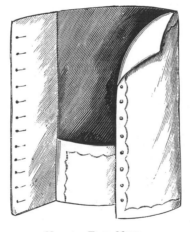

NO. 172. FOOT MUFF.

Made of crimson baize, 4 feet by 3 feet 6 inches, and grey baize 2 inches larger every way. To make: Fold the crimson baize in half the short way, and cut out from one end the two corners, measuring a square of 12 inches. Lay the two coloured baizes together, the grey undermost. Fold the grey baize over the crimson, to the depth of 2 inches, all round. Scallop the grey edges, and BUTTONHOLE them to the crimson baize. Turn up the flap left where the squares have been cut out, and form with it the pocket for the feet. Finish with wooden buttons and silk buttonholes. When the feet are in the Muff, it is buttoned to the knees of the wearer.

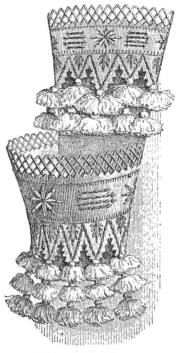

NO. 173. VIDE POCHE.

Foundation, a small wicker basket. Embroidery worked on bands of soldier's scarlet cloth. To work: Cut out the bands, and vandyke their edges. Work the stars, in pale blue Berlin wool, in RAILWAY STITCH, and the rest, with deep carnation-coloured purse silks, in BACK and FEATHER STITCHES. Make the tassels of the wool and silk combined, and BUTTONHOLE the bands to the foundation.

No. 175. SQUARE FOR COT QUILT.

The foundation is worked in CROCHET TUNISIAN with white Saxony wool, the design in pink or blue single Berlin wool, and with CREWEL STITCH. To work: CAST on 18 stitches, and work 18 rows in IDIOT STITCH. Border this square with a row of SINGLE CROCHET, worked with the coloured wool. Use the same coloured wool to form the flowers and leaves, and finish the flower centres with FRENCH KNOTS.

No. 174. WALL POCKET FOR LETTERS.

Foundation material, dark brown kid, embroidered with shades of bright brown filoselles, and ornamented with fine brown silk cords. To work: Cut a strip of leather or kid, 14 inches long, and 5½ inches wide, scallop out the top as shown, and work the running border in BACK STITCH, and the top medallion in SATIN STITCH, COUCHING the fine cord round the flowers and leaves and stems. Cut out three Pockets in kid, each 5 inches wide and 4 inches high, work the designs shown on them in Satin Stitch and Couching, sew them to the foundation, and border with the cord. Finish the Wall Pocket with a mill-board back, and sew a handsome cord on as an edging.

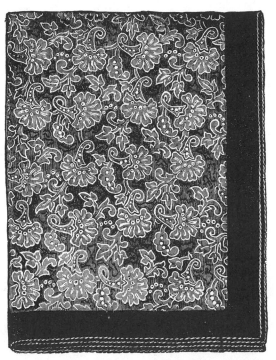

No. 176. GENTLEMAN'S SACHET.

The Sachet is of large size, and is intended for gentlemen's use. The cover is made of silk brocade, finished with a border of plush and a silk cord; the inside lining and pockets are of quilted satin. To work: Cut a piece of brocade, 18 inches long, and 8 inches wide. Outline the flowers on this brocade by COUCHING round them fine gold cord, and work in their centres, with FRENCH KNOTS and SATIN STITCHES, in coloured silks. Cut bands of plush, 2 inches wide, and sew these round the brocade. QUILT the lining and the pockets, sew them inside the cover, and hide the joins at the edges with a wide silk cord OVERCAST over them.

Plate LI. 581

NO. 177. KNITTED REINS FOR CHILDREN.

Needles No. 12, and coarse wheeling yarn of two
shades of colour, are required.   To knit:
CAST on 14 stitches, and knit 3 yards in
length in PLAIN KNITTING, to make the
Reins.   Knit four ½-yard lengths of the
same width, and sew these together to form
the cross-pieces and arms, and sew the Reins
to the latter.   Embroider the child's initials
with white filoselle, on the front cross-piece,
in CROSS STITCH.

NO. 178. KNITTING BASKET.

Foundation of wicker; ornaments, bands of cloth and ribbed ribbon, shown in No. 180.
To work: Cut the edge of the band into vandykes, and lay along its centre a
narrow piece of ribbon, cut into alternate diamonds and long squares.   Round
this narrow ribbon COUCH double Berlin wool strands, and work the centre
in SATIN STITCH and DOTS, with the same wool.   The side bands of the
Basket are worked in FEATHER STITCH, and their centre ornament consists
of a silk ribbon, cut in the shape of a leaf, and COUCHED round with
double Berlin wool.

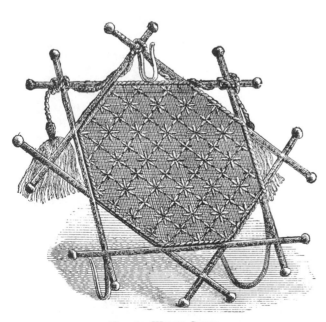

NO. 179. WATCH STAND.

Materials required: Bamboo stand, octagonal piece of Java canvas, brass
hook, silk tassels and cord of navy blue and crimson colours, and
filoselles matching the cord.   To work: Over the Java canvas embroider
alternate crosses and eight-pointed stars, in SATIN STITCHES.   Use the
crimson filoselle for the crosses, and the navy blue for the stars.

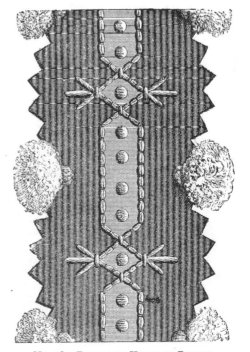

NO. 180. DETAIL OF KNITTING BASKET.

NO. 181. TOE OF CHILD'S SLIPPER.

Worked upon rough cloth, with crewel wools. To make: Cut the cloth to the size of the child's shoe, and work the toe in SATIN and ROPE STITCH with crewels of natural shades; sew the rough cloth to a slipper sock, and edge with a silk cord or narrow fur trimming.

NO. 182. CROCHET EDGING FOR A PINCUSHION.

Worked with coarse crochet cotton. First row: 6 CHAIN, 4 Chain to make a PICOT, 1 Chain, repeat from 4 Chain twice; 10 Chain,* cotton round the hook twice, and a LONG TREBLE into the seventh Chain; 4 Chain to make a Picot, and repeat from * twice, then repeat from the commencement of the row. Second row: Like the first, except that 6 DOUBLE CROCHET are worked over every 6 Chain of the last row, and the 3 Picots above the Long Trebles, the Long Trebles above the Picots.

NO. 183. PHOTO STAND SACHET.

Foundation and stand of strong millboard. Sachet, a square of ribbed silk. To work: Cut the square, as shown, into four flaps, embroider these with flowers in natural colours, and with filoselles in SATIN and DOT STITCHES. Sew three flaps together, surround with a silk cord, and carry the cord round the fourth, which open. Glue the back of the sachet, and the back of the extended flap, to the millboard mount.

NO. 184. HANDKERCHIEF BORDER.

Material for centre, fine white cambric; edging of white lace. To work: Trace the design upon the cambric, and work with French embroidery cotton in RAISED SATIN, OVERCAST, SATIN, and FRENCH KNOT STITCHES.

Plate LIII.

583

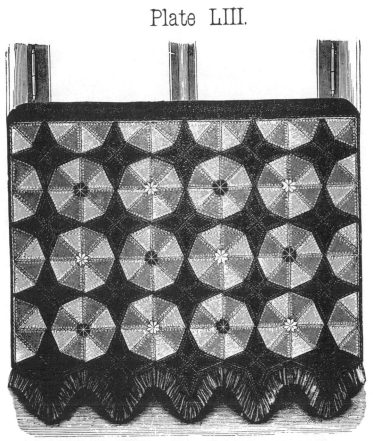

NO. 185. WINDOW SILL VALANCE OF PATCHWORK.

Materials required : Black velvet background, patches of silk and satin, and some filoselles. To work: Cut out the octagon stars, allowing two shades of one colour to each, such as two shades of grey, two of crimson, and two of olive green. TACK the patches together, and conceal the tacking threads with lines of FEATHER or CORAL STITCHES. BUTTONHOLE each star to the foundation velvet, and work connecting lines on that from one star to the other, as shown.

NO. 186. WHITE EMBROIDERY FOR UNDERCLOTHING.

Worked, with French embroidery cotton, on fine white linen. To work: Trace the design, and work it over in RAISED SATIN, OVERCAST, ROPE, and POINT DE POIS STITCHES.

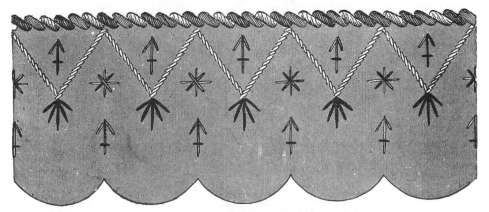

NO. 187. CLOTH EDGING FOR BOOK SHELVES.

The shelves are of plain wood, and, to hide their edges, strips of cloth ornamented with embroidery are used. To work the Edging, cut a strip of cloth the length of the shelf, and 2 inches in width; scallop one edge, and OVERCAST the other with double Berlin wool. Work the pattern with two distinct coloured filoselles, in CREWEL and SATIN STITCHES.

NO. 188. EMBROIDERY FOR TENNIS APRON OR DRESS APRON.

The Embroidery is worked upon a band of one colour, and then laid upon material of a contrasting shade. For a Tennis Apron it is worked on scarlet twill, and laid upon grey or white twill; for a Dress Apron, to the scarlet band blue stars are appliqué, and the embroidery is laid on a black foundation. To work: Cut out the stars in grey or blue materials, lay them on the scarlet band, and work them round with CHAIN STITCH. Finish their centres with FEATHER STITCH and BUTTONHOLE. Work on the scarlet material in HERRINGBONE, SATIN, and CROSS STITCH. Use old gold, pale blue, and deep crimson filoselles, for the Embroidery.

NO. 189. BRAIDED MANTEL BORDER.

This design is also suitable for a wood basket or a table border. It is worked on dark cloth, with fine gold-coloured braid, and the centre fillings made with purse silk. To work: Trace the design, and BACK STITCH the braid round the whole outline. For the fillings, make crossbars of the strands of purse silk, and secure the bars where they meet with a back stitch. The Border can be worked either upon maroon, navy blue, olive green, or black cloth, with black and gold, plain gold, or fancy braids.

Plate LV.

585

No. 190. D'Oyley of Muslin, Lace, and Tulle.

Cut circles, 5½ inches in diameter, in thin muslin and tulle; arrange on the muslin dried leaves and grass, and gum them down; sew the tulle circle over them, and trim with two rows of fine lace put on very full; sew a row of gold beads over the join between lace and tulle.

No. 191. Detail of Chair Back.

No. 192. Chair Back of Drawn Work, Lace, and Embroidery.

The border of this Chair Back is one-third of the length of the material, and is made by sewing insertion lace between wide rows of Drawn Work. The narrow edge round the Toile Colbert centre is of Drawn Work and Lace. For the Embroidery, work the detail shown in No. 191. Work, in Satin and Overcast Stitches, with Oriental silks.

No. 193. Edging for Muslin Window Blind.

The net foundation is bought with the white vandykes already arranged, and the work consists in sewing a line of Arrasene silk along these lines, working the stars, and hanging on the plush balls. To work: Overcast the Arrasene with filoselle to the foundation, work the stars in Satin Stitch, with Arrasene, and hang on the plush balls with loops of filoselle.

Plate LVI.

No. 194. Trimming for Children's Summer Frocks.

Materials required: Brown holland or white piqué for the foundation, crewel wool or ingrain cotton for the embroidery. To work: Trace the design upon the foundation strip, and scallop the edges, which work round with Buttonhole Stitch. Work the design, in two shades of one colour, in Crewel Stitch and Point de Pois.

No. 195. Border for Tablecloth or Perambulator Rug.

Materials required: For the centre, a piece of tapestry cloth; for the Border, a piece of plain cloth matching the darkest colour used in the centre, and double crewel wools and silks of a lighter shade, but of the same colour, as the plain cloth. To work: Cut one edge of the plain cloth in scallops, and Tack this edge to the centre piece. Work the spray design in Railway Stitch with the double crewels, and Couch down two strands of the same wool to form the curved lines. Use the silk to make the Couching stitches, and to fill in the centres of the rosettes. To make the tassels, wind strands of wool round a card, cut and tie them, ravel out some silk, lay this over them, and retie with the silk strands.

Plate LVII. 587

No. 196. D'Oyley in Roman Work.

Worked on fine linen, with French Embroidery cotton. To work: Trace the design, OVERCAST the outline, and connect it to the border with fancy PICOTS. Work the border in BUTTONHOLE STITCH, and cut away the spare linen.

No. 197. Knitted Quilt for Bassinette.

Worked in four shades of one colour, with Laine de Vienne or single Berlin wool, and needles No. 11. To work: For a perfect square, CAST on 40 stitches, and KNIT in Plain Knitting an exact square; for the border of half squares, cast on 40 stitches, and decrease by KNITTING 2 together at the beginning of every alternate row, until only 2 stitches remain on the needle. Sew the various squares together in the arrangement of colour given in the pattern, line the Quilt with thin silk, and sew a coloured cord round the edge, or make a long fringe with the spare wool.

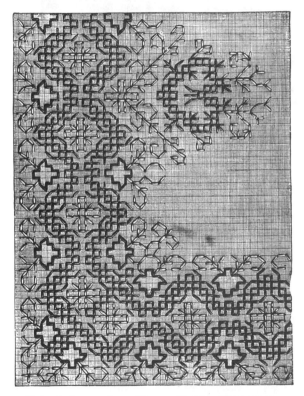

No. 198. Square Lamp Mat in Holbein Embroidery.

Materials, Java canvas, and ingrain silks of three shades. To work: Execute the entire design in HOLBEIN STITCH, and put in the three shades of colour as indicated by the dark or light printing. The same design worked on Toile Colbert is used for window blinds as in Holbein Stitch; both sides of the work are alike.

No. 199. Border for Baby's Head Shawl.

Foundation, either blue or scarlet flannel. Embroidery worked with white, unbleached silk. To work: Scallop out edge of shawl, and work it round with BUTTONHOLE STITCH; trace the design above it, and execute it in SATIN STITCH.

NO. 200. LAWN TENNIS SHOE CASE.

Materials used: American cloth of a thin make, brown holland, blue worsted braid, and blue crewels. To make: Cut a piece of American
cloth, and one of holland, 24 inches in length, and 12 inches wide. Round the edge of one of the lengths, and embroider the American
cloth with crewels in CROSS and VANDYKE STITCHES. Make two full holland pockets, and sew them to the holland. one on each side
of the length of the material, and at a little distance from each other. Bind the holland and the American cloth together with braid,
and make divisions by stitching down lines of blue worsted braid to the holland. Finish with a strap, or button and buttonhole.

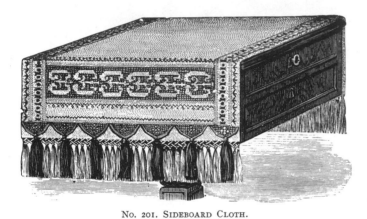

NO. 201. SIDEBOARD CLOTH.

NO. 202. DETAIL OF SIDEBOARD CLOTH IN HOLBEIN STITCH.

The foundation material is of crinkle cloth, or diaper cloth, with the border woven in the stuff. The embroidery is worked so as to bring
the pattern out in relief, by filling in the background at the sides of the cloth; at the long edges the embroidery is placed between the
woven lines. To work the sides, fill in the background with HOLBEIN STITCH, as shown in No. 202, with crewel wool. For the lines,
work in CROSS STITCH, in ROPE, CORAL, FEATHER, and DOT STITCH.

NO. 203. LEAD PINCUSHION.

NO. 204. EMBROIDERY OF LEAD CUSHION.

The foundation of the Pincushion is a square of lead, sunk in a wooden frame. Above the lead a cushion, stuffed with horsehair, and covered
with black velvet, is sewn, and the wooden frame is concealed with black satin, to which a panel of old gold-coloured silk is Appliqué.
To work: Cut out the panel, and work the pattern shown in No. 204 in FEATHER STITCH, with crimson purse silk. APPLIQUÉ to the
black satin, and COUCH a crimson silk cord round the panel.

Plate LIX.

589

NO. 205. WOOD BASKET.

Foundation, a black wicker Basket, with gilded handle. The sides of Basket are covered with a deep cloth valance, embroidered with single Berlin wools or crewels, and finished with wool tassels. To work: Cut out dark blue cloth to fit the side, and vandyke one edge. Work the pattern in POINT LANCE, BACK STITCH, and FRENCH KNOTS, in old gold and bronze colours, on the cloth. Finish with tassels of wool.

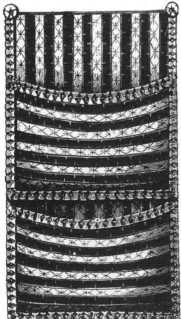

NO. 206. WALL POCKET FOR DRESSING-ROOM.

Made of striped red and white ticking, and used for holding toilet necessaries. Size of foundation, 12 inches by 7 inches; of Pockets, 4 inches by 7 inches. To work: Work stars, in SATIN STITCH, and with dark blue filoselles, down all the white stripes of the ticking. Line the Pockets with blue quilted alpaca, and finish the Pockets and edge with a ruche of blue ribbon.

NO. 207. WORK TUB.

Foundation, an American flour tub. The lid is covered with soldier's blue cloth, and a deep valance of the same material hides the Tub, while the wooden handle is also covered with the cloth. The cloth on the lid should be of a light blue, and that on the Tub of a darker shade. To work: On the lid cover embroider the pattern with SATIN STITCH, in shades of pale yellow and pink silks; on the Tub cover work in SATIN, CREWEL, and ROPE STITCHES, and with carnation-coloured silks. Make the tassels of Berlin wool, to which add strands of all the coloured silks used in the embroidery.

NO. 208. BOOT BAG.

Materials required: Brown holland,
scarlet braid, and scarlet ingrain cotton. To work: Cut
one piece of holland, 13 inches
by 6 inches, and another 16
inches by 6 inches. Round
both edges of the longest strip,
and one of the shortest. Work,
in HOLBEIN STITCH, the bordering shown, as an edging to
both pieces, sew them together,
and bind round with the braid.
Make a flap by turning the
long piece over the shortest,
and finish with a button and
buttonhole.

NO. 210. CIGAR CASE.

The materials used are two shades of grey kid, two shades
of ruby-coloured purse silks, and ornamental grey silk
cord. To work: Trace the design and initials on the
lightest coloured kid, and work in RAISED SATIN STITCH.
Appliqué to the dark kid, and surround the panel with
the ornamental cord. Work the design on the dark kid,
in SATIN STITCH, with the darkest ruby silk.

NO. 209. SPECTACLE RUBBERS.

Cut four pieces of thin card, 2½
inches long, and shape like
a pear. Cover two with dark
kid, and embroider them with
a butterfly in SATIN STITCH.
Pad the other two, cover with
chamois leather, and sew on to
the kid, to form the inside of
the Rubbers. Take a small
curtain ring, and cover it with
SINGLE CROCHET, worked in
purse silk. Sew the Rubbers
on each side of this ring, leaving enough space for a narrow
ribbon to be run through the
ring.

NO. 211. LUNCHEON CASE.

Materials required: Waterproof cloth, dark brown holland, and navy blue dress braid. To work: Cut out the waterproof cloth, and line it
with the holland. Make a large double pocket, to hold a nickel silver tumbler and a sherry flask; a wide pocket, to hold sandwich
case, and a strap for table napkin, and knife and fork. These pockets are all made of holland, bound with braid, and the articles
should fit them tightly. Ornament the braid with HERRINGBONE STITCH, worked in scarlet or white silk.

Plate LXI.

591

NO. 212. KEY BASKET.

Foundation of wicker, covered with cloth, and worked with CLOTH EMBROIDERY. The Basket is lined with silk, and finished with a frill of ribbon.

NO. 213. WATCH POCKET.

Foundation of millboard; lining ot pale blue rep silk; Bag of dark blue velvet, embroidered with SATIN STITCH; flowers edged with COUCHED lines of gold thread.

NO. 214. DOLL'S TROUSSEAU BASKET.

Basket of wicker; trimming of ribbon and lace; lining of blue sateen.

NO. 215. BOX PINCUSHION.

Foundation, a cigar Box; covering of German canvas, worked with CROSS STITCH; trimming, plush ribbon, silk fringe, and tassels and gimp.

NO. 216. WORK-BASKET.

Foundation, an ordinary wicker Basket, which is worked with HOLBEIN STITCH, and lines of coloured tinsel sewn on between the work; edging of fine wire, covered with BUTTONHOLE; lining of silk; ribbons of silk.

Plate LXII.

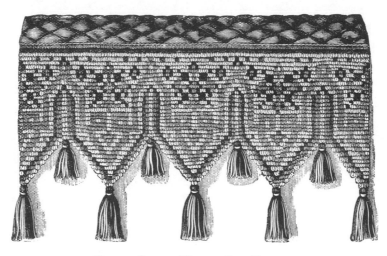

No. 217. Gobelin Window Seat Valance.

To work the Valance, *see* Gobelin Tapestry. Finish with tassels matching the colours used; and for the Window Seat use quilted satin sheeting.

No. 218. Tapestry Screen (*see* Tapestry).

Plate LXIII

593

NO. 219. HANDKERCHIEF BORDER OF MIGNARDISE BRAID
AND CROCHET.

To work: Sew the centre Braids together to form open diamonds, and connect
them together with CHAIN STITCH loops. Work the Borders in rows
of SINGLE CROCHET and CROSS TREBLES, and edge with Single Crochet
loops. The Braid is taken down the centre of the Handkerchief, as well
as round the sides.

NO. 220. CROCHET SOFA RUG.

Foundation, IDIOT STITCH; border of CHAIN STITCH,
worked in a darker coloured wool than is used for
the centre, and over the Idiot Stitch foundation.
To make the rosettes, work a round of Chain
Stitch in light wool, and fasten this down with
BUTTONHOLE STITCH, made with a dark coloured
silk.

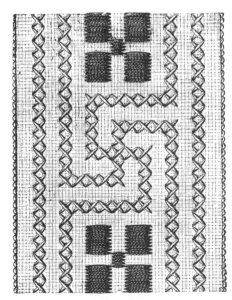

NO. 221. WINDOW BLIND BAND.

These ornamental Window Blinds are used to block
out an unsightly view. They are made with
alternate strips of Guipure Lace and Toile Colbert. Work the Toile Colbert in CROSS and
LONG STITCH, with ingrain cotton.

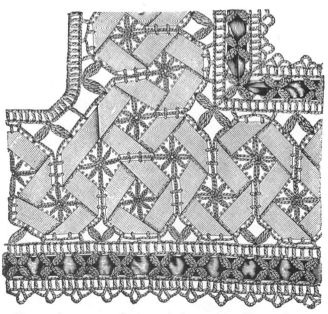

NO. 222. BORDER AND CENTRE FOR ORNAMENTAL PILLOW CASE.

Made with plain Mignardise braid and Crochet. To work: Sew the braid
together to form the centre pattern, and ornament with loops of CHAIN
STITCH and a border of Chain Stitch and SINGLE CROCHET. Rows of
Single Crochet and CROSS TREBLES form the edgings.

Plate LXIV.

No. 223. INSERTION FOR CHILDREN'S UNDERCLOTHING IN CROCHET AND
MIGNARDISE BRAID.

Foundation, a narrow row of braid. First row, CROSS TREBLES and 5 CHAIN
alternately; second row, 5 DOUBLE CROCHET into the centre of the first
Cross Treble, * PURL FOUNDATION STITCH for one loop, 3 Chain into centre
of second Cross Treble, 3 Chain back to Purl Foundation, draw through as a
loop, and repeat from * three times. Repeat from commencement of the row
to the end. Work both sides of the Insertion in this manner, and join them
together, as shown, with looped Chain Stitch.

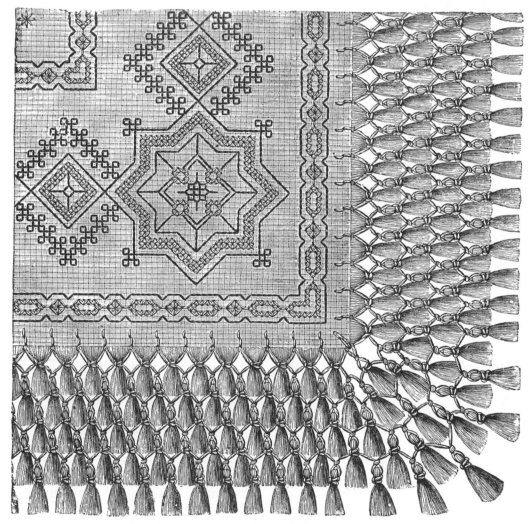

No. 224. TABLECLOTH FOR SMALL DRAWING-ROOM TABLE.

Foundation, ecru-coloured German linen, woven in squares. Design worked, in two shades of crimson ingrain cotton, in
CROSS STITCH, HOLBEIN STITCH, and RUSSIAN EMBROIDERY STITCH. Border made by drawing out the foundation
linen to a depth of 3 inches, and making tassels of the remaining threads, as shown, with the scarlet cotton securing them.

Plate LXV.

595

No. 225. Border for Book Shelves.

Foundation, seal brown cloth; embroidery in Oriental silks of yellow shades, and in Satin and Chain Stitch.

No. 226. Crochet Sofa Quilt Centre.

Worked with double Berlin wool, in strips (each strip of a different colour), and with Raised Cross Stitch.

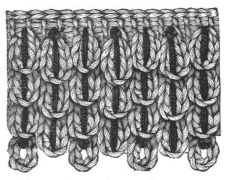

No. 227. Looped Crochet Border for Sofa Quilt.

Foundation, a strip of crochet, worked in Idiot Stitch. The loops are worked over the foundation, 9 Chain to each loop, and a dark coloured wool is fastened through them.

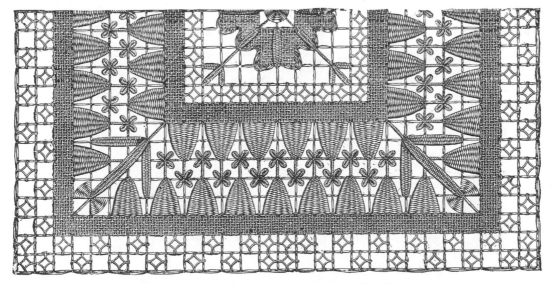

No. 228. Half Square of Guipure d'Art, for Sofa Cushion.

This Square is laid, when worked, upon a foundation of plush, and is edged with a broad band of satin, and finished with a wide frilling of satin and a Guipure Lace edging. Foundation, Square Netting, over which is worked, with fine linen thread, Point de Toile, Point d'Esprit, Point de Reprise, Guipure en Relief, Point de Venise, and Etoiles.

Plate LXVI.

NO. 229. CHAIR BACK.

Made with plush, satin, and fancy ribbon. To work: Cut out four squares of maroon-coloured plush, and five squares of old gold-coloured satin; size of squares, 6 inches. Cut five squares of plush, 1½ inches square. Sew the latter to the centres of the satin, and work the embroidery in SATIN STITCH and crimson silk. Edge the small plush centre with an old gold-coloured cord. Make up the various squares with the brocaded ribbon as connecting strips, and border with the same ribbon, concealing the stitches with an old gold silk cord. Finish with a bought tassel plush fringe.

NO. 230. GUIPURE LACE EDGING FOR BLINDS.

Foundation, SQUARE NETTING, over which is worked, with fine linen thread, POINT D'ESPRIT, filling in background; and on the design, GUIPURE EN RELIEF, POINT DE VENISE, and ETOILES. For the border, POINT D'ETOILE, POINT DE VENISE, and BUTTONHOLE STITCH, are required.

Plate LXVII.

597

NO. 231. LEAVES FOR BASKET.

Foundation, a fine wire, covered with SINGLE
CROCHET. Open part of leaf, TREBLE
CROCHET. Edging, a loop of 3 Chain and
Single Crochet alternately.

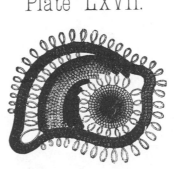

NO. 232. DETAIL OF BUTTERFLY.

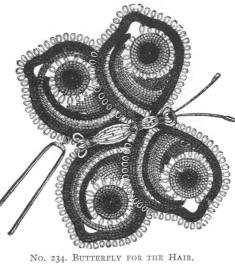

NO. 234. BUTTERFLY FOR THE HAIR.

Made of gimp and CHAIN STITCH; foundation of wings and body, fine wire. Lines of gimp
OVERCAST to wire, and worked round the edges with loops of silk.

NO. 233. ORNAMENTAL COVER FOR
BRADSHAW.

Foundation of satin, with corners embroidered with SATIN STITCH;
border of HERRINGBONE STITCH.
The foundation is crossed diagonally
with a piece of plush that is edged
with a silk cord and rosettes of embroidery.

NO. 235. WORK BASKET.

Foundation of wicker; leaves made with fine wire, worked
over with single Berlin wool in CROCHET. A satin
bag and pompons complete the trimming.

NO. 236. CLOTH EDGING FOR MANTELBOARDS. CHAIN
STITCH EMBROIDERY.

Foundation, plum-coloured cloth, worked in CHAIN
STITCH, with two shades of pale blue silks, and ornamented with spangles and bugles.

Plate LXVIII.

No. 237. TEACLOTH OF TOILE COLBERT BORDERED WITH LACE.

Centre of Tablecloth, CROSS STITCH, surrounded with DRAWN WORK. Embroidered border, of SATIN STITCH, finished with insertion and edging lace.

No. 238. ORNAMENTAL EIDER DOWN COVER.

Centre, a GUIPURE D'ART square, bordered with a puff and frillings of satin, edging of swansdown, and a frilling of double satin.

No. 239. CHAIR BACK.

Foundation, terra cotta-coloured plush, ornamented with BROCADE EMBROIDERY.

Plate LXIX.

599

NO. 240. CHAIR BACK.

Foundation, cheese cloth, on which is laid fancy braid
in strips. To work: Ornament the cheese cloth
with rows of DRAWN WORK, and the fancy braid
with CHAIN STITCH.

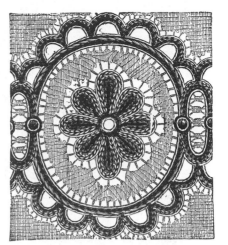

NO. 241. DETAIL OF ORNAMENTAL BRAID
FOR CHAIR BACK.

Work the outlines of the braid over with CHAIN
STITCH, using single Berlin wool.

NO. 242. CORNER FOR TABLECLOTH.

Foundation, German canvas. Background worked with two shades of single Berlin wool, in CROSS
STITCH; pattern outlined with HOLBEIN STITCH, in purse silk.

NO. 243. FOOT MUFF.

Foundation of velveteen and fur. APPLIQUÉ SILK EM-
BROIDERY upon the velveteen. A broad silk cord is
COUCHED round the Appliqué pattern as a finish.

NO. 244. POCKET HANDKERCHIEF SACHET.

Foundation of satin; trimming, a GUIPURE D'ART square, and
Guipure edging. Border, FEATHER TRIMMING. Bow of satin at
one corner as a finish.

No. 245. Italian Cross Stitch and Holbein Work-table Centre.

Foundation material, German canvas embroidery, executed with ingrain scarlet and navy blue purse silk.   To work: Fill in the
background entirely with Cross Stitch, and with the scarlet silk work Holbein Stitch round the outlines of pattern,
and, for the markings of the same, with navy blue silk.

Plate LXXI.

601

No. 246. HAND SCREEN IN FEATHER WORK.

Foundation of pheasant feathers.   To make the butterflies, *see* FEATHER WORK.   A spray of
artificial flowers finishes the Screen.

No. 247. EMBROIDERED PILLOW CASE.

Foundation, fine linen.   Design executed in fine white linen
thread, and with RAISED and FANCY EMBROIDERY
STITCHES.

No. 248. DETAIL OF EMBROIDERED PILLOW CASE.

Worked in RAISED SATIN STITCH, POINT DE
POIS, and SATIN STITCH.

No. 249. EMBROIDERED INITIALS FOR HANDKERCHIEF.

Worked on fine white cambric, with white embroidery cotton, in RAISED SATIN STITCH and
FRENCH KNOTS.

No. 250. Window Blind Strip in Guipure d'Art Lace.

Foundation, Square Netting, over which is worked, with fine linen thread, Point d'Esprit.

No. 251. Teacloth.

Foundation material, German canvas. Embroidery executed in Cross Stitch, with pale blue washing silks.

Plate LXXII.

Plate LXXIII.

603

No. 252. HOLBEIN TABLECLOTH.

Foundation material, fine German canvas. Embroidery, shown in full working size in
Detail No. 253, executed with scarlet and blue ingrain cottons, and worked
in CROSS and HOLBEIN STITCH.

No. 253. DETAIL OF HOLBEIN TABLECLOTH (No. 252).

NO. 254. SHOE THIMBLE CASE.

Foundation of cardboard, lined with crimson silk, and covered
with kid. Embroidery on kid worked in SATIN STITCH,
and with one coloured silk.

NO. 255. MULE SLIPPER.

Foundation, an ordinary kid Slipper, which is covered with a
pale coloured silk, and embroidered with SATIN STITCH
flowers of various colours, worked in silks. A long puffed
bow forms the heading.

NO. 256. PINCUSHION TOP.

Foundation of oatmeal cloth; embroidery in
red and blue ingrain cotton. To work:
Cut out and scallop the edges of the
cloth; work the border design in RAIL-
WAY, CHAIN, and CORAL STITCHES, and
the flowers and leaves in SATIN STITCH.

NO. 257. LETTER BRACKET.

Foundation of wicker; pockets of brown silk,
lined with brown twill. To make: Cut
out the silk to the size of the Bracket,
and embroider it with old gold-coloured
purse silk, and with SATIN, ROPE, and
CORAL STITCHES. Attach the silk to
the wicker with lacings of brown chenille.

NO. 258. WALL POCKET.

Foundation of wicker, the back of which is
covered with dark green quilted satin.
The valance to Pocket and finish to back
are of green silk. The pattern is worked
with RAISED SATIN STITCH, outlined
with gold thread. One shade of crimson silk is used for the embroidery, and
the fringe is of green and crimson silk.

Plate LXXV.

605

NO. 259. BOX PINCUSHION.

Foundation, an old cigar box, lined with satin. The lid of the box is then well stuffed to form a Cushion, and covered with blue cashmere, while a wide flounce of blue silk conceals the sides of the box, and a ruching of blue ribbon the opening. The embroidery for the top of the Cushion is worked on cream cloth, and is shown in working size in Detail No. 260. To work the embroidery: Trace it on the cloth, and line with Toile cirée. BUTTONHOLE round the centre star and each scallop with blue silk, and work plain BARS with the same silk, as shown, cutting the foundation cloth from beneath them. For the flowers, work in RAILWAY STITCH, CORAL, and FRENCH KNOTS, and with two shades of blue silk.

NO. 260. DETAIL OF BOX PINCUSHION (NO. 259).

NO. 261. EMBROIDERED STOCKINGS.

Foundation of silk. Embroidery executed in SATIN STITCH, with coloured filoselles.

NO. 262. ROLL BOOK MARKER.

The foundation is of fine blue cloth, embroidered, in HERRINGBONE and CREWEL STITCH, with silks. The Roll is stuffed tightly with cotton wool, sewn up, and finished with silk tassels.

NO. 263. SERVIETTE FOR EGGS.

Materials required : Red baize, plain and quilted satin, and filoselles. To make: Cut out five wedge-shaped pieces of silk, and embroider them with a small strawberry-plant design. Quilt up satin to form five separate linings, and sew the linings to each front. Sew each piece down the seams to a piece of doubled baize cut to the shape of design, but leave the outer edge of each unfastened in the centre of each wedge, to form the egg pocket. A bow of ribbon is placed in the centre of the Serviette.

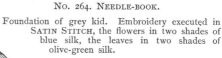

NO. 264. NEEDLE-BOOK.

Foundation of grey kid. Embroidery executed in SATIN STITCH, the flowers in two shades of blue silk, the leaves in two shades of olive-green silk.

NO. 265. MAT CENTRE IN GUIPURE D'ART.

Foundation, a square of netting. Pattern worked with linen thread, in Guipure d'Art stitches : POINT DE TOILE, GENOA STITCH, POINT D'ESPRIT, ETOILES, POINT SERRÉ, AND RONES.

NO. 266. BED POCKET.

Foundation of carmine cashmere, with Appliqué pattern of silk of a lighter shade, secured with a fine silk cord, couched round. To make : Cut out the shape of the back piece in millboard, and cover it with quilted satin. Cut out the front Pocket in cashmere, and APPLIQUÉ the design to it ; also work the little Watch Pocket in the same way. Sew the Pockets to the back piece, and finish with a ruche and bow of ribbon.

NO. 267. LETTER WEIGHT.

The Weight is of lead, the cover made of blue cloth, and the cords of silk. To make : Cut the cloth to fit the lead, and embroider the flower spray with pale blue filoselle, and in SATIN STITCH. Select the silk cord made of several bright strands of silk, and sew it to the sides of the Weight and bottom, and knot it together to form a handle.

Plate LXXVII.   607

NO. 268. EMBROIDERED BRAID FOR DRESS APRONS.

The foundation is of broad black llama braid, and the embroidery is worked with scarlet single Berlin wool. To work: Cover the braid with Berlin canvas, work the pattern in SATIN, CROSS, and DOUBLE CROSS STITCHES, and pull away the canvas threads.

NO. 269. NEEDLE-CASE COVER.

The foundation is perforated gold cardboard, and the embroidery is worked with single Berlin wools, shades crimson, and dark olive-green. To work: Attach the diagonal lines of wool to the cardboard with fancy CROSS STITCHES, and work the same stitches in the centre of each vandyke.

NO. 270. MAT CENTRE.

Foundation material, dark blue baize; Appliqué leaves of a darker shade of silk. To work: Cut out the leaves, and BUTTONHOLE them to the foundation. Work the small leaves and sprays with filoselle matching the silk, and with FEATHER and SATIN STITCHES.

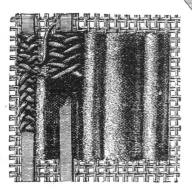

NO. 271. IMITATION FUR BORDERINGS FOR MUFF, COLLARS, AND CLOAK TRIMMINGS.

Foundation, fine Penelope canvas, covered with fine Saxony wool. To work: Cut a 2 inch wide strip of millboard, lay it on the canvas, and cover it with double HERRINGBONE. Leave a space of canvas, and lay on the canvas a second strip of millboard, 2½ inches wide.   Work a breadth of 6 inches in this manner.   Work a second row of Herringbone over the first, and a third over the second, all with white Saxony wool; then take a sharp pair of scissors, and cut down the centre of each Herringbone line, until the millboard is reached.   Remove the millboard, and comb out the cut wool.

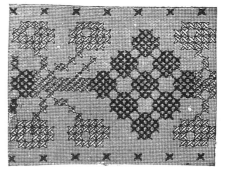

NO. 272. BORDER FOR TOILET COVER.

Foundation, scarlet canvas. Embroidery executed with black and white crewel wools, in CROSS STITCH.

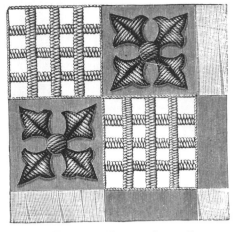

NO. 274. DETAIL OF FOLDING CHAIR (NO. 277).

NO. 273. INFANT'S SHOES.

Foundation material, pale pink silk, lined with flannel of the same shade. Embroidery shown in Detail No. 275 worked in SATIN STITCH, in pale blue silks of various shades. The fronts of the shoes are trimmed with a pulled out at the edges ruching of pink silk, and the straps are stitched with blue silk.

NO. 275. DETAIL OF INFANT'S SHOES (NO. 273).

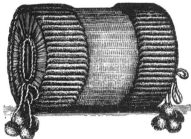

NO. 276. CHILD'S MUFF.

Foundation of PLAIN KNITTING, in white wool; size, 25 inches long, and 14 inches wide. This strip, forming the outer covering of the muff, is wadded and lined with white silk, and has its edges drawn together, to form the openings, with a white silk cord and tassels. The trimming is of imitation fur similar to that shown in No. 271.

NO. 277. FOLDING CHAIR WITH EMBROIDERED COVER.

Foundation of Chair, wicker. Cover of strong grey ticking, woven in squares of grey and white. To work : Embroider the grey squares, with crimson wool, in SATIN STITCH, and work the white ones, in DRAWN WORK, with white linen thread, as shown in Detail No. 274. Finish the cover with bands of crimson braid and a knotted wool fringe.

NO. 278. COLLARETTE FOR CHILD.

Foundation material, PLAIN KNITTING, in white wool, made to the shape of a collar cut out in paper. This knitting is wadded and lined, trimmed round the edge with the imitation fur trimming shown in No. 271, and finished round the neck with three rows of CROCHET TRICOTÉE and three rows of 3 CHAIN inserted as a loop into every second Tricotée Stitch.

Plate LXXIX.

609

NO. 279. WALL BASKET.

Foundation of wicker, lined with cashmere, and edged with ruchings of silk ribbon. The valance shown in working size in
Detail No. 281 is made with three distinct coloured strips of
cloth, having their joins concealed with narrow braids. For the
embroidery, cover rounds of cardboard with silk, and work
LEVIATHAN STITCH, in single Berlin wool, in their centres, to
hold them to the cloth, and work in SATIN STITCH, OVER-
CAST, and CROSS and RAILWAY STITCHES, in single Berlin
wool, for the set designs. Make tassels of wool as a finish.

NO. 280. COUVRETTE, OR CHILD'S QUILT.

Foundation strips, CROCHET TRICOTÉE, in Saxony wool, each strip
being 16 inches wide, with a narrow band, 6 inches wide, of a
dark shade, between each broad strip. To embroider the
flowers, work with SATIN STITCH and pale blue silk for the
petals, as shown in Detail No. 282, and with FRENCH KNOTS,
in maize silk, for the centres. For the buds, work the petals as
before; the calyx, with dark green silk, stitched with white
silk. Work a row of LEVIATHAN STITCH down the dark
small strips.

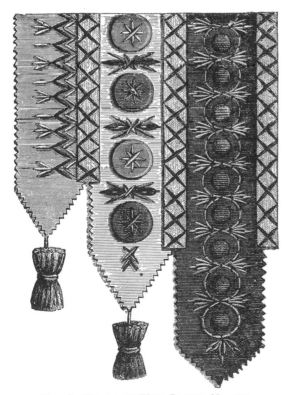

NO. 281. DETAIL OF WALL BASKET (NO. 279).

NO. 282. DETAIL OF COUVRETTE (NO. 280.)

Plate LXXX.

No. 283. Couvrepied.

Foundation of cricketing flannel or frieze. Embroidery executed with fleecy wool. To work : Cover the foundation with Berlin wool canvas, and work with FANCY BERLIN WOOL STITCHES, through the canvas on to the cloth, and with four shades of one colour. Pull the threads of canvas out, and edge the Couvrepied with a knotted woollen fringe.

No. 284. Garden Bag.

Foundation of strong grey linen. Embroidery executed in SATIN STITCH. The linen is mounted on cardboard, and stitched down in the machine to form four pockets. The Bag is lined with Turkey twill, and finished with handles and bows of scarlet braid.

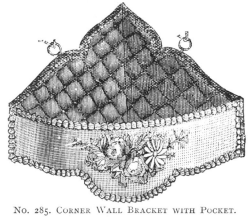

No. 285. Corner Wall Bracket with Pocket.

Foundation of millboard. The back part of Bracket is covered with dark blue satin that is quilted, and each cross line finished with a tuft of silk. The outer part of bracket is made of grey Java canvas, and embroidered in the centre with CHINA RIBBON WORK. A quilling of dark blue satin ribbon borders the Bracket.

Plate LXXXI.   611

No. 286. WORK BASKET.

Foundation of Basket, wicker, covered with Java canvas, and trimmed with bands of cloth and handsome worsted fringe. To work the bands of cloth shown in Detail *A* (No. 287), take a strip of dark chesnut brown cloth, and Berlin wool of a rather lighter shade, and work the spray, in FEATHER STITCH, on the brown cloth, and the bordering in SATIN STITCH, after the band is sewn to the Java canvas. For Detail *B* (No. 288), work directly on the Java canvas, with dark brown wool, in RAILWAY and FEATHER STITCH, finishing the flower centres with FRENCH KNOTS. Line the Basket with brown silk, and ornament with worsted fringe and tassels.

No. 287. DETAIL *A* OF WORK BASKET (No. 286).

No. 288. DETAIL *B* OF WORK BASKET (No. 286).

Plate LXXXII.

NO. 292. DETAIL OF LAMP SHADE (NO. 289).

NO. 289. LAMP SHADE.

Foundation material, coloured sarsenet, with black net shields. To work: Cut out six leaves in crimson sarsenet the size of Detail No. 292 ; fasten the black net to the centre of each, secure it firmly, and cut away the sarsenet beneath it. Ornament it with embroidery in silks of two colours, and with SATIN, OVERCAST, CREWEL, and POINT DE POIS STITCHES. BUTTON-HOLE the extreme edge of each leaf. Cut out the top of Lamp Shade in sarsenet, work it in Satin Stitch, and sew the six leaves and top together. Line the sarsenet with muslin before working it, and reline it with sarsenet when finished.

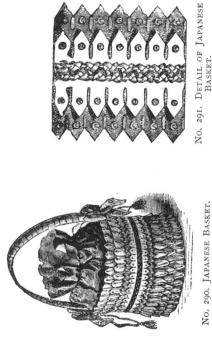

NO. 290. JAPANESE BASKET.

Foundation of straw, lined with a bag of crimson silk. Embroidered band shown in Detail No. 291 of white cloth, mounted on crimson cloth, and fastened down the centre with a row of fancy straw plaiting. Embroider each point of the white cloth with a FRENCH KNOT in crimson purse silk, and the crimson cloth with French Knots and SATIN STITCH in black purse silk.

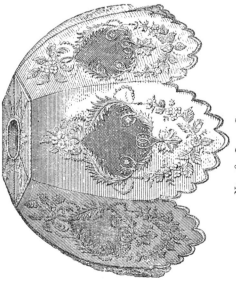

NO. 291. DETAIL OF JAPANESE BASKET.

Plate LXXXIII. 613

No. 293. DETAIL *A* OF WINDOW BLIND (No. 294).

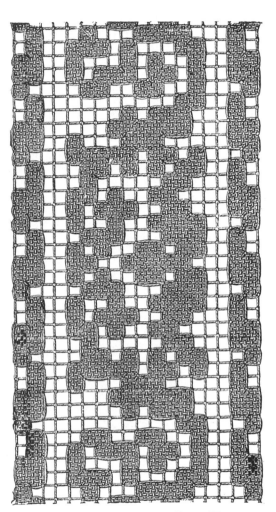

No. 295. DETAIL *B* OF WINDOW BLIND (No. 294).

No. 294. WINDOW BLIND.

Composed of alternate bands of Toile Colbert and Guipure d'Art. To work the Toile Colbert shown in Detail *A*, No. 293, use fine crewels; and outline the whole design in CROSS STITCH, and fill it in with FRENCH KNOTS, SATIN STITCH, and fancy Cross Stitches. To work Detail *B*, No. 295, NET the foundation, and use POINT DE REPRISE for the pattern. The Window Blind is finished with a cord edging and a handsomely knotted fringe.

NO. 296. BORDER FOR BRUSH AND COMB CASE.

Foundation, Java canvas. Embroidery executed, with two shades of one coloured Crewels, in CROSS and SATIN STITCH.

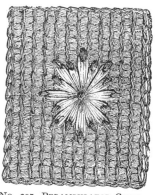

NO. 297. PERAMBULATOR COVER.

Foundation of CROCHET TRICOTÉE, worked with single Berlin wool, in strips 6 inches wide, and 1 yard long; different colours used for each strip. For the centre flower, work with maize-coloured wool for the flower petals in SATIN STITCH; tip each petal with a silk of the same shade, and with a RAILWAY STITCH, and make a FRENCH KNOT with the same silk for the centre. From six to eight strips are required for each cover.

NO. 298. NEEDLEWORK EMBROIDERY FOR CIGAR CASE.

Foundation of cashmere, with centre star an APPLIQUÉ of pale coloured satin. To work: Fasten down the Appliqué star by working it over with trellis work, and work the rest of the pattern in SATIN STITCH, POINT RUSSÉ, and FRENCH KNOTS. Line the cashmere before working, and reline with flannel when finished.

NO. 299. ASSYRIAN BORDER FOR TABLE NAPKINS.

Foundation of fine linen. Embroidery executed, with fine white linen thread, in SATIN, ROPE, and FANCY CROSS STITCHES.

NO. 300. EMBROIDERED STRIP OF OATMEAL CLOTH FOR EDGING DRUM-SHAPED WORK BASKETS.

Foundation material, oatmeal cloth, worked with scarlet Berlin wool, and edged with scarlet braid. To work: STITCH on the lines of braid, and work the pattern in HERRINGBONE and CROSS STITCH.

Plate LXXXV.

615

No. 303. LAMP MAT, DETAIL B.

No. 303. LAMP MAT, DETAIL B. Border, a bouillonée of silk, 2½ inches in width, crossed at regular intervals with cloth strips, given in full working size in Detail B (No. 303). To embroider these strips, work in CHAIN, RAILWAY, and CORAL STITCHES, with coloured Berlin wools, and finish each flower centre with a FRENCH KNOT.

No. 302. LAMP MAT.

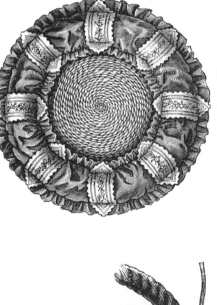

No. 301. LAMP MAT, DETAIL A.

No. 302. LAMP MAT. Foundation of cord, crocheted in circles, as shown in Detail A (No. 301, and measuring 10 inches in diameter.

No. 304. BORDER FOR A SMOKING CAP.

No. 304. BORDER FOR A SMOKING CAP. Foundation material, fine cloth. Appliqué design, silk of the same colour, but of a darker shade. To work: Cut out the leaves in silk, lay on the cloth, and secure with BUTTONHOLE STITCH, made with filoselle of the same shade as the silk. Work the small leaves and sprays with filoselles matching the cloth, and with SATIN and FEATHER STITCH and COUCHING.

NO. 305. BRAID DRESS TRIMMING.

Foundation material, dark blue or brown cloth. Sew fine black braid to the cloth, as in BRAIDING.

NO. 306. EMBROIDERED BAND FOR TABLECLOTHS.

This Band is laid on as a border to dark tablecloths, and is worked before it is applied. Foundation, a band of fine cloth, with edges pinked. Embroidery executed with single Berlin wools, in CORAL, close HERRINGBONE, and SATIN STITCHES.

NO. 307. CENTRE SQUARE FOR SOFA CUSHION.

Foundation, pale blue silk. Embroidery executed with filoselles matching the natural colour ot flowers and leaves, and in SATIN, CORAL, and CREWEL STITCHES. Bow of ribbon outlined with CHAIN STITCH, and filled in with FRENCH KNOTS. For Sofa Cushion and Border, see Nos. 309, 310.

Plate LXXXVII.   617

No. 308. EMBROIDERED BAND FOR CHAIR BACK.

Foundation, Surah silk, lined with muslin.   Embroidery worked, with Oriental silks, in SATIN and FEATHER STITCH.   Narrow silk ribbon is laid between each
embroidered Band, to form a bordering.

Foundation materials, pale blue silk
and dark green satin, the latter
being quilted and the former
worked over.   To work: For the
design used on the Centre Square
see No. 307, where it is given in
full working size, and the stitches
explained ;   for the outer Band,
see Detail No. 310, where it is

given in full working size.   Outline each strip of work with a silk
cord.   Gather the corners of blue
silk up, and quilt the green satin.
Sew these pieces to the work, and
hide the joins with a cord.   Line
the back of the Cushion with
green silk, and sew cord and
tassels round the sides.

No. 309. SOFA CUSHION.

No. 310. DETAIL OF BAND FOR SOFA CUSHION.

Work the set pattern with fine gold silk cord, which COUCH down ; work the rosebud and leaves in natural colours, with filoselles, and in SATIN and
CORAL STITCHES ; the centre ornament of set pattern work in the same stitches, in shades of brown silk.   For Centre of Cushion, see No. 307.

Plate LXXXVIII.

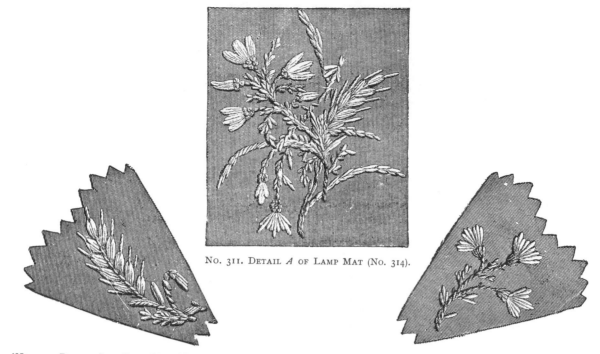

NO. 311. DETAIL *A* OF LAMP MAT (NO. 314).

NO. 312. DETAIL *B* OF LAMP MAT (NO. 314).

NO. 313. DETAIL *C* OF LAMP MAT (NO. 314).

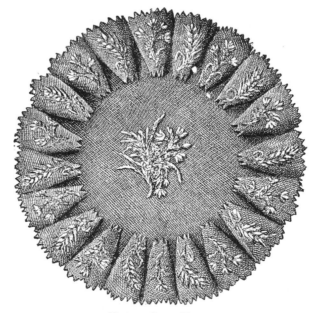

NO. 314. LAMP MAT.

Foundation of black cloth, worked in the centre with Detail *A* (No. 311), in SATIN STITCH, CHAIN, and FRENCH KNOTS, with silks matching the natural colours of the flowers. For the border, cut out twenty pieces of cloth rather larger in size than Details *B* (No. 312) and *C* (No. 313), and with enough cloth to turn under. Pink their edges as shown, and work them with natural shades for a blue cornflower and ear of barley, in Satin, ROPE, and RAILWAY STITCHES.

Plate LXXXIX.

619

No. 315. KEY BASKET.

Foundation of straw; lining of fine crimson cloth; outside decoration, a tassel fringe of brightly coloured wools. To make: Cut the lining the size of the Basket, and work the pattern shown upon it with black silks; sew it inside the Basket, and sew on the outside fringe.

No. 316. SOFA CUSHION COVER.

No. 317. DETAIL OF SOFA CUSHION COVER.

Materials: Fine cloth centre, puff of satin, and border of Guipure Lace. Embroidery executed with crewel wools and purse silk. To make: Work the initials shown in Detail No. 317 with purse silk, and in RAISED SATIN STITCH. Lay white Berlin canvas over the foundation, and work the border with crewel wools in CROSS STITCH; pull away the canvas threads when the border is finished. Attach the satin puffing and the lace together with a vandyke border worked in Cross Stitch.

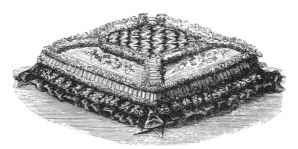

No. 318. HANDKERCHIEF SACHET.

Materials required: Blue satin and ribbon, Blonde Lace, filoselles, and a wooden box. To make: Line the inside of the box with quilted satin. For the outside, make a full puffing of satin for the centre of the lid, and ruches to mark out the four flat panels. Work these four panels with a flower design, in SATIN STITCH, with the filoselles. Make a deep frill with box-pleated ribbon, cover the upper part with Blonde Lace, and sew on round the bottom of the box, finishing with a ruche of ribbon above the lace.

No. 319. HANDKERCHIEF MEDALLION.

Foundation material, fine white silk. Embroidery worked in shades of old gold colour, in SATIN, CORAL, ROPE, and POINT DE POIS STITCHES.

No. 320. HANDKERCHIEF MEDALLION.

Foundation material, white cambric. Embroidery executed, with fine linen thread, in RAISED SATIN, OVERCAST, ROPE, and POINT DE POIS STITCHES.

No. 321. TOE OF CHILD'S SLIPPER.

Foundation material, fine blue cloth. Embroidery executed with white silk, in SATIN, CORAL, OVERCAST, and CREWEL STITCHES.

No. 322. CHINESE PENWIPER.   No. 323. DETAIL OF CHINESE PENWIPER.

Foundation of wire, strengthened with cardboard, and covered with scarlet cloth. Bright coloured birds' feathers are sewn to the cloth foundation. To make the Penwiper, cut out a piece of scarlet cloth the size of Detail No. 323, and work it in OUTLINE STITCH, as shown. Cut out several flaps of black cloth, rather larger than the scarlet, and pink their edges. Sew them all to the feather end of the Penwiper, and hang on tassels as a finish.

Plate XCI.

No. 326. EMBROIDERED WINDOW BLIND.

Foundation material, Toilé Colbert, on which are laid bands of fine white braid. Work the bands with a set design, and with crimson ingrain cotton, and the rest of the design with pale blue cotton. The coat of arms, work in crimson cotton, and in SATIN STITCH.

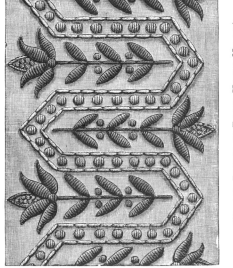

No. 325. DETAIL OF TOWEL HORSE (No. 324).

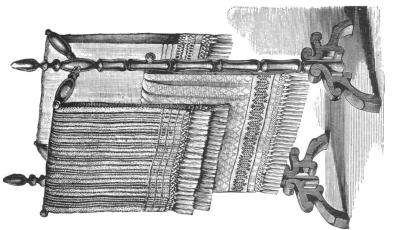

No. 324. TOWEL HORSE.

Embroidered bedroom towels in the Russian style are now fashionable. Some of these towels are adorned with straight lines of CREWEL STITCH and with DRAWN WORK insertion; others have elaborate borders like the one shown in working size in Detail No. 325. To work Detail: Work the parts printed a light colour in Turkey red cotton, in DOTS and laid lines; the leaf sprays, with dark blue cotton, in SATIN STITCH and FRENCH KNOTS.

Plate XCII.

NO. 327. SPRAY FOR COVER OF NEEDLE-
BOOK.

Materials required: A strong yellow silk
foundation, and two shades of chestnut-coloured Oriental embroidery
silks. To work: Trace the design on
the foundation; work the flowers
with the lightest colour embroidery
silk, and the leaves with the darkest,
and with fancy EMBROIDERY
STITCHES.

NO. 328. CIGAR CASE CENTRE.

Materials required: Ecru-coloured kid, and purse
silks. To work: Trace the design on the
kid, and work all the flowers in RAILWAY
STITCH, the light ones with maize silk petals
and brown FRENCH KNOT centres; the dark,
with pale blue silk petals and maize French
Knot centres. Work the stems and leaves
in CREWEL STITCH.

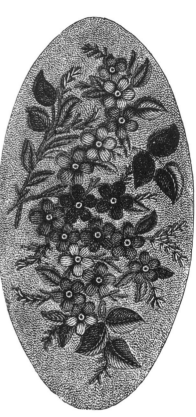

NO. 329. CIGAR CASE CENTRE.

Materials required: Rough brown kid, and purse
silk. To work: Trace the design on the kid,
and work all the flowers with two shades
of purple silk, and in SATIN STITCH, with
FRENCH KNOT centres of yellow silk.
Work the leaves with olive green silk of two
shades, and in Satin Stitch, and the sprays
in CORAL STITCH, with light brown silk.

NO. 330. MANTELPIECE BORDER.

Materials required: Rough oatmeal cloth,
dark crimson silk, and fine crewel
wools. To work: Trace the design,
and work it entirely in RAILWAY
STITCH, with two shades of crimson-
coloured wools. Scallop the edges
of the cloth, and pleat the silk as an
edging to the cloth.

Plate XCIII.

623

No. 331. Cover for Eider Down Quilt.

Foundation, an Eider Down Quilt, covered with blue or crimson-coloured satin.   Cover of Toile Colbert, with insertion and edging of
Modern Point Lace.   The initials and coronet in the centre are worked in Satin Stitch with coloured silks.

No. 332. Blotting Book Cover.

Foundation of claret-coloured velveteen.   Embroidery worked in shades of old gold-coloured filoselles, and in Satin, Coral, Point de Pois, and
French Knot embroidery stitches.

NO. 333. CHILDREN'S GARDEN TENT.

The Tent is bought ready made, and ornamented at the sides in BRAIDING, with scarlet worsted braid.   The valance of scarlet
twill, lined with ticking, is trimmed round the edges with braid, and embroidered with scarlet fleecy wool.

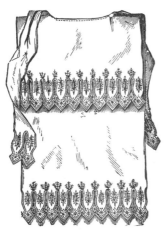

NO. 334. CHILD'S ITALIAN APRON.

Foundation of scarlet twill or white crash. Embroidery shown in Detail No. 335 worked
in RAILWAY, HERRINGBONE, WHEEL, and
FRENCH KNOT embroidery stitches, either
with black or scarlet cotton.

NO. 335. DETAIL OF CHILD'S ITALIAN
APRON (NO. 334).

Plate XCV.

625

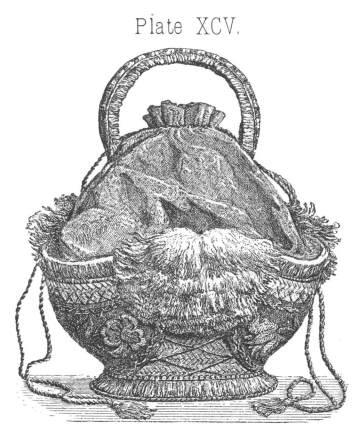

NO. 336. PANAMA WORK BASKET.

Foundation, an ordinary Panama basket. The bag is of Surah silk, and the outside embroidery worked upon red plush, in yellow silk, in SATIN and CORAL STITCHES. Worsted fringe and worsted tassels complete the ornamentation.

NO. 337. CLOTHES BASKET.

Foundation of wicker, covered with quilted satin for the lid, and with puffings of satin on the Basket. The lace bands are of Breton lace, run with lines of bright coloured silks.

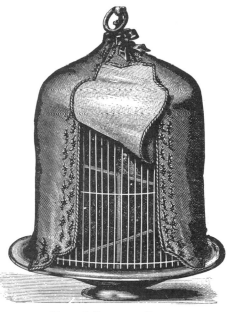

NO. 338. BIRDCAGE COVER.

Foundation of serge, cut into five pieces, four of which are sewn together, and the fifth joined to them at the top only. The opening and the flap are edged with a worsted cord. The Cover is embroidered round the sides with CREWEL STITCH, and with crewel wools.

Foundation of perfo-
rated gold cardboard,
which is OVERCAST
together, in the front
part of the Needle-

case, with blue silk.
The lining is of blue
cashmere, and the
stars are worked
with blue silk.

NO. 339. NEEDLE-CASE OF PERFORATED CARDBOARD.

NO. 340. CROCHET LAMP MAT.

NO. 341. DETAIL OF CROCHET LAMP MAT.

Foundation of blind cord, which is crocheted together, to form a flat round, with single Berlin wool, in DOUBLE CROCHET; over this plain round lines of wool are arranged, to form a star. The border is made with a series of leaves; the outside line of each leaf is worked over a fine cord. The leaves (shown full size in Detail No. 341) are commenced with a joined 8 CHAIN, into which 1 Chain and 1 Treble are worked fifteen times; at the end, join with 1 Treble on the first Treble, then 12 Chain, and commence the second leaf. Make ten leaves, and work the last two rows all round these leaves. Commence with 1 Treble over the first Chain, * 2 Chain, 1 Treble over the next Chain; repeat from * to the end. In the next row, work 1 Double Chain into every stitch, insert the wire, and work over it. In the last row, make PICOTS, with 5 Chain and 2 Single between each Picot.

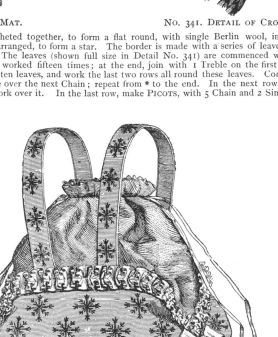

Foundation of cardboard,
covered with Java can-
vas; handles of the
same material. To
work: Cut the Java
canvas to the size, and
work the stars upon it,
in SATIN STITCH, with
brown wool. Make the
inside bag of brown
silk, and sew it to the

cardboard, so as to en-
tirely conceal the latter.
Work the handles and
line them, sew them to
the Java canvas, and
put a wide ruche of
brown ribbon round
the edge of the latter.
Finish with a draw
string and two hand-
some ribbon bows.

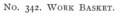

NO. 342. WORK BASKET.

Plate XCVII.

627

NO. 343. CENTRE MAT FOR TABLE.

Foundation of Java canvas, trimmed with narrow edgings, fringed out, and made into rosettes. Embroidery worked, with single Berlin wool of two colours, in SATIN STITCH.

NO. 344. ROMAN COOKING APRON.

Foundation of damask linen, whose ends are fringed out, and then knotted together as shown. Embroidery, bands of CROSS STITCH, worked upon scarlet German canvas, laid on the damask, and surrounded by lines of braid.

NO. 345. WINDOW BLIND.

This Blind is made to fit the window sash, and is mounted on canes. The foundation is Toile Colbert, and the design is worked in HOLBEIN STITCH, with scarlet ingrain cotton of two shades.

No. 346. BORDER FOR PINCUSHION.

Foundation material, plain Brussels net. For working pattern, *see* EMBROIDERY UPON NET.

No. 347. TRIMMING FOR A CAMBRIC DRESS.

Foundation of blue cambric, scalloped at the edges, and finished with BUTTONHOLE. In each scallop a small window-shaped piece of material is cut away, and the edges Buttonholed. A band of blue braid is secured in vandykes to these spaces. The embroidery, in RAILWAY STITCH and HERRINGBONE, is worked with dark blue ingrain cotton.

No. 348. SHIELD FOR HANDKERCHIEF.

Foundation material, fine cambric. Shield, of Brussels net, which is laid on the cambric, its edges secured with OVERCAST and POINT DE POIS STITCHES, and the cambric beneath it cut away. The embroidery upon the cambric is worked with fine French thread, in RAISED SATIN, ROPE, and Point de Pois Embroidery Stitches.

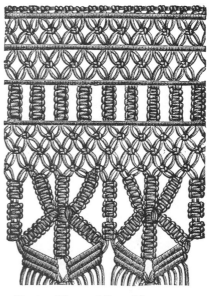

No. 349. MACRAMÉ LACE MANTELPIECE TRIMMING.

Worked with ecru-coloured linen thread, and in MACRAMÉ LACE KNOTS.

Plate XCIX. 629

NO. 350. BATH SLIPPER.

The foundation is of baize, and the embroidery worked, with two shades of gold-coloured purse silks, in SATIN and CREWEL STITCHES. The toe of the Slipper is sewn to a felt foundation, and no heel part is required.

NO. 351. SCENT SACHET OF JAVA CANVAS.

Made of double diamonds, formed of Java canvas or perforated cardboard, OVERCAST round with filoselles, and ornamented with stars. Before the diamonds are quite sewn up, powdered scent is put into them, enclosed in muslin bags. The diamonds are joined together with pearls, and finished with silk tassels.

NO. 352. BASKET FOR EASTER EGGS.

Foundation Basket of gilded or bronzed wire; bag formed of four pockets, sewn together. The bag is of Toile Colbert, and the top of each pocket is ornamented with a design worked, in OUTLINE STITCH, with filoselles. The manner of closing and opening each pocket is shown in the illustration.

NO. 353. NEEDLE-CASE WITH THREADED NEEDLES.

Case made of Toile Ciré, lined with scarlet flannel, and bound with black ribbon. The lower part of the Case is turned up to form a pocket, into which three reels of cotton are placed, and run through a knitting needle, whose ends are concealed with bows of ribbon. Rows of needles are inserted in the flannel, and threaded with cotton, and each needle can be used without the trouble of threading it, until the case is empty, when all are re-threaded.

Plate C.

The foundation is of old gold-coloured plush, and the parts printed black in the design of a claret-coloured plush, ornamented with FRENCH KNOTS, worked in old gold silk. The APPLIQUÉ pattern is cut out of pale blue cloth, and a silk cord of the same shade is COUCHED round its edges. Tassels and fringe, a mixture of all the colours, are used.

No. 354. PIANO STOOL COVER.

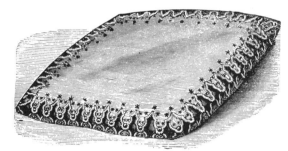

No. 355. PILLOW CASE.

Foundation, an ordinary pillow, over which a pink cambric cover is buttoned down, and removable. The outer cover is of fine Irish linen, made in two pieces, and buttoned together at each worked scallop. The pattern is worked in ENGLISH EMBROIDERY, in BUTTONHOLE and OVERCAST STITCHES.

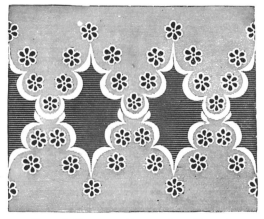

No. 356. DETAIL OF PILLOW CASE (No. 355).

Foundation of coarse straw plait, sewn together as an oval, and embroidered with red wool, in HERRING-BONE or LONG STITCH. The handle is made of straw, and embroidered like the foundation. The Bag is of moss-green plush, and is finished with a draw string of silk cord and tassels.

No. 357. STRAW WORK-BAG.

Plate CI.

631

NO. 358. FOOTSTOOL.

Materials required : Fine cloth of two shades of one colour, fancy braid, and embroidery silks. To work : Cut out three wide flounces of cloth, have their edges pinked, and ornament each scallop with a star worked in silk. Cut out of the darkest shade of cloth a Maltese cross, and have the edges of it vandyked. Ornament the fancy braids with CORAL and CHAIN STITCHES. Arrange them, as shown, over the Maltese cross, and sew firmly to the Footstool.

NO. 359. WALL BRACKET.

Foundation of cardboard ; lining of blue silk ; front of dark blue velvet, to which is Appliquéd sky blue velvet. To work : Cut out the design of APPLIQUÉ, and attach to the velvet foundation with lines of BUTTONHOLE matching the light blue velvet. Finish by COUCHING two rows of gold thread round the design. Make up the basket, with its lining, and attach handsome cords and tassels to the sides and round the pockets, and work the embroidery at the back in SATIN STITCH.

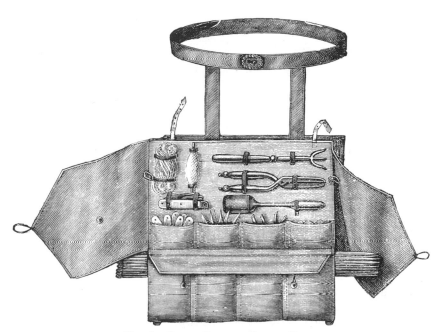

NO. 360. CANVAS BAG FOR GARDEN TOOLS.

Foundation of strong sailcloth, the centre part stiffened with cardboard. The two rows of small pockets in the front are used for labels, seeds, &c. The large pocket at the back of the front is made the entire length and width of the apron, and holds large tools ; it is fastened at the top with small straps. The waistband, and flaps to cover over the apron, are all of sailcloth, while wide elastic is used for securing the tools.

Foundation, plum-coloured cloth, on which a wide piece of Torchon Lace is sewn. The stitches shown in the illustration are worked, with uncut strands of coloured filoselles, over the lace pattern. See CRETE LACE.

NO. 361. IMITATION CRETE LACE FOR MANTEL BORDER.

NO. 363. SHIELD FOR HANDKERCHIEF.

The centre of the Shield is made of net, Appliquéd to the cambric foundation of the Handkerchief. To work: Lay the net over the cambric, secure the two together, work the design in SATIN, POINT DE POIS, and OVERCAST STITCHES, with fine white embroidery cotton, and, when the embroidery is completed, cut away the cambric beneath the net.

NO. 364. SEED EMBROIDERY FOR CIGAR CASE.

Worked upon brown rep silk. The flowers are formed of small seeds, and the sprays and leaves with green and brown chenille, worked in SATIN STITCH. See SEED EMBROIDERY.

NO. 365. MUSLIN PINCUSHION.

Foundation of Cushion, a pale blue satin. The muslin over the satin is ornamented with initials, and a spray worked in WHITE EMBROIDERY. A double ruche of old gold satin-coloured ribbon is placed next the muslin, beneath it a frill of Breton lace, and a wide box-pleating of pale blue satin. The corners of the Pincushion are finished with blue satin bows.

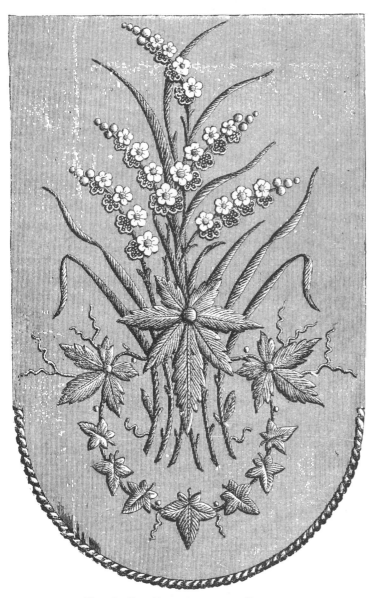

NO. 362. SILK EMBROIDERY FOR A BRACKET.

Foundation, of fine cloth of a dark shade. Embroidery of leaves and flowers executed, with coloured silks, in SATIN, RAISED SATIN, and POINT DE POIS. Edging to scallop, a wide silk cord.

Plate CIII.

633

NO. 366. RAILWAY RUG.

The foundation is of striped blanket cloth; the embroidery, of Braiding and Satin Stitch. To work: Outline the design with wide black silk braid, and work the centre stars, &c., with double crewel wool, in SATIN STITCH. Two shades of deep crimson colour are required.

NO. 367. CHAIR BACK.

NO. 368. DETAIL OF CHAIR BACK (NO. 367).

Material, Toile Colbert or French flax, bordered with dark blue plush, 3½ inches wide. Length of Toile Colbert, 23½ inches by 17½ inches. The tassels are of silk matching the plush and the colours used in the embroidery. To work: Use six shades of blue filoselles, and work in LONG STITCH, taking up six strands of material for each stitch. The correct placing of the various shades is shown by the numerals printed on Detail.

Plate CIV.

Material for foundation, écru-coloured German canvas; embroidery in washing silks of chocolate and dark blue shades. To work: Use the chocolate-coloured silks for all the straight lines, which work in double rows of CROSS STITCH; also outline the Vandykes with chocolate silk, in BUTTONHOLE STITCH. Work the rest of the design in Cross Stitch, with two shades of blue silks. The fringe is formed by unravelling the canvas, and ornamenting it with silk tassels.

No. 369. FOUR O'CLOCK TEACLOTH.

No. 370. RUSSIAN EMBROIDERY CENTRE SQUARE OF TEA-TABLE SERVIETTE.

Foundation material, fine white linen. Embroidery worked, in washing silks, in POINT RUSSE.

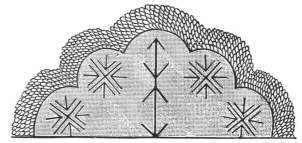

No. 371. OVAL TEA-TABLE SERVIETTE IN RUSSIAN EMBROIDERY.

Foundation material, fine white linen. Embroidery executed in washing silks, in POINT RUSSE.

Foundation material, white figured damask. Embroidery executed in white linen thread, in SATIN and RAISED SATIN STITCHES.

No. 372. DAMASK TEA-TABLE CLOTH AND SERVIETTE.

Plate CV.

635

No. 373. Detail of Hand Screen (No. 377) in Ribbon Embroidery.

Foundation of wickerwork, ornamented with silk tassels. Ribbon Embroidery worked with rose-coloured and green ribbons and green chenille, upon a black satin foundation. Embroidery shown full size in Detail. *See* Ribbon Embroidery.

No. 374. Border for Toilet Cloth.

Foundation, white German canvas. Embroidery executed in Cross Stitch, in two shades of golden brown crewel wools.

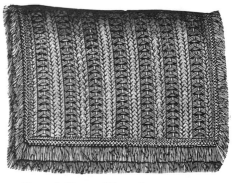

No. 375. Penwiper.

The foundation and top of Penwiper are cut out in millboard, which is covered with scarlet military cloth, and the cloth ornamented with Braiding, in fine black braid. The Penwiper is formed of rounds of black cloth, folded into four, and sewn, by the centre point thus formed, to a bought brass handle, which is passed through both pieces of millboard, and fixed, with an inch space between the millboards, to hold the black cloth.

No. 376. Drawn Work Antimacassar.

Foundation material, Toile Colbert or Butter cloth. The drawn threads spaces are run down the centre with crimson purse silk, and the plain spaces embroidered in Coral Stitch, with pale blue purse silk. *See* Drawn Work.

No. 377. Hand Screen in Ribbon Embroidery.

636

Plate CVI.

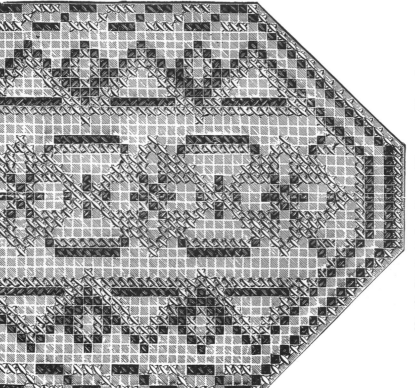

No. 380. Detail of Java Canvas Work-case (No. 379).

Take a strip of Java canvas, 12 inches in length, and 5 inches in width. Cut the flap as shown. Work the canvas in Cross Stitch, with single Berlin wools, in three distinct colours, and line with a bright-coloured sateen. Sew the Case together, and ornament sides and flap with a silk cord. See No. 379 for Case completed.

No. 378. Nightgown Sachet.

Materials used: Fine white linen, Valenciennes lace, coloured Persian silk, and 2-inch wide ribbon to match the colour of the silk. To make: Cut out a centre square of linen, and work the initials in Satin Stitch, with linen thread, in the centre. Surround the linen square with a border of Valenciennes insertion lace, then a border of white linen, and an edging of wide Valenciennes lace, put on full. Work round every seam with Coral Stitch. Make a bag of the coloured Persian silk. Sew the ornamental cover to one side of the bag, and tie the opening of the bag with the ribbons.

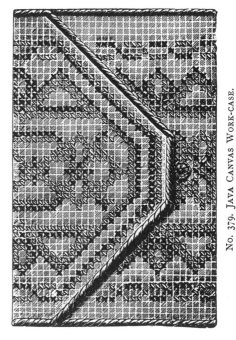

No. 379. Java Canvas Work-case.

Plate CVII.

637

No. 381. EMBROIDERED SOFA CUSHION COVER.

Foundation material, Java canvas. Embroidery executed in coloured filoselles matching the natural tints of the flowers. To work : Make long straight stitches across the spaces marked with very fine lines, and work round these laid stitches in SATIN STITCH. Work the rest of the design in SILK EMBROIDERY.

No. 382. BRACKET OF SILK EMBROIDERY AND APPLIQUÉ.

Foundation material, olive-green ribbed silk. APPLIQUÉ design, pale blue silk, surrounded with a double line of Japanese gold cord. Embroidery in SATIN STITCH, worked with fine floss silk, in shades matching the natural shades of flowers and leaves.

Plate CVIII.

NO. 383. ROMAN EMBROIDERY FOR END OF NECKTIE.

Foundation material, cream-coloured linen. ROMAN EMBROIDERY worked, with
ecru-coloured linen, in BUTTONHOLE STITCH and BARS with PICOTS.

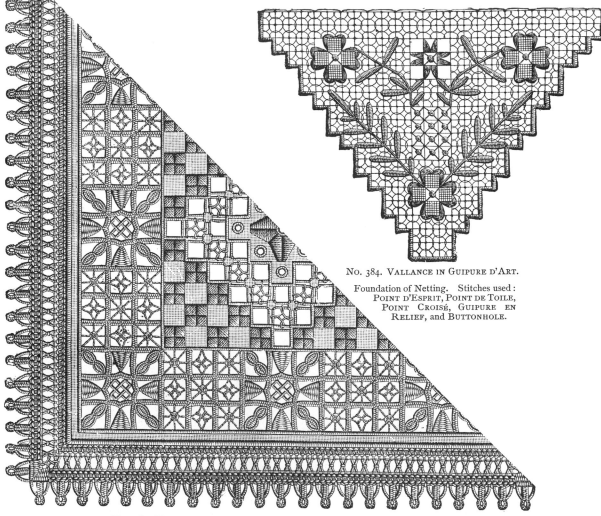

NO. 384. VALLANCE IN GUIPURE D'ART.

Foundation of Netting. Stitches used:
POINT D'ESPRIT, POINT DE TOILE,
POINT CROISÉ, GUIPURE EN
RELIEF, and BUTTONHOLE.

NO. 385. HALF OF TABLE MAT, IN GUIPURE D'ART AND DRAWN WORK.

Foundation of fine linen. Drawn Work in squares, with POINT DE REPRISE worked over the dividing threads, and Guipure stitches
in the open spaces. Stitches: WHEELS, POINT D'ESPRIT, POINT DE FESTON, OVERCAST, and BUTTONHOLE.

Plate CIX.   639

Foundation material, navy blue rep silk. Embroidery executed in Satin Stitch, with coloured silks. To work: Fill in the design with SATIN STITCH, and outline every part with a line of gold thread, COUCHED down; also sew small spangles in the centres of the embroidery. Trim the edges of the Cushion with a wide ruche of coffee-coloured lace, and ornament one corner with a long bow made with gauze ribbon —colours matching the embroidery.

NO. 386. DRAWING-ROOM PINCUSHION.

NO. 387. BRACKET VALLANCE—RIBBON EMBROIDERY.

The foundation material is dark terra cotta satin. The colours for the Ribbon Embroidery are two shades of blue for the large flowers, pale primrose with dark brown centres for the small flowers, and green for the leaf sprays. Dark green silk cord is COUCHED to the foundation as a finish.

No. 388. Tablecloth Ornamented with Appliqué.

Foundation material, ruby-coloured diagonal cloth; Appliqué, Eau de Nil-coloured silk brocade. To work: Sew the brocade to the cloth, and conceal the edges with an inner line of thick gold cord, and an outer line of filos. lle; use a thick strand of filoselle for this line, and slightly puff it out between each securing stitch; work the design on the Appliqué in SATIN STITCH, with coloured silks, and use dark green cord for the stems of the flowers, and other thick lines.

Plate CXI.

641

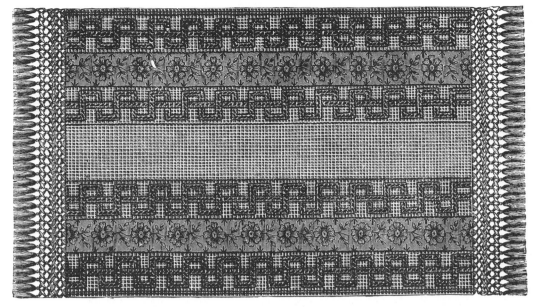

No. 389. Ornamental Window Blind.

Foundation material, Toile Colbert, to which two broad bands of brocaded ribbon are sewn. Upon the Toile Colbert work, in CROSS STITCH, with crewel wools, the conventional design, using the shades of wool that match the flower brocade. Finish the ends with a wide fringe.

No. 390. Ornamental Stool.

No. 391. Detail of Ornamental Stool (No. 390).

The foundation is of strong black wicker, to which a well-stuffed cushion is fixed. The cushion is covered with dark green plush, and finished round the sides with bows of ribbon. To work the embroidery shown in Detail (No. 391): Work the flowers in RAILWAY STITCH, and the stems and leaves in SATIN STITCH. Fill in the centres of the flowers with FRENCH KNOTS.

No. 392. PINCUSHION SQUARE IN CROSS STITCH.

Materials used: Berlin canvas and single Berlin wools. Colours: For the pattern, four shades of crimson; for the background, maize-coloured silk.

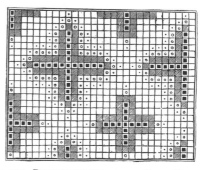

No. 393. PINCUSHION SQUARE IN CROSS STITCH.

Materials used: Berlin canvas and single Berlin wools. Colours: For the pattern, four shades of chocolate browns; for the background, sky blue silk.

No. 394. POCKET HANDKERCHIEF, SHOWING CORNER AND PART OF BORDER—APPLIQUÉ ON NET.

Foundation of Brussels net and fine cambric. *See* APPLIQUÉ UPON NET.

Plate CXIII.

643

No. 395. BERLIN WOOLWORK FOR A COUVREPIED.

The foundation is Berlin wool canvas; the wools used, single Berlin. The colours for the wide strips are shades of ruby upon a grey grounding; for the narrow strip, shades of blue upon a chocolate ground. The stitch is CROSS STITCH.

No. 396. BERLIN WOOLWORK FOR A SUMMER COUNTERPANE.

Foundation of Java canvas, with a band of strong braid inserted near the edge. Wools required: Five shades of single Berlin, in shades of russet browns for the centre, and five shades of blues for the bordering. Stitch: CROSS STITCH,

No. 398. WALL POCKET.

Plate CXIV.

Foundation material, cardboard, covered with Java canvas. Design worked in crewel wools, in SATIN STITCH. After working, the front and back of the Pocket are sewn together, and ornamented at the edges with a silk cord. The Detail (No. 397) gives the full working size.

No. 397. DETAIL OF WALL POCKET (No. 398).

Plate CXV.

645

No. 399. Detail *A*, showing Border of Reticule
(No. 400).

No. 400. Reticule.

Made with strong rep silk and German canvas, embroidered in Cross Stitch, with two shades of crimson purse silk. To work : Cut out the bag in navy blue purse silk, and make it up with a draw string and tassels. Work out the pattern on the German canvas, as shown in Details *A* (No. 399) and *B* (No. 402) ; line the canvas, and sew it on each side of the bag. Cut a straight piece of canvas for the handle of the reticule, work and line, and sew it to the sides.

No. 401. Table Mat.

Foundation of strong ornamental cardboard, lined with Persian silk. Corner of Table Mat and part of Border are shown. Design worked in Satin Stitch, with two shades of purple silk and one of old gold colour.

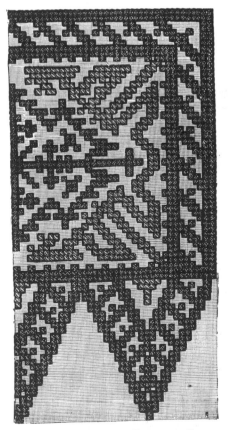

No. 402. Detail *B*, showing Centre of Reticule (No. 400).

Plate CXVI.

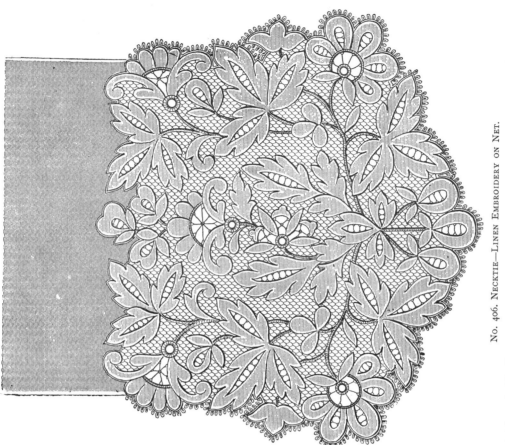

No. 406. NECKTIE—LINEN EMBROIDERY ON NET.

Materials used: Fine linen, open net, and lace cotton. To work: Outline the pattern on the linen, place the two materials together, OVERCAST round the edges of pattern, cut away the superfluous linen, and work the stems in Overcast, with WHEELS and CROSSES in the open spaces. Finish with a fine lace edging.

No. 403. EMBROIDERY ON NET FOR A DRESS FLOUNCE.

Materials: Fine Brussels net and muslin. *See* EMBROIDERY ON NET.

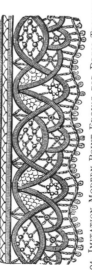

No. 404. IMITATION MODERN POINT EDGING FOR DRESS TRIMMINGS.

Materials required: Fine lace braid and edging, and lace cotton. Stitches used: WHEELS, POINT DE BRUSSELS, and POINT FESTON.

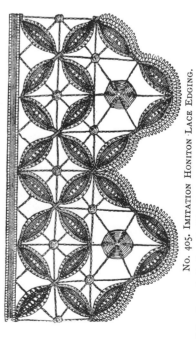

No. 405. IMITATION HONITON LACE EDGING.

Materials required: Lace braid and edging, and fine lace cotton. To work: Tack the braids to the pattern, using Vandyke lace braid, except for the plain border. Sew on the edging, and make the ornamental WHEELS and plain BARS.

Plate CXVII.

647

No. 407. Darning on Netting for a Curtain Border.

Foundation, netting; pattern darned with soft netting cotton. *See* Darned Netting.

No. 408. Cushion Centre—Darning on Netting.

Foundation, netting; pattern darned with soft netting cotton. *See* Darned Netting.

No. 409. Lacet Braid Chair Back.

To make this Chair Back, strips of lacet braid are quilled up, then sewn together to form open squares. Each open square is filled with a Wheel made with lace cotton.

Plate CXVIII.

No. 410. Serviette worked in Linen Embroidery.

Foundation, fine damask linen ; pattern of damask, embroidered with linen thread. To work : Outline the pattern with Cord Stitch, and work the centres with Single Coral and Feather Stitches, as shown in Detail (No. 411).

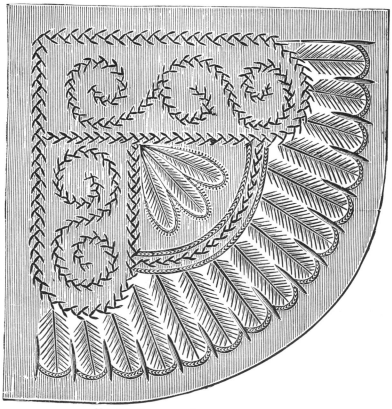

No. 411. Detail of Serviette (No. 410).

Plate CXIX.

649

NO. 412. PERFORATED LEATHER BRACKET VALLANCE.

The pattern is pricked on the leather, and the pricked lines are filled in with Pearsall's silks, of four shades of red. Three Vandykes are required to make the Vallance.

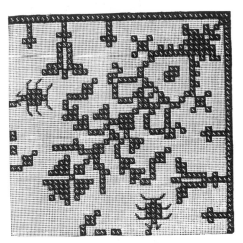

NO. 413. TEA-TABLE CLOTH.

Foundation of crash; embroidery in CROSS STITCH, in scarlet ingrain cotton.

Foundation of ècru-coloured linen; embroidery executed with linen thread of the same shade. To work: RUN the outlines of the design, then work the BARS and PICOTS, BUTTONHOLE round the outer and inner edges of the pattern, and cut away the superfluous linen.

NO. 414. NECKTIE IN ROMAN WORK.

Plate CXX.

No. 415. Appliqué Table Border.

Foundation material, seal-brown plush. Appliqué flowers and leaves of satin, in shades of brown and old gold. To work: Outline the Appliqué pieces with silk cord matching them in colour, and work the smaller leaves with chenille wools.

Plate CXXI.

Foundation material, olive-green velvet, lined with maroon silk. Embroidery executed with purse silks matching natural tints of flowers and leaves. Stitches used: SATIN, ROPE, and FRENCH KNOTS. Embroidery shown in full working size in Detail No. 417.

No. 416. LETTER CASE EMBROIDERED IN SILKS.

No. 417. DETAIL OF LETTER CASE (No. 416).

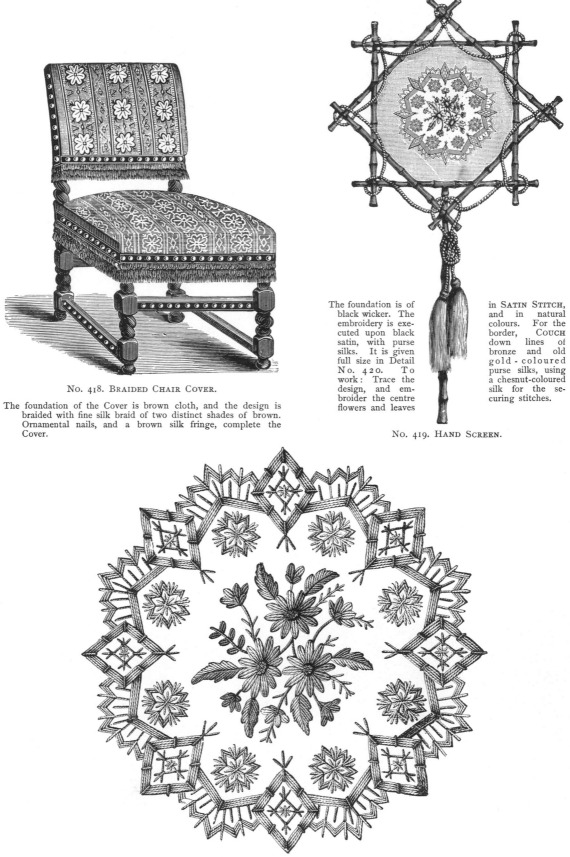

NO. 418. BRAIDED CHAIR COVER.

The foundation of the Cover is brown cloth, and the design is braided with fine silk braid of two distinct shades of brown. Ornamental nails, and a brown silk fringe, complete the Cover.

The foundation is of black wicker. The embroidery is executed upon black satin, with purse silks. It is given full size in Detail No. 420. To work: Trace the design, and embroider the centre flowers and leaves in SATIN STITCH, and in natural colours. For the border, COUCH down lines of bronze and old gold - coloured purse silks, using a chesnut-coloured silk for the securing stitches.

NO. 419. HAND SCREEN.

NO. 420. DETAIL OF HAND SCREEN (NO. 419).

Plate CXXIII.

653

NO. 421. DETAIL *A* OF WORK-BASKET
(NO. 424).

NO. 422. DETAIL OF CHRISTMAS-CARD BOX
(NO. 425).

NO. 423. DETAIL *B* OF WORK-
BASKET (NO. 424).

NO. 424. WORK-BASKET WITH ORNAMENTAL COVER.

Basket foundation of black wicker, lined and quilted with
rose-coloured silk.   Ornamental Cover is separate
from the Basket.   The Cover is of dark green plush,
embroidered with SATIN STITCH, with POWDERINGS
as shown in Detail *A* (No. 421).   The Border is of
Guipure lace, the netted foundation being worked with
POINT D'ESPRIT, and BUTTONHOLED to the plush.
The flower shown in Detail *B* (No. 423) is worked
with chenille, and the tassels are of chenille.

NO. 425. CHRISTMAS-CARD BOX.

The foundation is of millboard, with sides and
interior covered with dark blue silk, and top
and bottom with dark blue velvet.   The
velvet is embroidered in SATIN STITCH
with the design shown in Detail No. 422.

Plate CXXIV.

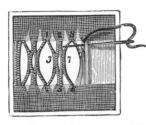

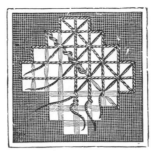

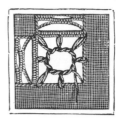

NO. 426. DETAIL *A* OF DRAWN WORK (NO. 430).

NO. 427. DETAIL *B* OF DRAWN WORK (NO. 430).

NO. 428. DETAIL *C* OF DRAWN WORK (NO. 430).

NO. 429. DETAIL *D* OF DRAWN WORK (NO. 430).

NO. 430. DRAWN WORK FOR TEA-TABLE CLOTH.

The foundation is of linen, with border and centre ornamented with DRAWN WORK. Detail *D* (No. 429) gives the outer border, with threads withdrawn, 1, 2, 3, 4, indicating the position of threads retained, and 5 the manner of securing them. The border partially completed is given in No. 430; 1 shows the overcasting of the side lines of the design. Detail *B* (No. 427) gives the manner of drawing out and overcasting the threads retained to form an ornamental centre to the Table-cloth, and Detail *A* (No. 430) the narrow border to surround it, 3 and 7 pointing out where the separate overcasts are connected together. Detail *C* (No. 428) is a WHEEL used in the corners alternately with the one shown in No. 430.

NO. 431. COLLAR POINT IN STRASBOURG EMBROIDERY.

Foundation material, white cambric, embroidered with linen thread. To work: Trace the design upon the cambric, make the BARS and PICOTS, BUTTONHOLE round every part of the design, also the edges of the Collar, and finish by cutting away the cambric beneath the Bars.

Plate CXXV.

655

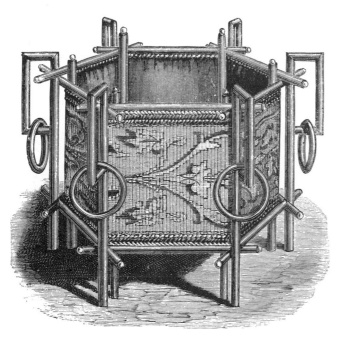

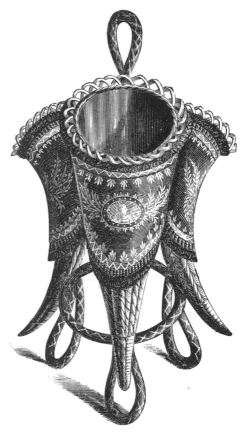

NO. 432. FLOWER-POT HOLDER ORNAMENTED WITH GOBELIN TAPESTRY.

Foundation of black wicker work, fitted with a tin lining to hold the Flower-pot. The ornamental covering to the tin lining is of GOBELIN TAPESTRY (which *see*). The pattern and number of stitches are shown in Detail No. 434. The ground colour work in a deep brown, the pattern in shades of green and crimson.

NO. 433. CORNUCOPIA FLOWER VASE.

Foundation of brown basket work. Each Cornucopia is fitted with a tin lining. The ornamental vallance to the Vase is of dark blue cloth, embroidered with fancy stitches, such as CORAL, SATIN, POINT DE POIS, and Vandyked lines.

NO. 434. DETAIL OF GOBELIN TAPESTRY FOR FLOWER-POT HOLDER (NO. 432).

NO. 435. TATTED EDGING FOR TOILET CLOTH.

This Edging is worked in pieces, then joined together.
Walter and Evans' crochet cotton No. 10 is
sufficiently coarse. *See* TATTING.

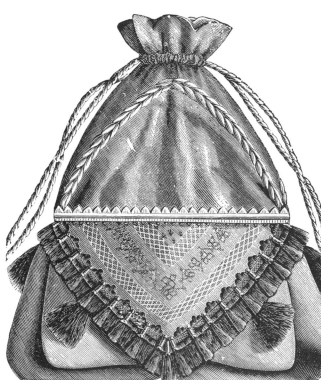

NO. 436. HAND BAG.

The Bag is of seal-brown plush, the Vandyke upon each side of the Bag of
seal-brown silk, embroidered with old gold-coloured silks.   Stitches
used, LATTICE and SATIN.

NO. 437. BRACKET VALLANCE.

Foundation of ruby-coloured cloth; ornaments, BRAIDING
and SATIN STITCH Embroidery.

Plate CXXVII.

657

No. 438. Lamp Mat.

Foundation of black cloth. Embroidery executed in Satin, Rope, Feather, and Point de Pois Stitches, with purse silks.

No. 439. Table Mat.

Foundation, white cricketing flannel. Embroidery in two shades of blue purse silk, in Feather, Lattice, Satin, and Buttonhole Stitches.

No. 440. Tatted Antimacassar.

The Antimacassar, when complete, is made with twenty-four rosettes and thirty-eight crosses. Walter and Evans' crochet cotton No. 10 is used. The crosses are worked with a double thread, the rosettes with a single thread.

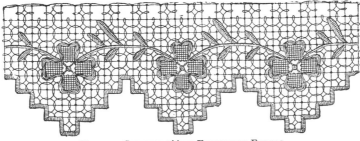

No. 441. Guipure d'Art Furniture Edging.

The foundation is netting. Guipure d'Art stitches used: Point d'Esprit, Point de Toile, Guipure en Relief, and Buttonhole.

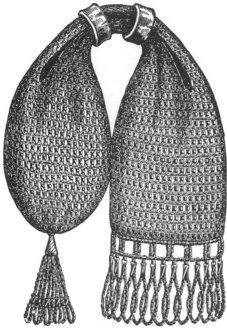

NO. 442. CROCHET PURSE.

Materials required: Steel beads, rings, and tassels, and skeins of garnet-coloured purse silk. To work: Use crochet needle Penelope No. 3, and Pearsall's purse silk. Thread the beads on the silk. Make a chain 5 inches long, work 1 DOUBLE CROCHET in the third chain from the needle, * 1 Chain, miss 1, 1 Double Crochet; repeat from * to the end of the row. Work a bead in with every Double Crochet. Make a length of 8 inches, sew up, leaving an opening 2½ inches long in the centre, which finish with Double Crochet. Add tassels and rings.

NO. 443. PINCUSHION—MACRAMÉ.

The foundation is an ordinary square Pincushion, covered with crimson satin. The ornamental cover is of MACRAMÉ LACE, surrounded with a wide and full quilling of crimson silk ribbon. To work the lace: Put on double threads that divide into eight. Work SINGLE DIAMONDS of eight threads each, and ornament their centres with SOLOMON KNOTS.

NO. 444. WATCH-STAND.

Foundation of black cane. The back is covered in with three shaped pieces of black satin, embroidered in SATIN STITCH, with coloured filoselles. A hook is fastened in the top of the centre-piece, to hold the watch. The base of the Stand is made with a round piece of black satin, embroidered with fancy stitches, such as CORAL, POINT DE POIS, VANDYKE, LATTICE, and FEATHER.

NO. 445. WORK-BASKET.

The Basket is of wicker; the tripod legs are of wood, covered with cloth, and finished with ornamental nails. The drapery of dark green plush round the outside of the Basket is caught up at intervals with green silk cord, and finished with plush balls. The inside of the Basket is lined with dark green silk, and fitted with pockets to hold cottons, &c. Wherever a plain space is left without pockets, it is ornamented with SATIN STITCH Embroidery.

Plate CXXIX.

659

NO. 446. SECTION OF LAMP MAT.

Foundation of marone-coloured cloth; embroidery, a combination of APPLIQUÉ, BRAIDING, CHAIN STITCH, and SATIN STITCH. The Appliqué pieces are of dark, marone-coloured plush; the Satin Stitch and filoselle, matching the cloth; and the Braiding and Chain Stitch, in two shades of old gold-coloured filoselles.

NO. 447. LETTER-HOLDER.

Foundation of millboard, covered with plush, and edged with fur. The initials of owner are embroidered with old gold silk, in RAISED SATIN STITCH, on the plush.

NO. 448. MACRAMÉ BASKET.

Made with white and scarlet string, in rows of SINGLE BARS and CORD. The owner's initials are worked in CROSS STITCH, with scarlet wool, in the centre of the Basket, and the red string is used for the two stripes.

NO. 449. SECTION OF LAMP MAT.

Foundation of blue cloth; embroidery, a combination of APPLIQUÉ, BUTTONHOLE, COUCHING, CHAIN STITCH, and SATIN STITCH. To work: Appliqué pale blue silk to the cloth, and work in Chain Stitch; Buttonhole round the pieces with filoselles darker than the cloth. Couch down lines of silk cord round the Satin Stitch embroidery, using dark blue shades, and work the Chain Stitch and Couched lines near it with two shades of ruby-coloured filoselles.

NO. 450. SIDEBOARD CLOTH BORDER.

Foundation of white German canvas, with woven, coloured
border lines, or pieces of scarlet braid, sewn down to the
canvas. Embroider in HOLBEIN and CROSS STITCH,
using ingrain red cotton on the white canvas, and white
linen thread on the border lines.

NO. 451. CURTAIN BANDS.

Foundation of thin cloth, with a pinked-out edge.
Execute the embroidery in CREWEL, POINT DE
POIS, TÊTE DE BŒUF, and POINT LANCÉ Em-
broidery Stitches.

NO. 452. CUSHION IN APPLIQUÉ AND LAID WORK.

Foundation of Cushion, light terra-cotta-coloured silk; Appliqué pieces, a darker shade of terra-cotta plush. To work: Round the
Appliqué pieces COUCH down thick strands of filoselle with old gold-coloured silk.   Outline the leaves and flowers of the
design in the same way, and vein the stems with gold cord. Work the border with LATTICE STITCH, and use SATIN STITCH
for the filled-in leaves, &c.

Plate CXXXI.

661

No. 453. BORDER FOR TABLECLOTH.

Foundation of fine cloth. Embroidery worked with purse silks of the same colour, but darker in shade than the cloth. Stitches: BUTTONHOLE, ROPE, TÊTE DE BŒUF, and SATIN.

No. 454. MAT IN RICHELIEU GUIPURE.

Foundation of écru-coloured linen. BUTTONHOLE Lines and BARS worked with écru-coloured linen thread.
See RICHELIEU GUIPURE.

NO. 455. BRAIDED TABLE BORDER.

Foundation of olive-green cloth. Braiding worked with fancy silk braids of two shades of green. *See* BRAIDING.

NO. 456. BRAIDED WATCH POCKET.

Foundation of marone cloth, pinked at the edges. Braiding executed with gold cord. LATTICE STITCH, BUTTONHOLE, and DOTS, worked with marone silk.

NO. 457. CHAIN STITCH SHELF BORDER.

Foundation of dark blue cloth. CHAIN STITCH and POINT DE POIS Embroidered Stitches worked with blue silk.

Plate CXXXIII.   663

NO. 459. WORK BASKET.

Foundation of plush or silk ; handle and sides of Macramé. Knots and Stitches
used : CORD, CHAIN BOULÉE, and SINGLE CROSSES. *See* MACRAMÉ.

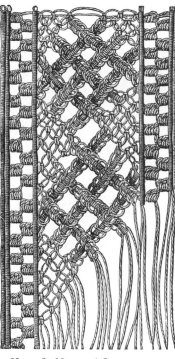

NO. 458. MACRAMÉ INSERTION FOR
SUMMER QUILT.

Knots and Stitches used : OPEN CHAIN,
CORD, SOLOMON KNOTS, and BUTTON-
HOLE. *See* MACRAMÉ.

NO. 460. MACRAMÉ INSERTION FOR PILLOW CASES.

Stitch used : SINGLE CROSS with eight strands.

NO. 461. INSERTION FOR SIDEBOARD CLOTH.

Knots and Stitches used : LEADERS, TREBLE CROSSES, CORD, and
FANCY KNOT. *See* MACRAMÉ.

NO. 462. MACRAMÉ LACE BORDER FOR
MANTEL BOARD.

Knots and Stitches used : SINGLE DIA-
MONDS, CORD, and SOLOMON KNOTS.
See MACRAMÉ.

NO. 463. MACRAMÉ WORK-BASKET.

Foundation, black wicker ; sides filled in with quilted satin and Macramé lace.
Knots and Stitches used : SOLOMON, SINGLE DIAMONDS, CORD, and
SINGLE SLANTING LEADERS. *See* MACRAMÉ.

Plate CXXXIV.

NO. 464. PINCUSHION.

Foundation of moss-green plush, embroidered with chenille of a lighter green than the plush; trimmings of pompons and fringe, matching the two greens. *See* CHENILLE EMBROIDERY.

NO. 465. DETAIL OF PERFORATED CARDBOARD FLOWER-POT STAND (NO. 467).

NO. 466. PERFORATED LEATHER WORK—SECTION OF TABLE MAT.

The Leather is embroidered with coloured silks, in SATIN STITCH.

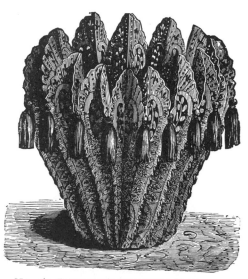

NO. 467. PERFORATED CARDBOARD FLOWER-POT STAND.

The sections of cardboard are sewn together with purse silk, and silk tassels are sewn on as a finish to each section. Detail No. 465 gives one section of the cardboard.

Plate CXXXV.

665

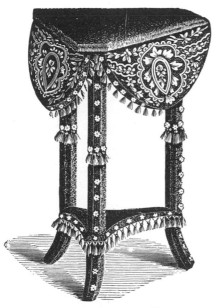

NO. 468. THREE-CORNERED OR TUCK-AWAY
TABLE.

Foundation of oak, covered with chesnut brown
    plush, fastened down with ornamental nails.
    The vallance is of chesnut-brown plush, orna-
    mented with SATIN STITCH and COUCHING.
    Colours used : Pale chesnuts. Detail No. 470
    shows pattern and manner of working.

NO. 469. CARD BASKET.

Foundation of cane and wicker. The lining is of dark
    blue silk, worked with coloured filoselles, in SILK
    EMBROIDERY.

NO. 470. DETAIL OF THREE-CORNERED OR TUCK-AWAY TABLE (NO. 468).

NO. 471. WORK-BASKET.

Foundation of wicker; vallance of plush embroidered with SILK EMBROIDERY, as shown in Detail No. 473, and finished with plush balls. The inside of the Basket is wadded, lined with quilled-up rep silk, and ornamented with a silk cord. The bottom is worked in Silk Embroidery.

NO. 472. WASTE-PAPER BASKET.

Foundation of open wicker-work; trimming of bands of velvet and plush balls. The bands round the top and base of Basket are ornamented with CORAL STITCH. The interior is lined with plain silk.

NO. 473. DETAIL OF WORK-BASKET (NO. 471).

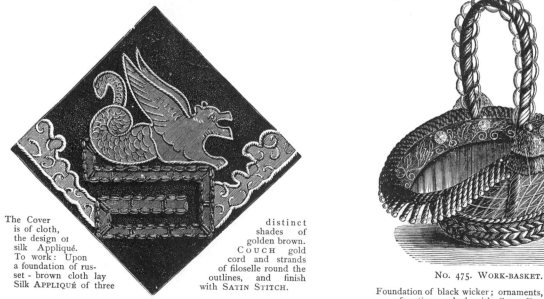

The Cover is of cloth, the design of silk Appliqué. To work: Upon a foundation of russet-brown cloth lay Silk APPLIQUÉ of three distinct shades of golden brown. COUCH gold cord and strands of filoselle round the outlines, and finish with SATIN STITCH.

NO. 474. CORNER FOR TABLE COVER.

NO. 475. WORK-BASKET.

Foundation of black wicker; ornaments, an inside band of satin, worked with SILK EMBROIDERY, and finished with a wide fringe of silk.

Plate CXXXVII.

667

NO. 476. CORNER FOR TABLE BORDER.

Foundation of Oriental silk. Design worked in LONG STITCH,
with gold cord COUCHED round the outlines. Colour of
foundation, ruby; of pattern, dark blue.

NO. 477. CORNER OF LAMP MAT.

Foundation of black ribbed cloth; APPLIQUÉ of pale blue silk. Embroidery executed with marone-coloured filoselles and
gold cord. Stitches used: COUCHING, SATIN, and DOTS.

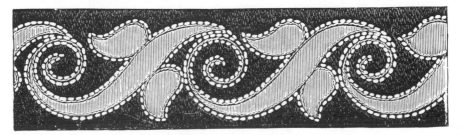

NO. 478. DESIGN FOR TABLE CENTRE BORDER.

Foundation of brown plush. Appliqué pattern, old gold silk, surrounded with lines of gold cord and pale yellow filoselle.

No. 480. PHOTOGRAPH STAND.

Foundation of wood; front of frame and doors covered with marone velvet, and embroidered in Satin Stitch. To work: Trace the design; work the leaves in SATIN STITCH, with green filoselle, the flowers with shades of pale blue filoselles, and in Satin Stitch.

No. 479. DETAIL OF WASTE-PAPER BASKET (No. 481).

No. 481. WASTE-PAPER BASKET.

Foundation of wicker overlaid with strips of cloth, perforated at the edges. The bands filling up the sides are shown in Detail No. 479; the one round the stand is simply vandyked at the edge, and ornamented with a row of FEATHER STITCH. To work Detail (No. 479): Take a piece of myrtle-green cloth, cut out the edges, trace the design, and work the tendrils and stem in CHAIN STITCH with chestnut-coloured purse silk; the leaves and centre flower in SATIN STITCH, with old gold coloured silk. Ornament the handles and top of Basket with woollen tassels of green and chestnut colours.

Plate CXXXIX.

669

No. 482. Portion of Toilet Cloth Cover.

Foundation of diaper pattern linen, embroidered with ingrain scarlet cotton. To work: Double the ingrain cotton, and work the trefoil in Cross Stitch, and the two straight lines in Single Coral Stitch.

No. 483. Oriental Chair Back.

Foundation of plush, overlaid with a band of Cross Stitch Embroidery, worked upon silk canvas. Silk fringes and tassels matching the colours used in the embroidery are attached to the sides. To work: Outline the vandykes with chocolate wool, and fill in their centres with sombre shades of blue wool. Work the flowers in Indian reds and browns, and the pendants from the vandykes in dull greens outlined with terra cotta. Work over the wools in the centres of flowers and vandykes with fine gold thread in Cross Stitch. Mix all the colours for the borders, and finish with Drawn threads and a line of Buttonhole Stitch.

No. 484. GERMAN LINEN THREAD EMBROIDERY FOR TABLECLOTH.

The foundation is of strong white linen, and the Embroidery is executed with two shades of blue ingrain cotton. To work: Trace the design, and work round every outline with the darkest shade of blue cotton, and in CREWEL STITCH. Fill in the centres with the light blue wool, as shown; the birds with FRENCH KNOTS and COUCHING; the leaves with HERRINGBONE, SATIN, CROSS, and DIAGONAL STITCHES; the figures with Cross, Diagonal, and Crewel Stitches.

Plate CXLI.

671

No. 485. MUSIC STOOL, WITH PATCHWORK COVER.

The stars are formed of patches made of shades of old gold silk, the six-sided pieces all of the same shade of seal-brown plush. To work: Cut out the patches, and turn the edges over neatly to the front of the work, as shown in Detail A (No. 486). Sew the patches together, as shown in Detail B (No. 487). Finish the Stool with tassels and a handsome fringe.

No. 486. DETAIL A OF MUSIC STOOL (No. 485).

No. 487. DETAIL B OF MUSIC STOOL (No. 485).

No. 488. STOOL COVERED WITH BROCADE EMBROIDERY.

Foundation of deep terra cotta brocade. To work: Outline the brocade pattern with a double line ot gold thread, and fill in the various centres with SATIN STITCH, worked with pale blue filoselle, salmon pink, and pale green. Outline each centre with lines of gold thread, and sew on small spangles as ornaments.

No. 489. BROCADE EMBROIDERY FOR A SOFA CUSHION.

The foundation is of woollen brocade, and the Embroidery is executed with filoselles. To work: Take a whole strand of filoselle, and
COUCH it down along the edges of the brocade. Form the finer inside lines with a few threads of filoselle, Couched down in the same
way. Fill in where indicated with SATIN STITCH. Select the filoselle for the Embroidery of the same colour, but a lighter shade
than the foundation material.

Plate CXLIII.

673

NO. 490. EMBROIDERED BELL ROPE.

Foundation material of fine claret-coloured cloth. Embroidery executed with purse silks, or Oriental silks, and in CHAIN, SATIN, ROPE, FRENCH KNOTS, and LACE STITCHES, in the following colours: a, pale yellow-green; b, a darker green; $c1$ and $c2$, two shades of dull blues; $d1$, $d2$, $d3$, shades of old golds; $e1$, $e2$, $e3$, shades of pale blue; $f1$, $f2$, $f3$, shades of pale greens; g, dark brown; $h1$, $h2$, $h3$, shades of rich reds, deepening to clarets for $k1$, $k2$, $k3$. The diagonal lines or open lattice, marked $e1$, are crossed with gold thread, and the Couched lines forming tendrils are worked with gold thread.

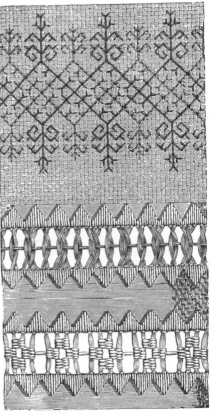

NO. 491. PORTION OF SIDEBOARD CLOTH.

Foundation of German canvas, embroidered with ingrain scarlet thread. To work: Pull out two lines of DRAWN THREADS, and work them over as shown. Execute the rest of the embroidery with SATIN and HEM STITCHES.

NO. 492. TEA-TABLE SERVIETTES.

These finely embroidered Serviettes are used for Five o'Clock Tea. The foundation is of fine Irish linen, with red or blue coloured borders. The embroidery is worked with ingrain thread matching the border in colour, and in HEM-STITCH. The designs used are given full working size in Details *A* and *B* (Nos. 493 and 494).

NO. 493. DETAIL *A* OF TEA-TABLE SERVIETTES (NO. 492).

NO. 494. DETAIL *B* OF TEA-TABLE SERVIETTES (NO. 492).

NO. 495. FIVE O'CLOCK TEACLOTH.

Foundation material of rough linen, with a wide diaper bordering. To work: Fill in the woven squares of the border with stars made with CROSS STITCH, and worked alternately in red or blue ingrain cotton.

Plate CXLV.

675

NO. 497. WASTE-PAPER BARREL.

NO. 496. DETAIL OF WASTE-PAPER
BARREL (NO. 497).

Foundation, a wooden flour barrel, set upon three gilt balls. Embroidery executed upon coarse German canvas, with single Berlin wools. To work: Lay down lines of olive-green wool to form the squares, and cover them with CROSS STITCH, worked in a lighter shade of green. Work the leaves in alternate shades of crimson, and the border lines in deeper crimson. Make the tassels and cord of a mixture of green and crimson. The Detail (No. 496) shows the design enlarged.

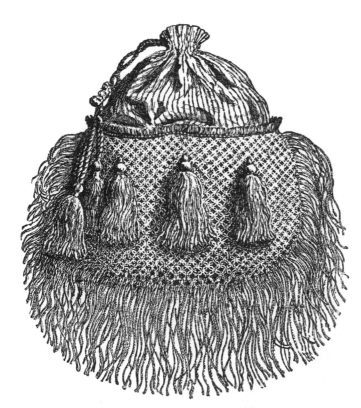

NO. 498. MACRAMÉ LACE GAME BAG.

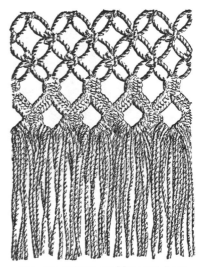

NO. 499. DETAIL OF MACRAMÉ LACE
GAME BAG (NO. 498).

Foundation of leather. Macramé executed with strong string. The manner of working is shown in the Detail (No. 499), and consists of single SOLOMON KNOTS of four threads. Make the border of double MACRAMÉ KNOTS, worked close.

NO. 500. CLOTH FOR SMALL TABLE.

Foundation of coloured damask, with a design woven upon it. The embroidery, which consists of working over this design, is shown enlarged in the Detail (No. 501). To work: Over the plain lines or bands work large CROSS STITCHES, and BUTTONHOLE to their edges thick strands of filoselle. Fill in the border pattern with SATIN STITCH, and work the centre pattern over with ROPE STITCH and FRENCH KNOTS.

NO. 501. DETAIL OF CLOTH FOR SMALL TABLE (NO. 500).

Plate CXLVII.

677

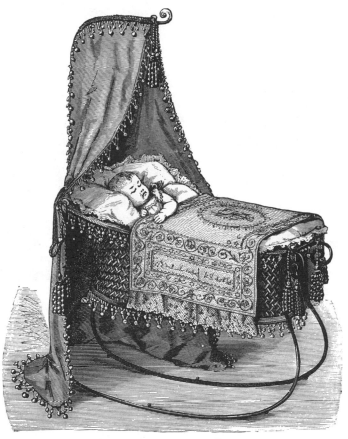

No. 502. Cot Quilt in Linen Embroidery.

Foundation material, pale blue cashmere, or fine cloth embroidery, executed with two shades of blue filoselle, and in SATIN and ROPE STITCHES. A part of the border design is given, full working size, in the Detail (No. 503). The child's monogram is worked in the centre of the Quilt, and a nursery rhyme in the centre of the border.

No. 503. DETAIL OF COT QUILT IN LINEN EMBROIDERY (No. 502).

NO. 504. ITALIAN APRON.

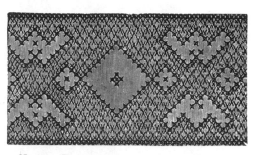

NO. 505. DETAIL OF ITALIAN APRON (NO. 504).

Foundation of white or grey crash. The design shown in the Detail (No. 505) is worked on the crash, and a row of insertion and an edging of Russian lace sewn beneath each band. To work the Detail (No. 505): Leave the parts forming the design unworked, and fill in the background with POINT DE CROIX, worked in irregularly, and with fine turkey-red cotton. Outline the design with CROSS STITCH, worked with black crewel wool.

NO. 507. EGG COSY.

This Cosy is made like a handkerchief case, with the four corners turned inwards, and forming a square. The outer cover is of striped, strong, grey linen; the inside of crimson silk, quilted and wadded. To work: Cut and fold the linen, and work with crimson arrasene, in RAILWAY STITCH, round the outer border. Work the inner border with the same coloured arrasene, in Railway, BUTTONHOLE, and CHAIN STITCHES. Make the FRENCH KNOTS of both borders with crimson purse silk, and also the centre ornament. The Detail (No. 506) gives the pattern in full working size.

NO. 506. DETAIL OF EGG COSY (NO. 507).

Plate CXLIX.

Plate CXLIX.

679

NO. 508. ANTIMACASSAR.

Foundation of plush embroidery, executed upon Toile Colbert, with coloured filoselles. To work: Cut the Toile Colbert in strips, work the design in SATIN STITCH, and outline each strip with laid lines of thick filoselles. Work DOUBLE CORAL STITCH as lines on the plush, and finish the edges of the Antimacassar with silk tassels.

NO. 509. WORK-BASKET.

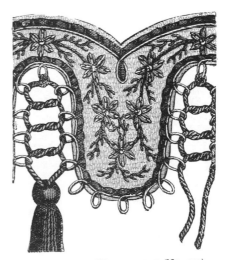

NO. 510. DETAIL OF WORK-BASKET (NO. 509).

Foundation of bamboo; inside lined with old gold colour, quilted; satin border of fine indigo-coloured cloth, worked with blue silks with RAILWAY and CORAL STITCHES. Each scallop of the border is edged with a fine yellow silk cord, sewn on in ovals; and through these ovals a thicker dark blue silk cord is laced, and finished with tassels made of blue and yellow silk. See Detail (No. 510).

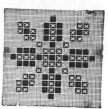

CROSS STITCH CORNERS FOR NAPERY.

Foundation of Irish linen; embroidery worked with two shades of blue ingrain cotton. To work: The squares marked with white crosses, work with pale blue cotton; the black squares, with indigo blue cotton; and both in CROSS STITCH.

NO. 511.

NO. 512.

NO. 513. SOFA CUSHION.

The centre of this Cushion is made with puffed, ruby-coloured satin, surrounded with grey cloth. The grey cloth is laid upon a large square of ruby plush, and trimmed with grey fur. The four ruby satin bands across the plush are also bordered with fur, and embroidered with Satin Stitch. Satin bows are sewn to the bands where they join the centre square. To work: Upon the grey cloth embroider a flower design, in CREWEL STITCH, and with two shades of blue filoselle; upon the satin bands, work a conventional design, in SATIN STITCH, with old gold coloured filoselles.

MODERN POINT LACE CORNERS FOR TABLE NAPERY.

Foundation of Irish linen. To work No. 514: Mark out a perfect square, draw out the side threads, and form the middle threads into a cross. Work POINT DE BRUXELLES at the four corners, and connect these to the centre cross with GUIPURE EN RELIEF. To work No. 515: Mark out the square, draw away the side threads, and work the centre threads to form a centre square. Work a WHEEL in the very centre, and POINT DE REPRISE where shown. Buttonhole round the outer edge of each square.

NO. 514.

NO. 515.

Plate CLI.

681

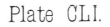

NO. 516. TABLECLOTH.

Foundation of strong German linen, with a pattern woven in it, forming the border.
Embroidery in CROSS STITCH, worked with ingrain blue cotton.

NO. 518. BASKET TO HOLD BABY LINEN.

The foundation is of wicker, lined with a washable chintz; the
pockets are made of the same chintz, lined with American
cloth, and tied up with blue ribbon. The hot-water bottle in
the centre keeps the linen aired. The outside of the Basket
is ornamented with handsome blue silk cords and Russian
lace.

NO. 517. WALL BASKET.

Foundation of wicker, lined with orange-coloured
silk. The vallance round Basket, and upon its
heading, is of seal-brown plush; the embroidery
upon the same, of SATIN STITCH, worked with
orange-coloured filoselle. Tassels of brown and
orange silks.

Plate CLII.

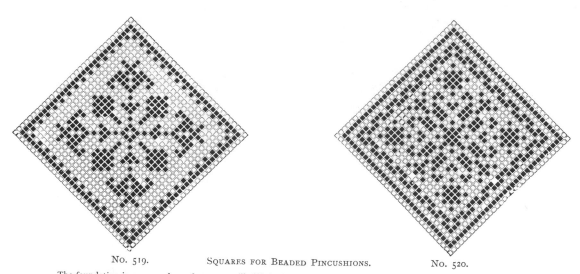

NO. 519. SQUARES FOR BEADED PINCUSHIONS. NO. 520.

The foundation is a square bag of strong twill, filled with bran, and covered with ruby velvet. The tops of the Cushions (shown in Nos. 519 and 520) are of Berlin wool canvas, covered with BEAD WORK. Colours used for No. 519, sky blue and indigo-blue beads; for No. 520, white, opal, and deep crimson beads. A fringe made with beads is worked round the squares after they have been sewn to the body of the Cushions.

NO. 521. GUIPURE D'ART CHAIR BACK.

Foundation of apricot-coloured Indian silk; trimming of Guipure d'Art squares and edging. To work: Upon the silk, work with olive-green filoselles, and in CROSS STITCH. Darn the netted edging with POINT DE TOILE, POINT DE REPRISE, and GUIPURE EN RELIEF. Work the five netted squares with coloured filoselles, in Point de Toile, POINT D'ESPRIT, RONES, and Point de Reprise.

Plate CLIII.

683

NO. 522. DRESS TRIMMING.

The foundation is of ecru-coloured holland, and the embroidery is executed with two shades of blue ingrain cotton. To work: The thick leaves and flowers work in RAISED SATIN STITCH, with the palest blue; the lighter parts in FEATHER STITCH, and with dark blue.

NO. 523. EMBROIDERY FOR A CIGAR CASE.

Foundation of rough kid. Work the flower design with purse silk, in colours matching the flowers, and with SATIN, RAILWAY, DOUBLE and SINGLE CORAL STITCHES, and FRENCH KNOTS.

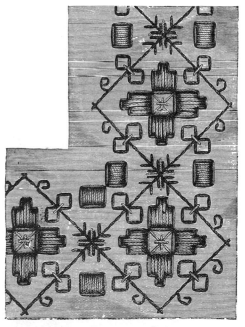

NO. 524. TABLECLOTH BORDER.

Foundation of fine indigo-blue cloth. Design worked with red, blue, and brown filoselles. To work: The diagonal lines work with CREWEL and HOLBEIN STITCHES, in blue, the centres in Holbein and SATIN STITCH, and in red, the detached squares with Holbein and Satin Stitches, and with brown filoselles.

NO. 525. CORNER FOR HANDKERCHIEF CASE.

Foundation of black satin; embroidery in SATIN
STITCH, FRENCH KNOTS, and SINGLE CORAL,
worked with yellow purse silk.

NO. 526. PINCUSHION AND WORK-CASE
COMBINED.

Foundation of wood, divided down the centre. The
Pincushion side is weighted with lead, filled with
bran, and covered with blue velvet. The Work-
case is divided into compartments, and lined with
yellow satin. The border is of black velvet,
worked in SATIN STITCH embroidery, with old
gold silk.

NO. 527. TRINKET BOX.

Foundation of wood, lined with quilted satin; outside covering of brown plush, ornamented with
APPLIQUÉ and Netting. To work: Cut out a bold flower design in chesnut-coloured plush;
appliqué to the brown plush foundation, and couch old gold coloured silk cords round the outlines.
Work the netting with old gold coloured silk, and make the tassels with chesnut-coloured silks.

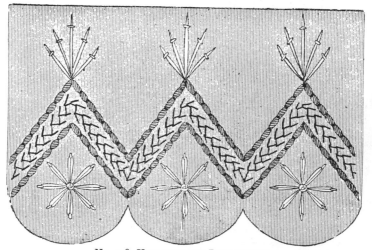

NO. 528. VALLANCE FOR BOOKSHELVES.

Foundation of fine dark brown cloth embroidery, worked with two shades of brown filoselles. To work:
COUCH whole strands of brown filoselles as bordering to the Vandykes; work the inside with
HERRINGBONE; make the stars with RAILWAY STITCH and FRENCH KNOTS, and the points
with SATIN STITCH.

685

Plate CLV.

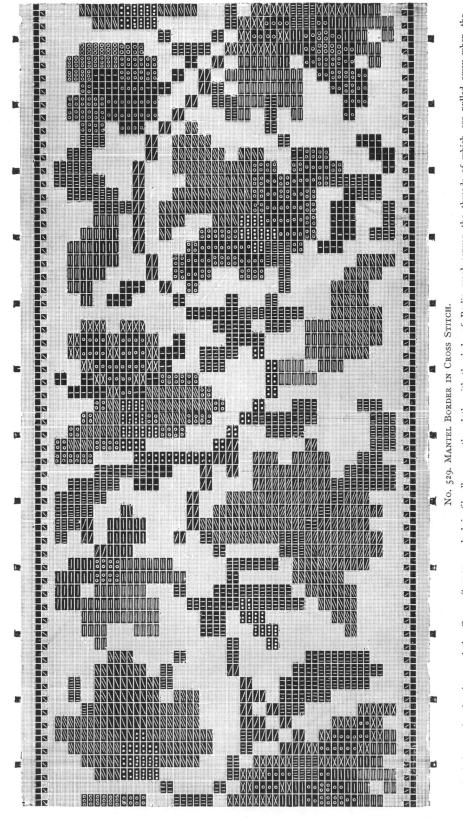

No. 529. Mantel Border in Cross Stitch.

Foundation, a chocolate-brown cloth; Cross Stitch worked in filoselles over the cloth, with the help of Berlin wool canvas, the threads of which are pulled away when the work is completed. Colours used : Spaces filled with white and open rounds (six in number) to be worked in crimson shades; spaces filled with diagonal lines, crossing right or left (six in number), in shades of indigo blues; spaces filled with horizontal lines (of four kinds), in deep-tinted olive-greens; spaces filled with crosses, in dark rich brown; spaces filled with perpendicular lines (three in number), in golden browns. There are twenty shades of filoselles requred in all.

Plate CLVI.

No. 530. CURTAIN BORDER IN APPLIQUÉ.

Foundation of deep indigo-blue cloth; appliqué cut out of olive-green silk for the leaves, and pale blue velvet for the flowers. To work: Lay down the APPLIQUÉ pattern, COUCH round the leaves with strands of green filoselle, and work CREWEL STITCH veins with the same colour. Surround the outlines of the flowers with fine blue silk cord, and work the centres and calyx with dark blue silk.

Plate CLVII.   687

No. 531. CHALICE VEIL.

Border, muslin appliqué upon net ; centre, white embroidery. To work the border : Trace the design upon fine muslin, lay the muslin on net, and OVERCAST the outlines with linen thread ; cut away the muslin foundation outside the overcast lines. To work the centre : Trace the design on fine linen, and work it over with linen thread, in Overcast, SATIN, LATTICE, and PETIT POIS.

NO. 532. HALF OF LAMP MAT IN APPLIQUÉ.

Foundation of brown furniture plush ; fleur-de-lys and round, cut out in old gold coloured furniture plush.   To work :
Cut out the appliqué, and BUTTONHOLE to the foundation with old gold coloured filoselle.   Work the CHAIN
STITCH, LATTICE STITCH, and FRENCH KNOTS, with brown filoselles.

NO. 533. ARRASENE EMBROIDERY FOR A
SACHET.

Foundation of pale blue silk.   Work the daisy
petals with pink arrasene, and the centres with
FRENCH KNOTS in yellow silk.   Make the
lines crossing the foundation with COUCHINGS
of gold thread.

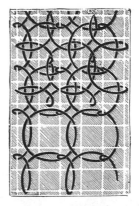

NO. 534. LINEN THREAD EMBROIDERY
FOR AN APRON.

Foundation of grey linen with a white
check woven in it.   Make the embroidery of interlaced rounds and loops,
with ingrain red and blue linen thread.

Plate CLIX.

No. 535. BOOKSHELF BORDER.

Foundation of dark green cloth. Execute the
embroidery with crewel wools, in natural
shades, in SATIN and SINGLE CORAL
STITCHES.

No. 536. POINT DE POIS EMBROIDERY
FOR A BUTTON.

Foundation of dark brown or indigo-blue
rep silk. Work the POINT DE POIS
in a lighter shade of the foundation
colour, with purse silk.

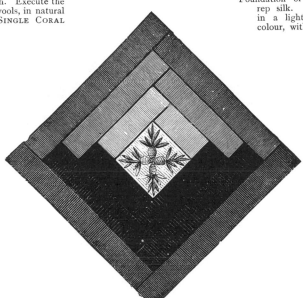

No. 537. LOGHOUSE QUILTING.

Colours used: three shades of old gold, three shades of russet-brown, and one shade of sky-blue.
To work: Make the centre square of pale blue silk, and work on it the design in SATIN
STITCH, with two shades of blue filoselles. Surround this centre with 1in. wide ribbon as
shown, keeping the lighter yellows and the darker browns to the centre.

No. 538. MACRAMÉ EDGING FOR A BRACKET.

Worked with Macramé twine, each pattern requiring
eight strands. First row—after the HEADING,
a CORD. Second row—a TREBLE STAR, with
ORNAMENTAL KNOT in the centre. Third
row—half a Treble Star, finished with an Ornamental Knot.

No. 539. MACRAMÉ EDGING FOR A BRACKET.

Worked with Macramé twine, each pattern requiring
eight strands. First row—after the HEADING,
a CORD. Second row—SINGLE DIAMOND,
made with eight strands, with a SOLOMON KNOT
centre. Third row like second. Fourth row—
upper half of a Single Diamond.

INDEX TO SUPPLEMENT.

Giving Alphabetical References to all the Subjects Illustrated in the One Hundred and Fifty-nine Special Plates.

----◆◆◆◆◆◆◆----